Twentieth Century Europe

ALEXANDER RUDHART

Villanova University

PRENTICE–HALL, INC., Englewood Cliffs, New Jersey 07632

Library of Congress Cataloging in Publication Data

Rudhart, Alexander.
   Twentieth century Europe.

   Bibliography: p.
   Includes index.
   1. Europe—History—20th century. I. Title.
D424.R83 1986   940.5   85-5674
ISBN 0-13-934662-7

Editorial/production supervision and
   interior design: **Marjorie Borden**
Cover design: **Diane Saxe**
Manufacturing buyer: **Barbara Kelly Kittle**

Printed in the United States of America

10 9 8 7 6 5 4 3 2 1

ISBN 0-13-934662-7   01

Prentice-Hall International (UK) Limited, *London*
Prentice-Hall of Australia Pty. Limited, *Sydney*
Prentice-Hall Canada Inc., *Toronto*
Prentice-Hall Hispanoamericana, S.A., *Mexico*
Prentice-Hall of India Private Limited, *New Delhi*
Prentice-Hall of Japan, Inc., *Tokyo*
Prentice-Hall of Southeast Asia Pte. Ltd., *Singapore*
Editora Prentice-Hall do Brasil, Ltda., *Rio de Janeiro*
Whitehall Books Limited, *Wellington, New Zealand*

To Kate and A.J.

Contents

Preface

As the twentieth century has entered its final quarter, the task of covering the history of twentieth century Europe in a single volume has become increasingly more complex and difficult.

Except for works dealing exclusively with European events since 1945, the tendency has been to concentrate on developments of the first half of the twentieth century and to add the history of post-World War Two Europe in shortened form. Given the degree of interest in more recent events, I have reversed the process and emphasized the post-war period with sufficient coverage of the pre-World War Two period to appreciate its significance in shaping twentieth century European history overall.

In this manner, it has been possible to give broader coverage to areas that may be of particular interest to the student and the reader—such as European integration, Commonwealth relations, the restoration of European democracy, the origins of the Cold War, the division of Germany, Eastern Europe, and post-Stalin Soviet Russia, to mention a few. I have given the history of the Second World War as much attention as space allowed, not merely from an interest in military history, but because of the war's role as a source of the division of post-war Europe and its symbolic significance in the struggle between human reason and unreason.

Even at the outset of the 1980s a final judgment on the meaning of the twentieth century for Europe would appear to be premature. Any such judgment might be as misleading as a final verdict on the meaning of the eighteenth century would have been if given at the beginning of the 1780s. What is certain is that the Europe of the 1980s is very different from what most Europeans might have thought probable or even possible when the twentieth century began. Under the impact of twentieth century revolutionary change in virtually every field of human endeavor, the dimension of time itself appears to have assumed a new and different meaning.

As in years past, I have been stimulated by student interest in the subject at hand. Special thanks go to Steve Dalphin, history editor at Prentice-Hall, who guided me through the preparation of this book. I am especially indebted to Bess Polkowski, who was kind enough to complete typing the manuscript even after her official retirement.

Alexander Rudhart

1

Europe on the Eve of War: Cultural Unity and National Conflict

Outwardly, European civilization at the opening of the twentieth century was a civilization in bloom, whose pride in the achievements of the past century was matched by its confidence in the prospects of the future.

The confluence of major advances in basic research and the sciences, on the one hand, and in engineering on the other, had given humanity a new mastery over matter, with revolutionary effects on transportation, communication, the manufacture of goods, and the technology of war. On land and on water, the steam engine (an invention of the late eighteenth century) had revolutionized transportation, much as the internal combustion engine (an invention of the late nineteenth century) would revolutionize transportation. The nineteenth century had been the century in which, thanks to advances in science and technology, the process of discovery of all the regions of the earth came to an end, with only the Polar caps yet to be explored and the highest peaks of the Himalayas to be scaled. As this process ended, man raised his eyes to the third dimension and fulfilled the age-old dream of flight, just as the twentieth century began.

MASS PRODUCTION AND THE MASSES

The application of machine power to the manufacturing process revolutionized past criteria of quantity and quality in the production of goods. It also became the principal lever of social change in the nineteenth century, as a result of the societal restructuring demanded by the economic imperatives of the new production methods. The mechanization of the production process promised great improvements in the material conditions of life, not only as a result of the substitution of machine power for human physical labor, but because it became possible to mass-produce articles of daily use at cheaper prices and in greater quantity than ever before.

At the start of the twentieth century the United States had already taken the lead in the mass production of consumer goods, and its methods began to be applied rapidly in Europe. Beginning with the mass production of rifles in the 1820s, American industry had expanded the process to clocks, watches, and farm machinery between the 1830s and 1850s, and to sewing machines, typewriters, and photographic equipment between the 1850s and late 1880s. The rationalization of mass production through time-and-motion studies and scientific management was an American invention, as was Henry Ford's moving assembly line. At the beginning of the twentieth century, American industry was setting new standards of precision in mass-produced articles, as evidenced in a demonstration before the Royal Automobile Club in Britain in 1908, in which three Cadillacs were completely disassembled and successfully reassembled from mixed parts, before being test-driven for 500 miles without mishap. The socially useful and, in a democracy, politically stabilizing effects of the new techniques of mass production were also first stressed by American observers such as architect Frank Lloyd Wright, who delivered his famous lecture, "The Art and Craft of the Machine," in Chicago in 1901. Another American, Christine Frederick, author of *The New Housekeeping* of 1912, was similarly influential in effecting changes in the interior design of European housing through the application of mass-produced implements and furniture.

Though Europe was lagging behind the United States in the social applications of the Industrial Revolution, European industry too was turning out an amazing variety of consumer articles as early as the 1890s, ranging from electrical appliances—including cooking stoves, vacuum cleaners, and flatirons—to bicycles, automobiles, furniture, and clothing.

The Industrial Revolution had vastly augmented Europe's wealth, but it had not distributed the increased wealth in a manner likely to preserve or to enhance social stability. Among the major threats to European stability at the outset of the twentieth century was the juxtaposition of inherited social and political forms with an economic system revolutionized by scientific and technological advances. The inherited social and political forms were still feudal or semifeudal in large areas of Eastern Europe— principally Russia—and parts of Central Europe—principally Germany and Austria-Hungary. But even in the politically advanced democracies, France and Britain, political progress had not resulted in comparable social gains for the mass of industrial workers. Indeed, semifeudal Germany possessed a more enlightened and progressive system of social legislation before the First World War than either France or Britain.

Yet the industrial age worked and lived under the pressure of time, more perhaps than had any previous age in the history of modern Europe. The pressure resulted from the fact that material progress was matched by a corresponding increase in the urgency of the social, cultural, and political problems which it had caused. The industrial age, more than any previous age, became the age of the mass, in part simply because of the sheer increase in the size of the European population. Having doubled between 1750 and 1850, the population of Europe was to more-than-double in the century following 1850, reaching 576 million by the middle of the twentieth century. The growth of population coincided with an increase in the literacy rate and the expansion of education. The industrial age became an age of mass literacy and, through increased social awareness and pressures, an age of mass movements and mass parties. Through the growth of newspaper circulation, early twentieth-century Europe also became a society of mass media which could influence and sway public opinion as never before. With the adoption of the military draft by virtually every major European power before 1914 with the exception of Great Britain, the industrial age also become the age of mass armies.

Marxism

A cataclysmic and revolutionary clash between the social classes created by the Industrial Revolution was deemed both desirable and inevitable by the doctrine of revolutionary Marxism. Of all the forms of nineteenth century socialism, that which called itself *scientific* became the most influential doctrine of European industrial labor. The appeal of revolutionary Marxism rested on its combined claim of being a philosophy, a science, and a practical guide to action. To this was added its claim of being the first correct interpreter of history, past, present, and future, and of being the vehicle and midwife of preordained progress and change. The appeal of revolutionary Marxism further rested on its filling an enormous spiritual and social void for the rapidly expanding industrial labor force of prewar Europe, which lived the existence of a segregated class. Society as a whole needed its labor; the state provided it with primary education, and demanded of it military service. But the doors to higher education, to affluence and social prestige, remained tightly shut by the guardians of social privilege, respectability, and wealth. The nations of industrialized Europe thus became compartmentalized societies in which the labor force led a separate social and cultural existence, with its own newspapers and clubs, and its own political party and ideology. Before the First World War, the German Social Democratic leader Friedrich Ebert once observed, not in jest but quite in earnest, that it was not possible for a German Social Democrat even to become imperial night watchman.

The segregation of the industrial labor force and the awareness of the identity or similarity of the conditions under which it was practiced in pre-1914 Europe lay at the root of the internationalism and antinationalism of revolutionary Marxism and its wide following. Karl Marx himself erred in assuming that identical social grievances would erase national allegiances among the working class of Europe, as the outbreak of the First World War was to show. He similarly erred in assuming that the economic model of mid-nineteenth-century European industrial capitalism was fixed and incapable of change in the direction of more enlightened social attitudes. It was this assumption, and the refusal of Marx's growing following of European workers to act on its strength before the First World War, that caused a rift between Marx and the various Socialist and Social Democratic parties of the 1870s and 1880s. The Socialist parties of prewar Europe failed to stage violent revolutions not only because they appreciated the armed strength of existing governments, but because they witnessed the beginnings of responsible social legislation on behalf of their constituencies by the state. Marx himself commented bitterly on the substitution of evolutionary for revolutionary attitudes on the part of Socialist parties by observing that he had ''sowed dragons'' but ''reaped a harvest of fleas.'' Marxism, nevertheless, remained the creed of the great majority of European workers because it had become a faith in social justice. The Christian churches of Europe had failed to turn this faith into a meaningful rallying point of social inspiration for the new proletariat because, to the extent that they *did* address themselves to the social consequences of the Industrial Revolution, they did so too late.

Colonialism

If social tension, resulting from social segregation, was a potential source of crisis in twentieth-century European developments, the policy of colonial conquest and overseas imperialism caused further potential problems. By the beginning of the twentieth century, the process of colonial conquest by European powers was virtually completed, with only certain areas of North Africa still nominally under Turkish rule, such as Morocco in the west and Libya in the center, not yet appropriated. In black Africa, Ethiopia was the sole area remaining outside European control after the Italian attempt to declare a protectorate had failed, following the Italian military defeat at Adowa in 1896.

The wealth of early twentieth-century Europe thus rested not only on the ingenuity and industry of its inhabitants, but also on the plunder and exploitation of the colonial world. But the morality of colonialism was not a topic of general concern in early twentieth-century Europe. It had formed the theme of stirring fiction, as in *Heart of Darkness* and other of Joseph Conrad's novels which depicted the corruptive influence of unlimited power over colonial peoples on the minds and souls of white Europeans. Other criticism of European brutality and colonial exploitation had come mostly from within the small states of western Europe, Holland, and Belgium, which owned huge colonial empires in Southeast Asia and Africa respectively. In the 1860s, the works of Edward Douwes Dekker, a former Dutch government official in the East Indies who wrote under the pseudonym of Muetatuli, attacked abuses in Indonesia and achieved a small measure of reform. Edmund D. Morel's *King Leopold's Rule in Africa* and *Red Rubber* castigated the methods of Belgian rule in the Congo under King Leopold, whom Mark Twain denounced as a "bloody monster."

THE ARTS

As an age which rapidly and decisively transformed the physical environment, the machine age had a powerful impact on the European arts. The latter part of the nineteenth century had produced a melancholy afterglow to an age of European art which had lasted nearly half-a-millennium since the beginning of the Renaissance and which, at the opening of the new century, was about to be superseded by a search for new forms and new expressions.

The afterglow had occasionally produced brilliant hues, especially in the field of painting and music. In painting, the French impressionists Claude Monet, Auguste Renoir, Paul Cézanne, Edgar Degas, Camille Pissarro, and Alfred Sisley gave the entire epoch a worthy farewell present with unprecedented bursts of color and a dream-like, transfigured portrayal of the beauty of the world. Transfiguration also may be viewed as the theme and effect of the music of the late romantics Claude Debussy, Tchaikovsky, Richard Wagner, Anton Bruckner, Gustav Mahler, and Richard Strauss. The music of the latter two straddled two ages, combining an emotional farewell to the romantic age with a somber premonition of the coming storms of the new century.

Architecture

The architecture of the nineteenth century, though imposing in scale, had remained unoriginal in style, developing and blending themes of earlier periods, from the Middle Ages to the Renaissance, the baroque, and the neoclassical. The Gothic revival of the early and mid-nineteenth century, as exemplified in the Houses of Parliament at Westminster and the Votiv-Church in Vienna, was followed by a vogue of neoclassicism, as shown in the massive Victor Emmanuel monument in Rome, the equally massive Reichstag building in Berlin, and the new museum architecture on Vienna's Ringstrasse. At the beginning of the twentieth century, Europe began to look for architectural inspiration to America, just as it had applied American techniques of industrial mass production. American functionalism in architecture, as expressed in the revolutionary styles of Louis Sullivan and Frank Lloyd Wright under the theme of "form follows function," excited the interest of some of Europe's most notable architects of the future, Walter Gropius, Mies van der Rohe, and le Corbusier.

Painting and Sculpture

The search for new styles, reflective of the spirit of the twentieth century, also dominated much of European painting and some of Europe's sculpture in the brief period between 1900 and 1914. The search was common to a host of new movements from Picasso and Braque's cubism, the fauvism of Matisse, Derain, Vlaminck and Dufy, Munch and Kirchner's expressionism, Klimt and Schiele's Vienna secession, and the futurism of Marinetti, Russolo and Sant'Elia, the architect, to mention but a few. The move towards total abstraction in painting, which was to dominate much of Western painting after the Second World War, was already foreshadowed before 1914 by the works of Wassily Kandinsky, Mikhail Larinov and Natalia Goncharova in Russia, Piet Mondrian in Holland and David Bomberg in Britain. Among the new movements, futurism not only worshiped speed and motion but also violence as admirable characteristics of the new civilization of the twentieth century; and it was perhaps ironic that some of its prominent exponents, such as Sant'Elia and the sculptor Umberto Boccioni, were killed in the First World War.

Futurism, as a predominantly Italian movement, was also to emerge after the First World War as one of the early roots of Italian fascism. Conversely, the dadaist movement, founded in Switzerland in 1915, by the painter Hans Arp and the poet Tristan Tzara among others, expressed the numbing effect that the First World War produced on the world of European art. The dadaist revulsion against the violence of early twentieth-century European civilization resulted in a total rejection of traditional art and a mocking of it by the elevation of everyday objects to the level of art. In 1917, Marcel Duchamp, who was to join the dadaist movement the following year, tried unsuccessfully to submit a urinal, which he titled *Fountain,* as a work of art in a New York art exhibition.

THE FACE OF EUROPE

Culturally, economically, and—with the growth of internationalist-minded Socialist parties—socially, the nations of pre-1914 Europe had developed a close and intimate relationship that overcame geographical distance and transcended national frontiers.

Yet the Europe of the early twentieth century had failed to develop a common European consciousness capable of subordinating individual national ambition to common peace and the common good. When Tsar Alexander II of Russia asked for a "European mandate" for the liberation of the Christian Balkan peoples from Moslem Turkish rule in 1876, German chancellor Otto von Bismarck observed sarcastically that *Europe* was merely a term of geography. The term *Europe*, Bismarck added, was most likely to be used by those leaders who wanted something for their own country which they dared not ask for in their own name.

Bismarck's Legacy

Not counting the Turkish Empire, there were some nineteen sovereign nations in Europe at the start of the twentieth century, and their relations were largely determined (as they had been since the sixteenth century) by written and unwritten alliances. The European state system had been restructured in 1870–1871 largely as a result of the unification of the German states under the leadership of Bismarck's Prussia. In the Peace of Frankfurt of 1871, which ended the Franco-Prussian War, Bismarck not only imposed a heavy war indemnity of $1 billion on defeated France, but annexed the border provinces of Alsace and Lorraine without the benefit of a plebiscite. Alsace-Lorraine was taken by Bismarck not because it had once belonged to Germany, but because of its strategic significance as a gateway for the invasion of southern Germany. In all likelihood, Bismarck would have annexed Alsace-Lorraine even if its population had not been predominantly of German ancestry.

After the Franco-Prussian War there was widespread fear, not only in defeated France but in Britain also, that the newly formed German empire would follow up its victory of 1871 with a series of new wars of conquest with smaller neighbors such as Holland, the likely early victims. This did not happen, at least not during the chancellorship of Bismarck between 1871 and 1890. More than most of his German contemporaries, Bismarck fully appreciated the external vulnerability of the empire he had created which stemmed from its central geographic position in Europe and the fears and anxieties which its very appearance had engendered among its neighbors.

Bismarck's appreciation of German vulnerability in Europe also explained his delay in entering the colonial race until the mid-1880s, out of fear that colonial rivalry in Africa and elsewhere would increase the likelihood of war in Europe. The overall objective of Bismarck's foreign policy was the preservation of the 1871 status quo. The aim was to be achieved through a system of defensive alliances between Germany and as many others of the *Great Powers* as Bismarck could get, with the exception of France. Bismarck took for granted the fact of French hostility and French desire for revenge. He thought it harmless and manageable, as long as France could not find allies among the Great Powers and thus remained isolated.

The threat of another French-German war was by no means the only threat to the peace of Europe in the age of Bismarck. Quite independent of the German factor, there existed sources of potential conflict old and new. Foremost among these was the imperial rivalry between Britian and Russia, which was global in scope. Its principal points of friction were the eastern Mediterranean, the Dardanelles, the Balkan Peninsula, Iran and the Persian Gulf, Afghanistan, Tibet, and, increasingly, China. A close second to Anglo-Russian rivalry as a potential cause of war was that between Russia and Austria-Hungary over the Balkans. The Russian-Austrian rivalry had sound strategic reasons, but it also contained historical ingredients and ethnic-racial passions which were to play an important role in the crisis of July 1914. Strategically, the Balkans were for Russia an access road to the Dardanelles, and for Austria a hinterland in which no other Great Power should be allowed to establish its influence. Historically, the Balkans were a region in which the Habsburg dynasty had been fighting the Moslem Turks long before the westward expansion of Russia under Peter the Great and Catherine the Great had also extended Russian power into southeastern Europe. Ethnically, religiously, and culturally, Russia claimed a much more intimate relationship with the peoples of the Balkans because they were predominantly of southern (Yugo-)Slav origin and were Greek-Orthodox Christian rather than Catholic.

The Balkans were a potential powder keg not only because of the conflicting aims of Austria and Britain on the one hand and of Russia on the other, but because of the progressive enfeeblement of the Turkish Empire, which still ruled a large part of the region. The description of the Austro-Hungarian Empire during the First World War by Wickham Steed, the foreign editor of the London *Times,* as a "carcass suffocating within the wrinkles of its parchment a number of young peoples striving to be born," could be equally applied to the Turkish Empire in the latter part of the nineteenth century. The Greeks had already secured independence from Turkey in the 1820s, but the Bulgarians, Rumanians, Serbs, Montenegrans, and Albanians were still striving to be born. Russia's aim was to accelerate the process of birth in order to eliminate Turkish power from southeastern Europe and to turn the newly independent Balkan states into allies and Russian client-states. The Austrian aim was the reverse, the upholding of Turkish power as a means of containing Russian expansion.

A further source of danger in Europe was the colonial rivalry between the major western powers—Italy, France, and Great Britain—principally as a result of the rival claims of Italy and France over Tunisia, and of France and Britain over Egypt and over commercial access to the interior of the Congo.

During the period from 1871 to 1890 crises and confrontations developed from all these sources, though with the exception of the Russo-Turkish War of 1876–1877, none culminated in an actual war. In the successful management of most of these international crises Bismarck played an important role, and in so doing he succeeded in advancing his own specific goal of assuring the continued isolation of France through an expanding system of alliances under his own leadership.

Bismarck's first effort at alliance building, in the form of the first Three Emperors' League of 1872 between Russia, Austria and Germany, became an early victim of the Russo-Turkish War of 1876–1877. When Russia intervened on behalf of Serbian and Bulgarian uprisings against the Turks in 1876, she expected at the very least a friendly German neutrality as a reward for her own benevolent neutrality towards Prussia in the Franco-Prussian War of 1870–1871. Instead, Bismarck issued a warning to Russia not to attack Austria-Hungary, as Austrian and British protests against Russian action made probable the expansion of the Russo-Turkish conflict into a Russian-Austrian-British war. Russian anger became greater still when the ensuing Congress of Berlin, convened under Bismarck's chairmanship in 1878, limited the war gains of Russia while conceding gains to Austria and Britain, neither of which had fired a shot in the war of 1876–1877. Against the background of deteriorating Russo-German relations, Bismarck concluded the Dual Alliance with Austria-Hungary in October 1879 as a defensive alliance against either a Russian or a joint Russian-French attack. The Dual Alliance was meant as a warning to Russia, but not as a final option against

Russia. After Russian anger had cooled off, Russia did consent to a renewal of the Three Emperors' League in 1881 on a stronger basis than that of 1872.

The Russo-Turkish War and its aftermath revealed the precariousness of the triangular relationship of Russia, Austria, and Germany against the background of the Balkan problem. The Balkans as such meant nothing to Germany, a fact forcefully expressed by Bismarck in his famous 1876 statement that Germany had no interests in the Balkans ''worthy of the healthy bones of a single Pomeranian grenadier.'' The specter of a Russian-Austrian war over the Balkans was, on the other hand, of vital concern to German security, because of the likelihood of an Austrian defeat and the subsequent dismemberment of Austria-Hungary. The disappearance of Austria-Hungary would, in Bismarck's view, have disastrous consequences for the European power balance overall, a view shared by the German government of 1914.

Nor did the Congress of Berlin establish conditions that would have satisfied the small Balkan nations themselves. The congress freed Serbia, Montenegro, and Rumania from Turkish rule without fully satisfying their territorial claims against Turkey. The congress partitioned Bulgaria, leaving its southern portion under Turkish rule. Both with regard to the Balkan problems and the related Austro-Russian rivalry, the Congress of Berlin achieved not a final settlement but merely a postponement of problems. It was over these problems that the second Three Emperors' League disintegrated, soon after it had been concluded, when the union of both parts of Bulgaria in 1885 provoked a new Austro-Russian confrontation.

Meanwhile, Bismarck had added Italy to his alliance system with the conclusion of the defensive Triple Alliance of May 1882 between Italy, Germany, and Austria-Hungary. The initiative for the alliance had originally come from Italy, which was angered over the French seizure of Tunisia in 1881. The prospect in early 1887 of a Bonapartist dictatorship in France under General Boulanger, with its implied threat of a war of revenge against Germany, prompted Bismarck to seek Russian assurances of neutrality in the event of such a war through the Reinsurance Treaty of June 1887. The Russians fully exploited their favorable bargaining position by extracting from Bismarck in return for their own neutrality pledge not only a promise of German neutrality, but a German commitment to active political support in a future Russian drive towards the Dardanelles. Bismarck would not have been Bismarck had he allowed such a commitment to stand without making provisions that it would in all likelihood never be invoked. This was achieved through his unofficial sponsorship of the Mediterranean League of 1887 between Britain, Austria-Hungary, and Italy, whose declared purpose of upholding Turkish territorial integrity lessened the likelihood of another Russian attack against Turkey. Bismarck's final project, shortly before his downfall in 1890, of drawing Britain into his defensive alliance system, failed over the polite rejection of Prime Minister Salisbury. Otherwise, Anglo-German relations were still friendly, having suffered only one setback in 1884–1885 at the time of Germany's first colonial venture in South West Africa.

Of all the major powers, France had had the least reason to be satisfied with developments since 1871, because Bismarck's goal of denying France any allies had been achieved. When Bismarck fell from power in 1890, the French press called the peace of Europe a *Pax Germanica,* a German peace, but the governments of Britain, Italy, Austria-Hungary, and Russia genuinely regretted Bismarck's going, just as they dreaded the prospect of a powerful Germany under the leadership of the inexperienced and vainglorious young William II.

PRELUDE TO WAR

The effectiveness of the Bismarck alliance system as an upholder of the 1871 status quo depended on the skill of its leader and the prestige he could inspire among the leaders of other nations. Bismarck's successors in pre-1914 Germany matched him neither in skill nor in prestige, and the alliance system, which contributed to the preservation of peace between 1871 and 1890, was turned between 1890 and 1914 into a factor contributing to war. The outbreak of the First World War, less than a quarter-century after Bismarck's fall, certainly cannot be solely attributed to the change of guard in Germany. The task of reconciling conflicts, resolving crises, and finding compromises became more difficult after 1890 as the scope of the European power struggle increasingly widened to a global scale, with new contenders such as the modernized Japan entering the stage as active participants. As European imperialism approached its zenith, the young generation of the early 1900s developed boundless energy and ambition. It looked upon the 1870s and 1880s as a mere beginning, and regarded the horizon of Europe as no longer sufficiently broad for the fulfilment of its destiny. Yet in the end it was in Europe that the foundations of European world power collapsed, and they collapsed over basically the same issues that had been the concern of the Great Powers before 1890.

The cornerstone of Bismarck's edifice, the isolation of France, was removed four years after Bismarck's fall when Russia, suspicious over the German nonrenewal of the secret Reinsurance Treaty, concluded a defense alliance with France.

Britain's Position

Within a decade after the Franco-Russian alliance, relations between Germany and Britain also had been basically altered. Anglo-German relations at the turn of the nineteenth and twentieth centuries were complex and by no means preordained to end up on a collision course. There was much in the new Germany that Britain admired, including German scholarship in the sciences and humanities. Some of Britain's leaders who dealt with German problems, such as her minister of war, Lord Haldane, and Eyre Crowe, the influential assistant secretary of state in the British foreign office, knew Germany well. Others, especially in the business world, found Germany a nuisance or worse, because of the impact of German competition, especially in the iron and steel industry. The sharpness of imperial rivalry with France over Egypt and with Russia over Iran at the turn of the century, on the other hand, forced British leaders to consider the possibility of ending Britain's traditional "splendid isolation" and of seeking allies on the continent. The sharp and virtually unanimous condemnation of British policy during the Boer War in South Africa enhanced the British sense of isolation and increased the desire to end British isolation. Britain's colonial secretary Joseph Chamberlain thought Germany the best choice, not only because of her continental power, but because Anglo-German rivalry, by comparison with that involving France and Russia, seemed small. Chamberlain dreamed of a Teutonic league which, in addition to Britain and Germany, would also include the United States. A trial balloon to that effect was launched by Chamberlain in his Leicester speech of November 1899. The Leicester speech and other British approaches between 1898 and 1902 failed to produce results because Germany distrusted British motives and because German chancellor Bülow thought that time was on Germany's side. Germany made it a condition of alliance that Britain become a member of the existing Triple Alliance of Italy, Austria, and Germany, an offer of no interest to Britain considering the scope of Triple Alliance commitments. Bülow's Germany also interpreted the British overtures as signs of British weakness. Assuming that Britain's conflicts of interest with France and Russia were insurmountable, Germany expected her own bargaining power to rise with time, as Britain would have no other option but to return with the request for an alliance.

Britain established a new imperial partnership with Japan in the Far East in 1902, and under the new foreign secretary, Sir Edward Grey, she quickly settled her old colonial disputes with France in the entente of 1904 and with Russia in the entente of 1907. The former conceded Egypt as a British *sphere of influence* in return for British recognition of French control over Morocco; the latter partitioned Iran into Russian and British spheres of influence with a neutral buffer zone in the middle.

The entente agreements of 1904 and 1907 were not, in themselves, military alliances, but they quickly acquired the strength and meaning of such alliances, especially in the minds of the French and Russian governments. The cohesion among the members of the Triple Entente increased in direct proportion to the pressures which a disturbed and alarmed Germany applied in futile efforts to break up the new power alignment of Britain, France and Russia. For the latter three, the upholding of the new entente henceforth became as vital a policy objective as the upholding of the Dual Alliance of 1879 was for Germany and Austria.

Germany's Ambition

The outlines of confrontation of 1914 were clearly established by 1907. These outlines had revealed themselves already in 1906 when, following the German-provoked crisis over Morocco in 1905, Germany and Austria were isolated by France, Britain, Russia, and even Italy in the Algeciras Conference dealing with the Morocco crisis. Beginning in 1911, when Germany and France again quarreled over Morocco, British and French military staffs concluded detailed secret agreements on the transfer of a British Expeditionary Force (BEF) of 170,000 men to France in the event of war with Germany. The final, decisive turn for the worse in Anglo-German relations developed over German naval ambitions. Under its new naval minister, Grand Admiral Alfred von Tirpitz, from 1900 onwards. Germany had embarked on an ambitious naval expansion program. If left unchecked or unanswered the German building program would have predictably destroyed the British *two-power standard,* upon which British naval policy was predicated since the 1880s. The two-power standard meant that the British considered a navy larger than the combined fleets of their two nearest naval competitors essential to the upholding of the integrity of their worldwide empire. Attempts at reaching a negotiated limitation of German naval armaments failed when, during the mission of British war minister Haldane to Berlin in 1912, the Germans demanded an unconditional pledge of British neutrality as a price for their voluntary limitation of naval armaments.

The German push for naval power reflected a trend which equated naval power with world power and which had been reinforced by publications such as *The Influence of Sea Power upon History* in 1890 by American author Alfred Mahan. The Germans also viewed naval power as a status symbol and a visible expression of their newly gained industrial might. Finally, naval power seemed in the early 1900s to be the most important strategic weapons system of the age, permitting the Great Powers to enforce their will over great distances, much as air power would in the 1930s and 1940s, or missile power in the second half of the twentieth century. What Germany failed to appreciate was the disconcerting effect its naval armaments were bound to produce on Britain. In British strategic thinking of the early 1900s, an unofficial balance existed under which Britain, the largest sea power in Europe, would forsake a draft army, and Germany, the strongest land power in Europe, would forsake a large navy. The combination of the strongest land force in Europe with a large German navy created such a strategic imbalance as to be unacceptable in its long-range implications from the British point of view. By refusing to impose voluntary restraints on its armed might, the Germany of the early 1900s gave yet another demonstration of its lacking sense of proportion, a lack which had been characteristically absent from Bismarck's policy. Bismarck had understood well the interrelationship between the restraints of power and foreign political dividends.

Italy

The foreign political isolation of Germany also grew in the early 1900s because of the disaffection and disillusionment of Italy under the old Triple Alliance of 1882, which was technically still in force. From the beginning Italy had predicated the viability of the Triple Alliance on the good relations of its members with Great Britain. Against the background of Germany's rapidly deteriorating relations with Britain, the Triple Alliance, from the Italian standpoint, became increasingly an unacceptable risk factor. Italy had also concluded the alliance in the hope that it would become an aid in the acquisition of overseas colonies. When this proved not to be the case, she turned secretly to France and Russia and sought and obtained the backing of these powers for the seizure of Libya from Turkey in the war of 1911–1912.

Austria-Hungary and the Balkans

By the early 1900s, Germany's sole reliable ally was Austria-Hungary. The Dual Alliance of 1879, which held the powers together, had also undergone significant changes, which turned it progressively from an instrument of peace into a potential cause of war. The change was in the gradual reversal of roles which the powers played within the alliance. Bismarck had never left any doubt in his ally's mind that Germany was the senior partner, and that the alliance could not be abused by Austria-Hungary as an insurance policy against all risks resulting from an aggressive Balkan policy. But that was precisely the use to which Austria began to put the Dual Alliance, especially from 1908 onwards, when she annexed the provinces of Bosnia and Herzegovina. Both provinces had been under Austrian military occupation since 1878 according to the terms of the Congress of Berlin settlement, but this did not, however, authorize annexation.

The nations chiefly affected by the Austrian move were Serbia and Russia, the former because of her own designs on the territory, the latter because of the shift in the Balkan balance of power. Neither country was in a position to effectively oppose the Austrian move, chiefly because of inner exhaustion and the poor state of Russian armaments following that country's defeat in the Far East in the Russo-Japanese War of 1904–1905. Both Russia and Serbia were determined not to let another Austrian-Balkan initiative go unchallenged in the future, when the improved state of Russian armaments allowed for acceptance of greater risks. Though war was avoided, the general effect of the annexation crisis was to incense Serbian nationalism and strengthen Russia's old enmity toward the Habsburg monarchy.

For a brief while Serbian nationalism was deflected in the direction of the Turkish Empire when Serbia, united with Bulgaria, Greece, and Montenegro in the Balkan League, attacked Turkey in October 1912. By December 1912 the Great Powers intervened in this first Balkan War through the instrument of the London Ambassadors' Conference, under the chairmanship of Britain's foreign secretary Edward Grey. The London Ambassadors' Conference, the first concerted Great Power action in the Balkans since the Berlin Congress of 1878, worked out a settlement in the London Treaty of May 1913, which essentially forced Turkey out of Europe, except for the capital of Constantinople and adjacent territory. The London Treaty failed to bring peace, however, and was followed by the second Balkan War, in which the erstwhile allies of the Balkan League fought each other over the Turkish spoils.

The overall result of the Balkan turmoil of 1912–1913 was that it whetted the Serbian appetite for further gains, this time at the expense of Austria-Hungary's own southern Slav territories, with a resulting rise in Austro-Serbian tensions. In October 1913 Austria-Hungary issued an ultimatum to Serbia after the latter had refused to comply with the demand of the 1912–1913 London Ambassadors' Conference that she evacuate Albania. As in the annexation crisis of 1908, Russia again advised Serbia to submit to Austrian demands, but only because Serbian action in Albania had been taken in defiance of all the Great Powers, not merely of Austria-Hungary. At the same time, Russia's foreign minister Sazonov advised Serbia in 1913 that her "promised land" was in the territory of present-day Hungary and that she should prepare for "the future inevitable struggle" with Austria-Hungary.

The Assassination of the Archduke

The "inevitable struggle" between Serbia and Austria-Hungary began with the assassination of Austria's Archduke Francis Ferdinand on June 28, 1914 by Gavrilo Princip, a member of the terrorist Black Hand in Sarajevo, the capital of Bosnia. The motivation of the deed was the fear that once Francis Ferdinand succeeded to the Austrian throne, he might actually solve the nationality problem of the Habsburg Empire by granting autonomy to the southern Slavs. If the southern Slav minority was ever given autonomy, its interest in joining Serbia might be diminished and the Serbian dream of a greater Yugoslavia would be destroyed.

Fundamental to the course of the European crisis which grew from the assassination was the determination of Austria-Hungary not to accept the mediation of others, and to destroy Serbia once and for all as a sovereign state on Austria's southern border. Austria-Hungary's foreign minister Court Leopold Berchtold felt quite clear that such a policy entailed the risk of a world war because of the likelihood of Russian intervention on Serbia's behalf, and through it the involvement of the entire network of Great Power alliances. Berchtold accepted the risk of world war because he equated the alternative of mediation with the abdication of Austria-Hungary as a Great Power, something he considered worse than a world war. The Austrian ultimatum of July 23, 1914, which if accepted by Serbia in all points would have allowed for a peaceful solution to the crisis, was never meant to accepted. Had it been accepted, it would have caused acute embarrassment in Vienna.

The only power capable of restraining Austria was Germany, by issuing a clear and early warning that Germany would not honor her obligations under the Dual Alliance unless Austria made at least an attempt at peaceful mediation. Bismarck would in all likelihood have given such a warning in similar circumstances. The German government of 1914 under Chancellor Bethmann-Hollweg came close to giving such a warning on July 30, 1914, at a time when the news of Russia's general mobilization was about to render futile any further efforts at crisis management. At the beginning of the crisis, on July 5, 1914, the Germans had instead encouraged Austria to proceed with the policy of force against Serbia, with Emperor William's famous "Blank Cheque" promise of loyal German support. The promise was given through a fatal miscalculation that the Austro-Serbian crisis could be kept localized and that the entente powers would not intervene.

Russia and France, on the other hand, were convinced from an early stage of the July crisis that the real issue was not between Serbia and Austria, but that Germany was merely using the Balkan crisis for the bigger purpose of wrecking the Triple Entente, much as she had tried to use the Morocco crisis of 1905 to destroy the Anglo-French entente of 1904. This belief was confirmed when the harsh terms of the Austrian ultimatum of July 23, 1914 became known.

Declarations of War

The view that Germany was manipulating the Austro-Serbian crisis for its own ends of damaging the Triple Entente also gained ground in London, especially among the two principal policy advisers of Grey, Undersecretary Nicolson and Assistant Secretary Crowe. Grey nevertheless attempted mediation, for which he judged Britain to be singularly qualified because Britain's hands were, in Grey's own expression, "free," due to the absence of a formal alliance commitment. The two major flaws of Grey's mediation were its late beginning, July 20, 1914 and his failure to appreciate fully both the motives and the determination of Austrian policy. From his own British ambassadors in the European capitals, Grey had been fully and exhaustively informed concerning both from a very early phase of the July crisis. His failure to take these warnings seriously before July 23, 1914, the date of the Austrian ultimatum, may well have reflected his own doubts as to whether Austria was actually capable of making the kind of policy which events subsequently revealed she did. Grey's most promising mediation proposal, the so-called halt-in-Belgrade proposal of July 29, 1914, was the first one which did take Austria's motive of preserving Great Power credibility into account. The proposal offered Austria satisfaction by allowing her to occupy the Serbian capital of Belgrade on condition that she accepted subsequent Great Power mediation of the Austro-Serbian quarrel. Like the German warning issued to Vienna on July 30, Grey's halt-in-Belgrade proposal came too late. News of the Russian general mobilization prompted the German declaration of war on Russia on August 1, and the mechanics of the German Schlieffen Plan, prepared in expectation of a two-front war against Russia and France, prompted the German declarations of war against France on August 3 and the German invasion of neutral Belgium on August 4, 1914. The German violation of Belgian neutrality prompted Britain's declaration of war against Germany on the same day.

The greatest folly of European leadership in 1914 and in the years preceding the July crisis consisted in the fact that Europe's leaders were conducting the business of international relations by the same methods and rules as those which had determined international relations in the seventeenth and eighteenth centuries. The new technology of the nineteenth century had profoundly altered the rules of war and it was no longer possible to define war as merely a continuation of politics by different means, as the strategist Clausewitz had done. At the same time, the industrial age had accumulated vast social problems, which a sustained modern war was likely to ignite into revolutions, especially among the losers of the war. Such an analysis may not have been readily apparent before 1914, but it cannot be said that there had been no warnings. Karl Marx understood the relationship of modern war and social revolution, because he had observed it in the Paris Commune uprising during the Franco-Prussian War. The Second (Socialist) International understood it because it had observed such a relationship in the Russian Revolution at the end of the Russo-Japanese War of 1904–1905. Britain's foreign secretary Grey among the foreign ministers of Europe in 1914 had a better appreciation of the likely consequences of a world war for Europe than most, but even he would have been appalled had be been able to foresee the actual state of postwar Europe in July 1914.

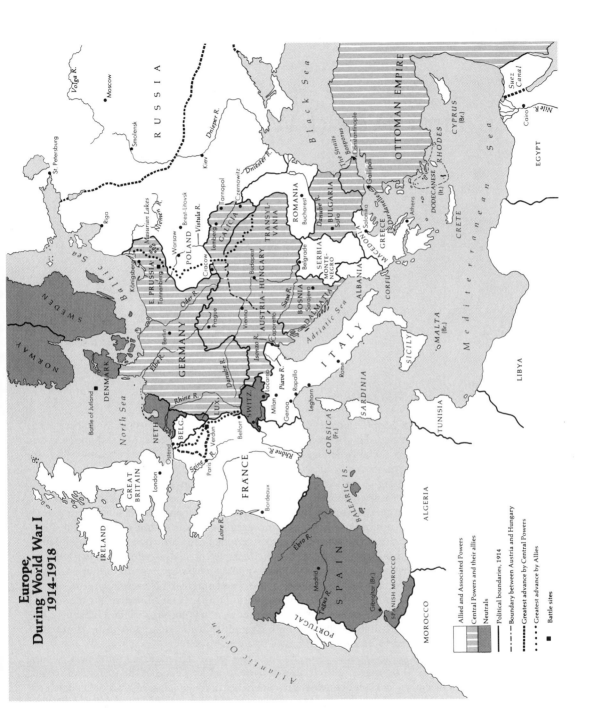

Europe,
During World War I
1914-1918

ATLANTIC Ocean

IRELAND

GREAT
BRITAIN

London

NETH.

BELG.

LUX.

FRANCE

Paris

Bordeaux

Loire R.

Seine R.

Verdun

Belfort

Rhône R.

SPAIN

Madrid

Ebro R.

Tagus R.

PORTUGAL

Gibraltar (Br.)

SPANISH MOROCCO

MOROCCO

ALGERIA

TUNISIA

LIBYA

NORWAY

SWEDEN

DENMARK

Battle of Jutland

North Sea

Baltic Sea

Riga

GERMANY

Berlin

Elbe R.

Oder R.

Rhine R.

Ostend

SWITZ.

Locarno

Milan

Genoa

Rapallo

Leghorn

CORSICA
(Fr.)

SARDINIA

BALEARIC IS.

Danube R.

Prague

Vienna

AUSTRIA-HUNGARY

Königsberg

Tannenberg

E. PRUSSIA

Masurian Lakes

Nemen R.

Warsaw

Brest-Litovsk

POLAND

Vistula R.

Cracow

GALICIA

Lemberg

Tarnopol

Czernowitz

Dniester R.

TRANSYL-
VANIA

BOSNIA

Sarajevo

DALMATIA

Isonzo R.

Caporetto

Piave R.

ITALY

Rome

Adriatic Sea

ALBANIA

CORFU

MACEDONIA

GREECE

Athens

Salonika

SERBIA

MONTE-
NEGRO

Belgrade

Bucharest

ROMANIA

Danube R.

BULGARIA

Sofia

Black Sea

Constantinople

Gallipoli

The Straits

Bosporus

Dardanelles

OTTOMAN EMPIRE

RHODES

DODECANESE
(It.)

CRETE

MALTA
(Br.)

CYPRUS
(Br.)

Mediterranean Sea

EGYPT

Cairo

Nile R.

Suez Canal

RUSSIA

Moscow

Volga R.

Smolensk

Dnieper R.

Kiev

St. Petersburg

SICILY

| Allied and Associated Powers |
| Central Powers and their allies |
| Neutrals |
| Political boundaries, 1914 |
| Boundary between Austria and Hungary |
| Greatest advance by Central Powers |
| Greatest advance by Allies |
| ■ Battle sites |

2

The First World War

THE NATURE OF THE CONFLICT

In its resolution adopted at the Basel Congress of 1912, the Second (Socialist) International had warned the governments of Europe that a world war would spell the end of the established social order and the beginning of proletarian revolution. The very thought of the "monstrosity of a world war," the resolution stated, would inevitably call forth the "indignation and revolt of the working class."

When war came in August 1914, the response was not social revolution but an outpouring of national and patriotic frenzy that united social classes and ethnic groups in all the major countries of Europe as no previous event within memory had done.

In Britain, the outbreak of war suspended the bitter controversy over Irish Home Rule, which had pushed the nation to the brink of civil war before August 1914. In France and Germany the Socialist parties quickly exchanged their traditional role of opposition to one of support, entering the government of "Sacred Union" in the French case and, in the case of Germany, voting for the first time ever for the defense appropriations of the government. In the multinational empires of the Habsburgs and of Tsar Nicholas II, habitually feuding nationalities pledged support to their monarch in what appeared to be the larger cause of common defense.

Of Europe's two great prewar conflicts—social strife and national rivalry—the latter controlled human emotions almost to the total exclusion of the former in August 1914. The causes of such behavior were the belief in the waging of a just war of defense as well as the sensation of equality which a common patriotic effort temporarily established among the divided classes.

The patriotic fervor of 1914 was not yet dimmed by the awareness of either the duration or the sacrifices of the coming struggle. The war was expected to be short, because of the weight and power of the new armaments. Some of the professional military knew otherwise and had said so as far back as 1890. German chief of staff Helmut Moltke, Sr. had prophesied in 1890 that a future war would not be decided in a few campaigns but might become a ''seven years' war,'' or even a ''thirty years' war.''

War and the New Technology

The length of the First World War was, in fact, largely the result of the new technology which produced the machine gun, rapid fire artillery, poison gas, the flame thrower and, in the final stages, long-range artillery which, in the German-invented ''Paris gun'' of 1918 had a range of seventy miles. The aircraft added a new dimension to war little more than a decade after the Wright Brothers' first flight in a heavier-than-air device in the United States. As a reconnaissance vehicle, the airplane played a significant role from the outset of the war, enabling, for example, the British to detect the vulnerable points in the German advance on Paris during the Battle of the Marne in September 1914. Subsequently, the airplane developed quickly into a tactical battlefield weapon of formidable strength, though its full strategic potential as a bomber of industrial and civilian targets was not fully realized until the end of the war. The submarine, an operational weapon since its fitting with the Diesel engine for surface cruising in 1910, proved to have a potency beyond all expectation. It also turned out to be a new weapon of momentous political consequences, providing the immediate cause for America's entry into the war in 1917.

The revolution in weapons technology was not matched by a corresponding progress in the mobility of armies on the battlefield. The armies of the First World War were still moving about on foot or horseback much as they had done during the Napoleonic Wars a century earlier. The disproportion between vastly enhanced firepower and unchanged mobility gave the First World War its peculiar quality of a war of siege, in which the opposing armies faced one another in unbroken lines of trenches across the face of entire nations. Defense in depth proved superior to attack owing to the inability of the attacker to turn a tactical breakout into a strategic breakthrough. The tank, conceived by the British as a ''trench-crossing machine'' and introduced into battle in 1916, might have broken the strategic deadlock but for lack of appreciation of its full potential at the time.

War Economies

The speedy changeover of the war of 1914 from a colorful, late-summer exercise into a grim and lengthy confrontation necessitated the mobilization of national economies for war purposes to an unprecedented degree. In the mobilization of human and material resources under various schemes of ''war socialism,'' the advanced industrial nations of Britain, France and Germany were most successful. The British Army, which entered World War I with 1,330 machine guns, eventually received 240,000 machine guns before the war ended, in addition to 28,000 artillery pieces and 55,000 aircraft. France, though she lost half her coal mines and two-thirds of her steel industry early in the war, increased daily shell output from 9,000 in September 1914, to 300,000 in 1915.

In Germany, industrialist Walter Rathenau rationed scarce strategic raw materials through the Raw Materials Board in order to counter the impact of the British blockade. By 1916 Germany had drafted all male labor between the ages of 17 and 60 for war purposes under the Auxiliary Service law. Although German armaments production performed great feats under the Hindenburg Program in the final years of World War I, the German war economy never succeeded in offsetting the impact of the British blockade on the food supply. Daily food rations in Germany were cut from 1,350 calories in 1916 to 1,000 calories in 1917, a starvation diet. The poor potato harvest of 1916 produced wide-spread hunger during the ensuing *Rübenwinter* (turnip winter), the turnip becoming the principal staple for the poor. Neither the German nor the Russian dynasty shared or even appreciated the hunger of the people in their cities, which explains their lack of popular support when events approached a crisis point, in 1917 in Russia and in 1918 in Germany.

The Role of Women

The war had a profound social impact on the role of women—first in Europe, then from 1917 onwards in the United States. Female industrial labor, though not unknown before 1914, became much more widespread under the conditions of total war. The British wartime government recognized the importance of female labor from the start, when including women in the provisions of the Defense of the Realm Act (DORA) in August 1914. The significant role played by women in the war economies had an appreciable impact on women's quest for social and political emancipation after the war. The granting of female suffrage after World War I in most European democracies, though not Switzerland, was one tangible gain. The social role of women in World War I was also reflected in fashion changes, particularly the raising of the hemline from prewar ankle length to postwar knee length. The prewar fashion styles were shown to be impractical and even dangerous in the operation of industrial machinery.

The Media

The First World War set trends also in the emergence of the news media as shapers of public opinion. World War I was the first European war in which the home fronts became eyewitnesses to the events on the battle front through photography and the newsreel. The press in all the belligerent countries played a major part in steering and influencing the public mood. In the propaganda war for influencing neutral, particularly American public opinion, the British were early and sure winners over their German competitors because of the common language and the adverse publicity of German occupation methods in Belgium. The report of Lord Bryce concerning German atrocities in Belgium, though unsubstantiated, had a powerful effect on American public opinion. In Britain Hugh Seton-Watson, in his capacity as foreign editor of the London *Times,* played an important role in the coming dismemberment of Austria-Hungary by his advocacy of independence for Austria-Hungary's Slavic nationalities.

FAILURE OF THE 1914 OFFENSIVE PLANS

By 1912 France and Russia had worked out a coordinated plan for attacking Germany from east and west. Russia was to invade Germany with an army of 800,000 men on the fifteenth day of mobilization, while France would attack Germany on either side of the fortified position of Metz in accordance with Plan XVII of the French general staff. French chief of staff Joseph J. Joffre had initially planned to invade Germany via neutral Belgium but was overruled on this issue by his own government, because of the predictably adverse response such an invasion route would have provoked in Britain. Britain had committed its Expeditionary Force (BEF) of six highly trained divisions to the defense of France since 1911.

The Austro-German Dual Alliance of 1879 had not resulted in a comparable coordination of military plans of the Central Powers, initially because Bismarck, the author of the Dual Alliance, did not wish Austria-Hungary to be tempted into a reckless Balkan policy on the basis of assured German military support. After the turn of the century, Austria and Germany disagreed on their military priorities, the former favoring a knockout blow against Russia, the latter deciding on a "France first" strategy.

The Schlieffen Plan

Judging France the more dangerous opponent, German chief of staff Alfred von Schlieffen developed a daring plan in 1905 which concentrated overwhelming German power against France, while leaving the German eastern borders virtually unprotected in the early stage of war. The idea was to beat France quickly in a campaign lasting no more than six weeks, during which time it was hoped that Russia would be unable to complete her mobilization. By the time Russia was fully mobilized, Germany would be in a position to shift her forces eastward and deal with the threat of a Russian invasion. Time, and the availability of excellent railroad communications permitting rapid troop shifts from one end of the country to the other, were of the essence to the success of the Schlieffen Plan.

As events soon showed, neither the French Plan XVII nor the German Schlieffen Plan succeeded. The French attacks on either side of Metz, which Charles de Gaulle was later to describe as an eyewitness, broke down in withering German defensive fire which claimed three hundred thousand French casualties in the first month of the war.

Meanwhile, four German armies had begun to execute the Schlieffen Plan with the invasion of neutral Belgium and Luxembourg. After an initial slowdown caused by Belgian resistance at Liège, the German advance gained threatening momentum from August 18 onwards. Having covered 180 miles in fifteen days, the Germans reached Amiens on September 1, 1914. The following day, the Geman First Army under Kluck and the Second Army under Bülow reached the Marne and German advance units could see the needle of the Eiffel tower on the horizon.

The Marne

By early September, General Joffre's countermeasure, which included the creation of a new army, the Sixth, under General Maunoury, and the purging of timid army commanders such as General Lanrezac, began to take effect. A flank attack by General Maunoury on the German First Army on September 5 forced the latter to open a thirty-mile gap with its neighboring Second Army, through which poured the forces of the BEF. German chief of staff Moltke (the younger), whose headquarters remained far to the rear in Luxembourg, ordered a general retreat from the Marne on September 8. The Allies had won the Battle of the Marne in part because Joffre, despite the defeats of August, had managed to achieve superior strength over his enemy at the decisive place and the decisive moment in early September 1914. By mid-

September, the German front had retreated behind a line running from the Aisne to Noyon and Verdun.

After the Battle of the Marne, the focal point shifted to Flanders and the North Sea coast, where both sides tried to outflank one another in the "race to the sea." The Germans failed in their attempt to seize the channel ports of Calais and Boulogne, which British forces had evacuated during the retreat of August 1914. The costly Battle of Ypres, a German-British clash lasting until November 11, 1914 extended the stalemate to the northern end of the western front. By the end of 1914, the western front ran from Nieuport on the North Sea to the Swiss border in an unbroken line of trenches and field fortifications.

The Eastern Front

In the east, too, rapid movement had given way to stalemate by December 1914. Although Russia had managed to mobilize only a third of her army by the end of August 1914, she made good on her promise of invading Germany. Between August 17 and 21, 1914, two Russian armies, the First (Njemen) and Second (Narev) under Pavel Rennenkampf and Alexander Samsonov invaded East Prussia, which was defended by one German army under Max von Prittwitz. Based on a plan worked out by one of Prittwitz' staff officers, Max Hoffman, the Germans left only a thin defensive screen in front of Rennenkampf's First Army, while encircling and destroying the Russian Second Army in the Battle of Tannenberg between August 23 and August 30, 1914. The Russian First Army escaped a similar fate through hasty retreat after the Battle of the Masurian Lakes in September 1914.

At the cost of 13,000 casualties, the Germans had won a brilliant defensive victory at Tannenberg, in which 125,000 Russian prisoners were taken. Tannenberg had a lasting demoralizing effect on the Russian army of World War I. It also established the military reputation of Erich Ludendorff and Paul von Hindenburg, who had taken over the command in East Prussia from General Prittwitz.

In the larger context of the war of 1914, Tannenberg had had a positive effect on Allied fortunes. News of the Russian invasion prompted the German High Command to withdraw two army corps from the French front to East Prussia, where they arrived too late to participate in the battle. Indirectly, the Russian invasion of East Prussia, though disastrous for the Russian army, may have saved Paris in 1914.

Russia's first encounter with the forces of Austria-Hungary was much more successful. An Austrian offensive, launched between the Vistula and Bug rivers on August 23, 1914 against four Russian armies, turned into a major Austrian defeat with the loss of 350,000 men and the abandonment of eastern Galicia and the Bukovina province. The Russian victory was facilitated by foreknowledge of Austria's plans, which had been betrayed to her before the war by the Austrian staff officer Alfred Redl.

Encouraged by these gains, the Russians mounted a second invasion attempt against Germany with the attack on Silesia in November 1914. It too ended in defeat for the Russians with the Battle of Lodz of November 11, 1914.

Austria-Hungary's attempts to crush little Serbia had meanwhile failed. After taking the Serbian capital of Belgrade on December 2, 1914, Austria's forces were evicted from Belgrade by Serbia's able General Putnik in mid-December 1914 as part of a general Austrian retreat.

Surveying the campaigns of 1914, General Falkenhayn, Moltke's successor as chief of staff, concluded that by the end of 1914 Germany would be in a position to inflict a decisive defeat on her enemies only if she secured a separate peace on one front first, either in the east or the west.

1915: THE HARDENING STALEMATE

French chief of staff Joffre concluded from the 1914 battles that Germany could be crushed, if the Allies increased their strength in artillery and manpower. With superior forces, Joffre intended to crush the so-called Noyon bulge, the German front line from Flanders to the Vosges mountains. Joffre predicted an Allied victory and the break-through to the Rhine by fall 1915.

The attack on the Noyon bulge was launched between February and October 1915. At the furthest point of penetration, the attack yielded 3,000 yards. For these gains, the British paid with 60,000 casualties in the single battle of Loos in September 1915, the French 150,000 casualties in the Champagne offensive of October 1915. After Loos, the British replaced BEF commander Sir John French with Sir Douglas Haig, but it was doubtful whether the change in command could, by itself, also change the nature of this war.

1915 witnessed the introduction of poison gas, which the Germans used on the western front for the first time in the Battle of Ypres of April 1915. The Ypres attack inflicted 70,000 casualties on the Allies, but the Germans, preoccupied with the eastern front in 1915, were not in a position to exploit their gains.

Gallipoli

The British had hoped to break the 1915 deadlock with an amphibious assault on the Gallipoli peninsula, guarding the entrance to the stategic Dardanelles straits. If successful, the Gallipoli campaign would drive Turkey out of the war, open a supply route to tsarist Russia for badly needed ammunitions, and conceivably contribute to an early collapse of Austria-Hungary.

The idea was that of Winston Churchill, the First Lord of the Admiralty. It was in the best tradition of British peripheral strategy, taking maximum advantage of su-perior British sea power and avoiding the costly head-on collisions, which had already claimed far too many lives on the plains of Western Europe.

The Gallipoli campaign, perhaps the Allies' greatest strategic opportunity to win the war, turned into an Allied disaster because of faulty execution and timid prose-cution. The Allies cast away the element of surprise by attacking Turkish positions with naval gunfire in February and March 1915 without immediate follow-up land-ings. The landings, when finally carried out chiefly with Australian and New Zealand divisions in April 1915, found Turkish defenses well prepared. Before long, the Gal-lipoli campaign developed into a smaller replica of the war of siege, so familiar from the western front. By November 1915 Britain's war minister Lord Kitchener ordered evacuation, which was carried out efficiently by January 1916. Britain lost another quarter-million casualties. Churchill was made the scapegoat and had to resign. A reputation for strategic amateurishness continued to haunt Churchill well into the Sec-ond World War. In the case of Gallipoli, it was undeserved.

German Operations in 1915

The Allied cause suffered setbacks elsewhere in southeastern Europe in 1915. Alerted by the dangers inherent in the Gallipoli campaign, Germany, supported by Austria, overran Serbia in October 1915. Bulgaria, which had been leaning towards Austria before the war, entered the war on the Central Powers side in September 1915. The defeat of Serbia and the addition of Bulgaria to the Central Powers cause established a direct link between Turkey and Germany for the first time since 1914. It also isolated and neutralized the Allied Expeditionary Force, which had been established under the command of General Maurice Serrail at Salonika, Greece in October 1915. As a force designed to strengthen Serbian resistance, the Salonika expedition came too late. It was to assume unexpected importance in the final stage of the war, when its breakout in September 1918 triggered the collapse of Bulgaria, Turkey, and Austria.

German operations against Serbia and German support to the successful Turkish defense of Gallipoli were secondary to the principal German aim of 1915, which was to drive Russia out of the war. Encouraged by the weak Russian showing at Tannenberg and Lodz in 1914, Hindenburg and Ludendorff wished to deal Russia a decisive blow in 1915 by cutting off the bulk of Russian forces in Poland. German chief of staff Falkenhayn, always concerned by the strength of the western Allies, did not release the strength required for such a sweeping strategy. The German-Austrian offensive of early May 1915, undertaken between Tarnov and Gorlice on the eastern front, was thus more limited in its scope. By August 1915 the Central Powers had taken both Warsaw and the Brest-Litovsk fortress, and by the end of the year all of Russian Poland, Lithuania, and half of Latvia was conquered. Russia lost 3,000 guns and 300,000 prisoners. The Central Powers had gained a major tactical victory. The strategic goal of driving Russia out of the war still eluded them.

Italy

Italy had joined the Allies on May 23, 1915, but it remained unclear for some time whether that fact constituted an asset or a liability for the Allied cause. Italy's sympathies had been on the Allied side from the beginning of the war, the history of the Triple Alliance of 1882 notwithstanding. In 1914 Italy did not join the Allies, in part because sizable Italian forces were still required for the pacification of Libya, which Italy had conquered in her colonial war of 1911–1912. Italy's continued neutrality was in part the result of negotiations with both the Allies and the Central Powers, in which Italy weighed the Allied offers for joining the war against the Central Powers offers for staying out of it. Germany, concerned by Austria's poor military showing in 1914–1915, urged Austria to make territorial concessions to keep Italy neutral. Reluctantly, Austria offered Italy the Trentino in March 1915, an offer the Allies easily topped in the secret Treaty of London of April 1915 with promises which also included the South Tyrol, Goricia, Trieste, and some of the Dalmatian islands.

Italy's first offensives of the war, undertaken in the four battles along the Isonzo river between June and November 1915, yielded no results. Italy's entry into the war did not divert sufficient Austrian strength to prevent the conquest of Serbia in October 1915.

1916: TOWARDS MUTUAL EXHAUSTION

At the Chantilly military conference of December 1915, French chief of staff Joffre drew up Allied plans for 1916, which were designed to deny the Germans the advantage of interior lines by attacking on several fronts simultaneously.

Verdun

German chief of staff Falkenhayn, in turn, decided to launch an all-out attack against the French fortifications at Verdun in early 1916. Verdun was chosen as a target for both psychological and strategic reasons. Verdun was the principal roadblock on the way to Paris and its successful defense was equated in the French mind with victory and survival. If Verdun fell, French military and civilian morale was likely to collapse.

The attack on Verdun might have succeeded if undertaken on the date scheduled, February 12, 1916, because French troop strength was not equal to the challenge at that time. Postponed for weather reasons until February 21, the Battle of Verdun quickly developed into the costliest battle of attrition of the entire war. At the point of maximum advance, the German offensive captured the key forts of Douaumont and Vaux, without being able to cut the lifeline to Verdun, the "Sacred Way," over which reinforcements continued to pour in, sometimes at the rate of six thousand trucks every 24 hours. In order to avoid the total destruction of the defenders, Marshal Philippe Pétain, the "hero of Verdun," rotated a total of sixty-six French divisions through the battle between February and July 1916.

With the Verdun attack, the Germans wrested the initiative from the Allies, and the relief offensives mounted by Britain, Russia, and Italy were dictated by German pressure, not Allied calculation.

The British army, reinforced by draftees since the adoption of the Military Service Acts of April 1916, took control of the larger sector of the western front from Ypres to the Somme. On July 1, 1916, Britain mounted a relief attack on the Somme, which was meant to draw German power away from hard-pressed Verdun. The first day of the Somme offensive claimed 58,000 British casualties. In the second Somme attack of mid-September, Haig committed the tank to battle for the first time, but with thirty-two vehicles the numbers were too small to have an appreciable impact on the battle overall.

The British Somme attacks had yielded very little ground, a six-mile penetration at the furthest point, but they had fulfilled their purpose of helping the French survive at Verdun. By October 1916 France recaptured both Douaumont and Vaux. French casualties at Verdun overall numbered 1.2 million, as against 800,000 German.

The Eastern Front

An Italian relief attack in the fifth battle of Isonzo between March 11 and 29, 1916 had failed. Austria attacked on the Trentino front in mid-May 1916, hoping to inflict a major defeat and force Italy to sue for peace. By June, Italy had suffered 280,000 casualties and the loss of 300 guns. The Germans, preoccupied with Verdun, had not sent the reinforcements which might have enabled Austria to turn the tactical victory into a strategic one.

Austria's gains in Italy were achieved at the expense of Austrian strength in Russia, where General Brusilov unleashed his powerful offensive against the thinned-out Austrian lines on June 4, 1916. In what was destined to become Russia's last successful operation of the war, the Brusilov offensive cost Austria 350,000 prisoners and the Bukovina province. Many of the Austrian prisoners came from units of Slavic nationality, whose support for the Habsburg cause had appreciably declined in the third year of the war.

The Russian gains of June prompted Rumania to enter the war on the Allied side on August 27, 1916. Rumania joined from motives of territorial gain at Austria-Hungary's expense. The territories promised Rumania by the Allies were Transylvania and the Bukovina, which contained ethnic Rumanian populations and which Rumania had coveted since before the war.

The sudden addition of a new enemy in the East took the Germans by surprise and compounded the Central Powers' crisis, which had been triggered by the gains of Brusilov's offensive. The crisis was mastered by December 1916 when Falkenhayn, dismissed as chief of staff in August, invaded Rumania in his new capacity as field commander. In early December the Rumanian capital of Bucharest was taken, together with the oil fields of Ploesti. With German help, the shattered Austrian front in Russia had also been rebuilt in October 1916 at a cost of over a million casualties to the Russians.

For both sides, the balance sheet of 1916 reaffirmed once more the stalemate of September 1914. In upholding it, the Allies and the Central Powers had had to reach ever more deeply into their national reserves of blood and treasure, with the limits of human endurance and the point of exhaustion rapidly approaching.

1917: THE LIMITS OF HUMAN ENDURANCE

By 1917, the war had not only killed and maimed millions of men, it had also shaken up the political and military leadership which had led its peoples into war three years earlier with the expectation of a brief conflict.

New Leaders

Lloyd George had replaced Herbert Asquith as British prime minister in December 1916 with the promise of more vigorous leadership. In Germany, the resignation of Chancellor Bethmann-Hollweg in July 1917 ended the contest between civilian and military authority and paved the way for a virtual military dictatorship under Ludendorff. In Austria-Hungary, the death of Emperor Francis Joseph in November 1916 left the tottering Habsburg Empire in the inexperienced and irresolute hands of Emperor Charles I, of whom it was said in Vienna that he was thirty years of age, looked like twenty, and talked like ten. In Russia, Tsar Nicholas II had assumed personal command of the Russian forces after the disastrous defeats of 1915, thereby identifying the dynasty with the reverses yet to come and preparing his own downfall in 1917. In Italy, Prime Minister Salandra, who had led his country into war during "glorious May" of 1915, had fallen from power after the Austrian victory in the Trentino attack of 1916. In France Aristide Briand yielded the prime ministership to tough Georges Clemenceau in 1917, when French spirits were at their lowest and need for strong leadership at its greatest. In the United States, Woodrow Wilson had been reelected to the presidency in November 1916 largely on the strength of his promise to keep the U.S. out of World War I.

The changes in military and naval command were scarcely less sweeping. In France, Joffre was replaced by Nivelle in 1916, in Germany, the Hindenburg-Ludendorff team replaced Falkenhayn after the German Verdun debacle. Haig stayed as commander of the BEF, but Kitchener was killed on June 5, 1916 on the cruiser *Hampshire* en route to Russia. Tirpitz, father of the German navy, resigned as naval minister in 1916 to protest his government's opposition to unrestricted submarine warfare. Italy's Cadorna became a victim of Italy's near-fatal defeat at Caporetto in 1917 and was replaced by Armando Diaz as chief of staff.

The Yearning for Peace

The question being asked by ordinary people in 1917 was why the war was being prolonged, if the original defensive aim had been accomplished by all the major powers. The yearning for peace combined with the suspicion that the governments of Europe were needlessly prolonging the conflict for reasons of territorial gain and greed.

To varying degrees all the belligerent powers revealed the strains of war and the limits of human endurance by 1917. In Russia, popular outrage over the high losses of 1916 combined with hunger and the conviction of tsarist incompetence to produce the revolution of March 1917. The Austrian naval mutiny at the Cattaro base in February 1917 had indicated both the social and national unrest in the Habsburg Empire. In France, the army suffered a collapse of morale in the widespread mutiny following the loss of 120,000 men in the Nivelle offensive of April 1917. French reserves that were marched off to battle issued shouts of ''bah-bah-bah'' to underscore their fate as helpless sheep being driven to slaughter.

In the United Kingdom, the Easter Rebellion of April 1916 had reopened the emotional Irish issue and had shattered the national unity of August 1914. There was restlessness among Commonwealth troops, the Australians attributing their high casualties at Gallipoli and at the Somme to poor British leadership. No less a patriotic and highly decorated soldier than Britain's famed World War I poet Siegfried Sassoon, a veteran of the murderous battles of Mametz Wood and the Somme, published his famous ''Statement to his Commanding Officer'' in 1917, in which he questioned the motives of the British government in prolonging the war and accused his government of deceiving the suffering troops.

In Germany, the Social Democratic party, a supporter of the war effort, broke up in April 1917 over the issue of war aims, and in July 1917 a majority of German Reichstag deputies passed a peace resolution calling for peace without annexation of foreign territory.

On August 1, 1917 Pope Benedict XV summed up the yearning for peace with an initiative of his own, proposing a ''just and durable'' peace, based on the ''moral force of right'' and urging the return of all conquered territory.

Spoils of War

The governments of Europe did not respond to these calls because, having invested so much blood and money in the war, they believed it to be an unalterable mandate for the strengthening of national security through the annexation of foreign territory, or the total destruction of the opponent. In addition, the European Allies had concluded several secret agreements among themselves for the distribution of territorial spoils. Russia had been promised Constantinople by Britain in 1915, Italy had been promised major gains at Austria-Hungary's expense in the London treaty of 1915, France and Russia had agreed on the severance of the Rhineland from Germany.

German annexationist aims increased as the war progressed. As early as September 1914 Chancellor Bethmann-Hollweg drafted the outlines of a German *Siegfriede* (peace based on victory), which included the annexation of the French channel coast all the way to Boulogne and the control of Belgium. In Africa, the German program called for the annexation of the Belgian Congo as well as French and Portuguese colonies. In the east, German ambitions increased from the goal of a "frontier strip" in Russian Poland to the much greater goal of the dismemberment of Russia. The latter goal was attained in the Peace of Brest-Litovsk of March 1918, following the collapse of Russia. Under the Brest-Litovsk peace, Russia lost 32 percent of her arable land, 75 percent of her coal and iron resources, 33 percent of her factories, and 26 percent of her railroads. The Brest-Litovsk peace was short-lived, to be sure, being overtaken and obviated by events in western Europe and Germany's own collapse in November 1918. Its significance as an indicator of German imperialist ambitions in World War I thereby was not diminished.

The annexationist war aims of the European powers also doomed the American peace initiatives which Woodrow Wilson had been undertaking since 1915. During his peace mission to Europe of 1915, the president's advisor Colonel House found the Germans intractable on the question of Belgium and Russian Poland, and the Allies not yet interested in a peace conference. In December 1916, the Germans issued a call for peace negotiations, stating their own war aims as the "existence, honor and freedom of development of the peoples of the Central Powers," a definition broad enough to cover any territorial annexation. When Wilson asked both sides to state their war aims in December 1916, the Allies cited aims such as the restoration of Belgium, which the United States also supported, without, however, mentioning their own annexationist objectives.

Wilson, satisfied with neither position, outlined his own ideas for peace in his Senate speech of January 22, 1917, which foreshadowed his *Fourteen Points* of January 1918. Central to Wilson's message was the theme of a "peace without victory." Despite the many signs of strain, such a peace was precisely not the aim of either camp in Europe. The American entry into the war only a few months later once more raised Allied hopes that the future peace would indeed be one of victory. The Germans, being similarly encouraged by the collapse of Russia in March 1917, entertained similar hopes for their own cause.

THE COLLAPSE OF RUSSIA AND THE UNITED STATES' ENTRY INTO THE WAR

The collapse of the Russian monarchy in March 1917 was initially applauded in the capitals of the Allies on the assumption, soon shown to be utterly false, that the revolution would energize the Russian war effort, just as the French Revolution of 1789 had given birth to a militant democratic nationalism in France. The collapse in July 1917 of the last Russian offensive of the war, named the *Kerensky Offensive* after the new head of the Russian provisional government Alexander Kerensky, revealed the true meaning of the Russian Revolution for the war. Russia was exhausted and eager for peace. The Germans gave it, strictly on their own terms, at Brest-Litovsk in March 1918.

While Russia was leaving the war, the United States was entering it. The immediate cause of American involvement in the European war grew out of the British-German naval contest. Until 1917, Britain had used her naval power against Germany with maximum effect and at minimum risk. When the war started in 1914, the British public expected an immediate Anglo-German naval showdown, a Trafalgar in the Nelsonian tradition, in which the superior Royal Navy would send the German imperial fleet to the bottom of the ocean. No such Trafalgar materialized. Instead, the British used their superior naval strength for a "distant blockade," in which the fleet blocked the North Sea route into the Atlantic by its mere presence at the home base in the Orkneys. Only once did the main bodies of the British and German fleets collide, in the Battle of Jutland of May 31, 1916. At Jutland, the British lost more ships and men than did their German opponents, a fact which did not in the least alter the strategic balance, which continued to be in Britain's favor. The German navy could not lift the British blockade after Jutland any more than it had been able to do beforehand.

The Submarine

By the end of 1916 the German High Command decided to use the submarine as a weapon of last resort. By using the submarine without restrictions in a declared war zone around the British Isles, against both enemy and neutral shipping, it was believed that Britain could be starved out before "the harvest of 1917."

Germany had employed unrestricted submarine warfare once before, in 1915, with the result of very nearly driving the United States into the war on Britain's side, following the loss of 128 American lives in the sinking of the British ship *Lusitania* on May 7, 1915. A rupture in U.S.-German diplomatic relations was narrowly avoided, when another British vessel with Americans abroad, the *Arabic,* was sunk by a German submarine on August 19, 1915.

Having suspended unrestricted submarine warfare in 1915, the Germans resumed it in January 1917. On February 4, 1917 the United States severed diplomatic relations, and on April 6, 1917 the Congress declared war. Whatever slim chances there were of avoiding open war after February were destroyed by the clumsy German maneuver of inducing Mexico into becoming Germany's ally with the promise of the recovery of Texas, Arizona, and New Mexico. The so-called Zimmerman Note which offered Mexico the deal (named after the German foreign secretary), was intercepted and deciphered by the British and subsequently published in the United States.

The German High Command thought the risk of an American entry into the war acceptable. Not only would Britain be starved out before the United States could enter the European war, according to the German estimate, but Admiral Holtzendorff, the German naval chief, gave his "word of honor" that no U.S. troopship could escape his submarine patrols.

American Opinion

The deeper causes of the American entry into World War I went beyond the violation of neutrality rights. The United States had, to be sure, acquired an economic stake in an Allied victory by 1917 through the advancement of loans and credits to Allied governments. As a "nation of nations," the people of the United States had, at the same time, many bonds of kinship and sympathy with peoples in Europe everywhere. Americans of Irish extraction were, on the whole, not sympathetic to the British cause. American-born Eamon de Valera, one of the instigators of the Irish Easter Rebellion of 1916, was saved from the gallows by U.S. intervention.

The ethnic German element in the United States was itself divided, because many German-Americans, descended from the refugees of the 1848 abortive German liberal revolution, identified the Germany of Ludendorff with the autocratic Prussia that had driven their forebears to American shores. The influence of ethnic Irish and German elements over the American elite of 1917 and its sources of influence and power was, in any event, not great. The elite identified closely with what it considered to be the kindred civilization of England, which it believed to be seriously endangered by the German threat. Americans of central and eastern European background welcomed the opportunity to advance the cause of national independence for their Czechoslovak and Yugoslav kin. The "Treaty of Pittsburgh" of May 1918, in which Czech nationalist Jan Masaryk promised equal status to the Slovaks in a future Czechoslovak state, was symbolic of this.

1917–1918: THE LAST BATTLES

Except for Russia's dropping out of the war, the fronts again remained stalemated in Europe in 1917. In France, the British carried the main burden of the war after the near-collapse of the French army in the Nivelle offensive of April. The British attempt to take the channel ports of Ostend and Zeebrugge, erroneously thought to be key German submarine bases, bogged down in the blood-drenched mud of Passachendaele. The British tank attack at Cambrai of November 1917, carried out with four hundred vehicles, yielded the biggest gains on the western front that year. It was celebrated in London by the ringing of churchbells. By November 30, the Germans had regained most of the ground lost because Britain lacked the infantry reserves necessary to exploit the breakout.

Italy came close to collapse after a joint Austro-German attack between Caporetto and Tolmino on October 24, 1917. By November 7, 1917, when the front stabilized again behind the Piave river, Italy had suffered 300,000 casualties, of which 260,000 were prisoners. British and French reinforcements, which neither country could afford to spare, were sent to Italy to restore confidence and morale.

The Middle East

In the Middle East, Britain could claim a major success when General Sir Edmund Allenby, nicknamed "The Bull," captured Jerusalem from the Turks on December 9, 1917.

The capture of Jerusalem climaxed British Middle Eastern strategy, which had skillfully combined defensive and offensive operations since the beginning of the war.

The operations, carried out over a vast region with relatively small forces, were to yield Britain major imperial gains after the war.

The first British forces had been landed in Mesopotamia in 1914 to protect the oil installations on Abadan Island in the Persian Gulf. From Basra, Britain pushed inland, aiming at the capture of Baghdad. The first attempt to take Baghdad failed because of insufficient numbers, and General Townshend, surrounded at Kut, had to surrender to the Turks in April 1916. With a much stronger force, Sir Stanley Maude took Baghdad on March 11, 1917. While advancing from the Persian Gulf, the British had successfully fought off all Turkish attacks against the Suez Canal, the first in February 1915, the second in August 1916. Turkish operations against Kut and the Suez Canal in 1916 enjoyed German support.

The War at Sea

All the land battles of 1917 took second place behind the German submarine offensive. Its outcome would decide whether American help could, or could not, reach Europe in time to help the Allied cause.

The battle against the submarine in World War I, like that of World War II, was a battle of statistics. In 1917 the Germans had 110 submarines, the Allies 21 million tons of merchant shipping. Britain considered a minimum of 15 million tons essential to her own survival. The German sinking rate of 880,000 tons for April 1917, would, if maintained, have destroyed Britain before the end of 1917. October 1917 marked the turning point in the battle, when sinking rates decreased as a result of the adoption of the convoy system and other effective countermeasures. Before long, the convoy system, which had been advocated by Britain's Admiral Beatty and Admiral William S. Sims of the U.S. Navy, reduced losses of merchant vessels to 1 percent. German submarine losses increased to 199 by the end of the war.

In combating the German submarine, the U.S. Navy, which was ready for action from the first day of war in 1917, played a major part. In 1917 the U.S. Navy laid a mine barrier of 70,000 mines between Scotland and Norway, thereby closing the passage from the North Sea to the North Atlantic to German submarines.

Ludendorff's Offensive

Although the German High Command had lost its submarine gamble, Ludendorff made yet another bid for total victory with the German spring offensive in France in 1918. The fall of Russia had enabled Germany to achieve superior numbers on the western front over the combined British-French forces for the first time in the war. Ludendorff's offensive hoped to break both the British and French armies before the Germans would once again lose their numerical advantage as a result of the arrival of American troops.

Between March and July 1918 Ludendorff delivered five major blows, which brought the war to its fiery climax. The first two blows at the Somme and Lys of March–April 1918 were mainly directed at the British. The British situation grew so desperate that reinforcements had to be rushed from Palestine and the Salonika front. The third, fourth, and fifth blows between May and July 1918 were aimed against the French, resulting in the German breakthrough to the Marne. In the second Battle of the Marne, German forces encountered strong American opposition.

By July 1918 Ludendorff had shot his last bolt, while American forces began to stream into Europe in record numbers. By September 1918, 29 U.S. divisions were holding one-fourth of the entire western front. From a small force of 200,000 in April 1917, American forces grew to over 4 million by the end of the war, of which more than two million actually reached Europe. Major General John J. Pershing, commander of the U.S. Expeditionary Force, had wisely insisted on creating a separate American army in Europe, rather than allow the distribution of individual American divisions among British and French troops, as the Allies had suggested.

On the German side, the British breakthrough of August 8, 1918, supported by 456 tanks, which Ludendorff called the "black day" of the German army, was considered the turning point. By late September the Germans had fallen back to the Hindenburg Line, which was not pierced until November 1, 1918. Unlike the German retreat from France during the Second World War in 1944, the German retreat of 1918 was orderly and not a rout.

The German Collapse

Ludendorff regarded the war as lost, nevertheless, and asked the emperor on September 29, 1918 to seek an immediate armistice. What drove Ludendorff into panic was the coincidence of events in France and the domino-like collapse of Germany's allies Bulgaria, Turkey, and Austria-Hungary.

The Allied bridgehead in Salonika, established since 1915, had been variously derided as an "internment camp" by the Germans and a "birdcage" by Allied cartoonists. In mid-September 1918 Allied forces under General Franchet d'Esperey broke out of the "birdcage" and defeated Bulgaria, which surrendered on September 30. A month later, on October 30, 1918 Turkey signed the armistice of Mudros, after Allenby had taken Damascus and routed the Turkish army in the Middle East. Austria-Hungary collapsed after an Allied offensive on the Piave of October 24, 1918, during which the authorities in Budapest, considering the war as lost, recalled the Hungarian divisions from the Italian front. On November 3, 1918, Austria-Hungary signed the armistice at Villa-Giusti.

The German armistice request had gone out to the United States on October 4, 1918. Before it was granted on November 11, 1918, the German empire had collapsed, on November 9, with a speed which amazed both friend and foe.

3

Collapse of the Old Order in Eastern and Central Europe

THE REVOLUTION IN RUSSIA

The Allied victory of November 1918 gave every appearance of a democratic triumph shortly to be enshrined in a permanent peace settlement. In a vast part of Europe, stretching from Russia to Germany and the Habsburg Empire of Austria-Hungary, revolutions were in varying stages of progress, the results of which outlasted and overshadowed much of the work that the Paris peace conference was about to accomplish.

The First World War had dramatically highlighted Russia's old dilemma, which derived from the fact that as a Great Power she was part of the European state system, but, because of her internal backwardness, she had remained a world apart from Europe.

The peoples of Russia were angered not only by the high cost of the war in blood and social distress, but by the awareness that the cost had been needlessly multiplied by the incompetence of the government and the ruling dynasty. At the front, nearly 2 million men had been killed in battles that were, for the most part, poorly conceived and badly directed. At home, both the production and distribution of food stagnated, resulting in an increase in food prices by 800 percent as against average wage increases of only 100 percent.

The fall of the tsar on March 15, 1917, in the wake of hunger demonstrations in Petrograd, unleashed not one but several revolutions, which resulted from a combination of the unsolved social and political issues of the prewar period and the war-weariness and hunger of 1917.

Liberal Russia

The liberal spearhead of the Russian Revolution of March 1917 developed out of the "progressive bloc" of the *Duma,* the legislature which the tsar had granted under the pressure of the revolution of 1905. The first provisional government under Prince Lvov was largely drawn from the liberal Cadet and the more conservative Octobrist parties which had vainly attempted to provide more efficient leadership during the war before 1917.

The aim of liberal Russia in March 1917 was the establishment of a Western-style democracy with the convocation of a constituent assembly serving as a first step. Though happy to break with Russia's autocratic past, liberal Russia, in a serious misreading of the public mood of 1917, continued to cling to the tsar's annexationist war aims. Paul Miliukov, the first foreign minister of the provisional government, wished to preserve and strengthen the alliance with the Western powers and to reap territorial rewards from the war. "Victory," in Miliukov's words, "is Constantinople and Constantinople is victory."

The Peasants

Peasant Russia viewed the downfall of the monarchy as an opportunity to satisfy its old land hunger, which all the measures and reforms of prewar Russia since the emancipation of the serfs in the 1860s had never fully satisfied. The prospect of seizing the land of the crown, the nobility, and the Orthodox church prompted some two million peasant soldiers to desert from the army by the summer of 1917.

The Ethnic Minorities

The non-Russian nationalities, Ukrainians, White Russians, the peoples of the Caucasus, and many others, saw in the revolution an opportunity to shake off the domination of the Great Russians, which had characterized the tsarist autocracy. The non-Russians aspired to change the empire into a multinational federation of autonomous peoples. The Finns and Poles wanted outright independence.

The Socialists

The aims of socialist Russia were initially shaped more by criteria of ideology than they were influenced by current pressures and opportunities. From the vantage point of Marxist historical analysis, the Russian Revolution of March 1917 marked the transition from feudalism to capitalism with socialist revolution an event for the distant future. The Socialist parties, the Social Revolutionaries (mostly of rural appeal) and the two wings of the formerly unified Socialist party, moderate Mensheviks and radical Bolsheviks, accordingly viewed their task in the revolution as supportive rather than directive—this despite the fact that the Socialist parties acquired a rival organ to the provisional government in the shape of the Petrograd *Soviet* (council). The Petrograd Soviet assumed very real executive powers with its "Order Number One" of March 14, 1917, which made all military orders of the provisional government dependent on its own approval. With the election of soldiers', workers', and peasants' soviets throughout the land, the Petrograd Soviet similarly enhanced its own position as the unofficial head of a nationwide soviet network.

The built-in rivalry that flowed from the dualism of power between government and soviets need not have led to rupture if there had been convincing evidence of the government's timely response to revolutionary expectations. However, the government's handling of the peace issue was the first clear indication that this was not likely to be the case. Its failure to respond to the other principal revolutionary pressures in the question of land reform, nationality policy and relief of urban hunger, quickly deprived it of its credibility and popular support. This failure to act shifted attention to Lenin and the Bolsheviks, both of whom had seemed unlikely leadership alternatives when the revolution began in March 1917. The provisional government's failure to hold early elections to the constituent assembly similarly deprived it of an important opportunity of institutionalizing the power of liberal Russia.

The Liberal Collapse

It was over the peace issue that the Petrograd Soviet and the provisional government first clashed. Reflecting broad popular sentiment, the soviet called for a peace without annexations in late March 1917. When Foreign Minister Miliukov persisted in continuing the war for the sake of territorial annexation, both he and the entire government, in May 1917, were forced to resign because of the extent of public criticism. The peace issue continued to haunt the provisional governments which followed, and it was to play a crucial part in the final collapse of the government in November 1917. Succumbing to Allied pressure, Alexander Kerensky, the minister of war in the second provisional government, mounted the ill-starred offensive of July 1917 which bore his name. After the defeat of the Kerensky Offensive, the Western powers' treatment of the provisional government rapidly shifted from support to impatience and thinly disguised contempt. After Kerensky had replaced Lvov as head of the government on July 21, 1917, the Western Allies conditioned their support on fresh evidence of Russia's unchanged loyalty and military effort in the common cause. This, and the failure of the Western powers to publicly renounce annexationist war aims, put Kerensky on the defensive at home and earned him the epithet of being merely a puppet of the Western bourgeoisie. The Petrograd Soviet did not expect or demand peace at any price, but it wanted to see its own government make a clear stand for a peace without annexations, independent of the Western Allies if necessary. The Allies finally promised to hold a conference on war aims in late November 1917, but they specifically barred any representatives of the Petrograd Soviet from attending. In any case, the promise came too late to be of any use to Kerensky, as did Wilson's *Fourteen Points* of January 1918. The latter might have been helpful to Kerensky at an earlier time because they came closest to the Soviet's own idea of a just peace, and because they also demanded the evacuation by German forces of all occupied Russian land.

The provisional government's inertia and its failure to effectively institutionalize power swept liberal Russia off the stage of history before it could even take its first steps towards realization. That the empty stage should be speedily occupied by a revolution, which called itself socialist, was largely due to a synthesis of ideological pragmatism and tactical realism in the person of Lenin.

Lenin

In less than a year, between April and November 1917, Lenin traversed the vast distance between near-total obscurity to leadership of the largest country in the world by tying together the most diverse opportunities and forces into a coherent pattern of single-minded revolutionary purpose. The difficult return from his exile in Switzerland, where he had spent the years since 1914, to his native Russia, was accomplished by putting German imperialism to his own good personal use. Though unknown to many others, Lenin was known to the German High Command, which gave him safe passage through Germany in the hope that his return to Russia would help topple the provisional government and hasten Russia's withdrawal from the war.

Lenin's *April Theses,* which he presented to a surprised following of Bolshevik party faithfuls upon his arrival in Petrograd in April 1917, represented a blueprint for immediate revolutionary action on the basis of a highly personalized adaptation of Marxist theory.

To the socialists of prewar Europe, Marxist theory had been more an impediment than a guide to revolutionary action because the precision of the Marxist socioeconomic analysis was not matched by an equally precise revolutionary timetable or directive for revolutionary tactics. Socialist revolution had become a subject of academic debate.

Lenin juxtaposed Marxist theory with the concrete revolutionary situation obtaining in the Russia of March 1917, and he did not hesitate to engage in the most extensive form of ideological pruning in order to preserve a claim to ideological legitimacy. Where Marx had viewed the transition to socialism as the result of both the weight of social and economic factors as well as the conscious effort of a revolutionary party, Lenin postulated socialist revolution by a revolutionary elite even if the social and economic conditions had not yet reached the level Marx had thought necessary for revolution. Socialist revolution in a precapitalist society such as Russia's was ideologically justified, in Lenin's view, because imperialism, as the highest stage of capitalism, had added a new dimension of capitalist exploitation in the form of colonial exploitation. The Leninist logic of socialist revolution in precapitalist societies rested on the argument that such societies, constituting the weakest link in the chain of capitalist exploitation, were likely to be the first ones to break. In so doing, they would trigger socialist revolutions in the more advanced capitalist societies under conditions that Marx himself had described and forseen.

Lenin's ideological somersaults might in themselves have remained irrelevant to the development of the revolutionary situation in Russia had they not also been accompanied by a guide to political action. The *April Theses* recognized the network of soldiers', workers', and peasants' soviets as ready-made instruments of power, which the Bolshevik party must first seize control of and which it must subsequently use for the overthrow of the provisional government. At the same time, Bolshevik propaganda must secure the necessary mass support through timely and unequivocal promises in all the vital areas in which the provisional government was temporizing and procrastinating; the issue of peace, of land reform, of autonomy for the non-Russian nationalities, of the urban food supply.

Rise of the Bolsheviks

When the first all-Russian congress of soviets met in Petrograd on June 16, 1917, the Bolsheviks were still outnumbered, with 105 delegates as against 285 Social Revolutionaries and 248 Mensheviks. By September 1917, however, Bolshevik strength in the soviets had increased from 10 to 50 percent, and the establishment of Bolshevik control over the two principal soviets, those of Petrograd and Moscow, was for Lenin the signal for launching an armed uprising against the provisional government.

While building his defenses against the rising power of the Bolsheviks, Kerensky failed to exploit the few remaining opportunities for weakening his opponent. He also failed to match the soviets, as instruments of Bolshevik power, with power centers of his own. The Bolsheviks become vulnerable in July 1917, partly because of the charge that Lenin was a German spy, a charge that seemed not implausible in the wake of the disastrous military defeat of the Kerensky Offensive. During the so-called July days of 1917 a number of Bolshevik leaders were arrested after the Bolshevik party unsuccessfully attempted to escalate antigovernment demonstrations in Petrograd into an all-out assault on the government. Lenin went into hiding in Finland. When General Lavr G. Kornilov attempted to overthrow the provisional government in a right-wing army coup on September 10, 1917, Kerensky called on all Socialist parties, including the Bolsheviks, to help defend the government. Lenin responded favorably, but the forces which crushed the Kornilov coup were the same ones that Lenin would soon be using against Kerensky himself.

During his final weeks of power, Kerensky tried to prop up his government with improvised and rapidly shifting assemblies such as the All-Russian State Conference during August, the Democratic Conference of September–October, and the Pre-Parliament, which was convened on the eve of the Bolshevik seizure of power. Far from strengthening the government's hand, the fleeting assemblies only mirrored the centrifugal revolutionary currents which the provisional government had failed to harness into a supportive force ever since March 1917.

The actual Bolshevik seizure of power on November 7, 1917, which was directed by Lenin's deputy Leon Trotsky, came as an anticlimax. In Petrograd, the Winter Palace, seat of the provisional government, alone became the scene of major fighting, before the disappearance of Kerensky's "pitiful, helpless, half-government," in Trotsky's words.

Lenin had achieved the improbable by November 1917, but it was far from certain whether his triumph would last. In the Peace of Brest-Litovsk with Germany of March 1918, Lenin traded land for time in order to consolidate the recently gained power. Whether the time gained would be only a brief respite or a lasting asset depended on events beyond Lenin's own control. The German High Command thought that Brest-Litovsk was a milestone to total German victory and William II characterized the peace as "the greatest success of world history." Lenin thought that, the Peace of Brest-Litovsk notwithstanding, the war would spur socialist revolution in Germany and in so doing would not only render the annexationist peace irrelevant but justify the Russian Revolution of November 1917 in terms of Marxist ideology.

THE GERMAN REVOLUTION OF 1918-1919

When revolution did come to Germany on November 9, 1918, its arrival was speedily hailed in Petrograd as the first step in the extension of the Russian Revolution into western Europe. Although the German Revolution paralleled that of Russia in certain external aspects, it sprang from different causes and it produced different results before very long.

The German Revolution was sparked by a sailors' mutiny at the Kiel naval base on November 3, 1918, in response to false rumors that the navy would be ordered on a suicide mission against Britain's Royal Navy. Imitating the Russian example, the mutinous sailors elected their own sailors' soviets, which carried word of the mutiny through Germany and thereby elevated it to the level of a revolution. By November 8, 1918, the revolution reached the Bavarian capital of Munich, and Berlin the following day.

In Russia, tsarism had collapsed in 1917 largely under the weight of its own incompetence. The Germany monarchy, by contrast, had managed its war successfully for as long as it had faith in its total victory over the Allies. It was only with the realization that the Ludendorff Offensive had been a failure that the military who had ruled Germany with an iron hand since 1914 lost faith in themselves and allowed a local mutiny to mushroom into nationwide political revolution. When a similar mutiny had occurred at the same naval base of Kiel during the summer of 1917, the authorities had suppressed it speedily and effectively.

After September 1918, the German High Command hoped to avoid a duplication of Russian events by a speedy democratization at home and the quick securing of an armistice abroad. The attainment of both objectives was left to the civilian head of the government, the newly appointed chancellor Max von Baden.

The Reforms of 1918

The comprehensive constitutional reforms which Max von Baden implemented in October 1918 conceded all that the Social Democrats had been asking for in vain since 1875, such as the abolition of the undemocratic Prussian three-class suffrage and the introduction of the parliamentary system. The attempt to preserve the Hohenzollern dynasty through the trauma of defeat by initiating controlled revolution from above would probably have worked except for the government's failure to secure a speedy armistice.

Woodrow Wilson neither could nor would grant an immediate armistice. He could not, because he had trouble convincing his own European allies that the *Fourteen Points* were indeed a suitable basis for peace. He would not, because he was not sure that the German constitutional changes of October meant what they said, and he preferred to deal with a Germany that had ousted William II.

The German public, appreciating the significance of William II to the attainment of peace, began to press for his removal. In this, the public and also the army were strongly influenced by a desire for peace which arose in response to the High Command's tacit admission of September 1918 that the war was lost. The first political demand of the mutinous sailors was the abdication of the emperor. On November 9, 1918, Max von Baden announced the abdication of William II, without having been authorized by anyone to do so. On the same day, Philip Scheidmann, a Social Democratic leader, proclaimed the German Republic, also without having been authorized to do so by his own party.

The abdication of the emperor was followed by the speedy and wholesale disappearance of all the other German princes and kings who had ruled in the individual German states. German conservative and middle-class politicians similarly left the stage, leaving it temporarily to the Left.

The German Left

The Left consisted of Social Democrats (SPD), and the Independent Social Democrats (USPD) who had split off from the SPD in 1917 over the issue of war aims.

The USPD also contained the old prewar far left grouped around Rosa Luxemburg and Karl Liebknecht, who had attacked the SPD for its moderate stand.

The SPD had remained a loyal supporter of the war effort even when territorial annexation became the undeniable aim of the High Command. Woodrow Wilson, who had previously viewed the SPD as a hopeful force of German democratic renewal, was sadly disappointed when the SPD failed to oppose the Treaty of Brest-Litovsk and merely abstained from voting during ratification.

The SPD did not want revolution. It placed itself at the head of the revolution on November 9, 1918 only because it was afraid that failure to do so would result in the seizure of power by the extreme left and the possibility of a Communist dictatorship, soviet-style. It was with such an understanding that Max von Baden had surrendered the chancellorship to SPD leader Friedrich Ebert on November 9, 1918.

The German extreme left consisted of two groups, the Spartacists around Luxemburg and Liebknecht and the Revolutionary Shop Stewards around Ledebour and Däumig. By December 31, 1918, both groups were to form the Communist party of Germany (KPD).

The Revolutionary Shop Stewards were the true German counterpart of Lenin's Bolsheviks, and they alone had made active preparations for the seizure of power before being overtaken by the spontaneous Kiel mutiny. Rosa Luxemburg, though a convinced communist until her violent end in January 1919, opposed Lenin's tactics of violence in Russia.

Ebert and the Social Democrats, who had not wanted the revolution, tried to keep it as short as possible and to lead it speedily towards a constituent assembly. Essentially satisfied with the democratization of the empire in October 1918, the SPD viewed the goal of the revolution as the fulfilment of the abortive 1848–1849 German liberal revolution.

The USPD and its extreme left wing wished to make the revolution as long as possible, in order to effect sweeping social-economic changes such as the nationalization of industry. The USPD viewed as the revolutionary goal not a liberal democracy but a system similar to Russia's, in which the German councils would play a leading role akin to that of the soviets.

Ebert's Coalition

Despite these fundamental differences, Ebert invited the USPD to join in the formation of a provisional coalition government of SPD-USPD on an equal basis. Ebert's offer was motivated by the desire to keep the USPD under control. The USPD accepted the offer on November 10, 1918, because it thought it could push the SPD further to the left.

Ebert secretly formed another alliance with the new head of the High Command, General Gröner, on November 10, in order to ensure military support against the far left should it become necessary. Gröner, in return, expected the SPD to function as an effective bulwark against communist revolution.

The precarious SPD-USPD alliance soon broke up after the meeting of the first all-German congress of soldiers' and workers' councils in Berlin in mid-December 1918. Reflecting the preponderance of SPD strength in the German councils, the congress of councils overwhelmingly endorsed the political goal of the SPD in the revolution and called for the election of a German constituent assembly. The date for the election was fixed for January 19, 1919. The extreme left, having been outvoted on its proposal for a German soviet dictatorship, carried the struggle into the streets. After the first armed clashes in Berlin, the USPD quit the coalition government in late December 1918. The Communist party, newly formed out of the USPD left wing on December 31, 1918, launched an armed uprising against the Ebert government on January 5, 1919.

The Communist Challenge

What soon came to be called the *Spartacist* (Communist) uprising collapsed after a week's bitter fighting. General Gröner, having observed during the disturbances of December 1918 the reluctance of regular troops to fire on civilians, even when armed, had raised a special volunteer force, the Free Corps, for the containment of the Spartacist uprising. Though crucial to the failure of the Communists, the Free Corps was itself to develop into a threat to the new German democracy because of its reactionary and violent spirit. The Free Corps volunteers executed both Luxemburg and Liebknecht during the street fighting in Berlin. Eventually, the Free Corps was to become a recruiting ground for Hitler's stormtroopers.

Communist-inspired violence and its suppression by the Free Corps continued into the spring of 1919, with a new round of fighting in Berlin in March and short-lived "Soviet Republic of Bavaria" in April–May 1919.

The German elections to the constituent assembly had meanwhile taken place as scheduled. Although the SPD failed in its effort to win an absolute majority, the election results were not without encouragement to the liberal-democratic cause the SPD espoused. Together with the Catholic Center party and the newly formed Democratic party, the SPD constituted a solid democratic majority in the constituent assembly which met in the city of Weimar in February 1919. The elections had also revealed the weak following of the USPD, which gained a mere 22 seats, as against 165 for the SPD. The Communists boycotted the elections.

Walter Ulbricht, the future head of the Communist regime of East Germany, was to declare after the Second World War that the German Revolution of 1918 had failed to follow the example of Soviet Russia becuase it had been lacking a "revolutionary party." The "revolutionary party" existed in the form of the Communist party. That its uprising of January 1919 produced different results from those of the Bolsheviks in Russia in November 1917 was rooted in the essentially different social-economic condition of Germany. Communist revolution failed in Germany, where it should have succeeded according to the prediction of Marx, because the German working class overwhelmingly identified with the preservation of the socioeconomic status quo. The question at the end of the German Revolution of 1918–1919 did not concern the threat of Communist victory, but the consolidation of its liberal-democratic gains against future nationalist and reactionary challenge. Such a challenge was very likely because of the coincidence of German democratic victory and national defeat in 1919.

THE DISINTEGRATION OF AUSTRIA-HUNGARY

After tsarist Russia and imperial Germany, the Austro-Hungarian Empire was the third great monarchy of central-eastern Europe to collapse under the strains of the First World War. Its disappearance in 1918 had no less a lasting effect on the course of twentieth-century European events than did the revolutions in Russia and Germany.

The Empire in Europe

Before 1914 the Habsburg monarchy had appeared both an anachronism and a promise, a threat to peace and a condition of its preservation. As a multinational and multilingual empire, it seemed an anachronism in an age of acute nationalism. As a cosmopolitan empire, it produced one of the great civilizations of Europe at the turn of the nineteenth and twentieth centuries, and inspired the continent with such artists and thinkers as Johannes Brahms, Anton Bruckner, and Gustav Mahler in music, Gustav Klimt and Egon Schiele in painting, Sigmund Freud in psychiatry, and Joseph Schumpeter in economics. Austria-Hungary seemed a threat to peace because it had blocked movements of national unification and had as a result contributed twice to war, once during the unification of Italy in 1859 and once during that of Germany from 1866 onwards. In 1914, it had provided the immediate cause for the outbreak of the First World War by attempting to prevent the unification of the southern Slavs under Serbian leadership. Germany's chancellor Bismarck, on the other hand, had considered the Habsburg monarchy a prerequisite for peace, because he was certain that its disappearance would result in the eventual domination of the Danube valley by Russia with a proportionate increase in Russian aggressiveness.

Internal Tensions

After the revolution of 1848–1849 had first indicated the strength of the national idea among the peoples of the Habsburg Empire, the monarchy had tried to reform itself. By 1914 it had not gone far enough to prepare itself for the severe stress of the First World War. The 1867 constitutional compromise (*Ausgleich*) with Hungary had granted the latter full internal autonomy, while preserving a common dynasty, foreign policy, and defense policy. The nationality policies in the two parts of the Dual Monarchy of Austria-Hungary subsequently followed different paths, being more liberal in the Austrian half and remaining repressive in the Hungarian. The Hungarian suffrage remained severely restricted before 1914 with only 6 percent of the people being enfranchised and only 50 out of over 450 parliamentary deputies being of non-Hungarian (non-Magyar) nationality. Ethnic Magyars, on the other hand, accounted only for 48 percent of the population of the Hungarian half of the empire, the remainder being composed of Austro-Germans, Slovaks, Rumanians, Ukrainians, Croats, and Serbs. The Austrian half introduced universal male suffrage in 1907. The hope that a democratic suffrage would ease nationality tensions through the formation of popular mass parties emphasizing social above national issues was not fulfilled. In March 1914 the parliament in Vienna, the Reichsrat, had to be suspended because of nationality conflicts. The depth of the friction between the ethnic German and Slavic elements was later demonstrated by Adolf Hitler, who grew to manhood in Austria before the First World War and whose nationalism and racism were deeply embedded in the attitudes of pre-1914 Austria.

Disaffection was strongest among the Slavic Czechs, who demanded autonomy similar to that granted Hungary in 1867.

On the eve of the First World War, various reform ideas were put forward, such as that of the Rumanian Aurel Popovici, for a "United States of Greater Austria," or the concept of "personal cultural autonomy" proposed by the Social Democratic leader Karl Renner. Popovici advocated the reorganization of the monarchy into fifteen federal states based on nationality, while Renner wished to grant each citizen special nationality rights regardless of place of residence. None of the proposals was adopted because there was insufficient time and because the Hungarians adamantly refused to extend the privileges of the 1867 compromise to any other nationality outside their own and that of the Austro-Germans. Archduke Francis Ferdinand, the one person who both desired such an extension, at least to the southern Slavs, and who might have had the strength to carry it through against Magyar opposition, was slain by a southern Slav nationalist in June 1914.

The Impact of War

The outbreak of war in 1914 rallied the Habsburg Empire around the old figure of Emperor Francis Joseph much as the outbreak of the War of the Austrian Succession in 1740 had rallied the nationalities of eighteenth-century Austria around the young person of Empress Maria Theresa. Despite losing the war to her foreign enemies, the empress was able to keep her empire largely intact precisely because she made timely concessions to the nationalism of the rebellious Magyar nobility. In 1917, after the death of Francis Joseph, the nationalities of twentieth-century Austria similarly looked to young Emperor Charles I for a great liberating gesture to reward their loyalty to the dynasty. They also hoped their new emperor might secure peace—a separate peace if necessary—especially after Russia, Austria's principal enemy, had collapsed in 1917.

On both counts Charles quickly proved to be a disappointment. His inconclusive secret peace feelers to the Allies via his brother-in-law Sixtus Bourbon became an acute embarrassment when revealed by French premier Clemenceau. The Germans responded by virtually subjecting Habsburg foreign and defense policy to their own control under the terms of the Spa Agreement of May 1918.

At home, Charles raised the hopes of the nationalities and as quickly dashed them by reconvening the Reichsrat in May 1917 without following through with structural reforms.

As late as January 1918 Britain's prime minister Lloyd George had declared that the breakup of the Austro-Hungarian empire was not a part of Allied war aims. Woodrow Wilson's call for the "freest opportunity for autonomous development" for the peoples of Austria-Hungary under Point Ten of his *Fourteen Points* was similarly not incompatible with the survival of the Habsburg monarchy in altered form. It was only after the Allies came to view Charles as a German puppet that they also made the destruction of the Dual Monarchy one of their chief aims in the war. In this they were also influenced by fears for their own survival under the blows of Germany's worst attack in the Ludendorff Offensive of 1918.

The nationalities concurrently changed their attitude from support to rebellion. As late as January 1917 the Czech Reichsrat deputies had reaffirmed their loyalty to Charles. After a year of disappointment, the same Czech deputies issued the *Epiphany Resolution* of January 6, 1918, which called for the union and complete independence of Czechs and Slovaks.

These changes gave new prominence to the various exile committees, such as the Paris-based Czech National Council, the Polish National Committee, and the London-based South Slav Committee. Until 1918, the organizers of these committees could not be certain either of majority support among their fellow nationals in Austria-Hungary, or of Allied endorsement of their cause. Among the leading Czechoslovak exiles were Jan Masaryk, Eduard Benes, and the Slovak colonel Milan Stefanik, who had been fighting on Russia's side until 1917. Ante Trumbic headed the South Slav Committee, while Ignace Paderewski, the Polish pianist, gained influential support for Polish independence in the United States.

The Rome Congress

Wickham Steed, the foreign editor of the London *Times,* helped pave the way for Austria-Hungary's dismemberment by organizing the Rome Congress of Oppressed Nationalities in April 1918. Attended by Polish, Czech, southern Slav, Rumanian, and Italian representatives, the Rome congress was intended to impress Allied governments with the exiles' unity and to gain Allied recognition of their aims. Towards that end, the exiles also organized volunteer units, composed chiefly of deserters and former POWs of the Habsburg armies. The volunteers fought alongside Allied troops in Italy and France. The most celebrated of such units was the Czech Legion, which had fought in Russia against the Central Powers before the Communist seizure of power. After the Bolshevik revolution, the Czech Legion soon became involved in the Russian Civil War. The French even thought of using the Czech Legion for the crushing of the new Bolshevik government of Lenin.

Dismemberment

Among the exiles' committees, the Czech National Council in Paris was the first to obtain Allied recognition in June 1918. Eduard Benes thereupon turned the council into a provisional government of the projected new state of Czechoslovakia. The United States too was rapidly moving towards a policy of dismemberment. On July 4, 1919 Woodrow Wilson, in his Mount Vernon speech, rejected "compromise" and "halfway decisions" as a solution of the Habsburg nationality problem. When the Dual Monarchy addressed an armistice request to Wilson on October 4, 1918, the president replied that not he but the nationalities of Austria-Hungary must be the judges of what action would satisfy their aspirations.

Emperor Charles' October Manifesto of October 16, 1918 and the formal repudiation of the Austro-German Dual Alliance of 1879 by Austrian foreign minister Andrassy on October 27, 1918, represented the last desperate steps to save the Dual Monarchy. Designed for the Austrian half of the empire only, the October Manifesto proposed a federal union of Austro-Germans, Czechs, southern Slavs, and Ukrainians. The Austrian part of Poland was to be joined with an independent Polish state, while Trieste, with its large Italian population, was to receive special status.

The American press ridiculed the October Manifesto as a "worthy production in the home of musical comedy." The manifesto certainly came too late to halt the process of disintegration, which had acquired a momentum of its own when the manifesto was issued. Czech nationalist leader Frantisek Stanek spoke for many when observing that the Slavic peoples, no longer satisfied with mere autonomy, desired a string of sovereign Slavic states, stretching from Danzig on the Baltic, via Prague, the capital of newly independent Czechoslovakia, to the Adriatic. In fact, the October Manifesto became the signal for the exiles' leaders to join forces with the numerous national committees which now began to be formed in the Czech, Slovak, Polish, southern Slav, and Rumanian parts of the disintegrating empire. It was from such combinations that governments were formed in Czechoslovakia on October 28, 1918, in Poland under Joseph Pilsudski on November 14, 1918, and in newly constituted Yugoslavia on December 1, 1918. The Rumanian national assembly proclaimed the union of Transylvania, previously a part of Hungary, and Rumania on December 1, 1918. Austria and Hungary, the nuclei of the once-sprawling multinational empire, emerged as separate states on October 30 and November 16, 1918, respectively. Amidst the turmoil of national revolutions, the formal abdication of Emperor Charles I had gone almost unnoticed. After several unsuccessful attempts at a political comeback as king of Hungary, Charles died in exile in Madeira in 1922.

4

The Peace Settlement

The First World War had been waged by the victorious democracies not only for the purpose of "making the world safe for democracy," but also for the even more important objective of making the world war the last of its kind.

Allied-American disagreements as to how best to achieve lasting peace had remained concealed while the war was going on. Woodrow Wilson had taken no official notice of the secret Allied wartime agreement concerning annexations. The Allies had endorsed the *Fourteen Points* for their usefulness as a means of weakening enemy resistance, as shown in the collapse of Austria-Hungary.

France, speaking through Premier Clemençeau, would have preferred the peace settlement to follow the past principles of European diplomacy and power politics, as symbolized in the Peace of Westphalia, which had ended the Thirty Years' War in 1648. The Treaty of Versailles, the centerpiece of the Paris peace structure of 1919, in fact specifically cited the 1648 Westphalia peace as a model.

WILSON'S FOURTEEN POINTS

Woodrow Wilson's *Fourteen Points* departed from past European practices in significant ways, especially in their objection to secret diplomacy, their demand for the freedom of the seas in war and peace, and their proposal of a permanent machinery for crisis management and mediation through the League of Nations. Against the traditional European concept of a balance of power, Wilson postulated the notion of a community of power, sustained and ordered by the shared commitment to liberal principles. The right of national self-determination constituted an important part of international Wilsonian idealism, though its problematic and potentially explosive impact was soon revealed when nations other than those of central-eastern Europe also demanded it as their birthright.

The armistice of November 11, 1918 had been concluded on the basis of the *Fourteen Points,* and, because of American pressure, it was subject to few reservations, despite Allied misgivings. The peace settlement as such, however, resulted from a compromise, reflecting both Wilson's stand and that of the principal European Allies.

FRENCH INTERESTS

The French approach to peace was overwhelmingly determined by considerations of national security. These considerations required not only a containment of German power, but the finding of a suitable substitute for Russian power, since the 1917 Bolshevik revolution had turned Russia from a French ally into a hostile and unpredictable entity. The Russian Civil War between Bolsheviks and Whites was in full swing while the Paris peace conference was in session in 1919. French premier Clemenceau and British prime minister Lloyd George would have liked to intervene on the side of the Whites, and preliminary steps towards intervention had already been undertaken with the sending of French troops under Marshal Franchet d'Esperey to Odessa in November 1918. Marshal Foch wished to mount a fullblown anti-Bolshevik crusade, using newly independent Poland and Rumania as a launching point.

Russia

By March 1919 Western plans for intervention in the Russian Civil War had been shelved and Allied troop withdrawal from Russia began the following April. The decision not to intervene was based, in part, on Woodrow Wilson's opinion that the Russian Revolution was an internal Russian affair whose outcome should not be influenced by external forces. In part, it derived from the Western governments' awareness of the unpopularity of intervention among the British, French, and Italian public, based on war weariness and sympathy for Lenin's cause, especially among the working class. The peace conference concluded its work with the future of Russia and her future relations with Europe still a question.

The Eastern Settlement

As a substitute for Russian power, France strengthened the states of Eastern Europe which either had been allied with the Western powers, such as Rumania, or whose independence the Western powers had sponsored, such as Poland, Czechoslovakia, and Yugoslavia. The borders of these states were drawn as generously as possible at the expense of the former Central Powers, and frequently in disregard for ethnic realities. The Versailles treaty surrendered the larger part of West Prussia and the province of Poznan to Poland, creating thereby the "Polish corridor" to the Baltic Sea and cutting off East Prussia from the rest of Germany. Mineral-rich Upper Silesia, originally ceded to Poland outright, was partitioned among ethnic lines, following a plebiscite in 1921. The port of Danzig, located in the corridor, was put under League administration rather than being given to Poland, because of its predominantly German character. The Peace of St. Germain with Austria recognized the Czechoslovak claim to the ethnic German Sudeten provinces, which were historically part of Bohemia, but whose population had expressed a preference for union with Austria or

Germany. The peace settlement more than doubled the size of Rumania through Rumania's gain of Transylvania (previously Hungarian), the Bukovina (from Austria), and the southern Dobruja (from Bulgaria). Rumania had also annexed the province of Bessarabia from Russia in 1918.

The new eastern settlement created sizable new national minorities of Germans, Hungarians, and Ukrainians, to mention but a few, whose opposition to the settlement was likely to spark future revisionist demands. Foreseeing this and doubting the long-range stability of some of the new states, Britain's prime minister Lloyd George had serious reservation about the eastern settlement.

THE GERMAN QUESTION

The future of Germany was the core of French security. After suffering two German invasions in less than half a century, France would have liked to undo the national unification of the German states of 1871, which it viewed as the original cause of both the Franco-Prussian War and the First World War. The United States and Britain barred such a solution out of fear that it would spark a new round of European wars. French premier Clemençeau himself conceded in 1919 that the dismemberment of Germany, however desirable from the French vantage point, was not feasible.

The Treaty of Versailles returned Alsace-Lorraine to France, but it did not detach the Rhineland from Germany. Instead, the left bank of the Rhine, together with a thirty-two mile strip on the right bank, was to be permanently demilitarized. Demilitarization meant a ban on all fortifications or stationing of troops. France also claimed the German Saar district with its rich coal mines, both on the grounds of compensation for French mines destroyed during the war and the fact that part of the Saar had belonged to France between 1793 and 1815. The Treaty of Versailles awarded the coal mines of the Saar to France but placed the territory under League administration. After fifteen years, the people of the Saar were to state their preference for a return to Germany or union with France in a plebiscite.

Little disagreement existed among the peacemakers on the need to disarm Germany, though the League proclaimed that German disarmament was only the first step towards general disarmament. The link between German and general disarmament was to cause friction soon after the peace was written.

The Versailles treaty limited German ground forces to a 100-thousand-man army of long-term volunteers and denied Germany possession of any of the weapons which the technology of World War I had developed or perfected, such as poison gas, tanks, large caliber artillery, aircraft, and dirigibles. The navy, reduced to 15,000 men, was denied submarines and limited in its capital ships to six pocket ships of 10,000 tons maximum tonnage. An Allied control commission was to have free access to all German military facilities.

Reparations

Reparations were a difficult subject for compromise among the Big Three because of the political and economic motives involved. The armistice had defined German reparations merely as compensation for "damages done to the civilian population of the Allies and their property." Yet the Allied public expected Germany to pay for more than that, in part because Allied leaders had promised she would. Lloyd George had won reelection by a landslide in the British "khaki elections" of December 1918 partly on the strength of his promise of "making Germany pay." Eric Geddes, Britain's minister of transport, called for Germany to be squeezed "like a lemon, until you can hear the pips squeak." All the European Allies had had to borrow from the United States during the war to the tune of some $10 billion, a sum Wilson was not prepared to either cancel or reduce. Most of the Allies had financed much of the cost of the war through internal borrowing, thereby vastly increasing the national debt. Britain, unlike France, had tried to cover as much of the war cost as possible through increased taxation and had managed to pay for 28 percent of the war expenditures in this manner. Britain's national debt was nevertheless fourteen times higher at the end of the war than before 1914. Britain's war loans to Russia, bigger than the £850 million debt owed to the United States, had to be written off once Bolshevik Russia repudiated the tsarist debt. At the peace conference, Lloyd George, supported by the Dominion governments, demanded the inclusion of veterans', widows', and orphans' pensions into German reparations, a demand the United States supported. Without the inclusion of pensions, Britain could claim few reparations because of the limited civilian damage she suffered. British shipping losses were compensated by the surrender of the bulk of German merchant shipping.

The Treaty of Versailles failed to fix a definitive sum on German reparations, however, because the Big Three were unable to agree on Germany's actual capacity to pay. A reparations commission, in which the United States initially had a seat, but in which she lost her voting right after failing to ratify the Versailles treaty, was to produce a final sum by May 1921. All German assets in the United States and Allied countries, valued at $2 billion, were meanwhile seized. The net worth of the German overseas colonies, which the Versailles treaty also took, was not deducted from the reparations sum. The final figure of $33 billion, though much lower than what had been demanded by France and Britain at the Paris peace conference, was still unrealistically high in the American estimate.

The resources lost to Germany under the Treaty of Versailles, permanently or, as in the case of the Saar, temporarily, represented 26 percent of her hard coal production, 75 percent of iron ore, 35 percent of pig iron, and 25 percent of steel production. The eastern territories lost to Poland represented 16 percent of the German grain-producing area, 18 percent of the potato-growing area, and 11 percent of her livestock.

By comparison, the resources lost to Russia under the short-lived Peace of Brest-Litovsk, imposed by Germany in March 1918, represented 32 percent of Russia's arable land, 75 percent of her coal and iron ore, 33 percent of her factories, and 26 percent of her railroads.

War Guilt

The German public was generally ill-prepared for the nature of the peace it was being offered in May 1919 in part because it mistakenly believed that the overthrow of the Germany monarchy and the conclusion of the Armistice on the basis of the *Fourteen Points* would cushion the impact of defeat. The Germans took particular exception to the statement of exclusive Central Powers war guilt, contained in Article 231 of the Versailles treaty. The Allies had included Article 231—the opening article in the chapter dealing with reparations—as a statement of legal liability from which the claim to compensate was derived. The Germans invested Article 231 with an aura of moral guilt and responsibility for what appeared, to the generation of 1919, the greatest atrocity in the history of western civilization to date: the world war with its loss of ten million lives. The war guilt issue was to preoccupy the German public for the following two decades and it was to play an important part in the growth of political extremism on the far right. In 1919, the Allies declined a German proposal to have the causes of the First World War examined by neutrals on the basis of the available documentary evidence of all belligerents. The Germans similarly objected to their exclusion from the League of Nations as another symbolic act of moral censure.

On June 28, 1919—the fifth anniversary of the assassination of Francis Ferdinand—the Versailles treaty was signed in the same Hall of Mirrors of the Versailles palace in which Bismarck had proclaimed the German Empire in January 1871.

BRITISH INTERESTS

For Britain, the defeat of Germany and the disappearance of German naval power seemed, in themselves, sufficient guarantee of security for a long time to come. The German navy, which had been scheduled for surrender to the British at Scapa Flow naval base in June 1919, had scuttled itself before the eyes of British sailors; but it had, nonetheless, ceased to be a threat. The war had raised the issue of British naval superiority in a new form, however, owing to the emergence of U.S. naval power at an equal level. The naval parity in capital ships, which Britain had denied Germany before the First World War, she had to concede in treaty form to the United States in the Washington Naval Agreement of 1922. The Washington Naval Agreement likewise signalled the shift in Dominion attitudes away from Britain and towards the United States with regard to Asian and Pacific issues. Australia, New Zealand, and Canada shared the American concern over the increase in Japanese power as a result of Japan's acquiring control, under the terms of the Versailles treaty, of the German island possessions in the Pacific north of the equator. Under joint U.S. and Dominion pressure, Britain was compelled to discontinue its 1902 alliance with Japan as part of the 1922 Washington Agreement.

The Middle East, by contrast, provided Britain with the opportunity to make major gains in the tradition of her past imperial policy of exploiting continental wars for the sake of colonial conquest. Militarily, the Middle East had been for Britain a "side-show" during the First World War, but the British Empire had traditionally "done very well" out of side shows, in the words of Prime Minister Lloyd George. In 1918, the collapse of the Turkish Empire opened up momentous possibilities in the oil-rich Middle East.

The dismemberment of the Ottoman Empire had been the subject of secret Allied wartime agreements, concluded between Britain, France, Italy and Russia during 1915–1917. The Russian Revolution in 1917 had eliminated that country as a claimant, but Greece, represented by Prime Minister Venizelos, appeared as a new claimant with British blessing. In May 1919 Greek troops landed in Turkey to make good the Greek claim on Smyrna.

Italy's share in the dismemberment of the Ottoman Empire was to have been the Dodecanese Islands and Adalia (Antalya) in Asia Minor. France and Britain had tentatively divided the Arab portions of the Turkish-ruled Middle East in the Sykes-Picot Agreement of 1916, which reserved Syria, together with the oil-rich Mosul territory, for France and Iraq for Britain. Palestine was to be placed under international administration. Prior to the peace conference, France had agreed to include both Mosul and Palestine in the British sphere in exchange for British backing of the French position on the Rhineland question.

While carving up the Middle East into spheres of influence, Britain also had made definite promises of independence to the Arabs during the war, in order to enlist Arab nationalism on behalf of the war effort against Turkey. Lloyd George, addressing the British Trade Union Congress in January 1918, had spoken of recognizing the separate "national condition" of Arabia, Mesopotamia (Iraq), Syria, and Palestine. Britain's high commissioner for Egypt, Henry McMahon, had similarly promised independence for the Arabs during the war. The Anglo-French declaration of November 8, 1918 likewise pledged assistance in the establishment of indigenous governments in Syria and Mesopotamia. The declaration of Britain's foreign secretary Balfour of November 2, 1917, by contrast, promised British support in the establishment of a national home for the Jewish people in Palestine.

The Mandate System

Woodrow Wilson opposed the outright annexation of the former Turkish Middle Eastern provinces by France and Britain as much as he had opposed the annexation of the German colonies in Africa and the Pacific by the Allies. The result was a compromise in the form of the *mandate system* whereby the Allied nations administered the areas in question not as their own property but on behalf of the League of Nations. Title to the mandates remained vested in the League with the overall intent of preparing the mandates for eventual independence. The final division of the Middle East into mandates was carried out by the Allied San Remo Conference of 1920, which followed the outline of the Sykes-Picot Agreement. Syria and Lebanon became French mandates, Iraq and Palestine, together with Transjordan, British mandates. Although the mandate system avoided annexation, it was strongly opposed in Syria and Iraq. The King-Crane Commission, which Wilson had dispatched to the Middle East, had clearly stated as much for Syria. The establishment of the British mandate over Iraq provoked a full-blown Arab revolt in June 1920, which Britain suppressed by force of arms.

TURKEY AND KEMAL

Turkish nationalists were resigned to the loss of the Arab Middle East, but not to the dismemberment of Turkey proper. Partial dismemberment was, however, the net effect of the Peace of Sèvres, which the Allies imposed upon the feeble government of the Turkish sultan, Mehmed VI in August 1920. The status of Smyrna and surrounding territory, which the Greeks had occupied in 1919, was to be decided by plebiscite after five years. The Dodecanese went to Italy and the Greek border in eastern Thrace was moved to within twenty miles of Constantinople. Cilicia became a French sphere of influence.

The ouster of the Greeks, Turkey's historic foes, and the revision of the Sèvres treaty became the object of the Turkish national revolution which Mustafa Kemal launched in May 1919 in response to the first Greek landings. Through a mixture of skillful diplomacy and inspired military leadership, Mustafa Kemal, the successful defender of Gallipoli in 1915, achieved his goal. Having defeated the Greeks at Sakarya in August 1921 and having successfully maneuvered both Italy and France out of Turkey, Mustafa Kemal confronted an isolated Britain in October 1922 with the threat of an armed clash at Constantinople, still under British military control. Lloyd George yielded, in part because the Dominion prime ministers were afraid of being drawn into another war, in whose making they had not been consulted and whose issues did not involve their direct interests. Following the Armistice of Mudanya of October 1922, Mustafa Kemal obtained a new peace conference, which produced, with Turkish participation, a new peace treaty, the Treaty of Lausanne of August 1923.

The Lausanne peace restored the territorial integrity of Turkey proper and abolished the humiliating "capitulations" which had granted foreigners special status. The Dardanelles remained demilitarized. A partial exchange of Turkish and Greek minorities was arranged in order to lessen old ethnic conflicts.

In pursuing his goal of treaty revision, Mustafa Kemal had enlisted the support of Soviet Russia in the Moscow treaty of March 1921. The alliance was pragmatic and did not permanently affect Turkish foreign policy. After the formal proclamation of the Turkish Republic in October 1923, Mustafa Kemal gradually moved toward the Western powers. He also implemented a program of Westernization and modernization at home which became one of the few successful programs of its kind in any Moslem country in the twentieth century.

ITALIAN DISAPPOINTMENT

Among the victorious Allies, the nation least satisfied with the peace settlement was Italy. Italy had entered the war in 1915 not as a result of foreign attack but from calculation of territorial gain. The cost of the war had proved to be far beyond expectation in blood, economic assets, and social stress. The Italian peace delegation under Prime Minister Orlando negotiated in Paris for maximum gain, even beyond what was promised in the secret wartime agreements, because it hoped to thereby neutralize both nationalist agitation and growing social unrest at home, which reached its first postwar climax in the general strike of July 1919.

The peace settlement gave Italy Trieste and the promised frontier with Austria along the Brenner pass, thereby surrendering the South Tyrol with 240,000 Austro-Germans to Italian rule without the benefit of a plebiscite. On the other hand, Italy received none of the German colonies in Africa and no part of the Turkish Middle East. Controversy broke out at the peace conference over the Italian-Yugoslav border and the port of Fiume on the Adriatic in particular. The latter, though not mentioned in the 1915 London treaty, was claimed by Italy despite its predominantly Yugoslav population and despite the fact that Italy was already assured of the port of Trieste, the largest and best seaport in the northeastern Adriatic. Italy's demand for Fiume rested on her jealousy of newly constituted Yugoslavia, which she viewed as a potential rival in the control of the Adriatic and the western Balkans. Italy's claim was chiefly opposed by the United States, in part because Point Eleven of Wilson's *Fourteen Points* had promised Serbia, the nucleus of Yugoslavia, a natural seaport on the Adriatic. The Fiume controversy prompted Orlando to boycott the peace conference temporarily and it gave rise to demonstrations against Wilson and the United States in Italian cities. Where Woodrow Wilson had been celebrated most recently as the "god of peace" during his visit to Italy before the opening of the Paris peace conference, he was now denounced as "Wilson the vile" (*vil sono*) with equal strength. Fiume became a symbol whose importance far exceeded the real importance of a relatively small seaport in a corner of an inland sea. To Italy it symbolized the unequal treatment which the established Great Powers had once again meted out to her, and it thus suggested that Italy's larger war aim, the attainment of coequal status with France or even Britain, remained unfulfilled. It was from this source of deep national bitterness that one of the roots of Italian fascism was to grow quickly into an all-embracing vine that sapped the strength of Italy's democracy, which was already weakened by war and hunger. The forceful seizure of Fiume by the black-shirted volunteers under the leadership of Italy's boastful and xenophobic poet Gabriele d'Annunzio in September 1919 was the first clear signal of the coming confrontation between inflamed nationalism and democracy in Italy.

The Peace and its Failings

The peace settlement overall came under attack soon after it was made and not merely by the spokesmen of the former Central Powers. Britain's famed economist John Maynard Keynes denounced the peace as "Carthaginian" in his *Economic Consequences of the Peace* of 1920. Keynes criticized the peacemakers for what he considered their neglect of economic issues and their preoccupation with frontiers and questions of sovereignty. The Europe bequeathed by the peace conference to the future was, in Keynes' view, an "inefficient, unemployed, disorganized" Europe.

That the peace of 1919 became a failure much sooner after its conclusion than did the peace of 1815 which followed the French revolutionary and Napoleonic period, was less the result of its provisions than of its faulty enforcement. The successful enforcement of the peace required the participation of its principal architects, including those of the United States. The war had established the outlines of a new Atlantic community for the first time. That community had enabled Western Europe to survive the German onslaught of 1918. It had also served the American national interest, which had been progressively endangered by European developments between 1915 and 1917. The peace conference was the logical extension of the Atlantic community of 1917. For the community to succeed in laying lasting foundations of stability, each of its members had to continue to carry part of its burden.

The precipitous American withdrawal from the enforcement of the peace through the repudiation of the league and, because of the league's organic connection to the peace settlement, of the peace treaties themselves, not only upset the basic security arrangements of the peace but deprived the liberal concept of its credibility and strength as a new force in international relations. By removing itself from the affairs of the League and of Europe, the United States deprived France of much needed reassurance, and it deprived the vanquished of much hope in the eventual readjustment of the harshest provisions of the peace.

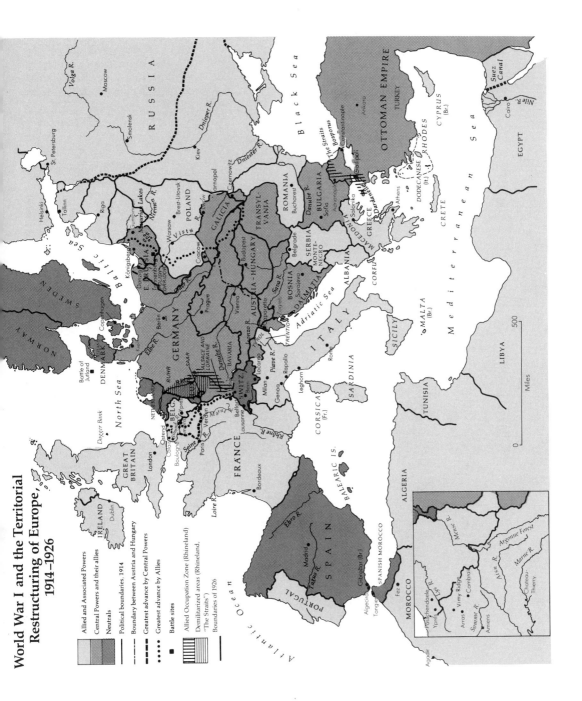

World War I and the Territorial Restructuring of Europe, 1914–1926

Allied and Associated Powers
Central Powers and their allies
Neutrals
Political boundaries, 1914
Boundary between Austria and Hungary
Greatest advance by Central Powers
Greatest advance by Allies
Battle sites
Allied Occupation Zone (Rhineland)
Demilitarized areas (Rhineland, "The Straits")
Boundaries of 1926

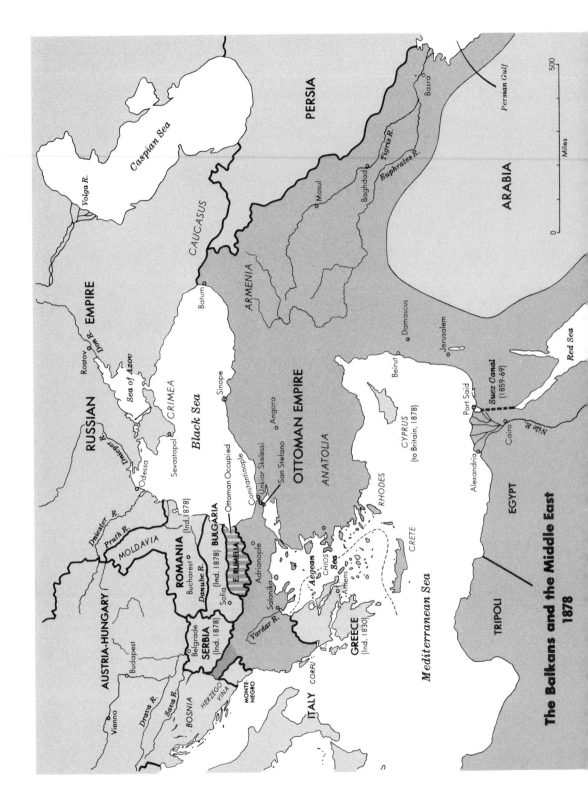

The Balkans and the Middle East
1878

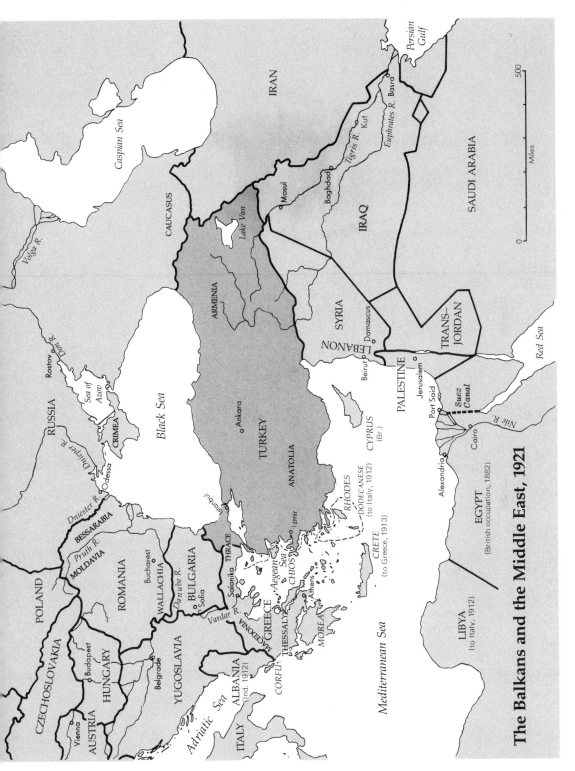

The Balkans and the Middle East, 1921

53

5

Enforcement of the Peace:
1919 to 1929

THE LACK OF ALLIED UNITY

After the peace settlement of 1919, France, in the words of Winston Churchill, "peered into the future in thankful wonder and haunting dread." The dread was occasioned not only by the American retreat into isolation but also by the lack of unity among the principal European Allies.

The American boycott of the League of Nations had sharpened Anglo-French differences on the purpose and the nature of the League. Britain, in the words of Foreign Secretary Lord Curzon, was satisfied with the League as a machinery which gave "practical effect" to the principles of international friendship and good understanding. Mindful of the failure of Sir Edward Grey's mediation effort during the July crisis of 1914 owing to lack of time and suitable machinery, Britain saw the League principally as a permanent organ of mediation and talk. France had seen the League as an extension of the wartime alliance for the enforcement of the peace, and she was dismayed to hear Canada and others object to the collective security obligations under articles 10 and 16 of the covenant at the very first League assembly meeting in Geneva in November 1920. French efforts to put additional teeth into the collective security provisions of the League through the Draft Treaty of Mutual Assistance of 1923 and through the Geneva Protocol of 1924 failed because of the refusal of Britain and the Dominions to assume additional guarantees.

Accordingly, France placed increased reliance on a tough policy against Germany and a strong alliance system in eastern Europe which was intended to help contain Germany and uphold the status quo. But even during the early postwar period, developments in Eastern Europe were not to French liking and raised misgivings for the future.

The Russian Threat

The question of Russia was answered by 1922, with the triumph of the Bolsheviks and the defeat of the White opposition in the civil war. War, civil war and the experiments of war communism had thoroughly weakened and exhausted the new Soviet Russia. They had, at the same time, destroyed none of the confrontational and revolutionary stances from which Lenin judged the long-term prospects of Soviet-Western relations. Speaking in 1921, Lenin observed that the first wave of world revolution had spent itself and the second had not yet arisen. At the same time, he viewed the existence of Soviet Russia side-by-side with "imperialist states" unthinkable for a protracted period of time. Instead, Lenin foresaw "a series of most frightening clashes" between Soviet Russia and the bourgeois states, until one or the other side had won.

France continued to regard Soviet Russia as a hostile power, as a potential threat to the states of eastern Europe, and as a likely source of mischief in conjunction with defeated Germany. The threat to eastern Europe was dramatically highlighted by the brief Russo-Polish war between April and October 1920. The Poles, not content with the "Curzon line," the ethnic border between Poland and Russia proposed by the Allies in 1919, had started the war in hopes of creating a Polish-Ukrainian-White Russian federation under their own leadership. After initial gains and the capture of the Ukrainian capital of Kiev in May 1920, the Poles were in turn thrown back to the outskirts of their own capital of Warsaw in a Soviet counterattack in August 1920. Warsaw was saved by the timely intervention of France, which sent a military mission under General Weygand.

Conflict in Eastern Europe

The Russo-Polish War likewise indicated a lack among the states of eastern Europe of the cohesion and solidarity essential to the stability of the region and the success of French policy there. Once freed from their former Russian, German, and Habsburg overlords, the new states of eastern Europe fell to quarreling over disputed border areas. These quarrels in many cases poisoned their mutual relations for the entire period of their brief independence between 1919 and 1939, and rendered a viable eastern European security system under French leadership impossible. Poland and Czechoslovakia remained conflicted for the entire interwar period over the disputed border area of Teschen, which even prompted an armed Czech-Polish clash before the Allies partitioned the area in 1920. Lithuania and Poland similarly quarreled over the possession of the city of Vilna, which Poland seized by force in October 1920. Polish-Lithuanian relations were subsequently severed and remained so. The Polish annexation of Vilna in turn jeopardized the regional security pact of the Baltic states, including Finland, Latvia, Estonia, Lithuania, and Poland, which had been under discussion in 1920 as a protection against Soviet Russia. A more limited regional pact between Finland, Poland, Latvia, and Estonia similarly collapsed in 1922 when Finland withdrew out of fear of being involved in Polish-Soviet tensions. The only east European country actually willing to help Poland during the Russo-Polish war of 1920 was Hungary, on account of historic ties of friendship and of the recent Hungarian experience with the Communist dictatorship of Béla Kun. Ironically, Hungary was barred from sending troops by Czechoslovakia, a nation on unfriendly terms with Poland. The Paris peace conference of 1919 had drawn Czechoslovakia's borders in such a way as to give Czechoslovakia and Rumania—but not Hungary and Poland— a common border.

Poland and Rumania, both of which had cause to fear Soviet revisionist territorial claims, did form an alliance in 1921. The effectiveness of the alliance was weakened by Poland's refusal to have it applied to a Rumanian-Hungarian conflict arising out of Hungarian revisionist claims on Transylvania.

Fear of Hungarian revisionist claims and concern over a possible Habsburg restoration there led Czechoslovakia, Yugoslavia, and Rumania to form the so-called Little Entente in 1920–1921.

France, eager to promote the unity of eastern Europe, attempted to combine the Rumanian-Polish with the Little Entente alliance systems. These efforts failed in the 1920s, as they were to fail again during the 1930s, because the obstacle of Polish-Czechoslovak hostility proved to be insurmountable. What remained was a system of bilateral alliances between France and the respective members of the eastern European blocs. The French-Polish alliance of 1921 was followed by a French-Czechoslovak alliance of 1924, a French-Rumanian alliance of 1926, and a French-Yugoslav alliance of 1927.

The French-Yugoslav alliance was largely a response to the mounting pressure which Italy had been exerting on the western Balkans and eastern-central Europe since 1919. Italian Balkan policy after 1919 was essentially a continuation of Italy's pre-1914 policy in the same region, only on a more ambitious scale since the disappearance of the Austro-Hungarian Empire. Although Italy had given her consent to the creation of the new Yugoslavia in 1918, she treated Yugoslavia as a rival from the start, once the war was over. The emotional quarrel over Fiume at the 1919 peace conference was an early example of the Italian-Yugoslav contest. In August 1923, less than a year after Mussolini's advent to power, Italy's Balkan policy assumed a more aggressive stance with the bombardment and temporary occupation of the Greek island of Corfu. The "Corfu incident" was in retaliation for the death of an Italian member of the Allied border commission, entrusted with the fixing of the borders of newly independent Albania. Albania itself soon ended up as an Italian satellite, first under the terms of the Pact of Tirana of 1926 and by 1927 through the Italian-Albanian "Unalterable Defensive Alliance."

Italian Balkan policy of the 1920s ran counter to the French design for eastern Europe because it ultimately aimed at the dismemberment of Yugoslavia and increasingly aligned itself with the "loser states" of eastern Europe: Hungary, Bulgaria, and Austria. The encouragement of Hungarian and Bulgarian revisionist demands in particular ran counter to the French purpose of keeping Rumania and Yugoslavia as strong as possible.

REPARATIONS, THE RUHR AND THE DAWES PLAN

The financial and economic legacy of the war was scarcely less onerous for the victorious Allies than it was for defeated Germany. Whereas the Napoleonic wars, a hundred years before World War I, had resulted in a great increase in British exports and foreign trade, notably to Latin America, World War I had resulted in a 50 percent drop in the value of British exports. While Britain's industrial economy was geared to the war effort, the Dominions, Japan, and the United States encroached on traditional British export markets. In France, war-related devastation and dislocation had resulted in a 34 percent decline in industrial output by 1920. The cost of rebuilding the war-devastated departments of eastern and northeastern France was estimated as high as $3 billion. Both Britain and France had extended huge war loans to Russia, the French loans being added to the prewar loans with which tsarist Russia had improved rail communications. The loans had to be written off following the Bolshevik repudiation of the tsarist debt. Allied attempts to alter the Bolshevik stand on prewar debts at the Genoa economic conference of April 1922 failed, as did Allied attempts to induce the United States to lower its claims for repayment of the $10 billion Allied war debt, or to cancel such claims altogether. In February 1922, Congress not only barred the U.S. government from cancellation of the Allied war debt, but further prohibited the acceptance of German reparation payments in lieu of Allied debt payments.

The German government accepted the Allied ultimatum of May 5, 1921 (the London ultimatum), which fixed total German reparations at $33 billion, because the alternative to acceptance was the Allied threat to occupy the Ruhr valley, Germany's principal industrial and mining center. A partial Allied occupation of the Ruhr, involving the cities of Duisburg, Ruhrort and Düsseldorf, had already been undertaken in early March 1921 in retaliation for Germany's not meeting delivery schedules for reparations in kind. By 1922, the German stand on reparations toughened, the German government pleading insolvency and demanding "first bread, then reparations." Specifically, the German government asked that the Allies advance Germany a loan for currency stabilization; that they grant a moratorium on reparation payments; that they have Germany's capacity to pay reparations reassessed by impartial bankers; and that they draw up a new and realistic payments plan, based on the experts' findings.

Both the United States, which had a major stake in the solution of the reparations crisis, and Great Britain, were basically sympathetic to the German stand. In April 1921, President Harding had rejected a German appeal for U.S. involvement in the German-Allied reparations quarrel. In December 1922, however, U.S. secretary of state Charles Evans Hughes delivered a significant address before the meeting of the American Historical Association, which dealt with the reparations issue and proposed, instead, assessment of German capacity to pay by experts and a payments plan based on the assessment. American bankers would participate in the assessment. The Hughes initiative was designed to forestall the policy of force, which French premier Poincaré was about to apply against Germany. It failed to prevent or even to delay the French occupation of the Ruhr, which began on January 11, 1923 with five French divisions and Belgian auxiliaries.

On the broader subject of French-German relations, two general attitudes had developed in France since 1919. The French Socialists, having quit the wartime government of "Sacred Union" in 1917 as a demonstration on behalf of a compromise peace, were also critical of the Treaty of Versailles. Socialist leader Leon Blum thought Versailles a betrayal of Wilsonian principles. To Blum, the world war had been a "great insomnia," filled with the "nightmare of hatred." The peace, Blum had hoped, would determine the "nature of the victory" rather than the victory determining "the shape of the peace." During the immediate postwar period from 1919–1924, Socialist influence on French foreign policy was minimal, however. The French elections of November 1919 had resulted in a significant drop in Socialist strength to 55 seats, as against 338 seats for the National Bloc, which set the course of foreign policy for the next five years. Advocates of reconciliation with Germany also existed outside the Socialist party, however, especially in Aristide Briand, the future French foreign minister of the mid-1920s, and Philippe Berthelot, secretary general of the French foreign office. Taking a long-term view of French-German relations in 1922, Berthelot thought that current French military supremacy was bound to be eclipsed by the superior industrial and human resources of Germany within half-a-century. In his view, it was therefore incumbent upon the French leadership of the early 1920s, while France was still the stronger of the two nations, to foster a permanent spirit of antimilitarism in Germany through a policy of French-German reconciliation.

This was not the view of Premier Poincaré, head of the National Bloc, who undertook the Ruhr occupation of 1923, At that time the Ruhr accounted for 85 percent of German coal, 90 percent of coke, 77 percent of pig iron, and 85 percent of steel production. By seizing the Ruhr, Poincaré pursued three main objectives: first, France would operate the mines and industries for reparations purposes; second, France would use her increased military presence to detach the Rhineland from Germany, an objective the United States and Britain had disallowed at the peace conference; and third, France would treat the Ruhr assets as "productive pledges" and not release them back into German ownership until the German government had given new and binding assurances of fulfiling its reparations obligations under the Versailles treaty. The official German pleas of insolvency, Poincaré dismissed as an evasion, unsupported by the real wealth of Germany.

The Weimar Republic responded to the Ruhr invasion with a policy of passive resistance in the occupied area, which amounted to a general strike. The strike was meant to deny France any economic gains from the occupation. At the same time, Germany hoped to increasingly isolate France internationally by mobilizing American and British sympathy on behalf of the German cause. The Soviet Union too could be relied upon to support German resistance, not only because of the recently concluded Rapallo treaty, but because Soviet foreign policy welcomed "contradictions," i.e. tensions, between the major powers of noncommunist Europe. During the Ruhr struggle, the Soviets, in fact, mobilized the propaganda apparatus of the Moscow-based Communist International to support German nationalist terrorists, such as Albert L. Schlageter, while denouncing Poincaré's policy as "imperialist" among the occupying French troops.

Both Britain and the United States were critical of the French policy of force and feared its consequences. King George V of Britain expressed the fear that France would "bankrupt Germany" and would "throw her into the arms of Russia." The U.S. government feared social revolution as a result of a German economic collapse under the weight of the Ruhr struggle. In addition, the United States suspected as a further French motive the intended fusion of the French and German coal and steel industries into a West European "supercartel" under French leadership, with consequences detrimental to U.S. economic interests.

By November 1923, Anglo-American pressure had succeeded in getting France to accept a conference of experts to reassess Germany's capacity to pay reparations.

The conference opened in January 1924 in Paris and very quickly produced an entire, new reparations plan, named the Dawes Plan after Charles G. Dawes, a U.S. banker and experts committee chairman.

Prior to the adoption of the Dawes Plan, Poincaré's policy of force had inflicted serious damage on Germany, some of it of lasting consequences, without securing proportionate advantages for France. The Ruhr invasion was essentially an economic failure. Although Poincaré succeeded in forcing the German government into abandoning its passive resistance policy by September 1923, the gains made afterwards were hardly sufficient to cover the cost of the military operation. Poincaré had to raise French taxes in early 1924, a fact which contributed to his fall from power in May of that year. The German economy and the German currency, in particular, had meanwhile collapsed and, just as Britain and the United States had feared, this had spurred social and nationalist upheaval. During "red October" 1923, the German Communists launched an abortive uprising in the states of Saxony and Thuringia, followed by Hitler's and the Nazi party's first unsuccessful bid for power on November 9, 1923. German inflation reached astronomical proportions in October 1923 with an official exchange rate of $1 to 2.5 billion marks. The inflation of 1923 further impoverished the German middle class and thereby increased its alienation from the democratic Weimar Republic.

Poincaré's policy of Rhineland separatism ended in failure through lack of support from the German population, and also through outside criticism, especially from Britain.

Being based on a bankers' examination of the German economy, the Dawes Plan had all the earmarks of a bankers' payments plan with sound guarantees and safeguards. As a first step, the Dawes Plan granted a $200 million (800 million marks) loan for German currency stabilization and recovery. Annual reparations were scaled down to 200 million marks for the first year to rise gradually to a standard 2.5 billion mark annual instalment. No final reparations sum was given, on the assumption that the Dawes Plan itself was an interim solution to be succeeded by a definitive settlement in the future. The plan thus left open the possibility of a future remission of part or all of the reparations debt. It identified the sources of German reparations such as specific taxes, the earnings of the German railroads, and the interest on industrial bonds. German reparation payments were to be transferred, or converted, into foreign currency only to the extent compatible with the stability of the German currency. The transfer of German payments was put into the hands of a newly appointed reparations agent, Parker Gilbert, an American.

The chief advantage of the Dawes Plan to the Germans was the lowering of reparation payments due in the near future and, more importantly, the restoration of foreign, chiefly American, business confidence in the German economy. The Dawes Plan thus opened a new phase in the economic development not only of postwar Germany, but of postwar Europe, with heavy U.S. investments streaming into Europe between 1934–1929. Although Charles Dawes and the other participating U.S. bankers had worked in a private, not official U.S. capacity, their role resulted from an official initiative and reflected official aims. Under conditions of returning prosperity in Europe between 1924 and 1929 the Dawes Plan worked well enough while prosperity lasted, and as long as U.S. loan capital continued to flow into Europe.

On the negative side, the Dawes Plan could not obscure the fact that it had vastly increased foreign controls over the German economy. In a sense, the Dawes Plan was a nonviolent application of Poincaré's policy of "productive pledges," expanded from the limited scope of the Ruhr economy to the national economy of Germany.

LOCARNO AND RECONCILIATION

In one way the Ruhr struggle had been the final battle of the First World War. Only after the battle was over was it possible to seek an improvement of French-German relations on a new basis. The setting was favorable in 1924, because of new leadership in France and Germany. The French elections of 1924 had brought to power the "cartel of the Left," composed of Socialists and Radicals. Premier Herriot and Foreign Minister Aristide Briand favored better relations with Germany than Poincaré had maintained.

Stresemann

In Germany, the Ruhr crisis had brought to the fore Gustav Stresemann, the most gifted political leader of republican Germany. Both in his domestic and foreign policies, Stresemann was a symbol of the democratic Germany that might have been, had it not been for the failure of the Weimar Republic after Stresemann's death in October 1929.

Originally identified with the annexationist policy of the German Empire during World War I, Stresemann came to accept the Weimar Republic as a desirable system under which postwar Germany could fully develop her domestic and foreign energies. He thought the confrontational policy of Germany between 1919 and 1923 a mistake, since it invited French military force, as in the Ruhr, and emphasized Germany's isolation in postwar Europe. Stresemann's alternative was reconciliation with the western powers as a prerequisite to the revision of the Versailles treaty by peaceful means. In the west, Stresemann hoped to regain the Saar and to secure an evacuation of the Rhineland ahead of the scheduled deadline of 1935. The principal revisionist aims concerned Germany's eastern borders with Poland, the return of Danzig and, conceivably, the union of Austria and Germany. Stresemann had little faith in the lasting value of a special relationship between Weimar Germany and Soviet Russia, such as the Rapallo treaty of 1922 had suggested. Although the Soviets had supported Germany during the Ruhr struggle of 1923, they had not hesitated to lend their full support to the German Communist uprising of October 1923, which had aimed at the overthrow of the German government. The lesson was one which Stresemann never forgot, because "red October" 1923 occurred during his own brief chancellorship of August–November, prior to his long-term tenure at the foreign office until his death in 1929. If the Soviets should ever reach Berlin, Stresemann privately observed, they will be content to "bolshevize Europe as far as the Elbe river," and throw the rest of Germany to the French.

The Germany of the future envisaged by Stresemann was a Germany restored to Great Power status, strongly linked to the west by economic and political ties. Stresemann's inspiration was not Bismarck, whose policy between 1864 and 1871 rested on military strength, but Prince Metternich of Austria. Just as Metternich had led defeated Austria back to Great Power status between 1809 and 1815 primarily through the skill of his diplomacy, Stresemann hoped to accomplish similar results for the Germany of the 1920s through a revision of the Treaty of Versailles by peaceful means. The Metternich biography by the Austrian historian Srbik, which was published in the early 1920s, served Stresemann as a guide.

Locarno

In order to achieve his goal, Stresemann relied on a strategy of multilateral agreements with the former Western enemies, designed to gain security for a disarmed Germany and to regain some of the lost territories. The Locarno treaty of October 1925, which resulted from Stresemann's initiative, was the first and most significant achievement of his multilateral approach. Concluded between Britain, France, Italy, Germany, Poland, and Czechoslovakia, the Locarno treaty guaranteed the French-German and Belgian-German borders and the demilitarized status of the Rhineland, with Britain and Italy acting as guarantors. France, Germany, and Belgium promised not to attack or invade one another's territory, nor to resort to war against each other. The treaty also included arbitration agreements between Germany, France, Belgium, Czechoslovakia, and Poland, as well as treaties of mutual guarantee between France, Czechoslovakia and Poland.

The German Locarno initiative resulted from an appreciation of the primacy of the security motive in French foreign policy. By voluntarily subscribing to the French-German borders, as drawn under Versailles, and by reaffirming the permanent demilitarization of the Rhineland, Germany renounced any revisionist claim to Alsace-Lorraine and hoped to satisfy French security concerns. The French were initially not satisfied with the German offer because they noted the absence of any corresponding German recognition of the German-Polish and German-Czechoslovak borders, implying German revisionist aims in the east. The French similarly feared a devaluation of the whole Versailles settlement by the selective German recognition of some of its provisions. Italy, too, raised objections at first, demanding that if the French-German border was to obtain a special guarantee, Italy's Brenner frontier with Austria must get comparable guarantees. Britain liked the German offer, because it promised German good behavior along the Rhine, which a succession of British foreign secretaries from Lord Curzon to Austen Chamberlain had declared the "outer frontier" and the real security zone of Britain on the continent. The British similarly did not quarrel with the German aim of revising the eastern frontiers, provided that such a revision could be accomplished peacefully.

British support and the addition of French-Polish and French-Czechoslovak guarantee treaties, which were meant to fill the gap in the German border pledges, made possible the conclusion of the Locarno pact. Briand's attempt to expand the Locarno treaty with an additional "eastern Locarno," guaranteeing the borders of Finland, Latvia, Estonia, Poland, and Rumania, failed in 1927 over British objections. At the time of its signing, Locarno was hailed as the real peace treaty ending World War I, as the "dividing line between the years of war and the years of peace," in Austen Chamberlain's words. Germany's entry into the league in September 1926 as a Great Power with permanent representation on the league council was a natural follow-up to the Locarno treaty. League membership represented yet another example of Stresemann's retreat from isolation through a policy of multilateralism.

Out of the Treaty of Locarno grew the "spirit of Locarno," which, at the time, was widely viewed as the dawn of a new and peaceful age, but which was soon revealed more as an afterglow of the spirit of hope and optimism of prewar Europe. The Kellogg-Briand Pact of August 1928, named after the U.S. secretary of state Frank B. Kellogg and the French foreign minister Aristide Briand, was symbolic of the Locarno spirit. The pact, which renounced war "as an instrument of national policy," was eventually signed by sixty-five nations, a number exceeding total league membership.

Briand and Stresemann, the architects of Locarno, were both awarded the Nobel Peace Prize in 1927. Yet even during its most optimistic phase, the "spirit of Locarno" represented different aims for France and Germany. Stresemann hoped to secure tangible revisionist gains quickly in order to justify his new approach before a critical nationalist audience at home. When meeting with Briand at Thoiry after the German entry into the league in September 1926, he asked for the withdrawal of the Allied disarmament commission, the withdrawal of Allied forces from the Rhineland by 1927, and the repurchasing of the coal mines in the Saar. In return, Stresemann promised to raise German reparation payment above the level required by the Dawes Plan. The Allies withdrew the disarmament commission from Germany in 1927, but they refused to yield on the other points.

The Young Plan

Seizing on the signing of the Kellogg-Briand Pact in August 1928 as a favorable opportunity, the Germans reopened their revisionist drive for an early Rhineland evacuation and a new reparations settlement to take the place of the Dawes Plan. The result was a compromise which fell short of Stresemann's expectations. The Allies promised to evacuate the Rhineland by June 1930, a full five years ahead of schedule. At the same time, Germany accepted a new reparations plan, the Young Plan, named after Owen Young, the American chairman of the financial experts who drafted it. Defined as a "complete and definite solution of the reparation problem," the Young Plan removed all foreign controls from the German economy, but it also instituted a payments plan, running all the way into the year 1988. In the event of U.S. remission of Allied war debts, Germany was to benefit by up to two-thirds of the remission prior to 1965 and to its full amount afterwards. Stresemann's original hope that the optimism engendered by the Kellogg-Briand Pact would allow for a complete cancellation of reparations was shown to be an illusion. In Germany, Stresemann's success in regaining full German sovereignty through the early evacuation of the Rhineland received little enough appreciation. On October 3, 1929, Stresemann died amidst a violent campaign against the Young Plan, which was organized by Hitler's resurgent Nazi party and Hilter's new allies in the conservative Nationalist party.

To Briand, the Locarno treaty had been but one approach to the question of French security, whose importance, relative to other safeguards, depended on the state of French-German relations at any given time.

French Security

Since 1924, French security had rested on a number of supports: on the eastern alliance system, which Briand expanded; on the collective guarantees of the Locarno pact, initiated by Germany; on the moral solidarity of the Kellogg-Briand Pact; and on what Briand called collective action in the case of "pressing risks." As late as September 1929, Briand had demonstrated his faith in the ongoing process of reconcilation and pacification by proposing a European federal union. The union was to have permanent supranational organs and was to achieve both economic and political integration. By 1930, with evidence of a much harsher international climate in the offing, Briand's union project had died a quiet death in the league-appointed commission of inquiry for European union. Britain cited her special relationship with the members of the Commonwealth as an obstacle to membership. The Germans suspected the union scheme to be a cover for French resistance to border revisions in eastern Europe. Italy wanted an agreement on disarmament to precede a European union. The small states of Europe generally supported Briand's scheme. From 1930 onwards, France was increasingly concerned with the new evidence of "pressing risks," as the high hopes placed upon the "spirit of Locarno" were found to be illusory.

SOVIET RUSSIA AND THE WEST IN THE 1920s

By the mid-1920s, Soviet Russia and the West began to coexist on terms neither had originally thought desirable or even likely. By the turn of 1923–1924 hopes of communist revolutions in the West as an immediate follow-up to the Bolshevik seizure of power in Russia had to be abandoned. In 1923 communist insurrections were crushed both in Bulgaria and the Weimar Republic. The abortive Estonian communist uprising in Reval of December 1924 marked the end of foreign communist uprisings, which had begun in ravaged postwar Germany and Hungary at the turn of 1918–1919.

Western attempts to overthrow the Bolshevik regime, first through direct military intervention, later through arms' aid and financial support to the Whites in the Russian Civil War, had similarly failed. After establishing full diplomatic relations with Weimer Germany in the Rapallo treaty of 1922, in 1924 Soviet Russia secured formal recognition from the principal powers of Western Europe, Britain, France and Italy, together with that of many of the smaller European states. Spain, Holland, Portugal, Belgium, Switzerland, Hungary, Bulgaria, and the nations of the Little Entente still withheld recognition.

Normalization of relations was important for reasons of trade and national security. The need for foreign trade increased especially towards the end of the 1920s with the beginnings of Stalin's industrialization program under the five year plans. By 1929, Germany supplied 22 percent of Soviet imports, the United States, which still withheld official recognition, 20 percent. Britain and France supplied 6 and 4 percent respectively. The total value of Soviet imports, though rising considerably between 1926 and 1928 from $346 million to $490 million, was still below the level of prewar imports, which had reached $700 million in 1913.

The normalization of trade notwithstanding, neither side forgot the other's hostile intentions and this continued to influence the policies of both.

After the end of foreign intervention and the civil war, it was essential for the Soviets to prevent, if at all possible, the coalescing of noncommunist Europe into an anti-Soviet bloc. The League of Nations appeared, in this context, an instrument of particular danger not only because it lessened the chance of war among the noncommunist powers, but because the league members might invoke the sanctions clauses of the covenant as a base for future military action against Soviet Russia. Among Lenin's motives in launching the Communist (Third) International in March 1919 was the intention of countering the League of Nations, which was, in the Bolshevik definition, an "antirevolutionary league of capitalist states."

Conversely, it was desirable from the Soviet standpoint to see German-French tensions of the postwar years prolonged in order to maintain the division of noncommunist Europe. The Rapallo treaty of 1922 between the Weimar Republic and Soviet Russia was intended to serve that larger purpose, for it did not merely establish normal relations between the signatories but laid the foundations of increased trade and secret, long-term military collaboration. The secret military collaboration was to last into 1932, enabling Germany to develop, in Russia, weapons whose possession the Versailles treaty had outlawed, and permitting Soviet Russia to share in the progress of German military technology and training.

The Soviet government was therefore dismayed at the prospect of improved German-Western relations at the turn of 1924–1925. The Soviets denounced the Dawes Plan of 1924 as the beginning of "German enslavement" by American capitalism and they urged Stresemann not to conclude the Locarno pact in 1925 out of fear that it would tie Germany politically to the West. Although Germany was still a disarmed nation when she joined the league in 1926, the Soviets feared the possibility of Germany's being used as a base for Western military action against the Soviet Union. It was for those reasons that in April 1926, the Weimar Republic and Soviet Russia concluded the Berlin treaty, which pledged the neutrality of both powers in the event of an unprovoked attack on either. Germany further reaffirmed the limitations of her own obligations arising from the sanctions clauses of the league, which the Western powers had accepted and agreed to prior to Germany's actually becoming a league member. These limitations virtually exempted Germany from any sanctions the league might impose on Soviet Russia in the future, in recognition of Germany's disarmed condition and her geographic proximity to Soviet Russia. As a further response to the newly created situation of the mid-1920s, the Soviets concluded a series of neutrality and nonaggression pacts with their immediate neighbors to the west and south. A Soviet-Turkish neutrality agreement of December 1925 was followed by a Soviet-Afghan treaty in August and a Soviet-Lithuanian nonaggression pact of September 1926. In October 1927 the Soviets concluded a nonaggression pact with Iran. In 1929, the Soviets applied the terms of the Kellogg-Briand Pact to the Litvinov Protocol, named after Soviet foreign minister Maxim Litvinov, which was signed by the USSR, Poland, Rumania, Latvia, Estonia, Lithuania, Turkey, Iran, and the Free City of Danzig.

Comintern Propaganda

The Western powers, principally Britain and France, remained deeply suspicious of Soviet intentions largely because of the activities of the Communist International in the western colonies and protectorates as well as areas such as China and Iran. In May 1923 Britain's foreign secretary Lord Curzon had demanded *per ultimatum* an end to Comintern propaganda in India, Iran and Afghanistan. In 1924, after Comintern agitation in support of national independence, was resumed in India, Egypt and Ireland, Britain's secretary of state for India, Lord Birkenhead, charged that Soviet policy was out to destroy the British Empire. Austen Chamberlain, upon becoming foreign secretary, sought common action with Premier Herriot of France in suppressing Comintern propaganda in the French and British colonies. In November 1924 the Conservative government canceled the Anglo-Soviet trade agreement, previously concluded by its Labour predecessor. The Conservative victory in the British elections of 1924 was due in no small measure to the so-called Zinoviev letter, which the British foreign office claimed to have discovered, and whose authenticity the Soviets denied. Zinoviev, head of the Comintern, was said to have called on British workers and soldiers to subvert national defense in the event of a Soviet-British war. In 1927 the Conservative government broke off diplomatic relations with Soviet Russia following the exposure of the Soviet trade mission in London, "Arcos," as a seat of Soviet espionage and Comintern propaganda. Soviet-British relations were not restored until another Labour government was in office in 1929.

Long-term Effects

The memory of Anglo-Soviet tension of the 1920s had a lasting effect on Conservative attitudes, and was still felt when the British government of the late 1930s had to choose between appeasement of the fascist dictators or effective collective security in league with the Soviet Union.

Soviet-French relations at the end of the 1920s were scarcely better than those between Britain and Russia. The Soviets were especially suspicious of Briand's project of European union, which they viewed as yet another French effort at rounding up an anti-Soviet European coalition. Stalin denounced the union project as a camouflage for upholding French hegemony in Europe and attacked France specifically as "the most aggressive and militaristic country among all aggressive and militaristic countries in the world."

6

The Crisis of European Democracy: 1919 to 1939

DEMOCRATIC PRESTIGE AND THE SOCIAL CHALLENGE

The victory of the democracies in the First World War had brought democratic prestige to an all-time high, a fact reflected in the adoption of democratic constitutions by the defeated Central Powers and by the newly emerged smaller states of eastern Europe. The German Weimar constitution of 1919 borrowed heavily from French, British, American, and Swiss models. The Weimar constitution, in turn, served as a model for liberal-democratic constitutions adopted by the small Baltic states, Latvia, Lithuania, and Estonia in the early 1920s. The 1921 constitution of newly independent Poland was liberal-democratic, as was that of Czechoslovakia of 1920. Rumania's first postwar elections of November 1919 were held under an expanded, democratic suffrage.

With liberal democracy the predominant form of government in the Europe of the 1920s, it was incumbent upon democratic governments to cope with the socioeconomic problems of the postwar era. The nature of these problems varied greatly from country to country and region to region, depending on the stage of development and on the prewar legacy of unsolved problems. In the advanced industrial societies of western and central Europe, full employment for the urban labor force and social safeguards against the hazards of old age, sickness, and accident were among the foremost social tasks.

The underdeveloped societies of Italy and Spain had inherited from prewar times a complex and explosive mixture of socioeconomic problems that included the pressing need for land reform, stark rural and urban poverty, widespread illiteracy, and lack of experience in the responsible uses of political power. The principal social issue of the newly independent states of eastern Europe was land reform and the breaking up of large feudal estates. Czechoslovakia was something of an exception in this, because its socioeconomic structure more nearly reflected that of the industrialized nations of western and central Europe. The social and political makeup of much of newly independent eastern Europe was complicated by the nationality problem, which had not been solved through national independence. In virtually every eastern European country dissatisfied national minorities persisted. In nations such as Czechoslovakia and Yugoslavia, friction between related and allied nationalities, Czechs and Slovaks, Serbs, Croatians, and Slovenes, resulted from rivalry and competition for national dominance. In situations of this kind, social action, such as land reform, was often employed not for social ends but as a weapon against rival nationalities.

Both in the victorious and the defeated nations of Europe, the First World War, with its revolutionary impact on social customs and longstanding social relationships, greatly heightened expectations among the traditionally deprived. The great and urgent question before the European democracies, old and new, was whether sufficient time was available for the solution of socioeconomic problems. What the Europe of 1919 did not know was that it would have to work against an invisible deadline, that of the world depression which struck a mere ten years after the democratic triumph of 1919. As a factor of social disruption and as a catalyst of national upheaval, the depression was soon to rival the First World War itself. Therein lay much of the cause of Europe's democratic failure so soon after its democratic victory.

BRITAIN: THE CHALLENGE TO IMPERIAL POWER

What was still called the British Empire had emerged from the First World War seemingly strengthened and greatly increased in size. The war had eliminated Germany as a naval threat and as a rival to British influence around the world. The German navy lay at the bottom of Scapa Flow, the base of the Home Fleet, where German sailors had scuttled their ships in order to avoid the humiliation of surrender. The 1917 Russian Revolution had similarly eliminated Russia as an imperial rival, at least for the time being. Although Britain and Russia had settled their imperialist rivalries under the 1907 entente agreement, there was no guarantee that such rivalries would not have resurfaced had tsarism survived the war. The British promise of Constantinople to Russia in 1915 would have made the return of Russian-British rivalry for control of the Middle East not unlikely, and very possibly inevitable.

The First World War had also produced a degree of cohesion in the Empire which prewar British imperialists had often dreamed of but never actually achieved in peacetime. The Dominions had sent a million soldiers to fight on behalf of Britain, and India had sent not only soldiers, whose help was crucial in the British conquest of the Middle East, but a "gift" of £100 million to help pay for the war. Britain, chronically short of trained soldiers because of the absence of the draft, possessed for the first time a huge standing army capable of advancing imperial interests worldwide.

Pressure from the Dominions

As against these strengthening factors, the First World War had also produced others which rendered the preservation of imperial grandeur more difficult, and which announced the beginnings of imperial retreat. Among these factors were the emergence of new world powers, principally the United States and Japan, as well as the strengthening of colonial nationalism and Dominion independence.

In the 1921 Washington Naval Agreements, Britain had to concede to the United States what she had always denied imperial Germany, parity in capital ships. American pressure had similarly forced Britain to abandon the 1902 alliance with Japan against Britain's wishes and against her better judgement. In this matter Dominion pressures also played an important part, because Canada, New Zealand, and Australia, sharing the American concern about the rise of Japanese power in Asia and the Pacific, also wished to see the Anglo-Japanese alliance ended. The defense of Dominion interests as distinct from British ones became a general feature of Dominion conduct between the two world wars. The Dominions were especially concerned over the possibility of another war starting in Europe, a war in which they would again be called upon to fight without having had any influence over the circumstances from which it sprang. Hence the Dominion restraint on British support for an expanded league commitment to collective security in the mid-1920s, and Dominion warnings addressed to Prime Minister Lloyd George during the Anglo-Turkish confrontation of October 1922. For similar reasons, the Dominions were to support Neville Chamberlain's policy of appeasement during the 1938 Munich Conference in the hope that the preservation of peace in Europe would enable Britain to increase her defense contribution to the Dominions in the Pacific area. Britain acknowledged the Dominions' desire for greater independence by securing them separate representation in the league and by defining them as *autonomous communities* equal in status to Britain in the 1926 Balfour Declaration. The 1931 Westminster Statute, which gave legal status to the declaration, made the application of British laws dependent on Dominion consent. The Ottawa Agreements on preferential tariffs of 1932 were intended to strengthen economic cooperation between Britain and the Dominions, especially in the emergency created by the depression. The agreements resulted in an increase of Empire exports to Britain from 24 to 37 percent of foreign trade between 1931 and 1937 and a rise in British exports to the Empire from a share of 32 to 39 percent.

Colonial Nationalism

The assertion of Dominion independence was matched by a rise in colonial nationalism in the nonwhite areas under British rule. Colonial nationalism and resistance to British colonial rule, though hardly a new phenomenon, were significantly strengthened after the First World War because Wilsonian idealism had created a new climate of international relations, as reflected in the League of Nations Covenant. This climate, which had its supporters also among British league advocates, could not but weaken and render obsolete prewar justifications of British imperialism. Such doctrine had rested on arguments of national interest, cultural mission, and racial superiority. Britain's prewar colonial secretary Joseph Chamberlain had claimed that half of England would starve if the British Empire were reduced to the size of the United Kingdom. Imperialist writers such as Benjamin Kidd attributed the success of the British Empire to the "superiority" of the "Anglo-Saxon race." Prime Minister Rosebery observed in the 1890s that the world, to the extent that it could be molded, should receive the Anglo-Saxon mold.

Nationalist challenge to British rule erupted almost immediately after the war in three widely separated, areas, Ireland, India, and the Middle East. Despite great regional and historic differences, the leaders of all three forms of nationalism viewed theirs as an interdependent struggle against the common adversary, Britain.

The Irish Troubles

British failure to apply the 1912 Irish Home Rule Bill at the time of the outbreak of World War I, and the suppression of the Easter Rebellion in 1916, had made the radical *Sinn Fein* (We Ourselves)—rather than the older, more moderate Irish Nationalist party—the leader of Irish nationalism. *Sinn Fein* leader Arthur Griffith, a student of the Hungarian struggle for autonomy under Habsburg rule, patterned Irish strategy on the Hungarian model, with Irish independence the ultimate aim. After capturing all seventy-three Irish House of Commons seats outside Protestant Ulster in the British elections of December 1918, the *Sinn Fein* deputies set up a separate Irish parliament (*Dail*) in Dublin, rather than claim their seats in Westminster. The *Dail* chose de Valera, *Sinn Finn* veteran of the 1916 Easter Rebellion, as president, and Arthur Griffith as vice president.

The British postwar government of Lloyd George faced the alternatives of compromise or military repression, the latter of which, in the judgment of the Imperial General Staff, would have required a force of one hundred thousand men. On the king's advice, Lloyd George reached a compromise in the form of the Anglo-Irish treaty of December 6, 1921. The treaty recognized the Irish Free State as having the status of a dominion with complete autonomy over internal matters. Predominantly Protestant Ulster was given the option of joining the Irish Free State, an option it promptly and predictably rejected in a plebiscite.

The 1921 Anglo-Irish treaty was not the end of the "Irish troubles." The *Sinn Fein* itself became split over the settlement, its more extreme wing under de Valera rejecting it and provoking a new round of violence, which claimed more lives than the first struggle had between 1919 and 1921. De Valera, upon succeeding to the Irish prime ministership in 1932, adroitly used the Westminster statute of 1931 to repudiate the Anglo-Irish treaty. The new Irish constitution of 1937 made southern Ireland (Eire) for all practical purposes an independent state.

India

While Britain witnessed the outbreak of national revolution across the Irish Sea in 1919, violence had erupted in faraway India at Amritsar in the Punjab, where some two thousand Indians were killed or wounded during a demonstration, on the orders of Britain's General Dyer. The Amritsar massacre opened up a new and much more violent phase in the long history of Anglo-Indian relations.

In August 1917 E. J. Montagu, the secretary of state for India, had given vague promises of increased Indian self-government after the war, in recognition of India's substantial contribution to the British war effort. The implementation of the Montagu promise in the 1920 Government of India Act fell short of Indian expectations. Under a system which the British called *diarchy* the 1920 Government of India Act opened up limited areas of provincial administration to Indian ministers. Throughout the interwar period, Indian nationalism, as organized in the India Congress party under Gandhi and Jinnah's Moslem League, expected and demanded to obtain Dominion status, identical with that of the self-governing "white" Dominions of Canada, Australia, New Zealand, and white-ruled South Africa. No British government between the wars was prepared to concede Dominion status to India, in part because of India's economic importance to Britain, in part because it was feared that Indian self-government would result in chaos and violence, especially between the feuding Hindu majority and the Moslem minority. In part, Dominion status was denied because of the unspoken prejudice of race, which reserved self-government for the white colonies.

Under the pressure of Indian nationalism, Britain broadened its concessions with the 1935 Government of India Act, which extended the system of diarchy to the federal level. The 1935 act still withheld Dominion status and it left defense and foreign policy matters in British hands. Despite strong initial objections, the India Congress party participated in the application of the new system until the outbreak of the Second World War. Incensed by the British viceroy's declaring war against Nazi Germany in 1939 without consulting anyone in India, the Congress party boycotted the institutions created by the 1935 act.

Egypt

In the Middle East, British rule proved to be sufficiently flexible to preserve appearances of Anglo-Arab cooperation for most of the region and much of the time, while assuring the continued presence of British military power and strategic control.

In Egypt, the first British response to organized demands for independence was the deportation of Saad Zaghlul, leader of the independence movement, to the island of Malta, and later to more distant places. After continued violence, Britain officially ended her protectorate over Egypt in February 1922, while retaining both her troop presence and her control over the Suez canal. Anglo-Egyptian relations did not improve until Egypt requested an alliance with Britain in 1936 because of the threat of Italian fascist aggression.

Iraq

The establishment of the British mandate over Iraq initially encountered strong opposition until the British wisely installed Feisal as king of Iraq, following Feisal's expulsion from Syria by the French. In 1931, Britain ended her mandate over Iraq, but the Anglo-Iraqi treaty of 1931 left Britain in control of the strategic air bases of Habbaniya and Shaiba, while also giving Britain a monopoly of the supply of arms to the Iraqi army. Under Feisal's successor, King Ghazi, Anglo-Iraqi relations worsened, reaching a low point in early 1941 when an Iraqi revolt attempted to oust the British and make common cause with Hitler's Germany.

Palestine

In the British mandate over Palestine, the clash between Arab nationalism and Zionism destabilized British control to a degree not anticipated by the British supporters of Zionism who had endorsed the 1917 Balfour Declaration. The latter had promised British support for the estabishment of a Jewish national home in—though not throughout—Palestine. Jewish immigration, which rose sharply after 1933 in response to Jewish persecution in nazi Germany, prompted both Arab resistance and British efforts to find a compromise. These efforts, made in the form of the 1930 White Paper on Palestine, the 1936 Peel Commission Report, and the 1939 White Paper of Colonial Secretary Malcolm MacDonald, suggested either curtailment of immigration, partition of Palestine, or both. The British proposals failed to win acceptance by either of the two antagonists. The outbreak of the Second World War merely suspended violence in Palestine without any solution having been found.

POLITICAL DEMOCRACY AND SOCIAL PRESSURE IN BRITAIN BETWEEN THE WARS

Few would have denied that British democracy was one of the freest systems of government, or that it was considered a model for democracy throughout continental Europe. The Reform Bill of 1911 had significantly reduced the powers of the aristocratic upper chamber, the House of Lords, by abolishing its veto over finance bills and by reducing the veto over other bills from absolute to suspensive. Women over thirty were enfranchised in 1918 and the Equal Franchise Act of 1928 gave the vote to all women over twenty-one.

The Class System

All this had done little to reform social structure or social privilege, however, so that while British society was one of the freest politically, it was at the same time one of the most restrictive socially. It was also one of the most unequal in the distribution of wealth, with 1 percent of the people owning two-thirds of the national wealth and 96 percent of the land in the hands of some 30,000 individuals. The barriers between the classes were reinforced by two distinct and unequal systems of education, both of which extended from the primary to the university level. The privileged and wealthy sent their children to the misnamed public schools, which were expensive private secondary schools, and it was mostly from these that admission to the two leading universities, Oxford and Cambridge, was secured. The political elite of the country, with the exception of Labour politicians, was drawn heavily from these elite schools.

The war had raised social expectations in Great Britain, as it had in other countries. The 1918 veterans expected a national effort in peacetime comparable to the national defense effort in wartime. They wanted improved educational opportunities, better housing conditions, and a rise in the standard of living of the working class.

The Economy

Prime Minister Lloyd George's reelection in December 1918 was due as much to his promise of "hanging the Kaiser" and "making Germany pay," as it was to his commitment to social improvement. In making this commitment Lloyd George was counting on a postwar economic boom. It turned out to be a miniboom without sufficient revenue to pay for sustained social programs. Its causes were suggestive of deeper structural problems that were to plague British economic developments throughout the interwar period. Britain had lost export opportunities in traditional markets to American and Japanese competition during the war, and continental Europe was too impoverished by the war to fill British export orders. The relative importance of the old staple industries of the nineteenth century, coal, steel, and textiles, began to decline while British progress in the newer industries, automotive, chemical, and electrical, was slow. Between 1907 and 1930 British coal exports declined from 82 to 70 million tons, while cotton exports decreased from 105 to 86 million tons. Even the Indian cotton market had shrunk due to increased native production by 42 percent in 1929, as compared to pre-1914 figures. Earnings from "invisible exports" such as shipping, insurance, and banking continued to cover balance of payments deficits until the depression. The 1929 balance of payments surplus of £103 million was followed by a deficit of £104 in 1931.

Unemployment

Industrial unemployment remained a persistent problem between the wars. Between 1920 and 1921 unemployment doubled, reaching the two million mark by June 1921. Even during periods of recovery, unemployment never fell below the 10 percent mark. The pattern of unemployment reflected regional differences. The areas hardest hit were those of the old staple industries, South Wales, Scotland, and the region north of the River Trent, as against the better-off areas of London, Birmingham, and south-central England, the centers of the newer industries.

Given the underlying economic problems, the social achievements of the Lloyd George government were meager. The 1919 Addison Act, after the minister of health, was an exception, resulting in the construction of 200,000 new homes between 1919 and 1922. The 1918 Fisher Act had initiated improvements in secondary education, many of which fell victim to the austerity measures of 1922, known after their sponsor, Eric Geddes, as the "Geddes axe." The 1920 Unemployment Insurance Act improved benefits, but it was a poor substitute for the steady employment which the veterans wanted. Parliament rewarded senior military leaders, such as Field Marshal Haig, who received £100,000, with substantial gifts of money. The rank-and-file veterans, who had returned from the mud and blood of the trenches of the First World War, did not do nearly as well, and many of them repudiated Lloyd George out of a sense of betrayal.

Lloyd George's Fall

In October 1922 Lloyd George fell as prime minister, after losing the trust of many veterans and the support of his Conservative coalition partners. The Conservatives were angry over his concessions to Irish nationalism in the 1921 Anglo-Irish treaty, and they thought he had impaired British prestige abroad by his handling of the Turkish crisis of 1922. In a wider sense, Lloyd George's fall reflected a shift away from the excitement of the war, in which he had ably led the country, and towards prewar "normalcy," whether such normalcy, in the old sense, was attainable or not.

Lloyd George's fall from power in 1922 also signaled the decline of the Liberal party as one of the two major political parties in Britain. Before 1914, the Liberals had been the most effective promoters of social legislation on behalf of the underprivileged. The First World War had polarized the electorate more clearly into property holders and wage earners, with the latter now voting in increasing numbers for the Labour party.

The Conservative decision to withdraw from the coalition under Lloyd George appeared to be vindicated by the Conservative victory in the parliamentary elections of November 1922. The Conservative government of Stanley Baldwin, who succeeded Bonar Law as prime minister in May 1923, regarded Britain's persistent postwar unemployment as the most pressing issue, and it hoped to cure it through a policy of tariff protection. Britain had, it is true, begun to impose selective import tariffs since

1914 and again in 1921, but the free trade principle was still very firmly entrenched in the public mind, in part because it allowed for lower food prices. Both Liberals and the Labour party opposed tariff protection, Labour calling it a "stomach tax." Because of the importance of the issue of tariff protection, Stanley Baldwin did not wish to impose it before giving the British public a chance to vote on it. The national elections of December 1923 were thus in the nature of a referendum on free trade and protection, and the Conservatives lost it. Though they emerged as still the largest single party, they were outnumbered by the combined strength of Labour and Liberals. With 191 seats, Labour was the second strongest party, but it was not strong enough to form a government of its own without the political support of Liberals in the Commons.

The First Labour Government

It was with Liberal backing that Labour party leader Ramsay MacDonald formed the first Labour government ever in the history of Britain on January 22, 1924, the twenty-third anniversary of Queen Victoria's death. The Conservative opposition was not a little shocked over Britain's being headed by a socialist government. During the election campaign the slogan "Baldwin for Britain, MacDonald for Moscow" epitomized both Conservative fears and Conservative smears, and the Conservative *Daily Mail* had warned that a Labour victory would threaten every man's home and every woman's clothes and jewelry.

The British Labour party was, in fact, overwhelmingly a nonideological and pragmatic party which continued to live and work by the rules of the British parliamentary system after its 1923 victory as it had done before. In practice, this meant the rejection of any extreme social or economic experimentation such as the Labour left wing under men like health minister Charles S. Wheatley might have favored, for fear of thereby losing the necessary Liberal party support. The social gains under the first Labour government thus remained limited to housing and education under the Wheatley Housing Act, and the reforms of education minister Trevelyan. The nationalization of the coal industry, which coal miners demanded, was not attempted because the Liberal party would not have tolerated it. In the field of Empire and defense policy there were no suprises, and Ramsay MacDonald, though himself a pacifist during the First World War, commissioned several new cruisers for the Royal Navy.

MacDonald's one significant departure from past practice was his extension of full diplomatic recognition to Soviet Russia, and it was Russia that proved to be his political undoing. When the Labour government failed to press charges of treason against the radical *Workers' Weekly* for calling on British soldiers not to turn their guns on "fellow workers" in a foreign war, it lost the support of the Liberals and had to resign. The elections of October 1924, in which "red scare" tactics played no small part, resulted in a Conservative landslide of 419 seats, as against 151 for Labour and 40 for the Liberals.

Baldwin, 1925-29

Stanley Baldwin's second, and much longer, administration from 1925 to 1929 coincided with the relatively stable and prosperous period during which postwar Europe seemed at last to have found lasting peace in the "spirit of Locarno."

The yearning for stability, normalcy, and peace of the mid-1920s was well symbolized by Baldwin's own unexciting character, which prompted the more illustrious Lord Curzon, his unsuccessful rival for the prime ministership, to dismiss him as "a man of the utmost insignificance." Baldwin was lacking in foreign policy interest and expertise, but he was a good party manager and he continued to be worried by the problem of unemployment. Overall, the British economy of 1925 showed a strong picture, with industrial production exceeding the 1913 level by 10 percent. British exports over the period from 1913 to 1925, however, had declined by a full quarter, with corresponding adverse effects on industrial unemployment. After the public had rebuffed tariff protection as a cure in 1923, Baldwin hoped to stimulate exports by lowering prices, which manufacturers intended to achieve by cutting not profits but wages. This also became official policy, and the attempt to cut wages, first in the mining industry, later in transportation and other areas, triggered the great British General Strike of 1926.

The General Strike

The General Strike was Britain's worst labor crisis between the wars and it began with a miners' strike. Working conditions in the coal industry were among the worst, and the industry itself was among the worst run. Fifteen hundred separate companies, operating some 3,000 mines, paid wages that ranged between two and four pounds per week. The miners' strike was intended to prevent a simultaneous cutting of wages and increase in working hours. Supported by the unions of printers, rail, transport, steel, construction, gas, and electrical workers, the General Strike effectively shut down the British economy for nearly two weeks in May 1926.

To the unions, the purpose of the strike was purely economic. To Baldwin and his government it was political, and even a threat to the constitutional order of Britain. Churchill, Baldwin's chancellor of the exchequer and editor of the *British Gazette,* the only newspaper to appear during the strike, called the striking workers "the enemy" and demanded their "unconditional surrender." Churchill's pugnacious antilabor and antiunion stand of 1926 was remembered by many, who turned Churchill out of office when he ran for reelection as prime minister at the end of the Second World War in 1945.

The General Strike collapsed without achieving its purpose, the miners' strike ending only by December 1926. Contrary to the strikers' slogan, "Not a penny off the pay, nor a minute on the day," many workers were rehired at lower wages for longer hours. The strike was predominantly peaceful. In 1927, the Baldwin government outlawed sympathy strikes with the Trade Disputes Act and Trade Union Act.

Social Welfare

The Baldwin years were not without social achievement. In Neville Chamberlain, Baldwin possessed an energetic and dedicated minister of health whose accomplishments in the area of social policy have been largely overshadowed by his failures as the architect of appeasement in foreign policy during the 1930s. In the first Baldwin cabinet, Chamberlain had sponsored the 1923 Housing Act, which was followed in the second Baldwin administration by the Widows', Orphans', and Old Age Contributory Pensions Act.

The elections of May 1929, reflecting the bitterness of the social strife of 1926, for the first time returned the Labour party as the strongest party, with 288 seats, without however giving it control over the Commons. When MacDonald formed his second Labour government in 1929 he depended, as in 1924, on Liberal support. Accordingly, Labour social policy was again cautious, being limited to a new Housing Act in 1930 and a reduction of working hours in the coal mines. Labour's attempt to repeal the 1927 Trade Disputes Act failed. The real crisis faced by the second Labour government was that of the depression. By December 1930 unemployment had climbed to 2.5 million and the Labour party became deeply divided over the best means of coping with the depression.

Britain in the Depression

During the 1929 election campaign, the Liberal party alone had come out with new ideas on how to combat industrial unemployment with Lloyd George's program, "We Can Conquer Unemployment." The program contained elements of John Maynard Keynes' theory, which subsequently appeared in more detailed form in Keynes' *General Theory of Employment, Interest, and Money* of 1936. Though upholding the free enterprise system in principle, the *General Theory* proposed that under the conditions of twentieth-century capitalism depressions should not be left to work themselves out through the self-regulatory mechanisms of a free economy. Instead, Keynes recommended recovery through government spending, even if such spending exceeded income from revenue, until recovery had been achieved and the rate of savings began to equal the rate of new investments. The 1929 Liberal party platform, breaking with laissez-faire concepts, advocated large-scale public works, financed through deficit spending if necessary.

The Labour government did not apply Keynesian cures, in part because Keynes' theories failed to win general acceptance, even in the academic circles of the 1930s and for some time thereafter. Instead, the Labour government attempted to fight the depression with the same deflationary measures, largely ineffectual, which other governments in Europe also tried.

As the "red scare" of 1924 had abruptly ended MacDonald's first government in 1924, the crisis of the British pound, triggered by foreign deposit withdrawals in August 1931, caused the fall of the second Labour government. The Bank of England attributed the crisis of the pound to the lack of confidence in Labour economic policy abroad. It therefore demanded a demonstration of austerity through a 10 percent cut in unemployment benefits, in order to achieve a balanced budget. Divided on this issue, the Labour government resigned and MacDonald, on the king's request, formed the National Government on August 25, 1931. The National Government was intended as an all-party government of Labour, Conservatives, and Liberals, but the Labour party split over the question of joining. The majority of the party, supported by the Trade Union Council, deserted MacDonald and only a minority followed him into the new government.

Through severe economies and the imposition of new taxes, MacDonald's National Government mastered the budget deficit, though not the pound crisis. On September 21, 1931 the pound went off the gold standard, resulting in a devaluation from $4.86 to $3.80 to the pound. After this, the Conservatives pressed for new elections, proposing a continuation of the National Government under the popular MacDonald, but hoping for an increase in their own strength through voter identification of the

Conservative party with the *National* label. The calculation proved to be correct, and the Conservatives gained 473 seats in the elections of October 1931, as against a mere 35 for MacDonald's Labour supporters. The outcome of the 1931 elections assured Conservative dominance in the National Government of MacDonald and, after his resignation in 1935, in that of Stanley Baldwin. Conservative influence was further strengthened when the Liberal members withdrew from the National Government in 1932 over the issue of tariff protection. In the elections of 1935, held under Baldwin's prime ministership, Conservative strength again prevailed, with 432 seats over 154 for the Labour opposition. Liberal strength declined to a mere 20 seats. The National Governments of the 1930s were thus, for all practical purposes, Conservative governments.

Communism and Fascism

Given the extent of social despair in Britain's depressed areas and given the spectacle of mushrooming political extremism in the depression-ridden industrial nations of the European continent, it was noteworthy that neither the British Communists nor Sir Oswald Mosley's British Union of Fascists gained a single seat in the elections of 1931. Between the wars, British Communist party enrollment never exceeded 10,000, that of the Fascists achieving about twice that number. In the elections of 1935, the Communists captured one seat, with William Gallacher being elected from West Fife. Oswald Mosley had run the full course from Conservative party member to Labourite to Fascist when he founded the BUF in 1931. Mosley's program for economic reform and Empire renewal was essentially a blend of prewar imperialist doctrine and postwar fascist ideology under the slogan, "Britain for the British." The appeal of Soviet communism among the British elite of the 1930s, including students of Britain's elite universities, was nevertheless not inconsiderable, with Soviet sympathizers eventually reaching high and influential positions in the British government, including the foreign service. The motivation for Soviet sympathy often was a revulsion against continental fascism and the belief that Stalin's Soviet Russia was the only effective long-term guarantee against a fascist triumph in Europe. The career of Soviet master spy Kim Philby was an example of British upper-class infatuation with Soviet communism.

Social disturbances in depression Britain were few and, by continental standards, mild. The National Unemployed Workers' Movement (NUWM) staged "hunger marches" on a large scale in 1934 and 1935 as well as a sit-down demonstration in the London business district on Christmas, 1938.

As a precaution against right-wing violence and Communist propaganda, especially in the armed forces, the National Government enacted the Public Order Act of 1936 and the Incitement to Disaffection Act of 1934. The former outlawed the wearing of political uniforms in public, the latter authorized search and seizure of seditious literature by the police.

The Road to Recovery

In fighting the depression, Baldwin and his successor Neville Chamberlain, who took over as prime minister in 1937, relied on a mixture of austerity, tariff protection, and limited government aid to depressed areas. As chancellor of the exchequer, Chamberlain lowered the interest rate on Britain's internal war debt from 5 to 3.5 percent and achieved thereby an immediate saving of £23 million. The Import Duties Act of

March 1932 put Britain firmly on the basis of tariff protection, with only foodstuffs and raw materials exempted. Empire imports were similarly exempted under the terms agreed upon in the 1932 Ottawa Agreements.

The National Government claimed industrial recovery by 1935, when industrial production again exceeded the predepression level of 1929. Low interest rates of 2 percent stimulated a housing boom, with 2.7 million new homes being built between 1930 and 1940.

National unemployment had peaked at 22 percent or nearly 3 million by 1932. Unemployment dropped below 2 million in 1935 and 1.6 million the following year. These gains could not obscure the often disastrous levels of unemployment in depressed regions and towns. Unemployment reached 27 percent in northern England, Scotland, and Northern Ireland in 1932. In places such as Jarrow in Lancashire, or the mining town of Crook in South Wales, unemployment ran as high as 68 to 70 percent.

Efforts to relieve the plight of the depressed areas under the Special Areas Act of 1934 were not overly successful, in part because the appropriations of £2 million were too low. The depressed areas and the national economy overall were greatly stimulated by rearmament, sparked by the government's White Paper on Rearmament of March 4, 1935. By 1937 annual expenditures on rearmament of £1.5 billion exceeded by far Chamberlain's own estimates of £120 million.

The official optimism surrounding the celebration of the twenty-fifth anniversary of King George V's accession to the throne on May 6, 1935 reflected a sense of national relief over what appeared to be the passing of the worst of the depression. At the same time, there was no denying a sense of pessimism and of cultural malaise springing from a fuller appreciation of the consequences of the First World War and an anxiety over new threats appearing on the continent. The crisis surrounding the abdication of George V's son, King Edward VIII, may be seen as indicative of the uncertainty of the 1930s. Edward's tired and dispirited renunciation of the British throne on December 11, 1936 for the sake of his future wife, the twice-divorced American socialite Mrs. Wallis Simpson, had all the appearances of an unconscious act of withdrawal from public duty such as would have been difficult to imagine for any of Edward's twentieth-century predecessors. The pomp and splendor surrounding the coronation of Edward's younger brother Albert, who assumed the title George VI, was meant to erase any impression of public pessimism. In fact, British democracy was about to meet its most severe challenge, as Neville Chamberlain entered upon his undertaking to salvage the meager socioeconomic gains of the interwar period through a policy of appeasement of the forces of external aggression.

THE THIRD FRENCH REPUBLIC

The victory of the democracies of 1918 had, for France, an even deeper meaning than it did for Britain, because the victory conferred upon the Third Republic a degree of public approval and prestige it had failed to achieve since 1870.

The Dreyfus Case

The basic political question before France ever since the defeat of 1870–1871 was whether the republic would endure or be replaced by either a restored monarchy or a Bonapartist empire. The republic survived the domestic battles over this issue more by default than by the strength of its supporters, for it seemed to be the form of government which least divided France. The basic controversy between royalism and republicanism also gave the terms *left, right,* and *radical* their special meaning in the context of Third Republic politics, connoting support for or opposition to the republic rather than any commitment to social change. Royalism and its allies, conservatism, the army establishment, and political Catholicism, suffered their worst defeat in the Dreyfus case, involving a French army captain who was falsely accused and convicted for espionage. The Dreyfus case of the 1890s and early 1900s became the most emotional and divisive of French prewar political scandals because of the symbolic significance of the two principal antagonists, the army and the Jewish captain. The army represented all those who identified the republican regime with corruption and treason and who traced the misfortunes of modern France all the way back to the revolution of 1789. Dreyfus symbolized republican, liberal, and progressive France, which tried to survive royalist plots and intrigues. The unmasking of the army's cover-up in the Dreyfus case, in large part through the efforts of the French liberal press, dealt royalism a blow from which it never recovered. At the same time, the Dreyfus case prompted the emergence of the *Action Française,* whose founder Charles Maurras wove the diverse strands of royalism, anti-Semitism, conservatism, and political Catholicism into a militant and sharp-edged ideology which some have viewed as a precursor of twentieth-century European fascism. Though never very large in its number of followers, the *Action Française* appealed to members of the French military and administrative elite and exerted a powerful influence over the affairs of the republic down to its end in 1940.

Internal Realignments

The First World War briefly reconciled the French Right with the republic because of the republic's success in organizing national defense and in regaining the lost provinces of Alsace and Lorraine. The *Action Française* would have preferred an even tougher peace with Germany than the one arranged under the Versailles treaty.

The war had also reconciled the republic with the French Socialist party (SFIO), though the reconciliation did not last the entire length of the First World War. Before the war, organized labor, especially in the form of the national CGT (*Confédération Generale du Travail*) had arisen as a new challenge to the republic on the far left through the adoption of syndicalist tactics, as advocated by Georges Sorel. Impatient with the gradualist approach of the French Socialist party, Sorel in his *Reflections on Violence* of 1906 had extolled the general strike as the most effective weapon of organized labor for bringing down "bourgeois France." The CGT adopted Sorel's syndicalist doctrine in the Charter of Amiens of the same year. After dealing its royalist adversaries a decisive blow in the Dreyfus case in the early 1900s, the republic braced itself for bitter social strife with syndicalist labor. The French Socialist party, a strong advocate of reconciliation with Germany under its prewar leader Jean Jaurès, joined in the government of Sacred Union at the outset of the war. Jean Jaurès himself was assassinated by unknown assailants.

Paralleling a similar crisis in other Socialist parties of Europe, the French Socialists quit the Sacred Union government in 1917 over the question of war aims. The SFIO suspected that France was no longer fighting for purely defensive aims and that it was needlessly prolonging the conflict in pursuit of territorial gain. The split between

Socialists and the republic widened after the war because of Socialist denunciation of the Treaty of Versailles as overly harsh, and because of the resumption of the prewar social conflict with organized labor. The republic and the labor Left were similarly strongly affected by the dilemma posed by Soviet communism, which had a special meaning for France.

Communism in France

In France, labor was far more sympathetic to the Bolshevik experiment than it was in any other European country with the possible exception of Italy. The workers' riots in Paris on May 1, 1919, which signaled a return to syndicalist tactics and violence, were sparked in part by labor opposition to Marshal Foch's project of an "anti-Bolshevik crusade." The sailors' mutiny in France's Black Sea fleet, incited by André Marty, was another indication of French proletarian solidarity with Soviet communism. On May 1, 1920, miners and railroad and transport workers called a general strike which was crushed by the government only after the seizure of CGT headquarters. In September 1920 at the Tours congress, the Socialist party broke up into a separate Communist party and the Socialists who, under the leadership of Leon Blum, retained the old SFIO party label. In July 1921 the unions broke up at the Lille congress into the Communist-led CGTU (*Confédération Generale du Travail Unitaire*) and the non-Communist CGT. It was significant that at both the Tours and Lille congresses, the Communists were in the majority. Other European Socialist parties underwent a similar split at about the same time but, with the exception of the Norwegian Socialist party, the Communists represented the minority.

French republican hostility to Soviet communism was reinforced by the memory of Lenin's separate peace with Germany at Brest-Litovsk in March 1918, when France was fighting for its life, and by the Bolshevik repudiation of the prewar tsarist debt, in which a large part of bourgeois France had put its life's savings. The vociferous opposition of French Communism to the French Ruhr invasion of 1923, and the strong support given by the Communist-sponsored newspaper *Le Paria* to Ho Chi Minh's colonial nationalism in French Indochina and to Messali Hadj in French Algeria during the 1920s further contributed to the republican appraisal of the French Communist party as a subversive agent serving foreign interests.

The National Bloc

The first French postwar elections of November 16, 1919 reflected the national self-confidence of the republic. With 338 seats the parties of the National Bloc easily defeated the Left, Socialist strength alone declining by nearly one-half as compared to its prewar strength. The National Bloc, which governed France during the period from 1919 to early 1924, and whose most forceful leader was Raymond Poincaré, faced the serious tasks of coping with the financial legacy of the First World War, of rebuilding the devastated areas of eastern and northern France, and of developing new social initiatives for the industrial labor force, which shared the heightened social expectations of industrial labor in other parts of postwar Europe. To a lesser extent than postwar Britain, the French republic also faced the challenge of colonial nationalism, both in its established overseas possessions and the newly acquired mandates of the Middle East.

These challenges were met by the traditional French republican system based on a weak executive and an all-powerful legislature. This system, which produced altogether fifty different cabinets between 1871 and 1914, was designed intentionally to prevent the recurrence of the abuse of executive power the country experienced under French Bonapartism. Emile Auguste Chartier, who wrote under the pseudonym of Alain, defined the political philosophy of the French republic as one in which resistance to the powers of government was essential to the safeguarding of individual liberty. In his *Eléments d'une Doctrine Radicale* of 1925, Alain argued that in a democracy not only does no party have real power, but there is no power, properly speaking.

There was serious doubt as to whether the French republican system, product of a specific situation in the nineteenth century, would be adequately equipped to meet the external and internal requirements of twentieth-century France. Both Socialists and Conservatives denied the suitability of the republican system of the 1870s to the problems of the 1920s and 1930s and both produced proposals for reform in the form of stronger executive action. In 1918, Socialist leader Leon Blum proposed such changes in his *Lettres sur la Réforme Gouvernmentale* and in the early 1930s Conservative leader André Tardieu was to make similar recommendations when the social plight of the depression called for energetic government measures. The fact that neither Blum's nor Tradieu's ideas were even taken up before the Second World War was testimony to the deeply entrenched republican spirit of social inaction, which contributed in no small measure to the overall failure of the Third Republic between the two world wars. Tardieu's reform proposals were suspect in the eyes of republican politicians for the additional reason that they favored a reduction in the number of political parties for the sake of greater executive stability.

The problem of finance remained the National Bloc's most pressing problem and it was over this that Poincaré's government fell in early 1924. When German reparations fell short of expectations, the National Bloc financed reconstruction through borrowing, not increased taxation, just as France had financed the war. The French budget was divided into an "ordinary budget," which was balanced, and a "German budget" to cover war pensions and reconstruction. Until German reparations were received, the "German budget" was covered by loans.

The financial difficulties prompted Poincaré into the risky venture of the 1923 Ruhr invasion, which isolated France politically and which yielded far fewer economic gains than had originally been hoped. When Poincaré had to raise taxes in 1924 to offset the cost of the Ruhr invasion, the National Bloc lost the elections of May 1924. The election of May 1924 brought a leftward shift in France, which paralleled similar developments in Britain at roughly the same time, but which differed in significant aspects. In Britain, it was the Labour party which formed a minority government with Liberal toleration. In France, Edouard Herriot's Radical Socialists, a party representing the radical republican tradition at its most typical, formed a government with the parliamentary support of Blum's Socialists under the Cartel of the Left.

The Cartel of the Left

Between 1924 and 1926 the Cartel of the Left engaged in much ritualistic confirmation of republican principles, but it made no real headway towards fiscal soundness. The postwar inflation continued unabated, largely because French business, lacking confidence in the cartel's economic policy, either shipped its capital to Switzerland or converted it into U.S. dollars and British pounds. By 1924 the French franc had fallen to 50 to the dollar, one tenth of its prewar value. Conservatives distrusted the cartel because of its suggestion that not only defeated Germany but the wealthy of France also should be made to contribute to the solution of the fiscal crisis. When finance minister de Monzie proposed a special tax on large properties, Herriot was ousted as prime minister.

Poincaré

On July 13, 1926 Poincaré was recalled as prime minister without the benefit of new elections for the overriding purpose of "saving the franc." Poincaré's government of National Union was more broadly based even than the Sacred Union government of August 1914, including as it did all parties except Socialists and Communists. Poincaré succeeded in "saving the franc" less through the adoption of unorthodox measures than the projection of an air of authority and the more forceful collection of taxes. His task of stabilizing the franc at 20 to the U.S. dollar was also made easier as a result of German reparation payments, which began to flow regularly during the prosperous mid-1920s since the adoption of the Dawes Plan in 1924. In addition, Poincaré availed himself of the expertise of French financial wizard Jacques Rueff, who was to assist Charles de Gaulle more than a generation later in the solution of a similar franc crisis. In 1928 France returned to the gold standard. By the time of Poincaré's retirement in September 1929, France had also largely completed the task of rebuilding the war-devastated areas, in which some 800,000 dwellings had been destroyed, thousands of factories gutted, and numerous coal mines flooded. The industrial index of France of 1930 was 40 percent above that of 1913, the agricultural index had increased by 10 percent. Reconstruction and public works had kept French unemployment at generally low levels during the 1920s. Before the depression, unemployment rarely rose above 100,000 in any one year. The low French birth rate and the high human losses of the war had forced France to import labor, chiefly from Poland, Italy and Spain. Despite increases in mechanized mass production, France retained a higher percentage of small-scale manufacturers than did most other industrial nations. In France, 1.4 million shops employed five workers or less as against 1.3 million enterprises employing over 500 workers. Among large industrial powers, France also remained the most rural, with more than half the population still in rural areas in the late 1920s. Near full self-sufficiency in agriculture and a high rate of domestic consumption of industrial output made France also less vulnerable to the fluctuations of the world market than was the case with both Germany and Britain. The depression was, partly for these reasons, slower in reaching France, but it also proved to be more persistent once it had taken root there.

FRANCE UNDER THE DEPRESSION

The external peace and the domestic stability which the Third Republic had at last attained under Poincaré's stewardship did not extend into the 1930s. As Briand's policy of conciliation towards Weimar Germany died a speedy death under the impact of impatient German revisionism between 1930 and 1932, the depression fueled fresh social turmoil and political disorder at home.

Tardieu

Poincaré's successor, Prime Minister Tardieu, though a Conservative, proposed to meet the challenge of the depression with a bold policy of public works, expanded social security, and the modernization of plants, all of which were part of his proposed five-year plan. The plan was coupled with a call for a simplification of the multiparty system, preferably in the direction of the Anglo-Saxon two-party system.

Tardieu's imaginative reform ideas fell victim to both partisan jealousies and the vested interests of the republican sociopolitical status quo. The Socialists accused Tardieu of stealing their own program, while others attacked Tardieu's political reform plans as an "authoritarian tendency." Pierre Laval, an ex-Socialist turned Conservative who succeeded as prime minister between January 1931 and February 1932, calmed Conservative fears by returning to an orthodox policy of balanced budgets and government austerity. By 1932, the depression had begun to hit France hard, however, with a drop in the industrial index of 34 points as against 1928 figures and unemployment climbing to 1.3 million by 1933.

Reflecting public anxiety, the French elections of May 1932 resulted once again in a victory for the parties of the Cartel of the Left with Herriot forming a new cartel government. Repeating also the pattern of 1924 to 1926, the cartel parties, Radical Socialists and Blum's SFIO, were lacking in a socioeconomic consensus which would have enabled the cartel government to develop a coherent and effective economic policy. Specifically, Herriot rejected as too extreme Blum's program of nationalizing the insurance business and the transportation industry, of introducing the forty-hour workweek, and of cutting the defense budget to 1928 levels.

The Stavisky Scandal

To the appearance of indecision in the economic field, the cartel added an impression of corruption, in the context of the Stavisky scandal. Serge Alexandre Stavisky was a shady financier with a long police record and good political connections in high places. Stavisky's sale of fraudulent bonds, based on the municipal credit of Bayonne, touched off a nationwide scandal which brought down the government. Like the Dreyfus case of the 1890s, the Stavisky scandal of 1933–1934 mushroomed into an emotional confrontation between supporters and opponents of the republic, with the deeper roots of antiliberalism and anti-Semitism exposed in the unfolding of the battle. The death of Stavisky, officially ruled a suicide, did not calm the outrage of defrauded investors, who assumed that Stavisky had been murdered in order to shield his presumed accomplices and protectors in the French parliament and, possibly, the cabinet. The severity of the crisis was enhanced by the coincidence of the scandal with the widening influence and appeal of European fascism in Italy, Nazi Germany and even in France herself. The Stavisky scandal and its aftermath thus triggered the biggest demonstration of French fascism to date, with the march of the French Fascist leagues, the *Croix de Feu, Action Française, Union National des Combattants* and others in Paris on February 7, 1934.

There was widespread fear that these Fascist demonstrations were the prelude to a Fascist overthrow of France's Third Republic. Although the resignation of a government under pressure of mob violence was unprecedented in the Third Republic, the February riots of 1934 actually fell short of overthrowing the republic. To accomplish this, the French Fascist leagues would have had to coalesce into a single party under a single leader, a situation not likely to develop in a country where factionalism even in fascism reflected the national passion for political division. The crisis thus passed after the speedy formation of a new government of National Union, which included Marshal Pétain, the hero of Verdun, as minister of defense.

The February 1934 riots nevertheless sufficiently frightened the parties of the Left to produce a coalition, albeit on a temporary and uncertain basis.

Union on the Left

Socialists and Communists, the most bitter of enemies since the split of 1920–1921, organized a common strike against the "Fascist plot" of February 7, on February 12, 1934. In July of 1934, the SFIO and the Communists concluded a "unity of action" pact in defense of "democratic liberties." The Socialist-Communist alliance was joined by Herriot's Radical Socialists in the Popular Front which won the elections of May 1936, gaining 378 seats, as against 236 for the center-right parties. The SFIO emerged as the single strongest party for the first time with 146 seats, while Communist strength soared from 10 to 72 seats.

The first Popular Front government, formed on June 4, 1936 with SFIO leader Blum as prime minister, raised widespread workers' expectations that meaningful social change and progress was on the way. By contrast, it caused a great deal of anxiety among the well-to-do and in financial circles, where it was feared that the new government might lean too closely towards Soviet Russia in foreign affairs and compromise the basic socioeconomic structure at home.

Blum gave an early promise of energetic leadership with the strike settlement of June 7, 1936, known as the Matignon Accord. Among its provisions was the right to collective bargaining for unions and wage increases ranging from 7 to 15 percent. Subsequent legislation granted annual paid vacations and the forty-hour workweek. The Fascist leagues were outlawed, though they managed to reappear in the shape of regular political parties.

The Popular Front government's promise of strong leadership soon yielded to the realities of infighting, and it suffered from the repercussions of the Spanish Civil War as well as the resistance which French capital and finance organized against Blum's commitment to social action.

French capital fought Blum's "New Deal" with the same weapon it had successfully employed against the cartel governments of 1924–1926 and 1932–1934, the flight of capital abroad. Between May and September 1936, 20 billion francs in gold, one-quarter of the French gold reserve, left the country. On September 25, 1936 Blum had to devalue the franc. When Blum announced a "pause" in the Popular Front's social policy on February 24, 1937 he was, in fact, announcing its end. In June 1937, Blum asked the French Senate for special powers to impose exchange controls and then, failing to obtain them, resigned the prime ministership. The Popular Front survived in name until 1938, with Blum himself briefly returning as prime minister early in that year. In spirit, the Popular Front was already dead, in part because of Communist disaffection. The Communists, who had supported Blum in parliament without actually entering his cabinet, were disgruntled over his failure to give the Spanish Republican government more direct aid in the Spanish Civil War. Blum might have liked to furnish such aid, but he was prevented from doing so for weighty foreign policy reasons, principally the reservations of the British government.

ITALY AND THE LEGACY OF THE FIRST WORLD WAR

If the Allied victory of 1918 had enhanced democratic prestige in Western Europe, it had no similar effect on Italy. The circumstances of Italy's entry into the First World War had fundamentally differed from those surrounding the entry of France and Britain, because Italy was not attacked when she entered World War I in May 1915. Rather, her entry resulted from careful calculation of territorial gain on the assumption that active participation on the Allied side would bring greater rewards than continued neutrality. Italy was thus lacking in the sense of national unity which sprang from the siege mentality which existed in virtually every other country at the outset of the war. It was significant for the development of postwar Italy that the opponents of intervention actually outnumbered its advocates and that the latter prevailed in large measure by identifying intervention with patriotism and neutrality with cowardice and treason. The motives of the opponents of intervention were diverse, ranging from the pacifism of Pope Benedict XV and of the Socialists, to the conviction of the Liberals that Italy could not afford to wage a war of such magnitude. Giovanni Giolitti, the long-term Liberal party leader and prewar prime minister of several Italian cabinets, also believed that Italy could do well at the peace conference without having to shed her blood or exhaust her resources. The interventionists, who included King Victor Emmanuel, the army leadership, and Nationalist agitators such as Gabriele d'Annunzio the poet and Benito Mussolini, a recent convert from Socialism, equated intervention with national honor.

The Nationalists

The 1919 peace settlement did not heal the 1915 divisions arising from the controversy over intervention. The Nationalists, who had pushed Italy into the war, denounced Italy's gains at the peace conference as insufficient, especially when measured against the high cost of victory, which included 600,000 Italian war dead and the bankrupting of the national economy. Although the peace settlement had given Italy essentially what she had been promised by the Allies in the secret London treaty of 1915, it had not given her either a share in the German colonial empire or a portion of the Turkish Middle East. In a broader sense, the 1919 peace settlement embittered Italian nationalism because the established Great Powers, Britain and France, had not, in the Italian view, accorded Italy recognition as an equal. The emotional controversy over the possession of the small Yugoslav port of Fiume was symbolic of the deeper injury to Italian national pride. Just as Italian Nationalists had denounced Liberal opposition to intervention in 1915 as cowardly, they now denounced Liberal Italy for having brought home a dishonorable peace, a "mutilated peace," *vittoria mutilata*. Hence the Nationalist applause when the eccentric Gabriele d'Annunzio, together with his legion of black-shirted volunteers, occupied Fiume in defiance of both the Allied peace conference and the government of Italy.

Social Problems Old and New

The Nationalist contempt for Liberal Italy was but one assault on the Liberal state after the war. The other developed out of the postwar social turmoil, which was itself the twin product of unsolved prewar social problems and those generated by the war itself. Among the unsolved prewar problems was an acute land problem, reflected in a huge rural proletariat, the landless laborers (*braccianti*), who accounted for nearly half the rural population. Sharecroppers (*mezzadri*), though better off than the laborers, demanded a bigger share of the crop than the customary 50 percent. Rural poverty was at its worst in the south, where inequality in land ownership was also at its most pronounced and where plantation-sized farms (*latifondi*), often owned by absentee landlords, predominated. Southern illiteracy ran as high as 70 to 90 percent in some areas. Social tensions in the industrial-urban areas of the north, in Italy's "industrial triangle" of Genoa, Milan, and Turin, were scarcely less pronounced, with syndicalist violence and the general strikes of 1904 and 1914 grim indicators of a near-revolutionary situation. The acuteness of Italian social problems, both rural and urban, was mirrored in the radicalism of the Italian Socialist party (PSI), which differed from Socialist parties in other west European countries in that it embraced both urban and rural social causes. It was also a strongly pacifist party whose pacifism was not confined to rhetoric but which had organized powerful demonstrations against Italy's colonial war of 1912 for the conquest of Libya.

Among Italy's prewar leaders, Prime Minister Giolitti had had the best grasp of Italian social and political problems, and he had launched important reform measures designed to direct revolutionary forces into evolutionary channels. These measures included the suffrage bill of 1911, which gave the vote to literate males above the age of twenty-one and to illiterate males above the age of thirty. The franchise bill of 1911 was followed by a series of social laws, referred to as "Giolitti's New Deal." Giolitti had also instituted a development program for the impoverished south. The broader aim of the pre-1914 Giolitti reforms was to integrate the broad mass of the population into the Liberal system, which had previously been the predominant domain of a well-to-do oligarchy, and to thereby lead Italian society gradually towards a functioning democracy with a basic social consensus. For this, time would have been required, and what might have become a successful transition was interrupted by the Italian entry into the war in 1915.

The postwar era added its own, new social problems, which stemmed from the exhaustion of the Italian war economy and the heightened expectation of returning war veterans. Reflecting the new "spirit of the trenches" (*trincerismo*) and the impatience of the spirit of "1919ism" (*diciannovismo*), the returning peasant soliders demanded land, and when they failed to get it, often enough took it by force. In the cities, angry workers rioted against war profiteers. The general strike of 1919 was in part organized as a protest against Western intervention in the Russian Civil War. In Turin, a dispute between FIOM, the metalworkers' union, and employers culminated in the seizure and occupation of hundreds of factories by striking workers in August and September 1920.

The postwar governments of Italy between 1919 and 1922 were predominantly governments under Liberal prime ministers, including veteran leader Giolitti, who returned briefly to the prime ministership between 1920 and 1921. Both the unsatisfactory peace of 1919 and the expanding postwar social chaos were thus laid at the door of Liberal Italy by angry Nationalists and frightened property owners. The latter lost faith in the Liberal state because the Liberal state failed to uphold law and order through a policy of tough police action.

Giolitti took a calmer view of the situation. He had chased d'Annunzio out of Fiume with a few salvos from the battleship Andrea Doria in late 1920 and had thereby exposed the hollowness of d'Annunzio's militant rhetoric. Giolitti also believed the

Turin factory seizures of 1920 to be the end, not the beginning, of the revolutionary wave which threatened social stability. The parliamentary arithmetic of postwar Italy was, on the other hand, singularly unfavorable to a calm riding out of the storm. The first postwar elections of November 16, 1919 had added a new force to Italian politics in the shape of the Catholic Popular party (*Popolari*), which gained a respectable 100 seats, as against 156 for the Socialists and 252 for the Liberal-democratic center. In combatting social chaos and Nationalist uproar, the Liberal center could not count on Socialist support, because of the fundamentally hostile and negative attitude of the Socialists towards the "bourgeois" state. The *Popolari* party of Alcide de Gasperi and the priest Luigi Sturzo was an unsteady and distrustful ally of the Liberals at best, as a result of social and religious differences. Parliamentary instability thus confirmed the impression of weak government in times of national emergency and contributed to the rise both of Mussolini and fascism.

Mussolini and the Rise of Fascism

As a political force, fascism reflected both the personal transformation of Mussolini from a militant Socialist into a militant Nationalist as well as the crosscurrents of embittered nationalism and social anxieties of postwar Italy. Mussolini's transition from the extreme Left to the extreme Right is less baffling if the chief motivation of his conduct is perceived not as a commitment to any particular ideology, or political philosophy, but as a yearning for personal involvement in "action." That Mussolini's activism was on behalf of the Left before 1914 was no doubt due to his own humble social origins and the proletarian legacy of his father Alessandro. With the fate of Europe hanging in the balance after August 1914, and Italy playing no active part in the drama, Mussolini joined the Nationalist interventionist cause, not merely because he may have been bribed, but because he genuinely disliked the prospect of a German-dominated Europe.

In December 1914 Mussolini had founded his first *fascio* (group) for revolutionary action on behalf of intervention in the war. After a brief stint in the Italian army during the war, he launched the *Fasci Italiani di Combattimento* on May 23, 1919 in Milan. The new movement combined the militant nationalism of the 1915 interventionists with demands for radical social change so characteristic of the "1919ism." Fascism, at the moment of its birth, also displayed the characteristic of physical violence toward opponents which was to remain central to its nature until its dying day at the end of World War II. The first action of the Fascists was the burning and sacking of the editorial offices of the Socialist newspaper *Avanti!* on April 15, 1919, for which Mussolini himself had served as editor-in-chief before his conversion to nationalism. Very quickly, fascism perfected violence into a regular technique, known as *squadrismo*, whose extensive use against Socialists and striking workers turned fascism into a de facto police force, serving the ends of frightened property owners in town and country.

By 1921 fascism had constituted itself as a regular party, whose "Rome program" shed much of the social radicalism of the incipient fascism of 1919 and thus advertised the party as an effective instrument for the preservation of the social status quo. By 1921 Mussolini had also been able to benefit from the less than heroic exit of d'Annunzio from the political stage, following the tragicomic Fiume incident. Until d'Annunzio's disgrace in late 1920, he had been the hope of Nationalist-reactionary Italy. Afterwards, Nationalist attention focused on Mussolini, who inherited d'Annunzio's mantle, style, and black-shirted uniforms.

The Fascists were still small in numbers. Having gained no seats at all in the 1919 elections, they picked up a mere 35 seats in the elections of May 1921, as against 123 for the Socialists and 108 for the *Popolari*. Fascist party membership was estimated at a quarter-million nationwide by 1921.

Insignificance in numbers was no more a deterrent to Mussolini's singleminded quest for power than it had been to Lenin and the Bolsheviks, whose technique in seizing power Mussolini admired as much as he admired the Bolshevik uses of force in the defense of power, once gained. After becoming Italian prime minister, Mussolini was to call the Bolsheviks "admirable teachers."

In 1922, fascism gained power through a two-pronged attack which came both from below, through the actual use of force and the threat of force, and from above, through the king. The king was persuaded that a legal and constitutional appointment of Mussolini to the prime ministership was preferable to either civil war or a continuation of the three-cornered parliamentary deadlock between Liberals, *Populari*, and Socialists. On October 30, 1922 the king appointed Mussolini prime minister, after Mussolini had threatened a "march on Rome" which would proceed from the scheduled Fascist party congress at Naples. The "march on Rome" took place only after Mussolini's appointment, its participants arriving by train and staging a victory celebration.

FASCISM IN POWER

The absence of any clear ideological definition of fascism before 1922 allowed it to appear as many things to many people. To some, fascism was simply a guarantee against the continuation of anarchy, and social violence did quickly and appreciably diminish after Mussolini came to power. To others, fascism was a promise of attaining Great Power status, and Mussolini went out of his way soon after gaining power to impress Italians, if not necessarily others, with their country's heightened prestige, by deliberate posturing at international conferences. To still others, fascism spelled the end of Italy as a civilized society, because of the undiminished brutality and violence, which fascism in power continued to direct against its enemies.

The ideological vagueness of fascism reflected both Mussolini's disdain for political philosophy as well as his calculated appeal to the greatest numbers, with himself as the perceived promoter of individual and group interest. Significantly, a definition of fascist doctrine appeared at a relatively late stage, in 1932, and in an offhand fashion, in *Volume XIV* of the Italian encyclopedia. Even then, the definition said more about what fascism was not than it did about what it was. Fascist doctrine defined fascism as antidemocratic, antiliberal, and anti-Marxist. The fascist doctrine of 1932 boasted of the "corporate system" as a new and significant system for the orderly settlement of social disputes in an industrial society, avoiding both the "anarchy" of economic liberalism and the abolition of private ownership of the means of production as under Marxism. Though launched with much fanfare under the Labor Charter of 1927 and implemented by law in 1934, the corporate system was, in reality, a façade for the preservation of an industrial-capitalist and semifeudal-agricultural economy. By 1930 one-half of 1 percent of Italy's rural population still owned 42 percent of the land, and land reclamation projects, such as the draining of the Pontine marshes, created no more than three thousand new farms. The corporations, twenty-two in number for the entire economy, far from becoming forums for social mediation, became organs for the preservation of the status quo.

The significance of Italian fascism consisted in the fact that it was the first successful example of institutionalized militarism in postwar Europe. Its symbols and gestures enshrined the memory of the marching armies of the First World War on a permanent peacetime basis, with the slogan of *Credere, Obbedire, Combattere* (Believe, Obey, and Fight) transplanting military virtues onto the civilian order of an entire country.

Soon, the political soldier in uniform was to become the symbol of an entire epoch in twentieth-century Europe. His shirt was of many different colors, beginning with the Black Shirt of Italian fascism and followed by the Brown Shirt of Nazi Germany, later by the Green Shirt of the Radical Union of Yugoslavia's prime minister Jan Stojadinovič, the Blue Shirt of the Spanish Falangists, the uniforms of Corneliu Codreanu's Rumanian Iron Guard, and many others. Despite the variations in color, the meaning was much the same. The political soldier was the visible symbol and reminder of a new order that rejected the free interplay of socioeconomic forces and the free expression of individual liberty as anarchic and detrimental to the common national interest. From this, the step towards a totalitarian system was not a very large one, once totalitarianism was accepted as a necessary element of an orderly status quo.

It was part of the Fascist reality that its claim to have "educated" society towards a higher level of law-abiding morality did not preclude a luxurious growth of corruption among party careerists and hangers-on. News manipulation and censorship, and the official promotion of an atmosphere of forced optimism, concealed the true state of public and private affairs from the eyes of the people both in Italy and, later, in the countries which borrowed the Fascist model.

Italian fascism was also carefully staged political street theater, in which the audience was made a participant through the choreography of emotionally frenzied mass rallies. Like Soviet communism, fascism was a pioneer in the effective uses of political propaganda, both at home and abroad. To Italian audiences, what Mussolini said was often as important as what he did. Mussolini's much advertized "battle for wheat" failed to reach the goal of self-sufficiency, and the campaign for a sharp increase in the birthrate, inaugurated in 1927, similarly fell short of the goal of raising the population figures to sixty million by midcentury.

The First Phase

The development of Fascist rule proceeded in two distinct phases. The first phase from 1922 to 1924 opened with a coalition government in which Mussolini still included representatives of the Liberal and *Popolari* parties, and it ended with the political scandal surrounding the murder of Socialist deputy Giacomo Matteotti. During this phase, on July 15, 1923, Mussolini enacted the Acerbo law which guaranteed Fascist control over parliament in the elections of April 1924. The Acerbo law assured any political party, which obtained a relative majority of two-thirds of the seats in parliament, provided the relative majority exceeded 25 percent. The remaining seats were to be divided proportionately among the other parties according to their relative strength.

The Matteotti Murder

After the elections of April 1924, the Socialist deputy G. Matteotti, on May 30, attacked Mussolini in a public speech on the floor of parliament for the Fascist violence during the election campaign, and demanded the invalidation of the results. On June 10, 1924 Matteotti disappeared. His stabbed body was discovered a few weeks later, murdered *squadristi*-style, in the woods near Rome.

The Matteotti murder touched off a tremendous political scandal, because there was still enough of a free press left in Italy to give vent to the public outrage. To most, Fascist responsibility seemed certain and the personal involvement of Mussolini quite possible. Anti-Fascist parliamentary deputies, led by Liberal leader Giovanni Amendola, himself destined to become a victim of *squadrismo,* staged a protest walkout from parliament. The participants of the so-called Aventine Secession, named after the Plebeian withdrawal to the Aventine Hill in ancient Rome, vowed not to reclaim their seats until the rule of law had been restored and a new government installed.

Mussolini's effort to ride out the storm with a mixture of cover-up and stonewalling might not have succeeded but for the silence of important individuals and groups in the affair. The king did not publicly assail Mussolini because he feared a relapse into the postwar disorders if Mussolini was forced out. Pope Pius XI, the recently elected successor to Benedict XV, had acquiesced in a Mussolini government in 1922 because he preferred such a government to a possible coalition of Socialists and Catholic *Popolari,* for which Luigi Sturzo had been working vainly. A Conservative, Pius XI had observed the Soviet invasion of Catholic Poland during the Russo-Polish war of 1920 while he was still Cardinal Achille Ratti, the papal nuncio. His fear of communism and Marxism still affected his attitude towards fascism when in 1924 Mussolini's fate hung in the balance. Italian big business, as organized in *Confindustria,* the Confederation of Industrialists, likewise dreaded the consequences for its own interests of a Mussolini downfall.

The Second Phase

When the anti-Fascist opposition failed to bring him down, Mussolini seized the moment to launch the second, totalitarian phase of fascism, begining in early 1925. After the dissolution of all political parties other than the Fascist between November 1925 and October 1926, Socialist and Catholic trade unions were also banned. The "Fascist laws" of 1925 and 1926 extended Fascist controls over the judiciary, the civil service, and the executive. In 1927, a special tribunal for trying crimes against the state was established, followed by a Fascist secret police (OVRA). New laws of 1928 and 1929 conferred constitutional status on the Fascist grand council, previously a party organ. Italian youth was militarized and politicized with the creation of Fascist youth organizations, the *Balilla* for ages 8 to 14, *Avanguardisti,* for ages 14 to 18, and *Giovani Fascisti,* for those between 18 and 21. The Fascist slogan for Italian youth became *Libro e moschetto, Fascista perfetto* (A Book and A Rifle Make A Perfect Fascist). Throughout, the aim of Mussolini was the closest possible identification of Fascist party and Italian state, a process called *fascistizzazione* under the motto, Everything Inside the State, Nothing Outside the State, Nothing Against the State. The process was extended to the schools, the universities, and the arts. The latter, under Italian fascism, nevertheless remained a great deal freer and more open to original experimentation than was the case in either Nazi Germany or Soviet Russia.

Fascism and the Church

Among the most popular and acclaimed policies of fascism was the reconciliation between state and church under the 1929 Lateran Agreements. There was a strong anticlerical tradition in Mussolini's personal background as a Socialist and in the early make-up of fascism. As a young Socialist, Mussolini had once attacked the priesthood as "black germs," as harmful to humanity, as "the germs of tuberculosis." The first Fascist party program of 1919 had called for the expropriation of church property.

Once in power, Mussolini found it politically expedient to seek a solution of the "Roman Question" in order to increase his own appeal among Italian Catholics. In Pius XI, Mussolini found a willing negotiating partner, in part because of the generous terms offered by the Fascist regime, in part because of the deep-seated anticommunist fears of the pontiff.

What was collectively termed the Lateran Agreements of February 11, 1929, consisted of a treaty of conciliation and a concordat. In the conciliation treaty Italy recognized the Vatican city as an independent, sovereign state and paid a compensation of 1.75 billion lira to the Vatican for the loss of the city of Rome, taken from the pope in 1870. The concordat gave Roman Catholicism a privileged position in Italian society, recognizing it as the religion of the state, extending the rules of canon law to marriage questions and instituting Catholic religious instruction in public schools.

Mussolini was hailed as the conciliator of an historic conflict between state and church, which all the prewar liberal governments had failed to solve. New conflicts between the church and the Fascist state did, in fact, develop soon after the 1929 agreements, principally disputes relating to the education of the young, but also because of the radicalization of Fascist ideology through its adoption of Nazi-style anti-Semitism. In response to these issues, the papal encyclical *Rappresentante in Terra* of 1929 stressed the educational mission of the church, while the encyclical *Non Abbiamo Bisogno* of 1931 condemned the Fascist theory of the all-powerful state.

Mussolini and Hitler

As the decade of the 1930s drew to a close, Fascist Italy, itself once the inspirer and model of Nazi Germany, increasingly copied the style and laws of its erstwhile pupil Hitler. The Italian imitation grew more pronounced the more Mussolini's role changed from partner to satellite of Nazi Germany in foreign policy. In 1937 Mussolini created a ministry of popular culture (*Minculpop*), in imitation of Goebbel's German ministry of propaganda. The "race manifesto" of July 14, 1938, drafted largely by Mussolini himself, marked the opening of a campaign of anti-Semitism, which surprised many Italians, because anti-Semitism previously had been largely absent from fascism. As recently as 1934, Mussolini had attacked nazism on the issue of anti-Semitism, denouncing it as "100 percent racism." Italian Jews such as Gino Arias, the theorist on corporations and Enrico Rocca, the organizer of the Fascist party in Rome, had occupied prominent positions in the early days of fascism. Mussolini's political education as a young Socialist before the First World War owed much to the guidance of his Russian Jewish friend, Angelica Balabanoff, the coeditor of *Avanti!* and Lenin's future collaborator in the Communist International.

The "race manifesto" was quickly followed by a number of anti-Jewish laws which followed the example of the Nazi Nuremberg laws of 1935, and which purged the Italian civil service, public schools, and universities of Jews.

With the Munich conference of September, 1938 Mussolini enjoyed one last upsurge of popularity among the Italian people precisely because the conference had saved the peace and Mussolini had appeared as arbiter among the Great Powers. His aping of the Nazi style in domestic policy and his chaining Italy to Nazi Germany in the Pact of Steel in May, 1939, increasingly isolated the star performer of Italian fascism from his own people, who had tired of perfunctory applause. When he led Italy into the Second World War in June 1940, he repeated, in essence—though on a grander and more deadly scale—the folly of d'Annunzio's occupation of Fiume in 1919. Like d'Annunzio, Mussolini had been the best audience of his own nationlist rhetoric which, after almost twenty years of power, had blurred his vision to the military and political reality of his time. As d'Annunzio's legionaries had dispersed at the first sound of gunfire in 1920, Fascist Italy, unprepared for serious war in 1940, staggered from one military defeat to the next. The Fiume occupation had ended on a tragicomic note; but d'Annunzio's inflated nationalism, which had inspired it, survived in the fascism that led all Italy to national disaster during the Second World War.

INTERNATIONAL FASCISM AND THE FAILURE OF SPANISH DEMOCRACY

Italian fascism, to Mussolini, was not "an article for export." The terms fascism and internationalism seemed indeed mutually exclusive because of the nationalist self-centeredness of fascism. In time, Mussolini came to view the Fascist system of Italy as a model for other societies which were beset by problems similar to those of Italy. With the declining role of democracy and the rise of right-wing dictatorships in depression-ridden Europe, Mussolini became convinced that fascist doctrine was rapidly becoming the doctrine of his age, just as liberalism had been the doctrine of the nineteenth century. Thomas Mann, Germany's distinguished novelist and Nobel Prize laureate, speaking of the 1930s, called fascism the "disease of the times" which was pushing Europe towards its perhaps most brutal phase in history. By the 1930s, Fascist or Fascist-type movements were indeed making rapid progress, seizing actual power in some countries or serving as the rallying point of a new and more militant force of nationalism. International fascism covered as wide and diverse a range as Oswald Mosley's British Union of Fascists, Hitler's Nazi movement, the *Action Française* of Charles Maurras in France, Jose Antonio Primo de Rivera's *Falange Española* in Spain, Corneliu Codreanu's Rumanian Iron Guard, Ferenc Szalasi's Hungarian Arrow Cross party, Stojadinović's Yugoslav Radical Union, Engelbert Dollfuss' Austrian *Heimwehr,* General Wallenius' Finnish Lapuan movement, Vidkun Quisling's Norwegian *Nasjonal Samling* (National Union), and Fritz Clausen's Danish Nazi party.

Despite the national diversity, the Fascist movements of Europe shared a broad-based consensus of antiliberalism and anti-Marxism, the latter reinforced by the spectacle of Stalinist Russia in the 1930s. Racism and anti-Semitism, though not an integral part of Italian fascism at its outset, became a central feature of fascism in Germany, Hungary, Rumania, and France. The anti-Semitism of Corneliu Codreanu, leader of the Rumanian Iron Guard, derived in part from the teachings of Codreanu's professor A. C. Cuza at the University of Jassy, with Cuza a disciple of Charles Maurras. The antiliberalism of Maurras had more distant and deeper roots than those of his contemporary fascist sympathizers, being embedded in Maurras' nostalgia for the preeminence and cultural distinctiveness of preliberal and prerevolutionary Bourbon France. Belief in the political ignorance of the common man was a widely shared feature of 1930s fascism, as was the conviction that democracy, in the hands of the mass, was destined to become an agent of destruction, politically, socially, and culturally. Maurras' observation that the only way of improving democracy was to destroy it, was representative of fascist thinking everywhere.

The failure of democracy in Spain in the early and mid-1930s assumed special symbolic significance because it occurred against the larger background of triumphant totalitarianism, and was widely viewed as a last-ditch battle between democratic and Fascist Europe. The Spanish drama also highlighted the dilemma of the common opposition of liberalism and communism to fascism, both in the arena of Spanish domestic politics and on the wider plane of European international relations.

Although Spain had stayed out of the First World War, its chaotic postwar social and economic situation bore striking resemblance to that of postwar Italy. Spain shared with Italy a high illiteracy rate, a serious land problem, as reflected in the revolutionary mood of the *braceros,* Spain's equivalent to the landless Italian *braccianti,* and syndicalist and anarchist violence in the cities. The divisions of Spanish society were aggravated by regional nationalism, especially in the economically advanced Basque provinces of Guipuzcoa, Vizcaya, Alava and Navarre, as well as in Catalonia.

The military dictatorship of General Primo de Rivera between September 1923 and January 1930 suppressed the anarchy of postwar Spain without addressing itself effectively to the underlying causes. When Primo de Rivera stepped down in January 1930 under the combined pressure of Spain's business community and leading intellectuals, such as Miguel de Unamuno, he also caused the downfall of the monarchy in the person of King Alfonso XIII, who went into exile in 1931. Outward appearances to the contrary, Primo de Rivera's dictatorship was not fascist, lacking in both ideological pretensions and an organized political mass movement.

The prospects of the Spanish Republic, which followed upon the exodus of Alfonso XIII, were slim enough, owing to the passions and divisions of Spanish politics and the inexperience of the newly elected constituent *cortes* of June 1931. The birth of the Spanish Republic also coincided with the broader failure of European democracy, a fact which overshadowed and deeply influenced its fate.

Between 1931 and 1933 the Republican government was a coalition of Socialists and Left Republicans, under Prime Minister Manuel Azaña, a doctrinaire liberal. Perhaps the main flaw in Azaña's sweeping reform policy in the areas of land ownership, illiteracy, and Catalan regional nationalism, was that it tried to solve long-neglected problems all at once. The Azaña government also needlessly antagonized the Catholic establishment of Spain and thereby contributed to the repudiation of the republic by a large part of Catholic Spain. The 1931 republican constitution, which declared Spain a "republic of workers of all classes," empowered the state to dissolve religious orders. In the words of Azaña, Spain had "ceased to be Catholic."

The parliamentary election of November 1933 registered a powerful Conservative reaction, spearheaded by the newly founded Catholic mass party CEDA, as well as the recently established *Falange Española* of Jose Antonio Primo de Rivera, the son of the dictator. The right-wing government which followed the 1933 Spanish elections undid many of the hasty reforms of its predecessor and thereby triggered mass violence, culminating in the uprising of Asturian miners in October 1934, in the course of which 900 workers and 300 soldiers were killed.

Franco Comes to Power

The elections of February 16, 1936, the last elections of republican Spain, witnessed the return to power of the parties of the Left in the form of the Popular Front. The Spanish Popular Front, which had the blessing of Moscow like its French counterpart of a few months later, consisted of Azaña's Left Republicans, Socialists, Communists, and Catalan autonomists, organized in the Catalan *Esquerra.* The victory of the Popular Front aggravated rather than healed the political divisions of Spain. Emboldened by their victory, the parties of the Popular Front demanded the outlawing of all opposition parties and newspapers. On April 7, 1936, the parties of the Left deposed Alcala Zamora, the moderate president of the republic, on dubious constitutional grounds, and put Azaña in his place. Parliamentary deputies attended the *cortes* sessions armed, while Falangists and Communists fought pitched battles in the streets. The murder of Calvo Sotelo, the leader of the Conservative opposition, on July 13, 1936 touched off the military insurrection under General Emilio Mola of the Pomplona garrison four days later. The following day, the forty-four-year-old Francisco Franco, former chief of staff and most prestigious officer of the Spanish army, joined the insurrection and assumed its leadership quickly thereafter. On October 1, 1936, General Mola's military junta at Burgos proclaimed Franco "chief of the Nationalist State." The Spanish Civil War between the republic and Nationalist Spain, destined to last until April 1939, was on. After a turbulent existence of fifty-seven months, the republic had come full circle from the high hopes of social and political reform to the challenge of a military dictatorship, allied with the Spanish version of European fascism.

THE FAILURE OF GERMAN DEMOCRACY:
THE WEIMAR REPUBLIC

The Allies had identified German autocracy and "militarism" as the chief sources of German misconduct and they had spent considerable effort during the First World War in defeating both. It is therefore perhaps surprising that they should have devoted so little effort or attention to the success of German democracy, which grew out of the German defeat and revolution of 1918. Bismarck, after defeating France in 1871, had not hesitated to apply pressure against the restoration of the French monarchy in the mid-1870s, because he equated a restored French monarchy with the likelihood of a French war of revenge. No similar effort on behalf of German democracy was undertaken by the Allied side during the brief fourteen-year existence of the Weimar Republic. Yet the success or failure of German democracy was not merely a concern of German domestic politics. It was bound to affect the stability of all Europe, because even in defeat Germany remained potentially the most dynamic and militarily powerful nation in Europe.

The consequences of the breakdown of the Weimar Republic by 1933 have tended to lend that failure an air of inevitability and preordained doom. Yet there existed, at the outset, both favorable and unfavorable circumstances for the development of German democracy, and it required the combination of successive and cumulative external and internal crises to bring the democratic experiment of 1919 to its end.

The Social Democrats

On the positive side there was the Social Democratic party, which had been a persistent agent of democratic reform since its formation in 1875 and which had grown into the largest single political party of the empire before 1914. Together with the Catholic Center party and the newly formed Democratic party, the Social Democrats, formed a stable democratic base in the first German postwar elections of January 1919, with 331 seats in the Weimar constituent assembly. Among the enemies of the republic, the Communists, having boycotted the 1919 elections, had no seats, while the promonarchist Nationalists captured a mere 44 seats. Among the positive factors must also be counted considerable political talent, coming mostly from the background of German municipal government, as exemplified by names such as Hans Luther, mayor of Essen, Hans Goerdeler, mayor of Leipzig and subsequent Resistance leader, and Konrad Adenauer, long-term mayor of Cologne. Gustav Stresemann, the Weimar Republic's most successful foreign minister during his long tenure between 1923 and 1929, was also noteworthy for his attempt, albeit unsuccessful, to reduce the large number of German political parties, much as André Tardieu tried to do in France's Third Republic.

The Legacy of 1848

On the negative side, the Weimar Republic suffered from the beginning from the historic weakness of German liberalism, rooted, in part, in the failure of the 1848–1849 liberal revolution to achieve German national unification. That failure had left a wide gap between the "people" and the "government" which the revolution of 1918–1919 had not been able to close. For this the continued functioning in the new republic of the old administrative, judicial and military elites was very largely responsible. Government, in the widespread German perception of the early twentieth century, was the business of experts, not the people at large. It was this deeply ingrained habit which prompted Hugo Preuss, the liberal drafter of the 1919 Weimar constitution, to observe in exasperation that the elected members of the constituent assembly did not seem to understand that the constitution must be "blood of their blood and flesh of their flesh."

The German political parties were also too many in number and too inexperienced in the responsible exercise of power. Except during the final months of the empire they had never served in a governing capacity as part of the imperial cabinet. Republican politics, though producing able men, failed to produce leaders of great national stature. In Weimar Germany, there was no Clemenceau or Poincaré. With mounting foreign policy failure and domestic socioeconomic crises, the impression quickly gained ground that the Weimar Republic was only an interim or stopgap solution.

The Kapp Putsch

Foreign policy failure triggered the first nationalist and military revolt in the shape of the Kapp-Lüttwitz *putsch* of March 12, 1920. Angered over Allied demands for the reduction of the army's size to the levels prescribed by Versailles, a portion of the army, under General Walter von Lüttwitz, supported by Wolfgang Kapp, a Prussian reactionary, tried to overthrow the Weimar Republic in a military coup. The attempt failed not because the majority of the army rallied to the republic, but because labor organized an effective general strike against the would-be conspirators.

Public disillusionment with the young republic was reflected in the outcome of the first regular parliamentary elections of June 1920, following the dissolution of the constituent assembly. As against a combined strength in the 1919 elections of 75 percent for the Weimar coalition of Social Democrats, Center party and Democrats, the coalition obtained less than half the Reichstag seats in 1920. The Weimar Republic threatened to become a "republic without republicans."

The Rise of Violence

Nationalist anger continued to mount over the partitioning of Upper Silesia by the League council in 1921 and the deepening reparations controversy in 1922. The anger was translated into violence directed against republican leaders, who were denounced as "traitors" and "politicians of fulfilment." In August 1921 the former minister of finance Matthias Erzberger was assassinated by Nationalist terrorists, followed by the murder of foreign minister Walter Rathenau in June 1922. Rathenau's murder, which also signaled the rise in German postwar anti-Semitism, stung the Weimar Republic into the adoption, on July 18, 1922, of protective legislative measures against political terrorism. The effectiveness of such measures remained doubtful because of the overt and covert sympathy of much of the German judiciary for the cause of Nationalist terrorists.

The climax of the reparations crisis with the Ruhr struggle of 1923, and the resulting twin uprisings of Communists in October and Hitler's Nazis in November 1923, very nearly brought the Weimar Republic to its collapse.

The Communist insurrection in Saxony, Thuringia and Hamburg resulted from both the social despair of the inflation-ridden proletariat and the basic change in tactics by the Moscow-directed Comintern. Having supported the German resistance to the French Ruhr occupation earlier in 1923, Moscow wanted to overthrow the newly formed government of Gustav Stresemann because of the latter's desire to change German-French relations from confrontation to negotiation. No sooner had Stresemann crushed the Communist insurrection than Hitler made his national political debut with his proclaimed "national revolution" of November 8, 1923 in Munich.

The "Beerhall" Putsch

The "national revolution," better known as the abortive "beerhall" *putsch* of 1923, failed because with the exception of General Ludendorff of World War I fame, Hitler's Nationalist-Conservative allies deserted him. Though a political failure, the "beerhall" *putsch* was an important propaganda gain for Hitler, because of the publicity accorded his subsequent treason trial in Feburary 1924. It was significant that

Hitler, still a foreigner with Austrian citizenship, was not deported and that he received the minimum sentence of five years, of which he served a mere eight-and-a-half months. For Hitler, the most important lesson of the events of 1923 was never again to attempt to seize power by the amateurish and violent methods employed in Munich.

Economic Recovery

Much to foreign surprise, the Weimar Republic recovered quickly from the turmoil of 1923. The runaway inflation was stopped by November 1923 with the issuance of a new currency, the *rentenmark,* under the supervision of finance minister Hans Luther and financial wizard Hjalmar Schacht. By 1924 the mark returned to the gold standard and interest rates, which had been as high as 100 percent per year, sank to 6 percent by 1926.

The 1923 inflation nvertheless left deep social and economic wounds which the short-lived economic boom of the mid-1920s obscured rather than healed. Among the wounds was the loss of middle-class savings and the identification of the Weimar Republic with what the middle class perceived to have been the third major disaster in half-a-decade, after the defeat of 1918 and the revolution of 1918–1919.

With the return of foreign loan capital in the wake of the adoption of the Dawes Plan in 1924, Germany experienced an economic boom comparable to that of the Hohenzollern Empire of the 1870s and 1880s.

With 76 billion marks, the German national gross product of 1929 was significantly above the prewar level of 45 billion. In 1930, German merchant shipping had climbed back to over 4 million tons, up from less than 700,000 thousand tons after World War I. There were significant gains in the mechanization and automation of the coal and steel industries, with resulting increases in productivity. The chemical industry, hard hit by the loss of German patent rights under Versailles, recaptured 28 percent of the world market by 1928.

Like Britain, the Weimar Republic continued to suffer from industrial unemployment even in the best of times. Unemployment was above 2 million in the winter of 1925–1926, dropping to 1.5 million at the turn of 1927–1928 and rising again to 2.6 million at the turn of 1928–1929. With projections of 600,000 unemployed, the unemployment insurance system was barely adequate to meet demands during the prosperous mid-1920s. It collapsed under depression conditions after 1929, when unemployment soared to 6 million.

The principal flaw of the 1920s boom was its reliance on the continued influx of foreign loan capital, chiefly from the United States. In addition, the Weimar Republic used foreign loans for the payment of reparations. With the withdrawal of foreign loans for both economic and political reasons, beginning in 1929–1930, Germany once again faced the dilemma of meeting both its reparations and commercial foreign debts from the diminishing returns of German exports. The prosperity of the mid-1920s proved to be short-lived and only a pause between the inflation of 1923 and the coming of the world depression in 1929.

The Bauhaus

Although social and political instability prevailed in the short history of the Weimar Republic, the republican period was among the most active and creative in the field of twentieth-century German cultural development. In this regard the republic benefited from the strong cultural roots of prewar Germany, as well as developing its own, often revolutionary styles in the 1920s. That decade witnessed the growth of the Bauhaus school, founded in Weimar in 1919 by the architect Walter Gropius, into a world-renowned leader of new architecture and industrial design. The novelty of the Bauhaus approach consisted in the interaction of artisans, artists and architects in a new synthesis of teaching and design. The Bauhaus style continued to influence architectural and design trends well into the post-World War II period under former Bauhaus leaders as Mies van der Rohe, who, together with other prominent Bauhaus members, left Germany after the political changes of 1933.

Writing, Music, and Film

In literature, the works of Thomas Mann, Hermann Hesse, and Alfred Döblin heralded a new era in the German novel, with Döblin's social-critical novel *Berlin Alexanderplatz* of 1929 the source of a recent and noteworthy West German television series depicting depression Germany. In music, Germany's most renowed pre-World War I composer Richard Strauss continued to excel with such new works as *Frau ohne Schatten* and *Intermezzo*. Arnold Schönberg explored new musical paths with the invention of the twelve-tone scale, and achieved fame with such works as *Verklärte Nacht*. Berlin became the center of a thriving motion picture industry and for a while the movie metropolis of Europe, with such productions as *The Cabinet of Dr. Caligari* and *The Blue Angel*, featuring Marlene Dietrich.

The burst of cultural activity in the Weimar period reflected the strength which flowed from the liberal spirit and institutions of the republic. Yet taken as a whole, the cultural community of Weimar Germany, with such notable exceptions as Thomas Mann, made little effort to strengthen the republican regime in the German public eye by any gesture or statement of support. Partly for that reason, the German cultural elite had little difficulty in adjusting to the new climate and conditions that were to follow the fall of the republic after 1933.

Weimar's Last Years

The domestic politics of the Weimar Republic closely mirrored the fluctuations of the economy. The elections of May 1928 gave a misleading impression of long-range political stability, the Social Democrats scoring an impressive gain with 153 seats. With Hermann Müller, the Social Democrats formed their first government in eight years, which expanded the traditional Weimar coalition into a "grand Weimar coalition" through the inclusion of Stresemann's middle-of-the-road People's party. Chancellor Müller's boast of 1928 that the foundations of the German republic were "sound and unshakable" might have proved truer if the favorable econmic conditions of 1928 had remained unchanged. Instead, the economic crisis of 1929 quickly reshuffled the political deck, diminishing the strength of the democratic center, augumenting the power of the republic's old enemies, and introducing new enemies whose mass appeal and vehemence eventually overwhelmed both the democratic center and the old antirepublican forces.

Parliamentary government collapsed with Müller's resignation on March 27, 1930 because his four coalition partners could not even agree on so minor a problem as raising funds to cover rising costs of unemployment insurance.

The deeper cause of the fall of Müller's government was the broadening anti-parliamentary consensus under the impact of the depression and of renewed Nationalist agitation, of which the noisy campaign against the Young Plan of October 1929, jointly organized by Hitler and Alfred Hugenberg's Nationalists, was the first sign. The antiparliamentary consensus included not only Hindenburg, who had been elected to the presidency in 1925, the Nationalists, the army establishment, and big business, but also elements of those parties, such as the Catholic Center and the People's party, which had previously been loyal and supportive of the republic. Before the elections of September 1930, the Nazi factor did not yet count in antirepublican calculations, because with a mere dozen Reichstag seats, it could still be relegated to the category of a lunatic fringe.

The principal architect of antirepublican strategy in the final years of Weimar became General Kurt von Schleicher, the army's man in charge of maintaining political contacts with the government.

Schleicher and his supporters wished to exploit the crisis created by the depression in order to effect a change from a liberal republic to a Bismarck-style semiautocratic system, which, given the inferior numbers of the antirepublican forces, they could not have attempted in normal and stable times. In effect, Schleicher wished to undo the results of the German Revolution of 1918–1919, with the restoration of the German monarchy also a possible option.

Between March 1930 and December 1932, Schleicher became the "kingmaker" of German chancellors, and operated behind the "throne" of Hindenburg in the manner of a "field gray eminence." The chancellors picked by Schleicher came to depend for their political survival less on parliamentary majorities than on Hindenburg's—and hence Schleicher's—endorsement. In this manner, the style of "presidential cabinets" approached the constitutional practice of the Bismarck empire, under which chancellors served at the pleasure of the emperor, not of the Reichstag majority.

Heinrich Brüning, forty-six-year-old leader of the conservative wing of the Center party, was Schleicher's first choice for the chancellorship. The choice proved to have serious consequences for Germany and, eventually, Schleicher personally. Brüning was not only an uninspiring leader who quickly earned the title of "hunger chancellor" from the growing army of the unemployed, but he displayed singularly poor political judgment in ordering the dissolution of the 1928 Reichstag and the holding of new elections in September 1930. The elections were intended to produce a more cooperative Reichstag. Instead, reflecting the social crisis under the depression, the September 1930 elections increased Nazi strength from 12 to 107 seats, that of the Communists from 54 to 77. The elections of September 1930 were the first decisive step towards the Nazi conquest of 1933.

NATIONAL SOCIALISM AND THE END OF WEIMAR

After the startling election results of September 1930, National Socialist strength continued to soar in virtually every national and state election until the Nazi party became the strongest party in the Reichstag elections of July 1932 with 230 seats, or slightly more than 37 percent of the vote. In the elections to the Prussian state parliament of April 1932, Nazi strength increased from 6 to 162 seats.

The sharp rise in Nazi strength was gained primarily at the expense of middle-class parties, especially the People's party and the Democrats, whose share of the popular vote declined from 25 percent in 1928 to five percent in 1932. At the same time, Nazi influence had grown in the armed forces, chiefly among young officers, as was revealed in the treason trial of Reichswehr officers in September 1930 for the dissemination of Nazi propaganda.

By contrast, Social Democrats and the Catholic Center remained largely immune to Nazi penetration, the SPD obtaining 133 seats in the elections of July 1932, the Center increasing its strength to 97.

In no national election did the Nazi party ever gain a simple majority of the vote, not even in the elections Hitler held in March 1933 after becoming chancellor. National Socialism was nevertheless a movement of unprecedented force and mass appeal in twentieth-century German politics, where the objective conditions of German postwar society were as much a determining factor as was the person of Hitler.

The German Conservatives and Nationalists hoped to fill the void of authority, which the collapse of the monarchy had caused in the German public mind, by a simple return to the pre-1914 status quo. The power of Hitler's appeal consisted in the fact that he correctly gauged the national discontent of the 1920s and early 1930s as not an ordinary longing for Conservative renewal, but as a search for national rehabilitation and social stability, which neither the Hohenzollern Empire nor the Weimar Republic had been able to provide.

Hitler's rise from anonymity to power was a slow process of mutual discovery between himself and his growing following, in which Hitler experienced the confirmation of the anxieties and hatreds of his own boyhood and young adulthood in the fears and resentments of postwar Germany. To Hitler the young Austrian, the prewar multinational Habsburg Empire was a world in decay, corrupted by agents of national and social division—Maxists, liberals, "the Jews." That these same elements had also been a prime cause of Germany's defeat in 1918 was a widely held opinion among German Nationalists and militarists long before most of them had ever heard of Hitler in the early 1920s.

Anti-Semitism formed a significant bridge in the encounter between Hitler and the German Nationalist constituency, in part because of the prewar writings of Nationalist publicists such as Paul de Legarde and Julius Langbehn. Both had criticized the Hohenzollern Empire for its alleged failure to follow up the external political unification with an inner unification through the creation of a distinctly Germanic culture and the overcoming of social conflict between the classes. Both attributed inner conflicts to the social and cultural power of German Jews, a sentiment echoed on a much more virulent scale by Hitler.

The Call for a Führer

DeLagarde and Langbehn, together with the publicist Moeller van den Bruck, who coined the term *Third Reich,* called for a new German leader, a *führer,* not in the person of a crowned head but in the form of an unknown from the depth of the people who would at last complete the work of inner unification as a prelude to unprecedented expansion of German power abroad. As his movement gained momentum, Hitler, to many, seemed a fulfilment of a prophecy. It was from roots such as these that the phenomenon of nazism grew in power and appeal, much more than as a result of the party's early program of 1920, which was amateurish and largely unknown.

The Divided Reichstag

Despite the stunning Nazi election gains of September 1930, the road to Nazi power was still difficult and long and Hitler could not have covered the distance without considerable tactical skill. The 1930 elections had given him no more than 18 percent of the vote and it was difficult to see how he could expect to gain power by constitutional means. His chance lay in the continued division of the non-Nazi Reichstag majority into mutually hostile blocs, as well as in the opening which the presidential emergency powers under article 48 of the Weimar constitution could provide in the hands of an unscrupulous leader such as Hindenburg.

The German Left remained divided between Social Democrats and Communists, just as it was divided during the revolution of 1918–1919. A Social Democratic offer to form a united anti-Nazi front was turned down by the Communists in 1931 on Moscow's orders. Moscow still viewed the prospects of Hitler's coming to power with equanimity, on the assumption that a Nazi seizure of power would hasten the collapse of German capitalism.

The Conservative coalition of Schleicher, Brüning, and Hindenburg also fell apart over the question of how to cope with the situation created by the Nazi election gains. Brüning, with the support of Reichwehr minister Gröner, was prepared to proceed with the implementation of Conservative strategy as initially conceived in early 1930. To minimize Nazi mischief, Gröner issued a ban on the public activities of Hitler's stormtroopers, the SA and SS formations.

The Brüning formula might have worked, if supported by Hindenburg. It failed to gain Hindenburg's support because of Schleicher's intrigues. Schleicher wished to include the Nazi mass movement in Conservative strategy, but for overwhelmingly Conservative ends and under strict Conservative control.

The question was on what terms, if any, Hitler was prepared to join the Schleicher cause. It is true that Hitler had been a willing and, according to eye witnesses, even a submissive ally of General Ludendorff in 1923. But the Hitler of 1930 was not the same man he had been in 1923. The hollow-cheeked streetcorner agitator of 1923 had matured into Germany's most successful orator, into an experienced party leader who had squashed rebellion in the ranks of his own party and who felt at ease with social notables and money-giving business leaders. After the elections of 1930 Hitler knew his own strength, and his goal was supreme power in the form of the German chancellorship.

Brüning's refusal to do business with Hitler prompted his removal from the chancellorship on May 30, 1932. His replacement was Franz von Papen, a hitherto little-known conservative Center party leader with backing in the business world.

Papen's Deals

Papen hoped to come to terms with Hitler by offering major concessions in return for Hitler's expected entry into his government as vice-chancellor. The concessions involved the lifting of the ban on Nazi stormtroopers, the ouster of the Prussian state government—the last major bastion of the Weimar coalition—on July 20, 1932, and the holding of new national elections on July 31, 1932. In these elections, Nazi strength soared to 230 seats.

Having accepted all of Papen's concessions, Hitler still demanded the chancellorship for himself when he met with Hindenburg in August 1932. Hindenburg refused. What followed in the final months of the Weimar Republic was a frantic and confused search for solutions by the original authors of the failed Conservative strategy, principally Schleicher himself, while Hitler watched and waited. Papen hoped to dent Nazi strength by holding yet another national election in November 1932, in which Nazi strength, in fact, declined to 196 seats. When Papen could find no other solution than to propose a military dictatorship, he too was forced to go. On December 2, 1932 Hindenburg appointed Schleicher to the chancellorship, compelling the master of intrigue to find a solution in the open. Consistent with past practice, Schleicher hoped to succeed by outmaneuvering his enemies on the Left and the Right by splitting their strength from within. For the benefit of the Left, Schleicher advertised himself as a "social general" who would reward Social Democratic support with an enlightened social policy. On the Right, Hitler was to be bypassed by an appeal to disillusioned Nazis who thought their *führer* had missed the boat by holding out for the impossible. To Nazis willing to desert Hitler, such as Gregor Strasser, Schleicher offered high office, including the vice-chancellorship.

The Left failed to rally to Schleicher's support because the Social Democrats had not forgotten Schleicher's role in the ouster of the Prussian state government in 1932. Hitler crushed the threat of an internal party revolt and kept control over the Nazi party. He never forgot the challenge which both Schleicher and Strasser had posed, and when the opportunity arrived, during the SA blood purge of June 1934, had both men executed without trial.

Schleicher's final failure opened the door to Papen's reentry. In January 1933, Papen offered Hitler a renewal of the 1932 scheme of Conservative-Nazi alliance with reversed roles, Hitler as chancellor, Papen as vice-chancellor. Counting on his own confidential relationship with the elderly Hindenburg, Papen thought the risk of a Hitler chancellorship acceptable. In a few weeks time, Papen boasted privately, he would have Chancellor Hitler "squeaking in a corner." On January 30, 1933 a reluctant and senile Hindenburg appointed Hitler as the nineteenth, and last, chancellor of the Weimar Republic.

THE SCANDINAVIAN MODEL

While democracy succumbed to the pressures of social fear and national anger in European nations large and small during the 1930s, Scandinavia remained an example of what Europe in the first half of the twentieth century might have become. Next to Switzerland, which Hitler was to characterize as a "small abscess on the face of Europe" during the Second World War, the Scandinavian nations were to remain the only survivors of European democracy before its restoration after 1945. Holland and Belgium, the other small democracies of western Europe, were overrun early in the Second World War, as were Norway and Denmark.

World War I

Externally, the Scandinavian nations had escaped involvement in the Great Power conflict of 1914–1918, but just barely. Despite repeated statements of Scandinavian neutrality, such as in the Malmö declaration of December 1914 and the Oslo statement of November 1917, these countries suffered heavy shipping losses due to naval action of the belligerent powers. Norway lost 1.8 million tons of merchant shipping, nearly half its fleet, Sweden lost over 200,000 tons. Sweden came under the joint pressure of Britain and Germany, the former requesting Swedish assistance in opening a short supply route to tsarist Russia, the latter demanding Swedish participation in the war against Russia. The timely collapse of Russia in 1917 freed Sweden from what might well have become an insoluble dilemma between neutrality and involuntary belligerency.

Scandinavism

It was the exposure to the common dangers of the First World War that bred a new spirit of cooperation among Scandinavian countries, called *Scandinavism.* Scandinavia became a model for peaceful international cooperation that others might have imitated in the interest of European peace generally. Scandinavism produced a peaceful settlement of the territorial dispute between Sweden and Finland over the Åland islands, in Finland's favor, in 1921. It also helped in the 1933 settlement of the Danish-Norwegian controversy concerning sovereignty over Greenland, with Denmark retaining sovereignty and Norway obtaining fishing rights. Scandinavism also produced the Oslo Convention of 1930 for economic cooperation among the nations of Scandinavia. All four Scandinavian countries adopted the principle of reciprocity in the disbursal of social security benefits for old people, regardless of their place of residence.

Scandinavian prosperity was helped by the absence of a large war debt and the keeping of defense budgets to an absolute minimum. The average armed strength of Sweden between 1919 and 1939 was 27,000 men, that of Norway 12,000, of Denmark 14,000, and of Finland 30,000.

The "Third Way"

All Scandinavian economies were pioneers in the development of cooperative enterprises, both rural and industrial. Denmark was a leader in farm cooperatives with 90 percent of the Danish milk industry organized on a cooperative basis by 1933. The cooperatives were privately owned and managed and were often admired outside Scandinavia as a "third way," avoiding the mistakes of either communist or purely capitalist economies.

Social Policy

The Scandinavian nations were leaders in the field of social policy. Norway's labor government under Prime Minister Nygaardsvold introduced annual paid vacations for workers and a "workers' protection" act in the mid-1930s, and this gave labor a voice in the setting of work rules. Sweden developed a system of "reserve work" during the depression which absorbed unemployment in public works projects such as highways and railroads. Sweden's Social Democratic prime minister Per Albin Hansson even developed a scheme for raising national purchasing power, under which the unemployed were to be rehired at full union wages by private enterprise and at government expense, the cost to be covered by a steep increase in inheritance taxes.

Common to the political development of Scandinavia between the two world wars was the emergence of the Social Democratic parties from opposition to governing parties. Social Democratic governments were first formed in Sweden in 1920, in Denmark in 1924, Finland in 1926, and Norway in 1928. On the eve of the Second World War, the governments of Norway, Denmark and Sweden were all under Social Democratic prime ministers, Johan Dygaardsvold, Thorvald Stauning, and Per Albin Hansson, respectively.

Communism and Fascism

The Scandinavian democracies proved singularly impervious to political extremism of the Left or Right variety. Before 1939, Sweden's Communists never gained more than 11 seats in parliament out of a total of 230. Denmark's Communists gained 3 seats in the last prewar elections of 1939. Norway's Communists failed to win any representation in parliament.

Of the Fascist and semi-Fascist movements in Scandinavia only Finland's Lapuan Movement gained any significance. The Lapuan Movement, named after the place of its origin, Lapua, succeeded in pressuring the Finnish government into outlawing the Communist party in 1930. After the unsuccessful Lapuan "march on Helsinki" of early 1932, the Lapuan Movement itself was outlawed and its leader, General Wallenius, was put in prison.

As racism and racial persecution descendend upon much of Europe during the Second World War, the Scandinavian countries again followed a different path. Sweden opened its doors in 1943 to Danish Jewish refugees who had escaped the Nazi dragnets in their own homeland by climbing aboard fishing boats and small craft of any sort. Finland, though a partner of Hitler's in the war against Soviet Russia, never surrendered one of its 2,000 Jewish citizens to Nazi Germany, despite urgent and repeated German requests.

7

Nazi Germany: 1933 to 1939

THE LEGAL FOUNDATIONS OF TOTALITARIANISM

Like Mussolini in 1922, Hitler came to power by legal means and as the head of a coalition government. The Nazi members of the coalition were outnumbered by their Conservative partners eight to three. Like the Italian Fascists, the German National Socialists accepted the coalition of January 30, 1933 only as a temporary arrangement, imposed by political necessity and useful as a screen for the implementation of dictatorship. The Nazi conquest of the machinery of the state proceeded much more quickly, however, and it produced more sweeping results than had been the case in Fascist Italy during the 1920s.

It was a unique feature of Hitler's and Nazis' technique of power that they were sticklers for legality in devising the foundations of a totalitarian system. In dismantling the legal and constitutional foundations of the liberal-democratic order of the Weimar Republic, Hitler observed the procedures enshrined in the Weimar constitution. The first assault on the democratic system came through the emergency decrees of February 4 and 28, 1933, issued on the basis of article 48 of the Weimar constitution. The decree of February 4 empowered the government to ban newspapers and public assemblies; the decree of February 28 ("Ordinance for the Protection of the Nation and State") suspended the constitutionally guaranteed civil liberties for an indefinite length of time.

The emergency decree of February 28, though less publicized than subsequent measures, nevertheless marked the decisive step in the transformation of Germany from a liberal democracy to a totalitarian police state. By suspending civil liberties, Hitler ended not only individual freedom but the political pluralism of Weimar Germany as well. Arbitrary arrest, indefinite detention without the benefit of trial, and the entire system of concentration and extermination camps which was to become the hallmark of the Nazi system in its final stage, grew from the powers granted under the emergency decree of February 28, 1933. As one of the cornerstones of the Nazi dictatorship, that decree remained in force until the end of Hitler's Germany in 1945.

The Reichstag Fire

President Hindenburg sanctioned the sweeping measures of February 28 on the strength of Nazi allegations that the burning of the Reichstag building on February 27 had been the work of Communists and was meant to act as a signal for a nationwide Communist uprising. The charge of Communist authorship of the Reichstag fire was generally disbelieved outside Germany, because of its timing and the obvious political benefits to the Hitler government. The Dutch ex-Communist Martinus van der Lubbe, the only person actually seized in the Reichstag during the fire and subsequently executed for the crime, steadfastly denied any connection with German Communists during his trial. Time-and-motion studies by German arson experts, on the other hand, indicated that no one individual could have set fire to so vast a structure in so short a time. Goering, who was strongly suspected of involvement in the Reichstag fire, denied any such role during the Nuremberg trials of 1946. His denial was not lacking in credibility, because Goering, unlike so many of his codefendants, did not deny responsibility for his actions under the Nazi regime. The origins of the Reichstag fire remained a mystery, but whatever its origins, Hitler immediately exploited the incident for his own benefit. The Reichstag fire not only served as justification for the suspension of civil liberties, but as an issue in the forthcoming elections.

The Elections of 1933

The Reichstag elections of March 5, 1933 did not produce the Nazi landslide that Hitler had hoped for. Despite the lack of genuine press freedom and the wholesale employment of SA stormtroopers as police auxiliaries, Socialist, Communist and Catholic Center party voters showed themselves surprisingly impervious to Nazi threats or Nazi promises. Compared to the elections of November 1932, SPD strength decreased from 20.7 to 18.3 percent, that of the KPD from 16.9 to 12.3 percent, while the Center party vote declined from 15 to 14 percent. The increase in Nazi strength from 33.1 to 43.9 percent was due less to voter defection from other parties than to the support of newly registered voters, as well as previous nonvoters. Voter participation was also unusually high at 89 percent. Though falling short of a simple majority, the Nazi party nevertheless secured control over the Reichstag with the support of its Nationalist allies, who polled 8 percent of the vote. For the first time since 1930, Germany had a government supported by a parliamentary majority, making Hitler less dependent on presidential support than Brüning, Papen, or Schleicher had been.

The opening of the new Reichstag on March 21, 1933 was a carefully staged ceremony in the Potsdam garrison church over the tombs of Frederick William I and Frederick the Great. The gathering of Hindenburg, the former crown prince, the senior army leaders, the new Nazi bosses, and the Reichstag in a shrine of Prussian history was meant to symbolize the union of aristocratic Prussia and dynamic nazism. The ceremonies of the ''day of Potsdam'' were symbolic of the Nazi claim both to the succession of past Prussian and German grandeur and to Conservative endorsement of the revolution which the Nazi regime was about to unleash on Germany.

The "Enabling Act"

The Potsdam rites successfully concluded, Hitler took the second major step towards personal dictatorship by usurping the legislative powers of the Reichstag. The ''enabling act'' (''law for terminating the suffering of people and nation''), passed by the Reichstag on March 24, 1933, conferred the Reichstag's legislative powers upon the chancellor for a four-year period. Since the enabling act was not a simple law but a constitutional amendment, it required a two-thirds majority for passage, a majority the Nazi-Nationalist coalition did not possess.

Hitler obtained the required majority through a policy of threats and false promises. Support of the Catholic Center was obtained through the false promise of revoking the emergency decree of February 4. The Communists posed no problem, since their 81 deputies were not even able to take up their seats. The SPD, in an act of courage that was as unique as it was politically futile, alone among the parties of the Reichstag voted against the enabling act. SPD leader Otto Wels, himself a veteran of many a battle with the Communists during the violent stage of the German Revolution of 1918–1919, attacked Hitler in a bold speech from the floor, citing lawlessness, persecution and repression as hallmarks of the Hitler government. With a courage reminiscent of Matteotti's attack on Mussolini in 1924 before his murder by Fascist *squadristi,* Wels warned Hitler that no enabling act would empower him to suppress "eternal and indestructible ideas." Hitler's response was a masterpiece of extemporaneous propaganda, which once again identified German Social Democracy with the defeat of 1918 and all the subsequent failures and misfortunes of the republican regime. When hurling at Otto Wels the statement: "He who loves Germany may criticize us; he who worships the International, may not," Hitler once more blurred the distinction between Social Democrats and Communists and identified both as Germans loyal to a foreign cause.

Fear and the belief in false Nazi promises may have played their part in gaining Hitler the necessary two-thirds majority in the crucial vote of March 24 but they were not the only factor. By the end of March the Nazi regime had staged a psychological campaign and succeeded in whipping up a nationalist frenzy that accepted Hitler as a savior and that equated support for his policy with patriotic duty. Not all Germans fell under the spell of Nazi propaganda and not all the non-Nazi parliamentary deputies did, excluding Social Democrats and Communists. Pressure for Nazi support had grown sufficiently by the spring of 1933, however, to convince many who had otherwise remained immune to Nazi persuasion that theirs was a lost cause in Germany. It was from such a sense of isolation that liberals like Theodor Heuss, the future first president of the West German federal republic of 1949, also voted for Hitler's enabling act in 1933.

The Unitary State

The dissolution of the political parties, either by their own decision or by order of the government, followed the self-immolation of the Reichstag in short order. The SPD was banned on June 22, 1933 and other political parties announced their voluntary dissolution in July. The law against the formation of new parties of July 14, 1933, declared the Nazi party the sole legal party in Germany.

Having destroyed the political parties, Hitler moved to dismantle Germany's federal structure. The first step in that direction had been taken in February 1933, when the national government took over the police powers of the states. In April 1933 Nazi governors were appointed to the federal states and in January 1934 the state legislatures were dissolved. In February 1934 the Reichsrat, the representative body of the federal states, was abolished. Germany had become a unitary state.

The Judiciary

Nazi control over the civil service was established by law of April 7, 1933, "for the restoration of the career civil service," which empowered the government to dismiss civil servants for reasons of past political activity or racial background. The integration of the judiciary into the Nazi system proved to be a more difficult task, however. Although Nazi Germany never formally abolished the independence of judges, it brought great pressure to bear on the courts to render decisions consistent with the Nazi slogan, Law Is What Is Useful to the German People. Despite the creation of a Reich commissioner for justice for the "renewal of the legal system," the coordination of the judiciary never quite succeeded. Hitler's distrust of the legal profession, and of judges in particular, persisted to the end of Nazi days. In April 1942, in the midst of World War II, Hitler threatened that henceforth judges would be dismissed if their decisions were not consistent with the "seriousness of the times."

Dictatorship

Within a year of coming to power, Hitler had removed all obstacles to dictatorship save the institution of the presidency and the armed forces. His Conservative coalition partners, pinning their hopes on Hindenburg as the last bulwark against a full-blown Nazi dictatorship, attempted to persuade the president to restore the monarchy. Prior to his death on August 2, 1934, Hindenburg privately told Hitler of his desire to resurrect the monarchy, but he did not make it a public issue. Hitler was loath to restore the monarchy, not only because he refused to share power with anybody, but because he regarded the example of Fascist Italy as a warning. Even at the height of Mussolini's power, the Italian king retained a certain independence, which eventually enabled him to assist in Mussolini's overthrow in 1943.

After Hindenburg died, Hitler quickly combined the powers of the presidency and the chancellorship in his own person under the new designation of Führer and Reichchancellor. In a new and personal oath, the army swore "unconditional obedience to the führer of the German Reich and people." The personal oath of loyalty gave Hitler a powerful means of moral and psychological control over an entire service steeped in traditions of loyalty sworn to the commander-in-chief.

HITLER, THE WEHRMACHT AND THE SA

The armed forces posed a special problem to the young Nazi regime because of the growing tension between the regular army and the Nazi-SA formations. In a sense, the army and the Nazi regime needed one another, though they had yet to work out the terms of their collaboration. Though largely of aristocratic background and disdainful of the proletarian element in the Nazi movement, the army leadership generally welcomed Hitler's chancellorship as an end to the political uncertainty of Weimar and a beginning of rearmament. The younger, more technologically minded officers, such as Heinz Guderian, who were eager to mechanize the army, were particularly impressed with the personal interest which Hitler showed in such matters at an early stage. In General Werner von Blomberg, Hitler found a minister of war eager to serve the new regime.

As a condition for its support, the army demanded the elimination of the SA as a rival and recognition of the army as the "sole bearer of arms." For Hitler, too, the SA had become a problem because of the ambitions of SA chief of staff Ernst Roehm and the revolutionary thrust of much of the SA leadership. Roehm wished to achieve instant rearmament by merging the nearly million-strong SA with the regular army, a plan which not only promised personal power and prestige for Roehm, but which would have politicized the German army to a degree unacceptable to the professional officers' class. In addition, the SA, as the veteran of hundreds of street battles and brawls with Communists, Socialists and regular police, expected substantial and speedy material rewards through social and economic revolution. Impatient with Hitler's legalistic approach to dictatorship and dissatisfied with his role as protector of private property, SA leaders could be heard observing by the end of 1933 that "Adolf will have to be taught a lesson."

The Blood Purge

On June 30, 1934, Hitler resolved the dilemma by a surprise attack on the SA in which hundreds of SA leaders, including Roehm, but also ordinary young SA men, were executed by the SS, Hitler's elite guard. The blood purge also claimed victims unrelated to the SA issue with whom Hitler wished to settle old scores. Among these was Gregor Strasser, ex-chancellor Schleicher and his wife, and Gustav Kahr, who had thwarted Hitler's 1923 "beerhall" *putsch.* Hitler justified the murders as an act of national emergency. The law of July 3, 1934 sanctioned Hitler's action ex post facto.

In striking a bargain with the German army, Hitler appeared to have paid the heavier price. In truth, June 30, 1934 marked the beginning of the army's submission to Hitler. Through its advance knowledge of Hitler's action and through its official silence afterwards, the army had made itself the accomplice of a policy of murder, which highlighted the true nature of the regime as no previous act had. The new loyalty oath of August 1934 and the appearance of the nazi swastika eagle on the German army uniform were outward symbols of the new submission. The opposition of the army leadership to Hitler's foreign policy designs in 1938 enabled Hitler to tighten his controls further through the abolition of the war ministry and its replacement by a new agency, the High Command of the Armed Forces (OKW).

Rise of the SS

The true winner of the contest between army and SA was the SS, since 1929 under the command of Heinrich Himmler. After June 30, the disorganized violence of the SA gave way to a system of SS terror, more centralized, institutionalized, and disciplined. In due course the SS developed into a state within the Nazi state. In 1936 Himmler became chief of all German police and by 1943 he had been appointed minister of the interior. The SS provided Hitler's personal guard with the *Leibstandarte A.H.* and administered the Nazi concentration camps through its deathhead formations. With the establishment of armed SS divisions (*Waffen SS*), Hitler broke his promise to the army that it alone would be the bearer of arms in Germany.

The Nazi Image

On the surface the Nazi system of government, based on the principles of "co-ordination" (*gleichschaltung*) and leadership, affected an appearance of great efficiency. The air of dynamism and efficiency was enhanced by the tangible economic gains of

Nazi Germany before the war, by the multitude of public projects and endeavors launched, and by the disciplined grandeur of the mass party rallies dramatically staged by Hitler's chief architect, Albert Speer. The official image of smooth and responsive government belied the reality of inefficiency, rivalry, and duplication of effort on the part of Nazi governors, SS empire builders, and governmental agencies. On the highest level, Hitler soon discontinued the practice of regular cabinet meetings and issued orders and directives without the knowledge of the minister in charge. During the Second World War, it was not uncommon for a minister of the Nazi government to learn of the existence of a new decree from the newspapers. Setting up rival agencies for an identical task became one of Hitler's favorite administrative devices for reserving ultimate decisions for himself and preventing any individual from amassing too much power. The absence of a free and critical press did not remove corruption from public life in Nazi Germany but merely made it less visible.

Nazi Corruption

Corruption luxuriated in high places more abundantly in Nazi Germany than ever was the case in the Weimar Republic, whose petty scandals Goebbels had delighted in castigating in his paper *Der Angriff*. As though obsessed with a desire to crowd as much high living and plunder as possible into the twelve years of Hitler's thousand-year empire, the high dignitaries of nazism outdid one another in the construction of palatial homes, the sequestration of art treasures, or, in the case of Goering, the collection of precious stones. Even the führer, spartan in his personal needs, found ways of supplementing his income by claiming royalties from the sale of postage stamps which bore his image.

That a civilized society such as Germany's could so rapidly acquiesce in the loss of its civil liberties and the public display of government by murder, as happened on June 30, 1934, served as a grim reminder of the fragility of constitutional safeguards against twentieth-century totalitarianism. In the Germany of the early 1930s the removal of such safeguards did not evoke a general public outcry, because individual freedoms did not occupy as central a position in the national history and consciousness as they did in the Western democracies. The Germany that supported or acquiesced in Hitler's terror of 1933–1934 was a country that regarded individual liberties as only the recent by-product of the unwanted revolution of 1918 or the legacy of the unsuccessful German revolution of 1848.

THE CHURCHES AND THE NAZI STATE

Hitler opened his chancellorship with reassuring words for the Christian churches of Germany. In his address of February 1, 1933, Hitler pledged to "protect Christianity as the foundation of our entire morality." Some years later, Hitler would privately call Christianity "a fairy tale invented by the Jews" and express the hope that Christian churches would "rot away like a gangrened member."

The Christian churches were a reality, however, which Hitler could neither integrate into the Nazi state nor openly antagonize for fear of adverse public repercussions. His initial intention of extending Nazi controls over German Protestants through the so-called German Christian church under "Reichbishop" Ludwig Mueller had to be abandoned in the face of strong opposition by such clergymen as Pastor Martin Niemoeller. Among Niemoller's followers, who organized the "confessional Church" in protest against Hitler's German Christians, was Dietrich Bonhoeffer, later to become a martyr of the Resistance during World War II and one of the most profound theologians among twentieth-century German Protestants.

The Catholic church, acting on the advice of former Center party chairman Kaas, concluded a concordat with Hitler on July 20, 1933. As in the case of Fascist Italy, the Church renounced political activities and organizations in exchange for concessions, including the right to maintain Catholic schools in Germany. The concordat raised Hitler's international respectability but it failed to secure a lasting peace between the regime and the Church. Individual churchmen, such as Cardinal Faulhaber of Munich and Bishop Galen of Muenster, publicly attacked the pagan attitudes and racist policies of Nazi Germany. Bishop Galen, in a public sermon, similarly attacked the euthanasia program which Hitler had secretly initiated on September 1, 1939 for the mass killing of German mental patients. Pope Pius XI attacked tenets of Nazi ideology in his 1937 encyclical *Mit Brennender Sorge* (With Burning Anxiety). In 1938 Monsignor Bernhard Lichtenberg of St. Hedwig's Cathedral in Berlin called on his congregation to pray for "Jews and inmates of concentration camps."

After the outbreak of the Second World War, Hitler maintained the truce with the churches because he feared the adverse effect a policy of repression and retaliation would have on the morale of the armed forces. Judging from his recorded private remarks, he had every intention of mounting a wholesale assault on the Christian churches once he had won the war. The attitude of the churches towards the Nazi regime, too, came under criticism, especially after the revelation of the full extent of the Nazi crimes in 1945. Among the critics was none other than future West German chancellor Konrad Adenauer. In his private correspondence during the post-World War II period, Adenauer complained that the German Catholic clergy knew more of Nazi crimes than it revealed and spoke up less against such crimes in public than it should have. A similar charge was made by West German playwrignt R. Hochhuth during the 1960s with regard to Pope Pius XII and the plight of the European Jews in his drama *The Deputy.*

ECONOMIC AND SOCIAL POLICY

The promise to end unemployment and restore a healthy economy was among the chief weapons in the Nazi propaganda arsenal. German unemployment stood at 30 percent towards the end of 1932 with no immediate relief in sight. By 1936 the unemployment rate had fallen to 2 percent, and by 1938 unemployment was virtually nonexistent.

Although there existed a scarcity of certain consumer goods owing to import restrictions and the tight rationing of foreign exchange, the economic situation seemed, on the whole, more encouraging to the German public under Hitler than it had appeared in the final years of Weimar Germany.

The Four-Year Plan

The economic upswing of Nazi Germany may be attributed to a variety of factors, not all of which were due to Nazi initiative or planning. To begin with, the world depression was levelling off at the time of Hitler's advent to power, and public works projects, funded by Hitler's predecessors, reached the stage of practical implementation only after January 1933. The Nazi regime added public works projects of its own with the launching of the four-lane superhighways (*autobahnen*) in September 1933. The beginning of rearmament in 1935, as well as the inauguration of the four-year plan in 1936, added new stimuli to the German economy. The objective of the four-year plan was the attainment of self-sufficiency in strategic raw materials as a prelude to war. By developing the low-yield ore fields of Salzgitter in central Germany, the regime hoped to reduce significantly the size of German ore imports, which accounted for 80 percent of German consumption. In the manufacture of synthetic rubber (*buna*), the four-year plan not only achieved self-sufficiency, but produced surpluses for export. Production of synthetic gasoline and lubricants, on the other hand, remained far below what was needed and planned for at the start of the Second World War.

Armaments

The scope of Germany's armaments production was far greater in official Nazi propaganda than in actual fact. The total impact of public spending upon the German economy through armaments, public works, and the projects of the four-year plan was nonetheless considerable, one third of the national income depending on government investment and spending.

Farm Policy

The farm program of the Nazi regime reflected the "blood and soil" mentality of Nazi ideology, which idealized the German peasantry as the foundation of racial strength. The peasant inheritance law (*reichserbhofgesetz*) of September 1933 declared medium-sized farms of up to twenty-four acres indivisible, and prohibited such farms from sale or mortgaging. The intention was to preserve a debt-free class of peasant proprietors and combat rural migration to the cities. The latter aim was only partially fulfiled, as the needs of German industry drew several hundred thousand farm laborers into the towns between 1933 and 1939. Nazi policy did not provide for land reform through the breakup of large estates and the resettlement of small farmers, such as the Weimar Republic had contemplated under Chancellor Brüning in 1932. Only with the conquest of Poland and the Ukraine during the war did Hitler initiate a resettlement program, at the expense of subjugated peoples. The scope and duration of the resettlement program remained necessarily small owing to the short period of German occupation.

Finances

The financing of Nazi economic policy was based on large-scale borrowing and deficit spending. Hjalmar Schacht, the wizard of the *rentenmark* of 1923, advanced 12 billion marks to Hitler between 1933 and 1939 in his capacity as president of the Reichsbank. Afterwards, the Nazi government resorted to forced loans from private banks and financial institutions to cover the rising costs of war and armaments.

Nazi economic policy was pragmatic rather than doctrinaire, bearing little resemblance to the economic tenets of the early Nazi party program. The class of petit bourgeois shopkeepers and artisans, which had supported Nazism on the strength of its economic promises, lost out to big business once Hitler was in power. The Nazi regime respected private ownership of the means of production, though it imposed a growing number of restraints through wage and price controls and the allocation of raw materials. Whenever big business was found wanting in effort or enthusiasm, the government launched enterprises of its own such as the Salzgitter steel works or the Volkswagen plant at Wolfsburg.

The Volkswagen Project

The Volkswagen project illustrated Hitler's resolve to have his own way even without the support of established industry, which was moving too slowly for him. It sprang from his own enthusiasm for automobiles and his desire to bring car ownership within the reach of ordinary people. Shortly after coming to power, he commissioned Germany's established car makers, including General Motors–owned Opel, to submit designs for a revolutionary "people's car" at low cost. Hitler found none of the designs acceptable because of high price and lack of engineering innovation. To the chagrin of established car makers, Hitler picked the design of Ferdinand Porsche, a fellow Austrian who, like Hitler, lacked a formal education. Apart from its advanced design features, such as an air-cooled engine and torsion-bar suspension, the Porsche vehicle was within the price limit of 1000 marks ($250) set by Hitler. When the German automobile industry refused to produce the Porsche-designed car, Hitler built his own factory with the funds of the Nazi recreational organization *Kraft durch Freude* (Strength through Joy). Hitler and Porsche remained friends thereafter, with Porsche designing some of Hitler's best tanks during World War II.

Though borrowing some of the terminology of Fascist corporatism, the Nazi economy was not truly organized along corporate lines. Farmers were organized in the Reich Food Estate, industry and trade in the Reich Estate of German Industry. All trade unions were abolished as of May 1933. The Nazi Labor Front (DAF) and its recreational affiliate *Kraft durch Freude* (KdF), became the sole official organs of labor. Apart from sponsoring the VW project, KdF organized cultural and recreational activities, including low-cost ocean cruises on its own vessels.

The Role of Women

Official Nazi social policy towards women was guided less by notions of emancipation than by the desire to reinforce the role which women had traditionally played in German society. Like Italian Fascism, German Nazism was eager to raise the birthrate, which had, in the German case, declined from 2 million births per year in 1900 to less than 1 million in 1933. By 1934 births were up to 1.2 million, climbing eventually to 1.4 million in 1939. Hitler remained opposed to the mobilization of female labor for war production long after Britain used its female labor resources, in large part because of Nazi population policy.

RAD

In 1935, the Nazi regime instituted a compulsory national labor service (*Reichsarbeitsdienst*, RAD), which drafted German youth above the age of eighteen for a six-month period. RAD men were used extensively in the construction of military fortifications and the new highway system. Among German youth of the 1930s, RAD service quickly acquired a deserved reputation for ruthless physical exploitation as well as intense Nazi ideological indoctrination, a fact which made even compulsory military service, which immediately followed, a more tolerable experience.

NAZI CULTURAL AND EDUCATIONAL POLICY

The book-burning ceremony of May 10, 1933, in front of the Berlin opera, in which students consigned the works of Jewish and other "undesirable" authors to the flames, was a fitting overture to the cultural policy of National Socialism. On March 15, 1933, Hitler had established the Ministry for Popular Enlightenment and Propaganda under Joseph Goebbels for the control of the press, literature, and motion pictures. The radio, previously under the administration of the postal ministry, was likewise seized by Goebbels. In due course Goebbels established professional chambers for the arts, the theater, literature, the news media, and the movie industry. The chambers were combined to form the Reich Chamber of Culture under his presidency. Exclusion or expulsion from the Chamber of Culture spelled the end of any professional career in those fields.

The editors' law of October, 1933 empowered the regime to remove newspaper editors on the grounds of political unreliability, and editors were exhorted to present the news not in "suicidal objectivity," but in a "positive" manner. As Minister of Propaganda, Goebbels kept a watchful eye over new publications, issuing weekly lists of "undesirable" or "forbidden" books. Paintings deemed "degenerate" were removed from public galleries, though not from the private collections of Nazi dignitaries such as Goering. The movie industry stressed the themes of anti-Semitism (*Jud Suess*), the Nazi struggle against communism before 1933 (*Hitlerjunge Quex*), or the excesses of nineteenth-century British imperialism (*Ohm Krueger*). Amidst the mass of Nazi propaganda films, German movie directors occasionally succeeded in disguising a ringing indictment of Nazi dictatorship and censorship in the context of historical subjects. In the motion picture *Die Entlassung* (The Dismissal), which dealt with Bismarck's career, the German Social Democrat leader August Bebel was shown delivering a stinging attack on Bismarck's policy of Social Democrat persecution in words which the viewer could easily apply to the political conditions of Nazi Germany. The device of attacking the present regime through historical parallels or Aesopean parables was also employed in the writing of fiction and even in historical scholarship.

Nazi Architecture

In architecture, Nazi Germany produced a style of its own of gradiose proportions, designed to bear witness to the Hitler era for future generations. Hitler, himself a frustrated architect who had failed to gain entrance to the Vienna Academy of Fine Arts as a youth, took a personal hand in determining architectural style, and in city planning. Albert Speer, Hitler's favorite architect and "inspector general of buildings," translated Hitler's sketches, some of which dated back to the 1920s, into reality. During the short period from 1933 to 1939 when Nazi Germany was still at peace, only a few of the planned buildings were actually completed. Among these were the House of German Art in Munich, the vast Nuremberg Zeppelin Field for party rallies, and the new Reich Chancellery, completed in 1939. The latter, bombed out during the war, served as a stone quarry for the huge Soviet war memorial in East Berlin after 1945.

Paris and Vienna were the European cities whose architecture Hitler most admired. Nazi plans for the redevelopment of Berlin, scheduled to be completed by 1950, were to outdo either city, however, at least in the dimensions of the projected public buildings and avenues. Berlin's "Grand Boulevard," more than twice the length of the Champs-Elysees in Paris, was to be flanked by a Soldiers' Hall as burial place of German field marshals, an arch of triumph over 500' wide and 386' high, and a domed hall with a cupola sixteen times the size of St. Peter's in Rome, reaching nearly 1,000' into the sky. Berlin, Hitler predicted, would be "changed beyond recognition," a forecast which proved to be accurate though not in the sense intended. Among other cities favored by Nazi town planning were Nuremberg, to receive a stadium large enough for 400,000 people, and Linz, the capital of Upper Austria and place of Hitler's boyhood. Nazi architecture was characterized not only by unprecedented dimensions in its public buildings, but by their occupants' safety from riot and mob violence. Hitler's palace on the Grand Boulevard of Berlin was to be equipped with bulletproof steel shutters for doors and windows. The masses, which Hitler's oratory whipped into frenzies of emotional abandon, apparently continued to inspire fear in Germany's most powerful dictator.

Artists and Writers

The German intellectual and cultural elite generally submitted to the Nazi regime or gave it its active support, though there were notable exceptions. As a group, German writers and poets constituted the largest single element in the cultural elite which put principle before opportunism, chosing exile rather than collaboration. Germany's best-known author, Nobel laureate Thomas Mann, headed the list of German literary exiles, many of whom found it difficult to work in their own language abroad, and some of whom ended as suicides. Germany's greatest contemporary composer, Richard Strauss, continued to reside and work in Nazi Germany, accepting its honors, as did Hans Pfitzner. The music of Gustav Mahler was banned from German concert halls during the twelve years of Nazi rule because of his Jewish background. Aspiring young conductors such as Herbert von Karajan joined the Nazi party on the assumption that it would further their musical career.

The Universities

The *gleichschaltung* of German universities proceeded with relative ease, and instances of open student or faculty rebellion against the regime were few. Careerism and the promise of promotion also played their part in influencing the attitude of academics such as Germany's renowned philosopher Martin Heidegger, who termed Hitler a "leader called by destiny." Isolated instances of student or faculty resistance, which was both courageous and futile, existed, as in the case of the Munich students Hans and Sophie Scholl, and Kurt Huber, professor of philosophy at Munich University. Appalled by Nazi atrocities on the eastern front during World War II, Hans Scholl, together with his sister Sophie, attempted to organize an anti-Nazi resistance cell at Munich University in conjunction with Kurt Huber, through the distribution of anti-Nazi mimeographed material. Discovered by the Gestapo, all paid with their lives for the courage of their convictions.

THE NUREMBERG RACIAL LAWS—PORTENTS OF THE HOLOCAUST

Much of the big-city liberal press of the Weimar Republic, the papers of the Ullstein, Mosse, and Sonnemann publishing houses, had been in German Jewish hands. The Nazi regime wasted no time in silencing that opposition by forcing the owners to sell, often enough at prices far below real value. It was not possible for Hitler to use similar methods against the foreign liberal press either in the European democracies or in the United States. The foreign liberal press was sharply critical of the new regime and it was quick to place responsibility for the Reichstag fire of February 1933 on the Hitler government. Hitler's response was to use the German Jewish minority as hostage, punishing it with chicanery and acts of violence for foreign criticism of the Nazi regime. This was the meaning of the official boycott of German Jewish businesses and shops which the government organized on March 28, 1933. Organized by local "action committees" of the SA throughout Germany, the "boycott" was in fact an official invitation to violence, vandalism, and personal abuse, which then occurred as the regime intended. Far from being an excess of SA rowdies on the fringes of the Nazi movement, the "boycott" of March 1933 reflected the most central and persistent feature of Nazi ideology, and to anyone prepared to face the truth it signaled the coming of a far greater terrror.

The 1933 civil service law, previously mentioned, represented a second logical step on the path of Jewish persecution. An enfeebled president Hindenburg protested especially against the dismissal of German-Jewish war veterans from the civil service, but his protest was not public and thus not even an embarrassment to the regime.

The Nuremberg racial laws ("laws for the protection of German blood and German honor"), announced at the annual Nuremberg party rally in September 1935, marked the third step in the policy of anti-Semitism. The racial laws outlawed mixed marriages, prohibited Jews from employing non-Jewish female domestics below age forty-five, and excluded Jews from virtually all professions. Jewish children were forbidden to have Christian surnames and had to be given first names authorized by the ministry of the interior. In effect, the Nuremberg laws stripped German Jews of their rights as citizens.

Kristallnacht

The Nuremberg laws' policy of humiliation and chicanery was followed by organized mass violence on an unprecedented scale during the night of November 9, 1938, known subsequently as *Kristallnacht* (Crystal Night, i.e. night of shattered glass). During Crystal Night synagogues went up in flames in German towns, some 7000 Jewish businesses were destroyed, and some 100 Jewish men and women killed. This orgy of violence, carried out by SA troopers—out of uniform, on Goebbel's order, so as to give it the appearance of a spontaneous mass uprising—was in retaliation for the assassination in Paris of German embassy counsellor Ernst von Rath by a German Jewish refugee, Herschel Grynspan.

Crystal Night was a significant step from legalized discrimination to the physical destruction of the Jews, those of Germany and eventually all of Europe. This was the meaning of the threat which Hitler uttered quite clearly in his Reichstag speech of January 30, 1939, when saying that if "international Jewry" plunged the world into war, the result would be "the destruction of the Jewish race in Europe."

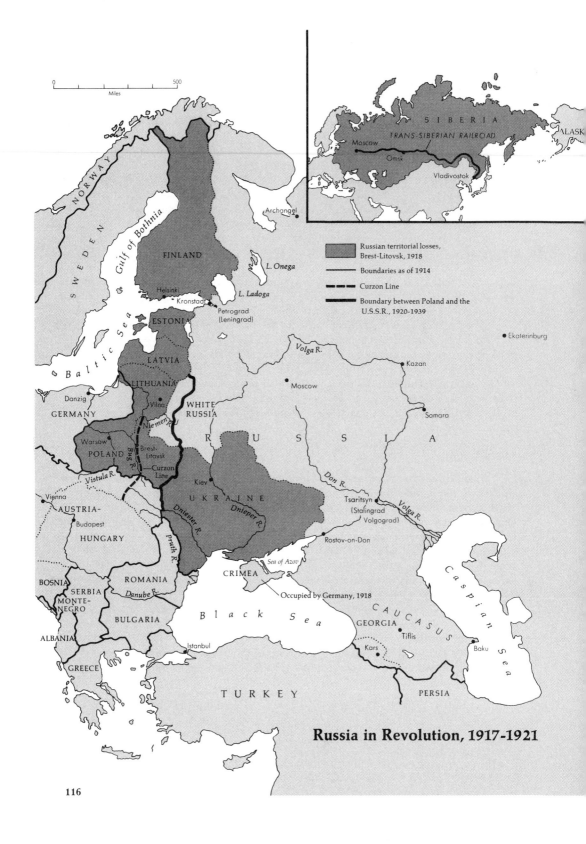

0 — 500
Miles

NORWAY

SWEDEN

Gulf of Bothnia

FINLAND

Helsinki

Kronstadt

Petrograd (Leningrad)

L. Onega

L. Ladoga

Archangel

Russian territorial losses, Brest-Litovsk, 1918

Boundaries as of 1914

Curzon Line

Boundary between Poland and the U.S.S.R., 1920-1939

• Ekaterinburg

Volga R.

• Kazan

Moscow

Baltic Sea

ESTONIA

LATVIA

LITHUANIA

Danzig

Vilna

WHITE RUSSIA

Niemen R.

GERMANY

Warsaw

POLAND

Bug R.

Brest-Litovsk

Curzon Line

R   U   S   S   I   A

Samara

Vistula R.

Vienna

AUSTRIA-

Kiev

UKRAINE

Dnieper R.

Dniester R.

Don R.

Tsaritsyn (Stalingrad Volgograd)

Volga R.

Budapest

HUNGARY

Pruth R.

Rostov-on-Don

BOSNIA

SERBIA

MONTE-NEGRO

ROMANIA

Danube R.

CRIMEA

Sea of Azov

Occupied by Germany, 1918

B l a c k   S e a

C A U C A S U S

Caspian Sea

ALBANIA

BULGARIA

GEORGIA

Tiflis

GREECE

Istanbul

Kars

Baku

T U R K E Y

PERSIA

Russia in Revolution, 1917-1921

SIBERIA

TRANS-SIBERIAN RAILROAD

Moscow

Omsk

Vladivostok

ALASK

8

Soviet Russia
from Lenin to Stalin

CIVIL WAR, WAR COMMUNISM AND THE NEP

Lenin's seizure of power in November 1917 was attributable in large measure to the effectiveness of Bolshevik propaganda, which addressed itself convincingly to the foremost issues confronting revolutionary Russia in 1917 and exceeded the promises made by Lenin's rivals. Once established, Bolshevik rule quickly aroused widespread opposition in Russia because of its addiction to violence, suppression of dissent, and nonfulfilment of past promises. Expanding domestic opposition constituted but one threat to Bolshevik rule, coinciding as it did with danger from without. Until the collapse of imperial Germany in November 1918, the external danger consisted in the possibility of a resumption of German hostilities. After the German collapse, the external danger derived from the possibility of foreign, Allied intervention in European Russia and that of Japan in eastern Siberia. The Allied decision not to intervene, which was reached in early 1919 for the reasons previously described, freed Lenin from what might otherwise have become the most formidable threat to his survival. American pressure on Japan, resulting in the Japanese evacuation of eastern Siberia in 1922 and of northern Sakhalin in 1925, enabled the Bolshevik regime to regain full control of the Far Eastern regions of the former tsarist empire. Foreign support of Lenin's domestic opposition, collectively called the Whites as opposed to the Bolshevik Reds, continued in the form of arms supplies and money even after foreign military intervention was discontinued. Though important at times, it failed to fill the gap created by the Allied military withdrawal from Russia in 1919.

Opposition to the Bolsheviks

At home, opposition to Bolshevik rule developed in response to Lenin's dispersal of the constituent assembly, whose election the Bolshevik government had tolerated on November 25, 1917, but whose first session was terminated under the threat of arms on January 19, 1918. The elections had clearly revealed the Bolsheviks as a minority, with 370 out of a total of 707 seats being captured by the Right Social Revolutionaries, as against only 175 for the Bolsheviks. The remaining seats were divided between Left Social Revolutionaries, Mensheviks, liberal Cadets, and lesser parties. The Bolshevik government had similarly instituted press censorship and launched the "All-Russian Extraordinary Commission" (CHEKA in Russian initials), as a new security police. The CHEKA and its successors, OGPU, NKVD and later, KGB, became a cornerstone of the Bolshevik regime, which retained the characteristic features first devised by CHEKA founder Felix Dzerzhinski.

By May 1918, the Right Social Revolutionaries openly called for the overthrow of the Bolshevik dictatorship in their Moscow party conference. The Left Social Revolutionaries, who were angry over both Lenin's peace of Brest-Litovsk with the Germans and the policy of coercion in the requisitioning of food from the peasantry, resorted to their prerevolutionary tactics of terrorism. On August 30, 1918 Michael S. Uritsky, chief of the Petrograd CHEKA was assassinated and Lenin himself seriously wounded by the Left Social Revolutionary terrorist Dora Kaplan.

Opposition to Bolshevik rule had also developed among the non-Russian nationalities. After witnessing the suppression of political freedoms, the nationalities were no longer content with autonomy in a federated Russia but opted for full independence. Before the end of 1917, the Ukraine, Estonia, White Russia, and the Caucasus states of Armenia, Azerbaijan, and Georgia together with Finland seceded from Russia. Bolshevik nationality policy, as redefined by Stalin in his capacity as commissar of nationalities in the first Soviet government, now distinguished between the "form" and "content" of autonomy. The Bolsheviks upheld the goal of autonomy for the non-Russian nationalities, provided its content was "proletarian," that is, under safe Communist control.

Military opposition to the Bolshevik government assumed its greatest strength in the outlying border regions of European Russia, in areas beyond effective Bolshevik control. In the Ukraine, the "Don Republic" was established under General Anton Denikin, while Victor Chernov, the leader of the Right Social Revolutionaries, installed himself at Samara. At Omsk, in western Siberia, Admiral Alexander V. Kolchak, former commander of the Black Sea Fleet, set up a predominantly conservative opposition government. An All-Russian National Conference at Ufa in September 1918, combining the opposition forces of Omsk and Samara, paved the way for the "Directory," an Omsk-based anti-Bolshevik coalition.

Bolshevik vulnerability to determined military attack was convincingly demonstrated by the actions of the Czechoslovak Legion in the summer of 1918. Composed of some 60,000 Austro-Hungarian deserters and former POWs of Czechoslovak nationality, the legion, under the command of General Stefanik, managed for a while to control the principal rail junctions in Siberia between the Urals and Lake Baikal. It was during the legion's Siberian campaign that the Bolsheviks executed Tsar Nicholas II and his family on July 16, 1918, to prevent the tsar's liberation from his imprisonment at Ekaterinburg.

The Red Army

By 1919 Trotsky, in his role as war commissar, had provided the Bolshevik government with a new and effective fighting force, the Red Army, launched in 1918 and numbering some 800,000 men. The Red Army included some 50,000 former tsarist officers whom Trotsky had drafted to provide competent and professional leadership. Some tsarist officers volunteered for Red Army service, including General Brusilov of 1916 fame, because they interpreted the civil war as a war of national defense against foreign powers. Poland's intervention in the civil war of 1920, and her attempt to annex the Ukraine, confirmed these impressions. The military initiative remained with the Whites until fall 1919. In the south, Denikin conquered the Ukraine with three armies and moved to link up with Kolchak at Saratov. Kolchak, in turn, prepared to cross the Volga with four armies in order to advance on Moscow. In the west, a third White army under General Nicolai N. Yudenich, operating out of the Baltic area and largely supplied by Britain, moved on Petrograd.

By July 1, 1919 strategic Tsaritsyn on the Volga, the future Stalingrad, had fallen to the Whites. Moscow was in serious danger after Denikin's capture of the cities of Kursk and Orel in September and October 1919. In the Baltic area, however, the first assault of Yudenich on Petrograd was checked in May 1919 by the superior artillery of Kronstadt naval base. The second attack of October 1919 failed largely through the personal intervention of Trotsky. By October 1919 the Bolsheviks had also retaken Orel, subsequently pushing Denikin all the way back into the Crimean Peninsula. By April 1920, Denikin had surrendered his command to Peter N. Wrangel, one of the most gifted White commanders. Kolchak's offensive, after initial gains in March 1919, was defeated when Tukhashevsky, Stalin's future chief of staff, captured the strategic Ural passes. By November 1919 Omsk, the seat of Kolchak's "government," was in Bolshevik hands. On February 7, 1920 Kolchak, a prisoner of the Soviets, was executed.

The Final Phase

The Russo-Polish War between April and October 1920 marked the final chapter of the Russian Civil War in its European phase. After evicting Poland from the Ukraine, the Bolsheviks drove the remnants of Wrangel's army off the Crimean Peninsula in November 1920. The Transcaucasian republics of Armenia, Azerbaijan, and Georgia were similarly retaken after a brief period of independence between 1918 and 1920. Following the Japanese evacuation of northern Sakhalin in 1925, the Bolshevik government, after nearly seven years of civil war and foreign intervention, had regained the tsarist patrimony, except for the western borderlands, Finland, Poland, and the Baltic states, Bessarabia, and the border provinces seized by Turkey.

Political and social factors weighed at least as heavily in determining the outcome of the Russian Civil War as did military factors. The White opposition was not only scattered over widely separated areas, allowing the Red Army to operate along interior lines, but it was also lacking in a coherent political and social program. In addition, it failed to develop leadership to match Lenin's resolve. The Omsk-based "Directory" of October 1918 vanished almost as quickly as it had been formed because Chernov's Social Revolutionaries and Kolchak's Conservatives failed to agree on the all-important question of land reform. General Wrangel, conscious of the importance of peasant support, did commission a land reform program, which was drafted by former tsarist minister of agriculture Krivoshein in June 1920. This came too late and Wrangel was, in any case, an exception. The preponderance of former tsarist generals and admirals among the Whites similarly aroused suspicion that a White victory might well mean the restoration of the tsarist status quo. Although Lenin had survived, Soviet Russia was in a deplorable state after the devastation of war, revolution and civil war. The social and economic disintegration of the country had been further accelerated by the "war communism" experiment, a policy aiming at instant communism by decree.

Bolshevik Social Policy

After seizing power, the Bolsheviks had nationalized banks, mines, factories and businesses, except those with fewer than ten workers. A supreme economic council was created in December 1917 for the overall direction of the economy. Bolshevik social policy reflected the views of A. V. Lunacharsky, the commissar for education, and of the economist E. A. Preobrazhensky, both of whom regarded the family as an undesirable relic of the bourgeois past. The right of property inheritance was abolished, as was the principle of communal property for husband and wife. Divorce was declared effective by the withdrawal of either spouse. A married woman no longer had to follow her husband if his residence was changed, nor did she have to assume her husband's family name. Abortion was legalized and the rearing of children by the state, not the family, propagated. The Bolshevik regime also departed from established practice when it engaged in an official campaign of antireligious propaganda. The clergy was deprived of civil rights, and the "Association of Militant Atheists," under the leadership of Trotsky at first, subsequently under E. M. Yaroslavsky, became the spearhead of such propaganda with the journal *Bezbozhnik.*

The Bolshevik party program of March 1919 had promised free education, the emancipation of women from the burdens of housekeeping, a leading role for trade unions in economic management, the six-hour workday, and the abundant production of goods in a planned economy.

The Realities

The socioeconomic reality of Soviet Russia at the end of the civil war bore little resemblance to these promises. The reality included a sharp decline in urban population, the city of Moscow alone losing half its prewar population, as people fled into the countryside in desperate search of food. Industrial production had fallen to one-seventh of the prewar level, and the great famine of 1920–1922 claimed an estimated five million lives. The Bolshevik goverment turned to noncommunist Europe and the United States for relief and the United States answered with the Hoover relief mission. Bolshevik family policy and the social dislocation engendered by the civil war had produced armed bands of homeless children, the *Bezprisornye,* contributing to a sharp rise in juvenile crime and despair.

Disillusionment was rife not only among ordinary people, but among Communist party members and unions. The party members assailed the increasing bureaucratization of the Communist party and the concentration of power in the hands of fewer and fewer men at the top. The unions deplored their effective exclusion from economic policy making. Discontent with Bolshevik rule and its results exploded in the Kronstadt rebellion of early March 1921 and in the proceedings of the tenth Soviet party congress of the same year. In the Kronstadt rebellion, Petrograd workers, angered by cuts in food rations, joined with rebellious sailors from the Baltic naval base of Kronstadt to demand a "third revolution" with freedom of speech, assembly and the press, and the removal of Bolshevik influence from the soviets.

At the Tenth Party Congress, a faction within the Bolshevik party under the name of "Workers' Opposition" demanded a division of power in soviet society between unions, soviets and the Bolshevik party. The unions were to exercise economic leadership, the soviets were to be invested with political authority independent of the Bolshevik party, and the Bolshevik party itself was to be limited to setting overall policy. Appreciating the gravity of the dual challenge within and without the Bolshevik party, Lenin responded with a policy which combined economic liberalization with a tightening of political controls and a redoubling of ideological vigilance. The Kronstadt rebellion itself was crushed by Red Army force. On March 18, 1921 Tukhashevsky and Trotsky completed the military operations which silenced the call for the "third revolution."

The NEP

On the economic front, Lenin substituted the coercion and experimentation of war communism with a policy of carefully defined liberalization under the so-called New Economic Policy (NEP). Adopted at the Tenth Party Congress of 1921, NEP ended the forceful requisitioning of food from the peasantry, authorized the leasing of farmland and the hiring of farm labor by individual peasants, and permitted the return of private enterprise to retailing and light industry. The "commanding heights of the economy," heavy industry, mining and banking, remained in state hands. Money, whose abolition the 1919 Bolshevik party program had confidently predicted, became respectable once more. In 1924 the Soviet currency was stabilized and put back on the gold standard.

The challenge of the "workers' opposition" at the Tenth Party Congress, on the other hand, was answered by a ban against "factionalism" which was adopted at the congress. Party rules, henceforth, prohibited the formation of "factions" between party congresses and their adopting a platform of their own. After 1921, Soviet party congresses rapidly developed into rubber stamp gatherings which approved the decisions made in advance by the highest party organs, the Central Committee and the Politburo. The latter, revived during the civil war, became the de facto leading organ of the party. As a further safeguard against dissent in the party ranks, Lenin instituted a major purge in 1921, resulting in the expulsion of 175,000 out of a total of 580,000 party members.

As an emergency measure to prevent economic disaster, the NEP was a qualified success. Recovery in agriculture was quicker than in industry, with three quarters of prewar farm output being reached by 1922 as against one quarter of prewar industrial production for the same year. The coal industry reached prewar levels by 1926. State-owned heavy industry continued to stagnate for want of investment capital, which Lenin failed to attract from abroad in sufficient amounts during the NEP despite his efforts and appeals.

The NEP also produced a class of *nouveaux riches* profiteers, which appeared almost overnight and which benefited from the unaccustomed economic freedoms of the new policy. The class of NEP profiteers disillusioned many Communist party faithfuls, to whom the privations and the sacrifices of the civil war now seemed to have been in vain. To Lenin and the party leadership, the NEP was merely a tactical retreat from communism, however, dictated by necessity and destined to be halted once circumstances would permit. As Lenin's health was failing, the final answer as to the length and duration of the NEP was being postponed. Lenin himself thought that a comprehensive industrial development plan, such as his successor Stalin was soon to unleash, was a "bureaucratic utopia" as long as the peoples of Russia were starving and poor.

THE STRUGGLE FOR SUCCESSION
AND THE STALINIST MACHINE

After suffering four strokes in less than two years, Lenin died on January 21, 1924, In theory, Lenin's death ought not to have provoked a major crisis in Soviet Russia, because Bolshevik party rule supposedly rested on the principle of collective leadership. In fact, Lenin had set an example of one-man rule, somewhat concealed by his personal modesty and opposition to what later came to be called the "cult of the personality." On the other hand, Lenin had neither designated a successor nor defined rules of succession. Lenin's memorandum of December 25, 1922, subsequently called his "testament," and the postscript of January 4, 1923, expressed no clear preference for any of his associates. Lenin was critical of Stalin, whose removal from the post of general secretary of the party he urged because of Stalin's "rudeness."

The unwritten rules of succession were shaped by the nature of the power struggle which unfolded after Lenin's death, and the nature of the struggle, in turn, has largely been determined by the practice of Bolshevik rule since 1917, which Lenin shaped.

Stalin's Power Base

The emergence of the Politburo as the de facto governing party organ logically limited the contenders to the members of that body. At the time of Lenin's death there were seven Politburo members: Zinoviev, Kamenev, Trotsky, Bukharin, Rykov, Tomsky, and Stalin. Each of these had a political power base of his own in accordance with his major function. Zinoviev headed the Communist International as well as the prestigious Leningrad party organization. Kamenev had taken Lenin's post as Politburo chairman, in addition to being head of the Moscow party organization. Trotsky was commissar of war, and Bukharin, who enjoyed great popularity in the party, was chief theorist. Rykov was head of the Soviet government, another position previously held by Lenin, while Tomsky headed the unions. The fact which soon emerged in the post-Lenin power struggle was that the post of party general secretary, the post held by Stalin at the time of Lenin's death, was by far the most important in the party hierarchy. It has remained so ever since this fact was first revealed in the 1920s. Before Lenin's death, few among the top Soviet leadership would have cared to fill the post, because it seemed dull and bureaucratic and because it offered few opportunities for the public display of brilliant oratory for which men such as Trotsky and Zinoviev were justly famous. The general secretary, on the other hand, had the power of appointment of regional, district, city and town party secretaries. This enabled Stalin to appoint trusted followers to key positions, officials on whose support he was able to draw later on when battling his rivals for supreme power. In 1922 alone, the party secretariat made some 10,000 appointments.

Control over party secretaries meant control over the party. Control over the party meant control over Soviet Russia, because the party, more than any other single instrument or institution of power, was regarded as the historical tool of communist revolution. This was almost an article of religious faith with Soviet Communists of the 1920s and 1930s, and it explains why many of Stalin's rivals preferred to sacrifice their own ambitions and even their lives once they had come to perceive their challenge to Stalin's rule as harmful to the strength and credibility of the Communist party. Underlying the power struggle were both issues and personalities. The issues revolved around the question of economic priorities and the social cost which these priorities would entail. Externally, the major issue concerned Soviet Russia's relations with the world and the likelihood of communist world revolution in the foreseeable future. Over those issues the lines were fairly clearly drawn between Left and Right, with Trotsky, Zinoviev and Kamenev heading the Left, and Bukharin, Rykov, and Tomsky the Right.

Left and Right

Embracing the views of the Soviet economist E. Preobrazhensky, as set forth in the *New Economics* of 1924, the Left was impatient to end the NEP as soon as possible and to launch Soviet Russia on the road to industrialization. The cost of industrialization, in this view, would have to be borne overwhelmingly by the peasantry. Preobrazhensky's thesis of "primitive socialist accumulation" called for the exploitation and even the expropriation of the peasantry to raise the necessary capital for industrialization.

The Left also continued to espouse the cause of revolution abroad. Significantly, Zinoviev supported and encouraged the German Communist uprising of "red October" 1923. Even after the failure of the German Communist uprising, Trotsky hoped for a Chinese Communist victory in 1927. The Right, by contrast, believed neither in the likelihood of imminent world revolution, nor in the practicability of an industrial crash program at home. Bukharin favored a continuation of the basic NEP pattern, which assured the Soviet peasantry of a reasonably comfortable living standard. Progress towards industrialization, in Bukharin's view, must necessarily be slow because of the weight of Russia's rural economy. In the debate over economic priorities, Stalin at first avoided identification with either the Left or the Right. By 1924, however, he did advance the thesis of "socialism in one country," which implied rejection of communist world revolution for the near future and which appealed to the patriotic pride of young Soviet Communists.

Stalin's Rise

Personal rivalries cut across the ideological divisions between the Left and the Right. Both Kamenev and Zinoviev, fearful of a Trotsky dictatorship supported by the Red Army, allied themselves with Stalin in a "troika" in order to contain the threat. By 1925 Trotsky was stripped of his post as war commissar. With Trotsky neutralized, Stalin abandoned his allies Zinoviev and Kamenev at the Fourteenth Party Congress in December 1925 and formed a new partnership with the Right under Bukharin. At the same time, Stalin's position in both the Politburo and the Central Committee was strengthened through the addition of new members who were personally loyal to him. In 1925 Molotov, Kalinin and Voroshibov joined the Politburo as full members. After Stalin's desertion of his Left allies, Kamenev, Zinoviev and Trotsky buried their past differences in a belated attempt to bloc Stalin's rise. With Stalin in control of the key party organs, the attempt came too late. In 1926 Trotsky was expelled from the central committee and Zinoviev lost his leadership both of the Leningrad party organization and of the Communist International. In November 1927 Trotsky and Zinoviev were expelled from the Communist party. In January 1928 Trotsky was deported to Alma Ata in Kazakhstan. Before long he went into foreign exile, first to Turkey, later to France, then Norway, and finally Mexico. From his foreign exile, Trotsky watched with mounting bitterness the course of Stalin's domestic and foreign policy during the 1930s. When Stalin withheld Comintern support from the German Social Democrats prior to Hitler's coming to power in 1933, Trotsky called for the formation of a new, Fourth International, without however being able to realize it. In his *Revolution Betrayed* of 1937, a book which anticipated the thesis of the Yugoslav reform communist Milovan Djilas of the 1950s, Trotsky condemned Stalin for having distorted the original aims of the Bolshevik party. On August 20, 1940, Stalin had Trotsky assassinated in his Mexican exile.

The Fifteenth Party Congress of 1927, which witnessed the destruction of the Left, was also the beginning of Stalin's attack on the Right. The Stalin platform of 1927 heralded the end of the NEP and the beginning of both wholesale industrialization and forceful collectivization of the farmland. The state planning commission (GOSPLAN) was directed to prepare the first five-year plan. Coercive measures against wealthy peasants (kulaks) were begun with the explanation that the state was short of 2 million tons of grain.

After 1927, the pattern of the Left's destruction was repeated as Stalin shattered the Right. Bukharin, the leader of the Right, made a futile effort to unite all the leaders of both the Left and the Right to defeat Stalin, whom Bukharin now termed a "new Genghis Khan." In fact, Stalin ousted Bukharin from the leadership of the Communist International, the post Bukharin had assumed after Zinoviev's fall. By 1929 Bukharin was also expelled from the Politburo. In the same year Bukharin's ally, Tomsky, was ousted as chief of the trade unions, and in 1930 was expelled from the Politburo. Also in 1930 Rykov, the third leader of the Right, was removed as head of the government and ousted from the Politburo.

Stalin's dictatorship was well established by the time of his fiftieth birthday on December 21, 1929. Many of the old Bolsheviks, more brilliant but less ruthless than Stalin, were exiled, silenced, or discredited. Portraits and busts of Stalin, larger in size than those of any other party leader, began to fill public places, and the old city of Tsaritsyn was renamed Stalingrad. From his western exile, Trotsky had called for a new revolution in Russia. A new revolution was, in fact, in the making, one in which Stalin applied the tested methods of his struggle for supreme power over the party to the whole of Soviet Russia.

THE STALIN ERA

The consolidation of Stalin's power in 1929 signaled the beginning of an economic, social and political revolution more sweeping in its effects than the two previous Russian revolutions of March and November 1917. Within only a decade after crushing the Left and the Right, Stalin would change Soviet Russia into one of the leading industrial nations of the world, uproot millions of peasants, and leave his personal imprint upon virtually every phase of Soviet life.

In method, the Stalin revolution of the 1930s followed the example of the war communism of the early 1920s. In its aims, the Stalin revolution appropriated some of Lenin's ideas prior to the NEP compromise as well as those advanced by the Left and its economic spokesman Preobrazhensky during the mid-1920s. Although Stalin adopted the economic program of the Left, he did so with a difference in emphasis and timing which gave his revolution a character all its own.

The Left had wanted speedy industrialization, but it had hoped that labor would be permitted to share its fruits. Under Stalin, Soviet labor lost its last vestige of independence, and industrialization aimed overwhelmingly at the creation of armaments, not goods for civilian consumption. The Soviet defense industry of the 1930s would expand two-and-a-half times as fast as Soviet industry as a whole. The Left had denounced the kulak as a parasite who fattened on the freedoms of the NEP, but the rural revolution it had in mind fell far short of Stalin's physical destruction of the entire kulak class. The Left had hoped to keep the human and social costs of the industrial revolution within tolerable bounds. The costs of Soviet Russia's revolution of the 1930s were to Stalin largely a matter of indifference, as long as they did not impede ultimate success.

Terror

Stalin's most significant departure from past Bolshevik practice concerned the uses of terror. The Bolsheviks had freely used terror against external foes and the "class enemy" during the revolution and the civil war. Stalin was the first to turn terror inward against the members and the leaders of the Bolshevik party during the Great Purge of the 1930s. Under Stalin, terror became an expedient for punishing scapegoats for the industrial failures of the regime, and it also became a weapon for settling personal accounts with enemies of the past and suspected future adversaries. Eventually the terror of the 1930s ended by debasing Soviet society as a whole and reducing it to a chanting chorus of frightened worshipers of Stalin's infallibility. The peasantry, the most numerous class of Soviet Russia, was the first to feel the impact of Stalin's rule. The size of the peasant population relative to the urban had actually increased between 1913 and 1928 from 65 to 72 percent. The number of individual peasant households had grown from 16.5 million in 1918 to nearly 26 million in 1929. Of these, some 2 million households were classified as kulaks, 15 million as middle income, and 9 million as poor peasants.

Collectivization

The growth of a class of well-to-do peasant proprietors in the midst of Communist Soviet Russia had been a source of discomfort and concern to Bolshevik leaders from the start, especially to Lenin. To him it seemed both abnormal and dangerous that capitalist modes of production on the farm should thrive in a society aiming to build communism.

Stalin solved the Soviet farm dilemma through a policy of ruthless collectivization. Collectivization was meant to yield economic, social, political and ideological benefits which were important to the overall success of his revolution of the 1930s. By reclaiming title to the land, which the Bolshevik regime had never actually abandoned, the state itself became the chief agricultural producer. It did not have to haggle over farm prices with 26 million individual peasant households and it could use the profits of the rural economy for investment purposes in industry. Political and social controls over the rural population were also far easier to establish under the collective farm system because of its administrative infrastructure and the establishment of binding rules for work and collective farm organization. Such rules were issued under the collective farm charter of 1935 and amended by new provisions in 1939 which defined the number of workdays to be spent on the collective. The state limited the time which collective farm workers were allowed to devote to their tiny individually owned garden plots, the last remnants of private farm enterprise. The "machine-tractor stations" (MTS) were a further aid in enforcing party controls over the countryside. As state-owned institutions, the MTS hired out mechanized equipment to collective farms while serving as a political listening post of the Communist party among the peasant population. Ideologically, collectivization terminated private ownership over the farm-land, which in the Marxist definition was as much a means of production as industry. The socialization of all means of production was, at the same time, an essential pre-requisite to the attainment of a classless society, as envisaged by Marx.

Stalin's initial call for a voluntary merger of farms into collectives evoked a very disappointing echo, with only 4 percent of the farms responding favorably by October 1929. A policy of massive coercion followed in which an estimated 1 million kulaks were killed. The surviving kulaks were driven off the land to form the first installment of a vast and growing army of forced labor. Children of kulaks were marked as "class enemies" and denied both a higher education and advancement in the urban economy.

The peasantry resisted forced collectivation by slaughtering livestock and refusing to plant crops. After the slaughter of an estimated 30 million head of cattle, 100 million sheep and 17 million horses, Soviet livestock figures for 1941 were still below the precollectivization levels. Failure to plant crops resulted in Soviet Russia's second great famine, after that of the civil war, with an estimated ten million people starving to death in the early 1930s. Despite much resistance, Stalin completed collectivization, which claimed to include 90 percent of the farmland in 1936 and 100 percent in 1940.

Industrialization

Concurrent with the revolution in agriculture Stalin launched his industrial revolution, beginning with the first five-year plan in 1928. He defined as its chief purpose the utmost increase in the defense capacity of the country. By assigning priority to the development of defense and capital goods as against light and consumer goods, Stalin's first five-year plan set a pattern that was to remain essentially unchanged in Soviet economic development in all the years following his era.

By the end of the first five-year plan, Soviet Russia claimed to have achieved a fourfold increase in the output of machinery and a doubling of oil production. At Stalingrad, Europe's largest tractor plant had been built, and at Dnieprostroi Europe's largest electrical power station was in operation with an output of 650,000 kilowatts. Between 1928 and 1937, steel production was said to have increased from 4 to 18 million tons per year, while hard coal output rose from 36 to 128 million tons. Entire industrial cities had been built in the Urals and Siberia close to ore and coal deposits, and new rail and water communications had been developed such as the White Sea and the Moscow-Volga canals.

The social cost of industrialization was high, because few provisions for absorbing the expanded labor force into the cities had been made. While the industrial labor force increased from 6 to 8 million people between 1932 and 1940, the percentage of total investment in housing was smaller after 1929 than during the preceding decade. Similarly, real wages in industry actually declined by as much as 43 percent between 1928 and 1940, the peak years of industrialization before World War II. Labor discipline was tightened and the issuing of "labor books" and internal passports effectively limited freedom of movement. By a decree of June 1940, lateness of as little as twenty minutes or sickness on the job became punishable by loss of one fourth of wages and imprisonment of up to six months. Beginning in 1936, workers in industry were urged to imitate the example of Alexei Stakhanov, a Donets Basin coal miner who had allegedly exceeded his work norm by 1,300 percent by mining 102 tons of coal in a single shift. The "Stakhanov cult" became a prominent feature of Soviet labor policy, which hoped to raise productivity through the incentives of medals and cash premiums. At the same time, Stalinist Russia increasingly relied on forced labor, especially for such projects as canal building. At the peak of the Stalinist purges of the 1930s, the size of the Soviet forced labor army was estimated as between 7 and 14 million, declining to an estimated 3.5 million before the Soviet entry into World War II.

THE STALIN CONSTITUTION, SOCIAL CHANGE
AND THE PURGE

Under Stalin, Soviet communism was rapidly acquiring a distinctly Russian national identity which differed in essentials from the internationalist, world-revolutionary make-up of the early Soviet period between 1917 and 1924. This, together with the need to create a more disciplined social climate as a background to the severe labor discipline of the 1930s, prompted the promulgation of a new constitution in 1936 and the enactment of conservative social legislation.

The Soviet constitution of December 5, 1936, soon to be called the "Stalin constitution," was meant to signal to the Soviet populace the end of the violent social struggle which had accompanied the launching of industrialization and collectivization. The "liquidation" of kulaks and NEP merchants, in Stalin's explanation, had ended the class struggle in the Soviet Union and laid the foundations of a new society in which only two "friendly" classes, workers and peasants, coexisted in harmony. The new constitution thus abolished the discrimination between urban and rural voters, which the first, rudimentary constitution of the Soviet Union of 1924 had still upheld. With an eye on the Western democracies, with which Stalin was in the process of establishing collective security against the fascist powers, the 1936 constitution also boasted an elaborate bill of "fundamental rights and duties" as well as a supposedly independent judiciary.

The Stalin constitution retained the federal structure of the 1924 constitution. The number of union republics was eventually increased to sixteen by 1940. A federal legislature was established with the bicameral supreme soviet, consisting of the soviet of the union and the soviet of the nationalities. In the former, one deputy was elected for every 300,000 Soviet citizens; in the latter, the union republics were represented by twenty-five deputies each, the autonomous republics with eleven deputies each, and the autonomous regions with five deputies each. The "Stalin constitution" was significant because it mentioned the Communist party by name and referred to its leading role in Soviet politics. Article 126 spoke of the Communist party as the "leading core of all organizations of the working people, both public and state."

Conservatism

Soviet social legislation of the mid- and late 1930s reflected the official intent to reverse the permissive and libertarian policy of the early 1920s. The social ethics of Lunacharsky and Preobrazhensky were now replaced by those of Anton S. Marenko, an educator experienced in the rehabilitation of homelesss children. Marenko praised the family as a collective in miniature, in which parents could impart values of duty, discipline and hard work. In the 1930s, abortion was again outlawed and heavy fines were imposed on divorced fathers for nonsupport of their children. Childbearing was officially encouraged through the granting of awards to prolific mothers. Divorce was discouraged under the new divorce law of June 1936 which charged progressive dues for repeated divorces.

The return of social conservatism in the mid-1930s coincided with an official campaign to stimulate Soviet patriotism with distinctly Great Russian nationalist overtones. The oficial stimulation and rehabilitation of Russian nationalism served the dual purpose of identifying Stalin and his policies with national pride and of preparing the Soviet populace for possible foreign conflict with Germany and Japan. In the Red Army, service ranks were restored, officers' pay was increased and the title "Hero of the Soviet Union" introduced. The new Red Army oath of 1939 pledged allegiance to the "homeland, the Union of Soviet Socialist Republics." By central committee decree of 1934, secondary school history texts were rewritten with greater emphasis on past Russian historical achievements. The Soviet motion picture industry and Soviet literature were similarly ordered to rehabilitate past heroes, including tsarist generals and even tsars. In the sympathetic Soviet film portrayal of Ivan the Terrible, fighting rebellious and scheming boyars, or that of Alexander Nevsky, defeating the invading Teutonic Knights, the Soviet moviegoer of the 1930s could easily detect the heroic qualities of Soviet Russia's current leader, Joseph Stalin.

Though undeniably ruthless, many of Stalin's policies were perceived to be rational and coherent. As such, they evoked Western sympathy and even admiration from intellectuals and writers such as France's André Malraux or, initially, Arthur Koestler of Hungary. The rationality and coherence of the Stalinism of the 1930s was put into serious question, however, by the Great Purge.

Purges

Touched off by the assassination of Sergei M. Kirov, Stalin's protegé and party secretary of Leningrad, on December 1, 1934, the purge first claimed the lives of former Left opposition leaders, such as Zinoviev, Kamenev and fourteen other old Bolsheviks, in the first big show trial of August 1936. A second show trial against seventeen old Bolsheviks followed early in 1937 with the improbable charge that the defendants had conspired with Nazi Germany and Japan to restore capitalism to Soviet Russia. The execution of the Soviet chief of staff Marshal Tukhashevsky in June 1937 was the signal for a massive purge of the armed forces. The military purge claimed the lives of 3 Soviet marshals out of 5, 13 out of 15 army commanders, 62 out of 85 corps commanders, 110 out of 195 divisional commanders, and 220 out of 406 brigade commanders. Communist party control over the army was increased by a decree of August 15, 1937, which declared political commissars equal to regular army officers.

In March 1938 a fresh show trial was staged, the "trial of the twenty-one," which eliminated the leaders of the former Right opposition, including Bukharin. Before the purge ground to a halt at the turn of 1938–1939, it had not only destroyed Stalin's old opponents, but many others who had actively supported his rise to power. Of the seventy-one members of the central committee, elected at the Seventeenth Party Congress of 1934, a total of fifty-five had been executed. Among the victims of the purge were also many foreign Communist leaders (such as Hungary's Béla Kun) who had sought refuge in the USSR after their own native countries had fallen under right-wing dictatorships.

It would appear that Stalin was determined to exterminate all Bolshevik leaders, and their followers, who had achieved fame before his own rise to power. A further motive, especially for the military purge of 1937, may have been to thwart any opposition from the senior military leaders, who had voiced alarm over the demoralizing impact of Stalin's ruthless policy of collectivization on Red Army peasant soldiers. That the purge simply got out of hand in its final stages is suggested by the fact that it also claimed the lives of two successive NKVD chiefs, Yagoda and Yezhov, who had previously supervised the mass arrests, the staged show trials, and the executions.

Stalin's industrial revolution had started at the beginning of the 1930s admist the widespread enthusiasm of young Communists at home and the applause of Western intellectual admirers abroad, who saw in Soviet communism both an effective barrier to fascism and a preferable alternative, in the depression, to bankrupt economic liberalism. By the end of the decade, the most tangible element in the atmosphere of Soviet Russia was no longer spontaneous enthusiasm but ill-concealed fear. Purge-related arrests had become so common, especially among people of professional background, that it was not unusual for Soviet families to keep a set of suitcases packed in anticipation of arrest. The packed suitcase, held in readiness for the dreaded pre-dawn arrest by the men of the NKVD, epitomized the spirit of Stalinist Russia of the 1930s more eloquently than did all the statistics of the five-year plans.

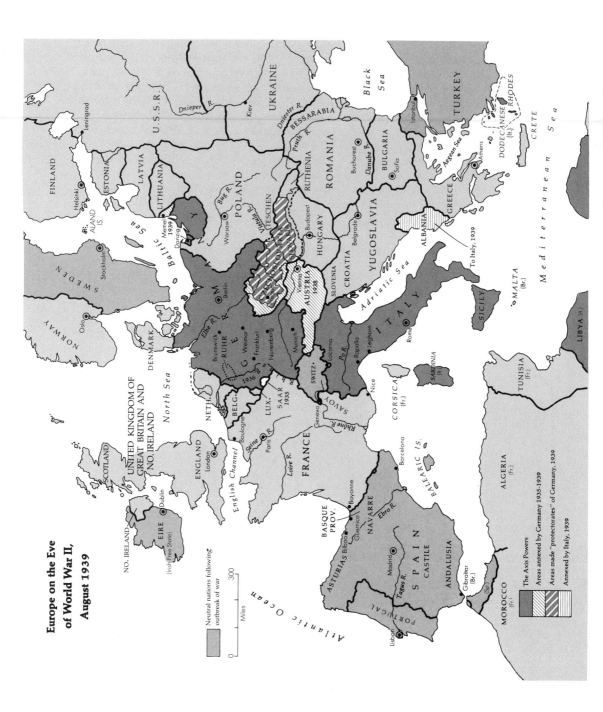

**Europe on the Eve
of World War II,
August 1939**

Neutral nations following
outbreak of war

Miles
0   300

The Axis Powers

Areas annexed by Germany 1935–1939

Areas made "protectorates" of Germany, 1939

Annexed by Italy, 1939

9

The End of European Sovereignty: 1930–1939

THE DEPRESSION AND THE END OF THE LOCARNO SPIRIT

If the term *European sovereignty* is taken to mean the ability of the European states to act on behalf of their national interest, either singly or collectively, without the inference of outside forces, the 1930s spelled the beginning of the end of that sovereignty.

The collapse of the European liberal-economic order in the wake of the New York Stock Exchange crash of October 1929 was a major cause of sharpened social strife, liberal-democratic failure, resurgent nationalism, and the loss of faith in international law and its chief symbol, the League of Nations. Both in domestic and in foreign relations, the depression prompted a search for alternatives to the accepted models of the stable mid-1920s, particularly in the fragile and recently established democracies of central and eastern Europe. The depression became the midwife of dictatorship in Germany under Hitler, in Austria under Engelbert Dollfuss, in Hungary under Gömbös, in Bulgaria under King Boris, and in Rumania under King Carol. Occurring as it did at the halfway point between the end of the First World War and the outbreak of the Second World War, the depression fell with special severity on the young generation of the early 1930s whose attitudes and outlook had not been shaped by participation in the First World War. There was, in the observation of Webster and Sydney Herbert, historians of the League of Nations, no guarantee after the end of the first postwar decade that peace would be maintained by the new generation, which had "its own ambitions, grievances, and unsatisfied energy."

The 1919 peace settlement, as John Maynard Keynes noted critically at the time, had failed to provide institutions for the promotion of international economic cooperation. Such cooperation as had developed was quickly replaced by a return to economic nationalism and protectionism when unemployment figures reached catastrophic levels, as they did in Germany, with 6 million out of work, and in Britain with 3 million. Between 1929 and 1932 European industrial production fell by 30 percent, while world trade declined by 20 percent between 1929 and 1931. Attempts at economic cooperation such as the London World Economic Conference of June 1933, or the economic conferences for eastern Europe at Bucharest, Warsaw, and Athens of 1930, were failures. Although the London conference paid lip service to tariff reduction, the governments of Europe in fact pursued precisely the opposite course. The United States had taken the lead in high tariff policy with the Hawley-Smoot Tariff Act of 1930. Britain followed the American example, first with the Import Duties Bill of February 1932 and the Ottawa Agreements of August 1932, which instituted a preferential tariff system for the Commonwealth. In Germany, import duties on rye and wheat were raised at the very time when the unemployed quite literally could not serve their families even the simplest of meals.

Japan in Manchuria

The policy of economic nationalism took its most extreme form in the Far East with the Japanese conquest of Manchuria in 1931. Although Japan had been maintaining a military presence in Manchuria since 1905, and her economic investment in Manchuria—accounting for 40 percent of all Japanese foreign investments—was considerable even before 1931, the actual conquest and the creation of the Manchurian puppet state of Manchukuo in February 1932 were clearly prompted by the depression and the effects it produced on Japanese foreign trade. With a decline of Japanese exports of nearly 50 percent between 1929 and 1931, Japan's "blood and iron" prime minister Baron Tanaka sought economic safety in foreign conquest.

For Europe, the significance of the Japanese conquest of Manchuria lay chiefly in the undermining of League authority and prestige. From the standpoint of the European democracies, Japanese action against Manchuria posed questions of both principle and national interest. Neither Britain nor France considered their national interest harmed by Japan's action. Japan also enlisted French goodwill in May 1932 by concluding a new trade agreement designed to improve commercial relations between French Indochina and herself. The British government tended to agree with Churchill's assessment that Japan's conquest of Manchuria must be viewed against the special background of China's unsettled internal conditions; China claimed sovereignty over Manchuria and had appealed for League help. Japanese control of Manchuria in the British view also represented a welcome check on Soviet power in Asia. Concerning the question of principle, the League-appointed fact-finding Lytton Commission concluded in 1932 that Manchuria was not a simple case of the violation of the frontiers of one country by the armed forces of a neighbor, because Japanese troops had already been present in Manchuria. The Lytton Report, nevertheless, also took note of the absence of Chinese popular support for the Japanese puppet regime of Manchukuo, and recommended the restoration of the "open door" principle to Manchuria. The League finally did not apply sanctions against Japan, and tried to disengage itself from the affair by refusing formal recognition of the puppet state of Manchukuo. Japan responded by quitting the League in March 1933, the first power to do so.

During the Manchurian crisis, Churchill remarked that the League had great work to do in Europe. That work, which would be urgently required in the Ethiopian crisis of the mid-1930s under circumstances not unlike those of Manchuria, would undoubtedly have been easier and possibly more promising if the League had not failed previously in its Asian efforts. That Japanese actions in Manchuria also constituted a violation of the Kellogg-Briand Pact was noted with greater anger in the United States than in Europe, because of the higher American stakes in the Pacific and Asian region.

Franco-German Hostility

In Europe, more pressing matters began overshadowing faraway Manchuria at the beginning of the new decade, such as a renewed distrust in French-German relations. The death of German foreign minister Stresemann in October 1929 was symbolic of the end of the brief period of Franco-German reconciliation of the mid-1920s. France, better than most, appreciated the significance of the enormous increase in Nazi strength from 12 to 107 Reichstag deputies in the German elections of September 1930. Equally disturbing to France was the lack of any sign of German appreciation for the premature French troop withdrawal from the Rhineland in June 1930. The impression of an unpredictable and potentially hostile Germany was reinforced by the noisy and chauvinistic campaign against the Young Plan, jointly organized by Hitler and his Nationalist allies in the fall of 1929.

Although France and Britain appreciated the efforts of Brüning, Papen and Schleicher, the last three chancellors of the Weimar Republic between 1930 and 1933, to contain the rising Nazi flood in Germany, France in particular had been alarmed by the stepped-up pace of German revisionist demands even before Hitler's coming to power. The last Weimar governments explained their foreign policy demands as a means of outmaneuvering Hitler's nationalist appeal and taking the wind out of Nazi sails. This could hardly sweeten the bitter pills which Brüning, Papen, and Schleicher expected France to swallow. Among them was the German demand for the French evacuation of the Saar before the scheduled plebiscite of 1935, the revision of Germany's eastern borders with Poland, and even the hint that the demilitarized status of the Rhineland, reaffirmed at Locarno, should be altered. When Germany and Austria without any advance warning announced the conclusion of a customs union in March 1931, France, supported by Italy and the nations of the Little Entente, reacted vigorously. Suspecting rightly that the customs union was intended to pave the way for eventual political union, France charged violation of the 1919 peace treaty of St. Germain with Austria as well as of the 1922 Geneva Protocol. The latter had been an international loan agreement conditioned on Austria's unchanged independence. Britain recommended adjudication through the Court of International Justice. Prior to the court's decision of September 1931, which concurred essentially with the French position, France retaliated by withdrawing bank deposits from Austria, thereby causing the collapse of the *Creditanstalt,* Austria's principal bank, in May 1931. The *Creditanstalt* collapse in turn caused a banking crisis of national proportions in Germany in July 1931. By September the projected Austro-German customs union was abandoned. The Brüning government had managed to achieve both a significant loss of prestige at home and a significant worsening of relations with France.

On the heels of the ill-starred customs union project, Chancellor Brüning announced in January 1932 what amounted to an end of German reparations. The Hoover Moratorium, announced by President Herbert Hoover on June 20, 1931 in response to the European banking crisis, had suspended debt payments between governments for one year. France had reluctantly accepted the proposal but only on condition that the principle of reparations be upheld. Brüning's announcement of January 1932 suggested that Germany could not resume reparation payments even after the end of the Hoover Moratorium because of her economic and financial plight. It did not escape French attention, however, that Brüning did not consider Germany sufficiently bankrupt to propose construction of another pocket battleship. As in the reparations crisis of 1923, Britain again supported the German position and for similar reasons. Sir H. Rumbold, Britain's ambassador to Germany, warned his government that failure to convene another reparations conference could result in the ouster of Brüning and the coming to power of Hitler. Walter Layton, editor of the *Economist,* had similarly recommended in the "Layton Report" of August 1931 that no further private loans should be advanced to Germany unless reparations were discontinued. The ensuing Lausanne conference of June 1932 in effect canceled German reparations, except for a final token payment of 3 billion marks. A French attempt to salvage at least part of the Young Plan by extending the Hoover Moratorium for another year failed. Likewise, a British project of tying the end of reparations to German promises not to raise other revisionist demands for a fifteen-year period, failed over French objections. The French government thought that a moratorium on revisionism would only weaken existing treaties and commitments for the preservation of the status quo.

The end of German reparations, far from constituting the end of German revisionism, coincided with a German drive for equality in armaments at the Geneva Disarmament Conference, which had opened in February 1932. As in the reparations question, the positions of Britain and France were not identical on the issue of German armaments. To British Conservatives, the continued disarmed condition of Germany was in itself a potential threat to peace because of the thrust of Soviet industrialization towards armaments under Stalin's first Five Year Plan. German rearmament might also boost sales of British arms manufacturers, especially tanks, which some British producers openly advertised in German military journals at the time. Britain was also not unsympathetic to the German government's argument that military expansion would absorb tens of thousands of young men who might otherwise flock to Hitler's stormtroopers. The French attempt to tie the arms issue to a new convention for compulsory arbitration of international disputes under the so-called Tardieu Plan failed over the opposition of Britain, Germany and Soviet Russia. By December 1932 a formula was finally found which seemed to meet both the German demand for equality and the French desire for more time to gauge German intentions and behavior. By conceding Germany "equality of rights in a system providing security for all nations," the formula fulfilled the equality pledge dependent on a system that would also have to be acceptable to France. Before the Geneva formula of December 1932 could be implemented, Hitler had assumed the chancellorship in Germany.

HITLER AND EUROPE

There is no doubt that many sources of friction existed in Europe during the 1930s, but it is very doubtful whether any of them would have led to war without the addition of the Hitler factor. Just at a time when most of Europe was eager to bury the memory of the First World War, Hitler burst upon the scene like a restless spirit from the trenches, determined to take his personal revenge on Europe for having spoiled his youthful dream of German greatness and glory. If the depression was the midwife of dictatorship and totalitarianism in Europe, then Hitler surely was the evil genius that tied together the contemporary elements of resentment and dissatisfaction, fear and frustration, aggression and arrogance, into an inextricable knot of conflict.

After the Second World War, Winston Churchill was to observe in his speech at Fulton, Missouri of March 1946 that no war in history could have been prevented more easily by timely action than the one which had just ended. It could have been prevented "without firing a single shot."

Churchill was justified in making such a statement because he was among the very few who understood the meaning of Hitler's coming to power and gave timely warning. French foreign minister Louis Barthou, who had studied Hitler's *Mein Kampf* and believed it to be a statement of Hitler's true intentions, also raised the alarm before his untimely death in October 1934. Most of the other prominent European politicians did not take Hitler seriously enough to see in him anything but an erratic and possibly dangerous figure, but one that could be integrated into the existing system by patient effort and affordable concession.

Hitler viewed the 1930s as an age of opportunity not likely to recur. The improbability of his own rise from obscurity to supreme power reinforced his belief in a providential mission and a duty to exploit opportunities to which others were blind. These opportunities derived from the fact that the victors of World War I were divided, that the leaders of the western powers wished to believe in their own illusions of perpetual peace, and that an effective coalition between the western democracies and Soviet Russia would founder on the rock of ideological suspicion despite strong individual efforts to the contrary. As Frederick the Great of Prussia had exploited the favorable power constellation of the mid-eighteenth century for the expansion of Prussia, and as Bismarck's Prussia had similarly exploited the opportunities of the 1860s and 1870s for the unification of Germany, so Hitler wished to exploit the 1930s for the realization of his own foreign policy ambitions before the victors of World War I had had time to awaken to the true threat of Nazi Germany.

Hitler's Foreign Policy

Hitler's foreign policy aims were very different from those of any previous leader of Prussia or of Germany, and they had been revealed quite frankly in *Mein Kampf*. The fact that the foreign policy passages of *Mein Kampf* were the best written and best organized parts of an otherwise poorly written and badly organized book demonstrates the prominence that foreign policy occupied in Hitler's thinking even in 1924. Once in power, Hitler was quite happy to delegate power in most domestic matters, but he jealously controlled foreign policy, excluding among others the professional diplomats from any real share of decision making or even meaningful consultation.

The most important foreign policy message of *Mein Kampf* was that Hitler was not a revisionist but a revolutionary. All the foreign ministers of the Weimar Republic had wished to revise the Treaty of Versailles and saw in the regaining of the 1914 status quo their ultimate objective. Hitler too wished to revise the Versailles settlement, not as an end in itself but as the starting position for German world power based on the conquest of Russia. Hitler dismissed both the aims of German pre-1914 foreign policy and the methods by which they had been pursued. The quest for German world power through overseas colonial expansion, world trade, and navalism was, in his view, outdated and self-defeating. It was outdated because colonial empires were like "pyramids stood on their heads," with only the summit in Europe. The future world powers of Hitler's vision were those with the pyramid "right-side-up," with a continental expanse providing the broad base of national power. German pre-war policy was defined as self-defeating because it allied Germany with the wrong powers, with "ancient states" such as Austria-Hungary which were already "pensioned off by world history." Navalism and expanded export had, on the other hand, needlessly antagonized Great Britain.

The mere regaining of the 1914 frontiers Hitler dismissed as "political absurdity." The future goals of German foreign policy were stated in categorical terms, the conquest of "living space" and the freeing of the German people from the danger of "vanishing from the earth or serving as a slave nation." Germany, Hitler observed, will either "be a world power or she will not be at all."

Hitler proposed Italy and Great Britain as Germany's future allies, the former because of its fascist ideology, the latter because of ethnic kinship and Britain's presumed role as "white policeman" in the colonial world. For Mussolini, Hitler expressed admiration. In order to win Italian friendship, he was quite prepared to renounce any claim to the former South Tyrol with its quarter-million ethnic German minority, which the 1919 St. Germain peace had awarded to Italy.

The idea of the Anglo-German alliance and German domination of Russia as a foundation of German world power was not entirely new. Britain's colonial secretary Joseph Chamberlain, whose son Neville was destined to become Hitler's partner in appeasement, had spoken of a "Teutonic League" of Germany and Britain at the beginning of the twentieth century. Ludendorff's peace of Brest-Litovsk had opened large parts of the former tsarist empire to German penetration before it disappeared behind the reality of Germany's own collapse of 1918. Hitler cast these earlier inspirations into a much more revolutionary mold, one shaped by his racist theories and the utter ruthlessness characteristic of all his designs.

The relevance of *Mein Kampf* as a source of Hitler's true foreign policy intentions was questioned by political leaders during the 1930s and again by historians during the 1960s. This appears plausible at least for the early 1930s because the early phase of Hitler's foreign policy in action seemed to bear little resemblance to the aims proclaimed in 1924. In foreign as in domestic policy, however, Hitler could be the most flexible of tacticians in order to achieve a fixed strategic goal. The foreign political reality of the 1930s was far too complex and Hitler's original position far too weak to permit an immediate execution of the aims of 1924. It was only after the Versailles system had been completely dismantled that Hitler possessed both the power and the opportunity to act on the strength of his convictions.

1933–1935: YEARS OF PREPARATION

The early phase of Hitler's foreign policy was characterized by prudence and a show of moderation which stood in sharp contrast to the belligerent rhetoric of the years before 1933. The foreign policy restraint of the early period was occasioned by his awareness of Germany's unchanged military weakness and the concern lest France and her Eastern allies, principally Poland and Czechoslovakia, be provoked into armed action against Germany. Hitler's "peace speech" of May 17, 1933, which evoked a favorable echo in Western capitals, sounded a note of reasonableness and moderation. Hitler expressed his "earnest desire" to avoid war and called a new war "infinite madness," which would only benefit communism.

His true intentions Hitler had revealed in secret conference with his army commanders on February 3, 1933. Once Germany had rearmed, Hitler told the generals, she should employ her new might for the conquest of "living space" in the east and its ruthless "Germanization." At the same time, Hitler took the first steps in 1933 and 1934 towards withdrawal from the multilateral foreign policy approach of Stresemann, and began to replace it with a policy of bilateralism. Stresemann's multilateralism, exemplified by Locarno and League membership, had been designed to gain security for disarmed Germany and to provide the means of treaty revision with the consent of the Allies. By contrast, Hitler used bilateral agreements in order to break up and neutralize the multilateral security arrangements of the 1920s in preparation for his intended victim's isolation.

The German withdrawal from the League as well as from the Geneva Disarmament Conference in October 1933 was the first example of the new policy. As an excuse, Hitler used the French demand that a four-year trial period should precede the implementation of the principle of German equality in armaments, which had previously been conceded at the disarmament conference. The German-Polish nonaggression pact concluded at Hitler's initiative in January 1934 was the second example of the new bilateral approach. Hitler induced Poland into concluding the 1934 pact by playing on the common theme of anticommunism and by appealing to the vanity of the Polish government, which interpreted Hitler's overtures as German recognition of Poland as an equal partner. As Hitler was to confess to his generals on the eve of the German invasion of Poland in 1939, the 1934 nonaggression pact had served the sole purpose of "stalling for time." In one stroke, and at no cost to himself, Hitler had weakened the French alliance system in eastern Europe and neutralized Poland in the coming annexation of Austria and dismemberment of Czechoslovakia.

Hitler's first reach into Austria, on the other hand, in conjunction with the Austrian Nazi uprising of July 25, 1934, ended in failure, and it temporarily threw Nazi Germany into isolation.

The Murder of Dollfuss

Democracy in Austria had perished at about the same time that Hitler came to power in Germany, following the parliamentary deadlock of Austria's two major parties, the Socialists and the Christian Social party. In February 1934 the last spark of Austrian democracy was extinguished as the opposition Socialists were wiped out by Chancellor Engelbert Dollfuss in a brief but bloody civil war. Though antisocialist, corporate, and authoritarian, the Dollfuss dictatorship was also strongly antinazi because of its close ties to the Catholic church. Before 1933, France had jealously guarded Austrian independence, as the customs union episode of 1931 had dramatically shown. As Dollfuss patterned his own regime closely after the Italian fascist corporate model, Mussolini's Italy took the place of France as the protector of Austrian independece. The Rome Protocols of March 17, 1934, signed by Austria, Hungary, and Italy and pledging the coordination of their foreign policies, signaled Mussolini's resolve to keep Hitler out of the Danube basin. Hitler's attempt to secure Mussolini's cooperation concerning German policy in Austria failed during their first face-to-face meeting in Venice on June 14, 1934.

Encouraged by its comrades in neighboring Bavaria, the outlawed Austrian Nazi party nevertheless, staged an uprising in Vienna on July 25, 1934, in the course of which Chancellor Dollfuss was brutally murdered. Mussolini responded by moving his troops up to the Brenner frontier with the implied threat of moving into Austria from the south should Hitler move into Austria from the west. Coming on the heels of Hitler's "blood purge" of June 30, 1934 against Roehm and the SA in Germany, the murder of Chancellor Dollfuss by Austrian Nazis isolated Hitler morally and politically in Europe. Hitler pulled back and disclaimed any part in the Austrian Nazi *putsch* of July 1934. In September 1934, Britain, France and Italy reaffirmed their common interest in Austrian independence. In March 1935 Hitler announced a policy of nonintervention and nonannexation regarding Austria. The appointment of Franz von Papen, previously Hitler's Conservative vice-chancellor, as the new ambassador to Austria, was meant as a gesture of reassurance. By the end of 1934, Hitler's foreign policy record seemed dismal enough. In less than two years after coming to power, he apeared to have destroyed the goodwill and friendly relations which the Weimar Republic had developed with the former World War I enemies during the preceding decade. Europe was sufficiently alarmed at the behavior of the new German government to take fresh steps toward the containment of its potential threat.

THE PROMISE OF COLLECTIVE SECURITY

Emboldened by the outcome of the Saar plebiscite of January 13, 1935, in which 90 percent of the voters opted for a reunion of the Saar with Germany, Hitler announced plans for creating an air force on March 10, 1935. On March 16 he announced the reintroduction of the draft with the stated objective of creating a peacetime army of thirty-six divisions, or 550,000 men. Both actions clearly violated the Treaty of Versailles. Hitler justified them on the grounds that the other powers had failed to reduce the level of their armaments and that the USSR, in particular, was expanding its armaments. Hitler's announcement of German rearmament provided the impetus for a realignment of powers, both in Western and Eastern Europe, which at first appeared to result in a new system of effective collective security against Nazi Germany.

Franco-Russian Rapproachement

France and Soviet Russia, the two powers chiefly concerned by German aggression, had taken the first steps towards containment even before Hitler's appointment to the chancellorship. As a precaution against a Hitler government, France and Soviet Russia had buried their own bitter strife of the 1920s and taken the first step towards rapproachement with the conclusion of a nonaggression pact on November 29, 1932. Soviet Russia, for its part, had also discontinued its long-term secret military cooperation with the German army, which dated back to the 1922 Rapallo treaty, by closing down German training facilities in the USSR in 1932. A major obstacle to effective Soviet-French cooperation was the security of the small states of eastern Europe, wedged between Soviet Russia and Germany. The French military alliances of the 1920s had been as much designed to protect eastern Europe against Soviet aggression as to uphold eastern European independence in the face of German attack. The Eastern European states, for their part, were equally afraid of their powerful neighbors to the west and east. France attempted to solve the dilemma of Eastern European security by urging the USSR to conclude nonaggression pacts with the small nations of the region. The Soviets complied by signing nonaggression pacts with Finland, Latvia, Estonia, and Poland in 1932. The Soviet-Lithuanian nonaggression pact, dating back to 1926, was renewed in 1931. A similar pact with Rumania failed because Bessarabia, annexed by Rumania in 1918, was still claimed as Soviet territory by the USSR.

In 1933, French foreign minister Joseph Paul-Boncour initiated negotiations towards a full-blown mutual defense pact with the Soviet Union. The project was vigorously pursued by Paul-Boncour's successor, Louis Barthou, prior to his assassination in October 1934. Both men had to overcome serious objections in their own country because the Soviet-French tensions of the 1920s were still remembered, and because there was evidence that communism was gaining strength in France during the 1930s. Barthou dismissed the ideological scruples and objections of the French by reminding them of the crucial role the Franco-Russian alliance of 1894 played in French survival during the first weeks of World War I.

Russia Joins the League

National security outweighed all other considerations on the Soviet side as well. Hitler's rise to power came at a particularly sensitive moment for the Soviet Union, because it coincided with the manifestation of Japanese imperialism in the Manchurian crisis. The Japanese annexation of Manchuria had made Japan the next-door neighbor of the USSR in Asia and it raised the possibility of a two-front war, one against Hitler's Germany in Europe, the other against Japan in the Far East. To the relief of the Soviet leadership, Japan had not followed up the conquest of Manchuria with aggression against Soviet Far Eastern territory. But Japan had, at the same time, turned down a Soviet proposal for a Far Eastern nonaggression pact in December 1932. In attempting to contain Japan, the Soviets could neither enlist the League, of which they were not yet a member, nor seek the aid of the United States, with which they had as yet no official diplomatic relations. So 1933 was from the Soviet standpoint as well a "junction of two eras." While Stalin's industrial revolution under the five-year plans was in full swing, the USSR needed, in Stalin's words, a "scheme of pacts" with the other status quo powers in order to discourage Nazi aggression in Europe and Japanese attack in the Far East.

The instruments which the Soviet Union had previously used to weaken and undermine the West, such as the Communist International, were now employed in the service of the new Soviet foreign policy line of collective security. Institutions such as the League of Nations, formerly denounced as tools of Western imperialism, now, in turn, were integrated into the policy of containment. Accordingly, Comintern propaganda of the mid-1930s shifted from its old message of class war and the inevitability of a Soviet-Western clash to the new theme of the "popular front," i.e., the alliance of Communist and democratic parties. In September 1934, the USSR joined the League of Nations. The Stalin constitution of 1936, in addition to serving certain purposes of Soviet domestic policy, was also part of the overall Soviet propaganda effort of depicting the USSR as a quasi-liberal power.

The Soviet effort of establishing collective security in the Far East was not successful. Although the new Roosevelt administration did establish full diplomatic relations with the Soviets in 1933, it declined a Soviet proposal for a Far Eastern regional nonaggression pact which would also include China and Japan. Without such a pact, the Soviets quietly abandoned their remaining interests in Japanese-controlled Manchuria by selling their share in the Chinese Eastern Railway to Manchukuo. Otherwise, the Comintern advised the Chinese Communists to shift tactics from opposing the Chinese Nationalist government of Chiang Kai-shek to supporting it in the common struggle against Japan. In August 1937, the USSR concluded a pact of nonaggression and friendship with the government of Chiang Kai-shek. The resumption of the Sino-Japanese conflict in 1937, which preoccupied Japan in China, served the Soviet purpose in the Far East well.

In Europe, France and the Soviet Union had meanwhile concluded a pact of mutual assistance on May 2, 1935, which was followed on May 16 by a Soviet-Czechoslovak pack of mutual assistance. The effectiveness of the USSR-CSR mutual assistance pact was conditional on France giving support to the country attacked.

Western Security

Just as common fear of Nazi Germany had helped remove past differences in Soviet-French relations between 1933 and 1935, a similar process of subordination of old national rivalries among the principal Western European powers seemed to be in the offing in 1934–1935 as a prelude to Western collective security against Nazi Germany. In the 1930s, Italian-French relations had been disturbed by rival policies in Yugoslavia and naval rivalry in the Mediterranean. Italy's chief grievance had been colonial, however, and the armed clash between Italian and Ethiopian forces at Wal Wal on December 5, 1934 signalled the imminence of a full-blown Italian attack on Ethiopia. In January 1935, French foreign minister Pierre Laval gave Mussolini a "free hand" in Ethiopia—without, however, defining the meaning of that phrase in the Ethiopian context. Mussolini reciprocated by promising joint Italian-French action on behalf of Austrian independence in the case of renewed German threats, in the Rome Accords of January 7, 1935.

The coordination of French and British policy seemed indicated by the Anglo-French "joint declaration" of February 3, 1935. Among other things, the "joint declaration" tried to contain Hitler through a multilateral air pact which was to have included Britain, France, Italy, Belgium, and Germany, and under which the signatories agreed to assist one another against unprovoked aerial aggression. When Hitler responded with the announcement of German rearmament on land and in the air, Italy, France and Britain issued the Stresa Declaration of April 11, 1935, which expressed the opposition of the three western powers "by all practicable means" to unilateral treaty repudiation. It reaffirmed western interest in Austrian independence as well as Italy's and Britain's obligations to France under the 1925 Locarno treaty.

THE FAILURE OF COLLECTIVE SECURITY

The Stresa Declaration of April 1935 and the signing of the Soviet-French pact of mutual assistance of May 1935 suggested the outlines of a successful policy of containment, provided the participating powers upheld national security as their most vital goal and provided further that they did not allow that goal to be compromised by the resurfacing of old rivalries or mutual suspicions. Sadly this proved not to be the case. Within a year-and-a-half of Stresa, Western and Soviet policy was thrown into disarray by old rivalries and mutual suspicions which shattered the common front and provided a watchful Hitler with openings and opportunities for further unilateral treaty revisions at minimum risk.

The 1935 Naval Agreement

The first breach in the Stresa front came with the signing of the Anglo-German naval accord of June 18, 1935, permitting the expansion of the German navy up to

35 percent of the British and allowing parity in German submarines under certain circumstances. As an agreement initiated by Hitler, the naval accord was a clever trap which damaged Allied unity under the guise of German deference to British special interests. By withholding German naval rearmament from his announcements of rearmament in March 1935, and by limiting German naval rearmament to a level acceptable to Britain, Hitler signaled his respect for Britain's position over and above that of the other powers. The impression of "reasonableness" on Hitler's part was reinforced by the memory of the Anglo-German naval race before 1914. When Britain had attempted to place limits on German naval armaments with the Haldane mission of 1912, Emperor William II had demanded the unacceptable price of an unconditional British neutrality pledge. In 1935, Hitler asked nothing in return for the limitation of German naval strength to 35 percent of Britain's.

In truth, the 1935 naval agreement was a strategic illusion and a serious political mistake. It was an illusion, because by 1935 the foremost strategic weapon in the arsenal of the Great Powers was not naval power, as before 1914, but air power. Concerning air power, Hitler had accepted no limitations and signed no agreements. Politically, the naval agreement was a bilateral breach in the multilateral collective security system of the Western powers. If Britain made exceptions to the principle of concerted action when it suited her national interest, what was to prevent others from doing likewise under similar circumstances?

The Ethiopian War

The second breach in the Stresa front developed out of the Ethiopian war, which began with Mussolini's invasion on October 3, 1935. When Mussolini joined the Stresa front in April 1935, he clearly believed that Italian support for the upholding of the European status quo, and of Austrian independence in particular, was being exchanged for tacit western consent to an Italian conquest of Ethiopia. The French, to whom Ethiopia mattered little, would have been only too happy to put their own policy in Europe on such a basis. Britain hoped to forestall an open Italian military attack by devising a number of compromise schemes which would have paved the way for a quiet eventual takeover of Ethiopia by Italy, but which would have avoided involvement of the League, of which Ethiopia was a member. War against Ethiopia was a very popular cause in the Italy of the mid-1930s, however, and not merely among Facists. Italy remembered the humiliating defeat her army had suffered at the hands of the natives at Adowa in 1896, when she had tried to take Ethiopia the first time. The war of 1935 was the revenge for Adowa. When Ethiopia appealed to the League in 1935, and Britain mobilized the League against Italy, Italy interpreted Britain's action not as the upholding of a principle but as an attempt to exclude Italian colonial power from East Africa.

The trouble with British policy in the Ethiopian crisis of 1935–1936 was that it ended up between two chairs. To the applause of the smaller League members, but also of the USSR, which had recently joined, Britain at first activated the League machinery of sanctions against Italy under article 16 of the covenant. The strong policy of the British government reflected the strong support which the League and the whole concept underlying it enjoyed among the British public at the time. But the British public of 1935 was also strongly pacifist and neither it, nor its government, possessed enough conviction to carry the issue to the point of war with Italy. For that reason,

Britain refrained from taking the very measures which would have been the most effective in actually stopping Mussolini: the inclusion of an oil embargo among League sanctions and the closing of the Suez Canal to Italian troop transports on their way to Ethiopia. In February 1936 Britain did propose the inclusion of an oil embargo into the sanctions policy, if other members of the League followed suit. But that, in truth, was only a face-saving gesture and a smokescreen to cover an ignominious retreat from the policy of tough opposition of October 1935. The policy of partial sanctions did not frighten Mussolini sufficiently to prevent him from completing his conquest of Ethiopia by May 1936. The League stood discredited as an instrument of collective security. Those who had believed in its power and usefulness, especially the small members and the USSR, took a second look. Mussolini was both angry and contemptuous of the western powers, and of Britain in particular, because they had obstructed his policy but had not had the courage and the will to see their policy through. For Mussolini, the Ethiopian War marked the decisive turning point away from a policy of collective security with the western powers and towards alignment with Nazi Germany. It was only now that fascist ideology began to acquire significance as a factor in Italian foreign policy, as Mussolini compared the "virile" fascist dictatorships with the "moribund" and "enfeebled" democracies.

Remilitarization of the Rhineland

Observing the change in British attitude, Hitler had seized the opportunity to remilitarize the Rhineland on March 7, 1936, against the advice of practically all the German military. The remilitarization of the Rhineland was not only a breach of the Treaty of Versailles, but also the Locarno treaty, which Germany had proposed and signed of her own free will. Hitler was unconcerned about the Treaty of Versailles, but he justified his violation of the Locarno treaty on the grounds that France had already deprived it of its "inner meaning" by ratifying the mutual assistance pact with Soviet Russia in February 1936.

What enabled Hilter to remilitarize the Rhineland with impunity was not a flimsy legal excuse but the lack of a coordinated policy among the democracies, as well as the sense of insecurity which characterized French policy from the mid-1930s onward. Hitler had correctly gauged the British reaction, which viewed Hitler's act almost as an internal German affair, since Hitler had only moved into "his own backyard" and had not threatened any foreign country with aggression. Hitler was equally correct in assuming that without British backing and approval, France, which better appreciated the significance of the action, would do nothing. The real meaning of the Rhineland remilitarization did not consist in the return of German troops and fortifications to positions along the French border, but in the unhinging of the whole French alliance system in eastern Europe. If Hitler applied political or military pressure to the small states of eastern Europe after 1936, France would be less likely to aid them because to do so her army would first have to fight its way through the new Rhineland defenses. That was, in fact, to be the pattern of French behavior during Hitler's dismantling of the eastern state system in 1938 and 1939. France did not move in defense of Austrian independence in March 1938, and she was only too glad to use the Munich conference of September 1938 as an excuse for not having to fight on behalf of Czechoslovak integrity. When Hitler invaded Poland in September 1939, the French army made no serious attempt to come to Poland's rescue.

Soviet Relations Deteriorate

Concurrent with the undermining of collective security in the West, the French-Soviet effort at collective security began to suffer irreparable harm between 1935 and 1938. The milestones along the road of Soviet-Western disillusionment were: the failures of British policy in the Ethiopian crisis; the failure of France to put military teeth into the 1935 mutual assistance pact; the resurgence of Western suspicion concerning Soviet intentions in the Spanish Civil War; the damage to Soviet military credibility as a result of the Stalin purge in 1937; and the loss of Soviet faith in Western sincerity as a result of the 1938 Munich conference dealing with Czechoslovakia.

The Franco-Soviet mutual assistance pact remained a pact without teeth because no intimate French-Soviet military collaboration developed comparable to that between the *Reichswehr* and the Red Army of the 1920s. The military effectiveness of the alliance also remained doubtful because no practical steps were undertaken for Red Army troop passage across the states of eastern Europe, principally Poland, in case of war with Germany.

The Spanish Civil War

In the Spanish Civil War, both sides, the Republican under Prime Minister José Giral and the Nationalist under General Francisco Franco, appealed for outside aid from the start. Nazi Germany and Fascist Italy responded to Franco's plea. Hitler provided Franco with a fleet of German transport aircraft and later a full-blown combat air contingent, the "Condor Legion." Mussolini provided both air power and ground forces, although the impact of the latter on the war was minor. In the battle of Guadalajara of March 1937, Mussolinis' *Corpo di Truppe Volontarie* suffered a humiliating defeat.

The principal foreign arms supplier to the Republican government became the Soviet Union, a fact which worried Western governments, Britain in particular. The Soviets not only sent tanks, airplanes, and military advisers such as Malinovsky, Konev, and Rokossovsky, all future marshals of the Soviet Union, but also staffs of NKVD men who eliminated opponents of the Republican government by the methods familiar from the Stalinist purge of the mid-1930s. The Popular Front government of France under Leon Blum would have liked to increase its support to the Republican government, but it was discouraged from doing so by Britain. To the British government, the alternative outcomes of the Spanish Civil War no longer appeared in simple terms of democracy or fascism, but rather as a choice between a Spanish Republic, possibly Communist-dominated, or a Nationalist Spain not necessarily tied to Hitler.

Hitler used the Spanish Civil War was a war game and a diversion. It allowed him to test his latest weapons in the air and to remind the western democracies that the destruction of Spanish civilian targets by German air power, such as occurred at Guernica, could be repeated in their own countries. Hitler also used the Spanish Civil War as a diversion. Western fears that the civil war would accidentally blow up into a general European war kept their attention riveted on Spain, and meanwhile Hitler dismantled eastern Europe. Hitler therefore carefully rationed out his armed support to Franco, never giving him enough air power to enable him to win quickly, but to assure Franco's survival never withholding aid in times of military crisis.

The Stalin purge of the mid-1930s weakened Soviet-Western collective security because its brutal methods belied Soviet efforts to advertise the USSR as a quasi-liberal state, and because among its victims were such first-rate officers as Marshal Tuk-hashevsky, the Soviet chief of staff. The French military, who had had great respect for Soviet military power in 1935, had a far lower estimate of their military capabilities by 1937–1938, after the Stalin purge had killed off thousands of officers.

APPEASEMENT AND AGGRESSION

The political and strategic situation in Europe had changed decisively by 1937–1938 compared to what it had been only four years earlier, and the change was not conducive to stability. The Ethiopian war had moved Mussolini away from involvement in western collective security and into partnership with Nazi Germany, this shift symbolized by the Rome-Berlin Axis of November 1, 1936. The Axis, though not yet a military alliance, clearly made such an alliance possible. By the time Mussolini signed a full-fledged military alliance with Hitler in the "Pact of Steel" of May 1939, the relationship between Germany and Italy had been reversed. At the outset Hitler had been the suitor, heaping flattery and praise upon the Duce. With German armaments approaching respectable proportions in 1937, the leadership and initiative within the Axis began to pass to Hitler. Mussolini's state visit to Germany in September 1937, during which Hitler impressed his guest with the might of German armaments and industry, may be regarded as the turning point in Nazi-Fascist relations. In November 1937, Mussolini joined the German-Japanese anti-Comintern pact which Hitler had concluded the previous year as a basis for possible future action against the Soviet Union. In December 1937, Mussolini also formally left the League. Fascist Italy, the chief obstacle to Hitler's annexation of Austria in 1934, was, after the changes of 1936–1937, not likely to pose similar problems in the future.

The last remaining threat to Hitler's aggression was the prospect of a strong united front of France and Britain. The record of Anglo-French policy since 1933 suggested that even this obstacle was not likely to be serious, because in every major crisis and on every major issue since 1933 the two countries had failed to achieve effective policy coordination. This had been the case in the German rearmament issue, the remilitarization of the Rhineland, the Ethiopian war, and the Spanish Civil War. By the late 1930s, leadership in the Western concert had decidedly passed to Britain, as France had repeatedly refrained from unilateral action for fear of displeasing her. Prime Minister Stanley Baldwin had allowed matters to drift during the crucial years between 1935 and 1937, in part because of his disinterest in foreign affairs, in part because of his failure to appreciate Nazi foreign policy goals. Baldwin, in Churchill's words, knew little of Europe and disliked what he did know. Baldwin's successor, Neville Chamberlain, by contrast, thought he understood the challenge of his time and hoped to meet it with a policy of appeasement. Appeasement, to Chamberlain, was both a choice and a necessity. It was a choice because Chamberlain, despite his personal dislike of Hitler, considered Nazi Germany a possible partner in the reoganization of Europe. The alternative of seeking cooperation with Soviet Russia, which the French had at least attempted, seemed, on the other hand, quite unthinkable to Chamberlain. The Conservatives had never forgotten the trouble the Communist International had given them in India and elsewhere during the 1920s, and they regarded the open display of Stalinist terror in the 1930s as final proof of Soviet Russia's incompatibility with western civilization. By comparison, Hitler's unleashing of mob terror against German Jews during Crystal Night, November 9, 1938 was, to the appeasers, more an embarrassment than an outrage. In seeking a partnership with Hitler, Chamberlain erred in judging Hitler's goals as compatible with the preservation of a European state system. Like others before him, Chamberlain believed that the revision of the Treaty of Versailles was the end, not just the beginning, of Hitler's true foreign policy program.

British Armaments

Appeasement also appeared as a necessity because of the unprepared state of British armaments. In 1938, London found itself in the awkward position of having fewer fighter aircraft for its defense than at the height of German air raids in the First World War. In the 1930s, Britain expected German air raids, should they come, to be carried out by hundreds of planes at a time, rather than by the small formations customary in 1917, which rarely exceeded forty aircraft. The fear of German air raids was heightened by the assumption that Hitler would not hesitate to use poison gas against civilian targets. Anyone viewing the newsreels of the Spanish Civil War could see what even conventional air raids could do to crowded population centers. In 1938, Britain's early-warning radar system, based on Watson Watts' 1935 invention, covered only the Thames estuary.

By September 1939 radar covered the approaches from the Orkneys to the Isle of Wight. British monthly aircraft production, which averaged 240 for 1938, rose sharply to an average of 660 in 1939. But Britain's military leaders did not expect completion of British rearmament until 1942, and they wished to postpone the outbreak of war with Germany, should it become unavoidable, until that date. Britain's chief of the air staff Sir Edward Ellington stated categorically in 1937 that there could not be war until 1942.

The Annexation of Austria

Hitler knew his advantage in armaments was only temporary. This fact dictated the timing of his aggressions, which he first announced in secret session to the three service chiefs, Goering, Fritsch and Admiral Raeder, along with War Minister Blomberg and Foreign Minister Neurath, on November 5, 1937. Recorded in the so-called Hossbach minutes, Hitler's statements mentioned Austria and Czechoslovakia as his likely first annexations, with a target date possibly as early as 1938 but not later than 1943–1945. The annexation of Austria followed on March 14, 1938, after Mussolini had responded favorably to Hitler's plea for Italian acquiescence. Afterwards, the Western powers refrained even from the ritual of condemning Hitler's treaty violation. The only power which still responded with concern was the Soviet Union, Foreign Minister Litvinov warning the Western powers that "tomorrow may be too late."

The ease with which the annexation had been accomplished emboldened Hitler to turn on neighboring Czechoslovakia even before he had had time to digest Austria. The aim of Hitler's policy in Czechoslovakia was, from the beginning, the total dismemberment of the country, not merely the "liberation" of the more than 3 million Sudeten-Germans from Czechoslovak rule. As a native Austrian, who had grown to manhood in the pre-1914 Austro-Hungarian Empire, Hitler had a special dislike for the Czechs, who had been the most vociferous critics of German-Austrian hegemony in the western part of the Dual Monarchy. Czechoslovakia was also a thorn in Hitler's flank, however, being the military ally of both France and Soviet Russia, and possessing a first-rate army and air force to boot.

Munich, 1938

As Hitler heated up his propaganda campaign against Czechoslovakia in the spring of 1938, the British appeasers were chiefly concerned with assisting in the transfer of the Sudeten provinces to Germany in order to avoid the outbreak of war by either accident or miscalculation. Such was the purpose of Neville Chamberlain's two trips to Germany, first to Berchtesgaden on September 15, and next to Godesberg on September 22, 1938. By 1938, Hitler was no longer content with a threat of force, but was eager to actually use the military power he possessed. He did not want the western powers to assist in the peaceful transfer of the Sudeten provinces, but instead to look the other way while he crushed the whole state of Czechoslovakia in a military operation, for which October 1, 1938 had been selected as the target date. When Hitler therefore declared himself no longer satisfied with Chamberlain's offer at Godesberg on September 22, war between a reluctant Britain and a determined Hitler seemed imminent, until Mussolini's last-minute intervention saved the peace. Acting on Mussolini's initiative, the four-power conference at Munich of September 29, 1938, attended by Britain's Chamberlain, Prime Minister Daladier of France, Hitler, and Mussolini, arranged for the peaceful transfer of the Sudeten provinces by Octrober 1, 1938. All of Europe, including Hitler's Germany, was immensely relieved at the peaceful outcome of the Czechoslovak crisis. Neville Chamberlain was welcomed as a peacemaker not only by the cheering throngs of London but by enthusiastic crowds in the streets of Munich. Hitler showed no signs of joy, because the Munich settlement was, for him, a half-victory at best.

The complete dismemberment of Czechoslovakia was, in fact, only a question of time. Poland and Hungary, Czechoslovakia's hostile neighbors to the east and south, had followed up the Munich conference with annexations of their own. On October 3, 1938 Poland seized the disputed Teschen area and, on November 2, 1938, Hungary's territorial claims against Czechoslovakia were partially fulfilled in the Vienna Award. Slovakia, egged on by Nazi Germany, declared its independence on March 14, 1939. Under threats of a German air raid against Prague, President Hacha asked for the establishment of a German "protectorate" over the Czech portions of the former Czechoslovak republic. On March 15, 1939 Hitler occupied Prague.

The final destruction of Czechoslovakia produced a reaction in Hitler that was in sharp contrast to the reaction of the appeasers. The seizure of Prague and the lack of any official Western response undermined whatever realistic sense of proportion Hitler may have had. By 1939 the unbroken pattern of success had so stimulated his arrogance that he deemed himself above the ordinary rules and hazards which ordinary leaders had always had to obey and guard against in devising foreign strategy. This resulted from both Hitler's flaw of character and lack of formal education.

The occupation of Prague had less exchausted the patience of the appeasers than that of the British public generally. Influential shapers of public opinion, such as the London *Times,* put increasing pressure on Neville Chamberlain to get tough with Hitler. When Hitler opened his next offensive against Poland on March 21, 1939 with demands for the return of Danzig and the building of an extraterritorial road and railroad across the Polish Corridor, Poland rejected the demands, and on March 31, 1939 Chamberlain issued a unilateral guarantee to Poland which was accepted at once. Having ordered the German army on April 3, 1939 to be secretly prepared for an invasion of Poland on September 1, 1939, Hitler had by the end of the month denounced both the 1934 German-Polish nonaggression pact and the Anglo-German Naval Accord of 1935.

Preparations for War

Between April and August 1939, the British government hastily put together what it hoped would be a credible policy of deterrence and collective security in Eastern Europe in order to make up for the omissions and errors of the previous twenty years. Among the measures of deterrence was the introduction of the draft in April 1939, the first such step ever undertaken in peacetime. Of the 200,000 eligible for the draft, only 30,000 were actually inducted by June 1939 and their training was not begun until mid-July.

The only power actually capable of providing effective military backing to the British guarantee to Poland was the Soviet Union. For the Soviets, however, the Munich conference of 1938 had been the most telling demonstration of western insincerity, because at Munich, the Soviet Union was among the uninvited. Between the Munich conference of September 1938 and early 1939 the Soviets, convinced that Hitler would strike before the year was out, sent signals to Berlin that they were prepared for an accommodation. Among the signals was the discontinuation of Soviet press attacks on Nazi Germany, the disengagement of the Soviet Union from the Spanish Civil War, hints in Stalin's speech before the eighteenth Soviet party congress of March 1939, and the replacement on March 3, 1939 of Maxim Litvinov, previously identified with the policy of collective security, by Molotov as Soviet foreign minister. Hitler did not respond to these Soviet overtures until May 1939, but from May onward it was he who tried to speed the pace of the Nazi-Soviet rapprochement in oder to secure a German-Soviet nonaggression pact before the invasion of Poland, originally scheduled for August 26, 1939.

The Soviet motive for the nonaggression pact, signed in Moscow on August 23, 1939, was to deflect German aggression away from the USSR and towards Poland and the Western powers. The longer the war between Nazi Germany and the West, the more time Soviet Russia would have to strengthen her own defenses. Hitler concluded the nonaggression pact because he hoped it might deter Britain from actually implementing its guarantee to Poland. Should Britain persist in doing so, the Nazi-Soviet pact would make the risk of war with the democracies acceptable. Although the news of the Nazi-Soviet pact exploded like a bombshell in the Western capitals, the pact had rather the opposite effect on Chamberlain from that which Hitler had intended. Hitler failed to appreciate that by signing with Soviet Russia he had destroyed the appeasers' last illusion that Nazi Germany, for all its other unpleasant features, was still valuable as bulwark against Soviet communism.

Conscious of German charges after the First World War that Britain's foreign secretary Sir Edward Grey had misled imperial Germany during the July crisis of 1914 with assurances that "Britain's hands were free," Neville Chamberlain reminded Hitler in his last communication of August 1939 that Britain's hands were not "free" in the present crisis and that Britain would stand by her commitment to Poland, regardless of the Stalin-Hitler pact. For a few days Hitler may have taken Chamberlain's warning seriously, because he postponed the scheduled invasion of Poland from August 26 to September 1, 1939. In the end, his contempt for the "men of Munich," whom he privately characterized as "little worms," prevailed.

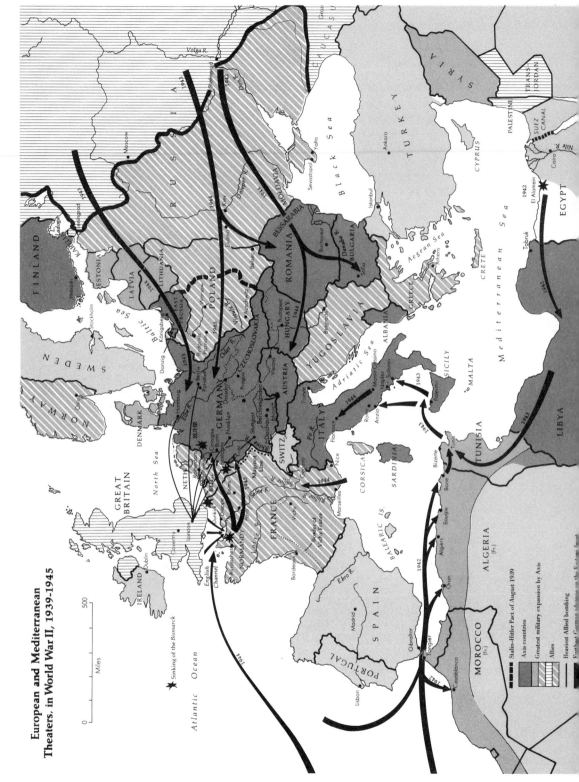

**European and Mediterranean
Theaters, in World War II, 1939–1945**

★ Sinking of the Bismarck

Stalin-Hitler Pact of August 1939

Axis countries

Greatest military expansion by Axis

Allies

Heaviest Allied bombing

Farthest German advance on the Eastern front

0   500
Miles

148

10

The Second World War

World War Two brought to a climax the crisis of twentieth-century European civilization which had become apparent in the First World War and which the interwar period had failed to resolve.

Initially, the Second World War seemed merely a repetition of the conflict of 1914, prompted by similar circumstances—the failure of the European states to devise an effective concert, the threat of German hegemony, the clash of two opposing ideologies—and waged for similar objectives.

But very quickly the Second World War developed into a battle on a grander scale, a deeper human challenge. The First World War, though it may have been the first total war in modern European history, had not been a war of totalitarian societies. World War Two was such a war, and it added a dimension to human suffering that would have appeared unimaginable to the generation of 1914.

Many of the questions raised by the First World War, but not answered in a definitive and conclusive manner, were to be answered in the course of World War Two or soon after: the future of European colonial power; the role of the United States in European and world affairs; the meaning of the Russian Revolution for the West and for the colonial peoples of the world; and the European claim to preeminence in the military, scientific and cultural realms.

The weapons of mass destuction introduced in the First World War had revealed to a startling degree the grim and suicidal alternatives of the industrial age. The scientific-technological breakthroughs of World War Two in the areas of nuclear fission and rocket propulsion raised the dilemma of self-destruction and intelligent progress to a new and awesome level of urgency. Never before had man's mastery over matter been propelled so far so fast as in World War Two, and never before had the moral challenge to use the newly gained knowledge for contructive ends been greater.

THE EUROPEAN PHASE, 1939 TO 1941

The Stalin-Hitler pact had been the key to the outbreak of hostilities on September 1, 1939, and it remained the key to the events which unfolded during the first or European phase of the war, between 1939 and 1941.

The Nazi-Soviet pact freed Hitler from the threat of a Soviet-Western coalition, but it did not free him from a two-front war. The reality of a two-front war in September 1939 was merely concealed by the speed of the Polish collapse and the lack of any serious military undertaking by the Western powers during the opening stage of the war.

Before the outbreak of hostilities, France had promised Poland an offensive on land and in the air on the sixteenth day after Polish mobilization. In fact, France launched only a local attack in the Saar region, which had little more than reconnaissance value.

Between September 1 and 17, the period of active Polish resistance, Hitler in fact committed the bulk of his army and virtually his entire air force to the Polish campaign, while leaving his western borders with France and hence the Ruhr armaments center essentially unprotected. Germany's western fortifications, much publicized in Goebbels' propaganda as the impregnable "Westwall," contained large uncompleted stretches. In 1939, it could not have repulsed a determined attack.

Poland Falls

Unaided by the West, Poland had little chance of sustained resistance. What little chance she had, she lessened by poor strategy. Rather than build strong positions behind natural lines of defense, the rivers San, Narev and Vistula, Marshal Ryz Smigly planned to launch an all-out offensive for the taking of East Prussia. Lacking in modern armaments, especially air power and tanks, Poland's infantry divisions, together with their horse cavalry, were quickly overwhelmed by an enemy with superior arms and a revolutionary war doctrine. During the Polish campaign, the Germans first applied the new doctrine of armored warfare conceived by British military historian Lidell Hart after World War I and later developed further by Germany's tank expert Heinz Guderian.

By September 19, 1939 the mass of the Polish army had been trapped and destroyed in a series of battles between the rivers Bzura and Vistula. On September 16, 1939 the Polish government had departed for Rumania. Warsaw, the Polish capital, surrendered after heavy aerial bombardment on September 28.

Resisting strong German pressure for an early intervention, the Soviets delayed their own invasion of eastern Poland until September 17, by which point effective Polish resistance had collapsed. A new German-Soviet "border and friendship agreement" of September 28 moved the German-Soviet demarcation line in Poland further east and closer to the old "Curzon line" of 1920.

For Poland, September 17, 1939 marked the beginning of her worst suffering at the hands of her neighbors to east and west. The methods of German and Soviet rule in partitioned Poland were remarkable for their similarity. Both aimed at the elimination of Polish elites in the professions, education, and the church, in order to deprive the Polish people of potential resistance leaders. The deportation and extermination policy of Nazi governor Hans Frank had its mirror image in that of Ivan Serov, Soviet police chief of the Ukraine, in eastern Poland. Under German-Soviet rule, one out of every five people living in Poland perished.

THE WESTERN STALEMATE:
THE BALTIC-SCANDINAVIAN INTERLUDE

Western strategy after the fall of Poland remained what it had been during the campaign. Neither in the air nor on the ground would there be any offensive action against Germany. After initial fears of German air raids on London and Paris proved unfounded, British and French civilian evacuees returned to their capitals and an unofficial truce in the air war materialized. British air raids even against purely military targets were suspended after a force of twenty-four Vickers Wellington bombers lost ten aircraft in a daylight raid on Wilhelmshaven on December 18, 1939.

Allied ground strategy proceeded from the assumption that time was on the Allied side. The Maginot line would shield France from any frontal assault. Should Germany attempt to outflank the Maginot line by invading Belgium, the German army would be met and destroyed in open field battle by the mass of French and British mobile forces in Belgium. Eventual victory over Hitler's Germany would be achieved through economic strangulation, or possibly as a result of internal revolution, sparked by hunger, just as in the Germany of November 1918.

Meanwhile, France was anxiously searching for new theaters of war, preferably in areas far removed from her own borders, in order to divert German strength. After Poland had lost its usefulness as a second front, France tried unsuccessfully to expand the French-British-Turkish mutual assistance pact of September 28, 1939 into an anti-Hitler Balkan alliance.

The Sitting War

Western inaction along the western front during the fall and winter months of 1939–1940 was matched by silence on the German side. After the fall of Poland Hitler would have preferred to launch an immediate attack on the West in October 1939, but was pursuaded by his generals to postpone the German offensive until the spring of 1940. After analyzing the Polish campaign, the German generals thought their army in need of further training and in need of more armaments, especially tanks. The lightning war (*blitzkrieg*) in Poland thus gave way to what the Western press quickly dubbed the "phony war" or "sitting war" (*sitzkrieg*) in the West, in which propaganda broadcast, rather than bullets, filled the air between the trench lines. The only real action was confined to the high seas. In October 1939 a German submarine penetrated the defenses of the British naval base at Scapa Flow and sank the battleship *Royal Oak*. In December 1939, Britain forced the scuttling of the German pocket battleship *Graf Spee* off Montevideo, after the *Graf Spee* had destroyed fifty thousand tons of British merchant shipping.

The Invasion of Finland

The autumn quiet of the European war was suddenly shattered on November 30, 1939 by the Soviet attack on Finland, which dramatically revealed the wider implications of the Stalin-Hitler pact for Eastern Europe.

After the Soviet occupation of eastern Poland, Soviet expansion in the Baltic had continued with the imposition of "mutual assistance" pacts on Latvia, Estonia and Lithuania between September 29 and October 11, 1939, which granted the Soviets air and naval bases. In due course, the Finnish government was asked to surrender the islands of Suursaari and Koivisto and to move the Finnish border near Leningrad westward by fifty miles.

Finland, though unaware that it had been assigned to the Soviet sphere of influence under the secret portion of the Stalin-Hitler pact, had mobilized its army on September 1, 1939, the day of Hitler's invasion of Poland. Rejecting all Soviet demands for Finnish territory in October 1939, Finland was not unprepared for the Soviet attack when it came on November 30.

Finnish resistance lasted much longer than it was expected to. With its small army of 300,000 men and an airforce of 150 obsolete aircraft, the Finns not only prevented a Soviet breakthrough between November 1939 and January 1940, but even managed to destroy several Soviet divisions in the winter battles of Suomossalmi. The Finnish cause enjoyed much sympathy in both the Axis nations and the Western democracies and Finland appealed for help from both. Hitler denied Finland any aid out of fear of jeopardizing the recently concluded Nazi-Soviet entente. The western powers, by contrast, were eager to help, all the more so as they hoped to combine a relief action on behalf of Finland with a military occupation of Scandinavia. An Allied seizure of Scandinavia would outflank Hitler from the north and cut off Germany's vital supply of Swedish iron ore from the Kiruna mines. On February 5, 1940 the Allied Supreme War Council decided to combine a relief action for Finland with a seizure of Norway and Sweden.

Had the Allied decision of February 5, 1940 been implemented in its full scope, it would very likely have resulted in a clash between the Western powers and the Soviet Union with serious long-term consequences for the entire Second World War. In fact, the Soviet Union and Finland decided to end their conflict quickly before an Allied intervention could materialize, the former fearing a head-on clash with the Western powers, the latter anxious to avoid becoming a Great Power battlefield. The peace of Moscow of March 13, 1940 cost Finland dearly, but it left the integrity and independence of Finland intact. Finland had to surrender South Karelia, the Karelian isthmus, Viborg, the Salla district, and a portion of the Fisher peninsula. Hanko and several islands in the Finnish Gulf were leased to Russia, but Petsamo with its nickel mines remained in Finnish possession.

Scandinavian Operations

After the peace of Moscow, the Allies scaled down their Scandinavian plans to a mining operation in Norwegian coastal waters in order to disrupt German iron ore traffic from Scandinavia. An Allied invasion force was kept in readiness, should the Germans retaliate with landings of their own in Norway.

Germany, for its part, had decided to seize Norway and Denmark as early as December 1939, quite independently of Allied plans. German and Allied plans for the occupation of Norway reached the point of implementation at virtually the same moment, although neither side had advance information of the other's intention.

When Germany launched *Weserübung,* the invasion of Denmark and Norway, on April 9, 1940, Denmark offered no resistance, buy Norway resisted to the limits of her capacity, sinking among others the heavy cruiser *Blücher.*

The Anglo-French response to the German invasion of Norway was poorly organized and badly executed. In theory, an amphibious operation on such a scale ought not to have been possible for Germany to execute, given the vastly superior naval power of Britain. Germany's quick seizure of Norwegian air fields, however, neutralized superior British sea power and doomed Britain's own landings near Trondheim. Although provided with reindeer saddles, the British expedition force had no skis and had to rely on tourist maps for orientation. At Narvik, in the far north, British naval superiority did have an effect, forcing German mountain troops to retreat on May 28 and causing the loss of the better part of the German destroyer flotilla. The ominous turn of events in the Battle of France, which had begun on May 10, 1940, compelled the Allies to evacuate Norway before long.

The Norwegian disaster claimed the political life of Prime Minister Neville Chamberlain, much as the Gallipoli debacle had driven Herbert Asquith from office in 1916. Leopold Amery, a fellow Conservative, hurled Oliver Cromwell's devastating words at Chamberlain in the House of Commons: "You have sat too long here for any good you have been doing. Depart, I say, and let us have done with you. In the name of God, go!"

Winston Churchill, who succeeded Chamberlain as prime minister on May 10, 1940, was never fully reconciled to the loss of Norway and repeatedly planned to retake it. The demands of other theaters did not allow these plans to be carried out. The Norwegian campaign yielded Germany important naval and air bases, from which Hitler was later able to intercept Allied convoys en route to Soviet Russia. It also netted the Germans the Vemork plant, at the time the only plant in Europe capable of producing heavy water, an item of significance in nuclear weapons research. Before long, British intelligence arranged for the destruction of the Vemork plant by Norwegian Resistance forces.

THE BATTLE OF FRANCE

When the long-awaited German offensive against France began on May 10, 1940, the opposing forces were roughly matched in the number of infantry and armored forces, though the Germans had a significant advantage in air power. In bombers, the Germans enjoyed an eight-to-one lead over France, in fighter aircraft four-to-one. The Royal Air Force (RAF) could not be wholly counted as a factor in Allied air power, because, as events were soon to show, a large portion of British fighter strength was withheld from action in France.

The Allies had also learned the date of the German invasion from members of Germany's own counterintelligence service, which was opposed to Hitler. Britain, it was only learned some thirty years after World War II, had the further invaluable advantage of having broken the German code by acquiring the German code machine "enigma." "Ultra," as the British deciphering of the German code was secretly called, gave Britain, and later also the United States, what was possibly the most potent weapon of the entire war against Germany. The full impact of "ultra" on the course of the war made itself felt only in the later stages, in North Africa in 1942–1943, Italy 1943, D-Day and Normandy in 1944, and the final battles on the western front in 1944–1945, when deciphering the German code had become routine. In 1940, surprises were still possible, and the principal surprise of the German spring offensive derived from successful strategic deception.

Operation Scythe

Based on a plan developed by Erich Manstein, among Hitler's most gifted strategists, the German invasion of Holland and Belgium was meant to draw the bulk of Allied mobile forces, the British Expeditionary Force (BEF) and the French First and Seventh armies, as far north as possible. This having been accomplished, the German main attack, supported by all ten German armored divisions, broke out of the heavily wooded Ardennes region, deep on the Allied flank. Between May 10 and May 20, Manstein's "Operation Scythe" cut through in a straight line from the breakout point at Sedan to the French channel coast at Abbeville, with all of Belgium and parts of northern France a sealed-off pocket.

Dunkirk

Dutch resistance had collapsed on May 14, 1940 after a devastating German air attack against Rotterdam. Belgium surrendered on May 28, 1940 after the principal Belgian fortress Eben Emael on the Albert canal had been stormed by German paratroopers, who landed on top of the fortifications. By late May Churchill feared the loss of the entire BEF and braced himself for an announcement of Britain's worst military defeat. Instead, 338,226 men, chiefly from Lord Gort's BEF, were miraculously saved from the beaches of Dunkirk on June 5, 1940, by ships and boats of all sizes. Six of the forty-one participating British destroyers were sunk by German air action.

The Fall of France

With the British army driven off the continent and the better part of the French armies destroyed, the German attack across the rivers Aisne and Somme signaled the opening of the second phase of the Battle of France on June 5, 1940. General Maxime Weygand, who had replaced General Maurice Gamelin as French supreme commander on May 19, 1940, hoped that a full commitment of Britain's RAF fighter squadrons might yet turn the tide of the battle. He also expressed vague hopes in an American intervention.

Churchill withheld the British fighter squadrons, because he considered the Battle of France already lost and because the RAF fighters were, next to the Royal Navy, Britain's sole defense against a German invasion. French hopes for an American Intervention were, in 1940, utterly illusory, given the degree of American military unpreparedness and the isolationist restraints on U.S. foreign policy. France was alone. In her final agony, Mussolini declared war on her as well as on Britain, on June 10, 1940. Militarily, the Italian intervention was inconsequential. However, Mussolini needed, in his own words, "a few thousand dead," in order to make good his claims on Corsica and French North Africa.

The French lines on the Somme had meanwhile broken and Paris fell on June 14, 1940. In the final stage, the Maginot line, previously bypassed in the north, was pierced in several places by frontal assault. The resignation of French premier Paul Reynaud and his replacement by the eight-five year old Marshal Pétain on June 16, 1940 signalled the imminent surrender of France.

Churchill would have liked to see France keep on fighting from French North Africa, if need be, much as he himself was soon to pledge a continuation of the war from the British Dominions, even if Hitler occupied the British Isles. Towards that end, he took up the suggestion of Jean Monnet, a man destined to play a leading role in European integration after World War II, for the constitutional merger of the French and British empires, the joint empires to have common citizenship and a common fleet.

Pétain and Weygand, for their part, took Britain's ultimate defeat for granted. No other course seemed likely to those who had regarded the French army the finest in the world before the Battle of France and who had seen that same army defeated in a campaign of forty-three days. Not all French officers shared Pétain's defeatist attitude. Charles de Gaulle, who had led French armored forces with distinction and who had served as undersecretary of state for war under Reynaud, did not consider the war lost after the fall of France. When Pétain surrendered, he tried to form a government in exile in order to carry on the struggle from London. The response of the French public, the armed forces, and the French colonies was disappointing at first. Only in Chad, the Cameroons, and French Equatorial Africa did de Gaulle gain a foothold. A Gaullist attack on Dakar was repulsed by forces loyal to Pétain on September 23, 1940 as were other such attacks on Syria and Lebanon.

Pétain asked for and received an armistice on June 22, 1940, the terms of which the French military regarded as harsh but not dishonorable. Under the terms, Germany would occupy three-fifths of metropolitan France, including Paris and the Atlantic coast. In the unoccupied southern part, soon to be called *Vichy France* after the improvised capital of Vichy, Pétain was permitted to maintain an army of 100,000, a figure exactly equal to that conceded the *Reichswehr* under the Versailles treaty. The French fleet was to be demobilized and kept in French bases for the balance of the war. Germany promised not to use the French fleet during the war nor to claim it in a final peace settlement. To the surprise of the French, the Germans did not ask for any overseas air or naval bases in any of the French colonies or possessions. This serious omission betrayed the hasty drafting of the terms and the continental limitations of German strategic thinking. Significantly, French North Africa was to provide the base for the U.S. entry into the European war in 1942–1943.

The armistice ceremony of June 22, 1940 was conducted by the Germans at Compiègne in the railroad coach in which the armistice of November 11, 1918 had been signed. Hitler put in a brief personal appearance to relish what was destined to be the high point of his power.

THE BATTLE OF BRITAIN

The defeat of France produced contrasting effects on Germany and Britain. In Germany, the fall of France was generally interpreted as the end of the war, with a resulting relaxation of psychological attitudes and economic efforts. German rejoicing was enhanced by the low German casualties. With 30,000 men killed, the whole French campaign of 1940 had cost Germany less in lives than many a single battle had claimed in the First World War in a week.

In Britain, the fall of France was regarded as the beginning of the real war after the failures of Norway and the near-disaster of Dunkirk. Accordingly, Birtain mobilized her war economy much more drastically in 1940 then did Nazi Germany through, for example, the drafting of female labor. In Hitler's Germany, similar measures were not adopted until fall 1944.

For Hitler, the most desirable course of events after June 22, 1940 would have been a negotiated peace with Britain, with Britain recognizing German continental hegemony and Germany recognizing British supremacy at sea and in the colonial world. Such a peace would also have given Hitler a free hand against Soviet Russia.

Churchill's Resolve

It was not likely that Churchill would make peace with Nazi Germany. Churchill had demonstrated his resolve by attacking the French fleet at Oran and Mers-el-Kebir on July 3, 1940, killing over 1200 French sailors and wounding another 351. Churchill's action was as much intended to impress President Roosevelt with Britain's unbroken fighting spirit as it reflected Churchill's total lack of trust in Hitler's word not to seize the French fleet at an opportune moment. In his speech of July 14, 1940 Churchill spoke of defending "every village, every town and every city." He would rather, Churchill said, see London "laid in ruins and ashes," than have it "tamely and abjectly enslaved."

There was hope in Berlin, however, that Churchill could be ousted and that a "peace party" might replace Churchill with someone more agreeable to a political solution on German terms. The Germans counted former prime minister Lloyd George as being among the "peace party" and, for a short while, even Lord Halifax, Churchill's foreign minister. It was for their benefit that Hitler issued his "last appeal to reason" in his Reichstag speech of July 19, 1940.

The negative reply of Lord Halifax of July 22, 1940, as well as President Roosevelt's renomination at the Democratic Convention in Chicago on July 19, 1940, strengthened Churchill's own position at home and dispelled any German illusions about an early peace with Britain. Hitler was forced to seek a military solution to his war with Britain. Before the fall of France the German army had not even made a hypothetical study of the invasion of England. An order for the preparation of a German invasion was not issued until July 16, 1940, but it too betrayed uncertainty and lack of confidence on Hitler's part. D-Day for an amphibious operation, code-named *Sea Lion* was finally fixed for September 21, 1940, with German landings projected along the south coast of England between Folkestone and Selsey Bill.

Throughout the planning of Operation Sea Lion the German hope remained that the air assault alone, preliminary to the actual invasion, would suffice to bring Britain to the negotiating table.

That air power alone can decide the outcome of a modern war was a thesis propagated by the advocates of strategic bombing such as Giulio Douhet in Italy and Hugh Trenchard, the British chief of the air staff, since the 1920s and early 1930s. The indiscriminate bombing of cities, according to Douhet, would be enough to crush an opponent's "moral and material resistance."

The assignment which Hitler gave his air force in the summer of 1940 was a multiple assignment and a large part of it was strategic. Within the very short space of time between August 13, 1940, the beginning of the air assualt, and September 21, the scheduled landing date, the German air force was to: destroy the British industrial infrastructure and communications; destroy British fighter defenses; and retain enough strength of its own to give effective ground support to the amphibious landings. At a later stage of the war, the combined air forces of Britain and the United States were to pursue identical objectives in their assault on Germany. For this they were given better than two years' time and they were equipped with true strategic bombers, the long-range, heavily armed, four-engined *Lancasters* of the RAF and the American B-17 *Flying Fortresses* and B-24 *Liberators*.

The German air force of 1940, by contrast, was not a strategic air force. When Hitler rearmed in the air in the mid-1930s, considerations of cost largely determined the nature of his air force as a tactical one, built and designed for battlefield support of infantry and tanks. German bombers were twin-engined medium-range aircraft with small bomb loads and inadequate defensive armament against the mass fighter attacks which they encountered during the Battle of Britain. The failure to provide adequate defensive armament partly derived from the experience of the Spanish Civil War as well. The high speed of German bombers had made them relatively immune to fighter attack in Spain in 1936 and 1937. This no longer held true in 1940 when the German bombers came under attack from RAF *Spitfire* and *Hurricane* fighters. Germany's own standard fighter of 1940, the Messerschmitt BF 109, was an easy match for the British *Spitfire* and, because of its fuel-injected Daimler-Benz engine it was in some ways superior. But its effectiveness as a bomber escort remained severely limited, because of its extremely short range.

Britain's Defensive Victory

The German air force began its assault on Britain with a significant numerical advantage of approximately 1,200 bombers and 1,000 fighters as against some 700 fighters of RAF Fighter Command under Air Marshal Sir Hugh Dowding. By September 1940 German losses had become so prohibitive, with some thousand planes shot down, that German air force chief Hermann Goering discontinued daylight raids. Having achieved none of the objectives of his air offensive, Hitler postponed Operation Sea Lion indefinitely on September 17, 1940. On October 12, Sea Lion was called off entirely for the year and postponed until spring 1941. British losses too had been severe, however, with nearly seven hundred planes lost, roughly the total RAF fighter strength when the battle began. Britain's defensive victory in the air was significantly aided by radar, a British invention which detected German bomber streams and directed RAF fighters where they were needed most. The Battle of Britain was also materially affected by British advance knowledge of German target selection, thanks to "ultra."

Before Hitler transferred 60 percent of his air power eastward in May 1941 preparatory to his invasion of Soviet Russia, Britain had yet to endure sustained night bombing throughout the fall and winter of 1940–1941. London was the hardest hit with seventy-six night raids. Coventry was attacked during the night of November 14, 1940, and 554 civilians were killed. Altogether, Germany dropped 67,000 tons of bombs on Britain during the Blitz, killing an estimated 40,000 civilians. The German aim of causing a collapse of civilian morale and of forcing Churchill from office was not accomplished.

RAF retaliatory night raids were still limited in 1940–1941, with only 15,000 tons of bombs dropped on German cities. It would be another two years before Churchill could make good his threat of 1941 of "meting out to the Germans the measure and more than the measure that they have meted out to us." Before the end of the war, RAF bomber command would drop 900,000 tons of bombs on Germany, in addition to the 600,000 tons dropped by the U.S. Air Force. Allied air raids would cause 500,000 German civilian deaths, sometimes as many as 30,000 in a single night.

THE AUTUMN STALEMATE OF 1940

While Hitler was searching vainly for ways of ending his conflict with Britain, the fall of France produced global repercussions suggesting an expansion of the war. Japan, which had benefitted from World War I by inheriting a poriton of the German Pacific empire, intended to reap even larger benefits from the weakness of the European democracies in the Second World War. After the fall of France and Holland, Japan pressured Thailand into signing a "mutual assistance" pact and forced Vichy France into granting military bases in French Indo-China. On July 25, 1940 the United States responded with an embargo of oil and scrap-iron exports to Japan.

American Support

Concurrent with the deterioration of Japanese-American relations, Churchill pleaded for greater American support for Britain. An American military mission to Britain under Major General D. C. Emmons, U.S. Army Air Corps, and Major General George V. Strong, assistant chief of army staff, concluded as early as autumn 1940 that an American military intervention in Europe was essential to Hitler's eventual defeat. Both officers were agreed that of the two probable future opponents, Germany and Japan, the former, being the more dangerous, must be defeated first. The "Germany first" concept was to become basic to Anglo-American strategy for the rest of the Second World War.

In 1940, actual U.S. arms aid to Britain was still slow and selective. During the summer Britain received American small arms and ammunition, a welcome relief after the BEF had left all its weapons on the beaches of Dunkirk. On September 3, 1940 Churchill obtained fifty U.S. destroyers, for which he had asked in June in anticipation of Italy's entry into the war. In return the U.S. got long-term leases of British bases from Newfoundland to the Bahamas. Churchill also pledged that the British fleet would sail for ports either in the United States or the Empire, should Hitler conquer England. The fifty U.S. destroyers, though of 1918 vintage, were vital to British sea defense because of high destroyer losses during the campaign in Norway and the Dunkirk evacuation. Also, the Royal Navy had not built a single new destroyer since 1938.

American arms aid to Britain had to be paid for, and when Churchill warned Roosevelt in December 1940 that Britain would soon have her dollar reserves exhausted, the president pushed the Lend-Lease Act through Congress on March 11, 1941. With an initial appropriation of $1.3 billion, the act empowered the president to "sell, transfer title to, exchange, lease, lend or otherwise dispose of" U.S. armaments.

The Tripartite Pact

As Britain was seeking ways and means of overcoming her isolation in the fall of 1940, Hitler was trying to increase it. In order to be effective, Hitler's policy required a coherent strategy embracing the United States, the Soviet Union, and continental Europe.

The Germans had been alarmed by the destroyers-for-bases deal of September 3, 1940, not only because it signaled a general shift from neutrality to intervention, but because of the suspicion that among the British bases leased to the United States, some might be in the Mediterranean. An American naval presence in Europe would increase the likelihood of a U.S. entry into the war, something Hitler was eager to avoid in 1940. The Tripartite Pact of September 27, 1940 between Germany, Italy and Japan was intended to discourage such a development. Apart from defining the respective spheres of influence of the three signatories, the pact pledged mutual assistance with all political, economic and military means if any one of the three should be attacked by a power not presently involved in the war in Europe or the Sino-Japanese conflict. The USSR was assured that the pact was not directed against it.

The Tripartite Pact was thought to be an effective deterrent, because it threatened the United States with a two-ocean war, should the United States intervene either in Europe or Asia. In 1940, U.S. naval power in the Pacific alone was outranked by Japan in every category of warship, especially aircraft carriers.

The Tripartite Pact was also intended as a platform for rallying continental Europe under German leadership, in order to deny Britain new allies among the nations of Europe. It was not difficult for Hitler to press the small nations of eastern Europe, Slovakia, Hungary, Bulgaria and Rumania, into Tripartite Pact membership. The difficulty arose when Germany also tried to integrate Vichy France, Franco's Spain and even Fascist Italy into its design. Hitler met personally with Franco at Hendaye in Spain on October 23, 1940, and with Pétain at Montoire, France, the following day. Apart from asking both Spain and France to join the pact, Hitler also requested Spanish support for a German assault on Gibraltar, planned for early 1941.

Both Franco and Pétain received Hitler politely, and both declined to join the pact. Both wished Hitler well with his unfinished war with Britain, but neither was prepared to accept the risks which an open association with Germany entailed. Pétain was prepared to follow a policy of passive collaboration with Nazi Germany, but his overall aim was for France, to "contract out" of the war and to save France further bloodshed. Pierre Laval, Pétain's deputy, was forced out of his position on December 13, 1940, when suspected by Pétain of moving too closely to a policy of open support for Germany. Franco excused himself on the grounds of the extensive damage caused by the Spanish Civil War, and he conditioned active Spanish support for Germany on the delivery of huge amounts of weapons, food and strategic materials which he knew to be beyond Germany's ability to provide.

Mussolini Attacks Greece

The failures of Hendaye and Montoire were followed by Mussolini's surprise attack on Greece on October 28, 1940, which upset Hitler's political concept yet further. Mussolini's motivation for attacking Greece was to gain glory and territory at little cost after being left out completely from any division of spoils in the Compiègne armistice of June 22, 1940. The Italian invasion of Greece was also intended to demonstrate the Italian, as distinct from the German, interests in the "parallel war" Mussolini intended to wage in the Mediterranean.

To Mussolini's intense embarrassment, the attack on Greece quickly bogged down, and the Italian troops, which had invaded Greek territory from their base in Albania were themselves threatened with a Greek invasion of Albania.

Mussoline's defeat in Greece provided Britain with an opportunity to reenter continental Europe, and it gravely complicated Hitler's relationship with the Soviet Union. The Greeks asked for British help and Churchill promptly gave it. By late October 1940 British naval and air units were installed on the island of Crete, which Churchill hoped to turn into a "Mediterranean Scapa Flow." The presence of RAF bombers on Crete meant that the Rumanian oil fields and refineries at Ploesti, Hitler's only source of petroleum other than Soviet oil, had come within Britain's striking range. Mussolini's Greek debacle thus spurred the Germans into drawing up a Greek invasion plan of their own for early 1941. In preparation for the German attack on Greece, Hitler dispatched troops to Rumania and Bulgaria, a move followed by the Soviet Union with mounting suspicion.

Nazi-Soviet Relations

Between the autumn of 1939 and the autumn of 1940, Nazi-Soviet relations had in fact undergone a significant change for reasons other than the Balkan developments. During what may be called the honeymoon in Nazi-Soviet relations, the Soviets had supplied Hitler with strategic materials, especially oil, a fact which largely nullified the British blockade. Soviet propaganda denounced the western war effort as "imperialist" and Molotov hailed the Stalin-Hitler pact as the product of Stalin's "historic foresight." The Germans paid for Soviet raw materials with armaments and military technology and during the Russo-Finnish War of 1939–1940 Hitler denied Finland any support, even of a diplomatic nature. This pleased Stalin sufficiently to prompt his announcement that the war with Finland had sealed Soviet-German friendship "with blood." Likewise, the Soviets had expressed no opposition to the German occupation of Norway in April–May 1940, because it lessened the likelihood of any western intervention in Scandinavia.

The fall of France abruptly changed the climate in Nazi-Soviet relations. Stalin had reason to fear the sudden surge in German power and the possibility of a negotiated peace in the west. A peace treaty between Germany and the western powers would set Hitler free to attack the Soviet Union. At the very least, such a treaty would make it well-nigh impossible for the Soviets to collect the remaining prize of the Stalin-Hitler pact. Stalin therefore proceeded to collect this prize in great haste. On June 15, 1940, the USSR occupied all three Baltic states and formally annexed them on August 1, 1940. The political leaders of the Baltic states—Ulmanis, Paets, and Voldemares—together with 150,000 of their fellow citizens, vanished into the interior of the Soviet Union. On June 23, 1940 the Soviet government demanded that Rumania hand over Bessarabia and northern Bukovina, the latter not having been assigned as a Soviet sphere of influence in the secret protocol of the Stalin-Hitler pact.

Hitler, however, began to extend his influence into parts of eastern Europe which, like Finland, had been expressly assigned as Soviet spheres or, as in the case of the Balkans, which the Soviets clearly regarded as being within their own security zone. In September 1940 Germany concluded a troop transit agreement with Finland, permitting German troops to pass in and out of Norway via Finland. In the Balkans, German troops appeared in growing numbers, both as a guarantee against a complete Soviet dismemberment of Rumania and a step towards the planned invasion of Greece. In the final months of 1940, Rumania increasingly became the central issue in the developing Nazi-Soviet confrontation. When Hungary and Bulgaria, Rumania's neighbors to the north and south, raised revisionist demands against Rumania with Soviet encouragement, Hitler countered with a joint German-Italian diplomatic intervention. In the "Vienna Award" of August 30, 1940 Hungary obtained northern Transylvania, while Bulgaria received the southern Dobruja in the Treaty of Craiova of September 7, 1940. Germany issued a territorial guarantee for Rumania after the border changes of August and September 1940. The Soviets openly ignored the German guarantee by seizing a number of Rumanian islands in the Black Sea delta of the Danube in November 1940.

Hitler had been following the Soviet moves in eastern Europe since mid-June with mounting anger, referring to Stalin as "blackmailer." In mid-July 1940 he spoke to his generals about invading Soviet-Russia in the current year, a proposal successfully opposed on the grounds of insufficient time. Hitler's inability to terminate the war with Britain quickly increased his fear of a Soviet surprise attack at a later stage of the war. A German conquest of Soviet Russia would, on the other hand, deprive Britain of her last potential ally in Europe and it would confer on Nazi Germany all the strategic resources for a war of indefinite length against Britain and even the United States. The destruction of Soviet Russia would also be consistent with the aims expressed in *Mein Kampf*, which Hitler had had to compromise in 1939 for tactical reasons. Before issuing final orders on what he was later to call "the most difficult decision" of his life, Hitler invited Soviet foreign minister Molotov to come to Berlin on November 12, 1940, in order to discuss possible Soviet membership in the Tripartite Pact of September 1940. The invitation may have served the purpose of finally confirming what Hitler regarded as Soviety duplicity. It may also have been Hitler's last attempt to give himself an option of extending the August 1939 arrangement with the Soviets, at least until Britain had been beaten.

As a price for Soviet membership in the Tripartite Pact of 1940 Hitler and Nazi foreign minister Ribbentrop offered Molotov generous portions of the British Empire which they did not, in fact, control. India, Iran, and the Persian Gulf were to be within the Soviet sphere of influence. Though not rejecting the vague German promises, Molotov returned persistently to the concrete issues which had disturbed Nazi-Soviet relations in eastern Europe over the past several months: Finland, Rumania, and Bulgaria. German troops were to be removed from Finland forthwith; Bulgaria would sign a mutual assistance pact with Soviet Russia; Soviet air and naval bases would be established in the Dardanelles; and Japan would be asked to relinquish her coal and oil concessions in northern Sakhalin. The Soviet government expressed the further desire of discussing the Jutland straits, connecting the Baltic and the North Sea.

Hitler was angered not only by the scope of Soviet demands, but by their fearless presentation by the pedantic Molotov, who showed himself not overly impressed by Hitler's victories of 1940. No foreign heads had talked to Hitler in similar fashion since the early 1930s, when Hitler had had to beat a hasty retreat following the Austrian Nazi debacle of 1934.

Hitler's reply to the Soviet demands of November 1940 was the secret directive of December 18, 1940 for the invasion of Soviet Russia, code-named *Barbarossa*. By the end of 1940, Hitler's political strategy for the isolation of Britain lay in shambles. The decision to invade Soviet Russia staked not only the survival of Germany, but also the fate of much of the rest of Europe, on the single card of military power.

MEDITERRANEAN DEVELOPMENTS: THE BALKAN INTERLUDE, SEPTEMBER 1940 TO MAY 1941

Concurrent with Hitler's failed political design for Europe was the emergence, in the fall of 1940, of the Mediterranean as a major theater of war. Britain scored her first great victories in ground operations there.

After the fall of France, it was fortunate for Britain that her enemies, Italy and Germany, failed to develop a coherent and offensive strategy in the Mediterranean, because British strength would have been inadequate to protect the entire region, from Aden in the Middle East to Gibraltar in the west. The stakes in the Mediterranean were high, however, and included imperial communications to India, Malaya and Singapore, and Middle Eastern oil, which fueled Britain's war economy and armed forces.

The German navy appreciated the strategic importance of the Mediterranean, and Hitler's naval chief Admiral Erich Raeder thought the "fall of Gibraltar" a more serious blow to British power than even the "fall of London." German plans for an airborne assault on Gibraltar had to be abandoned, however, in view of Franco's uncooperative attitude. Once Hitler had decided on the invasion of Soviet Russia, he lost the little interest he had had in the Mediterranean. To the extent that a German Mediterranean strategy materialized at all, beginning with the landings of the small Afrika Korps under Erwin Rommel in Tripoli in February 1941 and the German invasion of Greece and Yugoslavia in April 1941, its purpose was defensive, and corrective of Mussolini's mistakes and defeats. As a theater requiring a strategy of closely coordinated land, air, and sea operations, the Mediterranean never held Hitler's full attention.

Without major German support, Italy was, for Britain, an enemy of manageable proportions. Her navy, though large on paper, suffered from fuel shortages, and a lack of shipborne radar and aircraft carriers. The Italian army in North Africa, though much larger than the British army in Egypt, was lacking in motor transport and modern armor, two deficiencies of particular seriousness in a theater where mobility and tanks were decisive. Also, Mussolini failed to exploit Britain's weakness in the summer of 1940 by seizing the island of Malta, directly astride Italy's line of communications and supply to North Africa. Malta continued to disrupt Axis supply lines for the entire duration of the North African war and thus significantly contributed to the eventual Axis defeat in North Africa in 1943.

The Italian Invasion of Egypt

Mussolini did not attack until September 1940, when Marshal Graziani invaded Egypt with an army of 300,000 men. After taking Sidi Barrani on September 18, Graziani stopped to await fresh supplies. After this inconclusive beginning, Mussolini scattered his forces still further by invading Greece in October 1940.

On December 9, 1940 Sir Archibald Wavell, British commander in chief in the

Middle East, counterattacked and drove Graziani quickly out of Egypt. By early February 1941 British forces, numbering 25,000, had captured 113,000 Italian prisoners and driven westward all the way to the border of Tripolitania. During an otherwise cheerless winter, the desert victory in North Africa was cheerful news in London. Between January and May 1941 Mussolini also lost his empire in East Africa. Proceeding from Aden and Kenya, the British seized Eritrea together with its seaport of Massawa in January 1941. By May 1941 all of Ethiopia was in British hands.

Italian defeats on land were accompanied by naval disasters. On November 11, 1940 British torpedo bombers from the carrier *Illustrious* attacked the naval base at Taranto and put half the Italian battle fleet out of commission. The Taranto raid, being carried out in shallow waters, served as a model for the Japanese attack on Pearl Harbor almost exactly a year later. Italy suffered a further naval defeat in the Cape Matapan engagement on March 29, 1941, which facilitated the upcoming British landings on the Greek mainland.

The Balkans

Anticipating a German attack on Greece, Britain tried to mobilize several Balkan nations into a coalition against Germany. But the mission of Foreign Secretary Anthony Eden and General Sir John G. Dill of early 1941 failed because the small Balkan powers were afraid of German air power. Between November 1940 and March 1941, Hungary, Rumania, Slovakia, Bulgaria, and Yugoslavia had all been pressed into membership in the Tripartite Pact. A military coup of General Simovic of March 27, 1941 ousted the Yugoslav government, which had just signed the pact, but the coup came too late to be of any help to Greece.

When Yugoslavia signed a treaty of friendship and nonaggression with Soviet Russia on April 5, 1941, Hitler responded by including Yugoslavia in the German invasion of Greece the following day.

Yugoslav resistance collapsed by April 17, 1941 under the three-pronged German attack from Austria, Hungary and Bulgaria. Yugoslavia's collapse rendered the position of Greece also hopeless. The German invasion of Greece confronted Churchill with a difficult choice. British troop strength in the Mediterranean was insufficient to both continue the successful offensive in North Africa against Italy, and provide meaningful support to the Greek army. British field commanders in North Africa would have preferred to concentrate on the defeat of Italy in North Africa. Churchill decided otherwise, and dispatched an army of 57,000 to aid in the defense of Greece. The result was that Greece was overrun by the Germans regardless and that the British victory in the desert could not be fully exploited. Athens fell on April 27, 1941. Forty-seven thousand British troops were evacuated from the Greek mainland, some of them being used in the upcoming battle of Crete.

The Battle of Crete

The Battle of Crete of May 1941 quickly turned into one of the costliest and most bitterly fought of the entire Mediterranean war. The Germans had little choice but to take Crete, because without it the purpose of the Greek campaign, the eviction of British power from southeastern Europe, would have remained unfulfilled. Lacking in any sea power of their own, the Germans had to make the assault on Crete an airborne and parachute invasion. General Bernard Freyberg, the commander of the

British 42,000 man garrison on Crete, had precise foreknowledge of the German battle plan thanks to "ultra." Losses among German airborne and paratrooper forces, who were dropped by five hundred transport aircraft, were extremely high, so much so that Hitler forbade similar airborne operations for the rest of the war. The battle was decided by superior air power, however, and just as in the Norweigian campaign of 1940, the Royal Navy sustained heavy losses. British naval forces under Admiral John Cunningham lost six destroyers and three cruisers to German air attack. By June 1, 1941 Britain had pulled out of Crete after evacuating 17,000 of her troops.

Other Developments: Iraq and Egypt

The Greek campaign and the Battle for Crete coincided with other developments in the Mediterranean theater which were directly related to the situation in the Balkans. Emboldened by British reverses, the pro-German government of Iraq under Prime Minister Rashid Ali staged an anti-British uprising in May 1941, appealing for German arms aid. In North Africa, British troop withdrawals undertaken for the sake of Greece enabled Afrika Korps commander General Erwin Rommel to mount an offensive which aimed not only at the reconquest of Libya, but at the conquest of Egypt as well, with the Iraqi seaport of Basra the final goal. The naval situation was complicated by the breakout of a German task force consisting of the Battleship *Bismarck* and her escort, the heavy cruiser *Prinz Eugen,* into the North Atlantic, also in May 1941, forcing Churchill to withdraw naval strength from the Mediterranean in order to hunt down and destroy the German intruders in the Atlantic. After sinking the British battle cruiser *Hood,* the *Bismarck* itself was sunk in the North Atlantic in late May 1941.

While losing Greece and Crete, Britain mastered the crisis in Iraq and Egypt. Hitler gave little more than token support to Rashid Ali's rebellion. By July 1941 Britain was not only in firm control of Iraq, again but had ousted, in conjunction with Gaullist forces, the Vichy administration of Syria as well. In North Africa Rommel, after retaking Libya, invaded Egypt proper without being able to dislodge the British garrison at Tobruk, however. British control over Tobruk denied Rommel a supply port close to his front, forcing Axis supply lines to be extended over three hundred miles back to Benghazi and over a thousand miles to Tripoli.

In November 1941 General J. C. Auchinleck, who had replaced Wavell as chief of British Middle East command, counterattacked Rommel with the twin objectives of driving Axis forces from Egypt and of lifting the German siege of Tobruk. The climax came with the tank battle of Sidi Rezegh of November 23, 1941, which was turned into a British victory through Auchinleck's personal intervention. Towards the end of 1941 Auchinleck's twin objectives were realized, but the campaign had ended in a draw: the Axis had failed to take Egypt, the British had failed to trap and destroy Rommel. Regrouping in Tripolitania, Rommel planned to resume his attack for the conquest of Egypt in the spring of 1942. In a larger sense, Hitler had missed a major strategic opportunity by failing to fully exploit his gains in the Mediterranean in 1941. Without the tremendous diversion of the Russian campaign, which began on June 22, 1941, Germany might well have succeeded in following up the conquest of the Balkans with a seizure of the oil-rich Middle East at a fraction of the cost which Hitler later paid in his vain effort to reach the Soviet oil in the Caucasus region. Rommel attempted to enlighten Hitler as to the strategic possibilities of the Mediterranean, but he was rarely listened to. Instead, Rommel's Afrika Korp remained undersupplied and had to make do with captured Soviet weapons for its armaments in 1942. A large part of Rommel's motor transport, including his armored command vehicle, was captured British equipment.

THE GERMAN INVASION OF SOVIET RUSSIA

Numerous warnings began to reach the Kremlin during the spring of 1941 about an imminent German attack, some of which provided the exact date of June 22, 1941. The warnings came from British sources which had monitored German troop deployments in the east throughout the winter of 1940–1941, as well as from the Soviet Union's own intelligence sources, including the German Communist agent Richard Sorge, who operated out of Japan. Unlike Stalin, the Soviet military was inclined to take these warnings seriously. Stalin did not believe in a German attack in June 1941 precisely because the most emphatic warnings came from Britain, a nation Stalin suspected of wishing to embroil the Soviet Union in a conflict with Germany for her own ends. Stalin expected that Hitler might conceivably make fresh political demands after the Germans had established full control over the Balkans by May 1941. The Soviets attempted to break the ominous German silence after the Molotov-Hitler meeting of November 1940 through gestures of goodwill and even appeasement. The Soviets fulfilled all their trade obligations to Germany in full and on time, the last trainload of Soviet goods destined for Germany passing across the demarcation line in Poland just hours before the German invasion of June 22, 1941. Soviet gestures of appeasement included the expulsion from Moscow of diplomatic representatives of countries which Nazi Germany had recently conquered, and the official recognition of the pro-Nazi government of Iraq, which the British had ousted. In Moscow, Molotov asked the German ambassador for another meeting with Hitler, in order to learn the causes of Germany's apparent "dissatisfaction." When the German attack came, it found the Soviet Union leaderless during the first crucial days of the invasion, as Stalin had yet to recover from his shock and disbelief at the treachery of his partner Hitler.

"Germany's India"

For Hitler, the war against Soviet Russia was different from all previous German campaigns of the war. The war in the east was, from the beginning, an ideological war which Hitler intended to wage and to win without restraints of morality or international law of any kind. The long-term objective of Hitler's war in the east was the colonization of Russia, consistent with the proclaimed aims of *Mein Kampf,* together with the enslavement, deportation and extermination of the peoples of the Soviet Union. That Russia would be "Germany's India" was an observation Hitler frequently made. It was part of his scheme of preventing the resurrection of an independent Russian state at any future time that he ordered the complete destruction and levelling of both the cities of Lenigrad and Moscow, once they had been taken by German forces. Official Nazi policy towards the soldiers of the Red Army likewise reflected Hitler's personal racial attitudes and hatreds. The so-called commissar order of June 6, 1941 denied captured political commissars of the Red Army the status of prisoners-of-war and decreed their execution. But even ordinary Red Army soldiers were treated with contemptuous indifference, as evidenced by the death from hunger and exposure of 1 million soldiers out of 4 million Red Army prisoners taken by the German army during the first six months of the eastern campaign. In one of his early speeches during the eastern campaign, Hitler referred to the "eastern enemy" as an enemy "not of human beings, but of animals." The indifference and cruelty towards the Slavic peoples of the Soviet Union deprived Hitler of millions of potential allies, especially among the peasants of the Ukraine, who initially welcomed the invading Germans as liberators and who would have been quite prepared to lend active support to the overthrow of the Stalin regime.

In a purely military sense, Hitler approached the Russian campaign with a mixture of fear and contempt, the latter born of Nazi racial delusions. On the one hand, Hitler defined Soviet Russia as a mass of passive Slavs dominated by a Bolshevik elite. All that was necessary for the defeat of Soviet Russia, Hitler observed, was "to cut off the Jewish head," to "kick in the door," and the structure of the USSR would come "crashing down." On the other hand, Hitler had a sufficiently good grasp of the meaning of Stalin's industrialization of the 1930s to appreciate the productive capabilities of the Soviet armaments industry. When informed by General Heinz Guderian, Germany's tank expert, of Soviet tank output after the attack on Soviet Russia had begun, Hitler admitted privately that had he possessed such information before 1941 he "would not have started this war."

Soviet Armaments

The military potential of Soviet Russia was indeed the great enigma of 1941, in part because Soviet Russia had shielded its military secrets from foreign scrutiny better than any other Great Power. The available evidence was contradictory. The Red Army had performed poorly during the "winter war" against Finland in 1939–1940, but it had bested the Japanese army in every encounter during the undeclared border war in Manchuria in 1939. Soviet arms supplied to the Republican side in the Spanish Civil War had been noteworthy for their advanced technology, the Soviets introducing a fighter plane with retractable landing gear a year ahead of the Germans. Above all, the Soviets were about to surprise the invading Germans by the sheer mass of their armaments, Soviet tanks alone outnumbering German armor by better than three-to-one. With the T-34 tank, the Soviets possessed the most formidable tank of any country at the time, and its appearance in large numbers on the battlefield in 1941 demoralized German tank crews. The T-34's technology was so advanced that Hitler's own tank designer Ferdinand Porsche urged German industry simply to copy the Soviet design. A veteran of World War II, the T-34 was to fight again against the U.S. Army in the Korean War and was still active as a weapon of communist guerrillas in Angola in the 1970s.

Barbarossa

Hitler had studied Napoleon's Russian campaign of 1812–1813 before invading Soviet Russia in June of 1941, and he attributed Napoleon's defeat to the latter's preoccupation with Moscow at the expense of destroying the fighting power of the Russian army. Hitler's own strategic plan, Barbarossa, was intended to avoid Napoleon's mistake by assigning a lesser priority to the taking of Moscow than to the destruction of Soviet forces in western Russia and the Ukraine.

The army with which Hitler invaded the Soviet Union was not much larger than that which had conquered France in 1940, though German strength was augmented by Finnish, Slovak, Hungarian, and Rumanian troops. The three invading army groups under Leeb in the north, Bock in the center, and Rundstedt in the south were to trap and destroy the Soviet forces opposing them before the onset of winter. Hitler made no provisions for a strategic reserve either in men or equipment and none for winter fighting, should Soviet resistance persist beyond the expected collapse in 1941. Winter clothing was prepared for only one out of every five soldiers, a ratio deemed sufficient for an army of occupation. No margin was left for error, none for weather or the exhaustion that might befall the invader.

The actual clash between the three Germany army groups and the Soviet fronts opposing them under Voroshilov, Timoshenko and Budyenny led to battles as varied as the causes underlying Soviet strength and weakness. Soviet resistance alternated between a determination not previously encountered by Hitler's armies and the wholesale surrender of entire regiments and divisions, especially of Ukrainian units.

By early August 1941 the Red Army had suffered staggering losses, with over 700,000 prisoners being taken in the battles of Byelostok, Smolensk, and Uman alone. German gains had been greatest in the center, where the road to Moscow seemed open after the fall of Smolensk. At the same time, German casualties were on a much grander scale than during the French campaign of 1940, losses eventually exceeding 760,000 men by December 1941. During the first ten months of the Russian campaign German losses in aircraft numbered nearly three thousand, while German armored divisions were reduced to a quarter of their initial strength by the end of 1941. The new war in the east was turning quickly into a gigantic battle of attrition for which the German war economy was not prepared.

The high German casualties and the failure to prevent the mass of Soviet forces from retreating before the German onslaught forced the German leadership into changing the original battle plan. The German army urged Hitler to concentrate on the capture of Moscow because of the psychological impact which it was likely to have on both Soviet and German forces. Hitler rejected the advice of his generals and ordered the taking of the Ukraine instead, because the Ukraine was rich in minerals and because a huge Soviet force was still undefeated in the south.

The resulting battle of the Ukraine brought Hitler yet another major victory, the battle of Kiev alone resulting in the loss of over 600,000 Soviet prisoners in September 1941. Rostov, the gateway to the Caucasus, fell shortly thereafter. After the battle of Kiev, Hitler authorized the attack on Moscow, which began October 2, 1941. In the battles of Bryansk and Vyazma in early October 1941 the better part of six Soviet armies was shattered by Operation Typhoon, the German drive to Moscow. On October 2, 1941, Hitler publicly boasted that the enemy "was broken and will never be in a position to rise again." On October 3, the chief of the German press office announced that the war in Russia was over.

The Battle of Moscow

By October 1941 Hitler had, in fact, seized an area inhabited by 60 million people, nearly a third of the total population of the USSR, which accounted for 65 percent of all Soviet coal, 68 percent of iron ore, 58 percent of steel, 60 percent of aluminum, and 41 percent of railroad tracks. Overall Soviet industrial production had declined in the second half of 1941 by more than half, steel production by two-thirds.

For Moscow, the most critical time came in late November 1941. On November 20, 1941 German advance units entered the suburb of Yakhroma, prompting their commander Hasso van Manteuffel to observe that he could now ride into downtown Moscow if he had a subway token.

Inside Moscow, there had been signs of panic, looting and disorder in October. The Kazan railroad station was packed with eastbound trains carrying Soviet VIPs and their families to safety. Most government agencies had been evacuated to faraway Kuibyshev on the Volga. Stalin had stayed behind in Moscow and restored stability by threatening to shoot "provocateurs" on sight.

Before the turning of the tide in December 1941, the defenses of Moscow were pitifully weak. When General Vlasov, commander of the newly formed Soviet Twentieth Army, asked Stalin during a midnight conference on November 10, 1941 how many tanks he could provide for the immediate defense of the capital, the answer was "fifteen." The Soviet position had improved dramatically by early December, when Marshal Zhukov was able to commit his strategic reserve, drawn from Soviet Far Eastern units, to the battle of Moscow. On December 6, 1941, the day after the German drive on Moscow had ground to a halt, seven Soviet armies under Zhukov's command counterattacked with the aim of not only lifting the siege of Moscow, but of shattering the German front outside Lenigrad as well.

The Soviet winter offensive of 1941–1942 achieved significant results but fell short of the Soviet goal of driving Hitler out of Russia altogether in 1941. In the south, the Soviets recaptured Rostov, the first major city the German army had to abandon in the Second World War. In the center, the German front outside Moscow was pushed back all the way to Smolensk, whence the drive on Moscow had begun. In the north, the Soviets failed to lift the siege of Leningrad, which continued without interruption until January 1944. In the northern sector, the Soviets had also succeeded in encircling over one hundred thousand German troops in the pockets of Kholm and Demyansk. Supplied from the air, the German garrisons held out until relieved in the spring of 1942. The experience of Kholm and Demyansk encouraged Hitler to order the German Sixth Army to hold out after it became entrapped in Stalingrad exactly a year later, with results that were to prove disastrous for the Germans.

In its overall results, the Soviet winter offensive confirmed the defensive victory of the battle of Moscow. At the same time, the Soviet counterattack of 1941 represented an unparalleled example of military recovery after human and material losses which no western army could have survived.

The Soviets survived the initial German onslaught without any Western aid. Britain concluded an agreement with the Soviet Union on July 12, 1941, pledging mutual support and excluding a separate peace with Germany. Iran was jointly occupied by Soviet and British forces on August 15, 1941, in order to secure it as a future supply route to Soviet Russia and to prevent it from falling under German influence. Otherwise, Britain was not in a position to meet urgent Soviet requests for massive deliveries of war planes and tanks in 1941, nor could Churchill fulfil Stalin's demands for the immediate creation of a "second front" in western Europe through landings in France or Norway. Britain launched a carrier-borne raid against Petsamo in Finland on July 30, 1941, the significance of which was little more than symbolic.

The Soviets also turned to the United States with requests for military and industrial aid, valued at $2 billion, as early as July 1941. President Roosevelt responded by dispatching his adviser Harry Hopkins to Moscow the same month to ascertain

Soviet needs. At the Atlantic Conference with Churchill in August 1941, Roosevelt made public his decision to aid Soviet Russia, and in the Moscow Protocol of October 1941 the United States promised arms aid worth $1 billion for the coming nine months. Responding to Stalin's observation that motorization would determine the outcome of the war, Roosevelt promised an additional 10,000 American trucks per month. After the United States entry into the war, the USSR shared in the benefits of Lend-Lease, receiving a total of $11 billion worth of aid, including 13,000 tanks and 400,000 trucks. U.S. Lend-Lease aid greatly augmented the offensive power and mobility of the Red Army during the later stages of the war. The Soviet armies which approached Europe from 1943 onwards were rolling westward on American wheels. In 1941, the Soviet forces had to rely on their own strength for survival.

The eastern campaign of 1941 had also had a significant impact on German morale. The German army knew that it had given its best and that the best had not been good enough to achieve victory. Among knowledgeable German army leaders the conviction grew that a military victory was out of reach and that "Russia could only be defeated with the help of the Russians." This would have required an abandonment of Nazi racist policies and an appeal to the peoples of Russia to assist in the overthrow of the Stalin regime. As events were to show, there was still time and opportunity for such an appeal in 1942. The failure of "Barbarossa" had also created a deep crisis of confidence between Hitler and his generals. Hitler dismissed the leaders of all three army groups in Russia as well as the commander in chief of the army, Field Marshal Brauchitsch, and assumed personal command of the German army in December 1941.

THE JAPANESE ATTACK ON PEARL HARBOR

Although not formally at war, the United States had been committed since 1940 to a policy of containment of German power in Europe and Japanese power in Asia. In the Atlantic, the growing American involvement was indicated by the acquisition of British bases from Newfoundland to the Bahamas, the establishment of U.S. strongholds on Iceland and Greenland, and the adoption of Lend-Lease. The Atlantic Charter of August, 1941 had announced the moral principles of the undeclared war which the United States was waging against the Axis. August 1941, as noted earlier, also marked the beginning of American arms aid to Russia. Shortly after the Atlantic Conference between Roosevelt and Churchill, the United States assumed convoy duties in the North Atlantic, and on September 11, 1941, the president issued the "shoot first" order. The latter ordered American vessels to destroy German and Italian naval, land, and air forces "when encountered." Incidents in the Atlantic soon followed. At the end of October 1941, a German submarine sank the American destroyer *Reuben James*. The United States had fully become part of the battle of the Atlantic.

The Ten-Point Program

In the Pacific, the United States had responded to the Japanese penetration of Southeast Asia in the summer of 1940 with a policy of warning and pressure. On July 25, 1940, President Roosevelt ordered the control of American oil and scrap-iron exports, on which Japan depended heavily. In May, 1941, the president extended Lend-

Lease to Nationalist China, and on July 26, 1941, all Japanese assets in the United States were frozen. The aim of American policy was to persuade Japan to retreat from the war with Nationalist China, which had been raging full-scale since 1937. Specific American conditions for peace in Asia were presented to Japan in a ten-point program on November 25, 1941. These included the demand for a complete Japanese military withdrawal from China and French Indochina and the call for Japanese support of Chiang Kai-shek. Furthermore, Japan was invited to join a proposed multipower non-aggression pact between the United States, Great Britain, the Netherlands, Thailand, and the Soviet Union. Finally, Japan was asked to withdraw in effect from the Tripartite Pact with Italy and Germany. In return, the United States offered improved trade relations and future financial support of Japan.

The Japanese government, on the other hand, had reached a decision in principle, on July 2, 1941, to wage war against both Britain and the United States unless these powers acquiesced in Japan's defeat of China and the creation of a "Greater East Asian Coprosperity Sphere" under Japanese hegemony.

The conditions which General Hideki Tojo, the Japanese prime minister since mid-Octover 1941, presented to the United States for a peaceful solution of the Japanese-American confrontation in Asia were thus completely incompatible with the American ten-point program. Tojo demanded an Anglo-American pledge of noninterference in the war in China and a promise not to establish bases in China, Thailand, or the Dutch East Indies. The United States was even asked to lift the trade restrictions and thus, in effect, provide Japan with the means for further aggression. When Tojo's special envoy to Washington, Saburo Kurusu, was obtensibly still engaged in negotiations with the United States, a Japanese fleet struck Pearl Harbor with a carrier attack in the early morning hours of December 7, 1941.

In deciding on war, Tojo counted on a number of political and military advantages that seemed to minimize the risk of an open challenge to the United States in the Pacific. Manchuria was safe from Russian attack since the conclusion of the Soviet-Japanese neutrality pact of April, 1941, which Japan was careful not to break after Hitler's invasion of Russia. Neither Britain nor Holland could muster strong forces in defense of their rich Southeast Asian colonies. American naval forces, spread thin over two oceans since American involvement in the battle of the Atlantic, were outnumbered in the Pacific by Japan. Even before the American naval disaster of Pearl Harbor, Japan enjoyed a naval superiority in every category, especially in aircraft carriers, with ten Japanese carriers facing three American in the Pacific. The Philippines, America's chief outpost in Asia, were surrounded on all sides by Japanese strongholds, from Formosa to the Carolines and the Marianas.

Japan expected the war to be short and, therefore, failed to develop a long-range strategy in conjunction with Germany for the defeat of the Allies.

Technically, Hitler need not have followed up the Pearl Harbor attack with a declaration of war of his own, because of the defensive nature of the Tripartite Pact. Had Hitler not joined Japan in December 1941, he would have created a difficult situation for Roosevelt. U.S. public opinion, overwhelmingly turned against Japan, still would have had to be convinced of the need for an American delaration of war against Germany. Such a declaration would have been necessary, however, to implement the "Germany first" strategy, which Roosevelt had settled on some considerable time before Pearl Harbor.

Hitler relieved Roosevelt of such problems by declaring war on December 11,

1941. Italy and most of the Axis satellites, with the exception of Finland, followed suit. Until December 1941 the German military leadership had not considered the possibility of war with the United States and no operational plans existed for such an eventuality. In a complete underestimation of American strength, Hitler believed that Japan would sufficiently preoccupy the United States in the Pacific and in Asia to allow Germany to wage its own European war without undue American interference, at least for some time to come.

Japan, Germany, and Italy set up a joint military commission and signed a military agreement in January 1942. The military commission was not, however, the Axis counterpart to the Combined Chiefs of Staff of Britain and the United States, for it did not discuss joint strategy. The terms of the military agreement, referring mainly to Axis naval coordination, were so vague as to be meaningless. The few German submarines which operated from Japanese bases in Malaya were soon withdrawn for want of cooperation.

The extent of mutual confidence between the Axis partners can best be gathered, perhaps, from Hitler's own description of his Japanese ally: "They lie to beat the band; everything they say has always got some background motive of deception. . . If they've really got plans for something, we shall never hear about them."

THE MEANING OF THE U.S. ENTRY

With Pearl Harbor, the war which had begun in Europe in 1939 over the Polish Corridor was turned into a global conflict with every ocean and continent involved and every major power committed. By attacking the United States, Japan had added the world's leading industrial power with the most ample supply of raw materials to the Allied cause and had thereby dramatically altered the strategic balance of the war. The American economy soon produced nearly half of all the armaments of all the belligerents of the Second World War. In 1944, the United States turned out 96,000 aircraft as compared to Germany's 40,000. Whereas German submarines were to sink a total of 14 million tons of Allied shipping, U.S. shipyards produced 53 million tons of new shipping. U.S. farmers not only fed the armed forces of the United States, grown to over 12 million by 1945, but helped feed Soviet and British forces as well through Lend-Lease aid. The United States won the battle of production, before Allied and Soviet forces could turn the tide against Axis forces in Europe and Asia. What Britain's foreign secretary Sir Edward Grey had said of the American economy in the First World War still held true in the Second World War. The United States, Grey had observed, was like "a gigantic boiler. Once the fire was lighted under it, there was no limit to the power it could generate."

Superior American resources were also instrumental in the successful completion of the nuclear bomb project. Germany had had a head start in nuclear research before the war with the first splitting of a uranium atom by Otto Hahn in Berlin on December 17, 1938. During the war, the German nuclear program failed, in part because of inadequate resources which did not permit both a full-fledged nuclear project and the mass production of conventional weapons. In addition, the German and Italian dictatorships had driven some of the world's most renowned nuclear physicists to American shores, including Albert Einstein, Enrico Fermi, Edward Teller, Eugene Wigner, and Leo Szilard, all of whom made significant contributions to the perfection of an American nuclear bomb during the war.

The U.S.-British Partnership

The war effort of the United States and Britain was closely coordinated to the point where both powers fought practically as one. For purposes of military coordination and joint strategy the Combined Chiefs of Staff Committee was formed, consisting of the respective heads of the three military services. For purposes of pooling ammunitions, a combined Munitions Assignment Board and a Combined Raw Materials Board were set up in January 1942. Not counting the Atlantic Conference of August 1941, Roosevelt and Churchill met on seven separate occasions in places ranging from Washington, D.C., Hyde Park, Casablanca, Cairo, and Quebec, in addition to their joint meetings with Stalin at Teheran in November 1943 and Yalta in February 1945. Churchill's extensive travels during the war were conducted in an American-built long-range B-24 strategic bomber, which was converted into a civilian transport for that purpose.

Soviet-Western Strains

Soviet-Western strategic coordination was far less intimate because of the absence of any Soviet representative on the Combined Chiefs of Staff Committee. Effective strategic coordination was achieved in 1944, when the Soviet summer offensive was timed to coincide with the Normandy campaign, and again in January 1945, when Stalin advanced the date of his final assault on Germany in order to relieve German pressure on the western front during the "Battle of the Bulge." No effective scheme for the "shuttle bombing" of Germany was ever worked out, which would have enabled American bombers to land and refuel on Soviet airfields before returning to base in England. An attempt to develop such a scheme was soon abandoned by the U.S. Eighth Air Force, following an incident in 1944 when American B-17 bombers, which had landed on a Soviet air base, suffered heavy losses under German night attacks owing to lack of Soviet cooperation in organizing effective antiaircraft defenses.

The principal cause of Soviet-Western tension during the war was Soviet displeasure over the delay of a "second front" in western Europe. In 1943 the Soviet paper *Pravda* even attributed the delay to "small but influential groups in Britain and the United States, such as arms manufacturers and war suppliers, who place their private, selfish interests before those of the masses, to turn a bigger profit from the war." Soviet suspicion was mixed with Soviet anger in 1943 when the London-based Polish government-in-exile lent credence to the German charge that over ten thousand Polish officers had been murdered by the Soviets in eastern Poland between 1939 and 1941, whose mass graves the Germans claimed to have unearthed at Katyn. In early 1943 Stalin recalled his ambassadors from London and Washington. The strain in Soviet-Western relations may also explain why the Soviets sought to establish contact briefly with Nazi Germany in September 1943 via the Swedish capital of Stockholm. The purpose of these contacts may have been to explore the possibility of a separate German-Soviet peace, when the Soviets had doubt about the seriousness of the Allied war effort in western Europe. It also may have been simply a maneuver to scare the western Allies into a greater military effort. In any event, Hitler did not encourage the Soviet feelers, whatever their motive.

THE ASIAN WAR AND EUROPE, 1941–42

Although Germany and Italy did not coordinate their European strategy with that of Japan in the Far East, the Asian and Pacific war had an inevitable and appreciable impact on the war in Europe. The war in Asia forced both Britain and the United States to wage a two-front war. Although both countries directed their major resources towards Europe, consistent with the "Germany first" strategy, Japan absorbed sufficient Allied power, especially naval power, to affect the course of operations in Europe. The concentration of U.S. aircraft carriers in the Pacific, for example, materially affected Allied strategy in the invasion of Italy in 1943. The lack of carrier-borne air support dictated the choice of Allied landing sites in the far south of Italy, where land-based air support could be provided from North Africa and Sicily. Otherwise, the Allied invasion of the Italian peninsula might have been undertaken much further north, with appreciable savings in time and effort for the Allied campaign.

The war in Asia imposed an especially severe strain on Britain's more limited resources. Within weeks of Pearl Harbor, Britain lost Hong Kong, Malaya and Singapore, the latter surrendering with a garrison of 60,000 troops in February 1942. Japanese troops invaded Burma from Thailand in January 1942, capturing the capital of Rangoon in March. In March 1942 Japan also seized Borneo, Java, and Sumatra, following the defeat of a weak U.S.-British-Dutch-Australian force under the command of General Wavell. British naval disasters followed the defeats on land. On December 10, 1941 the battleship *Prince of Wales,* together with the battle cruiser *Repulse,* were sunk by Malaya-based Japanese aircraft. In April 1942 a Japanese carrier task force under Admiral Nagumo swept the Indian Ocean clean of British vessels, sinking two heavy cruisers, the carrier *Hermes,* and 130,000 tons of British merchant shipping. What were left of British warships hurried to the safety of British bases in East Africa. Britain's serious naval losses in Asia adversely affected her strength in the Mediterranean, a fact reflected in the new offensive gains of Axis forces in North Africa under Rommel in 1942.

Japan's ability to hold on to her vast gains in south and southeastern Asia depended on her ability to destroy American sea power, which had survived the Pearl Harbor surprise attack. This meant especially the U.S. carriers, which had been out of port on December 7, 1941. The American commanders, General Douglas MacArthur, in charge of the southwest Pacific theater, and Admiral Chester W. Nimitz, in charge of the central Pacific, mounted an aggressive defense against Japan with what little strength they had within a few weeks after Pearl Harbor. The defense included U.S. carrier raids against Japanese bases in the Gilbert and Marshal islands in February 1942 and General Doolittle's famous Tokyo raid with B-25 North American Mitchell bombers from the carrier *Hornet* on April 18, 1942. In the Battle of the Coral Sea of May 8, 1942, U.S. carriers clashed for the first time with their Japanese counterparts. The climax came with the Battle of Midway on June 4, 1942, in which a U.S. carrier task force under Rear Admiral Raymond A. Spruance sank the four Japanese carriers, *Hiryu, Soryu, Akagi,* and *Kaga,* which has spearheaded the attack on Pearl Harbor six months earlier. Midway marked the end of Japanese expansion in the Pacific. It also highlighted the American ability to wage war offensively on two fronts and on a global scale, quite contrary to the Axis assumption of 1940, which had produced the Tripartite Pact. U.S. global offensive capabilities were to be demonstrated even more spectacularly in June of 1944, when the invasion of Normandy was undertaken in the same month as was the successful U.S. invasion of the Mariana Islands in the Pacific. Both invasions signaled the approaching end of the war, both in Europe and the Pacific. Japan's loss of the Marianas brought all of Japan within striking range of U.S. strategic bombing. It was from the Mariana base at Tinian Island that the nuclear-armed B-29 bombers attacked Hiroshima and Nagasaki in August 1945.

THE GERMAN INVASION OF RUSSIA, 1942-43

Despite the heavy German casualties of 1941, Hitler still had eleven armies facing east in Russia, reinforced by Rumanian, Italian, and Hungarian auxiliaries.

The June Offensive

On June 28, 1942 Hitler launched his second major offensive in the east, the objectives of which were much more limited than those of 1941 in view of diminished German strength. The German aim of 1942 was to seize the oil-rich Soviet Caucasus between the Black and Caspian seas and possibly even to link up with Axis forces advancing eastward from North Africa, via Egypt, Iraq and Iran.

Though more limited in scope, the German aims of 1942 were still out of proportion with available strength, especially after Hitler had added Stalingrad on the Volga to his objectives. The taking of Stalingrad was crucial to the success of German plans, not only because of Stalingrad's importance for Volga river traffic, but because Stalingrad posed unacceptable risks, if left in Soviet hands, to the 1,200-mile-long German flank from the center to points furthest east. To cover the distance of 1,200 miles, Hitler had no more than two army groups available, each capable of controlling no more than a stretch four hundred miles long. The gaps had to be filled with satellite divisions, whose fighting power matched neither that of their German allies nor that of their Soviet opponents.

At first, the German June offensive covered ground rapidly between the rivers Don and Donets. On the Crimean peninsula, the fortress of Sevastopol, under siege since September 1941, fell on July 4, 1942. The Soviet retreat of 1942 was more flexible than in 1941, however, and fewer Red Army soldiers surrendered. By August 1942, the German spearhead branched out in two directions, one headed for Stalingrad, the other for the oil fields in the Caucasus. The force approaching Stalingrad, the Sixth Army and the Fourth Tank Army, was delayed by fuel shortages and did not reach Stalingrad until September 4, 1942. By the time the second army group, consisting of the Seventeenth Army and the First Tank Army, reached the Caucasus oil fields at Maikop, the retreating Soviets had thoroughly wrecked all installations. The Soviet oil fields of Baku and Grozny remained beyond German reach.

At Stalingrad, the Soviet sixty-second army under General Chuikov turned factories, houses, and cellars into such an effective system of defense that Hitler was forced to withdraw more and more strength from his armies in the Caucasus. Marshal Zhukov, successful defender of Moscow in 1941 and now in overall charge of the defense of Stalingrad, used the Soviet sixty-second Army as bait, in order to draw more German strength into the ruins of Stalingrad. Meanwhile, Zhukov assembled six Soviet armies north and south of the city for the coming battle of encirclement of the

German Sixth Army. For the Soviet defenders of Stalingrad, the crucial day was November 11, 1942, when the Soviet-held area was reduced to one tenth of the city and when the positions of the sixty-second Army were cut into three pockets. In far away Munich, Hitler had just delivered another boastful speech on November 8, 1942, claiming that Stalingrad was already his.

The Battle of Stalingrad

On November 19, 1942 the six Soviet armies north and south of Stalingrad broke through the weak flanking position held by Rumanian, Hungarian, and Italian auxiliaries. By November 22, 1942 the ring around Stalingrad was closed, trapping the German Sixth Army, its commander Field Marshal Paulus, together with twenty-four other generals and parts of the Fourth Tank Army. Hitler hoped to keep the Sixth Army fighting by supplying it from the air, much as the German troops had survived at Kholm and Demyansk the previous winter. In order to survive, the Sixth Army would have required a minimum daily supply of 700 tons. Goering promised to airlift 500 tons per day, but even this insufficient amount proved beyond Germany's reach. The actual daily airlift was no more than 95 tons. For a while, the encircled troops survived on the carcasses of the 50,000 horses, which were also trapped in Stalingrad. By February 2, 1943 the remnants of the Sixth Army, some 90,000 men, surrendered under Paulus.

Hitler had suffered his greatest defeat of the war to date, but the defeat was not as great as it might have been. The Soviets failed to trap the German troops in the Caucasus, which Erich Manstein safely evacuated by keeping the city of Rostov, gateway to the Caucasus, in German hands. Once clear, Manstein committed the evacuated armies to a counterattack which recaptured the city of Kharkov on March 12, 1943 and reestablished a stable front in the south of Russia.

Field Marshal Paulus, General Seydlitz and other captured German generals were so embittered by what they considered Hitler's betrayal of Sixth Army that they joined a Soviet-sponsored "National Committee of a Free Germany" at Krasnogorsk on July 13, 1943, which addressed propaganda appeals to German troops in Russia. After the war, Paulus was to play a leading part in organizing the army of Communist East Germany.

THE WAR IN NORTH AFRICA, 1942–43

Britain's serious naval losses in the Far East and in the Mediterranean between 1941 and 1942 had a direct effect on operations in North Africa, enabling the Axis powers to increase the flow of supplies across the Mediterranean. Apart from losing the *Prince of Wales* and the *Repulse* in the Far East in December 1941, the Royal Navy lost the battleships *Barham, Queen Elizabeth,* and *Valiant* as well as the aircraft carrier *Ark Royal* as a result of action by German submarines and Italian minisubmarines or "human torpedoes" at the turn of 1941–1942. By the end of 1941, Germany had twenty-six submarines operating in the Mediterranean.

On May 26, 1942 Rommel resumed the offensive in North Africa, which yielded the port of Tobruk, with vast stores of supplies, on June 21, 1942. Hoping to keep the British Eighth Army on the run, Rommel followed up the capture of Tobruk with an attack on Egypt on June 22, 1942. By June 30, the Axis had reached El Alamein, only a short distance from the Suez Canal.

The outcome of the battle for Egypt depended in large part on supplies. Rommel had begun his offensive in May 1942 with over 300 tanks, but his strength was down to fifty-five by the time he invaded Egypt in June. Due to increased British naval action, few fresh supplies reached Axis forces in the summer. The strength of Britain's Eighth Army under its new commander Bernard Montgomery grew by contrast to over 1100 tanks and 150,000 men by September 1942. On October 23, 1942 Montgomery attacked at El Alamein and by November 1, the Eighth Army had broken through the vast German mine fields following the heaviest artillery bombardment of the North African war. In the breakthrough, Montgomery had lost five hundred tanks, but he had six hundred left with which to pursue the beaten Germans.

Operation Torch

While Rommel retreated westward in North Africa, American and British forces carried out Operation Torch on November 8, 1942, the landing of 35,000 U.S. troops in Morocco, 39,000 U.S. troops at Oran in Algeria, and a mixed U.S.-British force of 33,000 at Algiers. "Torch" was under overall American command in the person of General Dwight D. Eisenhower because it was hoped that the French Vichy forces stationed in northwest Africa would not resist an American-led invasion. This proved not to be the case, at least not initially, as Vichy forces under Admiral Darlan put up a stiff resistance. When Darlan realized the scope of the invasion, he negotiated a cease-fire with Eisenhower and accepted the latter's appointment of himself as chief French civilian administrator in North Africa. On December 24, 1942 Darlan, previously a strong advocate of collaboration with Nazi Germany, was assassinated.

Hitler responded to the Allied landings in French North Africa by occupying Vichy France on November 11, 1942, and by rushing German troops by air to French Tunisia on November 10. The German attempt to seize the French fleet at Toulon failed when Admiral Delaborde scuttled all sixty-two French warships, including three battleships.

The Battle of Tunisia

The battle of Tunisia marked the final chapter in the North African war. Having taken Tripoli on January 23, 1943, the British Eighth Army under Montgomery broke through the German defenses in western Morocco, the Mareth line, in March 1943. Rommel's attempt to keep the two fronts in North Africa from closing in on him from west and east ended in failure after he had inflicted a defeat on American forces in the Kasserine pass in February 1943. By early 1943 the Allies had complete mastery in the air and on the sea in the western Mediterranean. Italian efforts to rush supplies to Tunisia resulted in the loss of fourteen destroyers and 325,000 tons of merchant shipping. Mussolini vainly pleaded with Hitler to conclude a separate peace with Soviet Russia, in order to permit the concentration of German power in the Mediterranean. The British capture of Tunis on May 5 and the U.S. taking of Bizerte on May 7, 1943 ended the battle of Tunisia and the North African campaign. The Axis lost nearly 250,000 prisoners, a bigger force than Hitler lost at Stalingrad. Among the prisoners was the bulk of the battle-hardened Afrika Korps with which Rommel had promised to defend Italy against all invasion attempts, if allowed to evacuate them from Africa in good time.

Tunisia marked the entry of U.S. ground forces into the European theater and the names of new commanders appeared, names which were soon to acquire fame on the battlefields of Sicily, Italy and France: Generals Mark W. Clark, George S. Patton, Jr., and Omar N. Bradley. Tunisia was significant also in that it provided an opportunity for U.S. and British fighting men to develop into a closely knit Allied team.

STRATEGIC DECISIONS AT CASABLANCA AND TEHERAN

With final victory in North Africa in sight, Roosevelt and Churchill, together with their staffs, met at Casablanca between January 12 and 25, 1943. Stalin too had been invited, but declined on the grounds that he was too preoccupied with fighting the battle of Stalingrad.

At Casablanca, Roosevelt and Churchill reached a compromise on the question of strategic priorities in Europe, which had previously caused considerable controversy among top U.S. and British military planners. Consistent with her tradition of peripheral strategy and mindful of her high losses in the World War I battles in France, Britain advocated a Mediterranean strategy. Following the conquest of North Africa, the United States and Britain were to concentrate on the invasion of Italy and eventually break into Germany from the south, via the "Ljubljana gap" in northern Yugoslavia and Austria. Churchill thought German defenses in southern Europe much weaker than those in France, hence his coining of the term the "soft underbelly" of Europe. A "Mediterranean first" strategy would have the further advantage of preserving and consolidating British political control over an area of historic British imperial interest. American strategists, headed by Chief of Staff George C. Marshall, strongly urged the earliest possible cross-channel invasion of the continent, in order to proceed as quickly as possible into Germany via France, with the conquest of the armaments center of the Ruhr and of Berlin the final strategic goal. Marshall would have liked to invade France as early as 1942. Angered over the British veto, he at one time threatened to abandon the "Germany first" strategy altogether and to concentrate American strength on the defeat of Japan.

At Casablanca, Roosevelt and Churchill agreed to follow up the Allied victory in North Africa with an invasion of Sicily, after which top priority would be given to the invasion of France. For the immediate future, first priority would be given to the defeat of the German submarine threat, because in early 1943 the Battle of the Atlantic was far from won. The Casablanca conference also issued directives for the intensified strategic bombing of Germany, the aim being "the destruction and dislocation of the German military, industrial, and economic system and the undermining of the morale of the German people to the point where their capacity for armed resistance was fatally weakened."

The "Unconditional Surrender" Doctrine

Following the meetings with Churchill, Roosevelt announced the "unconditional surrender" doctrine before a press conference, according to which doctrine the Allies would not negotiate terms of surrender with any of the Axis governments. The doctrine was criticized on the grounds that it tied the peoples and the dictators of the Axis powers together more closely than might otherwise have been the case, once the prospects of Axis victory began to fade, and that the doctrine therefore also discouraged internal revolt against the Axis dictatorship. Roosevelt himself emphasized that "unconditional surrender" did not imply the destruction of the populations of the Axis nations. His real motive may well have been to reassure the Soviet leadership that the Western powers would not make a separate peace with any Axis nation. He may also have wished to rule out a repetition of the experience of November 1918, when Woodrow Wilson had concluded the armistice on the basis of the Fourteen Points and was subsequently accused by the Germans of trickery and betrayal, because of the severity of the Treaty of Versailles. The decision of the Casablanca Conference to direct the main Allied effort towards the invasion of France was reaffirmed at the summit meeting of Stalin, Roosevelt and Churchill at Teheran in November 1943. Churchill's proposal to expand Allied military operations from Italy, which had meanwhile been invaded in September 1943, eastward into the Balkans, was overruled by Roosevelt and Stalin. The tentative date set for the cross-channel invasion of France was May 1944. The political implications of the decision to leave the liberation of eastern Europe entirely to the Soviet Union were clear enough to Churchill. Roosevelt was chiefly motivated by military considerations and the desire to end the war in Europe as rapidly as possible.

THE CONTAINMENT OF THE SUBMARINE THREAT; THE STRATEGIC BOMBING OF GERMANY

The decisions of the Casablanca Conference pertaining to the Battle of the Atlantic and the air war were implemented very soon after the conference ended.

During the early phase of World War II from 1939 to 1941, British merchant shipping had suffered chiefly at the hands of German surface raiders, such as the pocket battleships *Graf Spee* and *Scheer*. The sinking of the battleship *Bismarck* on May 27, 1941 ended German efforts to attack the North Atlantic sea lanes with heavy surface vessels. The fall of Norway and France in 1940 had meanwhile provided German submarines with excellent bases such as Brest, Lorient, St. Nazaire, and Bordeaux. Attacking from these bases, German submarines destroyed 2 million tons of merchant shipping between July 1940 and March 1941. Italian submarines, also operating in the Atlantic, added a further 130,000 tons during the same period. In 1942 Allied shipping losses for the first time exceeded Allied shipbuilding capacity with 7.7 million tons destroyed, as against 7.1 million tons newly built. The sharp rise in Allied losses was partly due to German submarine action against U.S. shipping along the East Coast of the United States and in the Caribbean, as well as against convoys bound for the USSR. One Allied convoy, sailing from Iceland to Soviet Russia on July 4, 1942 lost twenty out of thirty-three vessels when attacked by German aircraft and submarines operating from Norwegian bases.

The Battle of the Atlantic

The tide in the Battle of the Atlantic had begun to turn by May 1943, when one German submarine was being sunk for every 10,000 tons of Allied shipping lost, as against one submarine for every 100,000 tons of shipping in 1942. Altogether Germany lost 237 submarines in 1943, and the German goal of sinking 900,000 tons every single month of 1943 was never attained. Instead, German submarine chief Admiral Karl Doenitz had to break off the Battle of the Atlantic in 1944.

The Allied victory in the Battle of the Atlantic was due to improved command and tactics and a scientific lead in electronics. Airborne radar helped locate surfaced German submarines at night and thus deprived them of their principal advantage, that of surprise. Long-range aircraft, especially the U.S.-built B-24 *Liberator,* were able to close the "black pit," the area between Greenland and Northern Ireland in which submarines had previously been immune from aerial surveillance. The Allied ability to read the German code also contributed materially to the defeat of the German submarine. Having lost nearly 14 million tons of shipping, the Allies achieved victory in the Atlantic none too soon.

The "Combined Bomber Plan"

By the time that victory had been won, Allied strategic bombing of Germany also entered its decisive phase with the adoption of the "combined bomber plan" in June 1943. This plan subjected Germany to round-the-clock bombing, the U.S. Eighth Air Force under General Carl A. Spaatz and the U.S. Ninth Air Force under General L. H. Brereton attacking Germany by daylight, RAF Bomber Command under Air Marshal Harris attacking by night. The aim of RAF Bomber Command was to destroy residential areas by mass incendiary raids and thus to bring about a collapse of German civilian morale. Germany, in "Bomber Harris's" words, was to be bombed "city by city and ever more terribly in order to make it impossible for her to go on with the war."

The aim of U.S. strategic bombing was to destroy communications and the industrial and energy base of the German war economy. Before the availability of long-range fighter escorts in early 1944 and the arrival of the North American P-51 *Mustang,* the most outstanding long-range fighter plane of the Second World War, American losses were extremely heavy. U.S. strategic bombing in Europe had begun on June 11, 1942, when a force of thirteen four-engined *Liberators* attacked the Rumanian oil fields at Ploesti from the RAF base at Fayid in Egypt. On August 1, 1943 *Liberators* attacked Ploesti again from the Benghazi base in Libya, with 57 out of 177 B-24's lost. In an attack on the German naval base at Kiel on June 13, 1943, 22 out of 60 Boeing B-17 *Flying Fortresses* were shot down, and the famous B-17 raid on the ball-bearing industry of Schweinfurt on October 10, 1943 resulted in the loss of 60 planes, plus damage to another 138 out of a total attack force of 291 bombers. The British had meanwhile carried out some of the heaviest night raids of the war. On July 24–25, 1943 over 3,000 RAF bombers, dropping 9,000 tons of bombs and incendiaries, destroyed one-third of the city of Hamburg and killed 42,000 civilians.

For the U.S. Air Force, the tide in the air war turned with "big week" in February 1944, when nearly 10,000 tons of bombs were dropped, chiefly on German aircraft factories. Thanks to long-range fighter protection, the U.S. Air Force gained air supremacy over Germany by March 1944. Germany, in the words of German fighter chief Adolf Galland, had become "a home without a roof." By April 1944, American daylight raids concentrated on the Geman fuel industry, with paralyzing effects on the German air force and motorized and armored forces. Fuel shortage, the most serious strategic bottleneck of Nazi Germany in World War II, became critical in the fall of 1944 after the loss of the Rumanian oil fields at Ploesti with the Soviet invasion of the Balkans. The German synfuel industry, never able to supply more than 12 to 14 percent of need in the best of times, became Hitler's sole source of fuel. With concentrated strategic bombing of synfuel plants, this last source dried up too.

Although Germany produced 40,000 war planes in 1944, she had no fuel either to fly all these planes or even to train the pilots. Both in Russia, in Normandy and later in the "bulge," German armored forces literally ran out of gas. By early 1945 German air defenses had largely collapsed, with cities such as Dresden defenseless against attack. The Allied raid on Dresden in February 1945 caused more civilian casualties than the nuclear attacks on Hiroshima and Nagasaki combined. Strategic bombing, especially against industrial and fuel targets, contributed significantly to the German defeat in 1945.

New Weapons

German attempts to retaliate against Allied strategic bombing with revolutionary weapons, the V1 "buzz bomb" and the V2 rocket were, on balance, a failure. The V1, first launched on June 10, 1944 against London, was a primitive early version of a cruise missle, but its low speed made it vulnerable to both antiaircraft fire and fighter attack. The V2 rocket, a ballistic liquid fuel rocket, first fired against London on September 8, 1944, was, by contrast, a very dangerous weapon. Developed by the German army under the direction of General Dornberger, the V2 opened the missile age and provided the technology that was to lead to the first manned landing on the moon twenty-five years after its first appearance. Like so many other of Hitler's "miracle weapons," including the rocket-propelled, delta-wing and near-supersonic Messerschmitt ME 163 fighter and the jet-powered Messerschmitt ME 262 fighter plane, the first operational jet plane of the Second World War, the V2, came too late to have a strategic impact on the war. General Eisenhower thought that the German rockets, if introduced earlier, could have prevented the Normandy invasion of June 1944. Hitler, when first shown the films of V2 test firings in 1943, was so awestruck by the new weapon as to comment that such weapons would make war in the future impossible.

THE INVASION OF SICILY, THE FALL OF MUSSOLINI, AND THE ITALIAN CAMPAIGN

Based on the American experience in the island campaigns of the Pacific theater, the Allies expected the landings in Sicily, which occurred on July 10, 1943, to be difficult and costly. By July 1943, however, Italy had lost the stomach for war, once her colonial empire in Africa had been lost and her unprotected cities were exposed to Allied air attack. Hitler had lost his best forces in the Mediterranean with the defeat of the Afrika Korps in Tunisia. The best and strongest German forces were pinned down in the tank battle of Kursk and Orel, where the largest clash of Soviet and German armor was in progress at the very time when Allied forces landed in Sicily. German defenses in Sicily were thus weak and improvised. Having landed in the Gulf of Gela and in the vicinity of Syracuse, the U.S. Seventh Army under Patton and Montgomery's British Eighth Army fanned out across the island in an effort to trap the Axis garrison. After fighting a delaying action in Catania and around Mount Aetna, the Germans evacuated 45,000 of their own together with 60,000 Italian troops across the Strait of Messina.

The thirty-eight-day campaign for the conquest of Sicily yielded significant political and military benefits for the Allies. In Rome, the Sicilian campaign was the signal for the toppling of Mussolini on July 24, 1943 by a combination of forces, which included King Victor Emmanuel III, the former chief of staff Marshal Pietro Badoglio, and even members of the Fascist Grand Council. While professing unbroken loyalty to Hitler, Badoglio, the head of the new Italian government, sent out peace feelers to the Allies via Lisbon. The Allies failed to derive maximum strategic benefits from Mussolini's overthrow by delaying the invasion of Italy proper until September 9, 1943. The armistice agreement with Badoglio, signed in secrecy on September 3, 1943, was announced on the eve of Allied landings on September 8. Badoglio's hope of being able to hand over Italy to the Allies before Hitler had a chance of gaining control of the country was not fulfilled. Distrustful of Badoglio from the start, Hitler had prepared the disarming of all Italian armed forces under a plan code-named *Case Axis,* which was put into effect at the beginning of September 1943. By the time General Mark W. Clark's U.S. Fifth Army landed at Salerno on September 9, 1943, the Germans were waiting in strength. The landings were costly and, in Clark's words, turned into "near-disaster." By September 9, the Germans had also occupied Rome with the king, Badoglio, and their entourage narrowly escaping arrest. Mussolini, freed by German paratroopers from his confinement atop Gran Sasso mountain in the Abruzzi on September 12, 1943, was reinstated by Hitler as a German puppet in his new role as chief of the "Italian Social Republic" at the village of Salo at Lake Garda.

The Allied conquest of Sicily had, on the other hand, made the Mediterranean safe for Allied shipping for the first time since 1940. Churchill's attempt to exploit the conquest of Sicily by persuading Turkey to enter the war and thereby gaining a short and safe supply route to Soviet Russia via the Dardanelles, was unsuccessful. The Turks still feared the threat of German air power more than they trusted the Allies' ability to defend their capital city of Istanbul.

The Battle of Monte Cassino

The priority assigned to the preparation of the cross-channel invasion of France relegated Italy to a secondary theater with results that were costly and frustrating for Allied troops. Allied progress up the Italian boot was slow as the skillful German defense under Field Marshal Albert Kesselring withdrew from one prepared defense line to the next. After taking Naples on October 1, 1943 the Allies forced the "Volturno line" but came to a halt before the "Gustav line," which rested in its western flank on Monte Cassino. Before Monte Cassino all Allied attacks collapsed between November 1943 and May 1944 in what became the costliest and most bitterly fought battle of the entire Italian campaign. Among the casualties of the Battle of Monte Cassino was the anciet Benedictine abbey, which was totally destroyed by Allied bombing. The Allied attempt to unhinge the 'Gustav line' by amphibious landings behind the German front at Anzio and Nettuno in January 1944 eventually produced results by May 1944, but only at the additional cost of 59,000 Allied casualties. After the Allied capture of Monte Cassino, Rome, the first Axis capital, fell on June 5, 1944. The fall of Rome was largely overshadowed by the Allied invasion of France the following day. General Sir Henry Maitland Wilson, Eisenhower's successor as Allied supreme commander in the Mediterranean, would have liked to follow up the fall of Rome with an immediate pursuit of the retreating Germans before they had found time to consolidate a new defense line, the "Gothic line" in the Appenines. Wilson also wanted to land at Trieste and carry his attack into Austria via the Ljubljana gap. None of these schemes materialized because of the demands of the Normandy invasion and subsequent campaigns in western Europe. The "Gothic line" was pierced with the capture of the Giogo and Futa passes in September 1944, but the River Po in Upper Italy was not reached until the spring of 1945.

THE COLLAPSE OF HITLER'S "NEW ORDER"; THE HOLOCAUST

Hitler had found few active collaborators in conquered Europe when he was at the height of his power in 1940–1941, and he found even fewer willing to uphold German rule after the battles of Stalingrad and North Africa ushered in the defensive phase of the war for Nazi Germany at the turn of 1942–1943. Nazi collaborators such as Norway's Vidkun Quisling and his *Nasjonal Samling,* or Holland's Nazi leader Anton A. Mussert of the *National Socialistische Beweging der Nederlanden* were little more than German puppets without broad popular support. The strength of Pétain's Vichy regime derived less from its being perceived as a collaborator of Nazi Germany than as a protector of French interests when the majority of the French public was doubtful of eventual British victory. The most pronounced area of Vichy collaboration with Hitler was that of discrimination and eventual deportation of French Jews to Nazi extermination camps. Charles Maurras continued to publish the *Action Française* during the war, in which he hailed the increasingly virulent anti-Semitism of the Pétain regime.

Hitler's "new order" held no attractions for anyone in Europe save the Germans themselves, a fact even admitted by Mussolini in private conversation with his son-in-law and foreign minister Count Galeazzo Ciano. The traditional state system of Europe was, for Hitler, so much "rubbish," which he intended to replace with a Germanic empire reaching from Norway and the French channel coast to the Volga and the Crimean in the east. Britain might be tolerated as a "white policeman" in the colonial world. The United States, a country where, according to Hitler, "Europeans had once again become nomads," would be forever barred from the affairs of Europe.

Hitler's territorial aims in western Europe included not only the annexation of Norway, Denmark, Holland, Belgium and Luxemburg, but of the French channel coast as far as the mouth of the Somme, the Argonnes region and the Franche Comté as well. After Mussolini's fall in 1943, Hitler moved German administrations into the border areas of northern Italy, including the South Tyrol and Trieste, which were Italy's gains from the First World War.

Hitler's Plans for Russia

Nazi annexationist schemes reached their most bizarre extremes in the east, where Hitler began implementing his colonizing plan for Russia, first spelled out in the pages of *Mein Kampf.* "If we speak of new soil in Europe today," Hitler had written in 1924, "we are thinking primarily of Russia." Hitler's "eastern ministry" (*Ostmin-*

isterium) under Nazi ideologue Alfred Rosenberg drafted a *General Plan East* in 1941, which contemplated the deportation of up to 80 percent of the Polish population, 65 percent of Ukrainians and 75 percent of White Russians. Russians remaining among the German colonizers were to be kept in a state of near-illiteracy with sufficient knowledge of German to enable them to read road signs, according to Hitler.

Nazi policy in occupied Soviet Russia quickly turned the German image from that of potential liberator to certain enslaver, a fact which deprived Hitler of the support he might otherwise have obtained from both disaffected Ukrainian and anti-Communist Great Russians. Stalin's secret order of July 16, 1941 reflected his fears concerning collaboration with the German invaders when speaking of "many elements on all fronts" which "run to meet the foe and throw away their weapons on their first contact with him." The case of General Andrey Vlasov succinctly demonstrated both the degree of latent opposition to the Stalin regime as well as the extent of Nazi folly in failing to exploit that opposition. Having played a key role in the successful defense of Moscow in 1941, Vlasov, upon being taken prisoner in July 1942, proposed to German army leaders an alliance with anti-Communist Russians for the overthrow of the Stalin regime. It was Vlasov's insistence that such an alliance must be one among equals and Vlasov's damand for a "single and indivisible Russia," which doomed his scheme from the start. Hitler was determined to wipe out Russia as a political and military factor in whatever shape, under whatever leader. Vlasov was permitted to form a "Russian Liberation Army" (*Russkaya Osvoboditelnaya Armiya,* ROA) from among Soviet POWs in German captivity, but ROA's purpose was largely propaganda and its size was very small. Two ROA divisions were formed in Germany at Muensingen and Heuberg, one of which saw action against the Red Army at the Oder front in 1945.

Hitler's War on the Jews

Hitler's war against Soviet Russia set into motion another Nazi policy rooted in *Mein Kampf* and intended to be a corner stone of the "new order," the destruction of the European Jews. Since 1933, Hitler had held the Jews of Germany hostage for the "good behavior" of the Western press towards the Nazi government. In January 1939, he had been quite explicit in his threat to destory "the Jewish race in Europe," should the Western powers declare war on him. The invasion of Soviet Russia provided Hitler with new and vast areas, far removed from the attention and scrutiny of the outside world, in which to make good his threat of January 1939. By January 1942 Reinhard Heydrich, chief of the SS Security Service (SD) convened a conference of top government and SS officials at Wannsee, outside Berlin, for the purpose of coordinating mass arrests and deportations of European Jews to selected areas in the east.

The Nazi dragnet covered all of German-occupied Europe. The number of Jews who eluded it, such as those of Finland, because of the Finnish government's refusal to surrender its Jewish citizens, or those of Denmark, who were aided by their fellow citizens in their escape to Sweden, was very small. By far the great majority of European Jews were delivered to the extermination camps of Belzec, Sobinor, Treblinka, Maidanek, and Auschwitz, the latter the "greatest institution of annihilation of all times," according to Auschwitz commandant Rudolf Höss. The Nazi regime went to considerable lengths to conceal the most stupendous mass murder in history from public view, but the fact of mass killings of Jews was known to a larger number of people in wartime Germany than was generally admitted by Germans after the war. The Allied governments too, as evidence produced some forty years after the war has shown, had considerable knowledge of Hitler's "final solution," provided by sources inside Germany which had access to the facts and wanted the Allies to know them.

THE ALLIED INVASION OF FRANCE

Normandy, rather than the Pas-de-Calais, the area facing England at the narrowest point of the English Channel, had been chosen as the invasion site by British Lieut. General Sir Frederick Morgan, Eisenhower's chief invasion planner, because of the element of surprise and because of weaker German defenses in Normandy. While U.S. airborne forces descended behind Germain lines, American troops went ashore at Omaha and Utah beaches in the early morning hours of June 6, 1944, the British and Canadians landing further north on beaches code-named *Gold, Juno,* and *Sword.* The Allies enjoyed the advantages of complete mastery of the air, unlimited supplies and a unified command under Eisenhower's overall leadership, which included as deputies Air Marshal Sir William Tedder, Admiral Sir Bertram Ramsay, and Air Marshal Sir Trafford Leigh-Mallory.

Despite the vast Russian front and the Italian theater, Hitler could still muster some sixty divisions for the defense of France in 1944. The combat value of the German forces in France was not equal to that of the Allies because of the absence of any German strength in the air and the shortage of fuel for motorized and armored divisions. The German defenders were also successfully deceived into believing that the Normandy invasion was a mere diversion, to be followed by the "real invasion" of the Pas-de-Calais. Lastly, there was fundamental disagreement on the German side between Rundstedt, the commander in chief west and Rommel, in charge of coastal defenses. The former wanted to destroy the invasion forces in mobile battle in the French interior, the latter, mindful of Allied air supremacy, regarded the battle, and the war, as lost unless the Allies were pushed back into the sea on the first day of the invasion.

Events soon showed Rommel to have been right. In mid-July, 1944, Rommel warned Hitler of the imminent collapse of German resistance in Normandy. Two weeks later, the U.S. First Army captured Avranches and thereby opened the gap through which the First and Third Armies were able to break out into Brittany and Normandy. In the ensuing battle of Falaise 90,000 German troops were trapped and destroyed. While the U.S. First Army completed the destruction of the encircled German forces, Patton's Third Army raced towards the Seine, crossing it at several places by August 24, 1944. Paris fell the following day, the honor of first entering the French capital going to Jacques LeClerc's 2nd French Armored Division.

In the south, U.S. and French forces had meanwhile carried out Operation Anvil with landings on the Mediterranean coast on August 15, 1944. "Anvil" netted the Allies the port of Marseilles, which was essential for supplies, because seaports along the French Atlantic coast, like Cherbourg, had been either totally wrecked by the retreating Germans, or were actually still in German hands, defended by garrisons Hitler had left behind. Some of these garrisons held out until the end of World War II, denying the use of port facilities to Allied supply vessels.

THE AUTUMN STALEMATE; THE "BULGE" AND THE FINAL BATTLES IN WEST AND EAST

Towards the end of summer 1944 the war in Europe gave every sign of approaching its conclusion. Ever since regaining the initiative after the German defeat in the tank battle of Kursk in July 1943, the Soviets had advanced westward with few interruptions. The retaking of Kiev in November 1943 was followed by the lifting of the siege of Leningrad in January 1944 and the liberation of the White Russian capital of Minsk in July 1944. During the Soviet summer offensive of June–July 1944, twenty-eight German divisions, comprising 350,000 men, the bulk of the German Army Group Center, were destroyed. By August 1944 the Soviets had reached the eastern outskirts of Warsaw and by September 1944 both Finland and Rumania signed separate armistice agreements with the USSR.

The Plot against Hitler

Developments in Italy and the west had been no less promising for the Allies with the piercing of the "Gothic line" on the one hand and the capture of the port of Antwerp by Montgomery on September 4, 1944, on the other. It was against the background of the German military disasters in east and west that a conspiracy of high-ranking officers, including Field Marshal Rommel and former chief of staff Ludwig Beck attempted to assassinate Hitler in his East Prussian headquarters at Rastenburg on July 20, 1944. The attempt failed when the blast of the bomb, planted by Colonel Claus Schenk von Stauffenberg, was deflected from Hitler's person by the heavy wooden table in Hitler's conference room. In the aftermath of the abortive plot some 7,000 individuals were arrested, of whom 6,000 were executed. The leading conspirators were put on show trial before a "people's court" and subsequently hanged. "I want them to be hanged," Hitler explained, "hung up like carcasses of meat." Rommel, given the option of committing suicide by taking poison provided by the SS or standing trial for treason with dire consequences for his family, chose suicide.

Stalemate

Unexpectedly, the great advances made in east and west during the summer of 1944 were followed by a stalemate as a result of supply difficulties on both the Soviet and the Allied fronts. In the west, it was not possible to maintain the attack along the entire front, which now stretched from the North Sea to Switzerland. To maintain the momentum of the summer campaign, Montgomery proposed to concentrate available supplies and ammunition on the Allied left wing, his own, in order to break out into Holland and thence the Ruhr and Berlin. Eisenhower provided Montgomery with some, though not all, the support the British had asked for, including two U.S. airborne divisions, for the capture of the nine bridges across the Lower Rhine. Operation Market Garden, Montgomery's attack across the Rhine, ended in defeat for the Allies when the British First Airborn Division failed to take the ninth bridge across the Lower Rhine at Arnhem in September 1944. After the battle of Arnhem, the western front settled down to a war of siege with few changes in the front line. On October 21, 1944 the U.S. First Army took Aachen, on November 19, the U.S. Third Army captured Metz, and November 23, 1944 the U.S. Seventh Army occupied Strasbourg.

The Battle of the Bulge

On December 16, 1944 Hitler broke the stalemate on the western front with a surprise attack carried out by twenty-four divisions, including strong armored forces, along a narrow front in the Ardennes forest at the juncture between the U.S. First and Third Armies. The Ardennes offensive, or, as it soon came to be known, the "Battle of the Bulge," was carried out over exactly the same terrain as the successful German attack on France in May 1940, and like the 1940 offensive it achieved complete surprise. The aim of Hitler's last offensive of World War II was to recapture Antwerp and to inflict another "Dunkirk" on all Allied forced in Belgium. The larger political aim of the "bulge" was to inflict painful losses on the American army and thereby to persuade the U.S. government into granting Nazi Germany a separate peace. Then Hitler intended to shift all his weight eastward and defeat the Soviets, something he was confident of still being able to achieve, once freed from having to fight on three separate fronts. During the last months of the war, Hitler clung to the illusion that history would repeat itself, and that just as the Prussia of Frederick the Great had escaped almost certain destruction at the end of the Seven Years' War through the sudden withdrawal of Russia from the French-Austrian-Russian coalition, Nazi Germany too would miraculously survive the crisis of World War II.

After the initial shock of the German attack had worn off, Hitler's strategy speedily collapsed. The Germans failed to unleash the full power of their armored forces because they failed to capture important road junctions, such as Bastogne, which was stubbornly defended by the U.S. 101st Airborne Division under General Anthony C. McAuliffe. It was the latter who hurled his unorthodox "Nuts!" at the Germans when asked to surrender. The German attack also suffered from inadequate supplies of fuel, and it broke down completely under devastating Allied air attack once weather conditions changed from the fog of mid-December to clear skies after Christmas 1944. The "bulge" cost the U.S. Army 76,000 casualties. Hitler lost his last strategic reserve and thus the war.

The Soviets advanced the date of their last big offensive to January 12, 1945 at the request of the western powers, in order to ease German pressure in the Ardennes. There could be little doubt about the outcome of the Soviet offensive after Hitler had stripped his eastern front of its best units and had lost these units in the "bulge." By mid-February 1945, the Soviets had taken Upper Silesia, Germany's last great armaments center not yet gutted from the air. In the north, German resistance in East Prussia collapsed after the fall of Königsberg on April 9, 1945. In the south, the Austrian capital of Vienna was in Soviet hands by April 13, 1945. By mid-April 1945 the Oder, last natural obstacle on the way to Berlin, was also crossed by Soviet forces under the command of Marshal Zhukov as part of the final assault on Berlin.

The Death of Hitler

In the west, the Rhine had meanwhile been crossed after the U.S. First Army had seized the Rhine bridge at Remagen intact on March 7, 1945. Other Rhine crossings followed, by Patton's Third Army at Oppenheim and by Montgomery at Wesel. By mid-April 1945, the U.S. Ninth and First armies had destroyed the bulk of German forces in the Ruhr with 300,000 POWs taken. By April 25, 1945 Germany was cut in two when the U.S. First Army joined hands with the First Ukrainian Army at Torgau on the Elbe. After dictating his "political testament," which echoed his lifelong hatred for the Jews, and after appointing Admiral Doenitz as the new Reichspresident, Hitler shot himself on April 30, 1945 in his underground bunker in the center of Berlin. Eva Braun, his bride of less than two days, joined him in death, as did Joseph Goebbels with his family. The Soviet capture of Berlin was completed on May 2, 1945, on which day German forces in Italy also surrendered. The ceremony of unconditional surrender was carried out at Rheims on May 7, 1945 and repeated for the benefit of the Soviets at Berlin the following day. On May 21, 1945 the shortlived govenment of Admiral Doenitz was arrested at its seat in Flensburg on Eisenhower's order. The war in Europe had come to an end.

11

Europe from World War to Cold War

ILLUSIONS AND REALITIES OF THE GRAND ALLIANCE

The fashioning of a peace for Europe after 1945 was likely to be a much more difficult task than it had been in 1919 for two reasons: the lack of strong European representation in the councils of the Grand Alliance, and the ideological disparity between the Alliance's principal members, the United States and Britain on the one hand, the Soviet Union on the other.

A Federal Europe

Among European Resistance leaders who had fought the Nazi occupation on the European continent, there had grown up during the war a consensus on what the future Europe should be like. This consensus was extraordinary for it developed despite the great difficulties in communication between individual national resistance groups and because its supranational conception departed significantly from past patterns of European national thinking. Whereas the victors of 1919 had attributed the First World War almost exclusively to the errors and misdeeds of a single country, Germany, as stated in the "war guilt" clause of article 231 of the Versailles treaty, the Second World War Resistance viewed European fascism, the principal cause of the war, not as the product of a specifically Italian or German history but as a European malaise stemming from the excesses of twentieth-century European nationalism generally. The Resistance thus did not wish to see Europe rebuilt on the basis of the principles underlying the Westphalia peace of 1648, stressing the sovereignty of individual nation-states, but rather on the basis of integration and federation towards a new supranational European community. The projected new federal Europe was to embrace all the European states west of Soviet Russia, including Germany and its former European Axis partners.

The European federalists of the Resistance, conscious of the importance of timing, wished to exploit the moment of collapse of the old European state system at the end of the Second World War for the realization of their revolutionary project. It was therefore hoped that Europe-wide elections for a constituent assembly could be held immediately after the German collapse, before the European vacuum of 1945 could be filled by either a return to the traditional system of nation-states or by Soviet-American rivalry for control in Europe. Only by allowing the federal concept to take immediate root could the catastrophe of the Second World War be turned into an historic opportunity for renewal.

The brave new vision of a federal Europe, which was the vision of noncommunist Resistance leaders, required for its realization not only the faith of its advocates but power. The Resistance had had little enough power while it was active against the German occupation, and quickly lost what little power it had once the war was over. Lacking any larger, supranational organ or institution during the war, the Resistance had not been able to communicate its ideas to the wartime leaders of either Britain or the United States. Nor is it certain that its ability to do so would have had any significant effect on Churchill's or Roosevelt's own ideas concerning the future of Europe. Neither, for the most part, were the European exile governments which had taken refuge in the British capital concerned with federalist concepts, but merely hoped to return to the 1939 or 1940 status-quo. In this, the Polish government-in-exile in London was a significant exception, showing an early interest in postwar integration.

Spheres of Influence

The future of Europe was thus largely in the hands of the leaders of the Grand Alliance, and it was significant for Europe that this was neither an alliance of equals, nor one of shared values. The Grand Alliance fought under the common banner of antifascism, which signaled agreement on the common war aim but not, necessarily, on the nature of the postwar order for Europe or the world.

For most of the war, both the Western powers and the Soviet Union promoted the notion that the Grand Alliance was more than an alliance of necessity. Stalin deemphasized Communist global aspirations by the symbolic act of disbanding the Communist International in 1943. Western news media and the entertainment industry portrayed Soviet Russia not only as heroic ally, but as a system with a noble social purpose. In the United States, *Life* magazine produced a special issue in 1942 which advertised Soviet society in a manner appealing to Western liberal opinion. The Hollywood motion-picture industry uncritically adopted the official Soviet version of Stalin's Blood Purge of the 1930s in the film *Mission to Moscow,* which depicted key defendants in the Moscow show trials as agents of Hitler or the Japanese emperor.

It was an easy and not unnatural assumption that a country thus portrayed would also be a willing partner in the building of a postwar order based on western liberal ideas. The illusion of shared values was reinforced by the pronouncement of universalist, liberal-democratic war aims, such as those of the Atlantic Charter, by Roosevelt and Churchill, and their tacit as well as express acceptance by Stalin. At the same time, both the western powers and the Soviet Union had advanced a different concept in their mutual exchanges, that of *spheres of influence*. The juxtaposing of the *spheres of influence* and *universalist* concepts was fraught with potential friction once the victory over the common enemy had torn away the illusion of Soviet-western ideological and philosophical compatibility.

Roosevelt's proposal of the division of the world into four areas, to be under the four "world policemen," the United States, USSR, Britain and China, when made to Soviet foreign minister Molotov in 1942 was a spheres-of-influence concept. It may well have reminded the Soviet leadership of Hitler's proposal of November 1940 to expand the German-Japanese-Italian Tripartite Pact of September 1940 into a four-power pact through the inclusion of the Soviet Union. On the American side there existed, apart from the president, both supporters and opponents of the spheres-of-influence concept. Both Secretary of State Cordell Hull and Undersecretary of State Joseph Grew rejected the spheres-of-influence concept either as immoral, or, in Grew's case, as dangerous. Hull thought that the future United Nations would in and of itself eliminate the need for spheres of influence, and even of alliances or a balance of power as a means of safeguarding national security and promoting national interest. Undersecretary Grew thought that a Western recognition of a Soviet sphere of influence over Eastern Europe, such as Stalin had clearly demanded in his talk with British foreign secretary Eden in Moscow in December 1941, would merely encourage the Soviets to expand into Western Europe after the war. Secretary of War Henry Stimson and ex-vice president Henry Wallace, on the other hand, were prepared to recognize a Soviet claim to an East European sphere of influence on the grounds of national security. As a matter of practical policy, both the Western powers and the Soviets applied the principle of spheres of influence as their military forces began to conquer the European areas assigned to them by the Teheran conference of 1943. Britain and the United States excluded Soviet Russia from any effective role in the military government of Italy from 1943 onwards, though they did not bar Italian veteran Communist leader Palmiro Togliatti either from returning from his Moscow exile in early 1944, or from joining the Italian provisional government.

The Soviets, on their part, excluded the Western powers from any effective role in the military administration of Soviet-conquered Bulgaria in 1944. After crossing the old Soviet-Polish frontier in early 1944, the Soviets immediately took the first step towards the imposition of Communist controls over Poland by setting up the "Lublin Committee" under Polish Communist leader Boleslav Bierut. During the summer of 1944, the Soviets had watched the piecemeal destruction of the anitcommunist Polish Home Army by the Germans in the Warsaw uprising without giving any aid of their own or allowing western supplies to be airlifted into Warsaw.

As Soviet forces swept into Eastern Europe and the Balkans in the late summer and fall of 1944, Winston Churchill, together with Foreign Secretary Eden, flew to Moscow to salvage what little Western influence they could in an area of overwhelming Soviet military preponderance. Before 1944, Churchill had repeatedly assumed the role of spokesman of European interests, though his initiatives bore little resemblance to the federalist ideas of the European Resistance. Churchill thought in terms of a traditional European balance of power, which would be seriously disrupted by the disappearance of German power and the expansion of Soviet power. In 1943, Churchill unsuccessfully proposed the creation of a council of Europe as part of the projected United Nations organization. Significantly, the council of Europe was to have consisted of a bloc of western European nations, under British leadership, and another bloc of eastern European nations, designed to act as buffer between western Europe and the Soviet Union, much in the manner of the French-sponsored *cordon sanitaire* of the 1920s. Churchill's project of a Bavarian-Austrian-Hungarian federation, advanced unsuccessfully at Teheran in 1943, had similar ends in mind. It was in pursuit of a workable balance of power after the war that Churchill also promoted the restoration of French power. Towards that end, he succeeded in gaining for France a fourth occupation zone in Germany at the Yalta conference of February 1945.

During his October 1944 visit to Moscow, Churchill concluded his famous "percentage deal" with Stalin, which defined the relative Soviet and Western influence in the Balkan nations. According to the deal, Soviet influence was to predominate in Rumania and Bulgaria with 90 and 75 percent respectively, whereas British influence was to prevail in Greece with 90 percent. In Yugoslavia and Hungary, Soviet and Western influence was to be an even 50-50. The agreement, jotted down informally on a piece of paper, was silent on other eastern European countries, such as Poland and Czechoslovakia.

THE YALTA CONFERENCE

The lack of precise Soviet-Western wartime agreements concerning the future of Europe was not only occasioned by mutual fear that the attempt to reach such agreements might disrupt the wartime alliance. It also reflected a mutual awareness that postwar policy would be influenced by the relative power which each side had devoted to the common victory and which each would have at its disposal in support of postwar aims.

Until the summer of 1944 it was conceivable that the stupendous losses suffered by the Soviet armies in fighting Hitler between 1941 and 1944 would have so weakened Soviet Russia that her military power, relative to that of the United States and Britain at the end of the war, would be moderate and manageable. In such an event, the western powers would be in a much stronger position to insist upon Soviet compliance with Western, universalist, liberal-democratic principles, such as had been announced as a general war aim in the Atlantic Charter.

The actual course of military events between June 1944 and February 1945 quickly dispelled any such notion. The Soviets continued to absorb the bulk of German power on D-Day and throughout the Battle of Normandy, and it was the Western powers which asked the Soviets to carry out relief attacks in July 1944, in order to take the German pressure off their front in Normandy, and not the other way around. At the time of the Yalta summit in February 1945, the Soviets were already making deep inroads into Germany, while the western armies were still recovering from Hitler's last nasty surprise of World War II, the Battle of the Bulge.

The Yalta conference occurred at a time when, in Churchill's words, "the whole shape and structure of postwar Europe" was clamoring for review. It also occurred, however, at a time when the image of a tired Soviet army limping into Eastern Europe at the end of the war had given way to the reality of 11 million Red Army soldiers delivering the death blow to Nazi Germany and taking physical possession of Eastern and much of central Europe.

Still, the conclusions from this fact were not clearly drawn on the Western side, and the wartime fiction of the compatibility of Western universalist and Soviet sphere-of-influence aims was extended beyond the Yalta conference. Roosevelt himself, upon returning from Yalta, summed up the meeting as "the end of the system of unilateral action, exclusive alliances, and spheres of influence." In obscuring the contradictions between Western and Soviet aims, the agreements reached at Yalta provided much of the fuel of future disappointment and recrimination.

In its "Declaration on Liberated Europe," the Yalta conference pledged assistance to the peoples liberated from the domination of Nazi Germany and the peoples of the former Axis satellite states in the creation of "democratic institutions of their own choice."

Agreement was further reached on UN representation when the Soviets settled for three rather than the sixteen seats (one for each union republic) they had originally demanded in the UN General Assembly. The USSR's support for the first UN meeting in San Francisco in April 1945 similarly raised Western optimism concerning Soviet-Western postwar cooperation.

Poland

Regarding Poland, the western powers accepted a line, roughly equal to the Curzon line of 1920, as Poland's eastern border with the Soviet Union, with the city of Lvov and the oil-rich portion of Galicia also going to the Soviets. The conflict between the Moscow-backed Communist Lublin Committee and the Polish exile government was to be solved by compromise through a new provisional government of national unity, drawn from both. A commission of three, composed of Molotov and the American and British ambassadors to Moscow, was to aid in the formation of the new Polish government. Free elections were to be held as soon as they became feasible.

Germany

On the German question, the three powers upheld the principle of dismemberment without implementing it through a concrete scheme. France, which was not represented at Yalta, obtained an occupation zone as a result of Churchill's initiative. The French zone had to be carved out of the zones allotted to the United States and Britain by the three-power European Advisory Commission (EAC) in 1944. Agreement was reached on German reparations in principle, though not their extent. The United Stated, over British objections, accepted the sum of $20 billion, as suggested by the Soviets, as a basis for discussions.

The War against Japan

The question of Soviet entry into the war against Japan was principally discussed by Roosevelt and Stalin. Stalin had decided to enter the Far Eastern war as far back as 1941, because there was a prospect of recovering the Russian losses of 1905 to Japan. That Roosevelt asked the Soviet Union to come into the war against Japan made Stalin's position much easier. As a price, the Soviets demanded—and obtained—the recovery of all territorial losses of tsarist Russia to Japan, plus the Kurile islands, plus Soviet control over Port Arthur and the Manchurian railway. The autonomy of Outer Mongolia was to be guaranteed by international agreement. No promise was extracted from Stalin to discontinue support of the Chinese Communists.

The American request for Soviet support in the war against Japan was based on the assumption that Japan would have to be defeated through the use of conventional weapons. In February 1945 the nuclear bomb was still an untried weapon, its ultimate success still an uncertainty. Before Yalta, Japanese resistance had often been much tougher than anything encountered in Europe, with correspondingly high U.S. casualties. The taking of Iwo Jima in February 1945, the month of the Yalta conference, cost seven thousand U.S. casualties against 20,000 Japanese. American naval casualties suffered under kamikaze attack in the subsequent Okinawa campaign included thirty vessels sunk and ten battleships and thirteen aircraft carriers damaged.

With casualties of such magnitude and British power being limited to the secondary India-Burma-China theater, no responsible American leader could have avoided asking for Soviet help. That Soviet military power against Japan would exact a long-term political price from Asia as well was a prospect not faced with sufficient candor by those who sought to enlist it.

Soviet Relations Deteriorate

The official note of cordiality upon which the Yalta proceedings concluded was quickly supplanted by hints of treachery and charges of bad faith as the war approached its end in Europe.

In more ways than one there seemed a parallel between the change in Soviet-Allied relations during the year following the Yalta conference and the deterioration in Nazi-Soviet relations during the year following the fall of France in June of 1940. In both cases, the alliances were alliances of necessity which rapidly turned into confrontations once their original purpose had been fulfilled. In 1940 the reason for the alliance had been, on Hitler's part, the need to defeat France; and on Stalin's part, the need to keep Hitler preoccupied with the task of defeating France. Before April 1945 the need on both the Soviet and the western sides was the defeat of Hitler by joint effort. In 1941 the Nazi-Soviet alliance had floundered over Eastern Europe. In 1945 the Grand Alliance progressively disintegrated over Eastern Europe also, with Germany soon added as an even greater source of friction. Both the Stalin-Hitler pact of 1939 and the Grand Alliance of 1941 had subordinated past ideological differences to current imperatives of pragmatism; both rediscovered ideology as the source of incompatibility once pragmatism had served its immediate end.

After the fall of France in 1940, Hitler had commited a number of unfriendly acts towards the Soviet Union, including the German intrusion into the Soviet sphere of influence in Eastern Europe and the nonfulfillment of trade obligations. From early 1945 onwards the western powers committed a number of acts which, from the Soviet perspective, may have been regarded as similarly hostile. Among such acts was the termination of U.S. Lend-Lease aid to Soviet Russia before the conclusion of the war, and failure of the United States to respond to a Soviet request for a $6 billion loan for reconstruction purposes. To this were added bitter western complaints about Soviet nonfulfillment of the pledges made at Yalta concerning eastern Europe.

Soon after Yalta the Soviets had, in fact, prevented the Moscow three-power commission from making any progress towards the formation of a new Polish government, by sabotaging the commission's work and by arresting Polish leaders sympathetic to the exiled goverment in London. On March 28, 1945 fifteen leaders of the Polish Home Army were seized after being tricked into negotiations with General Ivanov of the USSR under false assurances of safe conduct. In Rumania, Soviet deputy foreign minister Andrei Vishinsky engineered a coup on February 27, 1945, resulting in the ouster of General Radescu's government and its replacement by a Communist puppet regime under Petra Groza.

These actions were incompatible with the principles of the Yalta "Declaration on Liberated Europe," if its interpretation came from a Western-liberal perspective. That the Soviet definition of *democratic institutions* had a different meaning was soon to be shown in the newly created "peoples' democracies" of Eastern Europe.

Stalin may have affixed his signature to the Yalta declaration because he thought such declarations necessary to satisfy public opinion in the Western countries. Crucial to Soviet Russia at the end of a long and costly war was the satisfaction of the Soviet security requirement, which, in the Soviet view, could not be met by Western-style liberal governments in Eastern Europe. Eastern European governments that were friendly to Soviet Russia without being Communist, as Churchill had suggested at Yalta, were governments that had yet to be invented, in Stalin's view. Given the disproportionately large Soviet military contribution to the common victory, the Soviets undoubtedly felt entitled to give priority to national security over western, universalist principles. The European Allies of the First World War had also subscribed to Woodrow Wilson's *Fourteen Points,* but they had not permitted these to become the sole determinant of the 1919 peace when vital interests of their own were at stake.

Soviet-Western disagreements reached a high point in April 1945. In that month the new U.S. president Harry Truman gave Soviet foreign minister Molotov his famous dressing-down over Soviet nonfulfillment of the Yalta pledges. Molotov's own account of the April 23 meeting at the White House, that he had never "been talked to like this before," may not have been wholly accurate, because at least one other foreign leader, Hitler, had talked to him in similar style during the Molotov-Hitler meeting of November 1940. The subject under discussion then had also been Eastern Europe, and the verbal clash of 1940 had been followed within a few months by the German surprise attack of 1941.

It is not likely that Stalin expected the Western powers to attack Soviet Russia after the defeat of Germany in the way that Germany had after the fall of France. What Stalin may have genuinely feared was a last-minute switch of alliances through a separate German-western armistice and a resulting transfer of all German forces to the eastern front. Such a turnabout would still have enabled Germany to drive the Soviets out of central Europe and thus deprive the Soviet Union of the hard-earned fruits of victory.

Stalin would not have suspected Roosevelt, whom he held in high personal esteem, of such treachery. But Roosevelt was dead in April 1945, and so was Hitler—with whom presumably no one in the West would have negotiated. The fact that Admiral Doenitz, Hitler's successor, and his government were not immediately arrested in British-occupied Flensburg was cause for grave Soviet suspicion, however. A further aggravating fact, not unknown to the Soviets, was the British policy of keeping all captured German forces and their weapons, including the large German garrison of Norway, in good fighting order. Churchill's German "ghost army," continued to vex the Soviet leadership as late as 1946 when it was finally disbanded in the British occupation zone. Lastly, Stalin's suspicions were reinforced by the separate armistice negotiations, conducted between the Western powers and the German military in Switzerland, concerning the surrender of German forces in Italy in April 1945. These negotiations, according to Soviet estimates, enabled the Germans to shift troops from northern Italy to the Eastern front.

The signing of the unconditional surrender document on May 7 and 8, 1945, and the voluntary withdrawal of American troops which had penetrated deeply into Saxony and Thuringia, the heartland of the future communist East Germany, dispelled whatever fears Stalin may have had concerning the faithfulness of his western allies. Stalin's relief may help explain the cordial reception he gave Harry Hopkins, Roosevelt's confidant and adviser, during the latter's Moscow visit in June 1945.

POTSDAM AND THE IRON CURTAIN

The Potsdam conference of July 1945 involving Truman, Stalin and Churchill, the latter soon to be replaced by newly-elected Labour prime minister Clement Attlee, briefly revived appearances of East-West cooperation. But within less than a year after Potsdam cooperation yielded to rivalry with Germany, Eastern Europe, the Greek Civil War, the Middle East, and Iran emerging as the focal points of controversy. Added to this, mutual ideological suspicion and Soviet fear of the American nuclear monopoly resurfaced as the broader, unifying elements of confrontation.

The Dismemberment of Germany

Germany was the principal subject of Potsdam but the decisions reached provided for an occupation of indefinite duration, rather than the framework of a final peace. Formal sovereignty over Germany had been assumed by the four occupying powers through the joint declaration of June 5, 1945. The declaration was silent on the subject of frontiers and it said nothing about dismemberment.

A partial de facto dismemberment of Germany had already taken place before the opening of Potsdam in the areas under exclusive Soviet control. The Soviets had annexed northern East Prussia, including the city of Königsberg, renamed Kaliningrad, and transferred Germany east of the rivers Oder and Neisse to Poland. Neither transaction came as a complete surprise to the Western powers, Roosevelt having agreed to the Soviet takeover of Königsberg as early as the Teheran conference of 1943. The Western powers withheld final recognition of the Oder-Neisse line, however, pending a final peace settlement.

The area surrendered to Poland accounted for nearly one-fifth of the total area of prewar Germany. It contained Germany's second largest industrial-mining complex in Upper Silesia, including valuable coal deposits. The transfer of so large and rich an area of prewar Germany to Poland was a shrewd Soviet move that was bound to tie any future Polish government closer to the USSR, on whose goodwill Poland would have to rely in defense against future German revisionist claims.

The rest of Germany, though divided into four occupation zones, was to be treated as a single economic unit. The Potsdam conference even made provisions for central German administrative departments of finance, communications, transport, foreign trade, and industry, to function as auxiliaries of the Allied high commissioners. Such central departments were never created, however, because of the mounting tension between the high commissioners and the resulting breakdown in the four-power government of Germany.

When advocating a uniform policy for all Germany, both the Western powers and the Soviet Union were acting from important economic motives of their own. The

Soviets, having surrendered mineral-rich Upper Silesia to Poland, wished to maintain access to the Ruhr, Germany's remaining large industrial-mining complex, which was situated in the British zone. The Western powers, having to feed the large urban populations of West Germany, which had been further increased by the stream of refugees from the East, hoped to be able to draw on the agricultural surplus of rural East Germany.

Reparations

Concerning reparations, the USSR was accorded a privileged position in recognition of its wartime losses. Each of the four powers was to satisfy its reparation needs from its own zone but the USSR would obtain an additional 15 percent of industrial equipment of the Western zones in exchange for timber, coal and foodstuffs from its own zone. Ten percent of West German industrial equipment was to be handed over to the Soviets outright.

The decisions concerning denazification, demilitarization, and the trying of German war criminals reflected common past objectives of the Grand Alliance and were the easiest to carry out. Very soon, even some of these objectives were being pursued according to different criteria in East and West as both sides began to mobilize the German potential for purposes of Cold War strategy.

Significantly, both Soviet and Western attempts to intrude into each other's spheres of influence outside Germany proper failed at the Potsdam conference. Soviet failure to change the status of the Dardanelles or to obtain a trusteeship over the former Italian colony of Libya was matched by the Western inability to commit Stalin to a halt in the Sovietization of Rumania and Bulgaria.

The Surrender of Japan

Japan, which had still been central to the Roosevelt-Stalin conversations at Yalta, appeared only on the periphery at Potsdam. The successful testing of the first nuclear bomb at Alamagordo, New Mexico on July 16, 1945, which Truman informed Stalin of at Potsdam, and of whose occurrence Stalin had knowledge from his own sources, made the surrender of Japan a foregone conclusion. On July 26, 1945, the day on which the U.S. cruiser *Indianapolis* delivered the first nuclear warhead to the Tinian base in the Marianas, the United States, Britain and China called on Japan in the Potsdam declaration to surrender unconditionally. The Soviets, having refused to renew the Soviet-Japanese neutrality pact of 1941 at the time of its expiration in April 1945, entered the Far Eastern war on August 8, between the first and second nuclear attack on Hiroshima and Nagasaki of August 6 and August 9 respectively. On September 2, 1945 Japan surrendered unconditionally.

Nuremberg

After Potsdam, East-West cooperation continued to function chiefly in the holding of the Nuremberg war crimes trials and the drafting of the Nazi satellite peace treaties.

In the Nuremberg trials from November 1945 to August 1946 twenty-four Nazi leaders were indicted on charges of conspiracy against the peace, crimes against the peace, violations of the laws of war, and crimes against humanity. Twelve of the defendants were sentenced to death, seven received prison terms, and three were acquitted, among them Franz von Papen and Hjalmar Schacht.

The trials suffered from certain legal flaws because of the ex post facto nature of the charges, and they were not devoid of irony because of Stalin's partnership with Hitler in the 1939 dismemberment of Poland and because of Soviet aggression against Finland in 1939 and the Baltic states of Estonia, Latvia, and Lithuania in 1940.

The Nuemberg trials nevertheless served an important purpose not only in the documentation of Nazi crimes, but also in the establishment of Nazi war guilt for the outbreak of the Second World War. Whereas the Treaty of Versailles had merely pronounced a judgement of German war guilt without either citing or admitting evidence, the Nuremberg trials produced extensive testimony and documentary evidence on the origins of World War II.

The Paris Peace Conference

The end of the Nuremberg trials in August 1946 coincided with the Paris peace conference, which was entrusted with the drafting of the peace settlements for Germany's World War II European allies and satellites, Italy, Bulgaria, Rumania, Hungary and Finland.

In the East European peace settlement following the First World War, frontiers had been largely determined on the basis of whether an individual state was designated ally or former enemy. In the 1946 Paris treaties, which were signed in a joint ceremony in February 1947, the chief criterion was the Soviet interest, with both "friendly" and "enemy" states having to make concessions.

The Soviets lost none of the gains they had made in Eastern Europe under the Stalin-Hitler pact and they added some new ones which improved their strategic position. Finland surrendered the nickel-rich Petsamo district, giving the USSR a common border with Norway. The USSR retained the gains of the 1940 Moscow peace in addition to obtaining a lease of the Porkkala naval base, subsequently returned to Finland in 1956. The Soviet annexation of the three Baltic states, though not expressly recorded in the 1946 Paris treaties, remained unaltered.

Czechoslovakia, though considered a friendly and liberated country, had to surrender its easternmost portion, Carpatho-Ruthenia, to the USSR after World War II. The surrender was to prove of strategic significance in August 1968 when the Soviets were able to move 600,000 troops and 4,000 tanks into Czechoslovakia across the common border, without having to cross Polish or Hungarian territory.

Rumania recovered northern Transylvania from Hungary, but had to confirm the Soviet annexation of Bessarabia and the northern Bukovina of 1940. The southern Dobruja, taken by Bulgaria from Rumania in 1940, remained in Bulgarian possession.

The Paris peace treaties imposed heavy reparations on all Eastern European Axis satellites. The reparation did not tell the full story of Soviet economic benefits, however, as other forms of economic exploitation, such as unequal trade agreements, were imposed on friend and foe alike.

The ethnic mosaic of Eastern Europe was somewhat simplified by the expulsion of most of the German populations from the newly gained provinces of western Poland, the Sudeten provinces of Czechoslovakia and Balkan nations of Yugloslavia and Rumania. The expulsions occasionally produced unforeseen economic consequences in places such as Czechoslovakia, where the ethnic German population had previously maintained a thriving glass-and-jewel industry.

The nationality problem of Eastern Europe, a cause of crisis and concern for all Europe before both World Wars, lost much of its earlier stridency after 1945, though it did not entirely disappear. The sharpness of old national antagonisms was blunted by the new factor of common opposition to Soviet Russia. Moreover, the Soviet Union itself would not tolerate national bickering in its newly-gained Eastern European sphere of influence any more than it would allow national dissent among its own ethnically diverse population, because of the weakening effect such quarrels would inevitably have produced on Soviet power. Communist ideology served as a convenient instrument of containment of national rivalry on the basis of the thesis that nationalism was a bourgeois phenomenon, now happily overcome in Communist Eastern Europe. This did not prevent the Soviet leadership from occasionally mobilizing existing Eastern European antagonisms after 1946, if the reactivation of nationalism could be made to serve Soviet hegemonic ends against disobedient satellites. Yugoslavia, after its break with Stalin in 1948, was to be a prime example of such tactics.

Italy

The peace treaty with Italy was heavily influenced by the emerging Soviet-Western confrontation and the division of Europe into hostile blocs. Although an enemy of the United States in the Second World War, Italy by 1946–1947 was being groomed by the United States as a Cold War ally. At the peace conference, the United States was thus the chief protector of Italian interests against the demands of the Soviet Union and of Yugoslavia in particular, in order, to strengthen the pro-American Christian Democratic party under Alcide de Gasperi in its struggle against Togliatti's powerful Communist party. For these reasons the United States successfully blocked any changes in Austria's favor in the Italian-Austrian border at the Brenner Pass, changes which France and Britain had originally supported. For identical reasons the United States denied Yugoslavia possession of Trieste and turned Trieste and surrounding territory into a separate entity under UN protection instead. Italian reparations too were kept at a relatively modest $360 million, with $100 million going to the Soviet Union. Britain, whose treatment of defeated Italy had been far less forthcoming than that of the United States ever since the armistice of September 1943, received temporary trusteeship of Italy's former colonies except for Ethiopia, which regained its status as a sovereign nation.

Soviet Expansionism

Germany, though not a subject of the Paris peace conference, had moved increasingly center stage by 1946. Both Molotov and Secretary of State James Byrnes of the United States were talking as much to German audiences as they were to each other when addressing German issues, in order to enlist German support for their rival aims.

By 1946, the United States and Britain had come to view Soviet policy in Germany as evidence of Soviet intentions in Europe generally. The question being asked in 1946 was whether Soviet European policy served legitimate security interests or whether it signaled expansionist designs.

In order to find answers to such questions, Secretary of State Byrnes proposed to Molotov at Paris a twenty-five year disarmament pact for Germany. The rejection of that offer by the Soviet Union was widely held as proof of an expansionist Soviet design which was believed to be aimed at the imposition of Soviet controls over all of Germany.

Byrnes' speech at Stuttgart in the U.S. occupation zone of September 6, 1946, signaled the coming shift in Western policy towards Germany, based on the new Western interpretation of Soviet policy. In the Stuttgart speech, held before a mixed German-American audience, Byrnes first announced the American commitment to stationing troops in Europe for an indefinite period of time; and second, recommended the economic merger of the Western occupation zones of Germany. Such a merger was accomplished for the British and U.S. zones by January 1947. The larger American objective of turning the Western zones into a separate West German state was foreshadowed by Byrnes' call for the moral rehabilitation of the Germans and their eventual reintegration into the family of free nations.

The Stuttgart speech marked an important milestone on the road towards the Cold War division of Germany, but it was a division very different from that desired by Roosevelt. Roosevelt and his wartime allies had envisaged the division of Germany in the service of their national security interest of preventing a revival of German power. The emerging division of Germany in 1946 reflected both soviet and American concern over each other's intentions in central Europe.

Soviet policy in Iran and Turkey and the revival of the Greek Civil War in 1946 reinforced Western impressions of an expansionist Soviet design. In Iran the Soviet Union refused to evacuate its military forces in conjunction with the withdrawal of British and American forces despite prior agreement on a joint evacuation within six months after the war. Soviet withdrawal was not effected until March 26, 1946 and only after strong Western protests. Turkey managed to resist Soviet demands for a revision of the straits convention and the surrender of Kars and Ardahan only with strong British and U.S. backing.

Dawn of the Cold War

In assessing each other's deeper motives, both East and West, by 1946, had recourse to ideology, which both had chosen to suspend in the interest of the alliance of necessity before 1945. The West reinterpreted Soviet policy as a manifestation of a communist world conspiracy, allowing for few exceptions or differences among individual Communist regimes. It was an interpretation which would require many years and much evidence to the contrary to be revised.

The Soviets undoubtedly labored under an ideological determinism of their own. To the Soviet leaders, American policy, as the policy of the world's leading capitalist power, appeared bent on global expansion through the inner forces of the system it represented. Aggressive expansionism, in the Leninist definition of imperialism, was as central to the nature of the capitalist system as communist world conspiracy was to Soviet communism in the interpretation of the noncommunist West.

Churchill's message in the "iron curtain" speech of March 5, 1946 at Fulton, Missouri, was that Soviet policy was "expansive and proselytizing." The Soviets, in Churchill's words, were responsible for splitting Europe "from Stettin on the Baltic to Trieste on the Adriatic," and they were in the process of building up a Communist regime in their zone of Germany, enabling the defeated Germans to put themselves "up for auction" between East and West. As he had once "thanked God for the French army" in the 1920s and 1930s as a defense against German aggression,

Churchill now thanked the United States for its nuclear monopoly, which had caused, in Churchill's words, no one in the world to "sleep any less well in their beds."

Stalin branded the Fulton speech as a "call to war with the Soviet Union." There was in Stalin's response both anger and frustration over the West's unwillingness to appreciate the Soviet security motive in Eastern Europe. Rumania, Hungary and Finland, Stalin reminded Churchill, had all shared in Hitler's attack on the Soviet Union in 1941. Any attempt to force the Soviet Union out of Eastern Europe, Stalin warned, would result in a defeat similar to that which the Western intervention had suffered during the Russian Civil War after the 1917 revolution.

By September 1946, Truman's secretary of commerce Henry Wallace observed, not without reason, that the "real peace treaty" now required was not between the Allies and the former Axis powers, but betweeen the Soviet Union and the United States. In the same month, Truman's special counsel Clark Clifford advised the president of the need to face up to the possibility of a future nuclear war against the Soviet Union. U.S. strategy, in Clifford's view, should include the use of a highly mechanized army capable of holding strategic areas in the Soviet Union. Such, basically, had also been the strategic concept of Operation Barbarossa, Hitler's plan for the invasion of Russia in June of 1941.

12

Soviet Russia after the War

THE RETURN OF STALINISM

The outside world's perception of Soviet Russia after 1945 was shaped not only by the conduct of Soviet foreign policy, but also by the nature of the society her leaders were building at home after the heroic exertions of the Soviet people in the Second World War.

The 1930s had ended on a general note of disillusionment for Western admirers of the Soviet experiment. Arthur Koestler's novel *Darkness at Noon*, which gave a fictional account of Stalin's Blood Purge, was a powerful literary monument to that disillusionment crowned by the Stalin-Hitler pact of 1939.

During the Second World War, Western fear of Hitler largely overshadowed disillusionment with Soviet Russia, and there was renewed hope within and without Soviet Russia that the war itself might somehow usher in a new and more liberal phase in the development of the country.

For this there seemed much evidence, both in Soviet foreign policy and in the relaxation of Soviet internal controls. Abroad, the Soviet Union appeared to have forsaken world revolutionary aspirations through the disbanding of the Communist International in 1943. At home, in an effort to mobilize patriotic sentiment, the Soviet government liberalized religious policy, deemphasized the collective farm system, and encouraged mass-enlistment in the Communist party, especially among young men and women of the armed forces. Moreover, the Russian Orthodox church was rehabilitated and Soviet Jews were encouraged to solicit Western financial support for the Soviet war effort through such agencies as the Jewish Anti-Fascist Committee of the USSR, under the chairmanship of Solomon Mikhoels. The Communist party lowered its admission standards and dispensed with the customary close examination of new applicants. As a result, 1.34 million new party members were admitted in 1942 alone and total party membership reached its highest level to date in 1945 with 5.7 million members.

Whether these measures were of a tactical nature, dictated by the contingency of war, or whether they signaled a basic change, was a question that had yet to be answered. The war had revealed deep social and ethnic fissures in Soviet society, as indicated by the early support given the German invaders by Ukrainian peasants. It was conceivable that Stalin relaxed communist orthodoxy in the midst of war merely for the purpose of preventing these fissures from reaching even greater proportions.

Retrenchment

An article appearing in *Pravda* as early as October 17, 1944, at a time when the outcome of the war could no longer be in doubt, suggested expediency, not a fundamental shift, as motivation behind the short-lived wartime liberalization. The *Pravda* article warned against a "poisoning" of Soviet consciousness and demanded a return to "socialist attitudes" among the Soviet people.

Against hopes of an improvement in the quality of life as a reward for the exertions of the war, there was retrenchment and a return to Stalinist conservatism on virtually all fronts, economic, social, intellectual, artistic and, above all, ideological.

The return to ideological orthodoxy was rooted in the twin need to repair the credibility of Soviet ideology, damaged by the events of the Second World War, and to provide new defenses in the developing Cold War with the Western powers.

The credibility of Soviet ideology had suffered because of the exposure of Soviet society to Western realities, which were at considerable variance with official ideology. On their westward march to Europe, millions of Red Army soldiers had seen with their own eyes that living standards outside Soviet Russia were incomparably higher than their own. The Soviet regime was sufficiently concerned about the effects of such observations to order returning veterans to be confined to special camps for extended periods of time before allowing their return to Soviet society.

Soviet society as a whole, however, not just Red Army veterans, was the object of ideological reeducation. The reeducation campaign aimed especially at the farm sector, while generally emphasizing the themes of antiforeignness (*inostranshchina*), anti-Westernism, and Great Russian chauvinism. The man in charge of ideological reeducation was Andrei A. Zhdanov, who, until his sudden death in 1948, was Stalin's right-hand man. A Politburo member since 1939, Zhdanov had long experience as a propagandist of pronounced Great Russian leanings.

The Farm Sector

In the collective farm sector, the lax discipline of the war years was quickly replaced by a return to tight controls and the enforcement of the provisions of the 1935 Collective Farm Charter. During the war, the Soviet regime had permitted peasants to enlarge their private garden plots at the expense of the collectives and to devote a greater number of workdays to the cultivation of the garden plots than would have been permissible under the law. The government's chief concern had been increased food production and the private garden plots yielded far more than did the inefficient collectives. There were even rumors in the villages during the war that the whole collective farm system would be quietly dropped after the war.

In fact, soon after the war a special council on kolkhoz affairs was created under the chairmanship of A. A. Andreyev, the Politburo's agricultural expert. The council seized 14 million acres of farmland from the private garden plots and restored them to the collectives from which they had been quietly appropriated. Certain provisions of the 1947 currency reform also singled out for punishment the peasant who attempted to become a private enterpreneur. Individual bank accounts were subjected to a ten-to-one exchange rate of the old for the new ruble, in order to skim off profits derived from black marketeering of farm produce. Collective farm bank accounts received a perferential exchange rate of five-to-four.

The reimposition of collective farm discipline was carried out with particular severity in the areas previously under German occupation, and those Soviet officials found wanting in zeal were made to feel the consequences very quickly. Leonid Brezhnev, in his capacity as newly installed party secretary of formerly Rumanian Bessarabia, pursued the policy of recollectivization apparently with sufficient vigor to have attracted the favorable attention of Stalin. Nikita Khrushchev, as first Ukrainian party secretary, by contrast was judged to be wanting in zeal, and found himself briefly out of favor in 1947.

If the economic cost of forced collectivization had been high in the 1930s, the cost of forced recollectivization after 1945 was also considerable. The great famine of 1946, though undoubtedly also the result of drought and war-related damages—which included the loss of 137,000 tractors, 17 million head of cattle, and 20 million hogs—was due in large part to the resurrection of an agricultural system of proven inefficiency and wastefulness. After the war, no less than before, Stalin was prepared to accept the economic cost of collectivization in the interest of doctrinal purity and political controls, both of which prohibited the growth of a socially independent class of well-to-do peasent proprietors.

Despite the greater efficiency of the private garden plots, there were efforts under way in Stalin's final years to have them eliminated altogether and to merge existing collective farms into even larger units. Between 1950 and 1952 the number of collectives was thus reduced from 252,000 to 97,000. It was part of the merger scheme to resettle the rural population from its traditional villages to new "agro-cities," consisting of city-type apartment blocks. From a Communist viewpoint, the "agro-city" scheme had the added advantage of atomizing the farm population into a rural proletariat and of thus erasing such social distinctions between country and town as had survived Stalin's agricultural revolution of the 1930s.

The "agro-city" scheme developed into a political issue in the Politburo, where it was advocated by Khrushchev but opposed by Andreyev. By 1952 Andreyev, who also favored smaller collective farmwork teams under the so-called *zveno* ('link') system, was dropped from the Politburo. Khrushchev's "agro-city" scheme was never adopted, however, apparently because of the strong opposition it had aroused among the peasantry.

In the arts, literature, and scholarship, Zhdanov instituted a purge, which soon bore his name as the *Zhdanovzhshina,* with exponents of non-Russian nationalism, especially those of Ukrainian background, special targets.

Great Russian Nationalism

Stalin's new crackdown on non-Russian nationalities was apparently rooted in his anger over instances of collaboration of non-Russians with the invading Germans. Some of the nationalities, such as the Crimean Tatars, Stalin had deported from their homeland as punishment. The Volga Germans were deported on the mere suspicion that they might become collaborators because of their ethnic background. Ukrainian support for the Germans so incensed Stalin that, according to Khrushchev's subsequent testimony at the Twentieth Party Congress of 1956, he would have liked to deport all Ukrainians except for the fact that their numbers were too great. By contrast, Stalin singled out the Great Russians for their "clear intelligence, firm character and great patience" in his victory toast in the Kremlin of May 24, 1945.

Promotion of Great Russian nationalism and fidelity to Soviet Communist orthodoxy became the criteria of Zhdanov's policy. The party journal *Bolshevik* denounced G. F. Alexandrov for insufficient emphasis on Russian philosophy prior to Karl Marx in his *History of European Philosophy.* N. Rubinstein's *History of Russian Historiography* was similarly attacked for inadequate coverage of Russian historians.

The attack against Soviet writers began with a Central Committee denunciation of the satirist Mikhail Zoshchenko and Anna Akhmatova, the poetess. Both were found wanting as serious communist writers, Zoshchenko being denounced as "hooligan," Akhmatova as "half nun, half whore." Alexander Fadeyev's *The Young Guard,* though previously awarded the Stalin prize, was now found deficient in its emphasis on the party's role in leading Soviet guerrillas against the German occupation.

That the Stalin prize was no protection against subsequent attack was dramatically demonstrated in the case of Shostakovich, the famed Soviet composer. Shostakovich's posthumous memoirs, published in the United States in 1979 under the title *Testimony, the Memoirs of Dmitri Shostakovich,* gave a grim account of the composer's lifelong difficulties under Stalin.

Stalin's personal interference in the Soviet sciences, especially the field of genetic research, had had disastrous consequences before the war and continued to do so afterwards. Trofym Lysenko, a Stalin favorite and self-styled geneticist, had his theory on plant heredity officially endorsed by the Soviet Central Committee in 1948, despite repudiation of his theory by all reputable geneticists inside and outside the Soviet Union.

"Antiforeignness" and "anti-Westernism" were the reverse side of Zhdanov's Great Russian campaign. Zhdanov's campaign was meant not only to extol Great Russian achievements, but to shut off Soviet Russia from all foreign and, by definition, harmful influences. Soviet legislation enacted between February and December 1947 thus prohibited marriage to foreigners and restricted contacts of Soviet civil servants, such as postal and railroad employees, with foreigners, to a minimum. Other decrees of 1947 banned the release of scientific and economic information that might be useful to a foreign power.

Anti-Semitism

The antiforeignness and national repression of Stalinism in its final stage provided a suitable atmosphere for the rekindling of Russian anti-Semitism in its new guise of anti-Zionism.

Between 1917 and 1947 Soviet Russia had gone full circle from the emancipation of the Russian Jews under Lenin to the beginnings of an officially orchestrated anti-Semitism of the aging Stalin. The founding of the state of Isreal in 1948 played a catalytic part in this development. Although Soviet Russia was the first power to recognize the state of Israel, it undoubtedly did so with the intention of damaging British influence in the Middle East.

Zionism was soon cast into an adversary role because of American support for the state of Israel. Soviet Jews, in turn, were quickly identified as potentially disloyal and subversive, because of their support for the new Zionist state. The actual strength and spontaneity of that support was demonstrated by the enthusiastic welcome given to Israeli foreign minister Golda Meir by Soviet Jews during her Moscow visit in 1948.

In an otherwise tightly sealed-off Soviet Union, the Soviet Jews thus emerged as the one group capable of maintaining strong bonds of loyalty to an outside force that Moscow regarded with utmost suspicion as an American ally. Accordingly, the Zhdanov campaign employed with mounting frequency the terms *cosmopolitan, cosmopolitanism,* and *rootless cosmopolitans* as epithets and code-words for the denunciation of Zionism and, by implication, of Soviet Jews.

How quickly the line between anti-Zionism and anti-Semitism was crossed was indicated by the Communist show trials in Eastern Europe, especially the Slansky trial in Czechoslovakia, in which many of the defendants were Jewish. The so-called Jewish doctors' plot in the Soviet Union shortly before Stalin's death was a further indication of the escalation of anti-Zionism into an anti-Semitic campaign.

RECONSTRUCTION AND ECONOMIC POLICY

For Soviet troops on occupation duty in Europe after the war it must have been a source of both amazement and frustration to witness the return of life, light and prosperity to war-ravaged cities such as West Berlin or Vienna at a time when living conditions in their own homeland had scarcely improved over the level of 1945.

The economic condition of Soviet Russia after the war was in large measure the result of damages sustained during the war, but it was also due to the priorities set by the fourth five-year plan, which Stalin launched in 1946.

Soviet statistics on war damages claimed the total or partial destruction of 1,700 towns and cities, 7,000 villages, 31,000 factories, 13,000 bridges, and 6 million buildings. Twenty-five million people were left homeless.

Leningrad, the most tragic of all battlegrounds of the Second World War, lost 600,000 civilian dead during its nine-hundred-day siege. Most of the historic buildings of the former Russian capital, such as St. Isaac's Cathedral or the Winter Palace had been reduced to ruins. Destroyed also were many of the great showpieces of the industrial revolution of the 1930s, the hydroelectric dams in the Ukraine and the huge Stalingrad tractor plant Red October, the site of bitter hand-to-hand fighting in 1942.

In the 1930s, when Soviet society transformed itself into an industrial nation, it had to generate the capital required for that purpose from its own resources. In the 1940s, when reconstruction was the foremost economic task, there were once again no foreign loans available to help finance the effort. Sweden and Britain advanced small reconstruction loans in 1945, but the hoped-for $6 billion reconstruction loan from the United States became an early victim of the Cold War. Cold War politics and Soviet suspicion of American motives also prompted the Soviet Union to reject the American offer of sharing in the bounty of the Marshall Plan of 1947, which contributed in a decisive way to the quick recovery of western Europe.

Eastern Europe and East Germany in particular were made to pay an involuntary contribution to the reconstruction of war-devastated Soviet Russia through the wholesale looting of their economies. The labor of German POWs, who were made to rebuild what they had come to destroy, was also an important factor in reconstruction. Much of the industrial equipment taken from East Germany was wasted, however, through careless handling in open-air storage in railroad yards.

Heavy Industry

Apart from the goal of reconstruction, the fourth five-year plan, covering the period from 1946 to 1950, set the same priorities which had guided Stalin's previous five-year plans. Investment and expansion were concentrated on the capital goods industries, providing the base for heavy industry and an armaments industry; on the energy industries, oil, coal and hydroelectric power; and on soil improvement, reforestation, and communications. Official Soviet statistics of April 1951 claimed fulfillment and overfulfilment of the plan targets, including annual production figures of 25 million tons of steel, 19 million tons of pig iron, 35 million tons of crude oil, and 250 million tons of coal. These figures, though modest by the standards of the 1980s, represented significant achievements in the early 1950s for a country as severely damaged as the Soviet Union.

The thrust toward heavy industry and armaments left few resources for the improvement of the quality of life for individual Soviet citizens. Food continued to be scarce and few consumer goods were available, a fact even admitted in some of the speeches of the Nineteenth Party Congress of October 1952, Stalin's last. The historic buildings of Leningrad were lovingly restored, and downtown Moscow witnessed the rise of several Soviet-style skyscrapers, including that of Moscow University, which gave the city a new skyline of arresting (though by western standards strange and uniform) beauty. The rebuilding of Stalingrad produced less happy results, though it was undertaken with the enthusiastic help of 20,000 Komsomol youth volunteers. Postwar Stalingrad made little progress over its prewar condition as a poorly laid out industrial city with few cultural amenities, few pleasant residential areas, and no efficient transport system. The city remained without a modern sewage system until 1975.

The quality of Soviet life left much to be desired in other ways. A decree of May 26, 1947 abolished the death penalty, giving as reason the "loyalty" of the Soviet people to their government during the war. The death penalty was restored, however, as of January 12, 1950, for "saboteurs, traitors and spies" in response, according to the official announcement, to "strong popular appeal."

THE CULT OF PERSONALITY

A wide discrepancy between appearance and reality had always been characteristic of the Soviet system and it seemed more pronounced toward the end of the Stalin era. The appearance then was that of the Soviet leader universally revered in his own country and in the socialist states established in the Soviet sphere of influence. Between the Elbe River in Germany and the Pacific there was scarcely a city or town that did not have a Stalin bust or statue or street or square named in his honor. Stalin made authoritative pronouncements in a field virtually without limit, including military strategy, economics, philosophy and the sciences, as well as in a number of other areas where his expertise had not been previously known, such as linguistics and philology.

The Nineteenth Party Congress of October 1952 marked the climax in the official adulation of the Soviet leader, with a proud recounting of Soviet achievements since the last party congress in March 1939 and with many of the East European satellite leaders, such as Poland's Bierut, Hungary's Rakosi, and Albania's Enver Hoxha paying tribute.

The reality of the final Stalin years was one of growing suspicion on the dictator's part, despite the universal applause. There were unmistakable signs shortly before Stalin's death of struggle and purging at the highest party levels with the sudden disappearance of three prominent leaders in the so-called Leningrad affair. Nicholas Voznesensky, head of the state planning commission *Gosplan,* Alexis Kuznetsov, a Central Committee secretary, and Micheal Rodionov, the premier of the Russian republic, were executed in 1950, a fact revealed only after Stalin's death. All three men had previously served in the Leningrad party organization under Zhdanov. Of the three, Voznesensky had been the most prominent. Appointed chief of *Gosplan* at the young age of thirty-five and honored with a Stalin prize for his book *The War Economy of the USSR* in 1948, Voznesensky seemed destined for a long and brilliant career.

By March 1949 suspicion had fallen even on such senior leaders as Molotov, defense minister Bulganin and foreign trade minister Mikoyan, all of whom lost their ministerial posts.

On January 13, 1953 both *Pravda* and *Izvestia* announced the uncovering of a plot masterminded by leading Soviet physicians, six of whom were Jews. The doctors were said to have planned the murder of prominent Soviet personalities, including the highest, as part of a plan of the Western intelligence services, supported by Zionists. As the Soviet population was bracing for the unleashing of another purge, Stalin died on March 5, 1953.

In the 1930s, Stalin's self-advertisement through what Khrushchev was to call the "cult of the personality" was dictated by considerations of power. In the 1940s and 1950s it may have been motivated by the additional desire to assure his place in history over and above that of all the other Bolshevik leaders, including Lenin. Although Lenin had founded the Soviet state, Stalin had turned that state from a weak institution into the world's stongest state and second largest industrial power. At the same time, according to his critics, Stalin had created a counterfeit communism in Soviet Russia which conformed to none of the ideas proposed by Marx and Engels. This charge was leveled against Stalin before the Second World War by the exiled Trotsky, whose murder Stalin ordered and, after the war, by Tito and his party theorist Milovan Djilas, whose criticism Stalin was forced to endure.

The Snake and the Rider

It was Stalin's historic achievement to have industrialized Russia and to have done it on a sufficiently large scale to enable him to win the war. He thus ranks among the great Westernizers of Russia, together with Peter the Great. In times past, periods of Westernization had been followed by periods of reaction in Russian history. The paradox of Westernization under Stalin was that Stalin was both its principal agent and chief adversary. Stalin changed rural Russia into industrial Russia but in enforcing the industrial revolution of the 1930s and 1940s he developed a system of terror that exceeded any violence known to medieval Russia. The age-old Russian dilemma of Westernization and reaction was well depicted in the equestrian monument of Tsar Peter the Great in Leningrad, by French sculptor Etienne Maurice Falconet. The Westward gaze of the Tsar was meant to symbolize Russia's yearning for Western ways, but the sculptor also placed a snake underneath the rider, representing the internal reaction, which tried to pull back the horseman. With Stalin, the rider and the snake became one.

13

Eastern Europe under Stalin

REFORM AND SOVIET CONTROLS

During their brief existence as independent states between the two world wars, the nations of eastern Europe had failed to solve three major problems characteristic of that broad region between the Baltic and the Adriatic seas. Those problems were land reform, industrialization, and a lasting settlement of nationality differences. The failure of land reform applied especially to the rural economies of the Baltic states, Poland, Hungary, and Rumania, but also to rural eastern Germany, where feudal land ownership had survived, often with unwholesome consequences for the political makeup of the states concerned. Industry was well advanced in the area soon to be known as the "iron triangle" of eastern Europe, Czechoslovakia, Poland, and the Soviet occupation zone of Germany. In eastern Europe overall, however, industrial employment had accounted for a mere 15 percent of the workforce before the Second World War, and was unable to absorb the large population surplus of the rural areas.

The national revolutions of eastern Europe at the end of the First World War had not resulted in the hoped-for pacification of a region habitually unstable as a result of unfulfilled and frustrated nationalism. Rather, the new state system of eastern Europe multiplied the nationalism factor, partly through rivalries among the states themselves, and partly through the scramble for influence over them by the established nation-states of western and central Europe.

Given the triple failure of eastern Europe before the Second World War, the Soviet presence in this region after the war could be seen as a force of social reform and order. Initially, such hopes existed among reform-minded eastern European intellectuals and leaders even outside the Communist establishment. A number of eastern European countries did enact sweeping land reforms soon after the arrival of Soviet power, beginning with the Polish land reforms of September 1944, with Yugoslavia, Rumania, Hungary, and East Germany following suit from 1945 onward. The land reforms were applauded by the peasantry, which benefited from the breakup of feudal estates. That land reform was meant to be only a halfway station between feudalism and Soviet-style collective farm communism was a fact not sufficiently appreciated until the imposition of full-blown Stalinism from 1947 onward.

The nationalization of basic industries, of banking, and of insurance, which accompanied land reform, was also a measure which enjoyed broad popular support outside Communist circles. Moreover, nationalization was neither uniform nor total in the immediate postwar phase, one-quarter of Hungarian heavy industry still being privately owned as late as 1948.

The economic and social reality of postwar eastern Europe was determined less by reform measures than by the mobilization of the region's economic assets and resources for Soviet reparation purposes. Together with occupied East Germany, eastern Europe was made to pay for the damages and losses suffered by Soviet Russia in the Second World War. Whether Soviet economic policy would have been less rapacious had the Soviets succeeded in obtaining the requested $6 billion reconstruction loan from the United States in 1946, is a matter of speculation. The Soviet failure to obtain such a loan was directly related to eastern Europe, however, as the opening up of eastern Europe to Western economic influence was among the conditions for obtaining it. By its own decision, the Soviet Union also cut itself and all of eastern Europe off from U.S. Marshall Plan aid in 1947, which was offered to the Soviets as much as it was offered to western Europe.

Economic Exploitation of Eastern Europe

The manner and method of Soviet economic exploitation of eastern Europe was varied. The former "enemy" nations—Rumania, Bulgaria, Hungary, and Finland— had had to make heavy reparation payments under the terms of both the armistice agreements of 1944 and the Paris peace treaties of 1947. "Friendly" nations, such as Poland, were made to sell coal from the newly acquired mines of Upper Silesia, for one-tenth the current world market price. Throughout eastern Europe, the Soviets confiscated "German assets," plants, factories and companies previously under German ownership, even if such ownership was itself the result of German confiscation during the period of German occupation. In many parts of eastern Europe the Soviets established "joint-stock" companies in choice areas of manufacture, such as the *Sovroms* of Rumania or the *SAGs* in East Germany. Joint-stock companies were formed in such areas as the East German watch, automobile, and uranium industries, and also in transportation companies, such as *Justa* and *Juspad* for Yugoslav civil aviation and inland shipping respectively. Top management of the joint-stock companies was predominantly Soviet and profits went predominantly to the Soviet Union, while working capital and facilities were provided by the host country. The various forms of economic exploitation, open and disguised, were a major factor in the growth of eastern European resistance to Soviet policy. Khrushchev recognized the depth of eastern European resentment of Soviet economic policy, admitting in October 1956 that "errors" had been made in the "relationship between socialist countries," without further identifying either the nature of the "errors" or the victims. Soviet economic policy contributed to Yugoslavia's break with the Soviet Union in 1948 and it was an important factor in the coming of the Polish upheavals and the Hungarian Revolution of autumn 1956.

Soviet Security

The second broad Soviet aim in eastern Europe, apart from the extraction of economic assets, was Soviet security. Soviet troops remained in all the countries of eastern Europe, which they had conquered in 1944–1945, except for Czechoslovakia, which was rewarded for the warm welcome given Soviet troops in 1945 and for its high Communist voter turn-out in 1946 by an early Soviet troop withdrawal. Soviet troops in Poland and in the Balkan countries remained, even after the signing of the 1947 Paris peace treaties, ostensibly for purposes of communication with Soviet forces stationed in Germany and Austria. Apart from the presence of troops, the Soviet security interest was served, even before the founding of the Warsaw Pact in May 1955, through a network of bilateral alliances. Of these, the Soviet-Czechoslovak alliance of December 1943 was the oldest, followed by the Polish and Yugoslav alliances of April 1945 and the alliances with Hungary, Rumania, and Bulgaria of early 1948. With East Germany, the Soviet Union was not to conclude an alliance until October 1955, when Soviet policy had failed both in its earlier attempt to extend Communist controls over all of Germany and in its more immediate effort to block the rearmament of West Germany.

The establishment of Soviet internal controls over the states of eastern Europe followed a two-stage pattern, with considerable variations being permitted during the first stage from 1945 to 1947, before the imposition of uniform Stalinist controls during the second from 1947 to 1953. Stalin chose not to annex the states of eastern Europe outright because such an option appeared as neither wise nor necessary. On the subject of the relationship of the USSR to other Socialist countries, Stalin had expressed his opinion as far back as 1920, when asked by Lenin to make a contribution to Lenin's *On the National and Colonial Question.* Stalin had distinguished between those states which had previously belonged to tsarist Russia, such as the Baltic states, and others, such as a "future Soviet Germany, Soviet Poland and Soviet Hungary." For the former, Stalin recommended "federation" with Soviet Russia, for the latter "confederation." The Baltic states were, in fact, annexed by the USSR in 1940 and remained so after 1945. In the other states of eastern Europe, other than Finland, the Soviets installed trusted Communists, sometimes in coalition governments with non-Communists during the initial phase, 1945–1947. Many of the east European Communists, who had sought safety in Moscow during the 1930s, such as Hungary's Béla Kun or Poland's Adolf Varski, Julian Lenski, Vera Kostrtseva and Henryk Valecki, had themselves been executed during Stalin's Great Purge. There was no reason to believe that those who had survived that purge would not obediently carry out Stalin's will in eastern Europe after 1945. Until Tito's break with Stalin of 1948, that assumption proved to be basically correct. In Hungary, the Soviets permitted relatively free elections in November 1945, with the non-Communist peasant party (freeholders) obtaining 245 seats against 70 for the Communists. Both the president and the prime minister, Zoltan Tildy and Ferenc Nagy, were taken from the dominant peasant party. In Bulgaria and Rumania the monarchy was retained in form until 1945 and 1947 respectively. In substance, Communists dominated the Bulgarian government under veteran Communist leader George Dimitrov and under Petru Groza in Rumania. Czechoslovakia constituted a unique case during the transitional phase. In Czechoslovakia, Soviet prestige was as high in 1945 as Western prestige was low, because of memories of the western sellout of Munich of 1938 and because of the liberation from the German occupation by the Russian "fellow Slavs." The warm reception accorded the Red Army by Prague in May 1945 reflected such sentiments. Czechoslovak Communists were strongly identified with Czechoslovak nationalism because of the Communists' leading role in the Resistance. Although the Czechoslovak government-in-exile under Eduard Benes had spent the war in London, not Moscow, it had signed a twenty-year alliance treaty with Moscow as early as December 12, 1943. Article 5 of that alliance precluded membership in coalitions directed against the other partner. According to the papers of Benes' long-term confidant Jaromir Smutny, Benes made even more far-reaching commitments to Stalin in private during the war, such as the pledge of full Czechoslovak support of Soviet foreign policy positions after the war. In the Czechoslovak elections of May 1946, which were free elections by western standards, the Communists emerged as the single strongest party with 38 percent of the vote. The coalition government under Communist leader Klement Gottwald contained twenty-six non-Communists as against nine Communists.

Poland and East Germany

Soviet internal control over Poland and East Germany, the other two members of the "iron triangle," were more direct and coercive. East Germany was an occupied country in fact and form before 1949 and remained so in fact afterwards. Poland, a supposed ally, posed greater difficulties because of its long tradition of fear and dislike of Russia, to which were added the more recent memories of Soviet treatment since 1939. The coalition government which Stalin had promised at Yalta ended up as Communist-dominated, despite the presence of peasant party leader Stanislav Mikolajczyk as deputy prime minister. After the manipulated elections of 1947, in which the peasant party, by far the strongest in the country, gained a mere 28 out of 444 seats, Mikolajczyk resigned. Even the Polish Communists presented problems for the Soviets, however, because of the memory of the Stalinist purge of the 1930s and the person of Vladislav Gomulka.

In 1942 Gomulka, who had been kept from going to the USSR in 1938 because of his imprisonment by the Polish government, had been elected general secretary of the Polish underground Communist party without Stalin's approval or support. After the war, Gomulka preached the "Polish road to Socialism," based on "Polish realities." By this Gomulka meant not only the preservation of a noncollectivist farm economy, but the retaining of a coalition with non-Communists on a more than fictional basis. Increasingly, Gomulka found himself at odds not only with Poland's Stalinist president Boleslav Bierut, but with Stalin directly, even before the phenomenon of "Titoism" had come to equate the search for a national road towards socialism with treason.

"TITOISM" AND THE YUGOSLAV-SOVIET BREAK

At the very time the Soviet Union began to tighten its controls over eastern Europe as part of a new and intensified confrontation with the West under the worsening Cold War of 1947–1948, serious trouble erupted from the unlikely source of Yugoslavia and its Communist leader Marshal Tito. The newly formed Communist Information Bureau (Cominform), launched in September 1947, had been designed to strengthen the Soviet hold over eastern Europe and to act as a common ideological platform from which to confront the West. The projected headquarters of the Cominform had been the Yugoslav capital of Belgrade, yet it was Yugoslavia that found itself indicted and condemned before the same Cominform less than a year after its founding.

To the uninitiated, Yugoslavia's swift transition from preferred Soviet ally to deadly enemy of all socialist states came as a stunning surprise, because the reality of growing Soviet-Yugoslav controversy and tension had been hidden behind the appearance of solid friendship. Since 1945, the appearance of Yugoslavia had been that of model Communist nation which had attempted to imitate the Soviet example ahead of anyone else and whose hostility towards the West, and the United States in particular, if anything exceeded that of the Soviet Union itself. Yugoslavia had been the first in eastern Europe to adopt a Soviet-style constitution in 1946, patterned after the 1936 Stalin constitution, the first to apply a Soviet style five-year plan in 1947, closely modeled after Stalin's five-year plans of the 1930s, and among the first and most ruthless promoters of agricultural collectivization. Tito delighted in criticizing other east European governments for their less precipitous policy of Soviet-style Communism and Yugoslavia even advocated closer bonds with the Soviet Union through some sort of constitutional association. Behind these appearances lay the reality of Yugoslav resentment of Soviet economic exploitation and Soviet concern lest Tito's unilateral provocations of the United States might land Soviet Russia into a dangerous confrontation over peripheral and nonessential issues.

Tito had displeased Stalin during the war by his public display of Communist zeal, when the soft-pedaling of Communism was deemed necessary by Stalin in the interest of Grand Alliance harmony. Tito continued to displease Stalin at the end of the war by emphasizing Yugoslavia's own primary role in its liberation from German domination, and by showing insufficient gratitude for Soviet help, which was, in fact, of moderate importance. Tito further displeased Stalin after the war by his independent foreign policy ventures, his confrontational behavior over Trieste, and the shooting down, in 1946, of unarmed U.S. transport planes which had strayed into Yugoslav air space. Soviet anger continued to be aroused over Tito's attempt to build his own armaments industry independent of Moscow, and over Tito's general ignoring of the unwritten first commandment of satellite good behavior: Before making major decisions, the opinion of the Soviet Union must be heard. The Yugoslavs, in turn, were upset by the quiet penetration of their military and intelligence leadership by Soviet agents, by the withholding of necessary aid for the implementation of the 1947 five-year plan, and by economic exploitation through such means as *Justad* and *Juspa*. The trouble surfaced when Stalin withdrew all technical and military advisers from Yugoslavia on March 18, 1948 in a move that Khrushchev was to repeat twelve years later in similar circumstances against Communist China. The Yugoslav inquiry as to the causes of the Soviet action prompted the ringing indictment by the Cominform of June 28, 1948. Although the Cominform served as the forum, the indictment bore all the features of Stalin's personal authorship.

The Cominform indictment was the overture to Soviet retaliatory action on a broad scale, covering the full range of ideological excommunication, economic blockade and attempted internal subversion. The vehemence of the Soviet response was prompted not only by the personal affront which Stalin clearly saw in Tito's behavior, but by the danger of east European insubordination, which Tito's Yugoslavia seemed to represent and to encourage. Accordingly, the attacks on Tito were also the signal for a general crackdown on the other states of eastern Europe in order to prevent the bad example from being imitated elsewhere. The attempt to topple Tito by internal Yugoslav subversion failed in large measure because among the many Soviet features Tito had borrowed was an excellent internal security and intelligence service. Potential Yugoslav quislings, such as Sreten Tsuyovich or Andriya Hebrang, were discovered and neutralized.

The Communist bloc blockade might have caused serious difficulties, especially since it coincided with a prolonged drought. Tito's attempt to enlist the help of the Chinese Communists in 1949 failed because the Chinese, whatever they might have thought of the Soviet Union privately, were still dependent on Soviet support after so recently winning victory in their own country. Communist China endorsed the Cominform resolution against Yugoslavia and rejected Tito's invitation to establish diplomatic relations in 1949. What enabled Tito to survive Stalin's wrath was not only the unity of his own country but the timely support of the United States in the shape of economic and military aid. After an initial $40 million Export-Import bank loan, the United States furnished Yugoslavia with an additional $578.5 million in non-military aid and $588.5 million in military aid by 1955. American aid to Communist Yugoslavia was neither automatic nor easy. The distinction between Yugoslav and Soviet Communism was not always understood nor was it always considered relevant, even under the existing Cold War climate of the early 1950s. Yugoslavia nevertheless represented the first real opportunity for the United States since 1945 for at least a partial limitation of Soviet power in eastern Europe. The outbreak of the Korean War of 1950 likewise made the protection of the "Ljubljana gap," the gateway from eastern Europe into northern Yugoslavia and northern Italy, an important task when U.S. defenses were spread thin under the twin demands of NATO and the Far East.

All other attempts at destroying Tito having failed, it is, in retrospect, perhaps surprising that Stalin stopped short of a military invasion, such as Khrushchev launched against rebellious Hungary in 1956 and Brezhnev against unstable Czechoslovakia in 1968. Stalin, whose authority was considerably greater than that of either of his two successors, undoubtedly refrained from military action against Yugoslavia for reasons of geography and recent history. With a long seacoast along the Adriatic, Yugoslavia was easily accessible to the West, and Western relief could have enabled Tito to carry on for an indefinite length of time the same kind of guerrilla war against Stalin as he had conducted successfully against Hitler during the Second World War.

Yugoslav Marxism

Tito's defiance of Stalin had begun as a revolt of Yugoslav nationalism against Soviet imperialism, without any initial Yugoslav attempt or intention to challenge Soviet leadership on ideological grounds also. Very quickly, however, the Yugoslav rebellion assumed ideological significance also, after the Yugoslav Communists began to study the original sources of Marx and Engels and found them to be at profound variance with the practices of Lenin and Stalin. Leading Yugoslav party theorists, such as Tito's long-term friend and fellow partisan Milovan Djilas, found Leninism-Stalinism not only at variance with Marx and Engels, but branded Soviet Communism a gross distortion and betrayal of the Marxist idea. The Yugoslav critique centered around the elitist and dictatorial nature of the Soviet Communist party, the all-powerful Soviet state under Stalin's "bureaucratic socialism" and the state monopoly of the ownership of the means of production under the Soviet system and its east European imitations.

All three aspects were, in the Yugoslav post-1948 interpretation, "un-Marxist" because Marx had: considered the "dictatorship of the proletariat" to be a brief and transitory phase, not a permanent condition of society after Communist revolutions; believed in the progressive elimination of state power (withering away of the state) under communism; and believed in direct workers' ownership of factories and other means of production.

Based on their reinterpretation of Marxism, the Yugoslav Communists instituted numerous reforms which were meant to correct past Stalinist mistakes and to bring the Yugoslav social, economic and political system into closer approximation with the Marxist vision of communism. Symbolically, the Yugoslav Communist party changed its designation in 1952 to "League of Communists," to suggest the character of a voluntary association, and also to revive a title Marx himself had used. In substantive terms, the Workers' Council Law of 1950 created elected workers' councils for factory management, the 1953 Decree on the Reorganization of Cooperatives ended forced collectivization, and the 1952 Law on People's Committees established elected local government. This was followed by the 1953 constitutional law which abolished portions of the 1946 Stalinist constitution, the 1954 General Law on Universities, permitting academic self-government at Yugoslavia's five universities, and the 1952 Law on Administrative Complaints, enabling ordinary citizens to file complaints against official abuse.

The Yugoslav charge of Leninism-Stalinism being a distortion and betrayal of Marxism was not, in itself, new. Similar charges had been made with regard to Leninism from the very inception of the Bolshevik state, by German and Austrian Socialists in 1917–1918, and by the majority of all European Social Democrats in 1919 and afterwards. Trotsky had made similar charges against Stalinism from his exile in *The Revolution Betrayed* during the 1930s. What was new about the Yugoslav charges and subsequent reforms was the fact that they were made by a regime of institutionalized Marxism which continued to regard itself not only as communist but more genuinely communist than the Soviet Union. However small and insignificant Yugoslavia may have been in resources and naked power by comparison with the Soviet Union, the Yugoslav reform ideas were a powerful attraction to Communist regimes everywhere in eastern Europe because they created fresh hope in the feasibility of a synthesis of communism and personal freedom, a "socialism with a human face." Such a synthesis was to be the goal of reform Communists in Poland and Hungary in 1956 and, after the defeat of the Hungarian Revolution of November 1956 and the ossification of Polish reform communism in the 1960s, it became the goal once more of Czechoslovak reform Communists in 1968. After the crushing of the Czechoslovak reforms in 1968, the search for the synthethis of freedom and communism was to be taken up in western Europe by the "Euro-Communists" of the 1970s. The question as to whether the desired synthethis was possible concerned the Yugoslavs themselves and none more than Milovan Djilas, who had triggered the ideological self-examination. In his book *The New Class,* Djilas attacked institutionalized Marxism for its inherent tendency to breed a privilaged class of functionaries and bureaucrats, which, in Djilas' view, exploited the "working class" no less than institutionalized capitalism was accused of doing. Whereas Djilas had still written as a reform Communist when drafting *The New Class,* he broke with Marxism altogether in his work *The Unperfect Society.* East European Communists, *The Unperfect Society* claimed, no longer believed in Marxism either but continued to cling to it as the sole remaining justification of power. The "renaissance of Marxism," Djilas concluded, was "a dream of Marxist professors."

Djilas, formerly a close friend of Tito's, broke with him over the question of political freedom and the multiparty system required to realize it. However willing Tito was to liberalize Yugoslav communism, he was never prepared to abandon the Leninist principle of the Communist political monopoly. It was not entirely without good cause that Khrushchev, when seeking a reconciliation with Tito after Stalin's death, maintained that the Yugoslav party had remained faithful to the "principles of Marxism-Leninism."

STALINISM AND THE SATELLITE PURGES

If Stalin was unable to assail Tito in his native Yugoslavia, he wished to make certain that "Titoism," both as an ideological and national challenge to Soviet power, could not spread to other parts of Eastern Europe. The period between 1948 and Stalin's death in 1953 was thus characterized by a comprehensive program of tightened political controls, orthodox Stalinist economic measures, heightened ideological vigilance, and the purging of political suspects, both Communist and non-Communist. In Soviet terminology, *people's democracies* described the coalition governments of Communists and non-Communists. In some of these people's democracies, such as Hungary and Czechoslovakia, power had been shared between Communists and non-Communists on a more than fictional basis. From 1948 onwards, the Communist monopoly of political power was speedily asserted where it had not already existed before. By 1954, the Great Soviet Encyclopedia thus characterized the role of Communist parties in the people's democracies as "the only leading force" in political life. The Communist parties, it was admitted, "cannot share leadership" with anyone else.

The Czechoslovak Coup of 1948

The most spectacular example of the elimination of "bourgeois influence" in the people's democracies occurred in the Czechoslovak Communist coup of February 1948. The Czechoslovak coup occurred against the background of diminishing Communist appeal nationwide after the spectacular Communist gains in the 1946 elections, in part because of resentment of the 1947 Soviet veto of her joining the Marshall Plan. The immediate cause of the coup was the resignation of twelve non-Communists from Gottwald's government in protest against the packing of the Prague police force with Communists by the Communist minister of the interior Vaclav Nosek. The non-Communists acted on the assumption that Gottwald would follow parliamentary custom and tender his own resignation with ensuing elections. Communist strength would, it was believed, greatly diminish from its 1946 high because of changes in public opinion since the last elections.

Instead of resigning, Gottwald mobilized numerous Communist front organizations, including the "Workers' Militia," in order to sustain himself in power. By June 1948 Gottwald replaced Benes as Czechoslovak president. The Czechoslovak coup was part of the larger Soviet design of consolidating Soviet power in Eastern Europe. Its coinciding with the Berlin crisis greatly strengthened Western impressions, not only in the United States but in the west European democracies as well, of an expansionist Soviet foreign policy, and thus contributed to the coming of NATO in April 1949 and the launching of a separate West German state in May 1949. The elimination of bourgeois relics in eastern Europe also included the dropping of liberal-democratic constitutions and their replacement by Soviet-style constitutions, based on the 1936 Stalin consititution, as occurred in Hungary. The example was repeated even on the level of local government, with the replacement of old, historic patterns by the Soviet-style *oblast* ('district'), each with its own "proletarian center" as the heart of Communist political power and social action.

The economies of Eastern Europe likewise imitated the Soviet-type five-year plans with overwhelming emphasis on capital goods and neglect of consumer goods industries. The building of a heavy industrial base was often undertaken without re-gard to need, resources, or an adequate energy base. Stalinist economics also dictated the forced collectivization of farmland from 1947–1948 onwards. The technique of collectivization was directly copied from the Soviet tactics of the 1930s, of carrying the "class war" into the villages with "kulaks," the owners of medium-size farms, the special target.

Stalinism in Eastern Europe also meant the duplication of Stalin's Great Purge of the 1930s. The East European purges of the late 1940s and early 1950s generally were divided into two categories, purges of leftover "bourgeois" politicians and purges of Communists suspected of disloyalty. Among the victims of the first category of purges were the Bulgarian peasant leader Nicola Petkov and the Rumanian liberal leader Jon Maniu. East European Communist leaders, in turn, fell into three major categories: those who had returned from Moscow exile after the war, such as East Germany's Walter Ulbricht, or Poland's Boleslav Bierut; those who had returned from Western exile, chiefly London, such as Czechoslovak foreign minister Vladimir Cle-mentis; and those who, like Poland's Gomulka or Czechoslovakia's Gustav Husak, had fought in the Communist underground during the war.

The satellite purges were chiefly directed against the second and the third cat-egories. Communists who had spent the war in the West, or who had acted as inde-pendent underground leaders, were clearly suspected either of having maintained ties to western governments or of wishing to imitate Tito's example of disobedience to Moscow. A fourth category of purge victims was added as a result of the expanding anti-Zionist and anti-Semitic hysteria which became so much part of the Soviet Union's own Zhdanov purge in Stalin's final years. Increasingly, satellite Communists were being put on trial simply because they were Jewish, regardless of any other aspect of their background. Among Polish Communists, the principal purge victim was Go-mulka. It was significant for Poland's subsequent development, however, that neither Gomulka nor the other leading purge victims were executed, because Polish Com-munists were able to bridge the chasm of factional hatreds by a common Polish con-sciousness, born out of common past sufferings at the hands of Soviet Russia.

By contrast, the Hungarian purge was ruthless and bloody, claiming the lives of Laszlo Rajk and many others. The memory of the Hungarian purge was to develop into one of the major causes of the Hungarian Revolution of 1956. In Bulgaria, Trai-cho Kostov was executed primarily because he had openly critized Soviet economic exploitation of his own as well as of other east European countries.

Rumania's top Communists Ana Pauker and Vasile Luca were purged simply because they were Jewish. The Czechoslovak show trials of November and December 1952 were similarly noteworthy for their concentration on Jewish Communists, with eleven Jewish defendants and eleven Jews being executed, among them Rudof Slansky, the former party secretary. The Slansky trial was followed by others, involving such leaders as Gustav Husak, subsequently rehabilitated and installed as Soviet puppet in Czechoslovakia in 1969. In Czechoslovakia, a country of 14 million people, 130,000 individuals were directly affected by the Stalinist purge through execution, imprisonment, or arrest.

Survivors of the 1952–1953 Czechoslovak purge were able to give details of the trials during Czechoslovakia's brief "Prague spring" of 1968. Former Czechoslovak minister of state security Bacilek told of the leading role of Beria's Soviet secret police in the show trials. The prison physician Dr. Sommer related the extensive use of drugs on prisoners.

The autumn of 1952 witnessed three events which were, each in its own way, symbolic of the state of eastern Europe under Stalin. One was the Slansky trial, the other the Nineteenth Party Congress and the third, the Sixth Party Congress in Yugoslavia. The Slansky trial was an accurate reflection of the suspicions and fears with which the Soviet Union still looked upon eastern Europe seven years after the Soviet occupation had begun. The Nineteenth Party Congress in Moscow adequately expressed the fear with which the satellite leaders, for their part, gauged the vicissitudes of Soviet rule in their own country. All satellite leaders present outdid one anther in praises for Stalin and the blessings of Soviet rule generally. Hungary's Stalinist Rakosi claimed that the poeple of Hungary enjoyed "freedom for the first time in history." Poland's Stalinist Bierut asserted that Polish workers owed "their liberty and national culture" to the Soviet Union. The Yugoslav party congress, in turn, reflected the yearning of the peoples of eastern Europe for genuine independence, and it indicated how far they were prepared to go in achieving it. Soon after these events, the peoples of Poland and Hungary were to demonstate in even more dramatic, but tragic, fashion their love of liberty and their courage in seeking it.

14

The Cold War and Central Europe

THE SOVIET APPROACH TO GERMANY

That Germany should have become the principal object of contention between the former members of the Grand Alliance so soon after their common victory over her will probably be viewed in future times as one of the major ironies of the twentieth century. For, having been the principal reason for Allied unity during World War II, the German problem quickly developed into the major cause and catalyst of the Cold War in Europe. The great strategic potential of even a defeated and divided Germany, and the appreciation of that potential by the Cold War contenders, meant that Germany in defeat was almost as much a threat to peace as she had been before the war. And so the German problem cast its shadow over East-West relations for a decade-and-a-half from 1947 onwards, culminating in the Soviet-American nuclear confrontation of 1962 over the interrelated issues of Cuba and Berlin and, in a wider sense, the issue of German reunification.

In retrospect, it would appear that the Soviets appreciated Germany's importance at an earlier stage and to a higher degree than did their Western adversaries. For what distinguished Soviet policy from that of the other occupying powers was a coherent design, concerned not only with the Soviet Union's own zone of occupation, but with the future of all of Germany.

Reparations

The first order of Soviet business was, to be sure, the extraction of reparations to the maximum degree and in the shortest time possible. Large scale dismantling of plants and factories began in the Soviet zone even before the formal establishment of the Soviet Military Administration (SMA) in Berlin on June 9, 1945. Between May and July 1945 the Soviets stripped West Berlin alone of 380 factories before handing over that part of the city to the Western powers. By June 1945, most of East Germany's railroads were reduced to single track as a result of Soviet requisitioning of rail tracks. By summer 1946 over two hundred of East Germany's principal chemical, paper, textile and shoe factories were shipped off to Russia. The optical Zeiss works at Jena had been moved eastward together with their entire German staffs. Reparations from current production continued until December 1953.

Overall, East Germany lost 50 percent of its factories to the Soviet Union. Twenty-five percent of those remaining were turned into Soviet–East German joint-stock companies (*Sowjetische aktiengesellschaften,* SAGs), which included the automobile and watch industries as well as the Wismuth uranium mines. During the 1950s most of the SAGs were sold back to East Germany, with the notable exception of the Wismuth mines.

Total Soviet reparations from East Germany were estimated at $12.5 billion. In effect, the people of East Germany were made to pay for the damages which all of Germany had inflicted on the USSR in the course of the Second World War.

Apart from the short-term goal of reparations, the Soviets pursued two long-term goals. The one, sovietization of East Germany, was certain of attainment. The other, extension of Communist controls over all of Germany, was possible of attainment and the Soviets attempted it at least until the early 1950s.

The Sovietization of East Germany

The groundwork of the sovietization of East Germany was laid immediately after the end of hostilities, but it was done in a manner which concealed exclusive Communist controls and which consciously struck a positive and optimistic note. Moreover, the Soviets were careful, then as later, not to offend German national sensibilities. At a time when western attitudes towards Germany were strongly influenced by the thesis of "collective guilt" of all Germans for Nazi crimes, Stalin carefully distinguished between the Nazi regime, now happily eliminated, and the German people. As early as May 1945 Stalin observed that "the Hitlers come and the Hitlers go, but the German people remain." Nor did it escape German public attention that Stalin censured Soviet novelist Ilya Ehrenburg for the latter's earlier anti-German outbursts.

Ahead of any other occupying power, the Soviets licensed "antifascist" political parties and trade unions in their own zone through Zhukov's Order Number Two of June 10, 1945. The German Communist party (KPD) under Walter Ulbricht was reestablished the following day, but it was not the only political party to appear in the Soviet zone, and the KPD party program of June 11, 1945 was notable for its restraint. The program said nothing about the socialization of either industry or the farmland and it called for a common antifascist front, together with other parties, in order to complete, it was stated, the German democratic revolutions of 1848 and 1918.

Ahead of the Western powers the Soviets also organized a functioning German administration in their own zone. By July 9, 1945, before the opening of the Potsdam conference, East German state (*Länder-*) governments were operating in Saxony, Thuringia, Saxony-Anhalt, Brandenburg, and Mecklenburg. By the end of 1945 an East German police force was established and by August 1946 an East German ministry of the interior was set up under the designation "German Administration of the Interior.'' The end of 1946 witnessed the appearance of an East German border police, followed soon afterwards by the paramilitary ''People's Police'' (VOPO).

The SED

In April 1946 East Germany's Social Democratic Party (SPD) and Communists (KPD) were merged into the ''Socialist Unity party'' (SED) on Soviet orders. The move was obviously inspired by the poor showing of the Communist parties in the Austrian and Hungarian elections in late 1945.

Initially, leadership of the SED was to be evenly divided between Social Democrats and Communists. In fact, effective leadership passed very quickly into Communist hands. As a mass party, the SED concealed the numerical weakness of Communists in East Germany while serving Communist ends of de facto control of the Soviet zone. As of 1946 the SED became the governing party of East Germany and it has remained so ever since. As early as 1946 the Soviets entrusted the SED with real state functions, such as the drawing up of a two-year economic plan.

By 1946, East Germany's Soviet zone had all the attributes of statehood save the name, long before any of the western powers had begun to contemplate similar moves in West Germany. The distinction was important because Soviet propaganda, directed at German nationalist audiences, was later to charge that the division of Germany had its beginnings in western initiatives.

By 1946 there were also numerous indications that the SED, apart from being the instrument of sovietization of East Germany, was intended to serve as the vehicle for extending Communist controls over the Western zones as well.

Significantly, the East Berlin ''unity congress'' of April 1946 which launched the SED had not been organized as an East German zonal event, but rather as a German national congress. Soon after the founding of the SED, some of its most prominent leaders were traveling freely through the western occupation zones in order to drum up West German workers' support for the new party. The SED advertised itself as the one new political force in postwar Germany which could realistically be expected to halt the drift towards the division of Germany which was already clearly visible in 1946.

The SED's attraction as the potential unifier of Germany rested on its appeal both to the working class and to German nationalists. The German working class of 1946 understood well the fateful consequences of its division into mutually hostile Communist and Social Democratic camps before 1933, and it was ready to heal these past divisions in the interest of working-class solidarity. The SED could be viewed as symbolic of that objective.

German "Neutral Nationalism"

German nationalism began to manifest itself after the war in the new guise of ''neutral nationalism.'' With the unfolding of the Cold War, in which the antagonists attacked one another with invective scarcely less vehement than that exchanged between the enemies of World War II, German nationalists derived satisfaction from the breakup of the Grand Alliance. They preferred to assume a neutral stance removed from the new Cold War battlefronts, appearing as critics of either side and obscuring in the process the memory of the horrendous Nazi crimes which the Nuremberg and other war-crime trials had so recently revealed.

Added to the newly discovered sense of moral superiority was the belief—widespread among German neutral nationalists—that the Soviets, not the Western powers, held the key to the reunification of Germany. That belief rested on the knowledge that the Soviets had made a considerably greater contribution to the defeat of Germany than had any of the Western powers, the United States included. The Soviet conquest of the capital, Berlin, was symbolic of that fact.

The German neutral nationalist constituency included many ex-*Wehrmacht* officers and ex-Nazis. In West Germany it was soon to obtain an influential spokesman in the weekly news magazine *Der Spiegel,* which was licensed in the British occupation zone in Hamburg in the late 1940s, and later in the illustrated magazine *Stern,* which was published in the same city and which maintained close administrative and staff contacts with the similar-minded *Der Spiegel.*

The Soviets skillfully exploited the German neutral nationalist capacity for self-deception and self-righteousness. The Soviet formula for reunification was an all-German SED-dominated government, supported by the neutral nationalists. In international affairs, such a government would be ostensibly nonaligned, but it would have to pay the price for restoring the unity of Germany with allegiance to the Soviet Union.

For an alliance of German nationalism and Soviet communism there existed many precedents, reaching all the way back to 1917. For an alliance of German nationalism and Russian (pre-Soviet) nationalism there existed an equal number of precedents, reaching back to Bismarck and even further, to the Russian-Prussian alliance of 1813 against Napoleon. When seeking to forge a new Soviet-German alliance after World War II under the altered conditions of a victorious Russia and a defeated Germany, the Soviets invoked memories of both categories of cooperation. The Treaty of Rapallo of 1922, which united Soviet Russia and the Weimar Republic, the two outcasts of post-World War I Europe, was invoked with particular frequency as a model and guide for post-World War II relations as well.

The basic pattern of Soviet wooing of Germany was set at an early stage. It was to remain essentially unaltered during all subsequent phases in the development of the German problem, during the emotional debate on German rearmament in the 1950s and down to the Euromissile debate of the early 1980s.

In its appeal to important West German interest groups, Soviet propaganda did not omit the academic, intellectual and artistic establishment. Noteworthy among Soviet-sponsored cultural fronts of the postwar period was the Cultural Federation for the Democratic Renewal of Germany (*Kulturbund*), which numbered 60,000 members in 1946 and which was active in both East and West Germany. No comparable Western-sponsored organization with access to the Soviet zone existed then or later.

Noted writers and artists accepted invitations to settle in East rather than West Germany upon returning from foreign exile, principally the United States. Among them were Bertolt Brecht, Gerhart Eisler, Karl Eduard Schnitzler, Stefan Heym, and Heinrich Mann, although the latter died before actually moving to Communist East Germany.

WESTERN ATTITUDES AND POLICIES

Success or failure of the Soviet design for Germany depended heavily on the nature of Western policy and the response which the peoples of West Germany themselves would develop.

What became generally true of Western policy in postwar Europe also applied to Western policy in Germany during its early stages. In contrast to the clear conception of Soviet policy, there was at first little coordination or cohesion in the Western approach to Germany and there were often enough contradictory purposes in the conduct of individual agencies of the same occupying power. For a considerable time, Western policy in Germany followed events rather than anticipating them.

The French Interest

France acted as the most independent-minded of all the Western powers, and Britain and the United States often regarded her, and not the Soviet Union, as the principal obstruction to effective four-power government. The French high commissioner exercised his veto power in the Allied Control Council more frequently than did his Soviet counterpart in the first year of occupation.

Not having been invited to Yalta or Potsdam, France did not feel bound by the decisions of either conference. Once installed as an occupying power, thanks in large measure to Churchill's initiative at Yalta, the French developed a policy specifically designed to serve French national interests.

As perceived between 1945 and 1947, the French interest was inspired by the distant memories of the Rhine-Ruhr policy of the 1920s and the more recent experience of the German occupation of France during World War II. As in the twenties, France aimed at the economic fusion of the Saar and the exclusion of German controls from the industrial and mining assets of the Ruhr. The separation of the Rhineland, as a policy goal, seemed only the natural counterpart to the separation of the German provinces east of the Oder-Neisse.

Otherwise, French policy was eager to get compensation for the damages and cost of the German World War II occupation and to erase, as far as possible, the memory of the French defeat of June 1940 from the minds of the Germans as well as from their own minds.

More than their British and American allies, the French felt the need to impress the Germans with the reality of their defeat by staging an expensive and highly visible occupation. French occupation costs were the highest of any Western power. Lindau castle on Lake Constance, the headquarters of General de Lattre's French "Army of the Rhine and Danube," became the scene of extravagant pageants and displays which attracted the unfavorable attention even of some of the Paris newspapers.

In the return of political power to German authorities, however limited, France remained by far the most cautious among the Western powers. Local government in the French zone remained under military control for fifteen months, longer than in any other part of Germany. The state (*Länder*) governments of Rhineland-Palatinate, Baden and Württemberg, which together constituted the French zone, were appointed by the military government, not elected. In the Saar, the French installed their own satellite party, the "Christian People's party" under Johannes Hoffmann.

Throughout its zone, France prohibited any label or institution that might have suggested the restoration of a national German government. The word *German* was stricken even from postage stamps.

Until 1947, the de facto dismemberment of Germany along zonal lines remained the long-term goal of French policy in Germany.

Consistent with the significance which France had traditionally attached to education as a vehicle for the spread of French civilization in the colonies and elsewhere,

French military authorities in Germany put great stress on educational policy. Among the Western powers, the French were the first to reopen schools and universities. Under the supervision of Raymond Schmittlein, chief of the Directorate of Public Education, new teachers colleges were organized and new textbooks were issued. A new university, the Gutenberg University at Mainz, was added to the older universities of Tübingen and Freiburg. The French authorities had little hope of molding the minds of young Germans over the age of fifteen, but they looked to those of younger age. The success of French-German reconciliation of the 1950s and 1960s must, in part, be attributed to the educational effort of the 1940s.

The American Zone

In the American zone, different agencies and individuals within the U.S. military government often enough pursued different policies. Some of these were motivated by the desire to purge German life of all traces of past Nazi influence. In the U.S. zone alone, there were 800,000 convictions in de-Nazification trials. Other policies were undertaken with an eye on enlisting German support against the Soviet Union.

Distrust of defeated Germany continued to guide the activities of the Psychological Warfare and Civil Affairs Division, while the Economic Division urged the rebuilding of the German economy as part of a larger reconstruction effort for all of western Europe.

U.S. military intelligence was the most pragmatic in the utilization and recruitment of information and personnel from the Nazi era to provide insights into Communist strength in Western Europe and Soviet military and strategic capabilities. Brigadier General Edwin L. Sibert recruited General Reinhard Gehlen, Hitler's top intelligence expert on the Soviet Union, as early as 1945. Gehlen, who had preserved his intelligence files through the vicissitudes of the German collapse of May 1945, was set up, together with many of his former aides, as head of a new intelligence unit in the village of Pullach, outside Munich, in early 1946. "Organization Gehlen" was soon able to provide the United States with proof of the expanding militarization of Communist East Germany by the Soviet Union. After the establishment of the Federal Republic of West Germany in 1949, "Organization Gehlen" became West Germany's official intelligence service under the title *Bundesnachrichtendienst*. That U.S. military intelligence also made use of former high Gestapo officials, such as Gestapo chief Klaus Barbie, stationed in German-occupied Lyon during World War II, became known only at the beginning of the 1980s.

Social Chaos

Along with de-Nazification and the recruitment of former staffs of the Nazi regime, there was the expanding problem of the economic misery and despair of West Germany's bombed-out urban population. The U.S. and British zones were the most heavily industrialized part of Germany and the most urbanized. They were also the most heavily bombed, in addition to being the principal gathering place of the huge stream of eastern refugees, numbering between 12 and 13 million. In some West German states, such as Lower Saxony, one out of every three residents was a refugee. Added to the 5 million homeless whose dwellings had been destroyed by Allied bombing, there were 6 million refugees without a roof over their heads in the U.S. and British zones during the winter of 1946.

The food situation was no less desperate. The Soviets had defaulted on the delivery of surplus food from their own zone, which they had promised under the Potsdam Agreement. Nor could sufficient foreign exchange be earned through industrial exports because of Allied-imposed production ceilings and the drop in industrial production in 1946 to one-third the 1936 level. Dismantling of plants continued at a hectic pace, especially in the British zone. The Volkswagen plant in Wolfsburg in the British zone escaped dismantling only because British automobile executives, when offered the VW plant by British military authorities, dismissed the Volkswagen beetle as a car without an economic future.

In the American zone, the near famine of 1946–1947 was somewhat alleviated by the generous help of private American charitable organizations and by the gifts of tens of thousands of individual American citizens, which often made the difference between survival and nonsurvival for the recipients. It was a humanitarian action on behalf of a former enemy which had no equal in the harsh world of postwar Europe. Germans born since the Second World War have difficulty visualizing the German reality of 1946. A not atypical response of young West Germans of the 1980s, when reminded of the social misery of the 1940s has been, "Why did not people protest?"

British efforts to subsidize food imports to their own zone were impaired by Britain's own balance-of-payments problems and the considerable financial commitments incurred through the financing of the anticommunist forces in the Greek Civil War as well as on-going Commonwealth commitments worldwide. Food rations in the British zone had to be cut to a thousand calories a day. This resulted in further drops in labor productivity and the danger of a tuberculosis epidemic in Hamburg.

To Rebuild West Germany

Fears that social chaos in West Germany might favor the course of Soviet policy, plus the perception of the interdependence of east and central European problems, prompted a coherent western policy response from early 1947 onwards. The two abortive foreign ministers' conferences of that year in Moscow and London revealed the Soviet-Western impasse over Germany. Each side accused the other of having broken the Potsdam Agreement of 1945. The Soviets denounced the economic merger of the United States and British zones, which had been in effect since January 1947. U. S. secretary of state George C. Marshall in turn attacked the Soviet-sponsored SAGs in East Germany as an infringement of the Potsdam Agreement. The western powers proposed to set up a federal government for all of Germany, with the fused Anglo-American zones of "Bizonia" to serve as a nucleus. The Soviets countered with a proposal for a strongly centralized German government, presumably under SED leadership.

After the failure of the 1947 foreign ministers' conferences, the Western powers attempted to build in a few months what Soviet policy had been establishing at a steady pace in East Germany since 1945: the outlines of a functioning German state. The West German political parties, which the Western powers had previously only tolerated, found themselves actively courted and enlisted in the task of West German state building. It was an assignment not always relished by West German political leaders.

THE GERMAN RESPONSE

Although the loss of German sovereignty was no less complete in West Germany than it was in the East, West German public opinion had more than passing significance for the success or failure of Western policy. In some important respects, the West German response to Soviet initiatives preceded that of the Western occupying powers with results that were crucial to the success of Western policy decisions.

Prior to the polarization of German politics under Cold War influences German emotions formed a complex mosaic, ranging all the way from resentment and ridicule of Western reeducation efforts to strong self-criticism. Another element in German thinking was the notion that the completeness of their defeat in 1945 gave them a unique opportunity not of rebuilding a destroyed social order but of creating an entirely new one, one that would avoid all the past mistakes of both institutionalized Marxism and established capitalism. The notion of a new and presumably juster social order ignored the unaltered realities of external political power, which were beginning to manifest themselves at record speed in the Soviet zone and which would soon play their part also in West Germany under the exigencies of Cold War imperatives. The notion of a "third way" was not altogether new to twentieth-century German history as the 1918 revolution had shown. Then too there were hopes that the idea of "soviet democracy," in its specifically German shape, might enable the Germans to build a genuine workers' democracy which would combine the elusive goals of a socialist economic order with personal freedoms. Some of the political instability that was to manifest itself later in West Germany during the 1960s was occasioned by a sense of betrayal, a sense that the longing for novel social and economic forms at "zero hour" in 1945 had been replaced by the realities of a reconstituted German capitalism in its familiar prewar form.

There also arose in 1945 a clash between the two cultural and intellectual communities that had been torn apart by the Hitler regime. The one, which had gone into exile if it could, had seen its books burned publicly in Berlin in 1933 and had seen its works branded as subversive, decadent, and alien to the German spirit. The other had made its peace with Hitler and had continued to function inside Germany, often at the price of its integrity.

There was, lastly, in the Germany of 1945 a deep-seated and genuine antimilitarist reaction, which was as pleasing to Allied education officers before 1950 as it would be problematic to Western governments soon afterwards, when a new West German army was suddenly found to be desirable in the service of a larger west European cause.

The resolution of the German intellectual-cultural conflicts of 1945 and the maturing of German antimilitarism should have required an extended period of time in order to leave a lasting imprint on German society. But just as world events had played their part in cutting short the German democratic experiment between 1929 and 1933, world events between 1945 and 1949 played a role in forcing internal German developments into new directions which they might otherwise not have chosen.

Explanations of Nazism

To German historians, the foremost question of 1945 was the explanation of the German catastrophe in terms of German history, both recent and remote. Gerhard Ritter, defending Prussian traditions, identified Nazism as an alien import from Austria and Bavaria. Friedrich Meinecke, in *The German Catastrophe* (1946), reversed the charge and blamed Bismarck's Prussia and its autocratic system for Hitler and the Nazi regime.

The Lutheran church expressed its readiness to accept part of the blame for the events of 1933 in the "Stuttgart Declaration of Guilt" of October 1945. Social Democrats, mindful of their collaboration with General Gröner during the 1918 revolution, did likewise, as did some German Communists even. The latter conceded their error in not forming a common antifascist front with Social Democrats before 1933, though they failed to point out that that error was principally Moscow's, not their own.

Thomas Mann

Few judged Germany as harshly as did Nobel Prize–winning German novelist Thomas Mann, and few could rival Mann's prestige as the most celebrated of German cultural emigrés. In his BBC broadcast of May 10, 1945, the last of several beamed to Germany during World War II, Mann called the hour of Germany's defeat also the hour of Germany's "return to humanity," though Germany, in his words, had contributed nothing to its arrival. Then, in his famous speech in the Coolidge auditorium of the Library of Congress on May 29, 1945, entitled "Germany and the Germans," Mann traced the roots of the German catastrophe of 1945 to her refusal to accept western concepts of freedom and democracy, while on the other hand contributing much otherwise to the western world from her own inner spiritual gifts. Thomas Mann warned his American audience not to equate the defeat of nazism with an automatic German change of heart in favor of democracy. As a distant future goal, Mann urged the Germans to seek a new "social humanism," transcending conventional "bourgeois democracy." The goal of "social humanism" continued to influence West German Social Democratic thinking for many years after 1945. In 1947, the Christian Democratic Union (CDU), soon to emerge as the midwife of restored German capitalism, postulated in its first party program of Ahlen the social ownership of basic industries.

In 1949, when Thomas Mann set foot on German soil for the first time since 1933, the Cold War had already split Germany in two. Mann found the mood in Germany arrogant, and indifferent to the memory of Nazi crimes. The Germans, Mann believed, blamed the Allies rather than their own Nazi past for their current woes. He spoke of the "unshakable arrogance" of German claims to preferential compassion and special consideration after a war in which Germany had inflicted suffering on countless others.

At the end of World War II Mann's views on Germany commanded wide respect in the United States. By the late 1940s they no longer reflected U.S. policy. In the approaching era of McCarthyism and Cold War rhetoric, Mann's views were found to be questionable on Soviet Russia, a country Mann never criticized, and obsolete on Germany. Soon he left his U.S. exile to settle permanently in Europe again, though not in his native Germany.

The SED Question

The political question that had intruded into the debate on Germany's future with mounting urgency was how to cope with the SED bid for West German support. In 1946 the Western powers were still largely indifferent to that challenge and until 1947 they forbade German newspapers to criticize any aspect of Soviet policy.

Opposition to SED activities in West Germany developed principally from the ranks of the West German SPD and its founder and leader Kurt Schumacher. When reestablishing the SPD in May 1945 at Hanover in the British zone, Schumacher had been careful to preserve the independence of the West German SPD as distinct from that of East Germany. When the SED merger occurred in 1946, Schumacher opposed it and he used his considerable moral authority among West German workers to follow his lead.

The SED's first attempt to eliminate the SPD as a rival ended in failure in West Berlin. In a grassroots vote held in 1946 among West Berlin SPD members on the issue of the merger, 20,000 votes were cast against the merger as against 3,000 in support of it.

Later, Schumacher often aroused the ire of Western occupation powers because of his independent spirit and outspoken criticisms. A courageous man who had spent twelve years in Hitler's concentration camps and whose health had been destroyed as a result, Schumacher believed it his duty to uphold German national interests, especially in the hour of Germany's greatest national crisis.

His opposition to the SED was motivated by his strong anticommunism but also by his desire, as a native of Kulm on the Vistula, to uphold the German claim to the territories east of the Oder-Neisse. His often strident German nationalism, which was critical of both Soviet and Western policy in Germany, was partly motivated by the belief that the SPD's neglect of national concerns before 1933 had contributed to its decline in the Weimar Republic.

Schumacher had serious reservations about the American initiative for the founding of a separate West German state because he feared that such an initiative might seal the division of Germany. Ironically, neither the establishment of West Germany nor its subsequent rearmament would have been possible without Schumacher's early and determined opposition to the spread of SED influence into West Germany. In this he had neither help nor encouragement from the United States, nor from any other western power.

THE BERLIN BLOCKADE AND THE ESTABLISHMENT
OF THE TWO GERMAN STATES

Soon after the economic fusion of the British and U.S. zones in January 1947, the United States developed the bizonal Economic Council into a West German de facto government with its seat in Frankfurt. The two leading parties, Schumacher's SPD and Konrad Adenauer's CDU were represented in the Economic Council in equal strength. The French zone was added to "Bizonia" only in 1949. The CDU monopolized the executive council, however, because of Schumacher's boycott, a fact which paved the way for Adenauer's future chancellorship.

West German popular support for the creation of the West German state was strongly motivated by the evidence of economic success of the zonal merger. As early as August 1947 the West German trade fair at Hanover suggested the great potential of the West German economy. What was needed was investment capital, a better food supply, and a stable currency. Within a year, these conditions had either been met or were in the offing. The currency reform of June 20, 1948, launching the new D-mark at the exchange rate of one-to-ten, was a significant milestone along the road to economic recovery, as was the inclusion of West Germany in Marshall Plan aid in the same year.

In January 1948 the Western powers further strengthened the German organs of "Bizonia" and in March 1948 the London six-power conference of the Western Big Three and Benelux (Belgium, Holland, Luxemburg) formally called for the creation of a West German federal government.

On March 20, 1948 Marshal Sokolovsky of the USSR walked out of the Allied Control Council in Berlin, ending even the appearance of four-power government.

The following month the Berlin blockade began, first as a "creeping blockade" of traffic interruptions and delays. As of June 20, 1948, the day of the West German currency reform, the blockade became total, except for the airways.

The official Soviet justification of the blockade was the need to close off East Germany and East Berlin to the expected flood of old German marks from West Germany following the introduction of the new D-mark on June 20. The true purpose of the blockade was to secure Soviet economic controls over all of Berlin and, more importantly, to force the Western powers into abandoning their plans for setting up a separate West German state.

Except for the still-unbroken U.S. nuclear monopoly, which was about to end, the Soviets seemed to be holding all the cards. The small Western garrison of West Berlin, numbering 6,500 men, faced 18,000 Soviet troops in East Berlin, plus another 300,000 in the surrounding East German countryside. American combat reserves, available for immediate duty in Europe, numbered a single infantry division. Food and fuel supplies for the twelve boroughs of West Berlin were scarcely enough to last for six weeks.

Advice to the U.S. president was mixed. Some urged retreat from West Berlin. Others, like Churchill, speaking as a private citizen, recommended the threat of nuclear weapons in order to force a lifting of the Soviet blockade.

General Lucius Clay, U.S. high commissioner in Germany, and Colonel Howley, U.S. sector commandant in West Berlin, proposed crashing through to West Berlin with an armed convoy, leaving the risk of war to the Russians. Both agreed that a Western surrender to Soviet Russia in Berlin would have disastrous psychological and political consequences for West Germany and all of western Europe.

The Air Lift

President Truman moved B-29 bombers to the old Eighth Air Force bases in East Anglia. Since they were thought to have nuclear weapons capability, an assumption later disproved, the move was intended to warn the Soviets not to interfere with the air lift being organized at the same time. The air lift, and its success, must have impressed Stalin with the ability of U.S. strategic air power to uphold Western interests in a Cold War confrontation with the Soviets.

From small beginnings, the air lift reached a daily peak of 8,000 tons, accomplished in fourteen hundred landings. Seventy-nine pilots and ground crews lost their lives in accidents. The Soviets did not interfere with air traffic.

Much depended also on the attitude of the West Berliners. The Soviets tried to drive a wedge between the Western powers and the people of West Berlin by asserting that the blockade was not directed against the latter. The people of West Berlin were being offered all the supplies of food and fuel they required, provided they registered for such relief in the Soviet sector of East Berlin. Fewer than 2.5 percent of West Berliners took advantage of this offer. The remaining 98 percent took their chances with the Western powers.

This meant the rationing of coal to twenty-five pounds per family per month and the cutting back of electrical power and gas to two two-hour periods in every twenty-four hour period. Unemployment in West Berlin soared to 150,000 during the blockade.

The blockade also ended Berlin's municipal government, which had previously functioned under SPD mayor Louise Schröder for all four sectors of Berlin. West Berlin constituted its own city government at Berlin-Schöneberg, with Ernst Reuter succeeding Mrs. Schröder as mayor.

Reuter, himself a Communist in the 1920s, became one of the staunchest SPD supporters of U.S. policy in Germany under the impact of the Russian blockade of West Berlin. Unlike Schumacher, Reuter strongly supported the founding of West Germany in 1949 and its rearmament in the 1950s. In this he hoped to uphold East German faith in eventual reunification under conditions of freedom. When the Western powers failed to give support to the East Berlin workers' uprising of June 1953, Reuter's own faith was shattered, and he soon died a broken-hearted man.

The Soviets lifted the blockade in May 1949 because they had achieved none of their objectives and because the Western-imposed economic counterblockade against Communist East Germany had begun to hurt the Soviets badly.

Towards West German Statehood

Meanwhile, West Germany had steadily progressed towards statehood, though not without encountering doubts and opposition among West Germany's own political leaders. On June 9, 1948 the Western powers had called on the prime ministers of the West German *Länder* to convene a constituent assembly for all West Germany as the first act towards statehood. Concurrently, they had outlined their own ideas concerning the nature of the projected state in the "Frankfurt Documents," which stressed federal structure, democracy, and human rights. German unity as a desirable goal was mentioned peripherally and nothing was said on the question of frontiers.

A formal West German constituent assembly was precisely what West German politicians wished to avoid, because such an assembly would have lent the appearance of permanence and finality to the West German state. If such a state was to be established, the West German leaders wished it to be perceived as a temporary and interim solution only, to be followed as soon as possible by a reunified Germany. Hence the choice of the little university town of Bonn as a "temporary" capital. Hence the modest "parliamentary council" which, as an organ appointed by the *Länder* governments, drafted the West German constitution, rather than a formal constituent assembly. The constitution too suggested its provisional nature by being called the "Basic Law." It had taken the impassioned pleas of West Berlin mayor Ernst Reuter at the Rüdesheim conference of *länder* premiers in July 1948 to move the latter even this far. The everpresent fear at the Rüdesheim conference and similar gatherings was that future generations might accuse the West German leaders of 1948 of having initiated the division of Germany.

In contrast to the Bonn-based parliamentary council, which included no representatives from East Germany, the East German "People's Congress" of May 1949 had one-quarter of its members drawn from West Germany. The "People's Congress" was presented as a genuine constituent assembly, which drafted the constitution of the East German "Democratic Republic," about to be installed.

The first West German elections under the "Basic Law" were held in August 1949. With 139 seats, Adenauer's CDU and its Bavarian affiliate, the CSU, won a narrow victory, followed by the SPD with 131 seats. The liberal Free Democrats (FDP) obtained 52 seats, the remaining seats being divided among lesser and regional parties, such as the German party (DP), chiefly from Lower Saxony. The West German Communists obtained 15 seats.

FDP leader Theodor Heuss was chosen first president of West Germany. Adenauer, previously chairman of the parliamentary council, was elected West German chancellor by the newly elected parliament (*Bundestag*) on September 15, 1949 by a majority of one vote, his own.

The DDR

In East Germany SED leader Otto Grotewohl became prime minister in October 1949, following the formation of East Germany's parliament, called the *Volkskammer*. The formal establishment of the East German "Democratic Republic" (DDR) was deliberately timed to follow, not precede, that of West Germany, in order to place the onus of the German division on the Western powers. Unlike West Germany, Communist East Germany did not stress appearances of the provisional or temporary.

Both German states began immediately to denounce each other as usurpers. To upgrade East Germany, the Soviets gave the DDR its own foreign ministry from the start, at a time when West German foreign relations were still conducted by the Allied high commissioners.

In failing to prevent the establishment of a West German state in 1949, the Soviets had lost a major battle in the German Cold War, but they clearly did not yet consider the war lost. Fresh opportunities of tempting the West German public with prospects of reunification at the price of cutting ties with the Western powers would soon present themselves with the arrival of the emotional rearmament issue.

In persuading West German political leaders to cooperate in the founding of West Germany, the sponsoring Western powers had had to support the goal of German reunification. To many West Germans, the Basic Law clause concerning the completion of the unity in freedom "of all of Germany" was the most important part of the West German constitution. How unsettling to the stability of postwar Europe the active pursuit of that goal would be, was soon to be revealed in the development of the German problem after 1949.

15

Towards a New Western Europe

WEST EUROPEAN DEFENSE

The state of western Europe immediately after the end of World War II inspired little hope that the vision of a federated Europe, championed by Resistance leaders during the war, would remain anything but a beautiful dream. Initially it had been hoped that Britain would assume the leadership of a "united Europe" movement because of Churchill's high personal prestige and because Britain was in a unique position as the only West European power undefeated and uncompromised by World War II. Such hopes were quickly dashed by Churchill's own position, which advocated integration as a desirable goal for the rest of western Europe but not for his own country. These hopes were also disappointed by the attitude of the Labour government under Clement Attlee, newly installed in July 1945.

Britain

Attlee and his energetic foreign secretary Ernest Bevin, it was quickly understood on the continent, followed the traditions of British foreign policy far more closely than either the Conservative opposition had dared to hope, or Attlee's fellow socialists in Europe thought they had cause to fear. The Labour party agreed with the Conservatives that Britain's role must remain more diversified than that of any other west European nation. Britain must remain both "in" and "out" of Europe by virtue of her Commonwealth connections and her "special relationship" with the United States, rooted in the World War II alliance. Churchill's characterization at the Conservative party congress of 1948 of Britain's role as a triple role, leader of western Europe, head of the Commonwealth, and preferred ally of the United States, was also shared by Bevin and Attlee. In this context, the leadership role in western Europe was understood in terms of traditional alliances, not untried schemes of integration involving loss of national sovereignty on the part of the participants. There was little faith in postwar Britain either in the feasibility or the need of European integration.

To such objections the Labour party added reservations of its own, rooted in specifically Labour partisan considerations. Labour viewed its landslide victory over Churchill of July 1945 as both an historic mandate and an opportunity to revamp Britain's antiquated class structure and create a new and juster society. This was a national task which Labour had not dared solve according to its own convictions between the wars because it had lacked the public mandate and the power. Now that it possessed both, Labour refused to have its goals compromised by the predictable complexities and challenges which integration with foreign cultures would impose. It was thus in the realm of traditional foreign policy, dealing with other sovereign nations on the basis of shared interests, that the Attlee government brought its power to bear on behalf of Western Europe. It was in response to events in Eastern and Central Europe between 1945 and 1947 and in response to eastern Mediterranean developments that the Labour government devised a policy of containment, before such a policy became identified with the American Cold War stance in Europe.

The Greek Civil War

Not surprisingly, British containment began in an area of traditional British influence and experience: the eastern Mediterranean. From Churchill, Attlee inherited Britain's involvement in the Greek Civil War between the Communist-led ELAS (People's Liberation Army) and the anti-Communist EDES under General Zervas. After the British-arranged armistice of Varkiza of February 1945, hostilities in the Greek Civil War erupted again in August 1946 with strong indications of a well-orchestrated Soviet-inspired plan. In the same month the Soviet government, acting through its Ukrainian UN spokesman, brought charges of Greek aggression against Albania and of Greek oppression of the non-Greek minorities in Macedonia and Thrace. The governments of Communist Bulgaria and Yugoslavia supported those charges with territorial demands for western Thrace and Macedonia. The fact that the Soviet government officially disowned the Greek Communists, was, to the Labour government, not sufficient guarantee that Soviet Russia would not take full advantage of a Greek Communist victory if it were allowed to happen. In its support of Greek anti-Communist leaders, such as prime ministers Papandreo and Tsaldares, who were often criticized in the American press as either corrupt or antiliberal or both, the Labour government was pragmatic. The Greek government which Britain had attempted to defend against German aggression in April 1941 had also been notable for its lack of liberal credentials.

The intensification of the German Cold War in 1947 extended the scope of British containment strategy to Central and Western Europe. Before 1947, Labour views on Germany had still been strongly influenced by past fears and resentments. From 1947 onwards, these gave way to new concerns over the prospect of a Germany reunited under Soviet auspices and firmly tied to Soviet Russia. By the end of 1947 Ernest Bevin had called for the creation of a far-flung Western alliance, ranging from Scandinavia to Spain and including both the United States and Canada. The events of 1948, the Czechoslovak Communist coup, the Berlin blockade, Soviet pressure on Norway, and the anxiety surrounding the crucial elections in Italy, lent a new sense of urgency to the Bevin project of a regional, west European alliance. The outbreak of the Korean War in June 1950 led Prime Minister Attlee to suspect that further Communist initiatives might follow soon in other parts of the world, including Hong Kong, Iran, and Greece. The British War Office was sufficiently pessimistic to consider the outbreak of a general East-West conflict as not impossible by 1952.

By 1947, the limits of Britain's leadership capacity had become clearly apparent. In 1946, the cost of maintaining overseas forces had been £225 million, a sum equal to more than half the total British balance of payments deficit. The adoption of the peacetime draft in 1947 under the National Service Bill added new expenses, as did the launching of Britain's own nuclear weapons program the following year. After the outbreak of the Korean War, the British defense budget climbed to 11 percent of GNP, a figure considerably above that of other West European nations. The limits of Britain's resources forced her into terminating her role in Greece and Turkey on March 3, 1947, and to seek replacements in American funds and arms. The United States responded with the "Truman Doctrine," pledging general support to the "free peoples of the world" and specifically filling the gap left by the British withdrawal from Greece and Turkey with an immediate aid package of $400 million. U.S. military advisers under the direction of General Van Fleet took over from their British predecessors in directing the counterinsurgency tactics against the Greek Communists. On October 16, 1949 the Greek rebel radio announced the end of Communist resistance. Containment in Greece had succeeded without the need to commit American ground forces. The defeat of the Greek Communists was also due in part to the Yugoslav-Soviet break of 1948, which resulted in an abrupt termination of Yugoslav aid to the Greek insurgents. The outcome of the Greek Civil War confirmed the Stalin-Churchill spheres of influence agreement of October 1944, but not until after the western powers had been tested in their determination to defend it.

The "Third Force"

Attlee's yielding to American leadership in Europe was strongly criticized by the left wing of his own party under Aneurin Bevan. In October 1946 twenty-one left-wing Labour members of parliament protested against the government's increasing alignment with the United States. In May 1947, the Labour left-wing pamphlet "Keep Left," coauthored by Michael Foot, the future Labour leader of the early eighties, renewed the attack on U.S. foreign policy and British support of it on a broader basis. Like west European Socialists elsewhere, the Labour Left was apt to blame the expanding Cold War in equal measure on the United States and the Soviet Union. The Labour Left dreamed of a socialist Europe, a "third force," which, under British leadership, would be independent of both the United States and the Soviet Union. This was an illusion on more counts than one because a socialist Europe, even if it had existed, would have been lacking in the economic and military resources necessary for recovery and a credible self-defense.

As it was, the governments which developed in the principal nations of Western Europe from 1947 onwards, France, Italy, and West Germany, turned out to be not socialist but right-of-center. They did not share Michael Foot's or Aneurin Bevan's conception of the future of western Europe. The European Socialists who did, Kurt

Schumacher in West Germany and Pietro Nenni in Italy for instance, were not supported by majorities in their own countries. Though vociferous in its anti-Americanism, the Labour Left failed to impose its view on its own government in matters of defense and foreign policy, particularly in Western Europe.

Foreign Secretary Bevin and Prime Minister Attlee merged their own concept of containment with that of U.S. secretaries of state George C. Marshall and Dean Acheson. It was in order to convince the American public of the sincerity of West Europeans to organize a regional defense against Soviet Russia that the Labour government sponsored the Brussels treaty of March 17, 1948 between Britain, France, and the Benelux countries (Belgium, Netherlands, Luxembourg). The Anglo-French Treaty of Dunkirk of March 1947 had not been adequate to that purpose, since it had been directed primarily against the revival of a German threat. The NATO alliance of April 1949 realized Bevin's 1947 design, with Article V the crucial part, stipulating that an attack on one or more members of NATO would be considered an attack on all.

WEST EUROPEAN INTEGRATION

The American leadership role in the defense of western Europe and its position as the strongest NATO member and the principal supplier of NATO arms during the early years was matched by its initiative towards the economic recovery of western Europe under the European Recovery Program (ERP), better known as the Marshall Plan. Though essential to the economic recovery of western Europe, the $13 billion in Marshall Plan aid did not, in itself, move western Europe closer to integration. The U.S.-sponsored Organization for European Economic Cooperation (OEEC) failed to break the pattern of individualized national economic policy. Marshall Plan aid helped restore the west European economies on a nation-by-nation basis, without a regional approach and with efficient industries being restored side-by-side with inefficient ones.

The Schuman Plan

Before 1950, European efforts to achieve integration were chiefly symbolic or undertaken for publicity purposes. When Britain launched the Brussels treaty in March 1948 as a step towards regional defense, France wished to expand the treaty's scope by proposing an economic and customs union with a joint European assembly. Britain successfully vetoed the French proposal. The Council of Europe, which was created under the Brussels treaty, was similarly denied any real powers because of British objections. The Council of Europe produced a European Convention on Human Rights in 1950, together with a Court of Human Rights but it remained otherwise little more than a sounding board for European-minded parliamentarians. The first realistic and practical step towards west European integration was taken with the European Coal and Steel Community (ECSC), or Schuman Plan of 1950. Named after French foreign minister Robert Schuman, the plan created a common market for coal and steel production among the six founding members, France, West Germany, Italy, and the three Benelux countries, through the elimination of tariffs and other trade barriers and through the removal of combinations in restraint of trade. The further aim of the community was the modernization of production and the improvement in the quality of coal and steel for all participants. The community was open to other European countries. Britain, though invited to join from the beginning, declined to do so.

Although the plan was named after Robert Schuman, its chief architect was Jean Monnet. Monnet had a distinguished prewar record as an international businessman, economic adviser to governments, and League of Nations deputy secretary general. In 1940, on the eve of the fall of France, it was Monnet who urged Churchill to propose an Anglo-French union with common institutions and common citizenship. After the war, Monnet played a key role in the economic reconstruction of the Fourth Republic as chief of the Commissariat for National Modernization. Monnet's effectiveness as one of the prime movers of west European integration rested on the fact that he believed with the fervor of an idealist in a federalist Europe, while recognizing that the goal of integration could only be achieved through a progression of practical measures, whose economic usefulness and political viability would have to be demonstrated in a tangible manner along the way. That Monnet chose coal and steel as the nucleus of economic integration had symbolic significance because both had, in the past, been the backbone of national armaments industries. There was the additional reason that France and West Germany, the two principal members of the six-member Coal and Steel Community, had complementary coal and iron industries. France, well endowed with iron ore, but short on coal, was in need of German Ruhr coal. West Germany had adequate coal resources, but was short on iron ore ever since the loss of Lorraine in 1919.

The immediate economic objectives of the Coal and Steel Community could have been achieved through conventional trade agreements between the six member nations. The Coal and Steel Community was, however, meant to be the first step towards a full-blown common market with common political institutions. Thus it also provided the model for those institutions, with a supranational high authority, a council of ministers, a common assembly, a consultative committee, and a court of justice. The members of the high authority, though chosen by the participating governments, were solely responsible to the community as a whole. The assembly, composed of representatives of the respective national parliaments, had power to remove the high authority if it rejected the authority's annual report by a two-thirds majority. The council of ministers had veto power over certain authority decisions. Both the mechanics and the institutions of the Coal and Steel Community were later taken over virtually without change when the larger Common Market (EEC) was formed in 1957. Eventually, the ECSC institutions themselves were merged with those of the Common Market.

Monnet's functional approach to integration was carried out against the broader background of a European consensus shared by the political leadership of France, West Germany and Italy in the persons of foreign minister Robert Schuman, Chancellor Adenauer and Prime Minister Alcide de Gasperi. Schuman and Adenauer viewed integration as a vehicle for lasting Franco-German reconciliation after centuries of war. Robert Schuman's own life and family background were symbolic of the tragic history of Franco-German relations between 1870 and 1945. His father, born in Lorraine when it was part of France, fought the Germans as a French soldier in the Franco-Prussian War of 1870–1871. Schuman, born in Luxembourg and raised in Germany, fought France in the First World War as a German soldier. A French citizen after Lorraine reverted to France in 1919, he entered French politics as a parliamentary deputy from the Moselle department. During World War II, he fought the Germans as a member of the French Resistance. In 1944 he became cofounder of the Christian Democratic MRP which, like Adenauer's CDU in West Germany, became the leading advocate of European integration in France during the fifties.

Italy's prime minister Alcide de Gasperi viewed the prominent role which the pro-Catholic political parties of France, Italy and West Germany, MRP, DC, and CDU, were playing in the implementation of European integration as a fulfilment of his long-nurtured hope of a "Catholic International" for the combating of international communism. In the 1930s, common Catholic efforts against communism had been compromised by the close association of some Catholic parties with fascist or protofascist regimes, as was the case in the Austria of Chancellor Dollfuss or the Spain of Generalissimo Franco. During the 1950s, the Catholic parties of western Europe no longer suffered from the stigma of fascist association but were themselves leading advocates of parliamentary government in Italy, France and West Germany.

The economic success of the Schuman Plan was by no means certain and its performance during the first few years after its implementation on July 25, 1952 was often disappointing. There was considerable suspicion on both sides of the French-German border that the plan would offer unfair advantage to the other side. German industrialists feared the flooding of their market with cheap French imports, while the French resented the monopolistic sales structure of the German Ruhr coal industry. France pressed for the rapid construction of the Moselle canal to facilitate German coal exports to France and French steel exports to Germany. West German industry opposed the canal project before it was finally launched in 1958. It was not completed until 1964. The overall performance of the Schuman Plan was also adversely affected by the general decline in steel sales at the turn of 1953–1954, following the end of the Korean War boom. In France, the elimination of coal and steel tariffs forced some uneconomical mines to shut down. The Schuman Plan, foreseeing such contingencies, had made provisions for the relocation, at community expense, of workers thus affected. When French coal miners of the Cevennes region refused to be relocated in Lorraine, the French Communist press, seizing on the issue, spoke of the imminent "deportation" of French miners to the German Ruhr coal mines.

The EDC

The disappointing early record of the ECSC coincided with the emotional debate over West German rearmament and its implementation through the European Defense Community (EDC). The advocates of European integration hoped to turn the necessity of German rearmament into a virtue of integration. Within the European Defense Community, as proposed by French Defense Minister René Pleven, a European army was to be formed by the six members of the Coal and Steel Community, including West Germany. No one contributing country would be allowed to maintain separate units of its own nationality beyond division-size level, and overall command of the European army would be completely integrated. These provisions were meant to put to rest the frequently voiced criticism that a new West German army would soon be dominating the armies of all the other members. The EDC also had a political dimension, however, built in by the European federalists in the hope that the pace of integration could actually be accelerated by the defense issue. The draft treaty of March 9, 1953, prepared by Belgian foreign minister Paul-Henri Spaak, thus proposed a political union for the members of the EDC, with a common executive council, a council of ministers, a court of justice, and a bicameral parliament. The latter would consist of a senate, chosen by the parliaments of participating member-states, and a "people's chamber," elected in direct voting. If realized, the proposed institutions of the EDC union were intended to replace those already operating under the Schuman Plan.

Since the EDC never materialized, its projected political institutions also remained stillborn. The EDC failed because Great Britain refused to join it for the same reasons that she refused, at the time, to participate in any other venture of European integration involving supranational institutions and goals. Without a British presence inside the defense community, the French, who had devised the whole complex defense structure of the EDC in the first place, also ended up feeling insecure opposite West Germany. Prime Minister Mendès-France allowed the EDC treaty to die a quiet death in the French Assembly on August 30, 1954, thus killing the entire project. Among Mendès-France's motives may also have been an unofficial deal with Soviet Russia whereby the latter would assist France in a face-saving withdrawal from Indochina at the 1954 Geneva Conference, in return for the defeat of the European Defense Community. Although the EDC was dead, West German rearmament, which had prompted the EDC in 1950, was realized, albeit in different form. It was Britain's foreign secretary Anthony Eden who came to the rescue with an imaginative plan, using the 1948 Brussels defense pact as a basis. The Brussels pact, initially signed by Britain, France and the nations of Benelux as a prelude to NATO, was expanded through the admission of West Germany and Italy. Renamed the "West European Union," the expanded alliance was given a British pledge to station four divisions, the "British Army of the Rhine," in West Germany for the duration of the West European Union (WEU). West Germany was admitted as a full NATO member, the WEU supervising her rearmament. West Germany would not be allowed to manufacture "ABC" weapons—atomic, bacteriological, or chemical.

The Eden plan, which was adopted in the October 1954 Paris Agreements, struck a careful balance between west European security needs, French anxieties over the long-term implications of German rearmament, and the British resolve not to compromise her own national sovereignty. From the perspective of the European federalists, the substitution of the WEU for the EDC was, however, a severe disappointment and a serious defeat. Because of the disappointing economic performance of the ECSC at roughly the same time, it began to be said at the end of 1954 that the Schuman Plan should also be scrapped. European integration, after all, appeared once more an unrealistic proposition, unable to solve the real tasks confronting western Europe's economy and security. Jean Monnet, as first president of the ECSC high authority, was now blamed for having overemphasized the supranational aspects of the Schuman Plan. He had also been a strong advocate of the EDC.

The integration momentum suffered a further setback at the turn of 1954–1955, owing to the change in leadership in Soviet Russia following Stalin's death in March 1953. With the first "thaw" in East-West relations, highlighted by the Soviet withdrawal from Austria and the Soviet-Western Geneva summit of 1955, the urgency of west European cohesion appeared to have gone. Belgium's foreign minister Spaak wisely observed in this context that the nations of Europe were acting like chicks, running together whenever they saw a hawk circling above, but scattering quickly in all directions when the hawk had gone.

16

The Return of Italian Democracy

DEMOCRATIC BEGINNINGS

Italy's liberation was not as speedy as that of France, and Italy's "unconditional sur-render" to the Allies in September 1943 did not have quite the same meaning as that of Germany in May 1945. The slow Allied advance up the Italian boot from Salerno in September 1943 to the Po valley in May 1945 created a unique political situation in Italy, for which there was no counterpart in any other European country in World War II. In the north, as Hitler's puppet, Mussolini vainly attempted to imbue his "social republic" with a radicalized antimonarchist, and also "anticapitalist" fascist ideology, as defined in the 1943 Verona Manifesto. There was hatred for capitalism among the workers of Italy's industrialized north, but it was chiefly directed against Mussolini's puppet regime at Salo, which itself had the appearance of a last crutch of Italian capitalism. Mussolini's last months between September 1943 and April 1945 were mainly spent wreaking vengeance on those Fascist leaders who had conspired with Badoglio and the king to bring about his downfall in July 1943. Eighteen such leaders were sentenced to death by the Verona special tribunal in January 1944, among them Count Ciano, Mussolini's own son-in-law. Otherwise, Mussolini turned what little power the Germans left in his hands against the growing Communist guerrilla or "partisan" movement, killing some 70,000 and wounding another 40,000. Cap-tured partisans were denied the status of prisoners of war, a fact which explained Mussolini's own execution by partisans after his capture in April 1945. Fascism left the stage of Italian history as violently as it had entered it and in so doing it bequeathed a legacy of fear and hate which made the restoration of democratic life in postwar Italy that much more difficult.

The "Kingdom of the South"

In the area under Allied control, soon to be called the "kingdom of the south," the Allied military government retained the king with Badoglio as his prime minister. The sovereignty of the king's government, installed first at Brindisi, later in Rome, was little more than nominal. The attitudes of the Allies and of the Soviet government toward Victor Emmanuel's government were not the same. Ironically, the Soviets were the first to extend full diplomatic recognition to the "kingdom of the south" on March 13, 1944 in an obvious bid for Soviet influence in postwar Italy. The United States extended full recognition on October 25, 1944, in a move which may not have been entirely unrelated to the upcoming U.S. presidential elections of November 1944 and the significance of the Italian vote to the outcome of these elections. Britain was the least forthcoming towards defeated Italy, in part no doubt, because she had old scores to settle, reaching all the way back to her humiliation in the 1935–1936 Ethiopian war. When Badoglio tried to upgrade his government's relations with the Allies by formally declaring war on Nazi Germany on October 13, 1943, Britain hastened to explain that such an act in no way altered Italy's condition as a defeated enemy nation.

The king, Badoglio, and the Allies worked together well enough, because all three pursued the identical aim of containing the social repercussions of the collapse of fascism and of preventing, in particular, an upsurge of Communist and other forms of radical social and political power. In this, they quickly encountered opposition in the newly formed "committees of national liberation" as well as among the political parties which began to reconsitute themselves in the "kingdom of the south."

The "committees of national liberation" (CLNs) often assumed de facto control over local government in the liberated areas and developed political initiatives independent of the Allies. This included not only forceful land seizures but the wholesale purging of the civil service of Fascists and Fascist collaborators. When a CLN congress held at Bari in January 1944 claimed for itself constitution-making powers for all of Italy, the Allies firmly rejected such a claim. The Allies kept a paticularly watchful eye on the two leading committees, the National Committee of Liberation in Allied-occupied Rome and the National Committee of Liberation for Upper Italy (CLNAI) in German-occupied Milan. The latter, directing the guerrilla operations against Mussolini and the German occupation, was a stronghold of Communist and other radical strength. Among CLNAI leaders was veteran Communist Luigi Longo, whose experience as a guerrilla leader reached back to the Spanish Civil War.

The resurrection of democratic life in the "kingdom of the south" was not an easy task. Twenty years of Fascist rule had left their mark, and the fact that the rebirth of democracy occurred in the southern and poorest parts of Italy also was not without effect. Moreover, many of the politicians returning from long exile, whom Churchill characterized as "old and hungry," were, in fact, overaged and none of them possessed the healing powers or the charisma of a Charles de Gaulle. Benedetto Croce, the respected liberal philosopher-historian, was often consulted by the Allied military government, but he was too old and scholarly to fill the role of an effective national leader. Besides, even if he had aspired to such a role, he would have found few followers among Italian workers.

Among the half-dozen political parties which emerged after 1943, the Communists, Socialists, and Christian Democrats were destined to play a leading part in shaping Italy's future.

The Italian Communist Party

The Communist party enjoyed many advantages which assured it of a commanding role after the war. The party could count on a mass following, especially among industrial workers of the northern cities and it played a leading part in the Resistance through its Garibaldi brigades. With fascism discredited and bankrupt, communism also had a considerable appeal to intellectuals, many of whom were greatly impressed by the *Letters* and other works of Antonio Gramsci, Italy's Communist leader of the 1920s. Written in Fascist prison and first published after 1943, the *Letters* claimed for Italian communism an original contribution to Marxism-Leninism. Gramsci called upon intellectuals to assume an active leadership role (*dirigente*) among the working class. The Communist party was also the only one to have maintained an underground network throughout the Fascist years and it was able to activate this network during the industrial strikes in northern Italy in March–April 1943, several months before Mussolini's overthrow in July. In Palmiro Togliatti, who returned from his Moscow exile in April 1944, the Communists possessed a skillful leader whose decisions were based on pragmatism more often than on abstract principle. Togliatti's pragmatism was reflected in his support of the king, when other political parties, including the Socialists, rejected the monarch because of his past association with the Fascist regime. When the Socialists quit the government of Prime Minister Bonomi, Badoglio's successor, in late 1944, Togliatti stayed on as deputy prime minister together with two other Communists, the veteran Stalinist Scoccimarro as minister for the (German-) occupied territories, and Antonio Pesenti as finance minister. For the Communists, the chief aim was to consolidate positions of power during the transition period from war to peace.

The Socialist Party

The profile and tactics of the Italian Socialist party (PSIUP), by contrast, were blurred by contradictions and unresolved internal dilemmas. The leadership was split between the hard-liners behind party leader Pietro Nenni and the moderates under Guiseppe Saragat, who was to break away from the party before long. The Socialists condemned the Communists for their pragmatism, as in the question of the king, but they were tied to the Communists under the "unity of action pact" which Socialists and Communists had concluded in 1934 while in exile. Before the end of the war the Socialists were also much more strident than the Communists on the subject of social revolution. In 1944 Nenni boasted that the "wind of the north" (*vento del nord*) would be sweeping down the Italian peninsula once the Germans were defeated.

The Christian Democrats

The Christian Democratic party (*Democrazia Christiana,* DC), soon to emerge as the largest party, had many diverse roots. In part, the DC was an outgrowth of the *Popolari* under Luigi Sturzo. Among the chief differences between the old *Popolari* and the new DC was their relationship with the Catholic church and the Italian hierarchy. Church influence in the DC was much greater, and continued to be so for many years after World War II, largely because so many future DC leaders had found shelter and protection in the church during the Fascist years. This was true as much of the young DC politicians, such as Aldo Moro, as it was of the older generation, such as Alcide de Gasperi. De Gasperi, after being released from Fascist prison, had worked as librarian in the Vatican and had written political commentaries in the Vatican bi-monthly journal *Illustrazione Vaticana* under the pseudonym *Rerum Scriptor* and *Spectator*. It was during these years that de Gasperi developed his perception of a future Catholic mass party. The weakening of European Social Democracy under the dual impact of fascism and communism during the 1930s opened up the way, in de Gasperi's view, for new Catholic mass parties, committed to both social reform and liberal principles. Among the leadership of the newly founded DC at the end of World War II, de Gasperi occupied the center. Others saw in the DC a mere bulwark against communism, still others wished the DC to go much further left than suited de Gasperi. During de Gasperi's leadership between 1945 and 1953, the "center" usually prevailed.

The Liberal Party

The Liberal party (PLI), which also reappeared in 1943, never regained the eminent position after World War II which it had occupied before World War I under Giolitti. The anticommunism of the post–World War II Liberal party made its relationship with the DC much closer than that between Liberals and *Popolari* of the 1920s, when the principle of separation of state and church had still divided the two parties.

The Action Party

A party with seemingly great promise was the Action party, launched by intellectual antifascist exiles in Paris under the leadership of Carlo Rosselli. The party was reformist without being Marxist and it professed adherence to the ideals of personal liberty. Although the Action party played an important part in the Resistance, it was soon shown to be without a major mass following and quickly evaporated after 1945.

Relations with the Allies

The year 1945 also marked the decisive moment in the relationship between the Allied military government and the newly formed or reconstituted political parties. Before 1945 the parties had preserved a semblance of unity and they had settled disagreements with the Allies by compromise. Yielding to the parties' opposition to King Victor Emmanuel, the Allies had agreed in April 1944 that the king would retire from public life after the Allied capture of Rome, the king's powers subsequently going to his son Umberto. In June 1944 the Allies again gave in to the pressure of the political parties and replaced Badoglio with Ivanhoe Bonomi as prime minister, a man who had briefly held power before Mussolini's coming to power in 1922. As the end of the war approached, Bonomi and the Allies were fearful that a coalition consisting of Communists, Socialists, the Action party and the Resistance forces fighting under the direction of the Milan-based CLNAI might seize power in northern Italy and launch a social revolution. The "Manifesto," published by the Action party in November 1944, seemed an indication of this, calling as it did for regional governments to be set up in the north under CLNAI direction for the purpose of socializing industries and organizing war crimes trials against Fascists. Cardinal-archibishop Ildefonso Schuster of Milan attempted to influence the course of events by negotiating with the Resistance, the Allies and the Germans shortly before the German surrender in northern Italy in May 1955, without, however, being able to secure binding agreements from anyone.

At the time of surrender, the Resistance briefly gained control over the "industrial triangle" of Milan, Turin and Genoa, as well as over a number of other cities such as Bologna, Forli, Ferrara, Ravenna, and Modena. There was some settling of old political scores, including the execution of Mussolini, but the Allies quickly assumed political control over all Italy north of Bologna. That control was not relinquished until de Gasperi was safely installed as prime minister in December 1945.

Before de Gasperi's assuming power, there was the brief interlude of the government of Ferrucio Parri, the leader of the Action party between June and November 1945. Parri promised a massive purge of Fascists and fellow travellers from the civil service and private industry, and he threatened big business with punitive taxes and other forms of punishment. The Parri government remained, however, chiefly an exercise in revolutionary rhetoric with little actual revolutionary change. When both the Liberal party and the DC withdrew from the government in November 1945, Parri too fell as prime minister. At the time of his ouster, Parri charged that he was the victim of the very same forces which had destroyed Italian democracy in 1922 and which had conspired to bring Mussolini to power. Few took these charges seriously, especially not the Socialists and Communists, who hoped to increase their own following at the expense of Parri's Action party. It was only after Parri's fall that UNRRA relief was sent to Italy in significant amounts. Likewise, Allied internal controls over Italy were not lifted until December 31, 1945.

DE GASPERI AND THE FOUNDATIONS OF POSTWAR ITALY

Pietro Nenni had proposed de Gasperi for the prime ministership in the certain expectation that the weight of Italy's postwar problems would damage de Gasperi to the point where voters would desert the Christian Democrats. In fact, de Gasperi utilized the period between 1945 and 1947 to lay the foundation of Christian Democratic rule that was to become a permanent feature of Italian postwar politics until the early 1980s.

His first government was a coalition that embraced most of the major parties, including the Communists and Socialists. De Gasperi's strategy was to keep Communists and Socialists in the government in order to share with them the responsibility for important or unpopular decisions, such as the adoption of a new constitution and the signing of the peace treaty, which was likely to be harsh. Moreover, de Gasperi was eager to have the Communists voting for the inclusion of the 1929 Concordat in the new postwar constitution, in order to preserve the privileges which the Concordat had bestowed upon the church under Mussolini. At the same time, de Gasperi proceeded to purge radical civil servants who had been recently appointed by the "committees of national liberation," and to restore professional civil servants, many of whom had functioned under fascism, in order to strengthen the power of the state against future left-wing attacks. De Gasperi was criticized for maintaining an "unnatural cohabitation" with Communists and Socialists, which ran counter to Christian Democratic principles. For de Gasperi, the "cohabitation" was a tactical necessity which would be abandoned once the foundations for Italy's internal and external developments had been laid and once the return of economic and social stability would provide a more suitable setting for Christian Democratic rule.

The 1946 Elections

The elections to the constituent assembly of June 1946, the first nationwide elections since 1924, revealed de Gasperi's Christian Democrats as the strongest party with 35.1 percent of the vote and 207 seats. The Socialists came in second with 20.7 percent and 115 seats, followed by the Communists with 8.9 percent and 104 seats. The Action party's poor showing of only seven seats signaled its imminent oblivion. The June 1946 referendum on whether or not to retain the monarchy had gone against the monarchy with 12.7 million against 10.7 million votes. The monarchists lost largely because of the personal unpopularity of the king, whose escape from Rome in 1943, without instructions to the civil service or the army, had, in the view of many Italians, all the attributes of an act of desertion.

Following the June elections, de Gasperi formed a new coalition government of the three major parties, DC, Communists, and Socialists, which also included the small Republican party. De Gasperi combined the prime ministership with the post of minister of the interior, a position which enabled him to continue the process of strengthening the power of state authority by tough police action, and by reinvigorating the civil service. Increasingly, de Gasperi used the police for breaking up strikes and suppressing social violence, such as occurred in September 1946 during the storming of the Mestre police headquarters by striking workers.

By February 1947 the peace treaty with the victors of World War II had been signed and by March 1947 the terms of the 1929 concordat, guaranteeing church privileges in Italy, had been safely included in Article VII of the new republican constitution. As de Gasperi had wished, the Communists had voted in support of Article VII for reasons of political expediency, not principle, in a bid for Catholic support.

The terms of the peace treaty caused considerable disappointment, though de Gasperi was not held personally responsible. The provisions deemed most objectionable concerned the border with Yugoslavia. Trieste was to be turned into a UN administered "free city," although it was actually divided into an Anglo-American-administered "zone A" and a Yugoslav-administered "zone B," which also included Istria. The arrangement lasted until 1954 when Trieste was partitioned between Italy and Yugoslavia, roughly along the earlier zonal border.

In a development whose timing closely paralleled events in France, de Gasperi began attacking the Communists in April 1947, preparatory to their expulsion from the government. The occasion for de Gasperi's attack was the Communists' own attack on the Truman Doctrine, which the Communists compared with Hitler's World War II aggressions. By May 1947, de Gasperi had terminated the coalition with the Communists, forming instead a government solely of Christian Democrats, with the exception of financial wizard Luigi Einaudi, the Liberal party finance minister.

Between May and December 1947 de Gasperi's one-party (*monocolore*) government made considerable progress in the solution of Italy's postwar economic and financial problems. Initially these problems had seemed far graver even than those left behind by World War I. During World War II 20 percent of all Italian industry had been destroyed and the level of industrial production of 1945 was only 25 percent that of 1939. Prices had increased twentyfold and inflation continued to soar into 1947.

Economic Policy

De Gasperi's economic policy aimed at preserving the strong economic role, which the Italian state had traditionally played and which had grown further under fascism through agencies such as the Institute for Industrial Reconstruction (IRI). Before very long, the state was to increase its economic role even further with the ENI trust, which was given a public monopoly for the exploration and development of Italy's considerable natural gas deposits. At the same time, de Gasperi was eager to help private big business, organized in *Confindustria,* to get back on its economic feet through U.S. economic aid. UNRRA aid to Italy was extremely generous, ranking third behind aid to China and Poland, with $435 million. The purpose of UNRRA aid was to combat starvation, however, and de Gasperi asked for investment aid, which he obtained from 1948 onwards through the Marshall Plan. As early as November 1947, however, price levels had dropped by as much as 20 percent, industrial production was back to 88 percent and agricultural production to 82 percent of the 1938 levels. Food rationing was gradually discontinued.

Other parties gave de Gasperi full credit for the economic improvements of 1947 and offered to join him in coalition. In December 1947, de Gasperi formed a new coalition government, which included Liberals, Republicans and the newly formed moderate "Socialist party of the Italian Workers" (PSLI) under Saragat, which had split off from the Nenni Socialists in January 1947.

The 1948 Elections

After the eventful year 1947, Italy went to the polls in April 1948 to elect her first parliament under the new republican constitution. The Italian elections coincided with the approaching Cold War climax surrounding the crises of Czechoslovakia and Berlin, a fact which heightened their importance in U.S. and British eyes. The western powers hoped to influence the outcome of the elections by supporting Italy's claim to Trieste and by promising economic aid under the Marshall Plan. With 48.4 percent of the vote, the DC won its greatest victory ever, gaining an absolute majority in the lower house with 304 seats and a relative majority in the senate. Saragat's Socialists did surprisingly well with 7.1 percent and 33 seats. The Nenni Socialists and Communists, running as a bloc, gained 31 percent and 183 seats.

De Gasperi could easily have ruled without coalition partners on the basis of the April 1948 election outcome. He chose, instead, to renew his coalition, chiefly in order to dampen the militancy on the right wing of his own party, which was inclined to interpret the election results as a mandate for conservative reaction.

DE GASPERI AT HIS ZENITH

The election results of 1948 enabled de Gasperi to lead Italy into NATO the following year. Togliatti strongly denounced the move, threatening to line up Italy's Communists alongside the USSR if it came to war. It was a remark he later regretted when the Soviet invasion of Hungary of 1956 prompted hundreds of thousands to quit the Italian Communist party.

Opposition to rearmament was not limited to the Communists, however. Both Nenni and Saragat Socialists objected to Italian rearmament with arguments that closely paralleled those of West German neutral nationalists. The Socialists perferred neutrality to alliance, as the Cold War was not, in their opinion, of Italy's making. There was also opposition from the nationalist Right, which was still angry over the terms of the 1947 peace treaty. West European integration did not stir Italy's imagination to the same degree that it did among many young people in France and West Germany. De Gasperi helped pave the way for the Common Market, whose establishment in 1957 he was not destined to see.

The "Economic Miracle"

At home, de Gasperi continued to concentrate on social and economic issues. Between 1948 and 1952 Italy obtained $1.5 billion in Marshall aid, of which one-fifth was used for plant and equipment modernization. Italy soon experienced its own version of the "economic miracle," which achieved its greatest momentum only after de Gasperi during the 1960s. As early as 1954 Italy's industrial production was 71 percent above the 1938 level.

With prosperity expanding, the question being asked by the Italian Left was, whether the new prosperity was merely a time for bigger profits, or whether it ought not also to be used for fundamental, long-range social reform. De Gasperi's answer to this question reflected his own centrist position in the DC as well as his political personality as a compromiser.

The left wing of the DC under Giovanni Gronchi, Amintore Fanfani and Giuseppe Dossetti favored a reform program, which was not far removed from that of the Socialists. On the Right, there was equally strong opposition in circles of *Confindustria,* and in Catholic Action under Luigi Gedda, to any economic change, such as socialization of industries, which might be construed as Socialist.

Social Reform

De Gasperi's principal program of social reform was in the area of land reform, Italy's oldest unsolved social issue. The land reform laws of May and October 1950 expropriated large estates, chiefly owned by absentee landlords, and redistributed the land among more than 100,000 beneficiaries. The new landowners, principally former *mezzadri* and *braccianti,* received title after thirty years, against payment of nominal annual installments of $25. The former owners were compensated by the state. A special development fund for the south (*cassa del Mezzogiorno*) was established by law of August 1950 for purposes of soil improvement, road construction, and the granting of loans. With an initial appropriation of 1,280 billion lire, funding was substantial. Lastly, de Gasperi encouraged private industry by tax incentives and other benefits to expand into the poorer regions of the south.

The land reform measures of 1950 were attacked by the Left as not going far enough, and by the Right for having gone too far. By granting land to only 100,000 peasants, as against 6 million land-seeking farm laborers, the measures of 1950 had certainly not gone far enough. De Gasperi considered them a promising beginning, however, upon which subsequent administrations might want to improve.

In fact, the industrial boom of the northern cities during the 1960s uprooted many of the southern peasants whom de Gasperi had settled in the 1950s. The rise in Italian prosperity during the 1950s thus remained uneven and relative. Where poverty persisted, it was usually more extreme than elsewhere in the west. In 1952 there were still 5 million illiterates. Over 92,000 families were still living in caves or primitive shacks with another 232,000 being crowded together in basements or attics.

The 1953 Elections

As new elections approached in 1953, de Gasperi was conscious of the diminishing appeal of his party, which was accused of doing too little or too much. Imitating a move made by the ruling coalition parties of France, de Gasperi pushed a new election law through parliament on March 29, 1953, one designed to help the Christian Democrats hold on to power. According to the new law, any party, or coalition of parties, obtaining 50.1 percent of the vote was to get 65 percent of the seats in the lower house.

The law, which was quickly dubbed *legge truffa* (fraudulent law), achieved the opposite of the desired effect because it aroused a storm of protest among the other parties, including some of de Gasperi's coalition partners. The law was also faintly reminiscent of Mussolini's Acerbo law of 1923, which had similarly served the purpose of assuring the Fascists of a parliamentary majority.

In the June 1953 elections, the Christian Democrats and their coalition partners, Saragat Socialists, Republicans and Liberals, together received only 49.8 percent of the vote, less than that required to keep control of parliament.

In part, the elections of 1953 were a repudiation of de Gasperi, especially on the part of conservative middle-class voters, who had been alarmed by his social initiatives. It was an ill omen for the policy of compromise and political stability so soon after the new beginning of Italian democracy.

De Gasperi, unable to find coalition partners among his old allies, briefly attempted a one-party minority government of the Christian Democrats in the tradition of his tactics of 1947. The effort failed in July 1953. Little over a year later he died, ending an era in Italian postwar history.

17

The Fourth French Republic

FROM VICHY TO LIBERATION

The shock of defeat for France in June 1940 was such as to produce a profound sense of failure in the adult generation that experienced it, those who had lived through the prewar years of social strife and economic stagnation of the Third Republic. Had it been possible to poll the French public in the summer of 1940, it is not unlikely that a substantial majority would have agreed with the conclusion of Marshal Pétain that Hitler had won the war and that it remained only for Great Britain to recognize that fact. It was a sentiment which Pierre Laval, among Pétain's most outspoken advocates of collaboration with Nazi Germany, was to remember during his own treason trial in August 1945, after liberation. In July 1940, Laval was to recall, no man "with any sense" in France could doubt a German victory.

Pétain, Laval, and the Vichy régime which they had created and served had a ready explanation for the French disaster of 1940. The principal cause, in their judgment, was the system of the Third Republic and its ideological underpinnings of liberalism, republicanism and anticlericalism. Ideologically and historically, Vichy France represented that opposition to republican-liberal France that had always traced the country's misfortunes to the revolution of 1789 and its aftermath. It was an aversion widespread among the monarchist-clerical-military establishment of nineteenth-century France, and it was newly propagated in the conservative and proto-Fascist movements of the early twentieth century, such as the *Action Fraçaise* of Charles Maurras. To Maurras, the defeat of 1940 was a "divine surprise" which permitted Conservative France, at long last, to reshape public institutions, morals and philosophy in accordance with its own ideas.

The formal transition from the Third Republic to autocratic Vichy France was legal, smooth and swift. On July 10, 1940 the combined vote of Senate and chamber authorized Marshal Pétain to produce a new constitution. The vote was 569 in favor, 80 against and 17 abstentions. Among those opposing the measure was Leon Blum, leader of the Socialists and prime minister of the Popular Front government of 1936. Among those who abstained was ex-prime minister Herriot, the leader of the Radical party. The constitutional acts of July 12, 1940 conferred on Pétain the highest legislative, judicial and executive powers.

Vichy Collaboration

The level of Vichy collaboration with Nazi Germany varied, depending on individual figures in the Vichy establishment and the stage of the war. Pétain's principal objective in dealing with the outside world was to "contract out of the war" and to spare France further damage and bloodshed. Hitler's invitation for a more active Vichy role was turned down by Pétain at the meeting at Montoire in October 1940. Laval wished to obtain a secure, albeit modest place for France in Hitler's "new order." After "parliamentary" France had, in Laval's opinion, insisted on fighting Germany in 1939 and had lost in 1940, it was incumbent upon "authoritarian, social and national" France to collaborate loyally with Nazi Germany. Collaboration went furthest in the areas of shared ideological values, such as the persecution of the Jews. The Vichy statute of October 1940 barred Jews from state employment in the tradition of Hitler's own Nuremberg laws of 1935 and Mussolini's decrees of October 1938. Beginning in November 1942—the month of Allied landings in North Africa—Vichy authorities readily collaborated with the Nazi policy of Jewish deportation. Drancy became the chief assembly point for the deportation of French Jews to German extermination camps in eastern Europe. Compared with the silent majority behind Pétain, de Gaulle's initial following was notable both for its small numbers and its absence of prominent names. No more than seven thousand men had joined de Gaulle's London-based Free French by July 1940, with senior military and naval commanders conspicuous by their absence. General Catroux and Admiral Muselier were the exceptions.

The Gaullist Vision

Opposition to de Gaulle was especially pronounced among naval officers, whose attitude towards Great Britain was influenced by old memories of naval rivalry and the more recent shock of the British naval attack on the French fleet at Mers-el-Kebir on July 3, 1940. Politically, the corps of naval officers was, if anything, even more deeply steeped in the traditions of the *Action Française* than were the senior army leaders.

The uniqueness of de Gaulle derived from two things: the fact that, despite the unpromising beginnings of his resistance, he was not crippled by the spirit of resignation which had gripped his generation in 1940; and that he was able to rise above both the broken spirit of the Third Republic and the reactionary vengeance of Vichy. With Pétain and the *Action Française* de Gaulle shared a low opinion of the Third Republic with its parliamentary instability and lack of partisan consensus. To de Gaulle, the political parties of the Third Republic—and before long, those of the Fourth— were reminiscent of the feudal anarchy of seventeenth-century France during the *Fronde* uprising against the youthful Louis XIV and his chief minister Cardinal Mazarin. Occasionally, de Gaulle would expressly refer to political parties as *feudalités*. De Gaulle differed from Pétain and the philosophy of the *Action Française* in his choice of an alternative to the republic which they all disliked. Whereas conservatives and reactionaries could visualize the regeneration of France only through the exclusion of certain people and classes from the mainstream of society, such as the "Jews" or the "working class," de Gaulle's mystical nationalism rested on the concept of a nation undivided and united by the grandeur of its superior civilization.

De Gaulle proposed to end the age-old division between liberal-republican and clerical-monarchist France by accepting the values of both as integral parts of French history and the present reality of France. Gaullist France, in the vision of its prophet, would be monarchic in the dignity and aloofness of its leader, democratic in the freedom of expression of its people, Catholic in the recognition of the special role of the church in its civilization, and pragmatic and innovative in its approach to economic and social problems.

Within such a vision, the French catastrophe of 1940 could be viewed against the wider background of past greatness and future promise, and so reduced to manageable proportions. What appeared to Pétain and Laval as the end of an era was, to de Gaulle, a temporary misfortune whose overcoming was assured by the purpose and the logic of history. That the greatness of France was a condition of world peace de Gaulle had stated as early as the 1920s. There was no reason to doubt that world peace would eventually return and with it, in de Gaulle's logic, the historic mission of the French nation.

His unshakable faith in the greatness of France sustained de Gaulle during the war as much as it was to support him during the years of self-imposed political exile after the war. What was needed, apart from a mystical faith, was the tactical skill to assert his leadership over the emerging resistance groups within France between 1941 and 1944, and to secure the recognition of his leadership role by sceptical and often hostile leaders of the Grand Alliance.

Assertion of Leadership

For de Gaulle, the former task was often easier than the latter. Resistance in metropolitan France, though widespread, was initially weak and ill-organized. Having created his own "national committee" in London in September 1941 as the nucleus of a Free French government-in-exile, de Gaulle proceeded to extend his authority over the scattered Resistance groups in metropolitan France. The effort succeeded in large measure because of the mission of Jean Moulin, who subsequently died under torture in German captivity. By May 1943 the National Council of the Resistance claimed leadership over all Resistance forces in France. Despite strong Communist influence, the NCR was loyal to de Gaulle under its leader Georges Bidault, the future founder of the Christian Democrats.

With the emergence of de Gaulle and the declining fortunes of Hitler Germany, Pétain and Laval too began to turn their attention to the Free French. When Hitler seized the territory of Vichy France in November 1942, Pétain intended to call for a constituent assembly to be elected after his own resignation for the purpose of blocking de Gaulle's accession to power after liberation. The announcement, planned for November 3, 1942, was overruled by the Germans.

Pierre Laval conceived yet another plan, one which would have included the sending of Pétain to Paris after the liberation for the purpose of calling a constituent assembly. Power was to be transferred thereafter from Pétain to ex-premier Herriot in a formal ceremony, in order to bar de Gaulle from accession to power. Laval even had Herriot released from prison at Maxeville near Nancy, where he had been confined after the Vichy show trial of Third Republic leaders at Riom. Herriot's refusal to have any part in Laval's scheme condemned it to failure from the start.

By 1944 de Gaulle's leadership over all Resistance groups, including the Communists, was well established, although there were indications of future difficulties even at this early stage.

The Assumption of Power

From articles which had appeared in the underground press, such as *Liberation* and *Défense de la France,* it was evident that the Resistance did not wish to see the institutions of the Third Republic resurrected, a desire with which de Gaulle could wholeheartedly concur. The Resistance press also intimated, however, that it expected France to have an all-powerful single-chamber legislature after the war, much in the tradition of the Convention of 1792. This was largely in response to the authoritarian makeup of the Vichy government with its concentration of the highest executive, legislative and judicial functions in the hands of a single individual, Marshal Pétain. In addition, there were demands for sweeping economic and social changes beyond those which Leon Blum's Popular Front government had attempted to implement between 1936 and 1938. Among the demands was the call for the nationalization of industries and banking and an active role for workers in management. The strong anticapitalist theme of the Resistance press was by no means confined to Communist publications, nor did it solely reflect Communist wishes. Rather, it mirrored a more general consensus that capitalism, in the form in which it had operated under the Third Republic, had failed to satisfy the social and economic needs of the country in general. The eagerness to break new ground, economically and socially, reached all the way into the camp of Christian Democratic leaders, soon to launch a new party under the label of MRP (*Movement Republican Populaire*).

On the eve of liberation, there was some anxiety among de Gaulle's followers that the Council of National Resistance (NR) might claim power for itself in the liberated areas, under the prodding of its Communist members. There was even greater concern over the attitude of President Roosevelt, whose relations with de Gaulle had remained strained. Roosevelt, apart from distrusting what he believed to be de Gaulle's Bonapartist ambitions, feared the outbreak of civil war in liberated France should de Gaulle claim exclusive power. This appeared as an unacceptable risk for no other reason than the safety of American forces fighting the Germans on French soil. The best solution from the American standpoint, and the one most wounding to de Gaulle's pride, would be the installation of an American-British military government, much as had been done in conquered Italy in 1943. It was in anticipation of such threats that de Gaulle created the "commissioners of the republic," who were to take actual control of the liberated areas as soon as they were in Allied hands. This first step was to be followed by the appointment of new prefects in the liberated departments. Also, de Gaulle warned the French public in a radio broadcast of April 4, 1944 not to obey any authority after liberation except that of his Committee of National Liberation.

On June 3, 1944, the committee reconstituted itself as the provisional government of France. The United States, Britain and the Soviet Union did not officially extend their recognition until October 23, 1944.

Far from provoking civil war, as some had feared, de Gaulle's assumption of power was greeted with great relief by most. The formation of a "government of national unity," drawn from both the Committee of National Liberation and the Resistance, including the Communists, permitted the illusion to take hold that the supporters of Vichy had always been a small minority and that France had rejoined the ranks of the victorious Allies overwhelmingly by her own effort. There was, nonetheless, a reckoning, both official and unofficial, with those who had exposed themselves as collaborators and Vichy activists. Pétain, who disregarded de Gaulle's advice to go to neutral Switzerland, was seized and tried, as was Pierre Laval. Both were sentenced to death, Pétain's sentence being commuted. An additional 2,071 death sentences followed, together with over 48,000 convictions resulting in prison terms. An unknown number of people were killed by the Resistance after liberation during a brief but violent wave of terror, the estimates of victims ranging anywhere from 10,000 to 100,000.

FROM LIBERATION TO DE GAULLE'S RESIGNATION

During the short period between liberation and his dramatic resignation as head of the government on January 20, 1946, de Gaulle gave many indications of his future policies as president of the Fifth Republic after 1958. In foreign and colonial policy, de Gaulle was eager to reassert the independence and power of France. At home, the honeymoon between Gaullists, Resistance leaders, and the newly constituted political parties became an early victim of disagreements over the constitution and the philosophy of government in postwar France.

Although France owed her liberation in 1944 chiefly to the United States and Britain, de Gaulle defied American orders on more than one occasion during the fighting of the last months of World War II. The French capture of the city of Stuttgart in early 1945 ran directly counter to Eisenhower's orders and de Gaulle had balked at the mere suggestion of evacuating Strasbourg at the height of the Battle of the Bulge.

De Gaulle's alliance with Moscow of December 10, 1944, the first alliance to be formed by France after liberation, represented an early move towards a position balanced between the United States and Soviet Russia. When de Gaulle encountered difficulties in restoring French influence in Syria in May 1945 and when Britain proposed an Anglo-American-French conference to resolve these difficulties, de Gaulle countered with a proposal to include the Soviet Union and China in such a conference.

In matters of colonial policy, de Gaulle understood the need for changes in form, but he was determined to restore the substance of French rule, by force if necessary. The 1944 Brazzaville conference had promised reforms in French colonial rule, including colonial representation in the French parliament and the formation of autonomous legislatures in the colonies. In his Washington, D.C. press conference of July 10, 1944, de Gaulle had also hinted at the possibility of a federal structure for overseas France.

In Indochina, de Gaulle installed Admiral Thierry d'Argenlieu as new high commissioner. Unlike General Leclerc of the French army, who advocated a negotiated political agreement with the Vietnamese nationalist and Communist forces under Ho Chi Minh from an early moment on, d'Argenlieu rejected negotiations and set the stage for the protracted Vietnam War of the French Fourth Republic, about to open in December 1946.

De Gaulle's social and economic policy between liberation and the end of 1945 went far to meet the expectations of the Resistance, but it was, as yet, lacking in a clear long-term concept. Mines and utilities were nationalized, as were the Renault motor works and the Gnome-Rhone aircraft company, which had openly collaborated with the Germans. The social security package of October 4, 1945 provided for improved health, accident and old-age insurance. Wages had been raised by 50 percent after liberation without regard to declining productivity and the sharp drop in industrial output. Industrial production after liberation was down to 40 percent of the 1938 level, steel production had declined even further. A proposal of de Gaulle's economic minister Mendès-France of early 1945 to institute a drastic currency reform as a first step towards controlling inflation, was rejected by de Gaulle.

The Elections of 1945

Friction between de Gaulle and the political parties developed quickly once the euphoria of liberation began to give way to problems of routine peacetime government, and once the political power base shifted from de Gaulle's wartime mystique to the measurable strength of the resurrected parties. Under these altered circumstances, de Gaulle's wartime leadership style, which had treated his aides as "auxiliaries," no longer sufficed as a suitable means of conducting peacetime government. De Gaulle fulfilled his promise of holding elections, which he had made in his "Algiers decree" of April 21, 1944, in October 1945. The elections of October 21, 1945 served the double purpose of electing a constituent assembly and of asking the voters to decide for or against a referendum on the constitution which the assembly would produce. De Gaulle thought such a referendum necessary as an additional check in case the constituent assembly, under Communist and Socialist influence, might produce an extreme, left-wing constitution.

De Gaulle won on the referendum, with 66.3 percent of the voters supporting it, but he had little cause for rejoicing in the election results as such. With 26.2 percent, the Communists emerged as the single largest party, followed by the newly formed Christian Democratic MRP with 23.9 percent and the Socialists (SFIO) with 23.4 percent. Of 586 seats the Communists controlled 151, the MRP 150 and the SFIO 139. The middle-class Radicals, most closely identified with the discredited Third Republic, obtained a mere 29 seats. The Catholic Moderates also fared badly.

The spectacular increase of the Communist vote of 11 percent since the 1936 elections was partly a tribute to the prominent Communist role in the French Resistance after 1941, though the Communists had sabotaged the defense efforts of the Third Republic in 1939–1940 while the Stalin-Hitler pact was still in force. Communist strength in 1945 was also an expression of the heightened social expectations of French workers, expectations which had been reflected in the underground Communist press during the war. De Gaulle's relations with the Communist party before the October 1945 elections had been cautious, dictated by tactical considerations. Neither side wished to offend the other and both wished to use the other side for its own ends.

The Communists and de Gaulle

After liberation, the Communists had permitted de Gaulle to disband their "patriotic militia," but they were careful not to surrender their own intelligence network. In September 1944 de Gaulle had taken two Communists, Francois Billoux and Charles Tillon, into his government as ministers of health and air respectively. But he denied them the key positions they desired, defense, and interior and foreign affairs. Otherwise, the Communist party cooperated with de Gaulle in restraining workers and unions from going on strike. The Communist argument, before 1946, was that such strikes would be harmful to the interests of the workers themselves, who would soon play a commanding role in the development of the French economy.

De Gaulle's Resignation

The election returns of October 1945 strengthened the hand of all three major parties, Communists, MRP and Socialists, in dealing with de Gaulle. Among the noteworthy new developments of postwar France was the emergence of much stronger party organizations than had been customary in the Third Republic. This fact was largely due to the belief of postwar leaders that weak party structures had been an important cause of the downfall of the Third Republic. After October 1945, the party leaders pressed for the adoption of a constitutional system that would give a major role to political parties, rather than a presidential system, as favored by de Gaulle. De Gaulle's irritation over a Socialist demand for military budget cuts was thus only a pretext for his abrupt resignation from office on January 20, 1946.

Public reaction to de Gaulle's exit was notable for its lack of excitement and even for a sense of quiet relief among party leaders. Like Churchill, de Gaulle had rendered his nation a wartime service of inestimable value. In de Gaulle's case, fortitude and personal courage accomplished the more difficult task of blurring the reality of actual defeat and of absolving France as a nation of the stigma of collaboration with the enemy, which de Gaulle knew to have been much more widespread among the French than was publicly admitted after 1945.

THE FAILURE OF *TRIPARTISME*

Despite growing friction, the three major parties, Communists, MRP and SFIO maintained the fragile coalition of *tripartisme* they had formed under de Gaulle. After de Gaulle's resignation, the three parties elected Socialist Felix Gouin as the new head of government on January 26, 1946. None of the three parties was prepared to let the other two monopolize the drafting of the constitution. The first constitutional draft, providing for an all-powerful single-chamber legislature and a president without real powers, was defeated by referendum on May 5, 1946, though only by a narrow margin. The elections for a new constituent assembly on June 2, 1946 confirmed what seemed to many a conservative reaction. The MRP now emerged as the largest party with 28.2 percent (166 seats), followed by the Communists with 25.9 percent (153 seats) and the Socialists with 21.1 percent (128 seats). Under the premiership of MRP leader Georges Bidault, the three parties produced a second constitution, which was endorsed by referendum in October 1946. Essentially a remake of the Third Republic, the constitution of the Fourth provided for a two-chamber legislature and a stronger executive, both with respect to the prime ministership and the presidency. In the hands of Socialist president Vincent Auriol, the presidency eventually acquired even stronger powers than the authors of the 1946 constitution had intended.

The three-party coalition of MRP, Communists and Socialists did not survive the constitution-making process for long. The elections of November 10, 1946 for the first regular parliament of the Fourth Republic had once more reversed the relative position of MRP and the Communists, returning the Communists again as the leading party. The election campaign had been waged with unprecedented bitterness, the MRP slogans exhorting voters to "vote French, not Communist." The Communists, in turn, demanded after the election the appointment of their leader Thorez as prime minister or, failing that, the key ministries of interior, defense, and foreign relations. *Tripartisme* was briefly revived in January 1947 under the Socialist prime minister Paul Ramadier, but it collapsed speedily as a result of the growing strike movement, now encouraged by the Communists, and the broadening controversy over French policy in Indochina. More generally, *tripartisme* became a victim of Cold War tensions, as French foreign policy changed from the earlier, independent approach of de Gaulle of 1944–1945, towards alignment alongside Anglo-American containment. In economic policy, MRP and Socialists opposed the Communists with a policy of wage restraints, which Jean Monnet, as architect of French economic recovery, demanded as part of an effective investment program. Regarding Indochina, the Communists blamed High Commissioner d'Argenlieu for the fighting which had begun full scale in December 1946 with the Viet Minh. By contrast, the MRP, together with Prime Minister Ramadier and the Socialist minister for Overseas France, Marius Moutet, flatly rejected the idea of negotiations with Ho Chi Minh at this early stage of the French Vietnam War.

The event which triggered the expulsion of the Communists from the French government was the Renault stike, which threatened to widen into a nationwide general strike. On May 5, 1947 Ramadier curtly decreed the "end of ministerial functions" of his Communist cabinet members. There followed no general resignation of the cabinet, nor were there new elections.

FRANCE UNDER THE "THIRD FORCE," 1947 TO 1951

The expulsion of the Communist party from the government in 1947 resulted in a growing isolation which was strengthened by its identification with Soviet policy. The presence of the French Communist party, together with that of Italy, at the launching of the Cominform in 1947 highlighted French Communist support for Stalinist Russia. It deprived French Communism of the support of many who had previously identified French nationalism and communism in the common cause of the World War II Resistance.

The RPF

The French Communist retreat into isolation coincided with de Gaulle's reentry into active French politics. Seizing upon the collapse of *tripartisme,* de Gaulle launched the "French Popular Movement" (*Rassemblement du Peuple Française,* RPF) for the declared purpose of revising the 1946 constitution and of "liberating" the nation from the control of the parties. The constitution of the Fourth Republic had become the target of de Gaulle's attacks after its publication in 1946, when de Gaulle offered his own counterproposal of a presidential republic in his speeches at Bayeux and Epinal. The president's role de Gaulle described as "arbiter above political contingencies." The newly created RPF won a resounding victory in the municipal elections of October 1947, in which it captured control of most of the big-city governments, including that of Paris. Encouraged by the 1947 municipal elections, the RPF demanded the dissolution of parliament and the adoption of a new constitution consistent with the ideas expressed in de Gaulle's Bayeux and Epinal speeches.

The RPF was skillful enough not to demand the dissolution of existing political parties. Calling itself a "movement" above parties, the RPF proposed dual membership for anyone belonging to a party but also wishing to support the Gaullist RPF. In practice, such dual membership would have weakened the parties, because the basic aims of RPF and the parties were essentially incompatible and contradictory. The Communists rejected the notion of dual membership as did the Socialists, the latter stressing that without parties "democracy cannot live." The Catholic MRP similarly forbade dual membership as it stood to lose the most from the RPF appeal because of its similar constituency. RPF gains in the 1947 municipal elections had been chiefly made at MRP expense. René Pleven of the small Radical party, by contrast, called for a broad union between the political parties supporting the Fourth Republic and the Gaullist RPF. Pleven wished to stabilize the Fourth Republic with the help of the RPF. The latter aimed at the removal of the Fourth Republic with the tacit support of the parties which actually represented it. Not until the advent of the major crisis of May 1958 over Algeria did a majority of party leaders resign themselves to the destruction of the Fourth Republic and offer their support to de Gaulle in what was perceived to be the overriding national interest. Until the national crisis of 1958 no lasting alliance of Gaullists and parties developed. By 1950 a disillusioned Pleven was to call the RPF a major obstacle to national unity.

The New Consensus

Although it was intended to hasten the end of the Fourth Republic, the RPF actually helped stabilize it for several more years. The alarm its appearance had caused among most parties forged a new republican consensus which helped bridge social, economic and other disagreements between the parties. The combined threat of the Communist Left, highlighted by the 1947 strike movement, and of the Gaullist Right, demonstrated by the 1947 municipal elections, joined the parties of the middle, MRP, Socialists, Radicals and Catholic Moderates into a new alliance for the defense of the republic. The parties of the middle, or, as they were soon called, "the third force," shared little besides their common fear of Communists and Gaullists. The chief differences were socioeconomic, to which was later added the issue of anticlericalism, thought long dead before its resurfacing in the fifties. Even the first "third force" government was difficult to put together under the respected MRP leader Robert Schuman on November 22, 1947.

The "third force" coalition governments, formed under a succession of prime ministers from Schuman to Pleven, lasted from 1947 to 1951. These governments made significant progress towards economic recovery and they achieved major gains on the road to European integration, a goal especially cherished by the MRP.

The Activist State

By 1950 Jean Monnet's first four-year plan, the *Plan de Modernisation et d'Equip-ment,* stressing investments in energy and basic industries, communications, and mechanization of agriculture, had produced good results, though not as good as had been hoped. Against the projected target of exceeding the 1929 GNP by 25 percent in 1950, the 1929 level was barely passed despite the influx of Marshall Plan aid and the investment of 2.2 billion francs.

The economic progress of the Fourth Republic, before and after 1950, was due in large measure to a far more activist role of the state in economic and social affairs than had been customary in the Third Republic. The activist state extended into the realm of population policy, encouraging larger families through family allowances and child subsidies. Efforts to raise the low French birth rate had already been launched by the Vichy government during World War II. French population statistics for the years 1945 to 1965 revealed an increase that was larger than the increase for the entire period of 1830 to 1945. The higher birth rate after 1945 also translated into increased productivity with the availability of more people of working age.

The good economic record of the Fourth Republic also reflected the innovative role of MRP leadership. When the party was first formed at the end of World War II it attracted many Catholic voters who saw in the MRP both a bulwark against communism and a convenient shelter against attacks which stemmed from the close association of the French church with the discredited Vichy regime. In due course, the MRP proved itself not only a pioneer in the promotion of European integration, but also an imaginative leader of domestic economic policy, mixing a strong commitment to free enterprise with government planning and *dirigisme.*

Among the parties of the "third force," the Socialists were the least satisfied with the economic progress, because they believed that the fruits of economic recovery were once again being divided unfairly. The SFIO therefore constantly pressured its coalition partners into granting higher wages to the workers, a demand often rejected on the grounds that the results would be inflationary. Disagreement over wage policy became the principal cause of government crises between 1947 and 1951.

The Elections of 1951

With the approach of new elections the parties of the "third force" enacted a new election law on May 9, 1951 which was designed to strengthen their own position and to weaken that of the Communists and the Gaullists. The election law facilitated electoral alliances among the coalition partners and strengthened the pluralist features over those of proportional representation.

Despite these measures, Communists and Gaullists together obtained nearly as many votes as did all the four coalition partners combined. In the industrial and economically more advanced regions, the combined vote of Communists and RPF actually exceeded that of the government parties. The Communists, with 20.1 percent were still the largest single party followed closely by the Gaullists with 17.3 percent of the vote. The MRP lost half its 1946 vote and emerged with 10 percent. SFIO, Moderates and Radicals obtained 11.3, 9.3 and 8 percent respectively. The combined strength of Communists and Socialists declined from its October 1945 high of 38.8 percent to 31.4 percent in the election of June 1951, a figure close to that of the May 1936 elections. Had the election law of 1945 still been in force, Gaullists and Communists together would have obtained an absolute majority of 324 seats as against the actual number of 120 for the Gaullists and 101 for the Communists.

THE DISINTEGRATION OF THE REPUBLICAN CONSENSUS

The governing parties of the "third force" did not interpret the 1951 election results as a close call and a warning that warranted a heightened sense of responsibility. Instead, they resumed their accustomed bickering over issues that were trivial compared with the great and dangerous challenges about to confront France in the arena of foreign and colonial policy. The socialists, apart from the wage issue, assailed their coalition partners over state aid to parochial schools. Not until August 1951 was a new government formed under René Pleven, one which no longer included the Socialists. After the Socialist withdrawal, the parties of the middle attempted to make the Gaullists their new coalition partner. The effort succeeded on specific occasions, such as when Gaullists supported the installation of Antoine Pinay as prime minister in March 1952, one of the most successful leaders in the realm of economic and fiscal policy. Gaullists also supported Prime Minister René Mayer in January 1953, and in May 1953 the RPF, having changed its name into *Union des Républicains d'Action Sociale* (URAS), entered the cabinet of Premier Joseph Laniel.

These actions did not signal a permanent change in the attitude of the Gaullist movement towards the Fourth Republic, in part because de Gaulle himself opposed some of them, in part because Gaullist support quickly evaporated when issues of European integration or colonial policy came up. This proved to be the case in the struggle over the European Defense Community between 1952 and 1954, when EDC was finally defeated in the French parliament.

The Colonial Issue

By the mid-1950s the colonial issue began to overshadow all others, including the emotional debate over German rearmament.

Some of the great issues confronting France in the mid-to-late 1950s were very similar to those confronting Britain. If these issues produced more tragic and violent results in the French case, it was in part a function of the different political mechanisms of the French parliamentary system and in part a function of the role played by the French military in deciding these issues. Decolonization in Britain after the Second World War was a process that enjoyed overwhelmingly bipartisan support and which never touched on fundamental questions of constitutional integrity. When the Conservative government of Anthony Eden suffered defeat in the 1956 Suez crisis, it produced a serious political crisis which could be overcome in a matter of weeks without permanent damage even for the ruling Conservative party.

The question of decolonization, for the French Fourth Republic, quickly turned into a question of survival, however, with the constitutional system itself on trial and with charges of treason and subversion of the national interest being leveled against the leaders of the republic. The memory of the defeat of the Third Republic of 1940, of which there was no counterpart in the history of Britain, quickly cast its shadow over the French colonial defeats of the middle and late 1950s, reviving old hatreds which the illusion of a French victory in 1945 had only temporarily concealed. The

French crisis of the late 1950s was compounded by the social disorientation of a frightened class of petit bourgeois shopkeepers and small entrepreneurs which saw itself threatened by the modernization of the French economy and which added its own sense of deep national frustration over colonial retreat to the swelling force of ultraright and antirepublican critics. The political reflection of this petit bourgeois economic insecurity and nationalist frustration was Poujade's *Union de Défense des Commerçants et Artisans* (UDCA), which captured an amazing 11.6 percent of the vote in the elections of January 1956.

Prime Minister Mendès-France attempted to face the French crisis of the mid-1950s with a new style of decisive leadership, expressed in his slogan ''to govern is to choose.'' But the choices he made, though often inevitable, were not accepted as such by the majority, whose support was essential to the survival of the Fourth Republic. Mendès-France extricated France from its Vietnam War in the Geneva Agreement of July 1954 after France had suffered 92,000 casualties, and after her defeat at Dien Bien Phu of May 7, 1954 had painfully demonstrated the uselessness of further military efforts.

The Army's Bitterness

Among those who watched the French retreat from Southeast Asia in official silence but with a sense of deep bitterness was the French army. The army saw a close parallel between the defeat of the Third Republic in 1940 and that of the Fourth in Vietnam in 1954. In both instances, the French Communist party had opposed the war effort. The army's bitterness was enhanced by the government's refusal to let anyone but volunteers fight in Vietnam and by the government's ban on the publication of citations for valor earned in the fighting in Southeast Asia. In their own minds, many officers put the Fourth Republic on notice that the policy of ''retreat'' would soon be answered by the same call to arms against the state which Charles de Gaulle had issued against Pétain on June 18, 1940.

The 1956 Elections

''Retreat'' followed, in short order, first in Tunisia in 1955, and later in Morocco, both French protectorates for many years. The government's promise to grant independence to Morocco resulted in the ouster of Prime Minister Edgar Faure by the assembly in November 1955. The public mood in France on the eve of the January 1956 elections was more uncertain than it had been five years earlier.

The Communists emerged once more as the largest party with 150 seats, followed by the Socialists with 94 seats. The once-mighty MRP got fewer votes with 11.1 percent than did the new Poujadist party with 11.6 percent. The supporters of former prime minister Mendès-France, gathered together in the newly formed Republican Front, obtained 75 seats. The Gaullists ended up with 21 seats. With the support of the MRP, the Republican Front, the Radicals and the Socialists, it was possible to resurrect a sort of ''third force'' government under the Socialist leader Guy Mollet. The Mollet government, the last effective government of the Fourth Republic, was surprisingly successful in some areas, notably European integration and Franco-German reconciliation. Mollet returned the Saar to West Germany after the 1956 Luxembourg agreement, and signed the Rome treaty in 1957, launching the European Common Market. Mollet's appointment to the prime ministership in January 1956 had been largely motivated, however, by the expectation that he would find a solution to the Algerian problem, which had given every indication of becoming the most explosive colonial issue ever since the beginning of the Algerian rebellion on November 1, 1954.

Mollet joined in Britain's unsuccessful Suez invasion in November 1956 chiefly in order to topple Egypt's President Nasser, whom Mollet rightly suspected of being the driving force behind Algerian nationalism.

Algeria

Algeria was, from the French standpoint, a problem very different from that of Vietnam, or even that of Tunisia and Morocco, because Algeria was administratively a part of France, it had a large European settler population (*colons*), and it was part of the NATO defense perimeter. The French army also rated its chances of winning the war in Algeria much better than its chances in Indochina. French troops fighting in Algeria were regular draftees and the French army had acquired considerable experience in counterinsurgency tactics as a result of the Vietnam experience. The French army had also assumed many social, educational and health functions in Algeria, especially through junior officers, which had brought it into close and often friendly contact with the Moslem population.

The widespread use of torture against prisoners soon became a significant aspect of the struggle between French troops and the Algerian FLN (National Liberation Front). It helped arouse strong opposition to the war among French intellectuals, journalists and representatives of the church. Before long, the Fourth Republic was trapped between a vociferous antiwar movement, a diehard and equally vociferous community of *colons* in Algeria, and an army leadership determined not to let the government abandon France's most important overseas possessions.

Among French army leaders in Algeria there was a strong element of former Vichy supporters, who shared with the Gaullists a deep resentment of the Fourth Republic. The strategy of the Gaullists was to put the Vichy element in Algeria to good use in order to open the door to de Gaulle's return to power. Gaullist emissaries, such as Leon Delbecque, went to Algeria in April 1958 in order to steer *colon* unrest into the right channels. On May 9, 1958 Algerian army chief Raoul Salan, a Vietnam veteran like his associate, paratroop general Jacques Massu, warned President Coty of the army's sense of outrage and "reaction of despair" should Algeria be abandoned.

The appointment of Pierre Pflimlin of the MRP as prime minister on May 13, 1958 was, to army leaders, a signal of abandonment because Pflimlin was known to be opposed to a "French Algerian" solution. May 13, 1958 also witnessed *colon* riots in Algiers and the formation of a "Committee of Public Safety" under General Massu. General Salan neither suppressed the riots nor arrested Massu. The rebellion of French army leaders in Algeria enjoyed the sympathetic support of senior army leaders in metropolitan France, including four of the nine commanding generals of the military regions of France. The seizure of Corsica by prorebel forces on May 24, 1958 was a clear warning to the Paris government. The army's trump was the threat of an armed invasion of Paris, for which plans existed under the code name *Operation Resurrection*.

De Gaulle Returns

Increasingly, de Gaulle emerged as the only person capable of saving France from civil war and of preserving the appearance of legality in the dismantling of the

Fourth Republic. For de Gaulle to fulfil his mission, he required the trust of the generals, which he possessed in 1958, as well as the collaboration of the political leaders of the republic, which he quickly obtained. President Coty, Prime Minister Pflimlin, and Guy Mollet, against strong opposition in his own Socialist party, offered de Gaulle all the help he needed. De Gaulle himself announced his availability on May 15, 1958. On June 2 and 3, 1958 de Gaulle obtained full powers from the French parliament for six months with the authority to revise the constitution. On June 3, parliament adjourned, never to return. Like the parliament of the Third Republic in July 1940, that of the Fourth had voted itself out of existence under the pressure of events it could no longer control but for which it could not entirely disclaim responsibility.

18

Britain after the War

THE SPIRIT OF 1940

It was often said that the great economic cost of the Second World War was among the major causes of the relative decline of British power in the 1970s, and that Britain somehow never fully managed to offset that cost by subsequent efforts.

How great the actual economic cost of the war—a full quarter of Britain's prewar wealth, if the sale of foreign assets is included—was probably not realized by the average person in 1945. What was well understood, however, was the fact that Britain's position in relation to other European powers was immensely strong, both in a material, political and psychological sense.

The sense of strength derived generally from what might be called the "spirit of 1940." It was the spirit of defiance in the face of seemingly impossible odds, when every major European power had accommodated itself to the fact of Hitler's power. France had done so out of necessity, Italy out of territorial greed, and Soviet Russia for what appeared to be valid reasons of expediency.

The results of World War II seemed to vindicate British policy in 1940, making her, in her own estimate, the first and major cause of Europe's liberation from the Fascist rulers. That the emerging superpowers, the United States and USSR, had made greater material contributions to the ultimate victory, and the fact that in the case of Soviet Russia, the suffering and the losses had been on an immensely greater scale, did not basically interfere with such sentiments. The memory of the moral fortitude of 1940 sustained a whole generation after the war, and it filled that generation with a sense of optimism and purpose which was not shattered by the war's damage.

During the Second World War, Britain once again seemed to have avoided the calamity of a revolutionary break with her past. On the continent the surviving or newly emerging governments had to settle accounts with those who had made their bets with Hitler. It was thus with the supporters of Vichy in France and the followers of Mussolini in Italy. Germany, having been liberated from her dictatorship by outside forces rather than her own, was awaiting judgment at the hands of the court at Nuremberg and countless historians both at home and abroad.

In Britain, there was no rupture with her past, despite the startling outcome of the elections of July 1945. Most basic values and perhaps even illusions of British life had remained unchanged. Such changes as the public wanted and expected could be safely carried out after the war within the familiar constitutional framework and political traditions. Whether the rules of continuity also applied to the development of foreign and Commonwealth relations was a question that was to intrude into the British consciousness soon after the war had ended.

DOMESTIC EXPECTATIONS AND ACHIEVEMENT: 1945 TO 1951

That Winston Churchill lost the elections of July 1945 to Clement Attlee and the Labour party so soon after winning the war against Germany came as a surprise more to people outside Britain than to the British public itself.

Churchill had been the right man at the right moment when he assumed the prime ministership on May 10, 1940, the day of Hitler's attack on France and the Netherlands. In rhetoric, imagination and resolve, he had no equal among Britain's wartime leaders.

There were those who still remembered Churchill's equally forceful rhetoric against striking British labor during the great General Strike of 1926, however, when Churchill, as editor of the British Gazette, had demanded the "unconditional surrender" of the striking workers.

There were others who might have wished or hoped that the British public would reward Churchill with reelection in July 1945 as it had rewarded Lloyd George with reelection in December 1918. But the parallel between Lloyd George and Churchill was limited. Both came to power in the midst of war and both were chosen for their wartime role on the strength of their resourcefulness and resolution. Lloyd George had a long record of social concern in British politics before 1914, however, which made his election promises of December 1918 to seek greater social justice effective and believable.

Churchill could not match such a record in his own pre-World War II career, he showed remarkably little interest in social questions during the war and his social promises during the election campaign, lacking in conviction, were uncertain at best.

Yet social expectations were high in 1945, higher than they had ever been in 1918. The heightened social expectations flowed partly from increased social services provided by the government during World War II, and partly from the fact of full employment and better living conditions for more of the population under the conditions of the war economy.

Infant mortality sank to its lowest recorded level in 1944, milk consumption for children doubled, and real wages rose faster than prices.

Heightened social expectations were also encouraged by official promises and demands voiced in the press, which stated as early as 1940 that a mere preservation of political democracy was not enough and that Britain should move towards the attainment of social democracy after the war.

The famous Beveridge Report of 1942 reinforced such demands with the proposal of a comprehensive social insurance system for after the war. Lord Beveridge's subsequent publication, in 1944, of *Full Employment in a Free Society* expressed the further hope that postwar unemployment could be kept to a level of 3 percent. In the same year, the Butler Education Act laid the groundwork for an expanded secondary school system with higher school-leaving age in order to broaden educational opportunities for those not able to afford Britain's expensive private schools.

The demand and the expectation of a more secure social existence for the postwar period was also deeply rooted in the memory of the depression.

The Labour Victory of 1945

That Britain would never again allow economic conditions to deteriorate to the levels of the 1930s was a bipartisan view. It was on how best to accomplish such a goal that the parties and their leaders differed. The Labour victory of July 1945 was a landslide victory with nearly 12 million votes cast for Labour, as against 10 million for the Conservatives. Since the last elections in 1935, Labour had picked up 3.5 million votes.

Apart from carrying a strong message in support of the welfare state as a permanent institution, the election results of 1945 could be interpreted in a variety of ways. Some saw it as a vote against the British class system, which Hugh Gaitskell, the future leader of the Labour moderate wing, defined as an "indefensible difference of status and income, distinguishing British society."

Others, on the Labour Left, such as Aneurin Bevan, saw in the Labour victory of 1945 a mandate for the socialization of key industries, especially mining and iron and steel, not as a means of increasing economic efficiency, but of achieving social justice. In addition, nationalization was, for the Labour left, a question of power in what was perceived to be an ongoing class struggle against British capitalism and its political tool, the Conservative party.

In actual fact, Attlee's Labour government strove towards the institution of a welfare state with a mixed economy. Its tactics relied on a maximum of pragmatism and a minimum of dogmatism. John Maynard Keynes, rather than Karl Marx, became the leading light of Labour economic policy, much as he remained the inspiration of future Conservative governments.

It was part of Attlee's pragmatic approach that he realistically took into account the impoverished state of Britain's economy before embarking on actual economic and social change. He also carefully balanced the demands of his domestic policy against those of preserving Britain's great power status in the world, which he and his forceful foreign secretary Ernest Bevin were by no means prepared to sacrifice or seriously diminish.

The first task was to set the economy right at home, to change it from war production to peace production in order to satisfy domestic need but, more importantly, to sharply increase exports.

During the war, the gap between falling earnings from exports and the rising cost of imports had drastically widened, the difference being made up by American Lend-Lease aid and by running up a rising debt with foreign suppliers, especially in the Commonwealth. In order to right Britain's balance of payments once again, it was estimated that she would have to raise exports by 75 percent above prewar levels. In 1945, Britain's foreign debt stood at £3.5 billion as against currency reserves of £500 million.

The American Loan

Like Russia, Britain too had hoped that American Lend-Lease aid would be extended beyond the actual end of the war, in order to facilitate reconstruction. When this proved not to be the case Britain, like Russia, applied for an American loan which, unlike Russia, she obtained.

The American loan of £3.75 billion nevertheless prompted strong criticism on the part of those who thought that it should have been given as an outright grant in recognition of Britain's wartime service. It was also criticized for the conditions attached to it by the lender, which was convertibility of the British pound within one year of the loan agreement. British experts considered the date too early by three years. Pound convertibility, in any event, had to be rescinded when it was first implemented on July 15, 1947 because of the run on the pound.

On the American side, congressional approval even of a loan agreement was not easy to obtain in 1946, so soon after the expenditure of huge sums for Lend-Lease and before the Cold War mentality had taken hold in 1947.

The overall social and economic record of the Labour government turned out to be not quite what had been hoped for in July 1945. In part, this was the result of the government's seeking to reach too many objectives in too little time, including those in the realm of foreign policy, which seriously drained British resources. In part, the Labour government came in for heavy criticism of its policy of nationalization. Such criticism may have been valid with respect to the iron and steel industry.

The nationalization of the Bank of England in 1945 was not a matter of serious dispute, nor was the nationalization of the airlines, BOAC and BEA, the railways, and long-distance trucking. Both the railway and long-distance trucking industries were in dire need of investment capital, which the private operators did not have.

Nationalization

The nationalization of the coal mines, effective January 1947, likewise did not occasion much controversy, given the generally disastrous labor and management record of the British coal industry since the end of the First World War. That nationalization was not a cure-all for economic difficulties was demonstrated in this case. The year of nationalization, 1947, also turned out to be the year of the worst fuel crisis within memory, which seriously affected the British export industries in their drive for increased foreign sales.

The status of the iron and steel industry was decided largely on ideological, even emotional, grounds. Aneurin Bevan charged the industry with having been concerned with profits during the depression to the exclusion of all other considerations, such as the welfare of the workers or even the need for capital investment. Attlee would have been satisfied with the regulation of the iron and steel industry through an Iron and Steel Board, without actual nationalization.

On this issue, the Labour Left triumphed when the nationalization of iron plants with over 50,000 tons yearly production and of iron and steel plants with over 20,000 tons output was decreed. As the decree on the nationalization of the iron and steel industry was not implemented before the parliamentary elections of 1950, the industry was left in a state of uncertainty which discouraged modernization and investment. As a result, the British steel industry fell behind the newly emerging competitors on the continent. During the 1950s British steel was lacking in capacity to fill the orders of even the native British automobile industry, which had to seek foreign suppliers.

Exports

The British Economic Survey of 1947 correctly analyzed the importance of earnings from export sales as the lifeblood of the British economy. It therefore stressed the need for competitiveness in pricing, quality, and design. This sound advice was too often ignored through the lack of market research and through the failure to build up strong overseas sales and service organizations. Too often, British industry produced for the tastes of its own domestic market, which were not always identical with those of foreign markets. That Britain's defense burden was excessive relative to her productive size under the Labour government soon became clear.

Social Welfare

Between 1945 and 1951 the Labour government built 1.5 million new homes. Much of the credit for this belonged to Aneurin Bevan who, as minister of health, defended the housing program against all efforts of the treasury to cut social expenditures.

The Industrial Injuries Bill of 1945, the National Insurance Bill for old age and unemployment of 1946, and the National Assistance Act of 1948 for the poor were key features in the realization of the welfare state. The National Health Service of 1946 was the keystone of Labour social policy, providing free medical, dental and eye care and establishing twenty regional hospital groups throughout the United Kingdom for a better distribution of medical doctors.

The application of the NHS in July 1948 was strongly opposed at first by the British Medical Association, which called the service an attempt at reducing medical doctors to the role of civil servants. BMA opposition was unsuccessful in the end because of Bevan's tough stand and the lack of political support from the Conservatives, which the medical profession had counted on. The public overwhelmingly endorsed the NHS with enrollment standing at 97 percent by the end of 1948.

To its critics, the Labour government had been more concerned with the redistribution of income than with the creation or stimulation of new sources of wealth. In any case, the cost of the NHS proved higher than expected and the taxes needed to cover it began to eat painfully into the earnings of not only the rich but also of those whom the NHS had been designed primarily to help.

With the end of Labour's term of office approaching, the party leadership was plunged into bitter strife over spending priorities and personal power. The high defense burden which Britain continued to carry, together with the cost of newly instituted social programs, forced a devaluation of the pound by 30 percent to $2.80 in September 1949.

In 1950 the Labour party narrowly won reelection with 13.2 million votes and 315 seats, as against 12.5 million votes and 298 seats for the Conservatives.

A Party Divided

The problem of spending priorities, which had divided the Labour leadership before the elections, reappeared in sharpened form after the elections, largely because of the Korean War. In January 1951 Attlee proposed to nearly double the defense budget with a projected increase over the coming three years of £4.7 billion. This was bitterly attacked by the Labour Left, which in addition to Bevan now also included Harold Wilson, the future prime minister. The high defense burden, Bevan charged, was causing Britain to "retreat from socialism." Together with others on the Labour Left, Bevan feared that Attlee was throwing away an historic opportunity which the British working class had been awaiting for forty years. For all its attacks on Attlee, the Labour Left failed to seize control of the party or its basic policy direction. Bevan was able neither to block the appointment to the treasury of Hugh Gaitskell, his rival on the opposite side of the party, nor to prevent the succession of the moderate Herbert Morrison to the foreign office after Bevin's resignation.

With the party leadership divided over both policy and power and the economy once more in a downturn, Attlee, his health failing, decided on new elections in October 1951. The Conservatives, led by Churchill, won a narrow victory with 321 seats over Labour's 295. In the popular vote Labour actually held a slim lead with 48.8 percent against 48 percent for the Conservatives.

COMMONWEALTH RELATIONS

European wars, in the past, had usually been exploited by Great Britain for colonial expansion at the expense of her continental foes. This still held true in the First World War, when Britain had seized the Arab Middle East before dividing it up with France. The strategic and political lesson of World War II for the Commonwealth was, on the other hand, that British power was inadequate to maintain it in its old, prewar form, much less increase its size.

At the end of World War II, Britain reoccupied all her lost possessions in Asia, from Burma to Malaya, Singapore, and Hong Kong. This would hardly spell the return of the imperial status quo, however, owing to two things: the encouragement which Asian nationalism had received through the events of World War II; and the opinion of the United States which, more than after World War I, would have to be taken into account. Britain's contribution to the defeat of Japan, though more than modest, had been less than decisive.

The independence of India was a foregone conclusion over which no disagreement existed in principle between Labour and Conservatives. There was, on the other hand, as yet no recognition of any linkage between India and colonial nationalism elsewhere. India was seen as a special case because of her long struggle for emancipation since 1920.

As for the rest of the Commonwealth and the Empire, the Labour government wished to concentrate on economic development on the assumption that it was the best means of satisfying both the needs of Britain and those of the peoples of the Commonwealth and of the colonies. This was reflected in the resumption of high capital investment in the Commonwealth, the enactment of a new colonial development and welfare act in 1945, and the expansion of the staffs of the Colonial Office. For Foreign Secretary Bevin, in particular, the Commonwealth was vital as an exporter of essential raw materials such as the tin and rubber of Malaya and the gold of South Africa, which brought in badly needed foreign exchange, particularly U.S. dollars. Hugh Dalton, the chancellor of the exchequer, preferred the opposite course and advocated imperial retreat as a means of saving money, a course which the Attlee government never seriously considered.

Indian Independence

Retreat from India, as noted, was a special case. Attempts to appease Indian nationalism with the "August offer" of 1940 and the mission of Stafford Cripps in March 1942 failed. On both occasions India was offered Dominion status for after the war. Before World War II, when British power was unchallenged in Asia, Britain had denied Indian Dominion status and the 1935 Government of India Act had retained Indian external affairs and defense under the British viceroy. The fact that Dominion status was being offered in August 1940, when Britain was fighting for survival in Europe, and then again after she had lost Singapore in February 1942, cast doubt on the integrity of British policy. The Simla conference of June 1945, arranged by Churchill between the viceroy and Indian nationalist leaders, also failed to secure compromise.

Churchill would have liked to delay Britain's departure from India a little while longer in order to extract an Indian promise of staying in the Commonwealth after independence. He would also have liked to safeguard the interests of the princes who, allied by treaty with Britain, had shown great loyalty in the past.

Labour too would have liked to stay at least until an acceptable frontier had been agreed upon under British mediation, once partition of the subcontinent into predominantly Moslem Pakistan and predominantly Hindu India had become a certainty.

Independence, originally fixed for June 1948, was nevertheless advanced to August 15, 1947, before any of the above objectives had been fully reached. The decision was taken on the advice of Lord Louis Montbatten, the last British viceroy of India. The outbreak of a naval mutiny in Bombay in February 1946 demonstrated Britain's rapidly diminishing authority even in circles such as the Indian naval and military, which had previously remained loyal despite Anglo-Indian political disagreements during the war.

India achieved independence admist great violence and turmoil. The number of people killed in the religiously mixed Punjab alone was some 200,000. Over 10 million people became refugees from fear or from actual experience of religious persecution. Churchill had foreseen much of this when giving sombre warning in the House of Commons only a few months earlier that with a premature departure of British authority the skies of India would be "darkened" and "reddened" with blood.

Yet Britain was not blamed for the tragedy and both India and Pakistan chose to remain in the Commonwealth as Dominions. India did so as a republic. Neighboring Burma, where the transition to independence was much more peaceful, quit the Commonwealth in 1948.

Economically, Britain retained a leading position in India up to the end of the 1950s through investments and trade patterns. It was also hoped that the full strategic implications of Indian independence could be averted by integrating Indian defense plans into Britain's own design for Asia. This turned out to be an illusion. During the Suez crisis of 1956 India was in the forefront of the attack against British policy. A coordination of Anglo-Indian strategic thinking occurred only on rare and isolated subsequent occasions, such as during the India-China border conflict of the early 1960s, when a common front was formed, with the United States included.

The Middle East

India had also been an essential link in the larger chain which reached all the way into the Middle East and North Africa. It was in large part with the support of the Indian army that Britain had conquered the Middle East from Turkey in the first place during World War I. It was with the support of the Indian army that Britain crushed the anti-British riots in Iraq at the time of the assumption of the British Mandate in 1920. It was with the support of the Indian army that Britain crushed the anti-British revolt of Iraq's prime minister Rashid Ali in April–May 1941, when German troops were pouring over the Balkans; and it was with the support of the Indian army that Britain stopped Rommel's thrusts into Egypt in 1941 and 1942.

The loss of India raised doubts about Britain's ability to hold on to the Middle East. Before 1947, the Labour government briefly contemplated contingency plans for a withdrawal to bases in Malta, Cyprus and Libya, should British resources prove inadequate for Middle Eastern defenses. If Suez were lost, Attlee thought of substituting Kenya with its large naval and air facilities at Mombasa for the Suez base. These proposals were strongly opposed by the British military chiefs, who threatened resignation in the event of their adoption. The military chiefs impressed upon the government that in the event of war with the Soviet Union, continental Europe might be overrun by the Soviets and Anglo-American strategic air power would require bases in the Middle East and North Africa exactly as in World War II against Hitler Germany.

The United States, sharing such views, was prepared to develop a coordinated Anglo-American Middle Eastern strategy by 1947, as it also was moving towards a joint policy of containment with Britain in Europe. At the same time, the United States advised Britain against the use of discredited modes of imperial policy and against the treatment of the Middle East as an exclusively British sphere of influence.

Palestine

The problem of Palestine intruded on the development of a joint Anglo-American Middle Eastern strategy, though the appearances of Anglo-American disagreement were greater than the substance of agreement on the larger issues.

The British had grappled with the Palestine issue unsuccessfully during the 1930s, when all their efforts to mediate between Zionists and Palestinian Arabs were rejected. The problems reemerged immediately after World War II, and in an atmosphere of far greater desperation because of the evidence of the Jewish holocaust in Europe and the resulting pressures for the establishment of a sovereign Zionist state.

Although the Labour platform of July 1945 had contained a pro-Zionist plank, Bevin's policy sided with the Arabs in the Palestine question. Britain opposed the UN plan for partitioning Palestine because it was also opposed by the Arabs. When the United States and the Soviet Union agreed on partition, Britain refused to help implement the plan, and quit its Mandate over Palestine in May 1948.

Like the British exit from India the previous year, the British retreat from Palestine was followed by violence, in this case in the form of open war between the new state of Israel and its Arab neighbors. Unlike the situation in India, Britain was fully blamed for the war of 1948, at least by the Arab states, which identified the beginning of Zionist immigration with the British Balfour Declaration of 1917. Conservatives, like Britain's future foreign secretary Selwyn Lloyd, thought the British retreat from Palestine a mistake, and attributed it primarily to American pressure.

The Labour government had hopes of establishing better relations with the Arab world by identifying itself with the leaders of popular nationalism rather than with the feudal princes and kings, such as Feisal of Iraq, with whom Britain had traditionally dealt between the wars. This proved to be an illusion, because relations with the feudal princes had been far easier than those with their spartan and xenophobic successors turned out to be. Also, the emerging revolutionary leadership of the Middle East showed no scruples in forming tactical alliances with Communist Russia, something which most of the Arab princes hesitated to do regardless of the strength of their anti-British sentiments.

Egypt

Anglo-Egyptian relations reached a deadlock even before the overthrow of King Farouk and his replacement by Colonel Nasser in 1951. In 1950, Egypt asked for the abrogation of the Anglo-Egyptian treaty of 1936, which was not due to expire until 1956.

The 1936 alliance had been originally concluded at the request of Egypt, which was afraid of Italian aggression after Mussolini's conquest of Ethiopia. In 1950, Britain hoped to persuade Egypt to renew the alliance by pointing to the present Soviet danger. In the event of war, Egypt was warned, the Soviet Union could invade the Middle East and Egypt in a matter of months. The Egyptians, not certain that the Soviets were a threat to them, still asked for treaty abrogation. Britain, in turn, proposed the inclusion of Egypt in a Middle Eastern regional defense pact, called MEDO (Middle Eastern Defense Organization), which would also include Britain, France, Turkey, and the United States. The Egyptian response was cancellation of the 1936 treaty and terrorist attacks against the British Suez garrison.

The Iranian Crisis of 1951

In 1951 King Abdullah was assassinated in neighboring Jordan and there was evidence also in Iraq of rising anti-Western sentiment. In Iran, the prime minister was assassinated in March 1951, after which a strongly nationalist government was installed under Mohammed Mossadek. Mossadek nationalized the Iranian oil fields and the refining facilities at Abadan which had previously been in the ownership of the Anglo-Iranian oil company.

The Attlee government denounced the nationalization as "illegal" and demanded damages and compensation. Herbert Morrison, Bevin's successor at the foreign office, thereupon contemplated the retaking of Abadan by force in July 1951. Attlee rejected force because he did not have a rapid deployment force available to do the job on short notice and because he feared the repercussions of such a policy on British influence elsewhere in the Middle East. What the Labour government refused to do in the Iranian crisis of 1951, the Conservatives were to practice in the Suez crisis of 1956 with very serious results.

Britain regained part of its influence through an American-inspired coup under General Zahedi in August 1953, which ousted Mossadek and restored the shah. Britain accepted the nationalization of the oil fields and refinery, which henceforth were to be operated by a consortium of eight foreign oil companies, with Britain's share being 40 percent. Iran was guaranteed 50 percent of the profits.

THE RETURN OF CONSERVATIVE GOVERNMENT

The margin of Conservative victory in 1951 was remarkably thin. What the election results seemed to mean was that the public wished to preserve the social gains of the past administration, especially the National Health Service, without also having to accept rationing and other forms of government control which were reminders of the war and of postwar austerity.

In certain areas, particularly in housing, the Conservatives had actually out-promised Labour, as with the pledge to build 300,000 new homes per year, for several years to come. Churchill and the Conservatives had pledged to do all that Labour had done, but to do it more efficiently, more economically, and without destroying private enterprise and initiative.

The choice of progressives for key cabinet posts, such as Butler for the treasury and Macmillan for housing, revealed the seriousness of the commitment to social progress under the Conservative government. Soon, the British *Economist* coined the term *Butskellism,* to emphasize the continuity in social and economic policy, as there seemed little difference between the policies of Labour chancellor of the exchequer Gaitskell and his Conservative successor Butler.

The social and economic record of the Churchill government between 1951 and 1955 was, in fact, more successful than most had expected. The economic crisis of 1951 was largely mastered by 1952, in part as a result of improved terms of trade, in part because of major dollar earnings of Commonwealth members, especially Malaya and South Africa. Churchill also significantly reduced defense spending from its all-time peacetime high of 1951.

The years 1952 to 1954 were the most stable economic period since the war, and rationing was lifted in 1953. Plans for the nationalization of iron and steel were scrapped, but the industry remained in a state of uncertainty, not knowing whether another Labour government might not try nationalization again.

Standards of living rose perceptibly in the early to mid-1950s, as reflected in a 50 percent increase in automobile ownership. To the welfare state the Conservatives seemed to have added the affluent society. Macmillan made good on his election promise and finished 300,000 new homes between November 1952 and October 1953.

When Churchill left office in April 1955 at the age of eighty for reasons of health, he had the great satisfaction of seeing unprecedented prosperity at home and restored power and prestige abroad.

Eden had used his diplomatic skill in obtaining a workable solution to the German rearmament problem and in getting a face-saving settlement for France in the Indochina war. Churchill's own initiatives in the realm of summitry, his eagerness to establish contact with the post-Stalin leadership of Soviet Russia before old age and infirmity would force him from the scene, were less successful.

Both in Russia's internal power struggles and in the continuing Cold War confrontation over Germany and eastern Europe, no final positions had been reached. Churchill may have possessed a sufficient grasp of history to understand the transitory nature of the gains achieved by Britain since the war, and it may have privately disturbed him that in the basic questions raised by World War II no final answers had been found at the time of his departure. That the situation in the Middle East was far from settled was also clear in 1955.

EDEN AND SUEZ

Eden held new elections after Churchill's resignation in May 1955, and he won them easily. Compared with the narrow victory of 1951, the Conservatives gained a comfortable lead of 59 seats. Their popular vote was nearly 50 percent.

The election results reflected both the prosperous times and the paralysis of Labour through its continuing internal struggle over power and ideology. To the old quarrels over nationalization was added the new controversy concerning the use of British nuclear weapons in a hypothetical war with Russia. Attlee and Bevan clashed over this issue in public debate in the Commons in 1955, which nearly resulted in the expulsion of Bevan from the party. Bevan and Gaitskell continued their battle over succession once Attlee resigned the leadership of the party.

But Eden's prospects, so bright at the outset, began to dim also, turning his prime ministership into a brief and failed administration. At home, there were new signs of a weakening economy with rising inflation and the highest rate of strikes since World War II. The death of Arthur Deakin, who had exerted a moderating influence on the unions under Attlee, was a contributing factor, as was the rise in consumer prices. In 1955 Britain lost 3.75 million workdays through strikes, more than all the workdays lost in the years between 1946 and 1954. Eden's appeal for wage restraints was rejected by the Trade Union Congress of September 1956.

The major challenge came from the Middle East. After Egypt had denounced the Anglo-Egyptian treaty of 1936, Churchill's Conservative government had succeeded in reaching agreement with the new government of Colonel Nasser on the evacuation of the Suez base. Under the agreement of October 1954 Britain promised to evacuate within twenty months, but retained the right of return in the event of an external attack on any member of the Arab League, or Turkey, except by Israel. An agreement had also been reached in February 1953 giving the Sudan the option of Egyptian rule or independence, an option exercised in favor of the latter. In July 1953 agreement had also been reached with Libya, granting Britain the use of bases for a twenty-year period, a settlement designed to offset the loss of Suez.

The Baghdad Pact

With British influence diminished in Egypt, British policy concentrated on Iraq, whose 1931 treaty with Britain was due to expire in 1957. Iraq still possessed a pro-British government under Prime Minister Nuri-es-Said. With Iraq, Britain concluded the Baghdad pact of 1955, which also included Iran, Pakistan, and Turkey. An additional Anglo-Iraqi agreement specifically secured for British use Iraqi air bases which Britain had used to good advantage between the wars and during World War II.

It was intended to expand the Baghdad pact into an even wider regional alliance, for the dual purpose of preserving British influence in the Middle East and keeping Soviet influence out. Britain attempted to draw the United States into open membership, the American role being initially limited to participation in special areas such as the counter-insurgency committee. The United States shunned open membership to avoid identification with "British imperialism." Britain also invited Jordan and Egypt to become members, as Iraq would have remained the only Arab participant otherwise.

The British invitation to Nasser to join the Baghdad pact rested on a basic misreading of Egyptian intentions after October 1954. Britain believed the October 1954 agreement to have been a concession which Nasser would reward with a policy of cooperation. Nasser interpreted the 1954 agreement as the beginning of full emancipation for Egypt and, eventually, for the rest of the Arab world under his leadership.

Britain and Nasser were also set on opposite courses with regard to Iraq, which Egypt regarded as its chief rival for leadership of the Arab world and whose pro-Western government Nasser did all in his power to undermine. It was therefore only logical that Nasser refused to join the Baghdad pact and that he pressured Jordan to do likewise.

In 1955 Nasser concluded his first arms deal with the Communist bloc, which was justified on the grounds that Israel had updated its air force with advanced French-built Mirage jet fighters. In the same year, Nasser recognized Communist China.

The Suez Crisis

The nationalization of the Suez Canal company by Egypt on July 26, 1956 thus represented the logical climax of a development which, in its more distant roots, took its cue from the abortive Iranian revolution of 1951 and which, in its more immediate setting, resulted from the attempt to subordinate Egyptian policy once more to British interests, though in a more subtle manner than had been customary in the 1930s and 1940s. The withdrawal of Anglo-American aid promises for the financing of the Aswan high dam project on July 19, 1956 was not, in itself, the principal issue.

Both the United States and Britain were agreed on the danger of Nasser's policy to Western interests, but they were not agreed on the type of response which that danger warranted. Failure to agree on a response was partly due to personalities, because Eden did not enjoy nearly as confidential a relationship with Secretary of State Dulles as Bevin had enjoyed with Acheson.

More important was a difference in perceptions of the challenge. If she left the challenge unanswered, Britain feared she would lose her remaining friends in the Middle East, who would dismiss her as an irresolute, perhaps cowardly ally. This would also directly reflect on Britain's claim to the role of world power, which she had only sustained at great cost and difficulty since 1945.

For Eden personally, there were the memories of British humiliation at the hands of Mussolini during the Ethiopian crisis of 1935–1936. Nasser was viewed as another Mussolini. Although recovery of the Suez Canal was seen as important in itself, the primary policy aim of Eden, and Macmillan, who had meanwhile moved to the foreign office, was the ouster of Nasser and his replacement by a more friendly successor.

American interests and American credibility were not on the line remotely to the same extent as were Britain's. The United States could therefore afford to wait and hope that time and the habitual bickering among Arab states would in the end blunt Nasser's purpose. The policy most likely to win support for Nasser, in American eyes, was a policy of force such as Eden was about to apply.

Within a week of nationalization, Eden had decided on armed intervention in partnership with France, which shared his eagerness to topple Nasser. The American attitude was assumed to be, at worst, one of passive neutrality. Eisenhower's urgent plea of October 30, 1956 for immediate consultation evoked Eden's airy response that the time for consultation was for "after the dust settled."

Apart from forgoing consultation with the United States, Eden's major fault was procrastination. As in the Iranian crisis of 1951, Britain did not have a rapid deployment force available for immediate action against Egypt. By the time such a force had been assembled, the Suez crisis had been allowed to expand into a major international uproar, with the UN, the United States, and the USSR all taking up fixed positions in anticipation of the Anglo-French strike.

The first to strike was the Israeli army, which Britain had reluctantly included in Operation Musketeer at the behest of France. Supported by Anglo-French air cover, the Israelis attacked on October 29, reaching all their objectives within days.

To conceal their own invasion, Britain and France issued an ultimatum to both Egypt and Israel, demanding the withdrawal of both armies to a line ten miles behind the canal. The joint Anglo-French attack, which followed on November 5, was undertaken on the false pretense of restoring peace between Israel and Egypt. On November 6, the day on which the joint British-French forces set out from Port Said to Suez, Britain halted operations, obeying the UN cease-fire resolution which had been adopted by sixty-four votes to five.

The United States, far from standing on the sidelines, mobilized the United Nations in the Suez crisis as Britain had once mobilized the League of Nations against Mussolini's invasion of Ethiopia in 1935. As Britain had then acted partly from moral, partly from political motives, so did the United States in 1956. Eisenhower opposed the Anglo-French action because it violated the principles of the UN charter, at a time when American influence in the UN still prevailed. He also opposed British policy because opposition was likely to enhance American prestige among Third World countries.

Suez also left Britain isolated in the Commonwealth, however, with only Australia and New Zealand supporting her. Canada's foreign minister Lester Pearson was among those leading the attack against Britain in the UN, and India's Nehru threatened to quit the Commonwealth he had so recently joined. In Britain, the question was raised, what was a Commonwealth worth under such conditions, which differed considerably from those of World War I and World War II, when all Dominions had given unstinting support.

With Suez turning into a disaster, domestic opposition also grew, with the division cutting across party lines. Not all cabinet members had been kept fully informed, and two members of the government resigned.

Within the Arab world, the repercussions of Suez ranged far and wide. Among the consequences was the coup of generals Kassim and Aref of July 14, 1958, which killed Iraq's prowestern king Feisal II and his prime minister Nuri-es-Said. The Iraqi coup spelled the end of the Baghdad pact which, following Iraq's withdrawal, had lost all meaning as a shield against Soviet penetration of the Middle East.

For Soviet Russia, the benefits of Suez were many, both in an immediate sense and on a long-range basis. Coinciding as it did with the Soviet invasion of Hungary and the crushing of the Hungarian Revolution in early November 1956, the Suez crisis served as a convenient diversion and cover for Khrushchev's own military action. Having crushed the Hungarians, the Soviets proposed joint action with the United States to stop the Anglo-French invasion of Egypt. Khrushchev, for good measure, threatened to send missiles against western Europe and volunteers to Egypt to dramatize the Soviet stand. Significantly, there was no similar American threat to unleash nuclear missiles against the Soviet Union or to send American volunteers into Hungary unless the Soviets evacuated Budapest. The UN, which had been effective in forcing Britain and France to evacuate their forces from Egypt, achieved no comparable results for Hungary under Soviet occupation either.

British, and in a larger sense, European power had been dealt a severe blow with the Suez debacle, which followed by only two years the French defeat in Indochina. European power had retreated under the joint pressure of the United States and Soviet Russia. Suez divided the United States from its European allies, who long remembered it when the United States itself became embroiled in the Vietnam War, a decade after Suez.

Given the parallel interests of Britain and the United States in the larger Cold War picture, the decisive weakening of British Middle Eastern power could not help but benefit the long-term Soviet interest. The time might even arrive when the United States would be the only power capable of upholding western interests in the Middle East against both regional nationalism and Soviet incursions from without.

19

Suez and the Revival of the European Spirit

THE FOUNDING OF THE COMMON MARKET

The twin crises of Suez and Hungary dramatically underscored European inability to effectively oppose decisions of either superpower in questions vital to the Europeans. In the Suez crisis, American pressure had forced Britain and France to retreat. In the Hungarian Revolution, west European reaction had to content itself with expressions of moral outrage and a sense of deep frustration. No other event had so sharply highlighted the full meaning of the outcome of World War II to Europe before. From the frustration of November 1956 grew a new spirit of hope, that was even to escalate to the level of enthusiasm, that European integration might indeed be the answer to the problems created by superpower dominance.

A new initiative for the revival of the European spirit had, in fact, been taken in 1955 by the small Benelux countries, even before the external stimuli of the Hungarian and Suez crises. Acting on a Dutch initiative of April 1955 the foreign ministers of Holland, Belgium, and Luxembourg, Johan Willem Beyen, Paul Henri Spaak and Joseph Bech produced the Benelux Memorandum, calling for a European Common Market and asking for a foreign ministers' conference of all six ECSC members to help launch the project. The Benelux initiative was well timed, because the Schuman Plan, after a poor start, showed clear signs by 1955 of becoming a major economic success. In June 1955, the six ECSC foreign ministers announced the beginning of a "new phase" in European integration at the Messina conference, one which would lead to the establishment of a European Economic Community (EEC) with common institutions. The Messina conference also installed an intergovernmental committee under Spaak's chairmanship to draft the framework of both the EEC and the projected European Atomic Energy Agency, EURATOM.

The intergovernmental committee produced its report (the Spaak Report) on April 21, 1956, and this contained all the essential features of the future EEC. Amendments were added concerning the association of overseas territories, a subject of major concern to France and Belgium, which still possessed large African colonies. Accordingly, the overseas territories of the EEC nations were to be given provisional association with the EEC for a five-year period, to be followed by new treaty arrangements. During the initial association period, a development fund for overseas territories was to be created in the amount of $581 million, Germany and France contributing $200 million each. The drafting of the treaty for a common nuclear agency (EURATOM) was preceded by the creation of a commission to investigate Europe's future energy needs in the wake of the 1956 Suez crisis. Composed of the Italian nuclear physicist Francesco Giordani, the French transportation expert Louis Armand, and the West German coal and steel expert Franz Etzel, the commission duly noted Europe's rising dependence on foreign energy sources and her backwardness in the research and application of peaceful nuclear energy as compared to the United States, the USSR and Great Britain.

The treaties for EEC and EURATOM were signed on March 25, 1957 at Rome. The fact that they were ratified by all members before the end of the year—in contrast to the drawn-out controversy over EDC several years earlier—attested to the new sense of urgency which the international crises of 1956 had created among the governments of western Europe. In January 1958, both agreements went into effect.

BRITAIN AND THE EEC

Britain had shunned a leadership role in European integration at the beginning of the 1950s for deep historical reasons and because she had doubts about the purely economic prospects of the integration venture. By the late 1950s, the economies of continental Europe had sufficiently recovered to suggest the great potential which western Europe was to actually achieve in the coming decade. The British attitude towards economic integration thus changed without a corresponding change in other basic British attitudes concerning Britain's role as a world power, her special relationship with the United States, and her commitments and privileges deriving from Commonwealth leadership. As before, Britain wished to be "in" and "out" of Europe. Although she was prepared to go "in" further than before, she still wished to determine the conditions of her entry in order not to jeopardize her position "out" of Europe.

The British dilemma between Europe and the world outside Europe derived from the fact that she had become both stronger and weaker by the end of the 1950s. She was stronger militarily since becoming a thermo-nuclear power in 1957 after the first successful hydrogen bomb explosion. The status of a thermo-nuclear power raised Britain to the level of United States and Soviet nuclear capabilities and enhanced her role as an American ally. Partly for that reason, the old "special relationship" with the United States could be quickly restored despite the disappointments and recriminations over Suez policy. The joint Declaration of Common Purpose of Eisenhower and Britain's new prime minister Harold Macmillan of October 25, 1957, announcing closer cooperation in the political-strategic field, was symbolic of the restored "special relationship." The Declaration of Common Purpose was soon followed by an agreement on the "cooperation on the uses of atomic energy for mutual defense purposes" of July 3, 1958, which among other things arranged for the sharing of nuclear test facilities in Nevada and British-owned Christmas Island. United States-British defense cooperation was further intensified when the United States provided Britain with a new nuclear-weapons delivery system in the form of the air-to-ground Skybolt missile, which filled the gap created by the closing down of Britain's own surface-to-surface Blue Streak missile for reasons of cost. Britain, in return, granted the United States a base for Polaris submarines at Holy Loch in the Firth of Clyde. Though stronger militarily, Britain had become weaker economically, relative to Western Europe. By 1959, West Germany overtook Britain in gold and foreign exchange reserves, Italy did so in 1961, and France in 1963.

Relations with Western Europe were increasingly determined on the basis of economic performance, not military strength, however, and it made very little difference in British–West European relations whether Britain was a nuclear power or not. Politically too the balance of power had changed or was in the process of being changed at the time of the Common Market's launching. In France, the unstable Fourth Republic soon gave way to the skillful and determined leadership of de Gaulle, closely allied with Adenauer's West Germany. The British goal of having economic integration on their own terms was not likely to be reached under these altered economic and political realities. British opposition to the Rome treaty of 1957 was centered on the fact that the Rome Treaty proposed the elimination of both industrial and agricultural tariffs, envisaged common external tariffs against nonmembers, and projected common organs with a supranational purpose, such as the EEC commission.

Britain preferred a European free-trade area without common supranational organs, without common agricultural tariffs, and without common external tariffs. The proposed free-trade area was to be built around the existing Organization of European Economic Cooperation (OEEC), in which Britain already enjoyed an established senior position. British hopes of changing the rules and the purpose of the EEC according to her own wishes and needs were quickly dashed as a result of the first Adenauer–de Gaulle meeting at Bad Kreuznach on November 26, 1958. The Kreuznach communiqué, which hinted at the coming of the drawn-out feud between de Gaulle and Britain, reaffirmed French–West German cooperation in the existing EEC without change. British tactics thereupon shifted to the creation of a rival free-trade association (EFTA), consisting of Britain, the Scandinavian countries, Portugal, Switzerland and Austria, which went into effect on May 30, 1960. EFTA was never intended as an end in itself, but as a means of pressuring EEC into changing its rules, opening the door to an EFTA-EEC merger. The tactic failed and when Britain's prime minister Macmillan threatened the creation of a new peripheral alliance directed against the increasingly intimate Bonn-Paris "axis," the threat had more the appearance of frustrated anger than a realistic policy option.

Economic necessity drove Macmillan to ask for British EEC membership in July 1961. The application was strongly criticized at the Commonwealth Conference at Accra in September 1961 by some Commonwealth members who depended on the British home market for their agricultural exports. During the ensuing Brussels negotiations between November 1961 and January 1963 Macmillan demanded "satisfactory arrangements" for the United Kingdom, the Commonwealth, and the other

EFTA members, which had been kept informed of British intentions. Britain's chief negotiator Edward Heath specifically asked for the exemption of Canadian aluminum, New Zealand dairy products and Indian tea from EEC external tariffs.

Economic compromise was not beyond the reach of Britain and the EEC. The reasons why the Brussels negotiations failed in the end were political. De Gaulle vetoed British membership in the EEC in his press conference of January 14, 1963 because Britain was, in his words, linked too much with "the most diverse and the most distant countries." It had angered de Gaulle, no doubt, that shortly before seeking EEC membership, Britain had reaffirmed her "special relationship" with the United States in a highly visible way through the conclusion of the Nassau Agreement with President Kennedy in December 1962. Under the agreement, the United States provided Britain with the Polaris submarine-launched missile, after the closing down of the Skybolt program by Defense Secretary Robert Macnamara for cost reasons.

INSTITUTIONS AND THE EARLY FUNCTIONING OF THE EEC

The institutions of the EEC and their functions represented a carefully thought-out compromise between the national interest of member-governments and the collective interest of the community. Great care was taken in devising formulas and keys that would bar discrimination against any one member-state in the distribution of power, staff positions, or influence over community institutions. In the distribution of power between individual community institutions, a system of checks and balances was worked out, the emphasis being on the community's ability to achieve its built-in purpose of supranationality. The institutions of the EEC represented a logical development from earlier efforts at European integration, less coordinated and comprehensive than the Common Market. Both EURATOM and EEC adopted the institutional concepts of the Schuman Plan—a council of ministers, an assembly, an executive body, and a court. The assembly and the court were shared by ECSC, EURATOM and EEC from the beginning, the Council of Ministers and the Executive Commission were merged only after 1965.

The Council of Ministers

The terms *Council of Ministers* and *Commission* were somewhat misleading, in that the former was the real legislative body, the latter the executive organ of the community. The Council of Ministers was the representative organ of the national governments of the community. By practice, though not by statute, the ministers were most often the foreign ministers, though their place could be taken by other ministers if the subject matter under discussion so required. Voting in the Council of Ministers was by majority vote in procedural and administrative matters. On substantive issues, the unanimity rule applied during the initial EEC stage. From January 1966 onwards, majority voting was to go into effect, a provision that was to prompt a major crisis in the EEC because of French opposition under de Gaulle.

Voting in the council was to be secret, chiefly to enable governments to change their position without having to face criticism or losing face before their own home parliaments.

The broad powers of the Council of Ministers, including that of widening its own prerogatives through treaty amendment, were limited by the provision that the council could act only on the initiative of the Executive Commission. The Executive Commission, or simply the Commission, was intended to function as a collegiate government for the community as a whole. It was the "real" government of the EEC which, through its power of initiative, would chart the future course. The Council and the Commission were thus the opposite poles of the community, the former representing the interest of individual governments, the latter that of the entire community. The Council could not act without the initiative of the Commission, but the Council was not bound by the recommendation of the Commission. In the often adversary relationship between the Council and the Commission, the latter enjoyed a purely technical advantage over the former, because the commissioners served the community full time. In addition, the commissioners acquired a more thoroughgoing technical knowledge of EEC issues through daily contact with their extensive EEC civil service staffs. The commissioners were thus often the better-informed party.

The Commission

After the admission of Britain, Denmark, and Ireland in the early 1970s, thirteen commissioners (originally nine) were appointed by the member governments, the major powers having two each, the lesser, one. Before the merger of the institutions of ECSC, EEC and EURATOM in the 1960s, the presidency of the EEC Commission went to West Germany, that of EURATOM to France, and that of ECSC to Italy. Afterwards, the Commission presidency was made a two-year rotating office, renewable for one additional term. Walter Hallstein, coauthor of the Rome treaties, was the first president. His administration was characterized by a very assertive stance by the Commission and the generally overoptimistic view that the integration movement had gained such momentum that the building of a European federal government was only a question of time, with 1970 being the often-mentioned target date. De Gaulle's veto against British membership in 1963 and his boycott of the community for six months in 1965, over the issues of common farm policy and Council majority voting, considerably dampened such optimism. Like the executive branch of a national government, the Commission was subdivided into administration departments, called *directions* in the EEC. Eight departments were organized for foreign affairs, finance, interstate commerce, antitrust policy, welfare, agriculture, transport, and foreign aid. Appointments of commissioners to the individual departments were made with an eye for either accommodating a special national interst in a given area, or of removing, in any event, the source of possible future friction. It was logical to assign the foreign relations department to Belgium, not only because Belgium was a small power, but because it displayed an excellent capacity for mediation when great-power interests collided, especially between France and Germany.

For similar reasons, the agriculture department went to Holland. Not only had the Dutch commissioner Sicco Mansholt, who also served as Commission vice-president, great experience as the long-term minister of agriculture in the Dutch national government, but the development of a common EEC agricultural policy was a subject so controversial that it was best to assign agriculture to a lesser power. France controlled finance and foreign aid because of her special interest in EEC aid to her own former colonies, the "associated territories." West Germany was put in charge of administration and antitrust policy, Italy of interstate commerce and welfare, and Luxembourg of transport. Through practice, though not by statute, these departments became "nationalized," that is, they remained in the hands of commissioners of the same nationality, though the "directors" serving directly beneath them were of a different nationality. The Common Market Assembly, or European Parliament, was by far the weakest institution of the community. Its function was advisory, though it was given the power to overthrow the Commission by two-thirds majority without, however, having any say about the selection of the Commission that would succeed. The power to remove the commissioners was more abstract than real, in any case, since the European Parliament, composed mostly of ardent federalists, was not likely to damage the cause of integration through drastic action of this kind.

The European Parliament

The members of the European Parliament were chosen by the national parliaments in a manner reflecting the strength of the various parties in the latter. Originally, France, Germany and Italy were assigned thirty-six seats each, Holland and Belgium fourteen each and Luxembourg four. Three major parliamentary groups developed, Christian Democrat, Socialist, and Liberal. By 1965 a fourth group was added in the form of the European Democratic Union party, which was actually a French Gaullist group and thus opposed to the supranational ambition of the European Parliament. Following a practice already developed in the assembly of the Coal and Steel Community, parliamentary deputies were not seated by nationality, but by party affiliation. The Rome treaty itself called for the eventual election of the European Parliament by direct suffrage in a provision not realized until much later in 1979. During the 1960s, the European Parliament proposed to the Council of Ministers that its size be tripled, with one-third of the members selected by the national parliament, two-thirds elected by direct suffrage. This proposal failed of adoption largely through the opposition of de Gaulle, who disliked the strengthening effect it would have had on the supranational aspects of the community.

Like the Council of Ministers, the European Parliament was a part-time institution, its members serving in the dual capacity as national and European deputies. The European Parliament suffered further from the fact that it had no permanent seat, its meetings being held in three different places. Full sessions of the parliament were held in Strasbourg at the *Maison d'Europe*, which was actually the headquarters of the Council of Europe. Parliamentary committees usually held their meetings in Brussels in close proximity to the Commission's offices. The secretariat of the parliament had its seat in Luxembourg. The chief function of the European Parliament soon became that of a major publicity and propaganda agency for the European movement. The parliament distributed more literature on the subject of integration than did any other EEC agency and it chose as its presidents well-known figures who symbolized the European idea. Robert Schuman was the first president of the European parliament. Among his successors in the 1960s was Gaetano Martino, formerly the foreign minister of Italy, who had hosted the 1955 Messina conference, where the EEC was born. The Court of Justice, composed originally of seven, later nine judges, after the EEC expansion of January 1973, was given powers unequaled by any previous international court. Acting on appeal, the court could rule against decisions of EEC governments, those of the Commission or the Council of Ministers, or even against the action of private individuals or companies which were deemed in violation of the Rome treaty provisions. In practice, however, court interpretation of the Rome treaty soon revealed itself as narrow, adhering to what was seen to have been the original intent of the treaty framers.

The Common Market

As had been the case with the Schuman Plan, there was some initial scepticism about the economic potential of the Common Market, especially on the German side. Economics minister Erhard believed that the EEC, as a customs union, would primarily benefit its weaker members, Italy and France, to the disadvantage of German industry, whose export structure was more strongly oriented towards the nonmember states of Britain, Scandinavia and overseas countries. Similarly, West Germany was fearful of the effects which Common Market rules might have on German economic performance overall, as it attributed its own economic progress since 1948 largely to the adoption of a neoliberal economic philosophy. Initially, the Common Market was often interpreted on the German side as the economic price West Germany would have to pay for improved political relations with France and Western Europe. Economic considerations also played a major part in West German support for Britain's project of a European Free Trade Area at the turn of the fifties and sixties. Soon after the first 10 percent tariff reduction went into effect on January 1, 1959, the Common Market developed in a manner few had foreseen. Between 1958 and 1962 West German industrial production increased by 35 percent, that of France by 23 percent. Both French and German trade with the other EEC partners doubled, while French-German trade nearly tripled. The EEC schedule for tariff reduction was accelerated, with a further 10 percent cut in tariffs going into effect by December 31, 1960. By the end of 1961 all import quotas on industrial goods were eliminated. By July 1968 the customs union was virtually completed, ahead of schedule.

The achievement of negative integration, i.e., the elimination of trade barriers, was generally an easier process than the achievement of positive integration, the development of a common policy in a particular area. The Rome treaty itself was more specific in devising rules and timetables for the former than for the latter. The greater difficulty in developing common policy reflected the deeper problem of national sovereignty versus community leadership. The ability to devise common policy was likely to depend on the ability of the central EEC institutions to assume a real measure of supranational authority. Much of the history and the development of the EEC during the 1960s, and later, was to revolve around this question. Relatively little progress was achieved in the development of a common transport and energy policy. The Coal and Steel Community had launched a free trade in coal in the early 1950s, when coal still accounted for a major portion of European energy needs. The growing reliance on oil in the 1960s did not result in a common oil policy, a fact dramatically highlighted in the energy crisis of the 1970s, following the 1973 oil boycott.

EURATOM

EURATOM, contrary to the high hopes initially placed on it, did not become a vehicle for a common nuclear energy program. Before very long, the national governments concentrated their efforts on national nuclear energy programs with jealously guarded nuclear technology and research. By comparison with national research efforts, those of the EURATOM research centers, such as in Karlsruhe in West Germany and Ispra in Italy, were of lesser importance. Among the noteworthy accomplishments of EURATOM was its policing of American-supplied enriched uranium against abuses for weapons programs.

CAP

The devising of a workable common agricultural policy (CAP) proved to be the most difficult of all challenges of EEC positive integration. The difficulty derived, in part, from the variations in farm efficiency and productivity between the participating member states, and in part it reflected the considerable political power which organized farming wielded within individual EEC countries. In order to please farming interests, CAP would have had to include a comprehensive and expensive system of price supports. CAP's difficulties also stemmed from the fact that it affected vital interests of the two strongest EEC countries, West Germany and France. The West Germans had the stronger industrial economy, but France had a more productive farm economy. The prospect of major farm exports to West Germany was one of the major reasons behind the French decision to enter EEC in the first place. The influx of cheap French food imports, on the other hand, was bound to affect less productive and marginal West German farms.

The first step towards CAP was a 5 percent reduction in farm tariffs on December 31, 1960. On January 14, 1962 agreement was reached on the organization of a communitywide agricultural market and on regulations for financing it. "Target prices" were fixed for specified farm products, which originally covered 53 percent of EEC agricultural production. If prices fell below the agreed minimum ("target") price in any given member country, the EEC as a whole would buy up surplusses, in order to restore price levels to the "target price." Price supports were to be financed through import levies and farmers were made eligible for direct subsidies. EEC agricultural exports to third countries would be financed through a common agricultural fund. CAP financing procedures were worked out for an initial transition period ending in June 1965. France pressed for an early agreement in the post-June 1965 period because of the importance of agriculture to the French economy overall and because majority voting was scheduled to go into effect in the EEC Council of Ministers as of January 1966. In a matter as vital as farm interests, France did not wish to take any chances on being overruled after that date. The twin issues of CAP and EEC progress towards supranationality, represented by majority voting, was to present the Common Market with its most serious crisis to date, because of de Gaulle's insistence on solving both issues overwhelmingly in the economic interest of France and in accordance with his conception of EEC's political purpose.

Superpower Reactions to the EEC

The considerable economic gains of the EEC and the prospect of its also attaining its larger aim of political integration, before de Gaulle dimmed such prospects by the mid-1960s, made the EEC a factor of considerable weight and interest for the superpowers. For the United States, the EEC represented something of a dilemma. On the one hand, European integration had been desired by the United States ever since the conception of an American regional approach to western Europe under the Cold War strategy of the late 1940s. The EEC also presented American private business with attractive investment opportunities. U.S.-based corporations, accustomed to the large

American domestic market, often recognized EEC business opportunities more quickly than did their European counterparts, still accustomed to small or medium-sized national markets. Across-the-border mergers of European national companies were at first a rarity until the success of such mergers had actually been demonstrated by, for example, the Dutch–West German aircraft manufacturers, or the West German–Belgian photo equipment companies. On the negative side, the EEC threatened American farm exports, because of the high EEC common agricultural tariffs. By 1964 U.S.-EEC trade relations threatened to assume the character of a trade war in connection with the "chicken war," following the imposition of EEC tariffs on frozen American chickens. U.S. farm exports to the Common Market actually increased after 1958, rising from $900 million to $2 billion by 1970. The solution sought by the United States was a liberalization of trade, not only between the EEC and themselves, but worldwide. Towards that end, the Trade Expansion Act was passed by Congress in 1962 and the Kennedy Round for the reduction of tariffs was launched in 1964. The Soviet reaction to the Common Market was rather the reverse of the American. European integration was unwelcome from the Soviet standpoint, because it was likely to strengthen Western Europe politically and strategically. The Soviet government and the impoverished economies of Eastern Europe nevertheless eyed the commercial opportunities which a wealthy West European market also offered to them with growing interest and appetite.

The official Soviet position was to deny legal recognition to the EEC and to refuse compliance with EEC foreign trade rules, while seeking to obtain on a bilateral basis economic advantages which otherwise were reserved to EEC members. This was the Soviet position taken in trade negotiations with France in 1962. In 1963, the USSR addressed separate inquiries, on a country-by-country basis, to EEC members, seeking most-favored nation treatment with each of them. The EEC replied as a unit, however, informing the Soviets that they should ask this kind of question to the appropriate EEC institution, which was the EEC Commission. In 1964, the EEC Council of Ministers informed the Soviet government of its basic willingness to lower tariffs, if the request was sent to the Commission. This the Soviet government refused to do, for to have done so would have been tantamount to recognition of the EEC as a separate entity under international law.

20

From Division to Rearmament: Consolidation of the Two German States

WEST GERMAN POLITICAL AND ECONOMIC RECOVERY

There was doubt at the beginning whether the Federal Republic of West Germany would succeed in any of the major purposes for which it had been formed. Many in Britain and France regarded the West German democratic experiment of 1949 with a mixture of anxiety and scepticism. To some, West Germany seemed little more than the premature child of U.S. Cold War politics which, having been given insufficient political and moral preparation, might not survive the nationalist and social stresses of the postwar period. François Ponçet, the newly appointed French high commissioner with a lifelong experience in German affairs, believed that sovereignty ought to be restored to the Germans much more slowly and in carefully measured doses. Others, like Britain's publicist Malcolm Muggeridge, judged West Germany's probable future on the basis of the known dismal record of the Weimar Republic.

There were obvious similarities between "Bonn" and "Weimar," both having grown out of defeat at the end of world wars and neither being reconciled to the permanent loss of German eastern territories. Yet the Germany of the 1950s was no more identical with the Germany of the 1920s than the Europe of the mid–twentieth century was the same as that of the post–World War I period. For the future of German democracy it was essential that Hitler, in the process of consolidating his totalitarian system, had also destroyed those reactionary-conservative elements which he had employed as allies in his final assault on Weimar between 1930 and 1933. In addition, the Second World War and the defeat of 1945 were events of such cataclysmic force as to discredit German nationalism, militarism and authoritarianism as no other event had in modern German history.

In the post–World War II search for the causes of the German democratic failure between 1919 and 1933, the Weimar constitution was frequently cited as a major contributing factor. To the extent that a constitution can provide safeguards against the repetition of past mistakes, the West German 1949 Basic Law attempted to do so. Thus it provided for indirect presidential elections, devised a "constructive vote of no-confidence" requiring a parliamentary majority to agree on a new chancellor before ousting the old one, and stipulated a minimum strength of 5 percent or three deputies for any political party to be elected to any legislature, state or federal. The electoral system itself was an ingenious compromise between direct and proportional representation, each voter casting two votes, one for a party list, another for a candidate of the voter's choice. The Basic Law also put great stress on civil liberties, which it entered at the beginning and which, unlike the Weimar constitution, it did not regard as mere recommendations. As a safeguard against dictatorship, the 1949 constitution made the multiparty system both a requirement and a guarantee.

Where the Weimar Republic had provided few inspiring leaders, Bonn was fortunate in having two powerful personalities at the start, Adenauer and Schumacher, both of whom could also point to a courageous and untarnished record during the Nazi years. Although the two principal parties CDU/CSU and SPD differed sharply on issues of economic-social and foreign policy, they shared a common commitment to the Basic Law, which gave the new state stability. Soon the Federal Republic moved in the direction of a two-party system, as its founders had intended. The number of political parties competing for seats declined from fourteen in the 1949 *Bundestag* elections to five in the 1953 election. During the twenty years following the 1949 election, the share of the two major parties increased from 60 to 89 percent.

Adenauer's long tenure as chancellor from 1949 to 1963 likewise lent stability to West German democracy, though it was not without its disadvantages. Among the disadvantages was the trend from a parliamentary to a presidential-style democracy. Although Adenauer's *kanzlerdemokratie* suited his own somewhat autocratic personality, it resulted in practice in the diminishing legislative initiative of the *Bundestag,* which ran counter to the intentions of the Basic Law.

The Federal Republic quickly developed an outstanding record in its economic policy, which further helped consolidate the new state. Never before in the twentieth century had Germans enjoyed equal measures of prosperity and personal freedoms at the same time.

The original SPD social and economic concept was a blend of traditional beliefs in central planning, socialization of key industries, and the yearning for the kind of social humanism of which Thomas Mann had spoken in his Library of Congress speech of May 1945.

Both SPD and West German unions were loath to end rationing and central planning in times of postwar scarcity out of fear that the result would be soaring inflation and a further reduction in the supply of goods.

The CDU's economic philosophy assumed the shape of the "social market" economy, devised by Adenauer's economic minister Ludwig Erhard. Erhard understood "social market" economy as a synthethis of unfettered free enterprise and the direction of public funds into areas most needful of assistance. In the specifically German situation of the late 1940s and 1950s, this meant primarily the refugees population and bombed-out families. In addition, there were efforts under way to integrate workers into the management process through "codetermination" and to help workers accumulate their own investment capital. The Emergency Aid Law of 1949 and the Equalization of Burden Law of 1952 were examples of the former type of social policy. The law of May 21, 1951, instituting workers' "codetermination" in management of enterprises exceeding one thousand employees, was an example of the latter.

The economic boom unleashed under Erhard's policy generated an optimistic climate in post–World War II Germany, for which there was no counterpart in Weimar. It was a boom greatly assisted by U.S. Marshall aid, of which, on a per capita basis, West Germany received half as much as Britain or France. The boom was also helped by the abundant availability of skilled labor, reinforced by returning POWs and, during the 1950s, by the unending stream of East German refugees.

West German unions were remarkably docile. The first major strike occurred only in 1956 with the metal workers' union strike in Schleswig-Holstein. Union membership declined between 1948 and the mid-sixties from 35 to 29 percent of the labor force, while the labor force itself increased from 16 to 22 million. Labor peace during reconstruction was undoubtedly aided by Adenauer's good personal relations with West German trade union boss Hans Boeckler.

Unemployment, the recurring scourge of the Weimar Republic, was not a problem for the Federal Republic for many years. Still near the 2 million mark in 1950, unemployment dropped below 3 percent by 1959. Average weekly earnings of industrial workers rose by 151 percent between 1950 and 1962, with a concurrent GNP growth from DM 97.9 billion to DM 355.1 billion. By 1953, West German living standards exceeded those of 1938.

THE QUEST FOR SOVEREIGNTY

At the beginning, West German sovereignty was only slightly more than nominal. The Occupation Statute, which went into effect on September 21, 1949, did not end Allied occupation, but merely modified its terms. The three western high commissioners, John McCloy (United States), François Ponçet (France), and Brian Robertson (Great Britian) continued to exercise exclusive power in such vital areas as foreign relations, reparations, de-Nazification, and numerous aspects of economic policy. The high commissioners also retained veto power over all *Bundestag* legislation.

Both Adenauer and Schumacher made the recovery of sovereignty their foremost objective, but they did so with considerable difference in style, motivation, and final purpose. Both shared a common desire to appear before the German public as leaders in their own right, not Allied puppets. Both defied and criticized the Allies. Both professed to uphold the claim for reunification, but Schumacher's was more strident and personal. Schumacher was a native of West Prussia, which was part of the area annexed by Poland in 1945. He had no illusions about Soviet policy in Germany and he had recognized the SED design for West Germany ahead of the Allies. His personal and partisan political bonds to East Germany continued to make him more susceptible to Soviet maneuvers on the reunification issue than was the case with Adenauer, a native of the Rhineland.

Adenauer had declared the broadening of West German sovereignty his foremost goal in his very first speech as chancellor in 1949. This meant not only the removal of the Occupation Statute, but the regaining of full controls over the Ruhr and the Saar. The industrial Ruhr had been placed under the control of the International Ruhr

Authority with the Ruhr Statute of April 28, 1949. The Ruhr Authority included Britain, France, the United States and Benelux, but not West Germany. The political future of the Saar, economically unified with France, was at best uncertain.

The ultimate uses of sovereignty regained differed for Adenauer and Schumacher. Adenauer wished to recover sovereignty so that West Germany might voluntarily part with some of it again in the larger interest of West European integration. The question of East Germany and the Oder-Neisse line was, for Adenauer, one of pragmatic politics, not emotional ties.

The Petersberg Protocol

Before 1950, Adenauer's progress in dealing with the Western powers was slow and often frustrating. The Petersberg Protocol of November 24, 1949 signaled the first gain, with West Germany being admitted to the Ruhr Authority and concluding agreements on the receipt of U.S. Marshall aid. Significantly, the Petersberg Protocol was immediately attacked in France, as going too far, and denounced by Schumacher and the SPD as not going far enough. It was during the Petersberg Protocol debate that Schumacher ridiculed Adenauer as "chancellor of the Allies."

Undaunted, Adenauer proposed a French-German economic union in March 1950, as a first step to reconciliation. It was an initiative which eventually led to the European Coal and Steel Community. In the midst of these developments the emotional issue of West German rearmament burst upon the political scene, following the outbreak of the Korean War in June 1950.

In 1950, the West German public showed great concern over events in Asia, and it identified far more closely with the fate of South Korea than it would identify with South Vietnam twenty years later during the Vietnam War. One reason for this, undoubtedly, was the fact that west European defense and collective security were in their infancy and had not yet acquired the credibility and strength they would enjoy two decades later. That West Germany might go the way of South Korea, if South Korea fell, was a sentiment not only widespread in West Germany, but it was a notion actively promoted by East German Communist propaganda. After the fall of the South Korean capital of Seoul in 1950, Ulbricht confidently predicted the imminent collapse of the "Bonn puppet government" of Adenauer. Adenauer was given public notice that he might soon have to stand trial for treason in an East German "people's court" lest he chose timely exile in a Western country.

Adenauer's "Security Memorandum"

The existence of a militarized "people's police" in East Germany, for which there was no West German counterpart, made such utterances a graver matter than a mere propaganda exercise. The military imbalance which had arisen in Germany since the end of World War II as a result of the Soviets rearming East Germany first, was a key factor behind Adenauer's "security memorandum" of August 29, 1950. The "security memorandum" offered U.S. high commissioner John J. McCloy a West German defense contribution. That Adenauer informed neither the West German parliament nor his own cabinet of such a decisive step became subsequently the cause of much controversy in West Germany. That Adenauer also appreciated the bargaining value of his initiative for his own quest for sovereignty goes without saying.

Rearmament

The issue of West German rearmament prompted no less an emotional and divisive debate in the Federal Republic than it did in neighboring France. The Soviets did everything they could to exploit antirearmament sentiment in West Germany. The West German opposition to rearmament covered a wide and diverse field, including pacifists on the Left, neutral nationalists, churchmen, ex-Nazis, neo-Nazis, former *Wehrmacht* officers, and SS veterans on the Right. The opponents also included Adenauer's own minister of the interior Gustav Heinemann, who resigned over the issue and who, after joining the SPD, ended up as West German president in 1969. Other opponents included former pro-Nazi academics such as Ulrich Noack, previously the author of panegyric tributes to Hitler, more recently a sympathizer of the Ulbricht regime, which actively courted him. Martin Niemöller, celebrated Resistance figure, took the occasion to denounce the West German state as such, calling it, in an allusion to Adenauer's Catholicism, a state "conceived in Rome" and "born in Washington."

Right wing opposition flowed from a mixture of German *Schadenfreude* (i.e., delight over one's enemy's embarrassment) and a "Hitler-was-right-after-all" stance. General Heinz Guderian, whom U.S. authorities had persistently shielded against Soviet extradition demands for war crimes, called rearmament unwarranted, because the West had "stabbed Germany in the back" when Hitler was fighting Soviet Russia. General Speidel, Rommel's chief of staff, and General Heusinger, Hitler's former chief of operations, supported rearmament. Both men had hoped that a German-Western alliance against Soviet Russia could be engineered in conjunction with the July 20, 1944 plot on Hitler's life.

Fears that the induction of thousands of former *Wehrmacht* officers into a new West German army would revive German militarism proved groundless. The West German army, soon after being launched in 1955, attained a high degree of military proficiency, but it never sought or obtained a role in West German politics. The draft was not popular with young West Germans, once it was adopted, and many of the older generation thought rearmament ludicrous, when the rubble of Germany's bombed-out cities had not yet been fully cleared away. Fear of Soviet Russia outweighed other considerations, however, and the election results of 1953 and 1957 showed that the rearmament issue had not hurt Adenauer politically. In the 1953 elections, held after West German ratification of the European Defense Community (EDC) treaty, CDU/CSU strength increased from 31 to 45.2 percent, whereas SPD strength dropped from 29.2 to 28.8 percent. In the 1957 elections, held two years after West Germany's admission to NATO, the CDU/CSU scored 50.2 percent of the vote, enabling Adenauer to govern without a coalition partner.

The Stalin Note

These results reflected also an endorsement of Adenauer's recovery of sovereignty. West German admission to NATO in May 1955 terminated the 1949 Occupation Statute. German sovereignty over the Saar was regained with the Luxembourg Agreements of 1956, following the Saar plebiscite of October 1955, in which 67.7 percent of the voters opted for a return to Germany. Soviet attempts to exploit the rearmament controversy as a lever for the neutralization of Germany had meanwhile failed. The Soviet note of March 10, 1952, subsequently known as the *Stalin note,* proposed German reunification on terms of ostensible neutrality. A reunited Germany was to be allowed to have its own armed forces, but it was not to be allowed to join any alliance that was directed against any power with which Hilter's Germany had been at war. A further Soviet note of April 9, 1952 even conceded free elections in both German states prior to reunification, but it was silent on the important question of international supervision of such elections. The Stalin note was skillfully timed, because by 1952 West German anxieties about the fall of South Korea had largely subsided and Germans could more calmly reflect on the long-term implications of rearmament for the future of their country. Also in 1952 West Germany had not yet ratified EDC.

The Stalin note thus evoked considerable interest in the West German public, especially among neutral nationalists and Social Democrats, for whose benefit it had obviously been drafted. Schumacher, before his death, urged a serious exploration of the Stalin proposal. Adenauer swiftly rejected the Stalin note as being of "no consequence." This earned him the lasting bitterness of neutral nationalists and also of some Social Democrats, who accused Adenauer of destroying what they regarded as Germany's only real chance of obtaining reunification.

What the Soviets really meant by a "neutralized" Germany was suggested by the reference to "peace-loving" and "democratic" parties, which alone would be permited to function in a reunited Germany. Given the Soviet definition of such criteria, a political party such as Adenauer's CDU would most probably not have qualified on either count. Adenauer's rejection was motivated primarily by the fear that a positive response would revive western suspicions and memories of the Weimar Republic's swaying back and forth between the Soviets and the west during the 1920s. This would have shattered the carefully laid basis for regaining western trust and of retrieving German sovereignty at least over one part of divided Germany.

THE CONSOLIDATION OF THE SED DICTATORSHIP

The failure of the Stalin note was followed very quickly by a change in Communist policy in East Germany. In May 1952 East Germany started construction of a "death strip" along its entire border with West Germany, complete with barbed wire, mines and machine-gun towers. In July 1952, East Germany disbanded its five federal states (*Länder*) together with their elected governments, and replaced them with fourteen districts under appointed SED leaders. At the same time, the regime stepped up its attacks on the East German Lutheran church and affiliated youth and student groups.

The "Construction of Socialism"

In July 1952 and second SED conference launched Ulbricht's new program of the "construction of socialism," which patterned East German economic policy closely after the Soviet model of the 1930s. The most drastic social dislocation occurred in the farm sector.

SED farm policy had begun in 1946 with the breakup of large estates and the redistribution of the farm land among poorer peasants. In this fashion one-third of the farm land was redistributed and 210,000 new homesteads were created. As of 1949 the sale or mortgaging of all farmland was forbidden. In July 1952 Ulbricht created the "Agricultural Production Associations" (LPGs in the German initials), the equivalent of the Soviet collective farms. Resistance to the spread of LPGs was severely dealt with.

Flight to the West

The immediate result of the "construction of socialism" was a flood of refugees to West Germany. In 1952 alone 60,000 East German farmers escaped to West Germany. In 1953 the number of refugees increased to 331,390. Before the Berlin Wall put an end to the mass exodus in 1961, East Germany lost the equivalent of the population of an entire village of between five and six hundred persons every single day, each year. Between September 1949 and September 1963 West Germany recorded the arrival of 2.7 million East German refugees, the majority of working age and many of them highly skilled and professional people including artisans, skilled workers, engineers, farmers, physicians, and teaching staffs of all levels.

The economic consequences of such a loss in trained labor and professional power were predictable and little short of catastrophic. Before long, the Soviets themselves intervened in Ulbricht's suicidal course. In 1953, soon after Stalin's death, Vladimir Semyonov, the new Soviet high commissioner in East Germany, urged Ulbricht to adopt a "new course." Ulbricht's failure to act on that demand quickly triggered the East Berlin uprising of June 17, 1953.

THE SEVENTEENTH OF JUNE AND ITS AFTERMATH

Soon after Ulbricht had set East Germany on a course of full-blown Stalinism, he became caught in the crosswinds of the Moscow power struggle following Stalin's death in March 1953. The principal figures in the Moscow struggle, Molotov, Beria, Malenkov and Khrushchev, held divergent views on East Germany. Beria and Malenkov were thought to be opposed to Ulbricht's militant course. Khrushchev was to claim in 1963 that Beria and Malenkov were even prepared to "liquidate" East Germany as a socialist state.

Ulbricht also faced a liberal opposition in the ranks of the SED in the person of Wilhelm Zaisser, minister of state security, and Rudolf Herrnstadt, editor in chief of the SED organ *Neues Deutschland.*

Far from implementing a "new course," Ulbricht upheld his decree of May 28, 1953, which had ordered an increase in working hours without a corresponding increase in wages. The protest strike of East Berlin construction workers, which followed as a result on June 17, 1953, quickly mushroomed into a political revolt that spread beyond East Berlin into other parts of East Germany. The lack of a firm Communist response during the early hours of the East Berlin uprising encouraged the rebels to air political demands such as the resignation of the Ulbricht regime, the holding of free elections and the release of political prisoners.

The very strength of the East Berlin uprising saved Ulbricht. It shifted responsibility for the upholding of Communist power to the Red Army, which moved T-34 tanks against rock-throwing East Berlin youths and which summarily dealt with the rebels through military tribunals. Ulbricht could not be allowed to fall, because his fall might have triggered unmanageable consequences in other parts of Eastern Europe.

After the SED had recovered its balance, the party organ *Neues Deutschland* attributed the events of June 17 to the influx of "Fascist scum," that is, Western intelligence agents from West Berlin. In fact, Ulbricht recognized the nature of the uprising as an act of despair of workers who thought they had nothing more to lose. Following Lenin's example in the handling of the Kronstadt Rebellion of similarly disillusioned Soviet workers in the 1920s, he eased economic controls while tightening political and ideological ones. The liberal opposition in the SED, headed by Zaisser and Herrnstadt, was purged. In this, Ulbricht, who always managed to be well-informed about "inside" Soviet politics, was aided by the outcome of the Moscow power struggle, with Beria executed in 1953 and Malenkov disgraced in 1955.

The NVA

When West Germany rearmed in 1955, East Germany also created, in addition to the VOPO, a "national people's army" (NVA). The NVA became a draft army only after the Berlin Wall went up in 1961, at which time chances of escape for potential draftees were no longer promising. The uniforms of the NVA, in an obvious bid for German nationalist sentiment, were a carbon copy of Hitler's *Wehrmacht* in color, cut and rank insignia, with only the swastika eagle missing on blouse and hat. The steel helmet was an ingenious hybrid of the old *Wehrmacht* and the Soviet army helmets. The goose step was entirely Prussian. East German soldiers, defense minister Willi Stoph said, were "German soldiers in German uniform."

Ulbricht weathered the crisis which swept Eastern Europe in 1956 after the Twentieth Party Congress of the USSR, as well as he himself, had survived the challenge of 1953. Once more an opposition had crystallized within the SED, this time in the person of Karl Schirdewan, Ulbricht's own deputy, and Ernst Wollweber, the minister of state security. Both men had contacts with West German Social Democratic leader Herbert Wehner, himself a former Communist. Together with Wehner, Wollweber and Schirdewan wished to explore the possibility of West German economic assistance in exhange for greater East German flexibility in the question of reunification.

Ulbricht purged Wollweber and Schirdewan while keeping a close watch on potential academic troublemakers, such as Wolfgang Harich, professor of philosophy at Humboldt University in East Berlin. Harich was sentenced to ten years imprisonment for attempting to "destroy the constitutional order of the German Democratic Republic." In East Germany, the dreaded alliance of disgruntled workers and disaffected intellectuals which had provided such an explosive combination in Poland and Hungary, did not materialize in 1956.

After the Hungarian Revolution, Ulbricht intensified the pace of "socialist construction," this time also in the arts. In the Bitterfeld conference of April 1959, the SED issued new guidelines for artists and intellectuals. The "Bitterfeld way" demanded greater identification of writers with the "working class" under the slogan "every book an instrument of the class struggle."

The result of this policy was, once again, an increase in the flow of refugees. To stop them, Ulbricht asked his Soviet ally with mounting urgency to adopt drastic measures, such as the expulsion of the Western powers from West Berlin. In this, he helped maneuver the Soviet Union into its most dangerous confrontation with the United States since the beginning of the Cold War.

21

Soviet Russia under Khrushchev

THE PROBLEM OF SUCCESSION

Periods of succession have traditionally been periods of stress in Soviet history, because it is then that external appearances and inner realities have been most difficult to reconcile. Lenin had established both the theory of collective leadership and the practice of autocratic rule, though his personal exercise of power was tempered by tact and modesty when dealing with his colleagues. Stalin, during his struggle for the succession, shattered even the appearance of collective leadership and degraded the highest organs of the party, the Central Committee and the Politburo (Presidium since 1952), to the role of sounding boards and instruments of personal dictatorship.

An essential difference between the power struggle after Lenin and that which followed Stalin's death lay in the character of the dead leader. Lenin died a man revered throughout the Communist world. There never was a "de-Leninization" in the history of Soviet Russia, and no one ever thought of renaming Leningrad. The tenure of Lenin's body in the glass coffin on Red Square in Moscow remained secure. Stalin died a man feared more than revered, and none feared him more than his closest subordinates, who knew how narrowly they had escaped extinction through Stalin's timely death. Stalinist terror had succeeded in erasing all vestiges of internal opposition, but it had also managed to take the life out of the Party, the initiative out of the bureaucratic elite, the creative spirit out of the artists, and the integrity out of the intellectuals. It had, above all, taken the joy out of living for millions of ordinary people in the Soviet Union and its string of Eastern European satellites. No system such as this could energize a people into greater effort, nor could it hope to advertise itself successfully as a preferable alternative to other systems or lifestyles.

The Need for Reform

There was agreement among Stalin's heirs that the Soviet system would have to reform itself, but wide disagreement persisted as to the extent, the nature and the overall purpose of that reform. On the economic front, there was urgent need to go beyond the stage of Stalin's "command-style" economy with its emphasis on capital goods and the armaments industry. Both the chemical and electronics industry needed expansion if the requirements of agriculture for fertilizer were to be met and if the technological gap with Western economies was to be narrowed. Ideologically, Soviet communism under Stalin had acquired an ethnocentric Russian quality both as a result of Stalin's doctrine of "socialism in one country" of the 1930s and as a result of the experience of the Second World War. In 1946 Stalin was fond of saying that World War II had proved the "superiority" of the Soviet system. There was much truth in such a statement, if applied to the organization of the Soviet war effort and to the feats of the Soviet armaments industry in the Second World War.

For the world of the 1950s, World War II was part of history, however, not a current experience. The viability of a socioeconomic system of the 1950s was measured by its ability to satisfy human aspirations for greater dignity through the satisfaction of material and spiritual needs. It was in these areas that the system developed by Stalin had revealed its greatest shortcomings.

The low Soviet living standards of the 1930s could be explained as the inevitable social cost of industrializing a backward country without foreign capital assistance. The low living standards of the 1940s could be explained as the inevitable result of war damages and the cost of reconstruction. It became increasingly difficult to explain Soviet Russia's, and Eastern Europe's, unrelievedly low living standards of the 1950s when other European countries had not only succeeded in repairing the damages of World War II, but were attaining living standards considerably above those of the prewar years. In some of these countries, such as West Germany, the devastation caused by war had scarcely been less than in the Soviet Union itself.

The death of Stalin also coincided with the beginning of a new phase in the colonial retreat of Western powers, which provided the Soviet Union with opportunities for expanding its political and ideological influence into Third World areas. For Soviet communism to exploit such opportunities, it had to shed its ethnocentric Russian image and to revive the internationalist appeal which Lenin had successfully projected in the early years of the Soviet experiment.

KHRUSHCHEV'S RISE

The first important step taken by Stalin's Old Guard after the dictator's death was the purging of the top party organs, the Presidium and the Central committee, of Stalin's recent appointees. This restored the exclusiveness of the Old Guard and it limited the power struggle, about to begin, to men from among the Old Guard itself. Although the new leadership was outwardly "collective," power rested initially with Beria and Malenkov, who attempted to create accomplished facts in early March 1953. Malenkov combined the post of first party secretary and prime minister in his own person, while Beria reunited the ministry of state security and the MVD (previously NKVD), which Stalin had separated in 1946, under his leaderhip. Beria, Molotov,

Kaganovich, and Bulganin, all members in the Presidium, also served as deputy prime ministers in Malenkov's cabinet. Marshals Zhukov and Vassilievsky were appointed deputy defense ministers under Bulganin.

By March 14, 1953 the lopsided arrangement of March 6 was overturned, with Malenkov resigning the post as first party secretary. Malenkov's resignation signaled the rise of Khrushchev, who was, as yet, not formally appointed first party secretary, however. By June 26, 1953 it was learned that Beria had been arrested. Both the charge that Beria had been a long-term "British agent," ever since 1919, and the announcement of December 17, 1953 of his execution seemed to suggest that the power struggle for Stalin's succession was being settled by Stalinist methods. In fact, according to Khruschev's subsequent claim, it was the common fear of a revival of Stalinist police terror which prompted Beria's execution. Beria's successor as chief of the state security service was denied a Presidium seat, while MVD power diminished notably throughout the country.

Khrushchev's formal appointment as first party secretary on September 13, 1953 signaled the opening of the Khrushchev-Malenkov struggle. Malenkov, the youngest of the Soviet leaders at fifty-two, had risen through Stalin's private secretariat. Western observers, who met him for the first time after Stalin's death, were impressed by his intelligence and polished manners. Khrushchev, born on April 17, 1894 near Kursk, had begun his career as a small party functionary in the Ukraine. An efficient and ruthless organizer, he had caught the eye of the Ukrainian party boss Kaganovich in the 1920s. In September 1929 Stalin brought Khrushchev to Moscow, and in 1934 Khrushchev headed the Moscow city party machine and was a member of the Central Committee. While in Moscow, Khrushchev made a name for himself as the builder of the Moscow subway system, the proud showpiece of Soviet urban development of the 1930s. After returning to the Ukraine in 1938 as Ukrainian first party secretary, Khrushchev became a full member of the Politburo in 1939 at the young age of forty-five. The appointment was a reward for his work as Stalin's agent in the Ukraine in the final stage of the Great Purge. During World War II Khrushchev served as a kind of political supercommissar with the rank of lieutenant general. His service in the field brought him into closer contact with ordinary people and their suffering, a fact, it was subsequently claimed, that gave him a greater sense of compassion and human understanding than was customary among the top men in Stalin's immediate following. Accused of insufficient vigor in restoring the collective farm system to the liberated Ukraine after the war, Khrushchev was suspended as Ukrainian first party secretary in 1947. Reinstated in 1948, he was recalled to Moscow in 1949 apparently to counterbalance Malenkov's and Beria's influence, which had grown since Zhdanov's death the previous year. Compared with other Soviet oligarchs, Khrushchev's development was more varied and more removed from Stalin's direct supervision. To the Moscow-based leaders, Khrushchev was an outsider, a country bumpkin, a *kukurudznik* (after the Russian *kukurudz,* corn), a Ukrainian *parvenu.* Indeed high office did not refine either Khrushchev's manner or his speech. His public conduct in the limelight of world attention, such as his desk-pounding with a shoe at the UN General Assembly, confirmed the worst of his rivals' fears and caused the Soviet Union considerable embarrassment.

Malenkov and Khrushchev were agreed on the need to reform the Soviet system but they disagreed in their choice of instruments for carrying it out. As prime minister, Malenkov wished to use the state bureaucracy, which also was his own principal power base. Khrushchev, as first party secretary, wanted to use the party *apparat,* his power base. Like Stalin in the 1920s, Khrushchev initially subordinated issues to personalities. Until Malenkov's downfall in 1955, Khrushchev sided with the conservatives, Molotov, Kaganovich and others. Later on Khrushchev himself emerged as the leading reformer, and his schemes often left the old conservatives baffled and embittered. Malenkov's reform drive opened with his "new course," announced on August 8, 1953 with the promise of higher living standards through better food supply and more consumer goods.

The "Virgin Soil" Project

Khrushchev answered with the speech of September 13, 1953, attacking the state of Soviet agriculture. Malenkov's speech was delivered before the supreme Soviet, an organ of the state, while Khrushchev's address was made before the Central Committee, an organ of the party. In February 1954, Khrushchev unveiled his dramatic "virgin soil" plan as a means of speedy and drastic increase in grain production. Under the plan, nearly 32 million acres of previously untilled grazing land in Kazakhstan and southwest Siberia were to be brought under the plow. The program was entrusted to the party, not the state bureaucracy, with an army of *komsomol* volunteers and 120,000 tractors being assigned the task. The "virgin soil" project had all the earmarks of a typical Khrushchev scheme, combining surprise, imagination, daring and above all, publicity. Launched with great fanfare, the "virgin soil" project, after initial successes, failed to produce the desired permanent results because of poor soil and climate. Khrushchev's own, somewhat subdued explanation of 1964 that the "virgin soil" scheme had merely been an emergency measure, did not correspond to his own vision ten years earlier of taking "these blessed lands away from the rabbits." Similarly, Khrushchev's hope of inducing the young *komsomol* volunteers into settling permanently in Kazakhstan was not fulfilled. Kazakhstan, an inhospitable place chosen by Stalin during World War II as a place of deportation for Volga-Germans, attracted few permanent residents among *komsomol* newcomers.

For the moment, the "virgin soil" project served Khrushchev's political purpose, however, in upstaging the rival Malenkov. On February 8, 1955 Malenkov resigned the prime ministership over the immediate issue of consumer goods versus armaments, in which Khrushchev sided with the conservatives and the military for tactical reasons. Malenkov's successor Bulganin was a man of the party's choice, not of the bureaucracy's.

THE DILEMMA OF DE-STALINIZATION

De facto de-Stalinization had been going on unobtrusively in a variety of ways since 1953 through a policy of gradual relaxation. In September 1953 the special courts of the secret police were closed and the release of political prisoners began. The Zhdanov ban on marriage with foreigners was lifted and non-Russian nationalities, accused by Stalin of collaboration with the Germans, were being rehabilitated. In literature and art new life was stirring in the more liberal climate of the "thaw," with the appearance of Ilya Ehrenburg's novel of the same name and such works as Vera Panov's *Season of the Year.*

Khrushchev's Attack

What had been a halting and gradual process was turned into a sudden and unprecedented attack on Stalin and Stalinism at the Twentieth Party Congress in February 1956. Following other speeches critical of Stalin's "cult of the individual," including one by party ideologue Suslov, Khrushchev's attack, delivered in secret session, was the most sensational and vehement. Khrushchev charged Stalin with having claimed for himself god-like characteristics, of having perverted party principles, party democracy and revolutionary legality, and of having many "honest Communists" killed during the Great Purge. Khrushchev cited the NKVD by name and denounced its methods of "lies, torture and fabricated plots." Stalin's wartime record was assailed for lack of nerve at the outset, incompetence and brutality, such as the deportation of entire ethnic groups merely because of individual instances of collaboration with the enemy. Though delivered in secret session, the text of Khrushchev's speech was in possession of U.S. intelligence by April 1956. Released by President Eisenhower, the speech was published in the *New York Times* on June 4, 1956. Khrushchev's attack, though unprecedented, was also selective. Nothing was said about Stalin's terror before 1934 and little was said about the terror against the people at large, not just against the party or the military. Khrushchev expressly praised Stalin for industrialization and the collectivization of the farmland. Yet it was the latter which claimed by far the greatest number of victims and which resulted in the great famine of 1931. Khrushchev was also silent on his own role and especially the part he had played in the Ukraine purge of 1938–1939 and that of eastern Poland during the period 1939–1941.

The indictment of Stalin, even before a select audience, carried with it grave risks, for it was bound to raise the question as to whether Stalinism was not, in itself, a logical outgrowth of the system rather than the personal aberration of an individual leader. So Khrushchev must have had important reasons, which, in his own mind, outweighed the risks. Among the reasons was Khrushchev's attempt to discredit his rivals by identifying them with Stalin's crimes and to pledge to the party elite that it would be safe from a relapse into Stalinist terror under his own leadership. Hence Khrushchev's reminder of the assassination of Leningrad party secretary Kirov in 1934, in which Molotov and Kaganovich may have been implicated, and of the "Leningrad affair" of 1948, in which Malenkov had been involved. De-Stalinization was also meant to set the stage for Khrushchev's own ideological pronouncements and reforms, such as the imminent Soviet transition to communism and decentralization of economic management as well as the upgrading of consumer goods industry. Such changes contradicted Stalinist precedents. To make them authoritative and acceptable, it was necessary to dethrone the godlike Stalin.

THE REVOLT OF THE "ANTI-PARTY" GROUP

Khrushchev's speech had a shattering effect on some of his listeners and it produced a revolutionary impact on parts of Eastern Europe. The Polish crisis between June and October 1956 and the Hungarian Revolution of November 1956 were triggered, in part, by the sudden change of the official Stalin image from hero to villain. In a larger sense, Khrushchev's denunciation of Stalin set into motion a Communist crisis of worldwide dimensions, ultimately effecting Soviet-Chinese relations in a decisive manner. Because of the close identification of Stalin with the reality of Soviet communism, the burial of Stalin's memory could neither be a simple nor a brief procedure. Rather, Khrushchev's own tenure in office until his removal in October 1964 remained filled with an ongoing see-saw struggle between Khrushchev himself and those who deemed his attacks on Stalin either unwise, unnecessary, or harmful. The struggle was carried out within the top Soviet leadership, it was duplicated in the satellite nations of Eastern Europe, and it became an important issue at Communist world gatherings, such as the Communist summits in Moscow of 1957 and 1960. Khrushchev's victories in the ongoing power struggle were never final, and his leadership had to reassert itself again and again after major policy failures at home and abroad. In attempting to remove terror as an integral part of the Soviet system, Khrushchev faced the dilemma of allowing the advocates of Stalinist terror to survive and to challenge his leadership.

The revolutionary upheavals of Eastern Europe in 1956 were sufficiently grave to prompt the Soviet leadership to make a temporary truce in its own internal strife, and to close ranks. Molotov, though dismissed as foreign minister, went to Warsaw in October 1956 in an effort to help stabilize the situation. In January 1957 both Malenkov and Khrushchev went to Budapest to restore stability in Hungary. There was retrenchment also at home, especially in the field of literature. Responding to such works as Vladimir D. Dudintsev's *Not by Bread Alone,* which denounced party corruption, Khrushchev threatened a general crackdown unless "slanderous" attacks on the party ceased. Boris Pasternak's Nobel Prize–winning novel *Dr. Zhivago* was strongly attacked by the official Soviet Writers' Union, precisely because it questioned the desirability of the 1917 Bolshevik Revolution itself. By May 1957 Khrushchev had regained sufficient bounce to launch a scheme for economic decentralization through the creation of "people's economic councils." Designed as a means towards more efficient management, the reform was bitterly resented by the Moscow central bureaucracy and its Stalinist allies, such as Molotov. Taking advantage of Khrushchev's absence from Moscow during a journey to Finland, Malenkov and Molotov called a Presidium (Politburo) meeting for June 18, 1957, in order to oust Khrushchev. If successful, the revolt would most likely have restored Malenkov to the prime ministership with Molotov taking Khrushchev's post as first party secretary. In the Presidium, a majority assailed Khrushchev for having undermined collective leadership as well as for failures in agriculture and the imbalancing of the economy in favor of consumer goods.

Though outvoted in the Presidium, Khrushchev survived the challenge by the unorthodox maneuver of appealing to the Central Committee, a lower party organ. In this, Khrushchev enjoyed the support of the armed forces in the person of Marshal Zhukov, who airlifted Central Committee members from the provinces to assure a pro-Khrushchev majority. The showdown of June 1957 was as much a clash between the party and the state bureaucracy as it was a contest between Moscow and the provinces, as well as between the liberal and the Stalinist wing of the party. Khrushchev's courting of army goodwill through the appointment of eleven new Marshals of the Soviet Union in 1955 paid off in 1957 when support of the armed forces was crucial to his own political survival. Zhukov personally supported de-Stalinization not only because of his own shabby treatment at the hands of Stalin after World War II, but because he, as senior Red Army commander, reflected the army's bitterness over the murder of so many of its finest officers during the Great Purge of the 1930s.

Having survived the challenge, Khrushchev purged his chief opponents. Malenkov was demoted to manager of a Siberian power station; Molotov, after being first assigned as ambassador to Outer Mongolia, was subsequently made Soviet representative at the International Atomic Agency in Vienna, Austria. Kaganovich became manager of a cement plant. Khrushchev's alliance with the army leadership was short-lived. Once safely back in power, Khrushchev dropped Zhukov from both the Presidium and the post of defense minister. What had divided the two men, and continued to divide Khrushchev from Zhukov's successor, Marshal Malinovsky, were defense appropriations and strategic doctrine. With the development of nuclear-armed missiles, Khrushchev favored cutbacks in conventional arms spending. Like President Eisenhower's secretary of defense Charlie Wilson, Khrushchev wanted a "bigger bang for the buck."

KHRUSHCHEV'S FALL

The period between 1957 and early 1960 was, in many ways, Khrushchev's most successful as a reformer, partly because of the absence of major Soviet foreign policy failures, partly because the Sino-Soviet conflict had not yet reached the stage of public name-calling. Soviet prestige soared in October 1957, and with it Khrushchev's personal reputation, with the successful launching of *sputnik,* the world's first earth-orbiting satellite. It was an event tailor-made to Khrushchev's style of showmanship, for it appeared to substantiate Khrushchev's boast of the "superiority" of the Soviet system.

Reforms

In education, efforts were made in 1958 to increase the supply of skilled workers. The secondary school system was changed from a ten-year to an eight-year curriculum and academic admissions policy was tightened up. University students were required to spend part of their time on physical work assignments. The Soviet theater and motion picture industry produced some works of outstanding quality between 1957 and 1960, with such films as *The Cranes are Flying* and *Ballad of a Soldier,* which were examples of enduring humanism unspoiled by communist political commercials. In agriculture, Khrushchev disbanded the Machine Tractor Stations (MTS) on the collective frams in 1958 and launched a new program for the manufacture of chemical fertilizers. The abolition of the MTS evoked criticism from conservatives, such as Suslov, because the MTS had been a cornerstone of Stalin's collective farm system. In the realm of industrial economy, the ambitious targets of the fifth (Stalin's last) and Khrushchev's own sixth five-year plan (announced at the Twentieth Party Congress) had remained unfulfilled. The failures of the sixth five-year plan were in part attributable to the East European disturbances of autumn 1956, which also adversely affected the Soviet economy. Khrushchev hoped to make up for lost production through the launching of a seven-year plan, which was noteworthy for its emphasis on chemical industry and its announced goal of overtaking American living standards within five years of its completion. The new seven-year plan was announced at the Twenty-first Party Congress of January 1959, officially labelled an "extraordinary congress" because it took place less than three years after the previous one.

The twenty-first congress was clearly intended to consolidate Khrushchev's position both with respect to the remaining opposition at home and the Chinese Communists abroad, who questioned Khrushchev's de-Stalinization and his policy of "peaceful coexistence" with the west. At the twenty-first congress Khrushchev announced a new party program, his own, and the first one to replace Lenin's largely forgotten program of 1919. The new party program was intended to reassert Soviet ideological leadership in the world communist camp and to enhance Khrushchev's personal prestige by setting guidelines for Soviet Russia's own social and economic development. The party program dismissed efforts to devise shortcuts to communism, such as the Chinese Communists had attempted with the "communes" of 1958. The Soviet Union alone was said to be at the threshold of communism as against the lower socialist stage, which other socialist countries, Communist China included, were still in the process of building. Consistent with Marxist theory, the organs of state power were said to be at the point of withering away in the Soviet Union, with the significant exception of the military. As the role of the state diminished, that of the party, Khrushchev's own power base, was said to be growing. As an example, Khrushchev cited the "comrade" courts, informal courts composed of *komsomol* and party activists, dealing with minor offenses. Chinese hopes for greater militancy in dealing with the west were answered by a new commitment to limited *détente*. At the twenty-first congress Khrushchev withdrew the time limit of his "Berlin ultimatum" of November 1958 as a down payment for the American invitation to meet with President Eisenhower in September 1959.

The U2 Incident

The U2 incident of May 1960 ushered in a new period of Soviet foreign policy failures which directly affected Khrushchev's domestic programs and ultimately contributed to his fall. The Soviet military, humiliated by the evidence of inadequate air defenses prior to the shooting down of the American U2 spy plane, demanded and got sharp increases in military spending. The U2 incident not only wrecked the Eisenhower-Khrushchev Paris summit of May 1960, but it very nearly destroyed Khrushchev's political position at home. Khrushchev's inflammatory language during his nighttime news conference in Paris after the failed summit was as much designed to placate Soviet defense minister Malinovsky, who sat at his side, as it was meant to embarrass Eisenhower.

At home, Khrushchev's foes, Suslov and Frol R. Kozlov, utilized Khrushchev's weakness to attack his handling of the broadening ideological conflict with Communist China, as well as his economic priorities and schemes of decentralization. It was against the background of renewed and bitter opposition to Khrushchev that the Twenty-second Party Congress convened in October 1961. Khrushchev hoped to weaken the opposition, which also included Marshal Voroshilov, the ex-president of the USSR, by publicly attacking Stalin and by identifying his opponents with Stalin's crimes. Among the crimes cited publicly this time was Kirov's murder in 1934, in which both Molotov and Voroshilov were said to have been implicated. It was also publicly claimed that Marshal Tukhashevsky's trial and execution in 1937 had been based on false evidence planted by the Germans. Power politics took on a note of the macabre when a Madame D. Lazurkina took the stand before the congress. Introducing herself as an old comrade of Lenin's who had also served time in Stalin's prison camps, Madame

Lazurkina told of a vision she had had in which the ghost of Lenin had complained of his discomfort because of Stalin's body in the glass coffin next to his own. Madame Lazurkina's appeal resulted in the removal of Stalin's body from the Lenin tomb and his reburial in a less conspicuous place nearby in the Kremlin wall. This act of ritualistic cleansing, which was followed by the removal of Stalin's name from cities and other places, failed to produce a lasting Khrushchev victory. The "anti-party" group, though condemned once more, was not actually expelled from the party.

The see-saw struggle between "dogmatism" (Stalinism) and "revisionism" (reform) continued. Works of Soviet literature aided Khrushchev's cause in 1962 with Yevtushenko's poem *Stalin's Heirs* and Alexander Solzhenitsyn's novel *One Day in the Life of Ivan Denisovich.* Yevtushenko's poem spoke of old Stalinists who, while cultivating roses, were longing for old times. Solzhenitsyn's novel gave the most shattering account of Stalin's slave-labor camps in Soviet literature to date.

The Cuban Missile Crisis

The Cuban missile crisis of October 1962, seen from the perspective of Soviet domestic politics, had all the appearances of an attempt by Khrushchev to recover all his losses in one great, risky gamble. If it succeeded, it would sufficiently enhance his prestige to deal in a conclusive manner with his domestic foes and to silence his Chinese Communist critics. The consequences of failure were proportionately grave and were, in fact, not long in waiting after Khrushchev's and the Soviet Union's humiliation of October 1962. "Adventurism" and "capitulationism" were the new terms of invective with which the Chinese Communists reacted to Khrushchev's Caribbean debacle. At home, Khrushchev had to grant new increases in the military budget. The establishment of a new Supreme Council of the National Economy in March 1963, under Dimitri Ustinov, the manager of the Soviet armaments industry, signaled a return to a strongly centralized economy with heavy emphasis on armaments. Although there were signs of yet another Khrushchev recovery even after Cuba, his removal may have been decided by a Politburo majority a considerable time before it actually happened in October 1964. With the signing of the Test Ban Treaty in 1963 as a symbol of limited détente, Khrushchev reopened the attack at home on all the familiar fronts. In a Moscow speech of July 19, 1963 during the visit of Hungary's Communist leader Kadar, Khruschev lashed out against Stalin once more in the strongest language yet. In April 1964 he had the satisfaction, shortly before his own downfall, of having "Molotov and others" at last expelled from the party.

At the beginning of 1964 Khrushchev had called for another Communist world summit to read the Chinese out of the Communist camp. In September 1964 he unfolded a "new plan" with increased emphasis on consumer goods production. On foreign policy, the outline of a deal with West Germany became visible which, if carried through, might well have affected vital East German interests.

Khrushchev Loses Power

In the second week of October 1964, while vacationing at the Black Sea, Khrushchev was removed from office by a Politburo majority, which included his own protégés, such as Leonid I. Brezhnev and Nikolai Podgorny. This time there was no rescue operation by the Central Committee, the armed forces, or any other source of power.

To those who engineered his downfall, Khrushchev had come to be regarded as too erratic and unpredictable for the national good and the interests of the party. The state bureaucracy had viewed him as an outsider and a danger to its vested interests from the beginning. Most importantly, Khrushchev appeared to have failed in the most difficult task of all, that of solving the dilemma of de-Stalinization. It was a task that any heir of Stalin's would have had to face and it was a problem which continued to preoccupy Khrushchev's own successors.

On balance, his failures appeared to outweigh his gains at the time of his downfall. Where there had been authority and unity at the time of Stalin's death, there was now division and the historic schism of the world communist movement through the break with China. The challenge to Soviet authority may have been recognized by the Soviet leadership as inevitable in the post-Stalin era but it had, in the case of the Sino-Soviet dispute, assumed the nature of a personal feud between Khrushchev and Mao. Khrushchev's removal, it was at first hoped in Moscow, might facilitate Sino-Soviet reconciliation. As a man who had been born in prerevolutionary feudal Russia, Khrushchev regarded the Communist party as the prime mover from feudalism to industrialism. He wished to retain for that party a leading role in a rapidly expanding and increasingly complex technocratic society. He also wished to make that society produce more for its own benefits and less for the needs of the Soviet industrial-military complex. Khrushchev's major political innovation in the Soviet system had been the expansion of the platform where issues of power were settled—at the broader base of the Central Committee, and even before the entire party congress. Khrushchev's fall resulted in an immediate retraction of the highest power base and thus the preservation of the Soviet oligarchy as a self-perpetuating elite. The resistance of entrenched Stalinism was greater than Khrushchev himself may have originally expected, compelling him, among other things, to embark on foreign policy adventures more hazardous than anything Stalin himself might have contemplated. Where Stalin had aimed at strength, Khrushchev aimed at a synthesis of strength and freedom, though the freedom he pursued was not identical with the western, liberal ideal. The desired synthesis eluded him, though not entirely. At best, Khrushchev had built new paths through the inherited terrain of Soviet totalitarianism, which his successors might wish to explore further in their search for answers to Soviet Russia's internal problems and external fears.

22

Eastern Europe after Stalin

IMPERATIVES AND DILEMMAS OF LIBERALIZATION

If de-Stalinization was for the Soviet Union a difficult and hazardous process, de-Stalinization entailed even greater risks for Eastern Europe. Soviet communism was more deeply rooted in Soviet Russia because of its identification with industrialization and national defense and because of its longer history, dating back to 1917. In Eastern Europe, communism had neither developed strong native roots, nor was it, as yet, in a position to point to major social or economic gains. By the mid-1950s communism in Eastern Europe was still regarded as a recent foreign import and widely associated with Soviet postwar plunder and the loss of national independence. The ruling Communist parties themselves were deeply scarred and bitterly divided in their leadership after the sensational and humiliating show trials against "Titoists" during Stalin's final years.

Liberalization and de-Stalinization in Eastern Europe was not merely a problem of domestic reform but also one affecting the relationship between individual states and the Soviet Union. Progress and improvements in both areas would undoubtedly have been much easier if Moscow had given clear signals and issued firm directives concerning the nature of liberalization and its limits. Such was not the case in Khrushchev's time because the Kremlin leadership was itself divided between reformers and conservatives during the ongoing power struggle of the fifties. The Moscow see-saw battle between Stalinists and anti-Stalinists was thus reflected and reenacted in the power struggles of many East European Communist parties, a fact which greatly contributed to the Polish and Hungarian upheavals of 1956. The East Berlin workers' uprising of June 17, 1953 had shown how quick and decisive Soviet reaction could be when Soviet rule itself was threatened. The use of military force in East Germany was determined by the special conditions obtaining in that country, in which the bulk of Soviet military power in Eastern Europe stood face to face with NATO and the United States. In other Communist nations of Eastern Europe there was more room for maneuver, however, and the use of force was the last, not the first option of Soviet policy.

"Collective Leadership"

The Moscow example of "collective leadership" was duly copied in Eastern Europe after Stalin's death, though with different emphasis and results. In Czechoslovakia, Klement Gottwald, symbol of Stalinism, had conveniently died in March 1953 following Stalin's funeral. Power was subsequently shared by the conservative Antonin Novotny, as first party secretary, and the reformer Antonin Zapotocky, as president. In Poland, the Communist party congress of March 1954 divided power between the Stalinist Bierut, as first party secretary, and the ex-socialist Cyrankiewics as prime minister. In Hungary, it required considerable Soviet pressure to force the Stalinist Rakosi into appointing the reform Communist Imre Nagy as prime minister in 1953, though this, as events were soon to show, was far from being the end of the Hungarian party strife.

In East Germany, Walter Ulbricht, having weathered the East Berlin workers' uprising of June 17, 1953 with the support of Soviet tanks, remained the calm center in Eastern Europe's gathering storm of national and social discontent.

Before 1956, the newly formed "collective leaderships" enacted few substantive policy changes, despite the announcement of a "new course" in several states. The rehabilitation of purge victims was, as yet, casual and off-hand. In Czechoslovakia's case, show trials against "Titoists" actually continued after Stalin's death with the Slovak Communist Gustav Husak the most prominent defendant. In other areas too, Czechoslovakia's liberalization produced few lasting results. Workers' demonstrations in Pilsen, Prague and the Ostrava coal mines against unpopular economic and fiscal measures were speedily suppressed in May 1953. Zapotocky's attempt to end the collective farm system was thwarted by the hardliner Novotny in August 1953. Czechoslovakia's de-Stalinization was brief and superficial, a fact of no small importance for the events of 1968.

In Hungary, Imre Nagy, the most prominent survivor of the Hungarian show trials against "Titoists," launched a "new economic policy" on July 4, 1953, which promised a fundamental change from Rakosi's earlier Stalinist industrial and agricultural program. Nagy pledged an end to the collective farm system and an increase in the supply of consumer goods. Political prisoners were to be amnestied and intellectual freedoms were to be restored. Nagy's promising reforms were cut short when Rakosi, in the continuing power struggle between Stalinists and reformers, succeeded in ousting him as Hungarian prime minister in March 1955.

SOVIET-SATELLITE RELATIONS

The examples of Czechoslovakia and Hungary suggested the unevenness of internal de-Stalinization, which mirrored the specific political and economic conditions of individual satellites. Soviet-Yugoslav relations, on the other hand, were symbolic of the problem which all satellites shared in dealing with the Soviet Union. In the improvement of Soviet-satellite relations, some sort of Soviet-Yugoslav reconciliation was a necessary first step. Reconciliation with Yugoslavia was also dictated by compelling reasons of Soviet security and ideology. The Stalin-Tito feud had given the United States its one major gain in Eastern Europe at moderate financial cost and without any political or military risk whatever. The 1953 Balkan pact between Yugoslavia, Greece, and Turkey was a warning of Yugoslavia's further foreign policy alignment with the West if reconciliation with Tito was not effected soon. The restoration of ideological unity was essential to a system whose external and internal policies officially derived from a single ideological premise.

The Soviet-Yugoslav Reconciliation

At first, Khrushchev seemed to have solid credentials as a peacemaker, because he was flexible in his tactics, more down-to-earth than Stalin and, as a populist, himself not far removed from Tito's idea that the Communist system ought to be made to serve the people, not merely the interests of the bureaucracy or the elite. There existed certain conceptual similarities between Khrushchev's new party program of 1959 and the aspirations of Yugoslav reform communism concerning the diminishing power of the state and the reinvigoration of the party in the pursuit of the communist ideal. Certain of the Yugoslav reform ideas, such as elected factory workers' councils, were dismissed by Khrushchev as unsuited to Soviet conditions, but there was much ground for compromise and agreement otherwise. Fundamental to the possibility of Soviet-Yugoslav ideological reconciliation was the fact that Tito had never compromised the political monopoly of the Yugoslav Communist party, now renamed "Communist League." This fact notwithstanding, the durability of Soviet-Yugoslav reconciliation also depended on the ability of both parties to reach a compromise on the question of competing national interests, the other root of "Titoism" after the 1948 break. At first, either side may have assumed that reconciliation could be achieved on its own terms. The East European crisis of 1956 quickly dispelled any such illusion and thereby revealed the problem of "Titoism" as one destined to endure beyond Stalin and, for that matter, beyond Stalin's successors of the 1950s and 1960s.

The Soviets took the first step towards reconciliation by exchanging ambassadors with Tito in the summer of 1953. Trade relations were restored the following year and in November 1954 Khrushchev toasted Tito during a visit to the Yugoslav Moscow embassy. The Sino-Soviet Declaration, issued during Khrushchev's Peking visit of October 1954, marked another significant step. By stressing the principles of equality, mutual respect, national sovereignty and territorial integrity in the relationship between socialist states, the Peking Declaration indirectly endorsed the position also taken by Tito. These overtures were climaxed in May 1955 by what had all the outward appearances of a Soviet pilgrimage to the Yugoslav capital Belgrade, undertaken by Khrushchev, Bulganin and Mikoyan. Khrushchev blamed the past Soviet-Yugoslav acrimony on the dead Beria and, having assured the Yugoslavs that they had remained faithful to the principles of "Marxism-Leninism," signed the Belgrade Declaration of June 3, 1955. The latter reaffirmed the principles of mutual respect and nonintervention in the internal affairs of socialist states for "whatever economic, political, or ideological reasons."

Khrushchev's attempt to give the Belgrade meeting the impression of a convivial and jovial social event was not reciprocated by Tito. Tito responded with great seriousness, for the wrath of Stalin had not been a laughing matter, either for him, or his people. Soviet-Yugoslav relations continued to improve for about a year after the Belgrade meeting. Tito welcomed Khrushchev's attack on Stalin at the Twentieth Party Congress and the subsequent disbanding of the Cominform. The Moscow Declaration of June 20, 1956, issued during Tito's return visit to the USSR, appeared to put the official seal on Soviet-Yugoslav reconciliation. Expanding on the Belgrade Declaration, the Moscow Declaration acknowledged a relationship between socialist development and the specific conditions obtaining in a given socialist country. The Moscow declaration even praised the diversity of form in the development of socialism as a positive factor. Tito called the diversity "pluralism." The Italian Communist leader Palmiro Togliatti was to name it "polycentrism."

The Moscow Declaration was immediately put to the test by the Poznan riots in Poland, which occurred little more than a week later, and by the chain of events set into motion in Poland and Hungary. Having given Tito satisfaction and having come as close to an apology for past injustices as they could, the Soviets may have hoped that Tito would now return to his earlier position of Soviet admirer and would conduct himself with the modesty becoming a satellite leader. Reconciliation remained, for Tito, reconciliation on his own terms, however, and he showed neither modesty nor sufficient support for the Soviet position to satisfy the Soviet leaders. In November 1955 Tito received Secretary of State John Foster Dulles of the United States at Brioni, and he continued to receive U.S. aid, though purely military assistance was discontinued at Yugoslavia's request in 1957. When, after the Hungarian Revolution of November 1956, the USSR and its satellites again cut off all loans to Yugoslavia, U.S. aid became crucial once again to Tito's survival during the period of the so-called second freeze. Between 1955 and 1958 the United States provided $105.4 million in military and $632.1 million in nonmilitary aid to Yugoslavia.

The nations of the Third World admired Tito for his balancing act between the blocs, and Tito found them highly useful allies. Third World solidarity gave Tito's voice far greater reach and volume than might justly be expected from the leader of an underdeveloped Balkan nation with a chronic balance-of-payments problem. Third World solidarity was also an important insurance policy at low cost against the threat of Soviet military action, should it materialize under conditions of a new Yugoslav-Soviet freeze.

THE POLISH CRISIS AND GOMULKA

De-Stalinization affected Hungary and Poland in a manner different from other East European states, partly because the scars left behind by Stalinist rule were, in Hungary's case, deeper, and partly because both nations shared a tradition of strong resistance to foreign domination. Though not always tolerant of their own national minorities, Poles and Hungarians fought for national independence more fiercely and frequently than most other East Europeans, even when the chances of success were minimal. The common national revolutionary tradition grew over the years into a strong bond of friendship, which also played its part in the upheavals of 1956.

In Poland, liberalization began in earnest after the death of Boleslav Bierut, who, having heard Khrushchev's attack on Stalin at the party congress in February 1956, died of a heart attack in Moscow. Bierut's successor Edward Ochab, though previously identified with Bierut's purge, had nevertheless avoided the excesses of both the Hungarian and Czechoslovak parties. In March 1956, the party released Gomulka and other prominent leaders, such as Marian Spychalski and Zenon Kliszko, from prison, followed by the release of non-Communist political prisoners. On April 25, 1956 an amnesty set free a total of 30,000 lesser political prisoners. Also in April 1956, party intellectuals, speaking through the paper *Po Prostu,* encouraged factory workers to elect factory councils in imitation of the Yugoslav model. Soon the first such councils were formed in the Fiat assembly plant of the Zeran motor works in Warsaw. The steady and measurable progress towards liberalization was shattered on June 28, 1956 by the riots in Poznan, which grew out of workers' discontent at the Cegielski locomotive works. Quickly, the riots turned into bloody demonstrations with strong anti-Communist and anti-Soviet overtones. The Ochab regime responded to the Poznan riots in two ways. First, it suppressed them with severe force, causing the death of eighty-eight demonstrators. Having restored order, the regime signaled its unbroken commitment to economic and political reform. The press was permitted to report the grievances from which the riots had sprung and the trial of leading rebels of September 1956 was open and resulted in mild sentences.

This outraged Poland's surviving Stalinists, such as Zenon Novak, and it disturbed the Soviet leadership. Most disturbing of all was the restoration of Gomulka as party leader, a move decided on by the Polish Central Committee on October 13, 1956. The Soviets distrusted Gomulka more than any other Polish leader. All other moves of keeping Gomulka out having failed—including a summons to the Polish Politburo to come to Moscow and the attempt of Poland's defense minister, the Soviet Marshal Rokossovsky, to arrest hundreds of Polish reform Communists—a Soviet delegation under Khrushchev and Molotov arrived in Warsaw on October 19, 1956. The Soviet delegation included Marshal Konev, the Warsaw Pact commander. Gomulka faced Khrushchev in a dramatic showdown which lasted many hours. Gomulka defied Khrushchev because of the strength of his arguments and the strength of his position. On October 19, 1956 he enjoyed virtually unanimous support because the Polish people regarded him at that moment truly as their national spokesman. As a veteran Communist party tactician, Gomulka had also assured himself of the support of all important centers of power in his own country: the army, the police, the security services, and the bureaucracy. Unlike in Hungary in November 1956, or in Czechoslovakia in August 1968, there were no Soviet quislings in high places in the Polish October 1956.

Gomulka demanded freedom to implement his domestic reforms but he gave his word not to quit the Warsaw Pact. He reminded Khrushchev of the Belgrade Declaration of 1955 and he could point to Chinese Communist support for his own person. He insisted on the ouster of Soviet Marshal Rokossovsky as Poland's minister of defense. Khrushchev departed for Moscow on October 20, 1956, willing to give Gomulka a try. Until Gomulka's own downfall in December 1970, under circumstances strikingly similar to those which had brought him to power after the Poznan riots, neither Khrushchev nor his successors had cause to regret the Soviet decision of October 20, 1956. During the Soviet invasion of Czechoslovakia in 1968, Gomulka was to support the Soviet position by sending troops of his own into neighboring Czechoslovakia. At the Fifth Congress of the Polish Communist Workers' party at Warsaw in November

1968, Brezhnev was to call Gomulka "the faithful son of the Polish working class and the greatest activist of the international Communist movement."

If the Soviets ended up hailing Gomulka, many of Gomulka's Polish supporters were to find him a disappointment after 1956. There was, to be sure, immediate relief in Poland's economic plight, with the Soviets cancelling Polish debts in the amount of 2.1 billion rubles and extending loans of 1.1 billion rubles. Moreover, the USSR promised higher prices for Polish coal exports and an increase in transit fares for shipments across Poland between East Germany and the USSR. Polish controls over Soviet forces remaining in Poland were increased in a new status-of-forces agreement of November 18, 1956.

Gomulka also effected important changes in farm and church policy. Forced collectivization was ended and the collective farm machinery centers, the so-called peasant circles in Poland, were disbanded. Cardinal Wyszynski was released and religious freedom promised on condition of noninterference in state affairs by the church. To the industrial workers, Gomulka had promised *socialist democracy* without, however, providing a definition of that term. It was soon revealed that the much-vaunted factory councils were, for Gomulka, far more an object of toleration than an instrument for social and economic renewal. Within a year of October 1956 the factory councils' role in plant management was done away with as "anarchist utopia." Poland's intellectuals were, in the long run, no less disillusioned with Gomulka's leadership than were the workers. Jerzy Andrzejewski, one of Poland's most prominent writers and author of the widely acclaimed novel *Ashes and Diamonds,* returned his Communist party membership card in November 1957, when the authorities banned a new liberal literary magazine, *Europa,* which he had helped found. By the 1960s, Poland's leading liberal Communist intellectuals, professors Leszek Kolakowski, Adam Schaff, and Stefan Zolkiewski, had either been purged from the party or removed from its leading organs. Kolakowski's *Man Without an Alternative,* Schaff's *Marxism and the Human Individual*, and Zolkiewski's *The Freedom of Marxist Culture* were too liberal to suit Gomulka's taste.

THE HUNGARIAN REVOLUTION

Hungarian Stalinism had been more severe than Poland's before the Twentieth Party Congress of February 1956, and Hungarian de-Stalinization remained more fitful and inconclusive afterwards. Unlike Czechoslovakia's Gottwald or Poland's Bierut, Hungary's Stalinist leader Matyas Rakosi continued to dominate events well into the crucial summer of 1956. Pressure for reform and rehabilitation continued to build up, on the other hand, on many levels of Hungarian society. At the top, survivors of the Stalinist purge of the late 1940s demanded revenge for Laszlo Rajk, most prominent of the purge victims. At the base of Hungarian society, resentment of the unchanged power of the secret police, AVH, called *Avos,* continued to smolder. *Csengöfrasz,* "bell fever," was a widespread state of mind in Stalinist Hungary, i.e., the fear of being rung out of bed in the middle of the night by agents of the AVH.

The Soviets had tried to induce Rakoski into softening some of his policies with little success, as evidenced by the quick demise of Imre Nagy, the reform Communist, during the Hungarian power struggle between 1953 and 1955. In an apparent appreciation of the explosiveness of the Hungarian situation, the Soviets dispatched a high-level mission under Suslov and Mikoyan to Budapest in mid-July 1956, which finally ousted Rakosi. The measure failed to defuse the Hungarian crisis because Rakosi's successor, Ernst Gerö, was no less a Stalinist and there was little noticeable progress in economic and political liberalization. The Polish example electrified the Hungarian public and provided the spark for Hungary's explosion. Where the Polish Communist party managed to achieve a considerable measure of unity with the public in the common confrontation with the Soviets, the Hungarian Communist leadership continued to lag behind public expectations. The concessions made were too few and too late to enable the party to regain the initiative and control the course of events.

Concessions

Among the belated concessions was the rehabilitation of purge victims and of Laszlo Rajk in particular, who was granted a state funeral on October 6, 1956. The state funeral became the occasion for the first great anti-Stalinist mass demonstrations in Budapest, and news of Gomulka's victory of October 19 provided the second. On October 22, 1956 the Petofi circle, a group of liberal reformers named after Hungary's freedom poet of 1848, Sandor Petofi, published a ten-point program for liberal reform. The program demanded Nagy's return to power, factory management by workers' councils, and the recasting of Soviet-Hungarian relations on the basis of "absolute equality." The ten-point program neither repudiated the Communist system as such, nor did it demand Hungary's withdrawal from the Warsaw pact. The student demands of Budapest University, publicized the same day, did both. Linking Hungary's cause to that of Poland, the students called for a rally of solidarity for October 23. The resulting demonstrations, beginning at the statue of General Bem, the Polish general who had supported the Hungarian revolution of 1848 against the Habsburgs, touched off the Hungarian Revolution of 1956.

Violence Erupts

Lacking clear leadership the demonstrations of October 23 quickly turned into violence with AVH strong points the principal target. Panic-stricken, Gerö made two contradictory decisions. Nagy was recalled as prime minister and Soviet forces were called to Budapest to restore order. On October 24, with street fighting between Soviet tanks and rebels in full swing, Suslov and Mikoyan returned to Hungary once more. They dropped Gerö and replaced him with Janos Kadar, himself a victim of the Rakosi purge. The Nagy-Kadar team, if installed several months earlier, would most likely have succeeded in stabilizing Hungary. By October 24, the rebels had had their first taste of victory, fighting the Russian tanks to a draw in the streets of Budapest. Although Nagy was still a popular figure, the rebels were no longer content with reform but demanded revolution instead. The goal of the Hungarian Revolution was the restoration of liberal democracy at home and the quitting of the Warsaw pact in foreign relations. The joint appeal of Nagy and Kadar to stop the fighting was drowned out in the roar of gunfire. From October 30 onwards, Nagy and Kadar followed opposite courses. Swept up by the patriotic wave, Nagy abandoned communism and placed himself at the head of the national revolution. Kadar denounced the "counterrevolution" of his fellow Hungarians and made himself the mouthpiece of Soviet intervention. On November 4, Kadar formed a new "Revolutionary Workers' and Peasants' Government'' and asked for renewed Soviet military intervention after the Soviets had pledged earlier to evacuate Budapest on October 30.

Soviet Intervention

The Soviet decision to use military force against rebellious Hungary was helped by two factors: first, the USSR had a mandate for military intervention from all the Communist regimes that counted, including Communist China. The latter had supported Gomulka because he was both a nationalist and a Communist. But it ceased to support Nagy when Nagy ceased to be a Communist. Even Tito, who had urged the ouster of Rakosi, now came to view Soviet intervention as inevitable, when the Hungarian Communist power base was in the process of complete disintegration.

Second, the danger of Western intervention, and of U.S. intervention in particular, could be safely discounted once world attention was divided between Budapest and Suez. The simultaneous Suez crisis blurred the sharpness of the East European tragedy and even allied the United States with Soviet Russia in common denunciation of the Anglo-French-Israeli attack. In the Suez crisis, Khrushchev threatened to send Soviet nuclear missiles against west European capitals and Soviet "volunteers" to Egypt, unless Britain and France evacuated Egypt. There was no similar U.S. threat to fire nuclear missiles against Moscow or to send U.S. "volunteers" to Budapest in order to force a Soviet withdrawal from Hungary. The Anglo-French expedition force was speedily withdrawn from Egypt. The Soviet forces in Hungary stayed. World opinion was likely to condemn Soviet military repression in Hungary, but world opinion was clearly judged a negligible factor where vital Soviet interests were concerned. The suppression of the East Berlin workers' uprising in June 1953 had also been condemned by world opinion, but it had not prevented the leaders of Britain, France and the United States from sitting down with the Soviet leaders at Geneva in 1955 or proclaiming thereafter a new "spirit of Geneva." The Soviet action in Hungary also produced hostile demonstrations in western Europe, but it commanded low attention among Third World countries in the UN in part, no doubt, because Hungary was a European country.

That Soviet action in Hungary set into motion a very critical movement within the Soviet Union itself among scholars and intellectuals, was something the outside world only began to realize during the 1970s with the surfacing of the Soviet dissident movement.

Repression in Budapest itself was brief, treacherous, and efficient. After the Soviet command had promised to withdraw from Hungary by October 30, 1956, General Pal Maleter, Nagy's youthful defense minister, upon being invited by the Soviets to negotiate the terms of withdrawal, was arrested by Khrushchev's security chief Ivan Serov on November 3. Both Maleter and Prime Minister Nagy were subsequently shot. Budapest was retaken by Soviet forces between November 4 and 7, 1956. As for Kadar's regime, it was installed by the methods of classical Stalinism, but it became far less Stalinist than had originally been assumed. As Gomulka's reform communism became increasingly doctrinaire, paternalistic and overbureaucratized, Kadar's communism became flexible, imaginative and consumer-oriented. Kadar allowed his factory councils far more real power than was the case in Poland, and Hungary even permitted non-Communists to stand for parliamentary elections, though not to form separate political parties outside the Communist party. After many years of patient reform, Kadar changed his image from hated Soviet quisling to popular leader, who, it was claimed by many in Hungary, could even risk a free election in his country. "Those who are not against us," Kadar was to tell his people, "are with us."

THE SEARCH FOR NEW BLOC CONTROLS

The official Soviet explanation of the disturbances in Eastern Europe between 1953 and 1956, covering the whole area from East Berlin to Warsaw and Budapest, was that these events were the result of "counterrevolutionary" activity, incited by Western, principally United States, sources. Western Cold War propaganda especially over the U.S.-sponsored radio stations in West Berlin (RIAS) and Munich (Radio Free Europe) certainly played its part in the East European upheavals. Western propaganda appeals would not have achieved such a broad and resounding echo, however, if conditions in Eastern Europe had not provided such a numerous and receptive audience. Whatever the specific cause that triggered the upheavals, they had shown the quintessential need for force as the criterion of Communist survival, reformed or otherwise. For the Soviet Union, the task now was to devise and to develop controls which would strike a more workable balance between the needs of security and the incentives for collaboration.

The Warsaw Pact, established in May 1955 between the USSR and the East European states, other than Yugoslavia, was the most important of these controls. Among the Warsaw Pact's two functions, defense against external attack and internal revolution, the latter was shown to be of greater urgency. Both in the suppression of the Hungarian Revolution in 1956 and in the future Soviet invasion of Czechoslovakia in 1968, the Warsaw Pact served as the legal base for Soviet intervention. The Council for Mutual Economic Assistance (*Comecon*) had been established by the Soviet Union in 1949 chiefly as a propaganda device against the Marshall Plan. In Stalin's time, *Comecon* had failed to develop into a genuine vehicle for economic integration or coordination of the planned economies of Eastern Europe and the Soviet Union. The evidence of successful cooperation of West European economies under the Coal and Steel Community and, after 1957, under the Common Market (EEC), prompted Khrushchev into efforts to turn *Comecon* from a paper institution into an instrument of effective economic coordination.

The 1955 Budapest *Comecon* conference took a first step towards plan coordination through the creation of study commissions. These early efforts were defeated by Soviet Russia's own abrupt cancellation of the five-year plan, adopted in 1956. Khrushchev's later attempts to persuade *Comecon* members to specialize in industries already established, encountered strong opposition especially among the less developed countries, such as Rumania. The Rumanians objected to the proposals of Soviet economist Valev, who favored greater investments in the industrial economies of the "Iron Triangle," East Germany, Poland and Czechoslovakia, while relegating underdeveloped nations, such as their own, to the role of food and raw material producers. The transformation of rural into industrial economies was, for East European Communist regimes, the most important and often the sole justification for their existence. Rumania's defiance of Soviet leadership in economic questions was an important factor in the evolution of Rumanian national communism during the coming decade. Inevitably, opposition to economic decisions broadened into opposition on other questions, including those of foreign policy and relations with the western world in general.

Economic cooperation remained low key even among the industrially advanced *Comecon* members. During Khrushchev's tenure, no *Comecon* central planning authority was established with binding powers. Joint ventures, such as the electrical *MIR* (friendship)-grid, or the ''friendship'' pipeline from the Ural-Volga region to Eastern Europe, required many years to complete. Joint planning and investment developed only after Khrushchev's fall and with the adoption of a convertible ruble for internal *Comecon* trade.

In his *Economic Problems of Socialism* (1952), Stalin had postulated the permanent division of the world into mutually hostile socialist and capitalist economies. In fact, Eastern Europe and the Soviet Union itself soon came to depend on outside, western technology and capital resources as an essential aid to their own continued growth.

23

From Illusion to Reality:
the German Cold War, 1955–1962

THE NEUTRALIZATION OF AUSTRIA; THE SOVIET TWO STATE THEORY

Within precisely a decade, between May 1945 and May 1955, the policy aim of the victors of World War II had dramatically shifted from the elimination of German power to its maximum utilization on behalf of one or the other of the Cold War antagonists.

In this, a stability of sorts had been achieved by 1955 with the rearmament of both Germanys and their integration in the respective military blocs, NATO and Warsaw Pact.

The arrangement of 1955 might have developed into a suitable basis for ending the German Cold War—as indeed it did with certain modifications after 1975. That it did not do so in 1955 or soon thereafter was due to the issue of West Berlin and the unchanged West German claim to reunification on its own terms.

The Two-State Theory

Once West Germany had entered NATO, as of May 1955, the official Soviet position on the German question was that there existed two German states and that both sides in the Cold War ought to recognize that fact. As the USSR was prepared to establish normal diplomatic relations with West Germany, the United States and its NATO allies, West Germany included, ought to do likewise with regard to Communist East Germany. Western recognition of East German sovereignty inevitably raised the issue of West Berlin, however, which was located inside East Germany 110 miles from the East-West German border. Stalin had attempted to drive the western powers out of West Berlin during the 1948–1949 blockade, in order to thwart American plans for a separate West German state and in order to discredit the American policy of "containment" before the public of West Germany and Western Europe generally. Khrushchev's motive for seeking a similar solution for West Berlin during the late 1950s was, if anything, more urgent. Unless the flow of East German refugees through West Berlin were stopped very soon, the economic collapse of East Germany was a certainty. Moreover, West Berlin had been developed by the United States into a highly effective center of Western Cold War propaganda and espionage as well as a visible showplace of Western living standards amidst Ulbricht's drab and coercive East German "construction of socialism."

The Soviets may well have deluded themselves initially into believing that the problem of Berlin could be solved, because they had made an unprecedented gesture of détente by signing the Austrian State Treaty on May 15, 1955, resulting in the complete Soviet evacuation of Austria. As the USSR had withdrawn from Vienna and the Soviet zone of eastern Austria, might not the western powers be expected to reciprocate with a voluntary retreat from West Berlin?

Although there were many outward similarities between the situations in postwar Germany and Austria, there were also fundamental differences. Both countries had been divided into four occupation zones, as were their capital cities, Berlin and Vienna, both of which had been conquered by Soviet forces and both of which were located inside Soviet occupation zones. In the Moscow foreign ministers' conference of 1943 the Soviets and the western powers had agreed to restore an independent Austrian state, however, and the Soviets had permitted a single government for all of Austria to be formed immediately after the Soviet conquest of Vienna in April 1945. Similarly, the Soviets had permitted free elections in all of Austria in November 1945, in which the Austrian Communists did very poorly and won only 4 out of 165 parliamentary seats. The Soviets had subsequently stalled on the Austrian State Treaty, partly in order to exploit Austrian economic resources in their own zone, especially oil, partly to use the issue of the state treaty as a bargaining chip in order to obtain concessions in the German question. With internal questions of power in the Kremlin still unsettled, Khrushchev courted American goodwill by finally agreeing to the Austrian State Treaty after three hundred futile negotiating sessions between 1945 and 1955. President Eisenhower, upon assuming office in 1953, had listed the conclusion of the Austrian State Treaty as one of the conditions for improved East-West relations.

Khrushchev's timing in granting the Austrian State Treaty may also have been calculated to impress West Germany with the rewards of neutralization. After the Soviet withdrawal, Austria's chancellor Julius Raab promptly declared his country's neutrality, similar to that of Switzerland.

The Soviet evacuation of Austria did make a profound impression on the West German public, but it did not alter the basic course of Adenauer's foreign policy. The Soviets invited Adenauer to come to Moscow and to establish full diplomatic relations with the USSR, something the West German government was reluctant to do, because normal West German–Soviet relations were, in themselves, an indirect recognition of the Soviet two-state theory. Contrary to the advice of West German foreign minister Heinrich Brentano, Adenauer did go to Moscow in September 1955 in order to establish relations with the USSR, because the Soviets had made the release of the remaining German POWs and civilian internees conditional on such a move. Immediately after Adenauer's departure from Moscow, the Soviets concluded a new "treaty on the relations between the German Democratic Republic and the Soviet Union" on September 20, 1955 as a visible demonstration of the existence of two sovereign German states.

The Hallstein Doctrine

The Adenauer administration, by contrast, denied the existence of two German states, maintaining, as it had ever since 1949, that the West German government, as the only freely elected government in Germany, spoke for all Germans, West and East. In order to defeat the Soviet purpose, the West German government devised the so-called Hallstein Doctrine, named after State Secretary Walter Hallstein, which threatened to sever diplomatic relations with any country, other than the USSR itself, which officially recognized Communist East Germany. As a means of isolating Communist East Germany in the non-Communist world, the Hallstein Doctrine was not without effect, largely because of the growing dependence of developing Third World countries on West German aid.

Adenauer's stand on reunification, together with his policy of boycott and non-recognition of the Communist bloc nations, helped to preserve and intensify the Cold War in central Europe well into the 1960s and past his own retirement in 1963. For this there existed powerful reasons, some rooted in the West German reality of the times, still others deriving from the Cold War attitudes of West Germany's principal ally, the United States. The West German governments of the 1950s and 1960s felt strongly committed to the goal of reunification, because the 1949 Basic Law had declared reunification the foremost goal and responsibility of the government. The 1955 treaties, which had rearmed West Germany, contained the promise of West Germany's new allies to support the goal of reunification. When West German foreign minister Heinrich von Brentano characterized the division of Germany as merely a "temporary disturbance," he was basically only echoing American Cold War rhetoric of the Eisenhower-Dulles era, which also considered the Soviet presence in Eastern Europe as reversible. The majority of the West German public expected its government to uphold the goal of reunification, just as it refused to recognize the permanent loss of the German territories east of the Oder-Neisse line. The millions of German refugees and exiles from these territories as well as from Communist East Germany proper were well organized in groups such as the BHE, the "Federation of Expellees and Those Deprived of their Rights," which formed powerful pressure groups. Lastly, the public Soviet image and that of Communist East Germany was that of the "enemy," with memories and sentiments still rooted in the Second World War and Cold War incidents such as the East Berlin uprising of June 17, 1953.

Mutual Subversion

The Cold War in central Europe was thus fought with particular bitterness between the two German states, each trying to weaken and subvert the other with the weapons of espionage, propaganda, and occasional terrorism. West Germany's General Gehlen succeeded in recruiting the chief secretary of East German prime minister Grotewohl, Elli Barczatis, for West German intelligence, while East Germany's state security service (STASI) scored major gains with the cases of Otto John and Alfred

Frenzel. The former, head of West Germany's "Office for the Protection of the Constitution," defected to East Berlin in 1954. The latter, a member of West Germany's parliament since 1953, was unmasked in 1960 as a top-ranking Communist spy with access to highly classified NATO defense secrets. Günther Guillaume, East Germany's master spy and eventual close aid to Chancellor Willy Brandt in the early 1970s, entered West Germany in the 1950s in the guise of an East German refugee. In West Berlin, kidnappings of prominent anti-Communists such as Walter Linse, a member of the "Committee of Free Jurists," by East German agents was not an unusual occurrence during the 1950s.

WEST GERMAN SOCIAL, ECONOMIC, AND CULTURAL DEVELOPMENTS

West Germany's economic picture continued to be bright during Adenauer's last term of office between 1957 and 1963, though there were signs of coming social unrest and a crisis in higher education.

With only 75 percent of the population and 52 percent of the area of prewar Germany, West Germany had, by 1955, exceeded the GNP of Hitler's Germany of 1936. By 1958 West Germany overtook Britain as an exporter of industrial goods. By 1960 West German steel production exceeded that of Hitler's Germany of 1939 by 50 percent. The rise in labor productivity allowed real wages to double between 1950 and 1965, while weekly workhours were cut over the same period by 20 percent. As in other West European industrial nations, agricultural income lagged behind industry in West Germany. The number of marginal small farms which went out of business between 1949 and 1963 was 400,000. Overall farm yield greatly increased, reaching more than double the amount per acre in wheat and barley as compared with pre-1939 figures.

The 1950s and 1960s witnessed significant changes in the lifestyles of average West Germans, away from the hunger and privation of the postwar years and towards consumer affluence. That the new and sudden affluence produced its own forms of materialism was critically noted by West German postwar writers, such as Heinrich Böll and Günther Grass.

The neglected areas of West Germany's "economic miracle" were cultural development and education. Some of the cultural statistics were impressive enough, the number of theaters in West Germany being nearly equal to that of all prewar Germany at over two hundred. The loss of Berlin, the once great metropolis of innovative theater and film during the 1920s, was never quite made up in West Germany. The official capital of Bonn never overcame its provincial image, though the city of Munich, the "secret capital" of West Germany, developed once more into a thriving center of the arts, and by the 1970s, also of a promising motion picture industry. Some of the best films of the immediate postwar years came out of East Berlin, including the 1946 picture *The Murderers Are Among Us,* which introduced the young Hildegard Knef. Some of West Germany's greatest talent among the new generation of stage and screen actors came from neighboring Austria, such as Oskar Werner, who made his Hollywood debut with an unforgettable portrayal of the character "Happy" in *Decision before Dawn.*

Education

The most seriously neglected area was education. East Germany, which proceeded from a much weaker economic base, devoted considerably more effort towards educational expansion and modernization. Among the drawbacks of East German education, however, was the adoption of admissions criteria based more on ideological preference than aptitude. Ulbricht consistently favored the admission of children of "proletarian" background to higher education over those of "bourgeois" background. Likewise, the selection of fields of study more often than not was dictated by the needs of the state, not the preference of the applicant.

West Germany made few preparations for the mass influx of students during the late 1960s and 1970s, which was in large part the result of the increased affluence of West German society. The political engagement of West German students was still small during the fifties. West Germany's academic Marxists, such as Wolfgang Abendroth at Marburg University or the leaders of the "Frankfurt School," Max Horkheimer, Theodor Adorno and Ernst Bloch, had an appreciable impact on the West German student generation only from the mid- and late 1960s onward.

The SDP

During the 1950s, criticism of West Germany's state of affairs, both external and internal, was still largely in the hands of the opposition Social Democratic party. Before the adoption of the new party program at Godesberg in 1959, the SPD had not yet jettisoned its Marxist economic legacy, a fact which diminished its voter appeal at a time when Erhard's social market economy was producing spectacular results. SPD criticism focused primarily on CDU defense and foreign policy. The Social Democrats not only opposed the equipping of the new West German army with tactical nuclear weapons, but the stationing of U.S. nuclear weapons on West German territory. Opposition to nuclear weapons became especially pronounced after it was learned that the first NATO maneuver held on German soil after 1955 included the simulated use of over three hundred nuclear devices with an assumed civilian "collateral casualty" rate of 5 million. The nuclear debate of the late fifties assumed great personal bitterness when the SPD charged that nuclear weapons served the purpose of gratifying a "lust for power" on the part of Adenauer's defense minister Franz Josef Strauss.

The Godesberg Program

On the subject of the Cold War, the 1958 SPD party congress blamed the United States and the Soviet Union in equal measure. In early 1959, SPD leaders Carlo Schmidt and Fritz Erler drafted the so-called *Deutschland* plan, calling for a step-by-step disengagement of both the United States and USSR from Germany. It was only after Khrushchev provoked a new Berlin crisis at the turn of 1958–1959 and after he rejected the *Deutschland* plan, that the SPD made a major shift to the right in the 1959 Godesberg program. The new 1959 party program discarded Marxism as the ideology of the SPD and endorsed the basic features of West German foreign policy since 1949: rearmament, NATO membership, and west European integration. The Godesberg program paved the way for the 1966 CDU/SPD grand coalition under CDU chancellor Kurt G. Kiesinger, and for the SPD-Liberal coalition under Willy Brandt in 1969.

THE BERLIN ULTIMATUM

Several factors combined to move the city of Berlin once more into the center of the Cold War stage between 1958 and 1962. Foremost among these was the problem of East German refugees, who continued to pour in record numbers into West Berlin by the simple means of the Berlin subway system, which still operated freely between East and West Berlin. Secondly, West Germany had aroused Khrushchev's ire in 1957 when the West German government, alarmed by Soviet space achievements such as *sputnik,* had asked the United States for tactical nuclear weapons and launchers. The United States had complied to the extent of supplying West Germany with the launchers by June 1958, though not with the nuclear warheads, which remained under U.S. control. The Soviets had denied their own Chinese Communist allies any help with nuclear weapons, and they clearly considered the American move, bringing West Germany closer to nuclear arms, a breach of an unwritten agreement. Lastly, by reactivating the Berlin issue, the Soviets hoped to dampen West German revisionism, to isolate West Germany from its own allies, and to sow confusion and discord in the NATO alliance.

The second Berlin crisis began with Khrushchev's "Berlin ultimatum" of November 27, 1958, which demanded a Western troop exit from West Berlin within six months and proposed the turning of West Berlin into a "free city." The ultimatum was followed by a Soviet draft peace treaty with both German states in January 1959.

The American reply of December 31, 1958 pointed to the nexus of Western troop presence in West Berlin and the Soviet presence in Saxony and Thuringia, the heartland of East Germany, which had been conquered in 1945 by American, not Soviet forces. If American forces were to be withdrawn from West Berlin, Soviet forces would logically have to get out of much of East Germany. Despite the strong American reaction, there was fear in the Adenauer administration of a softening of the Western stand on Berlin. The fear was inspired by British prime minister Macmillan's unilateral attempt to defuse the Berlin crisis by his journey to Moscow in early 1959, which yielded no results. It was also inspired by the Eisenhower-Khrushchev summit at Camp David in 1959, following which Eisenhower characterized the lifting of Khrushchev's six-months time limit as a Soviet concession, and called the Berlin situation "abnormal." For Adenauer, any change in the Berlin status quo was likely to be a change for the worse. The Paris summit fiasco of May 1960, following the U2 spy plane incident, destroyed whatever promise the short-lived "spirit of Camp David" may have held for Germany and Berlin. The Berlin crisis outlasted the Eisenhower administration and it presented the incoming Kennedy administration with its first serious challenge.

Adenauer was not entirely happy over the change of administrations in Washington, because he suspected the new president and key Democratic foreign policy advisers, including the Senate foreign relations committee chairman William Fulbright, to be less willing to support West Germany's inflexible positions on Berlin and reunification. West Germany's ambassador to the United States Wilhelm Grewe, who continued to think and talk in the Cold War categories of the 1950s, in fact so annoyed the new president that he had to be removed before very long.

Yet it remained for President Kennedy to face the hardest Soviet challenge over Berlin. The Vienna summit with Khrushchev of June 1961, intended to clarify the

Berlin situation, failed to do so. In July, the president compared the precarious position of Berlin with that of Bastogne during the "bulge" of 1944. Pledging to defend West Berlin with equal determination, Kennedy asked Congress for additional military appropriations. How pessimistic Kennedy really was concerning the likelihood of an armed conflict over Berlin was suggested by his private remarks to the then mayor of West Berlin, Willy Brandt, that war with the Soviets might become unavoidable.

The Berlin Wall

In Berlin itself, the crisis had reached fever pitch in July and August as thousands of refugees poured out of East Germany as if to avail themselves of the last opportunity to escape. On July 30, 1961 Senator Fulbright warned that the Western powers had no right to keep West Berlin open as an escape hatch, a remark that may not have gone unnoticed either in East Berlin or Moscow. On August 13, 1961 the Soviets effectively sealed off the escape hatch of West Berlin with the Berlin Wall.

Willy Brandt asked that the wall be dismantled, by force if necessary, a reaction the Soviets may not entirely have ruled out. In fact, the wall was put up by East German and not Soviet workers, who were guarded by East German and not Soviet troops. Although the wall was a clear violation of the four-power status of Berlin, no physical counteraction by the Western powers was attempted, because of the risk of war with the Soviet Union. The wall had a demoralizing effect on the people of West Berlin and all of West Germany and it contributed to the loss of CDU strength in the West German elections of September 1961. The shooting and killing of would-be escapers who tried to scale the wall, such as young Peter Fechter, who was killed on August 17, 1962, turned the wall into an even more emotional subject.

The wall was not the end of the Berlin crisis. When Soviet foreign minister Gromyko met with Kennedy in early October 1961, he again proposed the turning of West Berlin into a "free city" in exchange for a Western recognition of the Oder-Neisse line and the existing German borders, as well as the establishment of a nuclear-free zone in both German states. The Western rejection of these proposals resulted in Soviet harassment of Western air traffic into West Berlin through the blinding of Western radar and the practice of "escort" flights by Soviet fighter aircraft.

The Cuban Missile Crisis

Khrushchev's missile strategy in Cuba in October 1962 was intended as the final Soviet trump in the Berlin crisis. Had Khrushchev's plan of stationing medium-range missiles in Cuba succeeded, he could have offered to trade the removal of these missiles, an essential U.S. security concern, for a Western military withdrawal from West Berlin, an essential Soviet policy objective.

The withdrawal of Soviet missiles from Cuba, beginning on October 28, 1962, deprived Khrushchev of any bargaining asset in Berlin also. Kennedy was determined to stay in West Berlin, but there was equal recognition on his part of the vital Soviet interest to stay in East Germany.

Kennedy in Berlin

The peaceful reunification of Berlin and Germany, Kennedy observed in his speech at the Free University of West Berlin on June 26, 1963, would neither happen quickly nor would it be an easy process. Reunification would become possible only in a "new Europe," which would also be of attraction to the peoples of Eastern Europe. Kennedy's rousing *"Ich bin ein Berliner,"* was a pledge to uphold the freedom of West Berlin, but it was not a commitment to force the Soviets out of East Germany.

Khrushchev directly answered Kennedy in his Werner Seelenbinder Hall speech in East Berlin on July 2, 1963. The Soviet Union, Khrushchev said, did not wish to change the "situation now existing" in Europe, but merely wanted to legally fix the situation, which had arisen as a result of the outcome of World War II. Gromyko's UN General Assembly speech of September 19, 1963 echoed this with the plea of "legally anchoring" the borders between the two German states.

The threat of a nuclear exchange between the superpowers, which had been very real during the Cuban missile crisis, also helped to induce both the United States and the Soviet Union to accept the German status quo as a preferable alternative. With the German Cold War removed from center stage, it was possible to explore agreement in other areas. Kennedy's speech at the American University in Washington, D.C. of June 10, 1963, calling for "peace for all time" as the "reasonable goal of reasonable men," was a step in the direction of Soviet-American détente. The Nuclear Test Ban Treaty of August 4, 1963, was one of the first fruits of the new effort.

24

Eastern Europe in the 1960s: New Hopes and Old Patterns

EASTERN EUROPE AND THE SINO-SOVIET CONFLICT

On the surface, the 1950s seemed to have closed on a note of restored unity in the Communist world, following the post-Stalin challenges in Eastern Europe between 1953 and 1956.

In November 1960, only four years after the Hungarian Revolution, the Moscow summit of eight-one Communist parties proclaimed that the socialist system was free from "objective causes" for "contradictions and conflicts" between the peoples and states belonging to it. The capitalist system, by contrast, was given the customary Communist definition of a system characterized by "antagonistic contradictions" between classes, nations and states, "leading to armed conflicts."

"Antagonistic contradictions," which Soviet Communism habitually attributed to the West, were, in fact, about to surface during the coming decade with the utmost vehemence within the Communist camp itself.

In retrospect, the Soviet suppression of East European nationalism and reform Communism in 1956 appeared as a stopgap rather than a final solution to Soviet Russia's East European problems. Both in its internal development and external relations with foreign Communist regimes, the Soviet Union continued to be plagued by the dilemma of liberal imperatives and Stalinist repression. Neither the Soviet pilgrimage to Belgrade in 1955 nor the dethronement of Stalin in 1956 had provided definitive answers to the questions of national diversity and doctrinal unity under Communism.

The 1960s were likely to add fresh challenges because of the rising expectations of the peoples of Eastern Europe in a decade when Western Europe was moving from postwar recovery to affluence. Very soon, such rising expectations were to be frustrated by the heavily bureaucratized economies of Eastern Europe, unable to generate investment capital or to develop advanced technology on the required scale.

Above all else, the 1960s were to challenge Soviet dominance over Eastern Europe and Soviet ideological authority in the entire world of Communism as never before as a result of the Sino-Soviet conflict.

The Sino-Soviet conflict had deep and distant roots, reaching back to the 1920s. Reversing the classical Marxist-Leninist position that Communist revolution must emanate from the cities, Chinese Communist leader Mao based his revolutionary strategy on the peasant and proposed to conquer the cities from the countryside. The Chinese Communists similarly embraced the thesis of Indian Communist leader M. N. Roy, which Lenin rejected in the 1920s, that the triumph of Communist revolution in Asia was crucial to the success of Communist revolution in Europe. Chinese Communist independence from Moscow was again suggested in 1943, when Mao characterized Stalin's disbanding of the Communist International as having no meaning for the Chinese Communists in view of the latter's independent tactics.

The 1949 Chinese Revolution

Chinese Communist independence vis-à-vis Moscow turned into a potential threat to the Soviet leadership only after the triumph of the Chinese Communist revolution in 1949. It was for that reason that Stalin had not considered that triumph as an altogether desirable development and would have preferred a China divided between Communist and Nationalist governments. Friction between Soviet Russia and Communist China developed soon after Stalin's death in 1953, though it remained concealed from the outside world until 1960. In a process that reversed the sequence of the Soviet-Yugoslav quarrel, the Sino-Soviet dispute developed initially over questions of ideology and only later turned into a clash of national interests and nationalism, unrelated to ideological issues. The end result of the process was nevertheless identical to that of the Yugoslav-Soviet dispute, i.e., the assertion of the primacy of nationalism over ideology, quite contrary to the Marxist prediction of the disappearance of nationalism in the Communist age. That the Sino-Soviet conflict should also have stirred strong racial emotions among both Russians and Chinese, added a further element of poignancy to a poignantly un-Marxist development.

The Sino-Soviet dispute unfolded in three distinctive stages, between 1956–1957 and 1960, 1960 to 1963, and the period after 1963. The issues of the first stage revolved around de-Stalinization and its domestic and foreign political implications. De-Stalinization, a necessity to Khrushchev, was an error to the Chinese Communists, confirmed by the Hungarian Revolution of 1956 and the ongoing ideological vagaries of Yugoslavia's Tito. Yugoslavia became the symbol as well as the stand-in for the Sino-Soviet controversy over the relative dangers of *dogmatism* or *sectarianism,* Soviet codewords for Stalinism, or of *revisionism,* code-word for de-Stalinization and Communist liberalization. Both sides were still maneuvering for compromise. When Yugoslavia issued a new party program in 1958 which was too liberal for Soviet taste, both China and the Soviet Union condemned it and Soviet Russia, together with East Germany, suspended loans and economic aid to Yugoslavia as punishment. By 1958 Yugoslavia had become, in the Soviet definition, once again a "Trojan horse of imperialism." The "Moscow Declaration," issued by the Moscow Communist summit of November 1957, which was also attended in person by Mao, praised on the other hand the USSR as the "first and mightiest socialist power" in the world. The Soviets, for their part, ridiculed the Chinese attempt at achieving "instant communism" with the commune system and the backyard blast furnaces, and called it in so many words Communist infantilism.

The collision of Soviet and Chinese national interests was the result of the foreign political implications of de-Stalinization. Interpreting Soviet Russia's "first" in the space race with the launching of *Sputnik* in October 1957 as a sure sign of Soviet weapons superiority over the United States, the Chinese Communists expected not only a tougher Soviet stand against the United States worldwide, but active Soviet support in all foreign policy confrontations in which Communist China herself was involved. In fact, the Soviets failed to give such support in the U.S.-Chinese dispute over the Taiwan straits and the islands of Quemoy and Matsu of 1958, or in the Sino-Indian border dispute of 1959. Khrushchev's summit with Eisenhower in the United States in 1959 and the subsequent proclamation of the "spirit of Camp David" aroused, on the other hand, strong Chinese suspicions about Soviet-American collusion, with China the odd one out. By 1960 Mao perceived the USSR not only in ideological error, but as a power orchestrating an anti-Chinese policy where vital national interests of China were concerned. Mao began to compare Communist China's relationship with the USSR with that of Lenin relative to the Second (Social Democratic) International before World War I. Like Lenin, the Chinese Communists began to claim the inheritance of the true revolutionary movement. Before long, the Soviets found themselves accused of "parliamentary cretinism." In the article "Long Live Leninism" in the Chinese party paper *Red Flag* of April 16, 1960, Yugoslavia was strongly denounced for its "revisionist views" on war, coexistence and revolutionary violence. The real target was the USSR.

The USSR answered publicly with Khrushchev's attack on Mao at the Rumanian Communist party conference at Bucharest in June 1960, which acted as the curtain-raiser to the second, public stage in the Sino-Soviet conflict. Mao was accused of "nationalism," "adventurism," and even "Trotskyism." By August 1960, the USSR recalled 1,400 technicians from China and shut down 257 joint scientific and technological projects. Sino-Soviet trade declined from $2 billion in 1959 to $370 million in 1964. Khrushchev refused any aid in the development of Chinese nuclear weapons. At the Moscow Communist summit of November 1960, which Mao boycotted, the Soviets were no longer interested in finding formulas for compromise, but in isolating China from the rest of the Communist world. The "Moscow statement" of November 1960 stressed the superior position of the USSR over and above all other socialist states. The USSR alone was credited with building communism, all others were said to be still engaged in varying stages of socialism, a lower stage by communist definition.

At the 1960 Moscow Communist summit, Albania, acting as Communist China's mouthpiece, attacked virtually all of Khrushchev's policies since the 1956 Twentieth Party Congress in language previously not heard at gatherings of this kind. Accusing the USSR of deliberately withholding promised grain shipments to Albania, Albanian party boss Enver Hoxha observed that "Soviet rats" were being fed, while Albanians were starving. The logic of Albania's role as Communist China's mouthpiece derived, in part, from Khrushchev's earlier attempt to unseat Hoxha, an unreformed Stalinist, as Albanian party leader. It was also rooted in Albania's old fear of being absorbed by neighboring Yugoslavia, a heightened prospect the more Yugoslavia-Soviet relations were improved under the broadening conflict between China and Russia.

The publications of the Chinese Central Committee letter to its Soviet counterpart in June 1963 marked the opening of the third and most vituperative phase in the Sino-Soviet conflict. Prompted by the USSR's signing of the Nuclear Test Ban Treaty, the Chinese letter accused the USSR of having violated the revolutionary principles endowed in the 1957 Moscow Declaration and the 1960 Moscow Statement. With the call for the formation of new Communist parties in the name of "true revolution," the historic schism of world communism was complete. With the Soviet occupation of Czechoslovakia of August 1968, Chinese invective reached an all-time high. Communist China denounced the "Brezhev doctrine" of limited sovereignty of socialist states as a "gangster theory," while branding the Soviet leadership itself as "out-and-out Fascist gangsters."

The deepening conflict between China and Russia and the corresponding Soviet effort of isolating China in the Communist world, provided the nations of Eastern Europe with a new leverage which they had not previously enjoyed. Among China's charges the most welcome to East European ears was the charge of "Soviet Great Power chauvinism," of Soviet "subversion" and "Soviet national egotism." The desire to exploit the Sino-Soviet conflict for ends of East European emancipation from Soviet hegemony also increased in countries such as Rumania as a result of the awareness that a similar loosening-up process was taking place in Western Europe vis-à-vis the United States under the impact of the Vietnam War and Gaullism. The East European search for greater independence also increased as a result of economic need, as the East European nations turned increasingly to the West for capital assistance and technology which the USSR could not provide.

RUMANIAN NATIONAL COMMUNISM

Albania's insults hurled at Khrushchev and the Soviet Union at the 1960 Moscow Communist summit were only the opening shots in a development of East European Communist defiance, in which Rumania and Czechoslovakia soon followed with challenges of their own. Rumanian national communism grew out of a peculiar mixture of past Rumanian-Soviet hostility, rooted in World War II, and of current Soviet attempts of interfering in Rumania's internal political and economic developments. Past resentments derived from Rumania's prominent role as Hitler's ally in the invasion of the Soviet Union when the Rumanian army threw the Red Army out of Odessa in 1941. Soviet punishment of Rumania after World War II was correspondingly severe, including, as it did, the reannexation of Bessarabia and the imposition of crushing reparations burdens during the Stalin era. In the Khrushchev era, the Soviets attempted to oust Rumania's Stalinist party boss Gheorgiu-Dej in favor of a more liberal Communist in a move that paralleled similar Soviet efforts in other East European countries. At the same time, *Comecon* proposed to assign to Rumania the role of food and agricultural producer, while the established industrial nations of Eastern Europe,

East Germany, Poland and Czechoslovakia, would concentrate on further industrial development.

It was in response to these pressures that Gheorgiu-Dej forged a new alliance between Rumanian communism and Rumanian nationalism. By identifying Rumania's deeply rooted anti-Soviet sentiments with his personal political survival, and by equating Rumania's Communist leadership with industrial progress in Rumania's, not *Comecon's* interest, Gheorgiu-Dej created a unique brand of East European communism which was both nationalist and Stalinist. Rumania's collectivization of farmland, for example, which was nearly 100 percent complete by 1962, was not reversed or modified afterwards. By contrast, the assertion of nationalism in other East European countries usually went hand-in-hand with liberalization and the purging of Stalinist remnants in the ruling Communist parties. This had been the pattern in Poland and Hungary in 1956 and it was again to become the alignment of reform elements in Czechoslovakia in 1968. Because of Rumania's unchanged adherence to communist orthodoxy even in times of strident nationalism, the Soviets found it far more difficult to cope with the phenomenon of Rumanian national communism than was the case elsewhere.

Likewise, the Rumanian Communists were among the very first to enlist Chinese Communist support for Rumanian national interests. It was with Chinese Communist support that Rumania persuaded the Soviets to take their troops out of Rumania in 1958. With Russian troops out of the country, Rumania also displayed a new cultural nationalism with emphasis on Rumanian national identity. By 1963 Rumania had shut down the Maxim Gorky Institute, principal cultural center of the USSR in Bucharest, and dropped the Russian language as a required subject from Rumanian schools. In 1964 Rumania raised the question of the status of Besserabia, and received a prompt and positive echo from Peking. The Rumanian Central Committee "statement" of April 27, 1964 rejected both the subordination of one Communist party to another and the primacy of "superstate" organizations, such as *Comecon,* over the principle of national independence. Although more cautiously formulated than the famous Chinese Central Committee letter of June 1963, the Rumanian "statement" of 1964 was clearly inspired by it.

The trend set in motion by Gheorgiu-Dej was continued after the latter's death in 1965 by his successor Nicolae Ceausescu. Ceausescu replaced the 1952 constitution, a copy of the Soviet 1936 Stalin constitution, with a new one and scrapped Soviet educational and administrative models in 1967. In 1966 Rumania, still a member of the Warsaw Pact, demanded a rotation in the Warsaw Pact supreme command, traditionally in Soviet hands. This was followed by the demand that nuclear weapons be stored in Warsaw Pact countries only with the consent of the nation concerned. In 1967, Rumania, having received loans from West Germany, established full diplomatic relations with that country. Rumania's move violated a Warsaw Pact policy principle that normal diplomatic relations with West Germany must be preceded by prior West German recognition of Communist East Germany. In 1967, Rumania likewise was alone among the Communist nations of Eastern Europe in not severing diplomatic relations with Israel during the Arab-Israeli War. When Soviet Russia organized a bloc conference at Karlovy Vary in Czechoslovakia in April 1967 for the purpose of establishing a common front against Communist China, Rumania, together with Yugoslavia and Albania, boycotted the conference. Instead, Rumania offered her good offices to both the USSR and China, to "mediate" the conflict between the giants. When the Czechoslovak crisis approached its flash point in February 1968, Rumania walked out of the bloc conference at Budapest which had been intended to put joint pressure on the Czechoslovak liberal reformers. In 1969, Rumania invited the U.S. president for an official visit, which helped pave the way for the coming Sino-American rapprochement.

The Soviets had countered Rumania's defiant attitude by threats and unfriendly acts. Khrushchev, angered by the Rumanian "statement" of April 1964, had encouraged Hungary to revive old territorial claims against Transylvania, the Rumanian-Hungarian bone of contention since 1919. Brezhnev threatened a boycott of vital raw materials in 1965, to which Rumania responded by broadening its trade with western nations. When there appeared danger of a Soviet military invasion of Rumania, in conjunction with the Soviet occupation of Czechoslovakia in 1968, Rumania coordinated her defenses with those of Yugoslavia, and otherwise relied on the political support of both Communist China and the United States.

TITO'S "SECOND REVOLUTION"

The ultimate success of Tito's liberal reforms of the 1950s was far from certain a decade later. From the beginning, Tito's reforms had been under dual attack from conservative and liberal critics, the former attacking the changes as too radical, the latter as not going far enough. Milovan Djilas, the most extreme liberal critic, rejected Tito's reforms during the 1960s, once he lost faith in the feasibility of synthesizing individual freedom and a socialist economic order. Edvard Kardelj, who had coauthored many of the early reforms with Djilas, continued to uphold the ideal of a "nonparty socialist democracy" for Yugoslavia.

Yugoslav reform communism of the 1960s thus became a movement of advance and retreat, progress and retrenchment, with Tito holding the balance between the extremes. Yugoslav developments were further influenced by the state of the economy at any given time, by the changing relationship with the USSR and China, as well as by the resurfacing of national tensions between Yugoslavia's principal ethnic blocs, the Serbs, Croats, Slovenes, Macedonians, Montenegrans, and Albanians.

Tito and the Third World

In the area of Third World relations, Tito scored new triumphs, while also encountering some disappointments and failures during the 1960s. The 1961 Belgrade summit of twenty-five "nonaligned" nations marked a new high in Yugoslavia's and Tito's personal prestige, though it was noted with bitterness in the United States that Tito singled out the United States for criticism on the subject of nuclear testing. At the Belgrade summit of 1961 Tito also recognized the Algerian provisional government, a year before de Gaulle gave Algeria independence. Yugoslavia's relations with Castro's Cuba deteriorated in direct proportion to Cuba's growing alignment alongside the USSR. Having hailed Castro's victory in the Bay of Pigs invasion of 1961, Tito boycotted Cuba during his trip to South and Central America in 1963. Yugoslavia similarly stayed away from the Havana conference of socialist states from three continents which was attended by both the USSR and China. In 1966 Castro dismissed Tito as a "lackey of imperialism" and an "opportunist."

Market Socialism

At home, Tito moved from a centralized socialist economy towards an economy of *market socialism*. It was part of that shift that Yugoslavia lifted price controls, introduced commercial banking practices, and increased the role of the factory workers' councils in the distribution of income. The currency was sharply devalued from 300 to 750 dinars to the U.S. dollar.

The changeover to market socialism was welcomed by the economically more advanced regions of Slovenia and Croatia, but opposed by the poorer, underdeveloped regions, such as Montenegro, Bosnia, and Macedonia, which relied on subsidies from the government in Belgrade. It was among the latter regions that the by-products of Tito's economic reforms, unemployment and inflation, were felt with particular severity. The Serbs rated economically between the advanced and the poorer regions. As the dominant nationality in the state bureaucracy, the Serbs favored a centralized economy.

Challenge and Reform

Conservative opposition to the liberal economic reforms began to crystallize around the person of Alexander Rankovič at the turn of 1962–1963. A Serb, Rankovič was chief of the secret police (UBDA) and a favorite of the Russians. Rankovič's elevation to the vice-presidency in 1963 seemed to signal his being groomed for the succession. Tito's "Great Economic Reform" of 1965 marked, on the other hand, another victory for the liberal economic reformers, who blamed the economic setbacks of the early 1960s on too little, rather than too much reform. It was in response to these developments that Rankovič staged his unsuccessful coup against Tito in 1966, in which the UDBA even "bugged" the private apartments of Tito. Having squashed the coup, Tito reacted with characteristic restraint, so as not to add new divisions to Yugoslavia's historic internal divisions. Rankovič was fired as vice-president without being tried, and the role of the UBDA in the state was sharply diminished. As a gesture to the liberals, Djilas was released from jail and the influence of liberal party leaders, such as Edvard Kardelj, Veljko Vlahovic, and Vladimir Bakaric was increased by promotion into the party presidium. The constitutional reforms of December 1968, adopted under the impact of the Soviet invasion of Czechoslovakia, were similarly liberal in intent in addition to aiming at greater participation of the several nationalities in federal affairs. The Ninth Party Congress of March 1969 witnessed the incorporation of some of the reform ideas of the Czechoslovak liberals of the "Prague Spring" of 1968. The congress stressed the separation of the organization of party and state and it limited the tenure in party and state executive positions to two consecutive terms. The leadership of the party and the armed forces was opened up to a greater number of non-Serbs. The Politburo (renamed *executive bureau*) henceforth would be composed of two representatives from each of the six federal republics plus one from each of the two autonomous provinces, the Kosmet and the Vojvodina. Concerning ideology, the Ninth Congress promised freedom of conscience, permitting dissenters to resign from the party without retaliation.

The constitutional and party reforms of the late 1960s were designed to strengthen the unity among Yugoslavia's diverse national and ethnic groups in preparation for the post-Tito era. The Soviet invasion of Czechoslovakia of August 1968 strengthened internal Yugoslav unity, as external danger had always unified the Yugoslavs in the twentieth century, in 1914, 1941 and again in 1948. As a visible demonstration of Yugoslav unity Tito organized a great military exercise in 1971, code-named *Freedom 71*, which involved 80,000 regular troops and 320,000 civilian "partisans."

Dissidence

With the passing of the threat of Soviet intervention, the unity of the late sixties gave way, once again, to internal bickering, with dissident intellectuals and spokesmen of the nationalities in the lead.

Intellectual dissent had been centering around the academic journals *Gledišta* and *Praxis*. The latter included among its editors foreign Marxist theorists, such as Ernst Bloch, Herbert Marcuse and Jürgen Habermas. *Praxis* advocated what it called a "socialism without dictatorship" in preparation of a "socialism without a party." Objecting to the imposition of Marxism as an official doctrine, *Praxis* demanded an open critique of Marxist philosophy as a safeguard against totalitarianism. Rankovič had suspended *Praxis* before his own downfall in 1966. In 1975 *Praxis* was shut down again as part of a wider drive against instructors and professors of philosophy at Belgrade University. Academic criticism of the Soviet Union also prompted official reprimands, if the attacks were deemed too harsh. An article in the Belgrade periodical *Delo*, accusing the USSR of having built concentration camps long before Nazi Germany, promptly brought its author Mihailo Mihajlov, a Zagreb University instructor, a prison sentence in April 1967.

The demand of the Croatian Writers' Association of 1967 for the recognition of Croatian as an official language, and the Serbian counterdemand for the teaching of the Serbian Cyrillic alphabet to Serbian children residing in Croatia, threatened to reopen the old Serbian-Croatian national antagonisms.

Tito, sensing his own inevitable passing in the not-too-distant future, struck out against suspected or real dissenters on the Left and Right who might endanger his life's work of Yugoslav unity under his own brand of communism. Before its renewed suspension in 1975 *Praxis* called Tito a "moody and charismatic leader," whose passing the Yugoslav Communist League both feared and secretly desired.

CZECHOSLOVAKIA FROM NOVOTNY TO DUBCEK

When the 1960s opened, Czechoslovakia seemed the very model of a stable Eastern-bloc nation with a strong economy and loyal ties to Moscow. The new 1960 constitution proudly proclaimed the "achievement of socialism" and the imminent "transition to communism." Together with East Germany's Walter Ulbricht, Antonin Novotny, the Stalinist Czechoslovak party boss, had expressly approved the Soviet intervention in Hungary in 1956 and condemned "national communism." In 1957, defying current trends towards "collective leadership," Novotny had combined the presidency with his post as first party secretary. At 11.6 percent, Czechoslovak Communist party membership exceeded even the Soviet rate. Collectivization of farmland, at 92 percent, was nearly complete by 1960. The claimed industrial growth rate of 11 percent per year was among the Eastern bloc's highest.

Before the end of the 1960s, the Czechoslovak economy was in complete disarray, party unity had given way to factional strife, intellectual dissent, and ethnic tension between Czechs and Slovaks, while relations with Moscow had reached a crisis point which triggered the biggest Soviet military action in Eastern Europe since World War II.

Economic Problems

At the outset of Communist rule in 1948, the Czechoslovak economy was among the strongest in Eastern Europe. Czechoslovakia was highly industrialized before World War II and Germany had added several important new industries during the war, including aircraft, synfuel and armaments plants. By the early 1960s, industrial plants and equipment were old and in bad need of overhaul and new investment. Industrial exports, including entirely new plants, went chiefly to the Soviet Union, in exchange for energy and raw material imports. With an average annual output of between 25 and 28 million tons, Czechoslovakia was self-sufficient in coal, but completely dependent on Soviet imports for oil and natural gas. With the decline of Czechoslovakia's iron ore production from 3 million tons in 1960 to 1 million tons a decade later, dependence on Soviet ore also mounted. Collectivization had turned Czechoslovakia from near-self-sufficiency in grain to net importer with Soviet imports again filling the gap. By the end of the decade, the Soviet-Czechoslovak trade balance was heavily in favor of Czechoslovakia, however, the USSR owing as much as $1 billion.

Added to the problems of foreign trade and plant deterioration were those of mismanagement. At a time when other bloc nations, such as East Germany, had already applied reforms with an eye to management efficiency and market needs, Czechoslovakia's smug and overage Communist bureaucracy was still resisting modernization of management. In 1962, Czechoslovakia's third five-year plan was scrapped altogether; the 1963 industrial growth rate stood at zero.

The NEM

Novotny understood the need for economic reform, but he feared its effects on other areas once it was undertaken. In January 1967, Czechoslovakia introduced the so-called New Economic Model (NEM), which was similar to East Germany's *NÖS*. Ota Sik, the economist who authored many of the NEM reforms, was himself a strong believer in the regulating forces of the market under any economic system, the socialist system included. NEM reforms were carried out halfheartedly, however, or actively resisted by undereducated party bureaucrats, who feared the loss of power and influence to younger technocrats and economists.

As Novotny had feared, NEM stimulated political and intellectual dissent. In 1967 dissent crystallized around the issues of Slovak national opposition and cultural and intellectual freedom. The Slovaks, who comprised 31.1 percent of the population according to the 1966 census, felt traditionally discriminated against by the Czech majority in politics, the civil service, and the economy. The new 1960 constitution reinforced such suspicions because of its emphasis on the Czech-dominated central authorities in Prague. The Slovak share of industrial production had actually increased under Communist rule from 7.8 percent before World War II to 27.7 percent in 1966, but the Slovak yearning for cultural autonomy had remained unfulfilled. Such yearnings were dismissed in Novotny's Czechoslovakia as "bourgeois nationalism." Gustav Husak, himself a Slovak and future Soviet collaborator, had been sentenced in the show trials of the 1950s for "Slovak bourgeois nationalism." In 1967 Slovak nationalists looked to Alexander Dubcek, a senior Slovak Communist party leader, for the fulfilment of their aspirations.

Opposition to Novotny

The strength of intellectual and cultural opposition to the Novotny regime was revealed at the Fourth Congress of the Writers' Union in Prague on June 29, 1967. The congress denounced the party elite and bemoaned the lack of cultural freedom. Among the critics was Ludvik Vaculik, soon to emerge during the "Prague Spring" of 1968 as the author of the pamphlet "Two Thousand Words." The attacks made against the Novotny regime at the Writers' Congress reflected a deeper sense of nationwide disillusionment with Communist rule in its current form, which derived not only from the prevailing economic woes, but the failure of the Czechoslovak leadership to purge itself of Stalinist attitudes and practices. By the late 1960s the party had lost its appeal to the young, the average age of party members having risen to forty-five. It was in an attempt to rejuvenate Czechoslovak communism, rather than to destroy it, that a coalition was formed between Alexander Dubcek and other reformers, including such party leaders as Smrkovsky, Svermova, Pavel, and Kriegel.

For a brief while, Novotny attempted to enlist the help of Soviet party leader Brezhnev in the approaching showdown with the liberal reformers. At first, Brezhnev counseled against changing the leadership of the Czechoslovak party at a time when West Germany was thought to be seeking an expansion of its influence in Eastern Europe. When Brezhnev learned of the degree of Novotny's unpopularity, he did not back him unconditionally. On January 3, 1968 the Central Committee ousted Novotny as first party secretary and replaced him with Dubcek. By March 1968 Novotny had lost the presidency as well, to Ludvik Svoboda, and by May 1968 he had even lost his Central Committee seat, and his ordinary party membership was suspended.

The "Prague Spring"

Between January and July 1968 there unfolded what soon came to be called the "Prague Spring," a period of hope and faith in the feasibility of a synthethis of socialism and democracy. The aim of the Czechoslovak reformers was not, as Professor Goldstücker of the Writer's Union explained in March 1968, the restoration of "bourgeois democracy," but the achievement of a new sort of freedom under socialism. Such a freedom would begin with the internal democratic reform of the Communist party, and would lead to a broadening of parliamentary power and the readmission of political parties other than the Communist. The notion that the Soviet Union was an unsuitable model for "a developed socialist society," in the words of Josef Smrkovsky, the president of the Czechoslovak parliament during the "Prague Spring," was fundamental to the reformers' purpose.

On the economic front, Ota Sik, Dubcek's vice-premier and economic minister, implemented a reform program under the motto, As Little Planning As Necessary, As Much Freedom As Possible. With marketing, budgeting, and price calculation as new criteria of business management, the Sik reforms had already shown good results by the spring of 1968, especially in industries such as the electrical. It was not part of the Sik reforms, however, to restore private ownership to the means of production.

The Action Program

Dubcek's Action Program of April 6, 1968 recast the role of the Communist party and opened the door to a return of political democracy. The party's authority, the Action Program stated, could not be imposed from above, but had to be earned continually. The Action Program furthermore called for the separation of party and state, and it promised the creation of a "National Front" to which political parties other than the Communist would be admitted. Lastly, the program pledged rehabilitation and compensation for purge victims, an improvement in state-church relations, and the fulfilment of Slovak demands for equality through constitutional change. Freedom of the press and all other news media, including television, was guaranteed by the law of June 26, 1968. Henceforth, the news media became a powerful ally of the liberal reformers in attacking surviving Stalinists and exposing their past misdeeds.

The Soviet Reaction

It is not likely that the Soviet leadership would have allowed the Prague reforms to stand unchanged under any circumstances, because these reforms touched on some of the most important and basic principles of Soviet political practice and ideology. Most dangerous, from the Soviet standpoint, was the lifting of censorship over the news media and the abandonment of the political monopoly of the Communist party. In terms of Soviet strategic and foreign political interests, the Czechoslovak reformers reached the point of no return when the subject of quitting the Warsaw Pact was also aired. The late 1960s were, however, quite generally a period of reaction in the Eastern bloc and in the USSR's own internal development, a fact which left the events of 1968 in Czechoslovakia sadly out of step and which heightened the likelihood of forceful Soviet intervention. Liberalization had generally occurred in the Eastern bloc at the beginning of the 1960s, when the Stalinist Novotny was still firmly in the saddle. By 1967 Ulbricht had curtailed his NÖS and Gomulka of Poland began cracking down on students and dissident intellectuals. The new hard line of 1967–1968 in bloc politics was prompted, in part, by the solidarity of intellectuals with Israel during the Arab-Israeli war of 1967. Soviet reaction to events in Czechoslovakia in 1968 was also strongly influenced by the fear that Czechoslovakia might follow the example of Rumania and establish close trade relations with West Germany in exchange for political concessions to the West German government. The fact that the Dubcek government had begun sounding out Bonn with regard to a West German loan to tide over the Czechoslovak economy, only confirmed such suspicions. In the USSR itself, there was a fear that the liberal Czechoslovak reforms would encourage a similar reform movement in the Soviet Union. Ukrainian party secretary Shelest and Yuri Ilnitski, the party secretary of the Carpatho-Ukraine, were among those who warned against domestic repercussions in their own provinces of events in neighboring Czechoslovakia. June 1968 also witnessed the emergence of Andrei Sakharov as a major Soviet dissident with his potentially explosive manifesto, "Progress, Coexistence and Intellectual Freedom," which strongly supported the "democratic reforms" of Czechoslovakia. By 1968, the influence of the military on questions of foreign policy and bloc relations was also probably greater than in Khrushchev's time. With nine of the USSR's fifteen military district commanders present in the Soviet Central Committee, the warnings of the military against the strategic implications of a prowestern Czechoslovak government must have been both persistent and effective.

The Soviet Invasion

The Soviet military invasion of Czechoslovakia on August 20, 1968 with 4,000 tanks and 600,000 troops came as no surprise to those who had been following the warnings which the Eastern bloc had been addressing to Prague with mounting urgency between March and July 1968. On three separate occasions—at Dresden in East Germany in March, Moscow in May, and Warsaw in July 1968— the Warsaw Pact members, minus Rumania, had warned the Prague reformers about the dangers and likely consequences of their actions. The Warsaw meeting denounced the Prague reformers as "counterrevolutionaries" and threatened appropriate measures in support of the "sound elements," i.e., the remaining hard liners in the Czechoslovak Communist party. The Hungarian Communists, mindful of their own experience of a Soviet invasion in 1956, hoped to alert the Czech reformers to the danger of an imminent Soviet invasion through both the private warnings of Imre Nagy and the well-meant advice printed in the pages of the Hungarian Communist daily *Népszabadsa'g*.

Dubcek and the liberals did not view their own situation as similar or identical with that of Hungary, largely because the Czechoslovak Communist party of 1968, unlike that of Hungary of 1956, actually enjoyed growing popular support as the liberal reforms were being implemented. The Prague reformers also counted on the support of foreign Communist parties, notably those of Yugoslavia, Rumania, France and Italy, all of whom had hailed the "Prague Spring." At the same time, the Prague reformers deluded themselves into believing that their ideas would ultimately prevail throughout the Communist bloc, regardless of the nature of the Soviet reaction in the short run. *Pravda zvítezi* (truth will prevail), the slogan of the Czech national hero Jan Hus, also became the motto of Josef Smrkovsky. Dubcek, like Gomulka in Poland in 1956, was a national hero in the Czechoslovakia of 1968, but he was far less skillful in consolidating his own political power before challenging the Soviets. Although the liberal reform wing of the Communist party scored a major victory with the expulsion of the Stalinist Novotny from the Central Committee in May 1968, there remained a hard-core Stalinist opposition grouped around such figures as Bohumil Chnoupek, the deputy minister of information, and Pavel Auersperg, the chairman of the party's ideological commission. It was from the midst of the conservative and Stalinist minority that an appeal for Soviet intervention was sent at Moscow's behest.

The liberals had hoped to swamp the conservatives by calling for a new party congress, the Fourteenth Extraordinary Congress, for September 9, 1968. Before the congress could meet on the scheduled date, the Soviet invasion of August 20 had taken place.

The Moscow Protocols

When informed of the imminent Soviet occupation, Dubcek had given orders not to resist by force of arms, a decision promptly and strongly denounced by Communist China. Still, Dubcek hoped to be able to defeat the Soviet purpose of destroying the liberal reforms of the "Prague Spring" by uniting the party and denying the Soviets the collaboration of any party leader of first rank. The Fourteenth Extraordinary Party Congress was held immediately after the Soviet invasion and it elected a new central committee minus those leaders suspected of being compromisers, such as Bilak and Indra. The Soviets countered by bringing the recalcitrant Czechoslovak leaders, including Dubcek and President Svoboda, to Moscow and having them sign the "Moscow Protocols" of August 26, 1968. Though promising "noninterference" in Czechoslovak internal affairs, the Moscow Protocols, in fact, reduced the Czechoslovak government to little more than a puppet. The decisions of the Fourteenth Extraordinary Party Congress had to be declared null and void, the Czechoslovak government had to suppress "counterrevolutionary forces," censorship over the news media had to be reinstated, and government and party officials who were judged as having made "unacceptable" public statements had to be dismissed.

Zdenek Mlynar, former party secretary and a leading architect of the 1968 reforms, recounted the Moscow meeting between the Czechoslovaks and the Soviet Politburo. According to Mlynar, Brezhnev justified the invasion of August 1968 on the grounds that Czechoslovakia's borders, like those of the rest of Eastern Europe, were also those of the USSR, until "eternity." Dubcek was allowed to stay on as first secretary until mid-April 1969 when, following the anti-Soviet riots in the wake of the Czechoslovak ice-hockey victory over the USSR, he was replaced by Gustav Husak. Husak's assignment was to achieve "normalization" in Czechoslovakia, i.e., a state of mind and politics as though the events since August 1968 had been free of anything unusual or abnormal. To those who continued to assail him or his Soviet sponsors, Husak responded with the warning that if he failed, much worse was in store for Czechoslovakia.

Concerning foreign reaction to the Soviet invasion of Czechoslovakia, the situation of 1968 was both more complex and easier than that obtaining at the time of the Hungarian Revolution of 1956. The Soviet action of 1968 was bitterly assailed by Communist China, Yugoslavia, Rumania, and the large Communist parties of Italy and France. Italy's Communist leader Luigi Longo called the Soviet action a "tragic error." Albania formally quit the Warsaw Pact. Western reaction was largely neutralized by the ongoing Vietnam War, which Soviet propaganda used as a diversion, much as Khrushchev had employed the Suez crisis of 1956 as a cover for military intervention in Hungary.

25

Germany in the 1960s:
West Germany after Adenauer,
East Germany after the Wall

ADENAUER'S RETIREMENT

Adenauer's long term of office ended on a note of foreign disappointment and domestic blunder. In 1959, after the expiration of Theodor Heuss' second term as federal president, Adenauer had toyed with the idea of seeking the presidency himself. The effort was abandoned when he encountered serious opposition even among CDU faithfuls. In Adenauer's hands the West German presidency, limited under the 1949 constitution to a ceremonial role, might well have assumed the power and prestige of the French presidency under de Gaulle's Fifth Republic. A further blunder followed in 1960 when Adenauer, in an attempt to counter alleged left-wing tendencies in West German television news reporting, proposed to create a more progovernment, federally sponsored TV network. Mindful of the abuse of radio as a propaganda weapon under the Nazi regime, the SPD-controlled state governments of West Germany brought suit against the federal government in February 1961 and won their case before the supreme court.

In October 1962 Adenauer was accused of interfering with West German press freedom when ordering the arrest of editors of the news magazine *Der Spiegel*, for allegedly leaking classified defense secrets. The *Spiegel* affair prompted the resignation of defense minister F. J. Strauss, who had been the chief object of the magazine's attacks. The arrested editors had to be released and the charges of treason dropped. The Free Democrats temporarily quit the Adenauer coalition government and conditioned their return on the promise of Adenauer's early retirement. Abroad, Adenauer had seemingly crowned his historic achievement of Franco-German reconciliation with the signing of the Elysée treaty of January 1963. Before long, West Germany recognized the Elysée treaty less as a vehicle for the achievement of German equality than as an instrument of Gaullist hegemony in western Europe.

The unofficial Soviet-American truce, which had ended the twin crises of Cuba and Berlin in 1962, also raised questions about Adenauer's Eastern policy as a suitable basis for future West German–Soviet relations. The Berlin Wall had caused CDU/CSU voter strength to decline from 50.2 to 45.3 percent in the 1961 elections. The Adenauer era had fulfilled most of the short-term hopes and aspirations of the West German public of the late 1940s: prosperity, reconstruction, individual freedoms, security, and the rehabilitation of the German name after the horrors of the Nazi crimes. Few others in recent German history could claim to have accomplished so much in so little time after such universal devastation. Adenauer's life span covered a period of momentous change in European history and fortunes. He was born in the age of Bismarck and he left public office shortly before Khrushchev's fall in Russia. In between, his own native Germany had been both a major cause and a major victim of the collapse of the old European state system. The most astounding aspect of his role in German affairs was perhaps the optimism and confidence with which he assumed leadership after World War II, at an advanced age and amidst the physical and moral ruins left behind by the war.

The premises of West German foreign and domestic developments began to shift in the early 1960s, however, as indeed they did for much of the rest of the world, and the Adenauer formulas of the 1950s could no longer meet the requirements of the new age in all circumstances. Among the new premises was the appearance of a more restless and less docile young generation at home. Abroad, there were new strains in the western alliance as a result of global developments originating in Asia, and as a result of a new crisis in the European federalist idea. Against the background of these changes, West Germany had, above all else, to come to grips with the question of its own identity as a state not likely to achieve German reunification within the foreseeable future.

THE ERHARD INTERLUDE

Although Ludwig Erhard, widely identified with the "economic miracle" of the 1950s, ran a close second behind Adenauer in popular prestige, the outgoing chancellor had done his best to discourage Erhard's succession on the assumption that the latter's political gifts were not equal to his economic genius. At first, Erhard as chancellor seemed to disprove Adenauer's fears, because CDU/CSU strength increased in the 1965 elections from 45.3 to 47.6 percent under his leadership. Very soon, though, Erhard proved to be a luckless chief executive, unable to cope with a host of domestic and foreign policy problems.

The Erhard administration became engulfed by a serious economic recession, the first of its kind in West Germany since the beginning of the boom of the early 1950s. The rise in unemployment figures was quickly reflected in the gains of the SPD opposition, which won the state elections in the federal state of North Rhine–Westphalia. A more ominous signal of discontent was the rising strength of the National Democratic Party (NPD), which, its own denials notwithstanding, was widely regarded at home and abroad as neo-Nazi.

Foreign Policy

The economic anxieties of the mid-1960s were compounded by foreign policy failures in a number of areas. The brief Erhard administration from October 1963 to December 1966 coincided with the first stage of full-blown Gaullism in French foreign policy, which placed West Germany often enough in the middle of the French-American controversy. Adenauer's own growing intimacy with Gaullist France had been among the American motives in proposing a nuclear multilateral force (MLF) with prominent West German participation. Launched in the final stages of the Kennedy administration and in the last phase of Adenauer's chancellorship, the U.S.-sponsored MLF was designed to fulfil several purposes. In a strictly military sense, the MLF was to serve as a counterweight to Soviet medium-range missiles targeted on western Europe. The MLF was to be implemented through a NATO force of some twenty-five destroyer-size vessels, armed with two hundred medium-range missiles and manned by mixed NATO crews, including West German. The United States would retain a veto power over actual use of the MLF arsenal.

Politically, the MLF was meant to satisfy the West German yearning to share NATO's nuclear role. The West Germans also regarded the MLF as a possible bargaining chip in future negotiations with the Soviets, in which a West German renunciation of MLF membership could be traded for Soviet concessions on the reunification issue. The military importance of the MLF increased in West German estimation as a result of de Gaulle's quitting the NATO command in 1966 and his eviction of all U.S. nuclear warheads from French territory.

In return for U.S. cooperation on the nuclear issue, Erhard supported U.S. foreign policy positions in the face of de Gaulle's public criticism of such support. With the Sino-Soviet conflict going public in the early 1960s, West Germany would have liked to exploit it for its own ends by supporting Communist China. The Chinese Communist denunciation of Soviet rule in East Germany as a form of "colonial annexation" was clearly welcome in Bonn. Erhard wanted to develop economic and other contacts with Red China, and West German–Chinese negotiations towards that end were set to begin in Switzerland. In June 1964 President Johnson vetoed these contacts because of the expanding Vietnam conflict and China's adversary role vis-à-vis the United States. When the United States entered the Vietnam conflict on a large scale in 1965, Erhard publicly supported the American war effort, thereby exposing himself to the attacks of the West German New Left. Erhard similarly complied with U.S. requests for continuing West German purchases of U.S. military equipment to the tune of $2.5 billion, in order to offset U.S. troop expenses in West Germany. Against the background of these developments, President Johnson scrapped the MLF project suddenly in 1966 without prior consultation with the Bonn government. The American decision was prompted by the desire to reach agreement with the Soviet Union on the nuclear nonproliferation treaty, which was beng negotiated at the time. The American cancellation of the MLF undermined Erhard's prestige at home and materially contributed to his resignation from the chancellorship in 1966.

The strains in U.S.-West German relations were matched by similar strains in French-German relations. De Gaulle criticized and occasionally ridiculed Erhard for what he considered to be Erhard's excessive subservience to American wishes. At the same time, de Gaulle had issued statements on the question of reunification and had launched initiatives in Eastern Europe, which, from the specifically West German standpoint, were considered unhelpful or even unfriendly. Having recognized the Oder-Neisse line as far back as 1959, de Gaulle now publicly observed that the unification of Germany was not primarily a German concern but a concern of Germany's neighbors.

Eastern Europe

Regarding Communist Eastern Europe, Erhard and his foreign minister Gerhard Schröder (CDU) abandoned the sterile policy of boycott of the Adenauer years and tried to substitute a policy of rapprochement, supported by the incentive of West German economic aid. The ultimate aim of such a policy was to loosen up the Eastern bloc and to isolate both Communist East Germany and the Soviet Union from their East European allies. That Communist China was pursuing similar goals in Eastern Europe at the same time for reasons of its own, could only be helpful to the West German cause. The first steps towards the new Eastern policy had already been undertaken during the final months of Adenauer's term of office with the trade agreements of March, October, and November 1963 with Poland, Rumania, and Hungary respectively. At the beginning of 1966 Erhard addressed a "Peace Note" to the Communist bloc nations of Eastern Europe, which offered nonaggression pacts and the exchange of military observers with Warsaw Pact nations as a means of lessening tensions. Bonn's new approach to Eastern Europe registered its first significant gain with the establishment of full diplomatic relations with Rumania in January 1967, shortly after Erhard's resignation.

De Gaulle too embarked on a new policy towards Eastern Europe at the very time Erhard did, but his motive and purpose were not identical with those of West Germany. Where West Germany offered financial and economic inducements as a lever for political gain, de Gaulle offered similar benefits to both the Soviet Union and the satellites without attaching strings and for the chief purpose of demonstrating his independence from American leadership. The disarray of West German foreign policy since Adenauer's departure was reflected in the division of the CDU-CSU into "Atlanticists" and "Gaullists." The former continued to give priority to close relations with the United States, the latter, having become disillusioned with American leadership, put their hopes in de Gaulle and the Gaullist vision of a "European Europe." Erhard, Schröder, and Defense Minister Kai-Uwe von Hassel were counted among the Atlanticists, F. J. Strauss among the Gaullists.

The Social Democrats, though out of power, had also been strongly affected by foreign policy events since 1961. The Berlin Wall had had a similarly disillusioning effect on West Berlin SPD mayor Willy Brandt as the abortive East Berlin workers' uprising of June 17, 1953 had had on his predecessor Ernst Reuter. For Brandt, the lesson of August 13, 1961 seemed to be that given the permanence of the division of Germany, the people of East Germany and East Berlin were not going to be helped by an unchanged West German policy of confrontation. The people of East Germany had no choice in the nature of their government and that government was likely to remain Communist for a very long time indeed. In penalizing the Communist government of East Germany, West Germany was thus also penalizing the peoples of East Germany, who could no longer escape to freedom after August 1961. The task thus must be to ease the lot of East Germans through a policy of gradual rapprochement.

The basic elements of this reasoning were first publicly aired by Brandt's adviser Egon Bahr in his speech at the Lutheran Academy at Tutzing on July 15, 1963. Soon, the Tutzing speech would be remembered as a landmark which anticipated Brandt's new *Ostpolitik,* after Brandt's assumption of the chancellorship in 1969. Erhard's own coalition partner, the small FDP, also began to change its foreign policy views in a manner resembling those of the SPD. FDP chairman and vice-chancellor Erich Mende assailed Erhard for not having gone far enough in his attempt to normalize relations with the nations of Communist Eastern Europe. In its March 1965 party conference the FDP called for a modification of the Hallstein Doctrine in order to facilitate such a course. The FDP's withdrawal from the coalition in October 1966 prompted Erhard's own resignation from the chancellorship.

THE GRAND COALITION, 1966–1969

The Grand Coalition of CDU/CSU and SPD, which was formed under Chancellor Kurt Georg Kiesinger on December 1, 1966, was an unusual government, reflecting unusual circumstances in the history of the Federal Republic. After the resignation of Erhard, a coalition of SPD and FDP would have been feasible, both on the grounds of parliamentary arithmetic and with regard to a consensus on issues, especially those pertaining to foreign policy. Both parties had in fact collaborated in December 1966 on the replacement of state premier Meyers with SPD premier Kuhn in the big industrial state of North Rhine-Westphalia. An SPD-FDP coalition would have had a very small parliamentary majority, however, the SPD having received 39.3 percent and the FDP 9.5 percent of the vote in the elections of 1965.

The chief motive in forming the Grand Coalition in 1966 was, however, to protect West German democracy against what appeared at the time, because of the economic recession, a potentially serious threat, the frustration arising from an uncertain foreign policy and the existence of growing far Left and far Right extremism. Controlling 447 out of 496 *Bundestag* seats, the Grand Coalition seemed well equipped to handle any political crisis that might arise.

Kiesinger, who had a good administrative record as CDU premier of Baden-Württemberg, seemed a good compromise candidate for the chancellorship. His background in state, rather than national politics, had kept him out of the Atlanticist-Gaullist factional controversy of Bonn. Kiesinger's former membership in the Nazi party was a liability, though his cabinet also included a one-time prominent German Communist in the person of Herbert Wehner.

With the Grand Coalition, the SPD returned to national power in Germany for the first time since 1930. Nine out of nineteen ministerial posts went to the SPD, including the vice-chancellorship and foreign ministry under Willy Brandt. The Grand Coalition was most successful in attacking the economic crisis of 1966, which was largely overcome by 1968. For this, SPD economics minister Schiller and CSU finance minister Strauss could both justly claim credit. The economic recovery was particularly noteworthy in the export business, with industrial exports rising by 41 percent between March 1968 and March 1969 at the very time when economic developments in France, Britain and the United States entered a downward trend. The Grand Coalition was equally successful in barring political extremists from gaining entry into either state or federal legislatures. Although the neo-Nazi NPD had been elected to the state parliaments of Bavaria and Hesse, it failed to clear the 5 percent hurdle in the 1969 elections for entry into the *Bundestag.* After the 1972 elections, the NPD soon faded into oblivion.

The Communists and the New Left

The extreme Left appeared in West Germany in two forms. In 1969, a new West German Communist party constituted itself with the initials of DKP, and was generally regarded as a successor to the old KPD, which had been outlawed by the supreme court in Karlsruhe back in the 1950s. As a political factor, the DKP remained meaningless, never exceeding 3 percent in state elections and gaining a mere 0.3 percent in the 1972 federal elections. The extreme Left that mattered during the sixties was the New Left of the student body and its open and concealed sympathizers in university faculties, the publishing world, and part of the intellectual establishment. The West German student protest movement of the sixties was part of a larger international phenomenon; students were influenced by the writings of American and British New Left authors. Many of the roots of the student movement were native German, however. Prominent among these was the neglect of German higher education during the fifties, the autocratic structure of German universities, the limitation of regular parliamentary opposition to the small FDP and, more generally, the conflict between the youth of the sixties and the older generation. Among the causes of dissent in West German youth must also be counted a critical attitude towards the West German social reality of the sixties. To some, that reality had failed to fulfil the aspirations of the new "social humanism" that had been voiced before the beginning of the West German "economic miracle." The "economic miracle," to its critics, was based on the revival of prewar German capitalism without a basic change in social attitudes.

The older generation, having lived during the Hitler era, World War II, and the collapse of 1945 had, as a general rule, not spent much time or effort to explain its own role in these events to its children. The West German educational system had failed to act as a suitable parent substitute in this regard. Ignorance of twentieth-century European history, and of Germany's part in it in particular, was often appalling among West German youths, and continued to be so well into the 1970s. Paralleling similar developments in other parts of Western Europe and in the United States, the West German New Left quickly became a main center of agitation against U.S. policy in Vietnam, with the Free University of West Berlin student body in the lead.

The anti-American thrust of the West German student protest was quickly seized upon by influential neutral-nationalist publications such as the newsmagazine *Der Spiegel*. To Rudolf Augstein, *Spiegel* publisher, the United States became for West Germany an "ally suffered only with nausea."

As a political factor, the student radicals remained unimportant. As a social factor generating considerable publicity and occasional violence, the student radicals polarized West German society and introduced a new element into its fabric that was in sharp contrast to the optimism of the fifties. The self-styled "extraparliamentary opposition," or "APO" in its German initials, of student radicals also became the recruiting ground for West German terrorists of the 1970s, such as Ulrike Meinhof, editor-in-chief of the left-wing paper *Konkret*.

Foreign Policy

In the realm of foreign policy, the Grand Coalition failed to develop a coherent alternative to Erhard's muddled course of 1964–1965. In part, this was the inevitable result of basic foreign policy disagreements between the coalition partners CDU-CSU and SPD, whose prime motive for entering into a common government had been concern over domestic stability. Brandt, as foreign minister, was prepared to drop the Hallstein Doctrine as a cornerstone of West German foreign policy and he specifically called for the recognition of the Oder-Neisse line in the 1968 SPD party conference at Nürnberg. The imminent scrapping of the Hallstein Doctrine was, in fact, suggested by the establishment of diplomatic relations with Rumania in 1967 and the reestablishment of full relations with Yugoslavia in January 1968, both of which also continued to maintain full relations with Communist East Germany. Brandt and CSU finance minister F. J. Strauss sharply disagreed over the significance of the nuclear nonproliferation treaty, which was signed on July 1, 1968 by the United States, Britain and the Soviet Union. Brandt had no reservations about West Germany's adhering to the pact, while Strauss denounced the treaty as a "super-Versailles" that would permanently discriminate against West Germany as a nonmanufacturer of nuclear weapons.

Kiesinger's attempt to restore close relations with Gaullist France was only moderately successful because of de Gaulle's assault on the long-term goals of the EEC during the Common Market crisis of 1966. French-German relations took a new turn for the worse in connection with the French monetary crisis of 1968 in the wake of the Paris May riots and the serious social and political disturbance that followed. At the Bonn meeting of finance ministers of the non-Communists world's ten leading industrial powers in November 1968, West Germany refused to revalue its currency in compliance with the wishes of France, Britain and the United States. This cast West Germany in an adversary relation to her principal Western allies just when the Soviet invasion of Czechoslovakia of August 1968 had raised West German security concerns to new heights.

Soviet Relations

The Soviet stand on Germany had, if anything, hardened since Khrushchev's fall in 1964. While West German ambassador to Moscow, Kroll had still entertained hopes that Khrushchev might be amenable to a special deal at East Germany's expense, the new Brezhnev-Kosygin team left no doubt as to the clarity and aim of its German policy. Erhard's "Peace Note" of 1966 had been answered by the Soviet demand for West German recognition of East Germany and the renunciation of nuclear arms as a sign of West German sincerity. The Soviets had followed West German initiatives in Eastern Europe with mounting suspicion in 1967, and *Pravda* signaled its protest in 1968 over Kiesinger's statement that the aim of West German foreign policy must be to change the status quo in Europe while the Soviet aim was to preserve it. Thus the Soviet invasion of Czechoslovakia of August 1968 was also intended to squash West German initiatives in Eastern Europe hostile to Soviet interests. Significantly, the Soviet government reminded West Germany as early as November 1967 of the unchanged relevance of articles 53 and 107 of the UN charter, which excluded the "enemy states" of World War II from the procedures and provisions of the UN charter. The Soviets had invoked both articles before in the context of the 1948 Berlin blockade and the issue of German POWs in 1950. The 1967 Soviet note reminded West Germany that it could not claim for itself the same position as other European states because of the absence of a formal peace treaty. In Bonn this was interpreted as a thinly-veiled Soviet threat of intervention even in the affairs of West Germany, because West Germany qualified still as an "enemy state" in the Soviet definition.

After the Soviet invasion of Czechoslovakia of August 1968, the West German government sought assurances from its western allies that they did not share the Soviet interpretation of articles 53 and 107. The replies were not what West Germany had hoped for, because West German relations with the three major western powers were themselves strained for the reasons described. Britain answered that the "enemy state" clauses of the UN charter were "in this situation" irrelevant, France replied that the Soviet interpretation was "abusive" and "imprecise," and the United States informed Bonn that the relevant articles did not give the Soviet Union the right of "unilateral" intervention. None of the western powers said what Bonn most wanted to hear: that existing NATO defense commitments to West Germany outweighed any other legal formula that the Soviets might wish to produce to intimidate or threaten West Germany.

The Soviet invasion of Czechoslovakia left Bonn's Eastern policy of the mid-sixties in shambles and it enhanced West Germany's sense of isolation. The fear of isolation was further strengthened by the withdrawal of 75,000 U.S., British and Belgian troops in 1967. The United States promised to airlift reinforcements back to Germany in an emergency, but the Soviets had successfully demonstrated their ability to rush twenty divisions in almost total secrecy into the heart of Europe in a matter of days, altering thereby the strategic balance which had existed in central Europe virtually unchanged since the 1940s. From the West German standpoint, the most significant aspect of the Soviet occupation of Czechoslovakia in 1968 was the loss of a warning period, in the event of a Soviet attack on West Germany. Prior to August 1968, the Soviet Union would have had to concentrate its military forces in Czechoslovakia, a neighbor of West Germany, before invading West Germany herself. After August 1968, Soviet forces were poised against West Germany not only in the old bases of East Germany, but in Czechoslovakia as well. This new military fact had a very strong effect on West German foreign policy before very long.

The Reunification Issue

The *Bundestag* Declaration of September 25, 1968 was an attempt to uphold and reaffirm the principles upon which the policy of reunification had been based. The declaration stressed the unchanged resolve to uphold the right of national self-determination as the basis of all West German foreign policy dealings. It repeated the claim that the Bonn government was the only government in Germany freely elected and lawfully constituted. The declaration lastly rejected the recognition of the "other part of Germany" as a sovereign state. In fact, the Soviet thrust into Czechoslovakia, and the western acquiescence in that move, put an end to the illusion of change in the German status quo which West German governments had continued to uphold well into the late 1960s and long after the other western powers had lost any real interest. It remained for the new Social Democratic–Liberal coalition under Chancellor Brandt, which was formed after the 1969 *Bundestag* elections, to break with past illusions and fit policy to the altered circumstances of the post-1968 period.

East Germany after the Wall

Many of those who were young or enterprising enough to leave Communist East Germany before 1961 had done so. Those who had not, had often acted from a sense of loyalty to the land, their home, not out of a sense of allegiance to a regime they had not chosen. The population that had stayed behind was overaged, much more so than that of West Germany. With 19 percent of the people at retirement age, East Germany carried a heavy social burden.

By 1961, East and West Germany had been kept apart under different social and economic systems for a sufficient length of time to have developed very different social attitudes and a very different physical appearance, despite their common German nationality. The scars of World War II were still very much visible in East Germany, and it was possible to move through East Berlin for miles amidst the uncleared bomb-debris, as though the war had ended only yesterday. The East German regime developed, with what limited resources it possessed, would-be Communist show places like Stalin Avenue, renamed Karl Marx Avenue, and the downtown East Berlin Alexander Platz, an area of dubious social distinction before the war. The monotonous, Moscow-style apartment blocks of Stalin Avenue, reserved for the SED party faithful, were built of such poor material, however, that the tile facing had fallen off in many places soon after completion of the project.

East German refugees, on the other hand, though familiar with the affluent West German consumer society through their exposure to West German television programs, once they had begun to settle in West Germany often complained of the lack of social altruism and the preoccupation with personal gain they found there. The wall had a significant impact on the East German economy because long-term planning and projections became possible only after the future availability of labor became a calculable factor. Ulbricht was carried away with his own optimistic forecasts when boasting to Khrushchev in 1963 that East Germany would soon be overtaking West Germany in economic progress. The East German economy, in Ulbricht's words, would become sufficiently attractive even to West Germans to make them wish to move eastwards. Although these were exaggerated boasts, East Germany made remarkable economic progress during the decade from 1961 to 1971 and East Germany could justly claim to have accomplished an "economic miracle" of its own. Economic progress rested, in part, on the adoption of more enlightened management techniques in industry, which were announced in January 1963 at the sixth SED conference under the name of "New Economic System of Planning and Directing the National Economy" (NÖS).

The NÖS

Among NÖS innovations was also a major reform of industrial prices along more realistic lines. As a result, state subsidies to industry could be cut from 13.5 to 7.5 billion East German marks. NÖS even contained consumer-oriented features such as the establishment of an institute for market research in Leipzig. The Central Institute for Socialist Economic Leadership, an affiliate of the SED central committee, provided modern managment-training facilities. Academic research was closely coordinated with relevant branches of industry, as in the case of Rostock University and Rostock shipyards, Schiller University and the Jena Zeiss optical works, and the Leuna synfuel industry and the Merseburg Chemical Institute.

NÖS, despite its great success, failed to live up to its full potential for economic and political reasons. Foremost among economic reasons were the unfavorable terms of trade with the Soviet Union, from which East Germany, a country with a narrow soft-coal energy base, received virtually all its energy. Under the 1965 East German–Soviet trade agreement, East Germany pledged to deliver 339 ships, many of them ocean-going fishing vessels, over 8,000 railroad cars, 100,000 tons of rolling mill equipment, and many other items valued at a total of 60 billion East German marks. Erich Apel, NÖS coauthor and chief economics administrator, committed suicide after signing the 1965 trade agreement. In the same year, East Germany assumed additional commercial commitments to its *Comecon* partners Poland, Czechoslovakia, and Bulgaria to the tune of 27 billion marks for the delivery of textile, sugar refining, electrical equipment, and cement factories.

Moreover, in a futile bid to outmaneuver the Hallstein Doctrine in Third World countries, East Germany offered increasing foreign aid to such countries as Egypt, Syria and Ghana, which received 336 million, 100 million and 80 million marks respectively during the 1965–1966 period alone.

The principal political reason behind NÖS frustration was familiar enough to other Communist nations during the sixties. The entrenched SED bureaucracy, which knew little of economics, feared the power and prestige of the professional technocrats. By 1967 Ulbricht himself was forced to replace NÖS with the "Economic System of Socialism" (ÖSS), which restored some of the economic power of the party bureaucrats. The shift was quickly reflected at the SED top, with the technocrats Günter Mittag and Werner Jarowinsky falling behind party stalwart Erich Honecker among Politburo members likely to succeed Ulbricht. The economic achievement of the sixties remained impressive nonetheless. By the early 1970s, East Germany was producing in six weeks as much as it had produced in an entire year in 1949. Between 1949 and 1973 the GNP increased sixfold, foreign trade multiplied twentyfold. By 1969 East Germany produced as much in ten months as all of Hitler's Germany had produced in a whole year before World War II. East Germany, a country the size of the state of Ohio, had become the tenth largest industrial nation of the world, occupying a place between Canada and Italy. On a per capita basis, the East German GNP exceeded that of Great Britain. East Germany was the USSR's chief *Comecon* trading partner and the most prosperous nation in the Communist bloc.

Life in East Germany

East German living standards continued to lag considerably behind those of West Germany, regardless. The areas of chief neglect were housing, highway construction, mass transit and also consumer durables, especially automobiles. Refrigerators and appliances, often enough in short supply in East Germany, were frequently sold to West Germany, where they were marketed without identifying labels of origin. The Dresden-based computer industry, which Ulbricht claimed would enable East Germany to overtake West Germany without having to "catch up" to her first, failed to live up to expectations. The social benefits for the old remained meager. Old-age pensions were raised somewhat in 1968, and the five-day workweek was introduced for every other week. The quality of East German life continued to suffer for other reasons also. East Germany's new criminal code of 1968, prepared by justice minister Hilde Benjamin—better known as "Red Hilda"—threatened severe penalties for "political crimes," including "antistate propaganda." These provisions assumed special significance during the mass arrests of young people in connection with riots and rock concerts in East Berlin during the coming decade.

Religion

The relationship between state and church, especially the predominant Lutheran church, continued to be uneasy after the SED had unsuccessfully attempted to split the Lutheran clergy during the 1950s by launching the pro-Communist "Faith and Conscience" movement. Wherever possible, the SED tried to substitute socialist ceremonies for church rites at births, weddings, and funerals. State-church relations improved somewhat under Ulbricht's successor Honecker during the seventies and early eighties, especially in conjunction with the East German and worldwide observation of the five-hundredth anniversary of Luther's birth in 1983.

Culture

In the realm of cultural policy, an era of new repression began in 1965 after a relatively liberal interlude between 1961–1965. As of 1965 Honecker, Ulbricht's heir apparent, once more inveighed against "scepticism," "pessimism" and the pursuit of "abstract truth" among East German intellectuals. In 1966, well-known writers such as Stefan Heym, Werner Braunig, Peter Hacks and Manfred Bieler, were especially singled out for criticism. In 1966 Robert Havemann, a dissident since the 1950s was expelled from the Academy of Sciences, and Wolf Biermann, the singer, eventually stripped of his East German citizenship, appeared for the first time on the East German list of potential troublemakers. In 1966 Ulbricht once again invoked the "Bitterfeld-way" of socialist realism of the 1950s. The cultural crackdown of the mid-to-late 1960s clearly reflected the anxiety of the ever vigilant Ulbricht to prevent developments in "his" DDR from following the dangerous example of neighboring Czechoslovakia.

Ulbricht Resigns

On May 3, 1971 Ulbricht resigned as SED first party secretary. The resignation, which surprised many in the west, was Soviet-inspired and reflected both Soviet displeasure and Soviet pragmatism. Despite his undeniable achievements and unquestioned loyalty, Ulbricht may well have annoyed the Soviets with the cult of his own personality, which, even in the homeland of the personality cult, may have been judged excessive. Before 1971 the face and name of Ulbricht was to be seen and heard everywhere in East Germany, and Ulbricht often boasted of the achievements of "his DDR." As a Cold War relic, remembered in West Germany with bitterness because of the events of June 17, 1953 and because of the inhumanity of the wall, Ulbricht had become a liability for the Soviets, once they had decided on a friendlier course in dealing with the new West German Brandt government. By the time of his death on August 1, 1973, Ulbricht had become, in his own country, an "unperson."

26

De Gaulle
and the Fifth Republic

THE CONSTITUTION OF THE FIFTH REPUBLIC

The Algerian crisis and the disturbances it provoked in France revealed how little progress had been made towards overcoming inner divisions. These were aggravated by the bitterness over the long and futile colonial wars which France had been fighting since 1946. Once again, there existed a national sense of failure, as there did at the end of the 1930s, despite the respectable economic gains achieved under the Fourth Republic.

Before turning his full attention to Algeria, de Gaulle drafted the constitution of the new republic, aided by his longtime aide and follower Michael Debré, now the minister of justice. The constitution would not only provide the framework for the new government in accordance with de Gaulle's own, well-known philosophy, but it would also be a statement and a message to the outside world about the coming power and determination of the Fifth Republic. As such, the new constitution might, in itself, assist in the solution of the Algerian crisis and it might make France's allies more willing to comply with de Gaulle's foreign policy wishes. The constitution was also meant to safeguard France against the recurrence of past crises and disasters, such as befell the Third Republic in 1940.

In theory, the constitution of Fifth Republic was a synthesis between a parliamentary and a presidential system. The president, chosen by indirect election through an electoral college of some 100,000 local counsellors, appointed the prime minister and had power to dissolve the legislative assembly and to appeal to the voters directly through referendum. Article 16, conferring on the president special emergency powers, reflected both the recent experience of near-civil war in May 1958 and the more distant tragedy of June 1940, when the Third Republic succumbed to the German invasion. Article 16 was also drafted with an eye to the possibility of future nuclear war, with its demand for exceptional powers to deal with exceptional emergencies.

Debré wished to give the prime minister real stature, rather than make him the mere message-carrier of the powerful president. Ideally, the prime minister was to be both a link and a buffer between president and legislature. The parliamentary feature of the constitution consisted chiefly in the fact that parliament could overthrow the prime minister by a censure vote. In order to avoid abuse of that power, the procedure for a censure vote was rendered more difficult. A censure motion had to be signed by at least one-tenth of the Assembly with forty-eight hours elapsing between the original motion and a full vote. Members of Parliament were limited to a single censure motion for each half-yearly session of the Assembly. The Senate had no powers of censure.

The role of Parliament, previously central to the political systems of the Third and Fourth Republic, was diminished in many direct and indirect ways. The legislative sessions were shorter, and the number of members of both the Assembly and of the Senate was reduced. Members of Parliament were given no staffs of their own, and opportunities to question government policy were limited.

Actual constitutional practice, as developed soon after the adoption of the new constitution, further shifted the emphasis towards the presidency. The president not only appointed the prime ministers of the Fifth Republic, but he also dismissed them, though the constitution was quite explicit in not giving him such authority. Eventually, de Gaulle's prime ministers Pompidou and Couve de Murville did not even bother to seek a parliamentary vote of approval upon being appointed by the president. Moreover, de Gaulle changed the election procedure for the presidency from indirect to direct popular vote in 1962 simply through referendum, without seeking prior parliamentary approval, which the constitution expressly required for constitutional amendments.

Presidential influence over the judiciary was also enhanced compared to the Fourth Republic, through the institution of the High Council of the Judiciary. Composed of the president, the minister of justice and nine other members of the president's own choice, the High Council appointed the judges of France.

The Constitutional Council passed on the constitutionality of laws, amendments and treaties. It lacked any powers of independent initiative, however, being able to act only on appeal of the president, the prime minister or the presidents of either legislative body. In practice, the Constitutional Council quickly developed into a presidential watchdog over the legislature. During de Gaulle's tenure from 1958 to 1969 the council never once rendered an unfavorable decision against the presidency in a major case, though it did so against the legislature. The council did not develop into anything comparable to the U.S. Supreme Court, and its prestige was never very high under de Gaulle because of its subservience to the presidency.

De Gaulle often ignored the independence of the judiciary in conjunction with the special courts which were created for the treason trials of rebellious officers during the Algerian war. In one instance, de Gaulle disbanded a special court he had recently created because the court's withholding the death penalty from General Salan displeased him. The Court of State Security for crimes against the state, created under the special conditions of the Algerian war, became a permanent institution, chiefly concerned with espionage cases, until disbanded by François Mitterand after his election to the presidency in 1981.

De Gaulle's constitutional practice reflected his own superior faith in people rather than institutions. To the extent that the constitution was his own creation, he felt free to interpret it according to his own needs and views, without undue regard for the opinion of constitutional lawyers or political leaders.

The 1958 Referendum

The constitutional draft of the Fifth Republic was overwhelmingly endorsed by referendum in September 1958, with 17.7 million *yes* and 4.6 million *no* votes. The *no* vote was smaller by a million than the Communist vote alone had been in the last parliamentary election of the Fourth Republic in 1956. The size of the majority surprised everyone, the Gaullists included.

The first parlimentary elections of November 1958 confirmed the results of the September referendum. The Gaullist Union for the New Republic (UNR) obtained 200 seats, against 140 seats for the SFIO, the MRP, the Radicals and the Communists combined.

The Communists, though getting 3.8 million votes, ended up with a meager ten seats under the new majority voting system.

The first impression of both elections seemed to be that de Gaulle had routed the old republican parties. When his new prime minister, Michael Debré, presented himself to the Assembly in January 1959, he obtained a confidence vote of 435 against 56 with 29 abstentions.

The election results emboldened de Gaulle to launch an austerity program in December 1958, implemented by finance minister Antoine Pinay through the so-called Pinay-Rueff Plan. The Pinay-Rueff Plan was designed to restore the franc to a sound footing and to combat the balance of payments deficit, which had climbed to $300 million by 1958. The measures included a 20 percent devaluation, tax increases, and economies in many areas.

Although the Pinay-Rueff Plan produced the desired results in the currency and foreign trade picture, it also alienated many of de Gaulle's early supporters. The beneficiaries were the old republican parties, which did surprisingly well again in the municipal and Senate elections of early 1959. Both these elections set a pattern. The Senate became the new bastion of old party politicians, and the Gaullists never succeeded in capturing the Senate majority.

De Gaulle's early foreign policy initiatives likewise caused disappointment. His proposal of September 1958 to reorganize the leadership of the Atlantic alliance through a three-power directorate of France, Britain and the United States, evoked no response from either the United States or Britain. Though de Gaulle was not yet free to launch a foreign policy openly hostile to the United States and Britain, because of the unsolved problem of Algeria, he showed his displeasure by such acts as French withdrawal from NATO naval command in 1959.

ALGERIA

If de Gaulle had hoped to pressure the Algerian FLN into a speedy settlement by a demonstration of his personal popularity in France, he was soon disappointed. It is clear that de Gaulle opened his Algerian policy with the hope of retaining French influence in Algeria in some form, though he knew from the start that Moslem interests would have to be served more generously than seemed acceptable to French *colons*. A "privileged relationship" with Algeria might at least preserve French access to Algeria's recently discovered oil and natural gas, and it might enable France to maintain its nuclear test facilities in the Sahara desert.

The Colons

De Gaulle's first move was not directed at the FLN but at the troublesome European minority in Algeria, whose uprising had brought him to power. On the one hand, de Gaulle reassured the *colons* during his first trip to Algeria on June 4, 1958 with the words, "I have understood you." On the other hand, he stripped the *colons* of independent power by denying the committees of public safety any authority, by transferring General Salan out of Algeria, and by dividing power in Algeria between the Resident General and the military command.

The political parties in France did not, for the most part, cause serious trouble for de Gaulle's Algerian policy, even when that policy moved towards abandonment under the force of circumstances. George Bidault of the MRP, who had at first actively supported de Gaulle's return to power, turned into a bitter enemy over Algeria, but his hostility was not shared by the rest of the party. Jacques Soustelle, representing the right wing of de Gaulle's own UNR, was to do likewise, but the majority of the party, including Prime Minister Debré, placed personal loyalty to de Gaulle above its call for a French Algeria.

De Gaulle's first attempt to persuade the FLN to lay down its arms, through a policy of flattery, failed. His offer of a "peace of the brave" of October 23, 1958 was answered by the FLN's announcement of a Provisional Government of the Algerian Republic (GPRA). De Gaulle's second approach of searching for a rival Algerian nationalist force with which to conclude a compromise settlement, likewise failed when it was shown that no such force existed. By September 16, 1959 de Gaulle began to speak of "Algerian self-determination," which could be achieved either through total independence, through "integration," or through "association." It was the latter that de Gaulle hoped to achieve, leaving France in control of Algerian defense and foreign policy.

Sensing betrayal by their former idol, the *colons* and their right-wing allies in the army and the political parties mobilized their opposition. General Massu assailed de Gaulle's Algerian policy in an interview in the West German newspaper *Süddeutsche Zeitung* in January 1960, which prompted his dismissal. Massu's ouster, in turn, sparked the anti-Gaullist demonstrations in Algiers during the "Incident of the Barricades" between January 25 and February 1, 1960.

De Gaulle responded by purging the army of unreliable paratroopers in Algeria, while reaffirming his own commitment to the "most French" solution of the Algerian problem. At the same time, he used the "Incident of the Barricades" to toughen his stand opposite the FLN. When talks were begun with the FLN at Melun in June 1960, de Gaulle refused either to recognize the GPRA or to agree to an armistice conditioned on French recognition of Algerian independence. The French public expected the Melun talks to produce results, and it responded with disappointment when the Melun talks collapsed. During de Gaulle's last visit to Algeria in December 1960, both the hostility of the *colons* and the solid Moslem support for the FLN were evident.

The Decision to Withdraw

By the turn of 1960–1961, de Gaulle knew that the majority of the French public shared his own conclusion that the Algerian war had become a "bottomless swamp." It was the Algerian swamp that paralyzed French energies and prevented them from undertaking a sweeping modernization of the economic system at home, and from asserting French hegemonial claims in western Europe. Once the decision to withdraw from Algeria had been made in de Gaulle's own mind, the enemy was the enemy within, *colons* and their right-wing army allies. To defeat this enemy politically, de Gaulle used the weapon of the referendum, with which he had outmaneuvered other foes in France in other circumstances. In the referendum of January 8, 1961 on Algerian self-determination, 15.2 million voted *yes,* 5 million *no.*

Revolt of the Army

Not unexpectedly, the diehard army opposition revolted, with generals Salan, Challe, Jouhaud, and Zeller seizing power in Algiers on April 22, 1961. Predictably, the attempt to reenact the events of May 1958 failed, because of the prestige of Charles de Gaulle, the constitutional safeguards of article 16 of the Fifth Republic, and the generally altered state of public opinion, which no longer considered victory in Algeria worth the cost. By April 25, 1961 Challe and Zeller surrendered. Others went underground to join the terrorist Secret Army Organization (OAS), which very nearly succeeded in assassinating de Gaulle at Petit Clamart on August 22, 1962. In Algeria itself, French terrorism claimed the lives of an additional 12,000 Moslems before the war was officially over.

Algerian Independence

The final agreement, concluded at Evian on March 18, 1962, though granting Algeria independence, also safeguarded certain French interests. The last French troops were not to be withdrawn for another three years and the naval base at Mers-el-Kebir was to be leased to France for another fifteen years. Oil exploration was to be carried out jointly, and France would retain control over her nuclear testing facilities. *Colons* would have free choice in their citizenship, with full protection of civil and property rights if they chose to remain French citizens. Having no faith in the settlement, most *colons* settled as refugees in France. The Fifth Republic, in one of its most successful and least advertised social programs, resettled a total of 800,000 *colons* in metropolitan France. *Colon* bitterness towards de Gaulle persisted and expressed itself in both sporadic terrorist attacks and a consistent anti-Gaullist voting record.

A great many human lives would have been saved on either side had de Gaulle withdrawn from Algeria at the beginning of his presidency. Public support for an early withdrawal did not exist, however, in 1958, and it developed to the degree necessary only after the attempt to salvage French power had been made and had been demonstrated to be prohibitive in human and political cost. That de Gaulle managed to turn a defeat into a personal political asset by broadening the powers of the presidency in the course of managing the Algerian crisis was no small tribute to his political genius and the power of his personality.

THE CONSOLIDATION OF PRESIDENTIAL POWERS

Among the leaders of the old republican parties there was hope after the Evian agreement that de Gaulle, having helped his country in surmounting a national crisis, would once again step down and retire from public office as he had done in 1946. France could then return to politics as usual under the Fourth Republic. De Gaulle's own supporters, on the other hand, urged him to exploit his current popularity and hold new parliamentary elections. De Gaulle followed neither course.

With the Algerian war settled, de Gaulle concentrated on the regaining of a French Great Power position abroad and the modernization of French society at home. These goals he wished to achieve not in partnership with the old political parties, or indeed any party, but through the powers of an expanded presidency. Accordingly, he dismissed Debré who, as prime minister, had favored a division of powers between the "reserved areas" of the presidency, chiefly defense and foreign policy, and the prime minister's domain of day-to-day business in social and economic matters. At the same time, de Gaulle strengthened the presidency by changing the presidential elections from indirect to direct. The change was affected by referendum of October 28, 1962 with 13 million *yes* and 8 million *no* votes. This was a smaller majority than de Gaulle had achieved in his two previous referenda of 1958 and 1961. The change of the presidential election procedure by referendum was, strictly speaking, unconstitutional, because the constitution of the Fifth Republic required the consent of Parliament for such a change. Before the October referendum, Parliament, in fact, passed a vote of censure against Prime Minister Pompidou, Debré's successor, with 280 out of 480 votes. De Gaulle replied by dissolving the Assembly and holding new elections in November 1962. By tying the parliamentary elections to the issue of presidential powers, de Gaulle fought the elections on a ground of his own choosing and under conditions favorable to himself. Public sympathy was on his side after the several OAS assassination attempts of 1962. With 250 seats, the Gaullists and their allies registered a gain of 60 seats since the elections of November 1958. With the support of Giscard d'Estaing's Independent Republicans, the Gaullists had Parliament well under control. Both the referendum of October and the elections of November 1962 confirmed that the Fifth Republic was here to stay.

DEFENSE AND FOREIGN STRATEGY

For a man of de Gaulle's personalized vision of history, foreign policy was no doubt influenced by the memory of the personal slights which he must certainly have suffered at the hands of the American president in World War II. To interpret de Gaulle's foreign policy simply as an act of revenge would be mistaken, however. Rather, de Gaulle viewed the 1960s as a period of opportunity for affecting major changes in the European balance. France must exploit these opportunities before they passed into history without the likelihood of a return.

The possibility of change, in de Gaulle's view, derived from the fact that Asia had revealed the limits of superpower influence. With the United States bogged down in the Vietnam War and the Soviets no longer able to conceal their fury at Communist China, Europe might enjoy the first relaxation of superpower dominance since 1945. The Cuban missile crisis too had had its positive effects for Europe. Having backed away from a nuclear confrontation with the United States in the Caribbean, the Soviets were not likely to seek another one soon in Europe. As the likelihood of a Soviet armed attack on western Europe diminished, so did the urgency of U.S. military support, and with it, the weight of U.S. political power.

A "European Europe"

De Gaulle intended to exploit the new opportunities of the sixties by dismantling the blocs into which the Cold War had divided Europe. Originally, Gaullist France had sought a larger role in the leadership of the western alliance with de Gaulle's offer of a three-power directorate in 1958. As the United States and Britain had ignored the offer, they had refused to pay a special price for keeping France inside NATO command. The Soviets might now reward France for moving out of it. As de Gaulle lessened American influence in western Europe, the Soviets might reciprocate by loosening their grip on Eastern Europe. A new relationship between Europe and the Soviets might develop via détente into an entente based on mutual interests. Europe would regain a new identity and a sense of cultural independence, as a "European Europe," "*l'Europe Européenne.*"

The center of the new "European Europe" would be the Paris-Bonn axis, which in turn would be under French control. To de Gaulle, the Germans were not only not a threat to France, but, for the first time in the twentieth century, an asset. West Germany was economically strong but politically weak, because of the German division and Berlin, and it was morally sensitive on account of the horrors of the recent Nazi past.

De Gaulle may have found the prospect of reorganizing Europe under French leadership and without the interference of the United States and Britain an exhilarating one. He was old enough to remember the many times when France had had to bow to the pressure of Britain, the United States, or both. Many of de Gaulle's generation believed that there might not have been war in 1914 if Britain had declared her intentions in July, rather than on August 4, 1914. In 1919 it had been the United States and Britain which restrained France from writing a tough peace, without offering tangible guarantees of security in return. In 1923 France was forced to abandon the Ruhr policy under joint U.S. and British pressure. In the 1930s, France no longer dared take unilateral action against Germany, with the result that Hitler got away with his occupation of the Rhineland.

During the 1960s, on the other hand, there was little that either the United States or Britain could do to restrain France. Britain needed French goodwill to get into the EEC, which de Gaulle pointedly refused in 1963 and 1967. The United States could not punish de Gaulle for pulling out of NATO command in 1966, because it could not do without French cooperation in a real war crisis in Europe.

The "European Europe" which de Gaulle pursued was not the federated Europe, envisaged by the 1957 Rome treaty. Instead, it was a Europe composed of completely sovereign states, bound together by traditional alliances under overall French leadership. Political integration, to de Gaulle, was a "utopian myth."

De Gaulle and the EEC

While wishing to retain the economic aspects of EEC, de Gaulle deliberately set out to wreck its political purpose by proposing alternate schemes in the so-called Fouchet plans between 1960 and 1962, named after his adviser Christian Fouchet.

The first Fouchet plan proposed a "council of six," composed of the heads of government of the EEC nations, without a commitment to supranationality. The second Fouchet plan asked for the transfer of important economic functions from existing EEC institutions to the "council of six."

De Gaulle secured the tentative agreement of the leaders of West Germany and Italy, Adenauer and Prime Minister Amintore Fanfani, to the Fouchet reorganization schemes, though both men fully appreciated de Gaulle's purpose of destroying supranationality. Both men thought West European cooperation in any form better than none at all, however, especially in view of the tense situation involving the abortive Eisenhower-Khrushchev summit at Paris in 1960 and the Berlin-Cuba crisis of 1962.

Significantly, the Fouchet plan was thwarted by the small EEC powers Holland and Belgium, whose foreign ministers Joseph Luns and Paul Henri Spaak deadlocked the EEC conference at Luxembourg of March 20, 1962. Just as Holland and Belgium had revived the sagging spirit of European integration between 1955 and 1957, they refused to help bury it in the Gaullist 1960s.

What remained of de Gaulle's reorganization scheme for Western Europe was the much more limited bilateral French-German Elysée treaty of January 1963.

Having failed to replace the EEC with his own scheme, de Gaulle wished at least to neutralize the supranational aspects of the EEC, such as majority voting in the EEC Council of Ministers. De Gaulle's attack on majority voting, which was about to go into effect in 1966, resulted in a head-on collision between France and the other five EEC members. The 1966 EEC crisis was compounded by disagreements over community financing of a Common Agricultural Policy (CAP), whose principal beneficiary would be France. EEC Commission president Walter Hallstein of West Germany had proposed a compromise plan in 1965, which combined a new CAP system favorable to France with a strengthening of the Commission's powers towards supranationality. De Gaulle not only rejected the Hallstein plan but recalled all French staffs from the institutions of EEC, EURATOM and ECSC, in direct violation of the rules under the 1957 Rome treaty. De Gaulle's boycott, which was soon dubbed the policy of the "empty chairs," was more in the nature of a tantrum, rather than a final French farewell to the Common Market, as many feared at the time. A compromise was reached with the Luxembourg agreement of January 1967, which gave France the favorable CAP settlement it could have had without the "empty chairs." Although de Gaulle failed to alter the terms of the Rome treaty pertaining to majority voting, he succeeded in curtailing their effectiveness. Henceforth, unanimity was to be sought on important issues before an actual vote count in the EEC Council of Ministers. Most important, the entire EEC crisis of 1965–1966 had dampened the spirit of the European federalists, thanks to de Gaulle's opposition, and it had rendered the goal of European integration once again abstract, academic, and improbable.

As for Soviet Russia, it warmly applauded de Gaulle's attacks on U.S. policy, including that in Vietnam, without sacrificing a single interest of its own. The Soviet invasion of Czechoslovakia in August 1968 thus shattered de Gaulle's illusion of a Europe united "from the Atlantic to the Urals," which the Soviets had previously tolerated in silence. Even before the Czechoslovak crisis, de Gaulle had seen himself by-passed on major international developments. France had had no say in the Arab-Israeli war of June 1967, nor in the July 1967 meeting at Glassboro between President Johnson and Soviet premier Kosygin. Increasingly, de Gaulle's outbursts betrayed his frustration, as when he sharply assailed Israel in the wake of the 1967 war, or when he took up the battle cry of French-Canadian separatists, *"Vive la Québec libre!"* during his 1967 official state visit to Canada.

The French Nuclear Program

The practical results of de Gaulle's Great Power posturing were meager when compared with the great expense of his nuclear armaments program, which was an essential part of his foreign policy design. Following up on preparations made by the outgoing Fourth Republic, the Fifth Republic exploded its first nuclear bomb on February 13, 1960 at Reggane in the Sahara. Eight years later she exploded her first thermonuclear device in Polynesia. Both the nuclear program and the building of a delivery system, including solid-fuel medium-range missiles and nuclear-powered submarines, were undertaken without American help. The cost of nuclear arms increased the French defense budget to 5 percent of GNP by 1966–1967, forcing economies in other areas, including social spending and education. The student riots of May 1968, which very nearly toppled de Gaulle, could thus indirectly be traced to de Gaulle's defense policy.

Nuclear-power status nevertheless remained a must for de Gaulle, both for the assertion of French seniority in the Paris-Bonn axis and as the core of a possible future European nuclear strike force under French leadership. Nuclear arms were also intended to provide the French armed forces with a new sense of purpose after the bitter memories of two unsuccessful colonial wars.

ECONOMIC PROGRESS UNDER DE GAULLE

The process of moving France from a stagnant and self-contained socioeconomic condition into an expansive and competitive one, had in part already started under the Fourth Republic through the able leadership of Jean Monnet. The pace quickened under the Fifth Republic, assuming often enough the quality of a revolutionary change.

Consistent with the presidential style, economic policy under de Gaulle became more concentrated in the centralized bureaucracy than had been the case under the Fourth Republic. The political parties and Parliament played a far less important role in economic decision making, a fact which deprived the government of an important source of public opinion concerning social and economic issues at any given time. The bureaucratic aloofness of the Gaullist regime explains in part why the Fifth Republic was repeatedly faced with sudden and, often enough, violent social protest, of which the student riots of May 1968 were the biggest, though by no means the only example. De Gaulle's own economic philosophy was pragmatic, growth-oriented, and free of ideological encumbrances. He never identified with big business, though he favored bigness in industry on the assumption of enhanced efficiency. More than his prime minister Pompidou and the right wing of the UNR, de Gaulle took a keen interest in the social welfare of industrial workers, advancing such schemes as profit sharing and workers' participation in management.

The overall economic progress between 1958 and 1968 was substantial. With an annual increase of 5.5 percent, the French GNP rose faster than that of other EEC nations or of the United States. France became a major industrial producer and exporter in areas such as capital goods, automobiles, and armaments, where she had not been strong previously. Eight years after de Gaulle's currency reform of 1958, the balance of payments turned from a $300 million deficit into a surplus of over $6 billion. De Gaulle promptly used his newly gained financial strength to attack and weaken the U.S. dollar.

Energy Policy

De Gaulle's energy policy was less successful in the long run. In order to give French industry a competitive advantage, he eliminated all taxes on imported fuel oil, resulting in a reversal of coal and oil ratios between the 1950s and the early 1970s from 77 percent and 20 percent respectively to 16 percent and 72 percent respectively. The oil crisis of 1973, which followed de Gaulle's presidency, thus affected France more severely than other industrial nations.

Relations with Business

De Gaulle's relations with employers' interest groups, such as the *Conseil National du Patronat Français* (CNPF), were not as good as might be expected, in part because of Gaullist interference in the private sector through price controls and other measures. The CNPF did not support de Gaulle in the presidential elections of 1965, nor did it endorse de Gaulle's position in the crucial referendum of April 1969, which marked the end of his presidency.

Farm Policy

Gaullist farm policy favored large farms over small ones on the grounds of efficiency. The 1960 Orientation Law and the 1962 Complementary Law created regional agencies for buying up small, inefficient farms and reselling them to bigger farms. A newly created Social Action Fund served the purpose of aiding old or poor farmers driven off the land by the new policy. The major farm organization FNSEA (*Fédération Nationale des Syndicats d'Exploitants Agricoles*) supported the policy of farm consolidation, until it became clear that its chief beneficiaries were not medium-size but large farms. Like the CNPF, the FNSEA did not support de Gaulle in the 1965 presidential elections, a fact which may have forced him into a humiliating second ballot. De Gaulle's concern about farm support explains his stubborn defense of French farm interests during the 1965–1966 EEC crisis revolving around CAP, and it prompted him to appoint a new activist minister of agriculture in the person of Edgar Faure.

Housing

The Fifth Republic's record in housing was not spectacular under de Gaulle. The city of Paris received a new facelift with the cleaning and sandblasting of its historic buildings and monuments, which were brilliantly illuminated at night. No comparable effort followed in the upgrading of social housing. According to the 1962 statistics, over 61 percent of all houses had been built before 1914 and over 32 percent before 1870. Half of all apartments were lacking in indoor bathroom facilities and 28 percent had no shower or bath. In 1969, 15 million people were living in overcrowded conditions.

Education

De Gaulle and the university students got off to a bad start when the *Union Nationale des Etudiants de France* (UNEF), the left-wing student organization, clashed over de Gaulle's cuts in the education budget as part of his austerity program of December 1958. Yet it cannot be said that the Fifth Republic was blind to the need for educational reform. In 1963, education minister Christian Fouchet created the new common secondary school, whose curriculum contained an admirable liberal arts portion. In 1966 there followed the "university institutes of technology" (IUTs), created for the specific purpose of turning out medium-level technicians in two-year programs. IUT enrolment expanded between 1966 and 1968 from 2,000 to 12,000. Regular university enrolment more than doubled between 1960 and 1967 from 215,000 to 460,000. Student dissatisfaction continued, in part because of overcrowding, in part because of the sagging job market for graduates in 1967–1968. In higher education, the stage was set for a serious confrontation with the government, which had not kept sufficiently in touch to be prepared for it.

THE 1965 PRESIDENTIAL CONTEST

The pollsters gave de Gaulle a public approval rating of 60 percent as the presidential elections of 1965 approached and there seemed, in fact, no serious rival for the presidency in sight. On the left, the Socialist mayor of Marseilles, Gaston Defferre, appeared briefly as a challenger, but he was not taken seriously by de Gaulle or any other major politician for very long. Three months before the election, Defferre withdrew from the race. On the right, there was Tixier-Vignancour, who had made a name for himself among OAS sympathizers as the defense lawyer of General Salan. Tixier could count on the vote of several hundred thousand disillusioned *colon* refugees, but that did not make him a serious candidate for the presidency either.

Mitterrand and Lecanuet

The picture changed dramatically just a few weeks before the election with the appearance of two new candidates, François Mitterrand of the Socialists (SFIO) and Jean Lecanuet, the leader of the MRP. Both made a good impression in the televised campaign, the emphasis being on their relative youth, as compared with the aging de Gaulle. Mitterrand obtained the support of the Communists, Lecanuet that of disaffected farm and business groups.

On the first ballot, de Gaulle barely got 44 percent of the vote, while Mitterrand's strength equalled that of the entire left in 1962. Only in the run-off election did de Gaulle win with 55 percent and 12.6 million votes, followed by Mitterrand's 10.5 million. Both Mitterrand and Lecanuet hoped to turn the 1965 alignment into permanent groupings with which to challenge Gaullism in the future. The Democratic Center, which Lecanuet founded for such a purpose in April 1966, was not a long-term success. By 1968 it was out of business, largely because too many MRP members of parliament remained loyal to de Gaulle. The Gaullists rewarded such loyalty by forming electoral alliances which often enough made the difference between safe or doubtful seats.

Mitterrand's Federation of the Left, an alliance chiefly of Socialists and Radicals, fared little better between 1966 and 1968. The federation suffered from its uncertain relationship with the Communists, with whom it was at first allied, but with whom it later broke over such issues as the 1967 Mideastern war and the Soviet invasion of Czechoslovakia of 1968. After the federation had disintegrated in the wake of the 1968 May riots, Mitterrand launched a new Democratic Socialist party in July 1969, to take the place of the old Socialist party (SFIO). Mitterrand's strategy rested on the calculation that with the deterioration of the economic situation, a large bloc of left-of-center Gaullists might become sufficiently disillusioned to consider a Mitterrand-Socialist presidency a desirable alternative to entrenched Gaullism.

THE MAY RIOTS AND THE END OF DE GAULLE'S PRESIDENCY

As late as January 1968 de Gaulle could boast of the stability of French affairs in contrast to the instability of other, nameless countries, among which, it may be assumed, he also counted the United States with its nightly televised anti-Vietnam War demonstrations and social crisis in the inner cities. Yet in France too a groundswell had been building in 1967, fuelled by widespread social discontent over sharp price increases, cuts in social benefits, and persistent pockets of unemployment. If de Gaulle remained unaware of these developments, it reflected the smugness of Gaullist officialdom, which controlled radio and television (ORTF) and which had come to regard itself as above criticism.

The student protest of May 3, 1968 at the Paris Sorbonne against the closing of the Nanterre campus acted as a spark for a much wider protest, which gripped much of France for several weeks. The night of May 10–11 marked the crucial transition from local to national crisis. After the Paris police had stormed the students' barricades in the Latin Quarter, the sympathetic labor unions called a general strike for May 13, 1968, the tenth anniversary of the disturbances which had brought de Gaulle to power.

From May 11, 1968 onwards Prime Minister Pompidou, rather than de Gaulle himself, was in charge of coping with the crisis, de Gaulle leaving on a state visit to Rumania. After making speedy concessions to the students, Pompidou calmed workers' unrest with the Grenelle agreements of May 27, 1968, named after the street in which the ministry of social affairs was located. Reminiscent of the 1936 Matignon accord, with which Leon Blum had ended the French strike movement of 1936, the Grenelle agreements granted wage increases of up to 15 percent, while raising the minimum wage and social security benefits.

De Gaulle addressed the nation only on May 24, 1968 with a call for "a mandate for renewal" through another referendum. To many, this was not the de Gaulle of old but an aged and uncertain leader. The uncertainty increased as de Gaulle was rumored to have left France for parts unknown. Mitterrand announced his availability to form a new government, should the Fifth Republic fall.

De Gaulle's mysterious journey had taken him to Baden-Baden, West Germany, where he conferred with former general Massu. Massu pledged unquestioned army support in exchange for an amnesty of convicted OAS leaders. Upon returning, de Gaulle dissolved Parliament, ordered new elections, and organized a mass rally of nearly a million people on the Place de la Concorde in support of himself and the Fifth Republic. In the elections of June 1968 the Gaullists gained 358 out of 485 seats. With the crisis ended de Gaulle fired prime minister Pompidou, the man who had saved the Fifth Republic during the critical May days, and replaced him with Couve de Murville, a loyal but colorless administrator.

Although order had been restored, the events of May 1968 had shattered the Gaullist mystique as no previous events had. The great victory of the Gaullists in the Assembly elections of June was then less a vote of confidence in de Gaulle personally than it was a commitment to the Fifth Republic under its presumed future leader George Pompidou.

Educational Reforms

Before the end of his presidency in April 1969, de Gaulle instituted a number of administrative and educational reforms, which were designed to remove some of the underlying causes of the disturbances of May 1968. Among these was a scheme for decentralization, giving departmental prefects greater power, and creating regional councils, to be drawn from several departments. The Senate, a body de Gaulle disliked for many years because of its role as a rallying point of the opposition, was to be confined to a consultative role and to be combined with the Social and Economic Council into a kind of corporate upper chamber.

De Gaulle's education minister Edgar Faure expanded student participation in university education, promoted interdisciplinary research and teaching and reduced university size under the new Orientation Law of November 1968. The twenty-three universities of France were broken up into sixty-five university centers with further decentralization of the traditional major study fields. The so-called *grandes écoles* of France, including the *Ecole Nationale d'Administration,* which produced the administrative elite of the country, remained quite untouched by the educational reforms of 1968.

De Gaulle also had to cope with the financial repercussions of the May riots and the strikes which had disrupted the economy. Among the financial repercussions was an increase in the budget deficit from 5.3 to 12.8 billion francs and a loss of $3.5 billion in reserves by the end of 1968. In the early months of 1969 capital outflow continued at the alarming rate of $300 million per month. De Gaulle's financial advisers urged devaluation of the franc as a remedy for the financial crisis, which de Gaulle explicitly ruled out on November 23, 1968 for reasons of national prestige.

De Gaulle Resigns

There was little support in the country for de Gaulle's reform plans concerning the Senate, though there was much interest in the decentralization plan on the departmental level. Senate president Monnerville, whom de Gaulle had ostracized socially for many years for his outspoken opposition, stepped down in favor of the less controversial Alain Poher, who vainly attempted to change de Gaulle's mind on Senate reform. Instead, de Gaulle placed both regional and Senate reform on a referendum in April 1969, with the announcement that a rejection of the referendum would result in his resignation. The referendum was defeated with a 53 percent *no* vote. On April 28, 1969 de Gaulle resigned the presidency. In accordance with the constitution, the presidency passed to the Senate president Poher, with new presidential elections to be scheduled within fifty days. Pompidou had announced his availability as a presidential candidate in the event of a vacancy in early January 1969. On June 15, 1969 he was elected president of the Fifth Republic on the second ballot against Alain Poher. On November 9, 1970 de Gaulle died at his residence at Colombey, shortly before his eightieth birthday.

27

Britain and the Commonwealth in the 1960s

CONSERVATIVE GOVERNMENT UNDER MACMILLAN

The impact of the Suez debacle of 1956 on Britain was less sustained than might have been assumed, in part because British opinion itself was divided over the wisdom of Eden's action. Those who did not question his policy of force had cause to be dismayed over his lack of nerve under pressure. After Suez, Eden's resignation from the prime ministership was a foregone conclusion.

Of the two most likely successors, Harold Macmillan and R. A. Butler, the former won because he had wider support in the party and because he possessed greater experience in government. That Macmillan also knew Eisenhower well from the days of World War II could only be helpful in repairing the "special relationship" with the United States.

Macmillan's critics regarded him more a skillful politician than a statesman, one who knew how to conceal the root cause of long-term problems for the sake of short-term political gain. In fact, Macmillan well appreciated the magnitude of the challenges he faced, especially with regard to Britain's economic woes and the issue of expanding colonial nationalism in the Commonwealth. Although originally he did not expect to last in office for very long, he soon emerged as a powerful political personality, partly through the aid of Conservative party whip Edward Heath. He won the elections of October 1959 handsomely with a Conservative gain of half-a-million votes and a total of 13.7 million votes. The Labour opposition lost 107 seats in the Commons. Conservative strength was based in part on the strong economy of 1959, reflected in Macmillan's election slogan, You Never Had It So Good. With evidence that living standards, including those of the working class, were apparently rising even the Labour party under Hugh Gaitskell strove to shed its class image and appeal to a wider range of voters. Theoretical works such as John Strachey's *Contemporary Capitalism* or Crosland's *The Future of Socialism* downplayed traditional Marxist concepts and recognized the positive aspects of capitalism within the limits of Labour's unchanged commitment to social reform.

The British Economy

The economic record since 1957 was in fact mixed, with a major loss of gold and foreign exchange reserves in that year being followed by a recession in 1958. When the boom year, 1959, was followed by yet another crisis in 1960, Britain's economic problems were at last recognized as long term and recurring, rather than isolated and short range. Although Britain's GNP had expanded by 20 percent under Conservative rule between 1951 and 1959, it had increased at a lower rate than that of the Common Market average during the same time period. Prices and wages had risen faster in Britain than in Western Europe, but capital formation had progressed at a lower rate. Shipbuilding had dropped since the mid-1950s by a third while the share in world chemical exports had declined from 16 to 12%, with West Germany overtaking Britain in this particular area. The aviation industry, second only to that of the United States in the western world, had a poor earning record in proportion to the high investment in research. Although a pioneer in jet propulsion and the first nation to introduce a commercial jet airliner with the Comet, Britain lost out to American competition in the civil aviation business. After a spectacular start, the Comet had to be withdrawn as a technological failure. The nationalized coal industry, though increasing in productivity, was again a depressed industry with a decline in employment from 700,000 to 419,000 during the decade following 1957, as a result of the competition of oil.

Against the background of an economy in relative decline, British still shouldered worldwide defense commitments and the British pound sterling still acted as a world reserve currency just like the U.S. dollar. Macmillan warned that Britain was "living above her means," but he hoped that timely reforms and British EEC membership could still enable Britain to continue her triple role as leading power of Western Europe, leader of the Commonwealth, and special ally of the United States.

Among Macmillan's economic measures was the founding of the National Economic Development Council (NEDC) in 1961 as an agency for the stimulation of economic growth and the granting of tax cuts, amounting to 270 million for the year 1963 alone. The NEDC projected a 4 percent annual growth rate for the economy for the half-decade following 1961 on the assumption of British EEC membership by 1964. The actual growth rate turned out to be considerably lower and EEC membership was barred by de Gaulle's veto of January 1963. Macmillan also hoped to assist the depressed areas of Britain's northeast through the newly established Ministry for the North East under Lord Hailsham, and through passage of the 1964 Industrial Training Act. Anticipating the need for more university graduates in an expanding economy, the 1963 Robbins Report called for a doubling of university enrolment during the next decade. The number of university graduates had already doubled between 1938 and 1960.

MACMILLAN AND THE COMMONWEALTH

Britain had granted independence to India in 1947 because Attlee feared the alternative of an alliance of Indian nationalism and Soviet communism. After the experience of the Suez crisis of 1956, Macmillan feared a similar alliance between communism and colonial nationalism worldwide unless that nationalism were directed into "broader and safe channels." For Britain, this meant the granting of full independence to her former colonies with the option of voluntary dominion status in the Commonwealth on the Indian model. As an inducement, Britain not only offered military protection, but also various forms of economic assistance and the advantages of Commonwealth trade and finance. Between 1957 and 1967 British financial and technical assistance to Commonwealth nations increased from £18 to £208 million. As of 1964 Commonwealth aid was administered through the newly established Ministry for Overseas Development. By the early 1960s some 46,000 students from Commonwealth countries were enrolled at British institutions. "The sun," Macmillan was fond of saying, "was not setting on the British Empire. It was rising over the new Commonwealth."

Until the Second World War, dominion status had been reserved for white colonies, and the Commonwealth had been a white man's club. India, Pakistan and Ceylon (Sri Lanka) were the first nonwhite dominions after the Second World War, but they were still outnumbered by the white dominions of Australia, New Zealand, Canada and (white-ruled) South Africa. Ten years after Suez the number of dominions had vastly increased, the majority of them nonwhite. In addition to the old dominions there were Ghana, Malaysia, Nigeria, Sierra Leone, Tanzania, Jamaica, Trinidad, Uganda, Kenya, Malawi, Zambia, Gambia, Guyana, Botswana, Lesotho, Barbados, Malta, and Cyprus.

African Decolonization

The transformation of the colonial Empire into a commonwealth of self-governing equals raised the issue of race and race relations in Commonwealth affairs. Race became an issue in those British colonies where large white settler minorities existed, as in Kenya and Northern and Southern Rhodesia, which all opposed black majority rule and feared the loss of economic power and of their land holdings. The political and economic implications of black emancipation for white minorities had been indicated by the Maú-Maú rebellion in Kenya, which Britain crushed in a long drawn-out campaign between 1952 and 1959. The Royal Commission on East Africa, which had been installed in 1952 for the purpose of investigating the causes of the rebellion and of suggesting remedies, had produced recommendations that were generally applicable to the process of decolonization. In its appeal for "racial partnership," the Royal Commission on East Africa called for the avoidance of a "clash of culture and race" as a means of pacifying Kenya.

Macmillan announced the coming retreat from British black Africa in his "winds of change" speech delivered at Cape Town, South Africa, in February 1960. This speech, which was also meant to encourage the South African government into changing its own policy of strict racial segregation (apartheid), announced the intention of proceeding with the policy of decolonization in Africa regardless of the vested interests of white minorities. In fact, Macmillan attempted to safeguard such interests to the best of his ability prior to independence, just as he tried to maximize British influence overall through suitable arrangements for the postindependence period. In this endeavor, the "federation" was the preferred instrument. Federations were meant to hold together areas of strong British influence with those in which British power was likely to be weak or, as in the case of the British colonies in central Africa, the federation was intended as a cover for preserving white minority rule. The device of federation was also used in former colonial areas of Asia and the Middle East. The federation of Malaysia was created primarily to assure the dominance of pro-British Malaya over Singapore with its large ethnic Chinese population. The Federation of South Arabia was intended to uphold the power of the pro-British emirs over anti-British Aden and the Federation of Arab emirates in the Persian Gulf was similarly designed to uphold British influence in the Persian Gulf area.

British decolonization in black Africa was easiest in those colonies where no large white settler minorities existed, such as in the West African colonies of Ghana, Nigeria, Sierra Leone and Gambia, all of which achieved independence between 1957 and 1965. The absence of large white settler minorities in the two East African colonies, Tanganyika and Uganda, made emancipation easy there also, the former becoming independent in December 1961 under the name of Tanzania, the latter in October 1962.

Kenya

In Kenya, the European minority numbered some 65,000 settlers who owned, as a group, an average of 195 acres of choice land per head, as against 5.6 acres per head for the seven million blacks. After the outbreak of the Maú-Maú rebellion, Britain issued the Lyttelton constitution for Kenya in 1954, named after the British colonial secretary. The constitution, meant as a first step towards the goal of "racial partnership," still upheld the principle of white minority rule when allocating a single seat in the Kenya legislature to the black majority, while conceding two seats to the Asian residents of Kenya. In 1960, the Lyttelton constitution was replaced with a new one which, though broadening black representation, still attempted to uphold white minority rule. By 1962 Britain conceded universal suffrage to Kenya prior to the granting of independence in December 1963. In the end, Britain also bought out most of the white settlers in order to remove the issue of unequal land ownership. Macmillan imposed a political and economic settlement on Kenya's whites which most of them disapproved of, in the larger national interest of good relations with the black government of Kenya. Such a solution was possible in Kenya because the white settlers of Kenya, other than those of Southern Rhodesia, never enjoyed self-government prior to independence.

Southern Rhodesia

The whites of Southern Rhodesia, accounting for 5 percent of the population overall, were the largest white minority in British Africa, numbering about 215,000. As in Kenya, land ownership played an important role in Southern Rhodesia, where whites as a group owned 279 acres per head, as against 17 acres per head for blacks.

The whites of Northern Rhodesia were the second largest white minority numbering 75,000. Though not a self-governing dominion like South Africa, Southern Rhodesia had received autonomy in 1923 with exclusive white settler control over defense, police, and the civil service. Southern Rhodesia's prime minister also routinely attended Commonwealth conferences until 1964, when the protests of the Afro-Asian Commonwealth prime ministers ended the practice. In 1953 Britain launched the Central African Federation, composed of the two Rhodesias and Nyasaland. The federal government, based in the Southern Rhodesia capital of Salisbury, was, for all intents and purposes, an extension of the all-white government of Southern Rhodesia. It was as a federation under white minority rule that the British colonies of Central Africa were to be granted independence. There were some provisions for token black representation, but the number of blacks enfranchised in the 1958 election was fewer than one thousand, out of a total population of seven million. In response to black nationalist protests in Nyasaland in March 1959, Macmillan appointed two fact-finding commissions. The Devlin Commission of 1959 recorded the extent of black opposition to the federation scheme in Nyasaland, while the Monckton Commission of 1960 did as much for both Nyasaland and Northern Rhodesia. Against strong opposition from the colonialist wing of his own Conservative party, Macmillan abandoned the federation project in 1962. In 1964 Nyasaland and Northern Rhodesia became independent under black majority rule, the former under the name of Malawi, the latter with the name of Zambia.

Macmillan was prepared to grant Southern Rhodesia, now simply styled *Rhodesia,* independence under conditions of white minority rule, provided that at least some gesture towards "racial partnership" were made by Rhodesian prime minister Ian Smith and his all-white "Rhodesian front." This Ian Smith refused to do, putting the British government into an increasingly difficult position in the Commonwealth, the United Nations, and world opinion. In September 1963 Britain vetoed a UN Security Council Resolution demanding that independence be granted Rhodesia only after a government representative of all Rhodesians had been established. With decolonization in full swing throughout the African continent, the time for compromise in the Rhodesian problem was rapidly running out.

South Africa

The problem of South Africa, whose policy of apartheid was coming increasingly under attack from the Afro-Asian Commonwealth prime ministers, had meanwhile been taken off Britain's hands through South Africa's voluntary withdrawal from the Commonwealth in 1961. The withdrawal had very little effect on Britain's economic stake in South Africa, which was considerable. At the beginning of the 1960s British investments in South Africa totalled over £900 million, an amount equal to all British investments in the nations of the European Common Market. In 1961 Britain enacted legislation which preserved South Africa's economic, financial and tariff privileges, which had previously been part of South Africa's Commonwealth membership. Britain's strategic and military ties to South Africa remained similarly strong. The UN resolution of November 1963, calling for an arms embargo against South Africa, was ignored by the British government.

THE LABOUR EFFORT AT NATIONAL RENEWAL, 1964 TO 1970

Conservative rule ended in 1964, after thirteen years, on a general note of doubt and a sense of failure. The sense of failure derived less from decolonization than it did from Macmillan's inability to enter Europe via the EEC. De Gaulle's veto against British EEC membership was a brutal reminder of the realities of continental Europe less than twenty years after World War II. The war was still, in the British consciousness of the sixties, Britain's "finest hour," and it was difficult to grasp how the liberated Europe of 1945 could have developed so quickly into a new combination of states hostile to British interests. A 1963 editorial of the London *Times* reflected this mood accurately when observing that after the "historic and heroic exertions" of World War II, the people of Britain were deserving of "some easement."

Profumo

Macmillan's political standing was damaged also by the sex scandal involving his defense minister Profumo and Christine Keeler, a woman whose extensive social connections included Soviet diplomatic personnel. There was considerable disappointment over the choice of the successor, after Macmillan resigned the prime ministership for reasons of health in 1963. The Conservative party picked Sir Alec Douglas-Home, who was competent in the field of foreign affairs but was lacking in the excitement the public seemed to want and expect after many years of Conservative rule.

The Labour Alternative

The mood of Britain in the early sixties was also affected by the literary impact of the "angry young men," John Osborne, Malcolm Bradbury, Alan Sillitoe and others. The "angry young men" were attacking British society, its class system, and its imperial traditions in a manner often found irreverent and disconcerting by the older generation, which clung to prewar memories of external splendor and suppressed social conflict at home. To much of the younger generation of the early 1960s the Labour party held out a preferable alternative, the promise of leadership more vigorous than that of the Conservatives Macmillan and Sir Douglas-Home.

The Labour party itself had been deeply divided over such issues as unilateral British nuclear disarmament. At the Labour party conference in Scarborough of October 1960, the Labour left wing defeated the moderates under Hugh Gaitskell on the issue of unilateral nuclear disarmament, only to be defeated in turn at the 1961 Blackpool conference. After Gaitskell's sudden death in January 1963, Harold Wilson triumphed in the leadership struggle over his rivals George Brown and James Callaghan. It was thought that Wilson, with his ties to the Labour left, would be in a better position to reunite the party. Wilson ran an effective election campaign in 1964, advertising Labour as modern and efficient. John Kenneth Galbraith, rather than John Maynard Keynes, was said to be the party's new guiding spirit in economic theory. The Conservatives suffered their biggest voter loss since 1945, but the Labour majority of four seats was paper-thin nonetheless. The chief beneficiary of Conservative voter defection was the Liberal party.

The new Labour government under Wilson was immediately confronted with serious economic and balance-of-payments problems, which it hesitated to deal with effectively because of Labour's tiny parliamentary majority. Wilson preferred to strengthen his popular image first, in preparation for new elections which would hopefully return a bigger Labour vote. The opportunity for such elections arose in 1966 when the economy had somewhat improved and when Wilson, claiming credit, increased his majority to a comfortable 363 seats. Meanwhile, the British pound had come under heavy pressure and had had to be propped up by repeated rescue operations of European central banks and the U.S. Federal Reserve, which together loaned $3 billion in November 1964 alone. The currency crisis reflected the lack of foreign confidence in the British economy, which continued to be plagued by excessive union wage demands and inflation. Wilson's so-called Joint Declaration of Intent on prices, profits, productivity and wages, which was meant to stem inflation, was openly ignored by the unions. The formation of a special Department of Economic Affairs under George Brown and the publication of a National Plan in 1965, with a projected annual growth rate of 3.8 percent for 1964–1970, were little more than declarations of good intent. The 3.8 percent growth rate was soon shown to be unattainable.

Wilson's Domestic Policies

The second Wilson cabinet from 1966 to 1970 had much to its credit in the areas of social policy and education. In housing, Wilson maintained an excellent record with 400,000 new homes built annually between 1964 and 1968, a record that could not be sustained into the 1970s. Wilson took pride in the fact that his administration spent more on education than on defense. During the 1960s the number of universities doubled, as did university enrolment. The selection of study fields did not always correspond to the needs of the economy, however, with industrial engineers and managers still in short supply. On the secondary school level the Labour government made a not altogether successful attempt to introduce a single comprehensive school to replace Britain's three traditional types of school.

While there was social progress in many areas, there was no comparable improvement in the condition of the economy overall. After his reelection with a bigger majority in 1966, Wilson instituted austerity measures, including consumer credit restrictions and a £50 limit on foreign travel. Unemployment reached a twenty-seven-year peak in July 1967, partly as a result of these austerity measures. Domestic spending cuts were sharply criticized by the Labour left and the unions. Even moderate proposals of the Labour government for curbing excessive union power, such as were advanced in 1969 in the document *In Place of Strife,* were quickly opposed by the Trade Union Council (TUC). Prolonged strikes, such as the seamen's strike between May and July 1966 or the dockers' strike in September and October 1967, did serious harm to the whole national economy. The strike movement contributed to the crisis of the pound, forcing Wilson at last to devalue the pound from $2.80 to $2.40 on November 18, 1967. Devaluation went hand in hand with fresh foreign loans. By 1968 Britain's public foreign debt had climbed to £8 billion, the highest per capita debt of any Western nation at that time.

Wilson's efforts to strengthen the economy through further acts of nationalization and mergers of industries were not overly successful. The off-again–on-again approach to nationalizing steel was finally resolved in favor of nationalization in 1967, with the establishment of the British Steel Corporation, encompassing 90 percent of the industry. During the first ten years of operation the steel corporations's record in productivity, management and profits was not successful. On the assumption that corporate-size companies worked more efficiently than smaller plants, the Labour government favored mergers through the Industrial Reorganization Corporation (IRC) of 1966, which also provided loans. Among industries thus merged was British Leyland in January 1968, formed out of British automotive companies. Supported by an initial loan of £25 million, British Leyland was eventually 95 percent state-owned. Productivity of British Leyland workers was half that of auto workers in continental Europe. IRC carried out mergers in other industries as well, the most successful example that of the ball-bearing industry. After the Labour defeat in the national elections of 1970, IRC was abolished with the argument that it had been supporting inefficient industries with ever-expanding public funds.

Regionalism

The Wilson years from 1964 to 1970 also witnessed the surfacing of regional nationalism in the British Isles on a larger scale than usual, as well as a reopening of the Irish question. The nationalist agitation in Scotland and Wales was partly induced by economic conditions. Both areas were traditionally depressed, though the GNP of Scotland actually increased between 1964 and 1973 at a faster rate, at 2.8 percent annually, than did that of England. In 1967 the Scottish National party (SNP) gained one seat in Parliament. For Wales, the Labour government instituted a special secretary of state in 1964, and it granted the Welsh language equal footing with English in 1967. Like Scottish nationalism, Welsh nationalism produced its own political party, the *Plaid Cymru,* under the leadership of Gwynfor Evans.

Ulster

The crisis in Northern Ireland was triggered by the reforms of Prime Minister Terence O'Neill in the mid-1960s. Also seeking stronger ties with Southern Ireland, O'Neill and his reforms came under swift Protestant attack. This in turn prompted the formation of the Catholic Civil Rights Movement, which agitated against discrimination in jobs, housing and voting. In early October 1968 violence erupted in Londonderry, and in April 1969 the O'Neill government resigned. By August 1969 the Labour government had dispatched troops to Northern Ireland, where they were initially well received by the Catholic minority. By April 1970 armed clashes between British troops and members of the extremist "Provisional" wing of the Irish Republican Army had rapidly altered the situation. The election of the Rev. Ian Paisley, the Protestant spokesman, to the British parliament in June 1970 likewise signaled a long-drawn-out contest in which violence was apt to play a major part.

Race in Britain

The 1960s also witnessed the development of the race issue as a domestic political and social problem, to the point where government action could no longer be avoided. An Institute of Race Relations had existed in Britain since 1958, the year in which the first major race riots occurred after a half-decade of nonwhite immigration, chiefly from the West Indies. The Labour party, which was identified with a liberal policy towards nonwhite immigration, in 1964 lost four seats in the West Midlands, previously considered Labour strongholds, because of the issue of nonwhite immigration. In 1965 Wilson limited unskilled nonwhite immigration, while at the same time enacting a new Race Relations Bill, banning discrimination in public places. In April 1968 Enoch Powell, the enfant terrible of the Conservative party, delivered his much-publicized speech in Birmingham, which warned the British that they might become "strangers in their own country," because of the allegedly higher birth rate of the immigrants. Powell's stance on nonwhite immigration was matched by his attacks on the Commonwealth which, consisting in its majority of Afro-Asian states, had ceased to be of any use to Britain, in Powell's view.

LABOUR AND THE EEC

Though himself originally lukewarm on the idea of EEC membership, Wilson applied for admission to the Common Market in May 1967 for what seemed to be compelling economic reasons. Trade with EFTA and the Commonwealth had proved not to be a suitable substitute for EEC membership, despite the EFTA decision of May 1963 to eliminate industrial tariffs in 1966, three years ahead of schedule. By 1966 the EEC accounted for 38 percent of British exports, versus 32 percent for the sterling area.

Commonwealth ties had become weaker since Wilson's accession to power for reasons other than the purely economic. Wilson came under increasing attack over the issue of Rhodesia. When India and Pakistan settled their 1965 war solely through the mediation of the USSR at Tashkent in early 1966, with Britain playing no part whatever, it angered Wilson and strengthened his resolve to give Europe greater priority.

The Common Market's internal developments since 1963 also seemed to favor a British admission by the late 1960s. The Paris-Bonn axis had become less intimate after Adenauer's retirement from office in 1963, and de Gaulle's attacks on EEC supranationality agreed with Britain's own distaste for the wider political aims of the 1957 Rome treaty. De Gaulle's second veto of British membership on November 27, 1967 came therefore all the more as a surprise. As in 1963, the real reasons behind de Gaulle's veto were political, not economic. Having herself quit NATO command and shut down NATO bases on her territory in 1966, France expected the Labour government to follow suit. If Britain also quit NATO command, de Gaulle would quickly compromise on the economic terms of British entry. Those were the outlines of a deal proposed confidentially by de Gaulle to the British ambassador to France, Christopher Soames, in February 1967. Implied in de Gaulle's scheme was a subordination of Britain to French leadership in western Europe. In fact, Britain pursued the exact opposite course. As Britain was forced to wind down her global strategic role and her presence "East of Suez" for economic reasons, she intended to upgrade her role in Europe with NATO serving as an important instrument. This was not a partisan issue, because Labour, having been a cofounder of NATO in 1949, still regarded the alliance as an essential part of British foreign and defense strategy in Europe.

WILSON AND COMMONWEALTH RELATIONS

Before the balance of payments crisis of 1967 and the resulting devaluation of the pound, the Labour government was no less determined to uphold Britain's global defense commitments than its Conservative predecessor had been before 1964. In 1964

Wilson confidently predicted "a very big role" for Britain "East of Suez." In 1965 the prime minister again spoke of Britain's frontiers being "on the Himalayas," and in 1966 Britain strengthened her presence in the Indian Ocean by jointly developing with the United States the island base of Diego Garcia. In Southeast Asia British forces succeeded in thwarting the efforts of Indonesia's Sukarno to destroy the recently established federation of Malaysia and to evict Malayan power from former British Borneo, now part of the federation.

During the second half of the decade British military power was rapidly withdrawn from the vast perimeter stretching from Aden in the Middle East to Singapore in Southeast Asia. The retreat from a role "East of Suez" was occasioned in the first place by inadequate financial resources which, even after the end of the draft in 1962, were insufficient to pay for modern air and naval weapons. With a balance of payments deficit of £540 million and military appropriations of £230 million for British forces in Asia, the "East of Suez" strategy had become unaffordable. Wilson could not have defended the necessary domestic spending cuts in the wake of the devaluation crisis without, at the same time, drastically cutting defense spending. The date of withdrawal from Singapore, originally set for the mid-1970s, was advanced to 1971 after the pound devaluation.

The decision to wind down the crucial base of Aden within two years was taken by Wilson in February 1966, largely in response to political developments and the nationalist agitation in South Yemen. Only after the pound crisis in 1967 was it decided to withdraw British strength from the Persian Gulf altogether, in part on the assumption that Saudi Arabia and Iran could fill the military vacuum with forces of their own.

There was unhappiness in the United States, Australia, New Zealand, Singapore and some of the Arab sheikdoms over the scope and speed of Britain's withdrawal east of Suez. There was also criticism from Conservative party quarters, though the Conservatives, once back in power, carried out the policy of strategic retreat for the same compelling economic reasons which had prompted the decision under Labour in the first place.

Britain's diminishing military posture in the Commonwealth during the 1960s was suggestive also of weakening economic and political ties. India and Pakistan received about 90 percent of their foreign aid from non-British sources, including the Soviet Union, which emerged as a major arms supplier to India, and licensed the manufacture of Soviet war planes in Indian factories.

British exports to Commonwealth nations, which had still accounted for 40 percent of all British exports in the 1950s, declined to 26 percent in 1966. Commonwealth exports to Great Britain declined from a share of 20 percent in 1962 to 12 percent in 1969. Japan made major inroads in the trade of Australia, Malaysia and several African states, including oil-rich Nigeria.

The Rhodesian Crisis

In Africa, the Wilson government was unable to solve the Rhodesian crisis and found itself involved in a new crisis in Nigeria, following the secession attempt of Biafra. Though it is doubtful whether agreement on Rhodesia could have been reached even if the Conservatives had returned to power in 1964, it is certain that the Labour victory stiffened the attitude of the all-white government of Ian Smith. Wilson may have committed a tactical blunder by declaring in March 1965 that his government was not prepared to use force against Rhodesia, except in the case of a general breakdown in law and order. On November 11, 1965 Rhodesia issued its unilateral declaration of Independence (UDI).

At the Commonwealth conference in Lagos in January 1966, and at the one in London in September 1966, Wilson came under increasing pressure from the Afro-Asian Commonwealth members to use military force against the Smith government in Salisbury and to recognize Rhodesian independence only on condition of black majority rule.

Despite the bitter attacks of Zambia and Tanzania at the UN Second Assembly session of October 1966, Wilson refused to consider the use of force. The concurrent Vietnam War was a good illustration of the hazards and costs of a war connected with a former colony. Politically, Wilson's slim parliamentary majority before the elections of 1966 ruled out any such extreme measure as the application of military force against a white minority government with powerful friends in the Conservative party. Wilson's policy was then confined to the application of sanctions, whose effectiveness was doubtful from the start because South Africa acted as a loophole. Otherwise, Wilson still hoped to affect a Rhodesia compromise through personal diplomacy in his two meetings with Ian Smith on the British warships HMS *Tiger* in December 1966 and HMS *Fearless* in October 1968. Wilson's compromise proposals included limited enfranchisement of blacks; a pledge not to alter the Rhodesian constitution arbitrarily once such enfranchisement had been granted; the inclusion of two blacks into the government; and British recognition of Rhodesian independence, once those conditions were met. In the sixties, Smith found even these proposals, which essentially upheld the principle of white minority rule, unacceptable.

Biafra

In the Nigerian civil war, which broke out in 1967 following the secession of the Ibo region in the east under the name of Biafra, Wilson supported the federal government despite strong criticism at home and abroad. British policy was motivated by the fear of Soviet involvement on the side of the federal government and subsequent loss of British investments of some £200. By the late 1960s Nigeria was also supplying Britain with 10 percent of her oil imports. British arms were instrumental in helping the federal government restore its power over all of Nigeria by January 1970.

28

Democracy and Dictatorship in the Mediterranean: Crisis of the 1960s and 1970s

POST-DE GASPERI ITALY

The policy of Western containment had had its beginnings in the Mediterranean with the British intervention in the Greek Civil War in 1944–1945. By the 1960s and 1970s the Mediterranean area was still far from achieving stability. In post–de Gasperi Italy the industrial boom of the late 1950s and 1960s produced new social stresses in the northern cities, which the increasingly rigid and often corrupt system of Christian Democratic rule was ill equipped to deal with. In Greece, post–Civil War Conservative rule under Field Marshal Alexander Papagos and his successor Prime Minister Constantine Karamanlis failed to develop an effective response to nationalist demands concerning the island of Cyprus and social pressure for improving the lot of the Greek urban and rural proletariat. In Spain and Portugal, the aging dictatorships of Franco and Salazar were drawing to a close, raising serious questions about the nature of their successors and, in the Portuguese case, the future of a vast overseas colonial empire.

The Boom

Italy's economic record during the first decade after de Gasperi's exit from the political stage in 1953 was spectacular. With annual growth rates of between 9 and 13 percent, Italy's economic gains between 1952 and 1962 exceeded those made during the entire first half of the twentieth century. Steel production increased between 1959 and 1962 from 6.7 to 9.4 million tons, while automobile production rose from 470,000 to 877,000 units over the same period.

Population Shift

The industrial boom was partly due to the availability of abundant surplus labor from the rural south. Northern industrial cities, such as the automobile center of Turin, counted as many as 260,000 persons of southern origin among a total city population of 1.1 million.

Neither industry nor municipal or national governments provided the social infrastructure necessary to accommodate and integrate such large population shifts. Substandard housing, discrimination and the spread of urban crime were often the by-products of the social changes produced by industrial demand. After de Gasperi, the Christian Democrats were even more uncertain and less united in their response to urgent social challenges than they had been under de Gasperi's administration.

The Christian Democrats After De Gasperi

The Conservative wing of the Christian Democratic party believed that de Gasperi's social policy had gone as far as it should and perhaps even further than that. The Christian Democratic governments felt little need to implement long-term social programs for housing and other services, when the appeal of left-wing parties, principally the Communist, seemed diminished in times of rising earnings and high employment. Since the mid-fifties, the influence of Communist-led unions among Fiat auto workers had decreased. The long-term hazards of a policy of social neglect in boom times revealed themselves during the decade of the 1970s, however, when high unemployment among the transplanted southern poor in times of recession created a climate of social unrest from which sprang the phenomenon of Italian urban terrorism.

The left wing of the Christian Democrats under Giovanni Gronchi and Amintore Fanfani would have preferred a more enlightened social policy, based on long-term projections. Although Gronchi managed to win the Italian presidency, against the bitter opposition of the Christian Democratic right wing, and although Fanfani became DC party secretary, the majority of de Gasperi's Christian Democratic successors in the prime ministership during the half-decade following 1953, were Conservative. Among Giuseppe Pella, Mario Scelba, Antonio Segni and Adone Zoli, Fanfani was the only progressive.

The Christian Democrats continued the aid program to the rural south, instituted by de Gasperi under the *Cassa,* but they failed to implement the so-called Vanoni Plan, which called for the development of a southern ''industrial triangle'' of the cities of Brindisi, Taranto and Bari.

As early as the late 1950s, Christian Democratic rule came under attack for corruption and was often compared unfavorably with the generally efficient and clean record of Socialist and Communist administrations in city and local government. The Christian Democrats nevertheless secured another long-term lease in office because of the twin issues of the collapse of France's Fourth Republic in May 1958 and the Soviet invasion of Hungary in November 1956. After Khrushchev's denunciation of Stalin in 1956, Italy's Socialist leader Nenni openly divorced himself from the Communists by returning the Stalin Prize. The failure of the French Fourth Republic, in turn, strengthened DC rule, because the Christian Democrats at least seemed to guarantee continuity, stability and prosperity, however unevenly distributed. In the elections of May 1958, the Christian Democrats increased their strength by 1.7 million votes over that of 1953, capturing 273 seats against 140 for the Communists.

The Apertura a Sinistra

Nenni's break with the Communists in 1956 raised the possibility of a Socialist–Christian Democratic coalition. Such an "opening to the Left" (*apertura a sinistra*) was also desired by Gronchi and Fanfani, whose social policy aims were not dissimilar to those of Nenni. The Christian Democratic party congress in Florence of October 1959 approved of such an alliance in principle after a bitter fight in which the left wing under Aldo Moro triumphed over the Conservatives. In 1961, such an alliance was concluded on the municipal level in Milan, Genoa and Florence. On the national level it was achieved after the elections of 1963, with Moro as prime minister and Nenni his deputy. Moro's willingness to serve as head of a coalition that also included left-wing parties made him the target of extreme-left-wing terrorism, which declared war on the democratic system during the 1970s, unwilling to see it function as a corrective to Italy's social ills. Hence Moro's abduction and murder by Italian terrorists, which precipitated Italian democracy's greatest crisis since its 1945 resurrection.

Italy's *apertura a sinistra* at the beginning of the 1960s was helped by the role of the new pope. John XXIII's encyclicals *Mater et Magistra* of 1961 and *Pacem in Terris* of 1963 addressed themselves to social and foreign affairs issues in a manner encouraging to the Christian Democratic party's left wing. *Mater et Magistra* rejected the laissez-faire concept and demanded wages to be based on "justice and fairness." *Pacem in Terris* was a strong call for lessening international tensions.

Italy's powerful Communist party was dealt a severe blow by the East European events of 1956, and it did not recover until after its condemnation of the Soviet occupation of Czechoslovakia in 1968. For the remainder of Togliatti's leadership, the Italian Communist party was divided into left, center and right factions. The right faction, under Giorgio Amendola, son of the liberal leader murdered by the Fascists, advocated a course of renovating the party's position in favor of an open and full acceptance of the parliamentary system. It was a position adopted only in the 1970s by Enrico Berlinguer, the new party leader and one of the principal spokesmen of the west-European "Eurocommunists." Amendola's call for "renovation" was also an attempt to prevent the Nenni Socialists from concluding an alliance with the Christian Democrats and thus of paving the way for a Communist-Socialist coalition government. Togliatti, occupying the center, rejected Amendola's position, without being able to offer a realistic alternative. The left wing in turn attacked Togliatti, and derided him in its pamphlet *Viva il Leninismo* of 1962, which reflected the Chinese Communist position in the current Sino-Soviet conflict.

GREECE FROM PAPAGOS TO PAPANDREOU

Although a small and underdeveloped country, Greece played a key role in both world wars and in the beginning of the Cold War, because of its strategic location at the foot of the Balkan peninsula. The breakout of the Allied expeditionary force at Salonika under General Franchet d'Esperey in September 1918 had triggered the chain of events which began with the collapse of Bulgaria and ended with the defeat of imperial Germany. Hitler's invasion of Greece in April 1941 delayed his attack on the Soviet Union for a crucial month and a half, which may have contributed to the survival of Soviet Russia as much as any other single factor. In 1944, Greece became the first country in Europe where political forces supported by the Soviet Union exchanged gunfire with political forces supported by a major Western power, thereby setting the stage for the coming Cold War.

Greek history before World War II held out little promise of stable democratic government even after the defeat of the Greek Communists in 1949. Republican and monarchist forms of government had followed one another in rapid succession, ever since the establishment of a Greek monarchy in 1832. In the struggle between monarchy and republic the army had often held the balance. Between the two world wars Greek governments were headed by the military, either active or retired, during three separate periods, from 1922 to 1924, 1925 to 1926, and 1935 to 1941.

During the periods when Greece did have a functioning democracy, she failed to develop stable and strong political parties. Greek parties often assumed the character of a personal following of charismatic leaders rather than that of an issue-oriented structure based on broad consensus. Greek parties were also numerous. Between 1946 and 1950 ten political parties were represented in Parliament and in the elections of 1950 over forty parties competed.

Papagos

Field Marshal Alexander Papagos headed the first stable post–Civil War government in 1952. Papagos' conservative Greek Rally (ES) was patterned after de Gaulle's Rally of the French People (RPF).

Papagos ushered in a long period of conservative rule, which continued after his death in 1955 until 1963. The Papagos years were characterized by close ties with the United States, which liberally subsidized Greece with financial and economic aid and began to operate military bases on Greek soil on a permanent basis from 1953 on. Papagos' 1953 currency reform was a major factor in economic recovery, but progress was uneven and high defense budgets left few funds for social spending.

Cyprus

Even during the period of close Greek-Western relations of the 1950s, the problem of Cyprus began to introduce a note of discord. Greek agitation for union (*enosis*) with Cyprus, a British possession since 1878, had been conducted before 1955 by the National Organization of Cypriot Combattants (EOKA), a terrorist group founded by Col. George Grivas, a Cypriot-born Greek army officer. EOKA supported Archbishop Makarios, the political head of the *enosis* movement.

Britain refused to withdraw from Cyprus, partly through concern for the fate of the Turkish minority, constituting 18 percent of the population, partly because of the strategic significance of Cyprus. In the pursuit of *enosis*, Greek governments, no matter how conservative or anticommunist, did not hesitate to seek the support of neutralist or even Communist bloc nations, in order to force Britain into a withdrawal.

The Zurich and London agreements of 1959–1960, which did grant Cyprus independence, did not satisfy Greek nationalism either, because they left Britain in possession of her military bases and because they protected Turkish minority rights under the new Cypriot constitution. The agreements also made Britain, together with Greece and Turkey, guarantee powers with the right to unilateral action in case of violation of the 1960 status quo.

The emotional Cyprus issue, combined with mounting social problems of the early 1960s, fostered new parties in opposition to the government of Prime Minister

Constantine Karamanlis, Papagos' conservative successor. Leading among the new parties was the United Democratic Left (EDA), which included former Communists, as well as the Center Union of George Papandreou. The political struggle of the early 1960s revolved principally around the contest between Papandreou and Karamanlis, the former determined to end Conservative rule in Greece, the latter equally concerned over the prospects of a left-of-center government under Papandreou. Karamanlis' resignation in 1963 over King Paul's official visit to England, the country denounced by *enosis* advocates, was followed by new elections in November 1963 and the formation of a Papandreou government.

Papandreou

Once in power, Papandreou confirmed the fears of the Conservatives, the army, and the king. Spending priorities were shifted from defense to social programs, left-wing political prisoners were released, and Communists reentered the political process. The death of King Paul in 1964 occurred at a critical moment, the crown passing into the hands of his inexperienced twenty-three-year-old son Constantine II. The old Papandreou and the young king became quickly deadlocked over the army's role in politics and the king's power over the cabinet. Papandreou charged the army with having rigged the 1961 elections through a plot based on the "Pericles Plan." The army charged Papandreou's son Andreas with involvement in a left-wing conspiracy, the "Aspida group," which was said to plan the overthrow of the monarchy. After the resignation of Papandreou, Greek politics remained deadlocked between 1965–1967 under a succession of weak governments. The army feared that Papandreou's Center Union might easily win the elections which the king had scheduled, after several postponements, for May 1967. Both the king and senior army leaders were surprised by a colonels' coup on April 21, 1967, headed by Colonel George Papadopoulos, which was designed to prevent the scheduled May elections.

The Military Coup

The military junta, which called itself the National Revolutionary Council, justified its action as an emergency measure, designed to protect Greece from a Communist takeover. Junta rule entailed the detention of opposition leaders other than just the Communists, however, including both Papandreous. American pressure secured the release of both father and son before the end of 1967.

The junta did not regard itself as an interim or emergency system but rather as the beginning of a lasting change of government, which would be patterned after the Gaullist model. In this, it failed to obtain the support of prominent pre-junta political leaders. The junta remained opposed as much by Conservative leaders, such as Karamanlis, as it was by left-of-center leaders such as the Papandreous. Andreas Papandreou was sharply critical of the United States for maintaining relations with the junta and even charged that the colonels' coup of April 1967 had been carried out in collusion with the United States.

The junta's relations with Western Europe remained complex. Relations with NATO, which Greece had joined in 1952, were close. The Common Market showed its official disapproval of the Greek military dictatorship by suspending negotiations for full Greek EEC membership. Actual trade between Greece and the EEC increased, as did private West German investment. The U.S.-imposed partial arms embargo was more than offset by increased arms sales to Greece by Britain, France and West Germany. Greece withdrew from the Council of Europe when it became evident that it would be expelled. She also withdrew her ambassadors from the Scandinavian countries and Belgium, which were particularly vocal in criticizing the military regime.

What caused the eventual downfall of the junta in 1974 was not external pressure, but the failure of its economic policy, internal squabbling among the junta leaders, and the folly of a military invasion of Cyprus, as a last-ditch junta effort to rally nationalist support on its behalf. The ambitious economic goals of the junta's 1972 five-year plan became largely a victim of the 1973 oil crisis and the ensuing devaluation of the U.S. dollar, to which the Greek currency was closely linked.

In 1973 Papadopoulos abolished the monarchy because of the king's involvement in an unsuccessful effort to overthrow the junta. But Papadopoulos' own hold over the junta was beginning to weaken, as a result of the jealousy of his fellow colonels and the extent of opposition to his repressive measures. In November 1973 General Phaedon Ghizikis replaced Papadopoulos as president of the Greek Republic. On July 20, 1974 Ghizikis launched an ill-advised military invasion of Cyprus.

The Invasion of Cyprus

Initially, the junta would have been satisfied with a partition of Cyprus along ethnic lines and the union of the Greek and Turkish parts of the island with their respective sponsoring nations, Greece and Turkey. "Double-*enosis*" came to naught because it was opposed by Cypriot president Archbishop Makarios, who preferred Cyprus's independence under his own leadership to partition. The Greek attack of July 20, 1974 was more directed against Markarios than it was against the Turks.

Fall of the Junta

Turkey nevertheless responded immediately with a military invasion of its own, which resulted in the capture of 40 percent of the island, an area considerably larger than the Turks might have received in a peaceful partition. The Greek junta compounded its blunder by ordering general mobilization as a response to Turkish action. By late July, Greece and Turkey, both anchors of the eastern NATO flank in Europe, were exchanging gunfire across the Evros river. In the end, it was the Greek army itself that brought down the junta. After a Greek-Turkish cease-fire, General Ghizikis asked Karamanlis to return from his Paris exile to head a new civilian government. On July 24, 1974, Karamanlis was sworn in as prime minister in Athens.

PASOK

The widespread hope that post-junta Greece might at last develop a stable two-party system with shared ideological consensus was not entirely fulfilled. Andreas Papandreou's newly founded Panhellenic Socialist Movement (PASOK), which emerged as the principal opposition to Karamanlis, advocated widespread nationalization of industries and the confiscation of the wealth of the Orthodox church. In foreign affairs, Andreas Papandreou, prior to his election as prime minister in 1981, advocated Greek withdrawal from NATO, Greek withdrawal from the EEC, which Greece had recently joined in January 1981, as well as close ties to Third World "liberation movements." He similarly supported the Arab position against Israel in exchange for Arab support of the Greek position on Cyprus. His stance was often characterized by a critical attitude towards the United States and the charge that Greece had sunk to the level of an "American satellite." This anti-Americanism was doubly interesting as Papandreou was Harvard-educated and, upon receiving U.S. citizenship during World War II, was commissioned a U.S. naval officer. Andreas Papndreou's friends often asserted that he was less anti-American than "pro-Greek." Once installed as prime minister after PASOK's election victory in October 1981, he proved to be considerably more moderate in his domestic and foreign policy than his preelection rhetoric had suggested. Greek nationalism and opposition to U.S. military bases had been duly reflected in the new Greek constitution of 1975, which stated that foreign military forces were "not acceptable" on Greek territory except when endorsed by the "absolute majority" of the total number of members of parliament. Although denouncing the U.S. military presence on Greek soil before 1981, Papandreou quietly renewed the American base agreements in 1983, albeit on a provisional basis.

SPAIN: FROM FRANCOISM TO DEMOCRACY

The often-quoted Spanish saying that "Spain was different from Europe" never seemed more justified than during the period following the end of World War II. Whereas democratic government was being restored to the rest of Western Europe, from the Rhine to Italy and France, the Franco dictatorship continued in Spain with little outward change. Spain was morally and physically isolated, to be sure, with the British Labour party frequently denouncing Franco, and France keeping her common border with Spain closed until 1948. Spain's isolation decreased largely because of the strategic interest which the United States showed in her as the Cold War intensified. The 1953 U.S.-Spanish defense agreement granted the United States air and naval bases on Spanish territory. To Franco, the 1953 defense agreement was more than a means of overcoming Spain's isolation: it was to him a belated vindication of his own struggle against communism during the Spanish Civil War. Franco called the 1953 U.S.-Spanish defense treaty his "real victory" in the civil war.

Franco abhorred communism, but he disliked in equal measure liberal democracy, upon which the postwar Atlantic alliance rested. Spain's link with the Atlantic alliance was thus meant to reinforce the principles of "Francoism," not to prepare the liberalization of the Franco system.

Democracy and communism were judged in the context of recent Spanish history and they were identified by Franco and his followers as "anti-Spain," that which the Spain of Franco had defeated in the civil war. Francoism postulated the incompatibility of "Spain" and "anti-Spain" and hence denied the possibility of a gradual evolution of the Franco system towards democracy.

The Pillars of Franco's Spain

Franco's Spain was authoritarian but not totalitarian. Its system of government rested on several pillars, among which the *falange* movement was but one, the Spanish church, the army, and the monarchists being the others. After World War II the Catholic lay order *Opus Dei* joined as an influential supporter of the regime, especially in higher education and among the technocratic elite which administered Spain's economic development from the late 1950s onward.

The relative strength and influence of the individual props of the Franco regime shifted with time and the changing conditions within and without Spain. There existed, under Francoism, a political pluralism at the top within carefully defined limits of the system.

Falangist and army influence were at their height during the civil war and the Second World War. With fascism discredited after World War II, the relative influence of the church and the monarchists increased. Both were useful to the regime's effort to overcome its isolation after 1945 and to gain international respectability. In 1947 Franco proclaimed Spain a monarchy without crowning a king or even suggesting who the future king of Spain might be. In 1953 Spain concluded a concordat with the Catholic Church which granted the latter extensive privileges, but which gave the state the power to nominate the bishops.

Economic Recovery

The 1950s also marked the beginning of Spain's economic recovery from the ravages of the civil war and the damages inflicted by the post-1945 isolation. Not until 1948 was the 1929 level of industrial production regained. Without the generous help of Argentina, Spanish postwar hunger would have been worse than it actually was. Reconstruction was generally completed by 1956, with Spain financing it from its own meager resources. The postwar isolation had denied Spain access to international credit facilities and she was not invited to join the Marshall Plan.

Before the 1950s, Franco's economic and social policy had been strongly influenced by the Fascist corporate model. The 1938 Labor charter (*Fuero del Trabajo*) had divided the economy into "vertical syndicats" with compulsory membership of workers, managers and owners. The syndicats continued to be a stronghold of falangism, but real economic growth and development from the 1950s onwards occurred outside them.

Franco and the EEC

1957, the year of the founding of the EEC, had much the same meaning for the Spanish economy as 1953 had had for her foreign policy. From 1957 onwards, Spain strove to establish close contact with the free enterprise economics of Western Europe. Eventual EEC membership, for which Spain first applied, unsuccessfully, in 1962, henceforth remained a policy objective.

Francoism hoped to derive similar political benefits from its quest for economic association with Western Europe, as it expected a strengthening of the regime as a result of the 1953 U.S.-Spanish defense treaty. Prosperity, it was hoped, would erase the class-consciousness of Spanish workers, which the Fascist-style syndicalist system had been designed to accomplish without actually achieving that purpose. A prosperous Spain would then facilitate the task of institutionalizing Francoism on a lasting basis, as Franco began to give serious thought to the problem of succession. Under conditions of greater affluence, the regime was also prepared to liberalize its social and cultural policy. Workers received the right of collective bargaining, and the new press law of 1966, though still restrictive by western standards, was considered progressive by those of Spain. What the Franco regime was not prepared to do was to crown the sum total of economic progress and liberalized social and cultural policy with a decisive political step from Francoism to a pluralist democracy.

The Future Constitution

Rather, it remained the illusion of aging Francoism that progress and liberalization in some carefully selected areas of public and private life could be safely used as an inducement for the public acceptance of the unchanged political and philosophical essence of Francoism. The permanent framework of Francoism had begun with the proclamation of the monarchy of 1947. To this was added the 1958 "Law of the Principles of the Movement," which reaffirmed the monarchist form of government. The candidate for the throne, chosen privately by Franco, but not publicly announced, was Juan Carlos, the son of Don Juan and grandson of the last ruling king of Spain, Alfonso XIII. On January 10, 1967 Franco added the "Organic Law of the State" (LOE), which was endorsed by popular referendum. The Organic Law, a synthesis of several previously enacted laws, was intended as the future Spanish constitution. To the question, "After Franco, what?", the regime replied, "After Franco, the institutions." Juan Carlos, having been publicly announced as royal candidate on July 22, 1969, took the solemn oath to uphold the "Principles of the Movement."

The economic policy of the Franco regime during the 1960s was quite successful, with annual growth rates sometimes as high as 7.5 percent. From a heavily rural economy, Spain moved towards ninth place among Western industrialized nations. Foreign investment, the earnings from foreign mass tourism, and the remittances of Spanish workers employed in France and West Germany provided the capital required for the modernization and expansion of the Spanish economy. The aim of combining the strategic-economic integration of Spain into democratic Western Europe while preserving undemocratic Francoism at home, eluded the regime however.

Regionalism

Originally, the guarantors of Francoism after Franco were to have been Juan Carlos—the future king—and the conservative Carrero Blanco, whom Franco installed as prime minister in June 1973. On December 20, 1973 Carrero Blanco was assassinated in a bomb attack, for which the Basque terrorist group ETA claimed responsibility.

The resurgence of Basque terrorism was symptomatic of the broader unrest which gripped Spain during Franco's last years. Many of the forces that Franco believed to have been permanently silenced reappeared, some with greater strength and boldness than before. Among such forces were Catalan and Basque regional nationalism, labor unions, Communists, Socialists, liberals and, to Franco's personal embitterment, even leading figures of the Spanish church.

Franco and the Church

The older bishops, such as Archbishop Morcillo of Madrid, the head of the Episcopal Conference of Spain, continued to support Franco. Among younger priests, some supported Basque and Catalan nationalism. Monsignor Cirarda, bishop of Bilbao, even invoked Franco's own 1953 concordat to deny the state permission to prosecute Basque priests in his own diocese.

The liberal pronouncements of Pope John XXIII and of his successor Paul VI had a strong effect on Spanish state-church relations. Encouraged by the spirit of liberal reform within the church, Catholic liberals in Spain gathered around the monthly review *Cuadernos para el Diálogo* as a possible rallying point of a Spanish version of

Italy's DC, or West Germany's CDU. From 1964 onwards, the Vatican also appointed younger and more liberal bishops in Spain, including Monsignor Tarancón, who succeeded the conservative Morcillo as archbishop of Madrid. Tarancón and the liberal wing of the Spanish hierarchy wished to disassociate the church from the Franco regime in expectation of its eventual downfall.

The 1974 Statute

There was hope, for a brief moment between Carrerro Blanco's assassination in December 1973 and Franco's death on November 20, 1975, that the Franco regime might be willing to seek a compromise with liberal forces, in order to save the country from disturbances after the dictator's death. Such a compromise would have had to include the legalization and readmission of political parties. The statute of December 16, 1974, prepared by the new prime minister Carlos Arias Navarro fell far short of liberal expectations, however. The "associations" permitted under the 1974 statute had to function within the official "movement" and their membership had to be drawn from at least fifteen separate provinces, in order to deny the rebellious Basques or Catalans their own regional associations.

The outbreak of the Portuguese Revolution in April 1974 also dampened whatever willingness there may have been among Franco supporters to concede reform of the Spanish political system.

Juan Carlos

Franco's funeral was notable for the lack of attendance by foreign dignitaries. By contrast, the coronation of Juan Carlos was attended by the Duke of Edinburgh, the presidents of France and West Germany, and Vice-President Rockefeller of the United States. The thirty-seven-year-old king was encouraged to lead his country through a difficult transition towards democracy. From all available evidence, it was a course supported also by the majority of the Spanish people, provided it could be achieved peacefully and without bloodshed.

The king's first approach was democratic reform through the existing institutions. On January 28, 1976 Carlos Arias, whom the king had retained as prime minister, promised constitutional reforms, the legalization of political parties, other than the Communist, and a bicameral legislature. Since the promise included no guarantees of a democratic franchise or any specific election date, it failed to satisfy the opposition and was answered by a new round of violence in early 1976.

Arias' successor, Adolfo Suárez, himself also a former servant of the Franco regime, succeeded in implementing the king's strategy of step-by-step transition to democracy between November 1976 and June 1977.

Reforms

The Law of Political Reform of November 1976, establishing a bicameral legislature, was followed in March 1977 by the readmission of free trade unions. The Francoist "syndicates," together with the "movement" itself, were disbanded at the same time. The Basque flag, banned under Franco, was legalized in January 1977 and in April 1977 even the Communist party was legalized. The general elections of June 1977, the final act in the democratic transition, produced as positive a result as anyone concerned with the success of the Spanish democratic experiment had a right to expect.

The Elections of 1977

The party most closely identified with the Franco regime, the "National Alliance of the 18th of July" received less than .5 percent of the vote. The Communists received 9 percent, and the Socialists under Felipe González, 28.5 percent. Suárez' own Union of the Democratic Center (UCD) emerged as the strongest with 34.3 percent.

After the elections, Suárez as head of the UCD government presided in October 1978 over the implementation of the new constitution, which defined Spain as a social and democratic state ruled by law. Parliamentary monarchy became the form of government with guaranteed autonomy rights for the individual nationalities.

Spanish democracy had cleared its first major hurdle, but it was far from permanently safe. Among the remaining obstacles was a serious economic recession, which reached Spain full force in 1976–1977. Spanish democracy also continued to be opposed by Basque terrorism in the shape of the ETA, which, like its Italian counterpart of the 1970s, the Red Brigades, wished to destroy democracy by forcing it into a Fascist-style response. Democracy also remained bitterly opposed by some army leaders, who thought that King Juan Carlos had broken his oath to Franco to uphold Francoism. In February 1981 right-wing army leaders staged an unsuccesful coup, whose failure was in large measure due to the skillful leadership of the king.

Democracy in the 1970s

Both externally and internally, the chances for success were better for Spanish democracy in the 1970s than they had been during the brief and unhappy period of the Spanish republic of the 1930s. In the 1930s, Spain's democratic experiment coincided with the high tide of European fascism, with Hitler and Mussolini actively supporting the antidemocratic forces of Franco and the *falange*. In the 1970s democracy was the preferred form of government in Western Europe and the west European democracies were eager to help Spanish democracy with advice, support, and financial assistance. In the 1930s, Spanish doctrinaire liberalism, personified in prime minister Manuel Azaña, had deeply divided the Spanish public through its anticlericalism. In the 1970s, the democratic consensus of Spain was broad, with important elements of the Spanish church also supporting the post-Franco democratic experiment. In the 1930s, the Spanish Communist party had functioned as an extended arm of the Soviet-directed *Comintern*. In the 1970s, the Spanish Communists under Santiago Carrillo, embracing the Eurocommunist concept of parliamentary government, no longer followed Moscow blindly. The Spanish Socialists under Felipe Gonzales even went so far in their October 1981 Madrid party conference to repudiate Marxism as their ideology. After Franco, both Socialists and Communists supported the Spanish king, because they saw in him the best guarantee against the return of military rule.

PORTUGAL IN TRANSITION

The trigger of change and revolution in authoritarian Portugal of the 1970s was the long and costly colonial war, which Portugal had been waging in Africa since 1961.

Ever since the early 1930s Portugal had maintained the fiction that her overseas territories were not colonies but extensions of the "whole territory of Portugal." The 1930 Colonial Act, coauthored by Portugal's long-term strongman Antonio de Oliveira Salazar, placed "Overseas Portugal" under the direct control of Lisbon. The inhabitants were divided into "natives" and "non-natives," the latter consisting of Europeans and mixed-blood and "assimilated" Africans. The "natives" remained subject to forced labor, which was not outlawed until 1955.

Salazar's Portugal at first seemed quite untouched by the trend of European decolonization of the 1950s and early 1960s. Belgium's retreat from the Congo, Macmillan's "Winds of Change" speech in Cape Town, and de Gaulle's disengagement from Algeria in 1962 failed to induce Salazar into adopting a similar policy in Portuguese Africa. When India seized the small Portuguese enclaves of Goa, Diu and Daman in 1961, Salazar called the seizure a temporary occupation, not a final loss.

The Colonial Wars

The Portuguese colonial wars began in northern Angola, Portugal's richest colony, in February 1961. In Angola, guerrilla forces were divided between Holden Roberto's non-Marxist Union of the People of Angola (UPA) and Mario de Andrade's Marxist Popular Movement for the Liberation of Angola (MPLA). Better armed than its rival, the MPLA became the dominant opposition force to Portuguese rule. In Mozambique, Eduardo Mondlane's Front for the Liberation of Mozambique (FRELIMO) began its attacks on Portuguese authorities in 1964. In Portuguese Guinea (Bissau), Amilcar Cabral's African Party for the Independence of Guinea and Cape Verde (PAIGC) had been operating since 1952, claiming for itself a model role for anti-Portuguese guerrilla movements throughout Africa.

Portugal answered these attacks with counterinsurgency tactics of mounting effectiveness, as well as belated reforms. The 1961 Code of Rural Labor guaranteed equal pay for equal work regardless of race. The old category of *asimilados* was abolished and full Portuguese citizenship granted to all. Portuguese economic development in the colonies also gave signs of promise in mineral-rich Angola, where considerable oil deposits were discovered, and in Mozambique, where the giant Cabora Bassa dam promised to generate enough electrical power for export to South Africa. In a strictly military sense, the Portuguese were winning the war in Africa, though at the high cost of having to allocate over 40 percent of the entire budget to the African war. In no Portuguese colony were the guerrillas able to disrupt the major flow of the economy.

Portugal's war in Africa was lost in Portugal itself, as a result of the attitude of the very military leadership on whose shoulders the burden of the war had rested.

Spinola

In early 1974 a book by General António de Spinola, entitled *Portugal and the Future,* startled the Portuguese public. Spinola had successfully directed the Portuguese military effort in Angola and later in Bissau in his capacity as governor general. *Portugal and the Future* rejected a purely military solution to the African war, acknowledged the legitimacy of the African quest for emancipation, and advocated the speedy granting of autonomy. Portugal, in Spinola's view, should continue to play a major role in postindependence Africa. Spinola even proposed an enlarged "Lusitanian" community, to be formed out of the countries of Portuguese civilization, including Brazil. For Portugal's own future, he proposed basic reforms of the Salazar regime, including the return of popular consultation and the end of official secrecy.

Spinola's book provoked an immediate and hostile response from Portugal's ruling conservative circles, including President Thomáz. The clash between the general and the ruling conservatives brought into the open the ultrasecret Armed Forces Movement (MFA), a conspiracy that had been planning a coup d'état against the Salazar regime headed by prime minister Marcello Caetano since Salazar's death in 1970.

On April 25, 1974 the MFA staged a well-planned and executed coup in Lisbon which quickly ousted president Thomáz and the government of Prime Minister Caetano. The chief organizer of the coup was Major Otelo Savaiva de Carvalho, a veteran of Spinola's Bissau campaign.

Spinola, though aware of the MFA's existence before April 1974, did not share its extremist views, both with regard to its Marxist commitment and its desire for an immediate Portuguese withdrawal from Africa. Although the newly formed military junta picked him as president in May 1975, differences between Spinola and the leftist MFA members resulted in a quick break by September 1974, when Spinola resigned the presidency. The junta granted full independence to the colonies, beginning with Bissau in September 1974, followed by Mozambique and Angola in June and November 1975 respectively. Independence often occurred amidst considerable violence between Europeans and Africans, especially in Luanda, Angola.

At home, Portugal was plunged into a period of experimentation, precipitous change, and ultimate anarchy, which did not end until the election of General Antonio Ramalho Eanes to the presidency in June 1976.

Junta Rule

Between September 1974 and June 1976 Prime Minister Lt. Col. Vasco Gonçalves, who was hand-picked by the leftist junta, instituted a drastic land reform and nationalized 60 percent of all Portuguese industry. The result was that Portugal, which had achieved self-sufficiency in wheat under Salazar, had to import food to the tune of $775 million by 1976. The overall trade deficit, resulting from the general economic dislocation, climbed to $1.2 billion by 1976. The Portuguese Communist party under Alvaro Cunhal experienced a significant comeback under junta rule. In 1975 the Communists seized the Socialist newspaper *Republica,* which caused Socialist leader Mário Soares to resign from the post of foreign minister in the Gonçalves government. Unlike his Spanish counterpart, Santiago Carrillo, Cunhal was not a "Eurocommunist." Staunchly loyal to Moscow and the Soviet political model, Cunhal rejected the notion of parliamentary government for Portugal on the grounds that the social and economic structure of Portuguese society was not, in his view, suited to democracy.

Eanes and Soares

Upon his election to the presidency, General Eanes appointed Socialist leader Mário Soares to the prime ministership. Together they tried to undo the damage of junta rule through a policy of "disintervention," i.e. the return of illegally seized farm land and factories. Eanes tried to exert the same moderating influence on post-Salazar Portugal which King Juan Carlos was applying to post-Franco Spain. When Portugal applied for EEC membership in September 1976, she did so not only for reasons of economic need, but in the knowledge that democratic Western Europe would lend its moral support to the fragile new democracy which Eanes and Soares were attempting to preserve in Portugal.

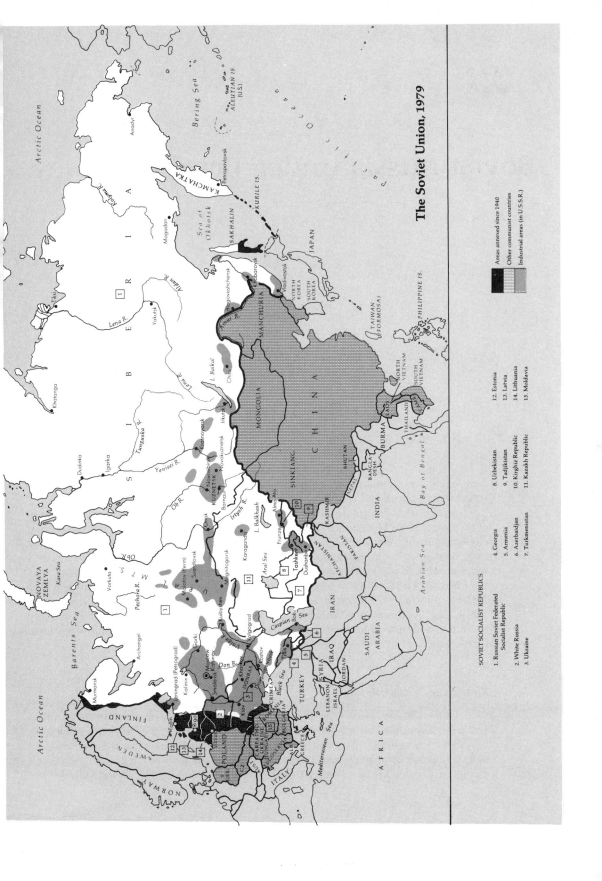

The Soviet Union, 1979

Areas annexed since 1940
Other communist countries
Industrial areas (in U.S.S.R.)

SOVIET SOCIALIST REPUBLICS

1. Russian Soviet Federated Socialist Republic
2. White Russia
3. Ukraine
4. Georgia
5. Armenia
6. Azerbaidjan
7. Turkmenistan
8. Uzbekistan
9. Tadjikistan
10. Kirghiz Republic
11. Kazakh Republic
12. Estonia
13. Latvia
14. Lithuania
15. Moldavia

29

Soviet Russia under Brezhnev

REACTION AND "REAL" SOCIALISM

If Krushchev had been preoccupied with overcoming the Stalinist legacy, Khrushchev's heirs were similarly concerned with correcting what they perceived to have been Krushchev's errors and excesses in trying to liquidate Stalinism.

As a restless reformer, Krushchev had disturbed the privileged lifestyle of many of the Soviet elite. His decentralization schemes, undertaken for efficiency's sake, had often meant the relocation of party and state bureaucrats into the provinces and far from Moscow, the preferred place of residence in the Soviet Union. In Khrushchev's time, the elite of party and state bureaucracy, known as the *nomenklatura,* was no longer the obedient class it had been under Stalin, nor was the Central Committee of the 1960s as pliable as the terror-stricken Central Committee of the Stalinist purges of the 1930s. The overthrow of Krushchev reflected not merely a power struggle at the very top but a widespread anxiety among the elite about the immediate and long-range consequences of the Khrushchev course.

Khrushchev's 1961 Program

In this, Khrushchev's party program of 1961 played a pivotal part for, if taken seriously, it would mean a serious threat to the accustomed role of Soviet bureaucracy.

The Khrushchev program had declared the socialist phase in the development of the USSR as completed, and announced the beginning of the "highest" phase, that of communism. This was further taken to mean the end of the "dictatorship of the

proletariat'' and the transition of the USSR towards a Communist "people's state."
Like the Yugoslav reform Communists of the fifties, Kardelj and Djilas, Khrushchev
wished to see Soviet society evolve along lines which Marx had predicted, rather than
those laid down under the Stalinist bureaucratic socialism of the thirties. This meant,
among other things, the "withering away" of the state. With the attainment of communism, Soviet society would witness the progressive reduction of state functions and
their transfer to autonomous social organizations under Communist party management. The most significant departure of the 1961 program from past practice was the
thesis that society itself, not the Soviet state, was destined to be the creator of the
communist order. By implication, the 1961 program also pointed to the citizen, not
the state, as the ultimate purpose and rationale of the Soviet system.

Whatever the motive of Khrushchev's party program, the impact was clear. In
the eyes of his successors, Khrushchev had not only jeopardized Soviet external security and prestige, but he had threatened the inner stability of the system as well.
The "hare-brained" schemes, cited in Khrushchev's official condemnation, probably
alluded as much to his ideological ambitions as to his foreign policy adventures.

The danger of the Khrushchev program of 1961 was soon revealed by the liberal-
Communist experiment undertaken by Czechoslovakia during the "Prague Spring"
of 1968. Many of the Czechoslovak reformers subsequently testified that their ideas
had been derived from the Soviet Union's own party program of 1961. In contrast to
Khrushchev's 1961 party program, of which little was subsequently heard, Brezhnev
introduced the concept of "real" socialism.

"Real" Socialism

The pragmatic concept of "real" socialism rested on the undiminished and expanding power of the Soviet state, its centralized bureaucracy, its military establishment, and its monopolistic Communist party. Eventually, the 1977 "Brezhnev
constitution" enshrined the exalted role of the Soviet state under "real" socialism.
The constitution's preamble specifically identified the Soviet state as the creator of the
"material-technical foundations of communism" and the promoter of the "education
of man in Communist society." It is the state, not some ill-defined future social organ,
that is given the task of "strengthening social equality," of "overcoming the differences between town and country," and of furthering the "development and integration of all peoples and nations of the USSR."

Where Krushchev had attempted to expand the power of the party at the expense
of the state, Brezhnev's "real" socialism was aiming at an increased identification of
party and state. The Czechoslovak reform Communists of 1968 had tried again to
separate the functions of party and state. Brezhnev's 4,000 tanks and 600,000 men
saw to it that they would remain closely tied together.

The state concept under Brezhnev's "real" socialism, if not an actual relapse
into Stalinist practice, was more of a logical outgrowth from the Stalin model than
what Khrushchev had had in mind in 1961. The reassertion of the governing role of
the state had immediate practical consequences. Between 1964 and 1965 Khrushchev's
decentralization measures were quickly discarded. Central economic planning was restored to the State Planning Committee (*Gosplan*) and the industrial ministries in Moscow, whose staffs had been cut by as much as 80 percent, resumed their accustomed

role. The economic reforms of Liberman, Kantorovich and Novozhilov, advocating increased freedom for individual plant managers and adoption of the profit motive, were quickly deemphasized by the late 1960s.

Cultural Policy

The conservative thrust of "real" Socialism soon affected cultural policy as well. Solzhenitsyn, widely known through his publication of *One Day in the Life of Ivan Denisovich* in 1962, was no longer permitted to publish *First Circle* and *Cancer Ward* in his homeland. Soon he was expelled from the official Writers' Union as well. Alexander T. Tvardovski, the editor-in-chief of the magazine *Novy Mir,* which had published Solzhenitsyn in 1962, was removed from the Central Committee in 1966. By 1970 he was also dropped from *Novy Mir.* The trial and imprisonment of the writers Andrei Sinyavsky and Yuri Daniel in 1966 likewise suggested a return to cultural and intellectual repression.

The Succession

The reaction to the Khrushchev era was also manifested in the style of the succession struggle and the manner in which the fallen leader was relegated to political oblivion. Khrushchev's heirs clearly regarded his style of leadership as embarrassing to Soviet prestige, and they were loath to repeat the spectacle of the post-Stalin power struggle of the mid-1950s. Despite the obvious clash of personalities, the public airing of differences was kept to a minimum after 1964. There was no dramatic purge after Khrushchev's fall, no startling revelations of treachery and treason in high places, such as had accompanied Beria's removal in 1953. Khrushchev's son-in-law Abzhubai lost his job at *Pravda,* and Polyakov, the Central Committee secretary for agriculture, was dismissed. There was a tightening-up of party membership at the lower levels, annual admissions being cut from an average of 760,000 to 600,000 between 1966 and 1971. Khrushchev, though permitted a reduced pension, became officially an "unperson." His death in 1971 and his burial at Moscow's Novodevichy cemetery merited a six-line notice in *Pravda.* No public recriminations followed. The party leadership was anxious to demonstrate the maturity of the system by arranging for a dignified succession.

BREZHNEV'S RISE

As was the case after Stalin's death in 1953, the new leadership presented itself as "collective" in 1964. This signaled less a permanent commitment to the principle as such than the existence of several contenders for the top position of first party secretary. The election of Prime Minister Kosygin by the Central Committee in October 1964 was unanimous; that of Brezhnev as first secretary was not.

Among the likely Brezhnev rivals in the Politburo was Nicolai V. Podgorny, a Central Committee secretary since 1961. By 1965, Podgorny, replacing Mikoyan, had been pushed into the politically unimportant post of the Soviet presidency. Frol R. Kozlov, a potential Brezhnev rival and Khrushchev's deputy since the Twenty-second Party Congress, was eliminated by ill health, and he died in January 1965.

Shelepin

The most serious challenger turned out to be Alexander Shelepin, younger than Brezhnev and enjoying strong backing in high party organs. In a fast-moving career Shelepin had risen from Moscow *Komsomol* (Communist youth) secretary to chairman of the KGB. Upon becoming Central Committee secretary in 1961 he handed the KGB leadership to his trusted friend Semichastny, who had previously filled Shelepin's post as *Komsomol* secretary. That Shelepin and Semichastny played an important part in Khrushchev's fall seems well established, and some have even pointed to Shelepin as the instigator of a plot. Shelepin was duly rewarded with full Politburo membership in 1964 without the customary "apprenticeship" as a nonvoting candidate member. From 1965 onwards, signs of a growing rivalry with Brezhnev became unmistakable, in which Shelepin steadily lost ground.

In 1966, at the Twenty-third Party Congress, Shelepin's followers organized noisy demonstrations on his behalf, an unusual event in Soviet politics, and one which had not occurred in this form since the launching of the Stalin cult at the Fourteenth Party Congress in December 1925. In 1967 Shelepin was ousted from the Central Committee secretariat, however. Among those who warned the party leadership against the "ambitious young man" was the old and experienced Mikoyan, survivor of many purges and servant to many Soviet masters.

Shelepin's ouster from the Politburo did not occur until 1975, following a well-planned intrigue. While visiting Britain in his capacity as trade union council chairman, he became the target of hostile demonstrations because of his role in the assassination of exiled Ukrainian leader Stephen Bandera by one of his KGB agents in Munich in 1959. The Politburo seized upon the embarrassment of the London demonstrations as an excuse for stripping Shelepin of both his seat in the Politburo and his chairmanship in the trade union council. KGB boss Semichastny shared his mentor's banishment into political obscurity.

Slower than Shelepin's, Brezhnev's rise began in the 1930s, when Stalin's purge had created many vacancies. Brezhnev's rise was typical in that it combined the career of a young technocrat with that of party activist. While training at the metallurgical institute at Dnepropetrovsk in the Ukraine, Brezhnev also became a party organizer among his fellow students. After graduation he rose to deputy mayor and party secretary of the Dnepropetrovsk party committee.

From his Dnepropetrovsk home base, Brezhnev was to carry many personal followers along as his career developed. Among these were the future premier of the Ukraine, Korochenko; the future first deputy prime minister under Kosygin, Nikolai A. Tikhonov; Brezhnev's own future deputy in the Politburo, Andrei P. Kirilenko; the future Ukrainian party boss, Vladimir Shcherbitsky; the future minister for internal affairs, Nikolai A. Shchelokov; and the future deputy KGB leaders, Viktor M. Chebrikov and Georgi K. Tsinev. The significance of the Dnepropetrovsk region to Brezhnev's political strength was similarly revealed by the membership of the Central Committee, newly elected at the party congress of 1976. Among the 287 elected members, the Dnepropetrovsk region enjoyed the largest single representation. In World War II Brezhnev, like Khrushchev, served as political commissar, with the rank of major general. His commanding officer in the Eighteenth Army was General Grechko, who also became Soviet defense minister in 1967. In May 1945 Brezhnev entered Prague with the Red Army, a city destined to play an important part in the shaping of the future "Brezhnev doctrine." After the war he became first party secretary in the Moldavian Republic (the former Rumanian Bessarabia). His performance was apparently deemed satisfactory by the aging Stalin, who rewarded him with appointments to the Secretariat and a candidate membership in the Politburo at the Nineteenth Party Congress in October 1952.

Stalin's death, at first, threatened to cut short Brezhnev's rise. Along with several other younger men, he owed his appointment in 1952 to Stalin's effort to outmaneuver the old guard of Molotov, Voroshilov, Mikoyan and others. After Stalin's death, Brezhnev was purged from his high posts. In 1954 Khrushchev sent him to Kazakhstan to implement the "virgin soil" project. Had the project failed it would undoubtedly have spelled the end of Brezhnev's career. Though a failure in the long run, the project was sufficiently successful at the outset to enable Brezhnev to claim credit at the 1956 party congress. Brezhnev regained both his seat in the Secretariat and his candidate membership in the Politburo. In 1957 he advanced to full Politburo membership.

In 1966 at the Twenty-third Party Congress, two years after his election to first party secretary, Brezhnev assumed the more resounding title of "general secretary," which only Stalin had held before him. In 1969 Brezhnev's portraits in public began to be featured a size larger than those of the other ten members of the Politburo, a sure sign of his enhanced power. Before long, it was Brezhnev, not Kosygin the prime minister, who presided over official state functions and the signing of international treaties, such as the SALT I agreement of 1972 and the SALT II agreement of 1979. Still, the late sixties to early seventies were not without their challenges to Brezhnev's leadership, particularly over foreign policy.

Opposition to Brezhnev's course of détente with the United States came from the Ukrainian first party secretary and hardliner P. Shelest, who objected to the Nixon visit in 1972, and also from G. Voronov, premier of the Russian Federal Republic (RSFSR). Voronov's demise began in July 1971, when he lost the premiership of the RSFSR; Shelest's demise began in May 1972, when the latter was driven from his Ukrainian post. In 1973, a year of foreign and domestic gains for Brezhnev after his successful visit to the United States and a good grain harvest, both Shelest and Voronov were expelled from the Politburo. Shelest's replacement as Ukrainian party leader and Politburo member was Shcherbitsky, a trusted Brezhnev lieutenant.

Changes in the Central Committee membership closely followed the shifts of power in the Politburo between 1971 (Twenty-fourth Party Congress) and 1976 (Twenty-fifth Party Congress). Of the 287 Central Committee members chosen at the 1976 party congress, 86 were elected for the first time, whereas 40 who had been elected in 1971 were not reelected. Of all the delegates chosen for the Twenty-fifth Party Congress, one-quarter had joined the party only since Brezhnev first became party secretary in 1964.

The Brezhnev Constitution

Brezhnev's attempt to combine leadership of the party with a strengthened Soviet presidency failed when first tried at the 1971 party congress. It succeeded only after President Podgorny was ousted in May 1977 and the "Brezhnev constitution" was adopted in October of the same year.

Like the Stalin constitution of 1936, which it superseded, the Brezhnev constitution of 1977 was both a party leader's statement of personal power at the end of a protracted power struggle, and a declaration of intent for Soviet domestic and foreign policy.

From 1977 onwards, Brezhnev's power seemed supreme and free from challenge. Official propaganda began to inflate his World War II role out of all proportion, conferring on him the title, "Hero of the Great Patriotic War." In February 1978, already honored with the rank of marshal since 1976, Brezhnev also received the "Order of Victory," the highest military decoration. In 1980 he was awarded the Lenin prize for his memoirs.

The constitution reflected the philosophy of "real" socialism by stressing the function of the state and by identifying the state, not society, as the sum total of the people, and the real object of Soviet Communist policy. Had Khrushchev been able to stay in power, the ideological thrust of the constitution might well have been different, for it was he who launched the project of a new constitution as far back as April 1962, following an announcement before the Supreme Soviet.

If the Brezhnev constitution marked a regression from Khrushchev's spirit of reform communism, it also attempted to take a cautious step forward from its Stalinist predecessor of 1936. The 1977 constitution was distinctly milder in its language than was the constitution of 1936, especially with regard to the penalties listed for infractions of Soviet law. The 1977 constitution also spoke for the first time of the "personal freedom," "honor and dignity of the individual" (article 57), while barring "hatred with respect to religious faith" and protecting the individual against abuses of official power. The Brezhnev constitution mentioned the Soviet Communist party as the "leading and determining force of Soviet society," but, like its forerunner, it failed to identify or even refer to the Central Committee or the Politburo as the real centers of power.

In fact, the Central Committee of the party, technically elected by the party congress, has come to assume a role not too dissimilar from that of the old state council under the tsar. Its 287 members, chosen at the 1976 party congress, faithfully reflected the major interest groups of the Soviet hierarchy, with party and state bureaucracy occupying 125 seats each. The party bloc included the five editors-in-chief of the principal Soviet news media. The state bloc included, apart from the heads of the central ministries, the highest judicial functionaries, thirteen of the USSR's most important foreign ambassadors, five of the leading scientists and two of the most party-faithful Soviet writers. The army was represented with twenty men, eight of whom were marshals. The "people" had to make do with the few remaining seats, divided between trade union leaders, kolkhoz farmers, and ordinary factory workers. Of the 287 Central Committee members eight were women.

THE GROWTH OF ARMS

If Khrushchev's tinkering with ideology had given his successors cause for worry, his defense and foreign policy legacy, itself interwoven with ideology, may have been an even greater source for concern.

Khrushchev's premature strategic challenge of the United States in the Cuban missile crisis had revealed the inadequacy of both Soviet ICBM and naval power. The escalation of the Sino-Soviet ideological dispute into a Great Power confrontation in

Soviet Asia and the Far East had added a new and potentially formidable foe. The blossoming of some of Khrushchev's own reform ideas in the "Prague Spring" of 1968, combined with the pressures of West German revisionist policy in Eastern Europe, threatened once more to unseat Soviet power in Communist Eastern Europe.

All three challenges spurred the post-Khrushchev leadership into a vast program of arms expansion, which claimed, according to Western estimates, anywhere from 11, 13, or even 20 percent of the Soviet GNP by the 1970s.

As a result of these efforts, the USSR had by then grown into a military power of much greater capabilities than it had been under Khrushchev. In the strategic arms race against the United States, the USSR had increased its intercontinental missiles from 225 to 1,600 between the mid-1960s and mid-1970s and had, according to western estimates, begun to overtake the United States in the majority of strategic weapons categories by the late 1970s. In submarine-launched ballistic missiles (SLBMs) Soviet strength grew over the same period from 29 to over 700, exceeding the American arsenal of 655.

Naval Strength

The expansion of Soviet naval power proceeded apace under the direction of Admiral Serge Gorchkov. After a decade of expansion, the Soviet navy exceeded the U.S. navy in its number of vessels, though not in overall tonnage. Between 1961 and 1975 the USSR constructed 57 new naval vessels of 3,000 tons or more as against 122 for the United States, whereas Soviet vessels between 1,000 and 3,000 tons over the same period exceeded American by 83 to 2. In submarine strength the Soviets maintained their lead of 408 over 110 U.S. submarines. The addition of Soviet aircraft carriers of the 45,000-ton Kiev class was a further significant indicator of the Soviet navy's advancement from a coastal to a "blue ocean" fleet between the sixties and the seventies. The week-long Soviet naval exercise "*Okean*-1975," in which 220 warships participated in five oceans simultaneously, was meant to demonstrate to the world the USSR's newly developed global naval reach.

Soviet conventional armed strength facing NATO in Europe and Communist China in Asia experienced a similarly spectacular growth both quantitatively and qualitatively. Between 1964 and the mid-1970s Soviet ground forces increased from 3.4 million to 4.4 million, compared to a decline in American military manpower from 3.5 to 2.1 million. Soviet conventional strength included 50 armored and 7 airborne divisions, with 1.1 million men, 36,400 tanks, and 3,825 aircraft facing NATO alone. An additional 44 Soviet divisions were drawn up along the Sino-Soviet frontier.

The expansion of Soviet military power during the decade following Khrushchev's fall was helped by a number of political and geopolitical developments in Europe, Asia and America.

The general impact of the second Berlin crisis from 1958 to 1961, and the Cuban missile crisis which followed in 1962, on Western and American policy, had been to introduce a new element of caution, especially where Germany was concerned. Although it took the West German governments of the 1960s longer than most to appreciate the basic shift in Western policy, West Germany too recognized the futility of its revisionist policy in Eastern Europe, once Soviet Russia had sounded its brutal warning with the Czechoslovak invasion of 1968.

West Europe Divided

Otherwise, Western Europe was deeply preoccupied and often divided against itself over the issues of Gaullism, Britain's unsuccessful efforts to join the Common Market, and a slowly rising West European resentment against West Germany's newly gained economic and monetary power. By the end of the 1960s, the USSR had little to fear from united Western European action.

The Chinese Threat

The Chinese threat was of a different order. The fact that Communist China exploded its first nuclear bomb in October 1964, two days after Khrushchev's ouster, was itself not lacking in irony, considering the fact that Khrushchev had done his best to thwart China's nuclear program. By 1966, the Chinese successfully tested their first nuclear-armed intermediate missile. In 1967 the first Chinese hydrogen bomb was exploded and in 1970 the first Chinese ICBM was launched. March 1971 witnessed the first Chinese-built earth-orbiting satellite—less than fourteen years after *sputnik*. The long-term implications of Chinese nuclear power for Soviet Russia were obvious, and there is reason to believe that at least the Soviet military urged their government more than once during the 1960s to deliver a preemptive strike against Communist China's budding nuclear weapons industry.

The advances in the USSR's own nuclear weapons technology during the 1960s, as well as the expansion of Soviet nuclear operational strength were such, however, as to keep the Chinese threat within acceptable limits. Despite its spectacular progress, the Chinese nuclear arsenal of the 1970s posed no greater threat to the USSR than did that of the French *force de frappe*.

The United States in the 1960s

American domestic and foreign policy developments were of special importance to the undisturbed growth of Soviet strategic power during the 1960s. In a general sense, that decade marked the decisive turning point in American postwar power in many of its strategic, economic and psychological aspects. More often than not, the American elite which reached maturity and power during the 1960s, was apt to view the shortcomings of its own society and of American policy abroad as at least as serious, if not more serious, than those of its principal Cold War adversary, Soviet Russia. The 1960s witnessed a reassessment of the Soviet image in the West, and this was not particularly disturbed by even the Soviet invasion of Czechoslovakia.

The revisionist interpretation of the Soviet Cold War role essentially assigned the Soviet Union a mirror image of the United States, without allowing for any distinction of underlying values in either society. To its own domestic critics, American power in the 1960s seemed not only excessive, but "arrogant." It seemed only fair and logical to allow the Soviet Union to draw even in strategic weapons on the basis of such a reassessment. Whether the Soviet Union would halt the expansion of its own nuclear arsenal once it had attained parity, or whether it would continue its growth momentum to the point of decisive strategic superiority, was a question few cared to raise in the Western world when the Soviet Union still had a very long way to go before even attaining parity.

Vietnam

That the Vietnam War also greatly aided the undisturbed growth of Soviet military power during the 1960s cannot be doubted. In strictly monetary terms, the $150 billion spent on the Vietnam War represented a diversion of funds which, even if only partially applied to the American strategic and conventional arsenal, would have assured U.S. armed superiority over the Soviet Union for the decade of the 1970s. The less tangible psychological and political benefits of the Vietnam War to the Soviet Union undoubtedly exceeded those measurable in strictly monetary terms. Among these benefits must be counted the strengthening of American isolationism, the alienation of western Europe from the United States and thus, overall, an important step towards the Soviet goal of gradual accommodation of western Europe to Soviet hegemony.

New Relations

Enhanced Soviet military power soon paid important political dividends in Europe and in Soviet-American relations. In Europe, the first benefit came in the turnabout of West German foreign policy from the revisionism of the mid-1960s to Brandt's *Ostpolitik* after 1969, itself a form of West German accommodation to Soviet dominance in central and Eastern Europe. With the United States, the Soviet Union was enabled to enter into a new relationship, different from that under Khrushchev, with U.S. recognition of Soviet strategic parity in treaty form, and the prospect of American technology and capital assistance. These goals seemed all the more attainable as the United States, anxious to extricate itself from the Vietnam conflict, was more in need of Soviet goodwill and support on this matter than the other way around.

ECONOMIC STRAINS AND CHALLENGES

In the West it was often assumed during the 1960s that Soviet military spending would not impede significant social progress of the ordinary Soviet citizen. Indeed, it was not unusual to find highly optimistic accounts in American publications commemorating the fiftieth anniversary of the Bolshevik Revolution in 1967, which cited Soviet health statistics as evidence of major social advancement and which announced that in the Soviet Union, the "family car" was "on its way."

The sharp rise in military spending under Brezhnev was undertaken by an economy, however, whose GNP, according to generous western estimates, amounted to about 52 percent of the American. Soviet productivity likewise lagged considerably behind that of western Europe and the United States, with Soviet output being estimated at 41 percent of American levels in industry and only 11 percent in agriculture.

That the Soviet economy was facing serious difficulties at the end of the sixties and the opening of the seventies was also suggested by the postponement from 1970 to 1971, of the party congress whose job it was to launch the ninth five-year plan.

That the Soviet economy would soon overtake the American in industrial production, or agricultural output, or both, had been a stock-in-trade prediction of Soviet leaders since Khrushchev.

At the time of the launching of the ninth five-year plan at the Twenty-fourth Party Congress in 1971, Prime Minister Kosygin boasted that the USSR would exceed

American industrial and agricultural production by 1975, a year whose grain harvest turned out to be the Soviet Union's lowest in ten years with 140 million tons. In 1976, a year with a good harvest, Soviet planning chief Nikolai K. Baibakov again predicted that under the tenth five-year plan (1976–1980) the USSR would exceed U.S. industrial figures of 1975 by 9 percent in 1980 and would match the U.S. 1975 agricultural production by the same date.

That the USSR, starting from a lower economic level than the United States after World War II, had achieved a faster and more steady growth rate, was not disputed in the West. Soviet statistics claimed a ninefold increase in Soviet industrial output for the quarter-century from 1950 to 1975, as against a threefold increase for the United States. There was less willingness to accept Soviet claims for a Soviet GNP of 62 percent of the American by the mid-1970s. Moreover, the Soviet economic gains were achieved by a labor force half again as large as the American, with a larger agricultural area and abundant mineral resources.

Soviet economic growth rates were high under the eighth five-year plan, which had been launched in 1965 after the expiration of Khrushchev's extraordinary seven-year plan. The plan succeeded in reaching its upper limit of 41 percent in the growth of overall national income, and very nearly attained the projected upper limit of a 52 percent growth rate in heavy industry with an actual growth of 51 percent. In the consumer goods sector the growth rate of 51 percent actually exceeded the projected rate by 1 percent.

The reversal of growth priorities in the last years of the eighth five-year plan, with consumer goods output rising faster than the growth of heavy industry, was due, in large measure, to the good performance of agriculture. The reversal was temporary only and was not repeated under the ninth and tenth five-year plans, which relegated consumer needs to their accustomed secondary position behind capital goods. Under the tenth five-year plan the projected growth rates for capital goods industry were fixed at between 38 and 42 percent as against 30 to 32 percent for consumer goods.

The Soviet industrial growth rate under the ninth five-year plan (1971–1975) was lower at 43 percent than that achieved under the preceding plan. The drop in growth rates of the 1970s was rooted in such factors as a mounting shortage of skilled labor, a drop in productivity, insufficient investment capital, especially in the expanding energy industry, a shortage of advanced technology, and the continued imbalance between older, established, industries, such as steel, and newer ones, such as electronics.

The ninth and tenth five-year plans attempted to attack and overcome these problems in a comprehensive approach which also included significant steps in foreign policy. The ideological imperatives of Brezhnev's "real" socialism continued to impose their limits on pragmatic economic reforms as a cure for Soviet social and economic ills, however.

PROBLEMS OF AGRICULTURE

The sixties and the seventies continued to show the familiar zig-zag pattern of Soviet agricultural performance, with years of low yield being followed periodically by record harvests. After the poor crops of 1963 and 1965, there followed high averages under the eighth five-year plan from 1966 to 1970.

The poor grain harvest of 1972, reaching 168.2 million tons, was followed in 1973 by a record crop of 222.5 million tons. 1974 yielded a respectable harvest of 195.5 million tons, only to be followed by the crop disaster of 1975 of 140.1 million tons, barely two-thirds of the planned 215.7 million tons. The pattern was repeated in 1976–1977, 1976 yielding a bumper crop of 223.8 million tons, to be succeeded in 1977 with 194 million tons. The latter figure, though not a disaster, nevertheless fell significantly below the target of 213.3 million tons.

The rising need for foreign grain imports, principally from the United States, to cover the Soviet Union's own shortfalls, undoubtedly played its part in the search for improved relations with the United States under the new course of détente of the early 1970s. After the poor harvest of 1972, Soviet grain imports totaled 40 million tons, of which 19 million, one-fourth of the American wheat crop, came from the United States.

Among the factors contributing to the Soviet grain dilemma was the emphasis placed on the expansion of livestock under both the ninth and tenth five-year plans. Because of the inadequate crops of animal feed grain, soy beans and corn, as much as one-third to one-half of Soviet grain was fed to livestock. The Soviet wheat harvest, ordinarily twice the size of the American, would, in itself, be sufficient to cover human needs.

Sharp drops in the grain harvest, such as that of 1975, thus usually resulted in large-scale slaughtering of livestock, limiting supply and pushing up prices in the free farmers market. Soviet livestock in early 1976 reportedly declined by 20 percent.

The grain dilemma was compounded by the Soviet Union's assumption of export commitments of its own to such Communist nations as Cuba, North Korea, Vietnam, Czechoslovakia and even Poland, which, taken together, have run as high as 5 million tons annually. Such commitments were usually discharged through direct Soviet purchases from Canada and Australia.

The Soviet leadership spared neither capital nor effort to increase the efficiency of food production and food distribution. To alleviate the bottleneck of transportation, which often resulted in huge waste and spoilage, the ninth and tenth five-year plans launched the world's largest truck plant at Kama, built with West European and American technology and components.

A great deal of money went into soil improvement under both five-year plans of the 1970s, especially in European Russia. The tenth five-year plan earmarked a spectacular $225 billion for both soil improvement and improved farm mechanization.

Labor productivity on the USSR's roughly 48,000 collective and state farms continued to lag far behind labor productivity on the tiny private garden plots which collective farmers are allowed to keep as private property. The garden plots yield on the average two-thirds of the potato crop, one-third of all meat and milk, and half of all the eggs, though their total acreage is no more than 3.3 percent of the arable land. The paradox of Soviet agriculture still remains that its socialist sector, upon which the state lavishes investments, is the least productive, whereas the private sector, least favored officially, remains the most productive.

In the farm sector, bureaucratic socialism was not infrequently outwitted by peasant deception, which turned official rules to its own advantage. As collective farmers were more liable to obtain feed grain from state sources if they could offer eggs in exchange, Soviet farmers were known to have bought eggs in the cities and to have subsequently offered them on the collective farm in exchange for grain.

During the 1970s Soviet planners also attempted to streamline food production and processing through the so-called agro-industrial associations. Patterned after similar successful examples in Bulgaria, the agro-industrial associations combined several collective farms with storage and, sometimes, food processing facilities into a single unit. Soviet claims quoted savings in production costs by as much as 50 to 65 percent, especially among associations specializing in a single crop. By the late 1970s some six thousand such associations were in operation, many of them concentrated in the Moldavian Republic, Brezhnev's scene of action in the mid-1940s.

PROBLEMS OF ENERGY AND THE DEVELOPMENT OF SIBERIA

Like the industrial nations of the West and Japan, the Soviet Union encountered a growing energy problem during the 1970s. Unlike the Western nations and Japan, the USSR had expanding energy resources at its disposal, whose output began to taper off only at the end of the decade after years of spectacular growth.

During the 1960s Soviet oil production rose from 147.2 million tons in 1960 to 348.8 million tons in 1970. By 1974 the USSR surpassed the United States as the world's leading oil producer with 458 million tons. The tenth five-year plan originally called for a production goal of 640 million tons for 1980, a figure not likely to be attained, however, because of diminishing growth rates in the Soviet oil industry in the latter 1970s. During the 1980s the Soviet Union is likely to become an oil importer itself with as much as 80 million tons per year imported, a figure higher by 1 million tons than Britain's annual North Sea oil production of 79 million tons.

The increase in Soviet natural gas production from the sixties to the seventies was even bigger, rising from 45.3 trillion cubic meters in 1960 to 320 trillion cubic meters in 1975.

The increases in Soviet oil and natural gas production were matched not only by increasing domestic demand, but by demand from the USSR's East European partners in *Comecon* as well. Moreover, with the growing energy shortage in the West, Soviet oil exports to nonsocialist countries assumed far greater significance than before, becoming the Soviet Union's principal source of Western currency. The Soviet oil revenue, obtained from nonsocialist customers rose from $550 million in 1972 to $2.7 billion in 1973 and nearly $8 billion in 1974. In 1974 Soviet oil exports accounted for 40 percent of the total value of Soviet exports. By 1976 Soviet oil exports to nonsocialist countries exceeded those to socialist countries for the first time.

The expansion of Soviet oil and natural gas production was overwhelmingly due to the opening up of new reserves in western Siberia, which, beginning in the 1960s, far outdistanced the older production centers in the Caucasus and the Caspian Sea. The latter areas, which had accounted for nearly 70 percent of all Soviet oil output at the end of World War II, had declined to a share of only 4 percent by 1973.

The west Siberian fields, by contrast, accounted for over two-thirds of the entire increase in Soviet oil output between 1967 and 1977. All in all some 150 new oil fields were developed in western Siberia, of which those at Urengoi, Samotlor, Surgut, Tobolsk and Tyumen were the largest.

With the slowing down of the growth rates in the Soviet oil industry by the end of the 1970s, Soviet planners began to focus on alternate energy sources, especially coal and nuclear energy. In 1960, coal still accounted for 70 percent of all fuel consumed in the USSR, as against 45 percent in 1974. The combined share of oil and natural gas increased over the same period from 20 to 50 percent. From 1975 onwards there was a renewed emphasis on coal, whose output was scheduled to rise from an annual 700 million tons to 1.2 billion tons by the year 2000. Soviet production statistics for the late 1970s again suggested, however, that the ambitious targets for increased coal production were not likely to be reached. Between 1977 and 1978 coal production increased by a mere 2 million tons from 722 to 724 million tons.

Beginning in the mid-1970s, the Soviet Union embarked on a determined nuclear energy program. Under the ninth five-year plan nuclear power represented 6.5 percent of all newly added electrical capacity, a figure scheduled to rise to 20 percent under the tenth five-year plan. Total Soviet nuclear power capacity by 1980 was scheduled to reach 19.4 million kilowatts, an amount equal to that projected for West Germany or France, but only about one-fourth of U.S. capacity. Soviet plans call for nuclear power to meet 20 percent of all energy needs by the year 2000, and to supply all electrical energy for European Russia by that time.

The safety factor of nuclear power in the USSR was debated in a well-known article in the authoritative party journal *Kommunist* in September 1979 by Nikolai Dollezhal, the leading Soviet expert on nuclear energy, and Yuri Koryakin, an economist. The article recommended the transferral of nuclear power plants from the vicinity of dense population centers and their concentration in "nuclear parks," as planned in Western Europe. The USSR itself suffered a serious nuclear accident in the Urals in 1958, which went unreported at the time. There were also nuclear accidents on a lesser scale involving Soviet-built reactors in Finland and Czechoslovakia, at Lovisa and Yaslovke Bohunice respectively, in the late 1970s.

Siberia continues to hold the bulk of the USSR's untapped energy and mineral reserves, though their exploitation has become increasingly difficult for reasons of cost and transportation. Kysyl Syr in eastern Siberia contains the largest known reserves of natural gas. Norilsk in northern Siberia is a principal site of platinum deposits, the USSR's biggest copper deposits are located at Udokan, while Magadan in the Soviet Far East is a major gold-producing area.

The high labor cost rendered the development of Siberia's mineral riches exceedingly expensive. To attract workers, wages had to be doubled on the average, and workers spending fifteen years in Siberia may retire five years ahead of the legal limit—age fifty-five for men, fifty for women.

It was partly for reasons of economic development that the USSR launched in 1974 the BAM (Baikal-Amur-Mainline) railroad project covering 2,000 miles and scheduled to be open by 1980. Running from Ust-Kut on the Lena river to Komsomolsk on the Amur, the BAM railroad is the first rail line to cross Siberia since the building of the trans-Siberian railroad under Tsar Nicholas II.

INDUSTRIAL MANAGEMENT AND PLANNING

The dynamics of Soviet economic growth and its increasing relationship with non-socialist economies under the changing trade patterns of the 1970s raised once more the question of the efficacy of the inherited system of planning and management.

During the 1970s a controversy began to emerge between orthodox Soviet economists, such as *Gosplan* chief Nikolai Baibakov, and the "mathematical economists," such as Nikolai P. Federenko, head of the Central Economic Mathematical Institute at the Soviet Academy of Sciences. Baibakov and the orthodox economists favored the retention of the system of fixed five-year plans, introduced by Stalin and programmed for definitive production goals for the entire plan period. The mathematical economists, on the other hand, suggested an alternative system known by its initials of SOFE (System of Optimal Functioning of the Economy), which would combine growth projections over a period longer than five years, with annual options for plan revision according to variables such as foreign trade or the availability of advanced technology.

The trouble with SOFE was not only its radical departure from orthodox economic tradition, but its implications of power and politics. Not only did the mathematical economists reject *Gosplan* as an agency suitable for the implementation of their ideas, but their built-in system of annual plan revision would, if adopted, undermine both the customary penalties for nonfulfilment and the traditional rewards for plan fulfilment or overfulfilment. Most troublesome, from the orthodox viewpoint, would be the prospect of an economy functioning increasingly through direct contacts between industries, rather than along well-supervised and predetermined bureaucratic lines. Such trends, if permitted to thrive, would erode the foundations of bureaucratic socialism under conditions of broadening market socialism.

The issue of mathematical economics was not entirely new to the Soviet Union. Though allowed very limited application under Khrushchev in such areas as capital investment and price formation, it had never been recommended on as broad a scale as it was under Brezhnev.

During the 1970s, however, the orthodox Soviet economists, such as Nikolai Baibakov, speaking through the *Gosplan* journal *Planovoye Khozpaist* (Planned Economy), prevailed over the mathematical economists. What the orthodox economists resented most about the mathematical economist viewpoint was the thesis that modern industrial economies, whether Soviet or capitalist, were confronting similar problems which were soluble by similar methods. What the orthodox economists did attempt in the late 1960s and 1970s was the modernization of the Soviet economy through massive imports of Western technology and machinery as well as through increased application of scientific techniques. The funding for research at such bodies as the Soviet Academy of Sciences and the State Committee for Science and Technology increased from $18.2 billion in 1971 to $21.7 billion in 1973. Dzherman M. Gvishiani, deputy chairman of the State Committee for Science and Technology urged, in his book *Organization and Management,* that the Soviet economy adopt that which was best in Western, principally American, management techniques, within the limits of the Marxist-Leninist system.

During the 1970s Soviet planners thus looked especially towards the western-style corporation as a model whose management efficiency had not escaped their attention. The result was the creation of "production associations" and "industrial associations." Under the former, for which precedents existed under Khrushchev, several related plants were placed under single management. The latter type aimed at the merger of an entire branch of a given industry. The "industrial associations" concept again came under attack from the ministerial bureaucracy, which feared loss of influence and power. With declining labor productivity, the Soviet Union also witnessed during the 1970s a revival of the slogans, titles and propaganda techniques, so familiar from the Stalinist thirties and forties, including the "Stakhanov cult." 1974 was officially designated "year of the shock work," 1975 "year of production records." Conversely, there was an increase in official attacks on "loafers, idlers, and drunks."

THE SOCIAL PROMISE AND THE REALITY

Consistent with similar claims in the past, the ninth and tenth five-year plans called the achievement of the "classless society" and the "attainment of higher living standards" for all their principal objectives.

Among the festive speeches given at the Twenty-fifth Party Congress of 1976, which launched the tenth five-year plan, there was one which asserted that in the Soviet Union there existed only one privileged class, the "class of the children."

The Nomenklatura

In truth, Soviet society has remained the highly differentiated social body it was under Khrushchev, with living standards, incomes, and conveniences sharply divided between ruling elite and the people. If anything, the privileged position of the *nomenklatura* remained more of a centerpiece of Brezhnev's "real" socialism than it might have been under Khrushchev's egalitarian party program of 1961. With average incomes and benefits of the elite running as high as thirty times those of average wage earners, the *nomenklatura* lives a life of social and economic apartness from the rest of Soviet society. This apartness embraces all aspects of social life from shopping, housing, and vacationing to medical care. The social differences between classes and individuals are, no doubt, even higher in western, nonsocialist societies. These societies do not, however, officially proclaim the attainment of a classless society as their goal, nor do they proceed from the low social level of ordinary citizens which is still widespread in the Soviet Union.

Social Welfare

Official Soviet statistics claimed major achievements for the 1970s in health care, education and social progress. Infant mortality was down to 26.4 per thousand live births and the average life expectancy was increased to seventy years. For every 10,000 citizens there were 30.5 physicians and 116 hospital beds. In education, there were 180 students enrolled at universities and higher institutions of learning for every 1,000 citizens. In a nation with an illiteracy rate of 76 percent at the time of the 1917 revolution, there existed 130,000 libraries with some 100,000 new books published every year in the 1970s. In housing, the Soviet government claimed the construction of between 2.2 and 2.3 million new apartments per year. Each Soviet citizen was said to be entitled to nine square meters of living space, though the reality more often was a minimum of four square meters.

In the early 1970s both *Pravda* and the trade union paper *Trud* criticized social abuses, especially the employment of minors and pregnant women in hard physical labor. In 1973 maternity benefits were raised and in 1974 every child under eight became eligible for a monthly assistance of twelve rubles, if the family income was below fifty rubles per person. In 1974 minimum wages were raised to seventy rubles per month (one ruble to $1.30 at the official rate) and the minimum income for a family of four was fixed at two hundred rubles per month. By the end of the 1970s the official average wage was given as 163.5 rubles per month, compared with an average 450 rubles for a member of the party and state bureaucracy.

Whereas wages had risen by over 30 percent on the average during the 1970s, official Soviet claims deny the existence of inflation in the USSR. Such claims are accurate for some though by no means all prices and costs.

Apartment rents remained constant at between 10 to 18 rubles a month for a two- or three-room apartment, for those fortunate enough to have one. Similarly the price of basic food staples, such as beef and potatoes, remained stable at $1.36 and 8 cents a pound, respectively, in government-run stores, if available. If they were not, the Soviet consumer had to rely on the private farmers markets, where *kolkhoz* farmers sold the produce raised on their garden plots. Food prices at the farmers markets were usually three to five times those charged at state-operated stores. As much as 80 percent of income went for food for average working families. The price of luxuries, especially automobiles, has, on the other hand, risen sharply. In 1974, the price of a Soviet-built Fiat sedan (Zhiguli) was 5,500 rubles. By 1979 the price had risen to 9,300 rubles, or the equivalent of four years' wages for a construction worker.

As in most Western societies, in the Soviet Union the old and the retired are worst off. Old-age pensions for factory workers were fixed in the 1970s at forty-five rubles per month. The pensions of retired collective farm workers, which were not included in any pension plan before 1964, were fixed at twenty-eight rubles per month. In terms of purchasing power, forty-five rubles buys a pair of new shoes. The price of a turkey at the farmers market is around fifty rubles.

The Soviet Consumer

The high growth rates of the Soviet economy during the late sixties and the still-respectable growth rates of the 1970s—the Soviet growth rate for the 1971–1975 period was, at an average annual increase of 4 percent, more than twice as high as the American—did not primarily benefit the consumer. In a non-market-oriented economy even the consumer goods produced often failed to satisfy demand, because type and quantity of output were not determined by market mechanism but by bureaucratic fiat. The inability to sell unwanted goods has then resulted in sales practices which, if attempted by private Western enterprises, would no doubt be the cause of wonderment or worse.

One such practice in the Soviet Union is the "combination sale." A desired article is sold only in conjunction with another which the buyer may not want, but which the state cannot otherwise unload. A motorcycle may be sold only if the buyer also agrees to purchase another item such as a crate of spoiled eggs. A railroad ticket may be purchased only in conjunction with a lottery ticket, whether the traveler cares to gamble or not.

The Soviet economic dilemma of the 1970s derived from the fact that the state-run economy was able to produce enough consumer goods, automobiles, washing machines, refrigerators and the like, to stimulate consumer appetites, without being able to really satisfy those appetites for the average wage earner. Internal Soviet propaganda thereupon attempted to solve the problem through a campaign discrediting "consumerism" and "commodity fetishism" as Western-inspired, depraved, and vaguely associated with other evils generally attributed to the West, such as moral decadence and pornography. The campaign did little to discredit Western living standards, for "to live like in the West" has remained a consumer wish for millions under Soviet socialism. The privileged few of the Soviet *nomenklatura* have, in fact, fulfilled that wish for their own class, although they have spared few efforts in concealing their accomplishment from those they rule.

DÉTENTE AND IDEOLOGICAL VIGILANCE

Periods of opening to the West have also traditionally been periods of heightened ideological vigilance in Soviet history. When Lenin opened the doors to Western economic cooperation under the New Economic Policy (NEP) of the 1920s, he did so for compelling economic reasons after the devastation of the Russian Civil War and the dislocation of Communist experimentation.

The NEP, at the same time, coincided with a party purge and the suppression of dissent within the Soviet Communist party.

Stalin's more liberal attitude toward the West during World War II, as symbolized by the dissolution of the Communist International in 1943, was prompted by military and political necessity. It was followed shortly afterwards by the renewed suppression of dissent inside and outside the party during the Zhdanov purge.

Brezhnev, it may be reasonably assumed, did not accept Western overtures of détente at the end of the sixties and the beginning of the seventies because he regarded the ideological struggle against the West as ended, but because he needed Western economic cooperation in order to maintain both a maximum growth of Soviet armaments and a minimum growth of living standards for the Soviet populace.

Under the Helsinki Accord, the Soviet leadership likewise committed itself to a greater flow of ideas between the blocs in exchange for Western de facto recognition of the Soviet dominance over Eastern Europe.

Within carefully drawn limits, the pledge of internal liberalization may have suited Brezhnev's purpose of dealing with the remaining diehard Stalinists in his own party, such as Shelest in the Politburo, or such Stalinist writers as Vsevolod Kochetov, for whom even Brezhnev's "real" socialism was not conservative enough. The fact that the full text of the Helsinki Accord, including those provisions pertaining to personal freedoms, was published in the Soviet press could not but have had domestic political significance. There were, and continued to be, signs of a revival of the Stalin cult in the 1970s, as reflected in Kochetov's novel *What Do You Really Want?*, which appeared in 1970, or Ivan Stadnyuk's novel *War* of 1974, which extolled Stalin's leadership in World War II. At the same time, there was a vast ignorance among Soviet youth of the 1970s as to the true dimensions of the Stalin terror of the 1930s. The Soviet poet Yevtushenko related in 1974 that Soviet youngsters believed the number of purge victims of the 1930s to have been only a few thousand at worst.

While using détente as a weapon against its own Stalinist opposition, the Soviet leadership nevertheless wished to remain in full control of whatever limited liberalization it had in mind. This required a campaign of heightened ideological vigilance against Western influences, which penetrated Soviet life more deeply in the 1970s than in previous times.

The ideological task of the 1970s was thus to assure the integrity of a multitude of interdependent factors, such as the credibility of Communist orthodoxy, the dominance of the Great Russian nationality, and cultural, social and intellectual conformity, all of which were facing varying degrees of challenge in a society grown too large, diversified and complex to fit comfortably into the molds essentially formed by Stalin in the 1930s.

Heightened vigilance expressed itself in many forms. It included Brezhnev's address to the seventeenth *Comsomol* congress of April 1974, as well as the Central Committee reprimand of June 1974 directed against the administrators of Saratov University and the Moscow Baumann Institute for neglecting the teachings of Marxism-Leninism. Ideological vigilance manifested itself also in the ostracism of leading Soviet academics, such as the renowned linguist Igor A. Melchuk, for refusing to publicly condemn Soviet dissidents.

The official siege mentality against Western ideas manifested itself in the denunciation of U.S. educational TV programs, such as "Sesame Street," which was branded as U.S. "cultural imperialism." Western newspapers and correspondents, who reported frankly and sometimes unfavorably about internal Soviet conditions, became a special target of Soviet attack. Among the Western papers singled out for attack were *Le Monde,* the London *Times,* the *New York Times,* the *Washington Post,* and the *Los Angeles Times.* Some leading Western correspondents were expelled, beginning with Ennio Caretto of the Italian *La Stampa* in 1970 and David Bonavia of the London *Times* in 1972. By the late 1970s the Soviets accused leading U.S. correspondents of being spies for the CIA, including Christopher S. Wren of the *New York Times,* George A. Krimsky of the Associated Press, and Alfred Friendly Jr. of *Newsweek.* In June 1977 *Los Angeles Times* correspondent Robert C. Toth, an acquaintance of Soviet dissident Anatoly Shcharansky, was arrested in Moscow.

THE REVIVAL OF GREAT RUSSIAN CHAUVINISM

Soviet population statistics of the 1970s revealed a much faster increase in the birth rate of the non-Russian nationalities than for the Great Russians, who comprise roughly one-half of the USSR's 261 million people. The increase was particularly notable among the Moslem population of the central Asian Soviet republics, which, having doubled between 1960 and 1980, numbered 50 million in 1980. It is expected to double again over the twenty-year period following 1980. The population share of the Great Russians in the central Asian republics declined, falling from 12.5 percent to 10.8 percent in Uzbekistan alone, between 1970 and 1979.

The declining share of the Great Russians among the roughly 120 different nationalities which make up the Soviet population raised the worrisome prospect of the loss of Great Russian dominance over the USSR. That dominance had been assured in a variety of ways thus far, including control over the top organs of party and state, the Politburo, the Central Committee, and the Council of Ministers. Even in union republics where the post of premier and party general secretary were in the hands of non-Russians, the Great Russians retained strong influence by occupying the deputy posts below premier and general secretary as well as retaining control of local KGB and military command.

The unfavorable population trends of the 1970s were accompanied by a stepped-up campaign of Russification, which was clearly intended to counter any new manifestation of nationalism on the part of the non-Russian nationalities. The campaign included the purging of the party chiefs of the Ukraine, Georgia, Armenia, and Lithuania between 1972 and 1974, all of whom had apparently been found wanting in the suppression of non-Russian nationalism. The new replacements, V. V. Shcherbitsky, E. A. Shevardnadze, K. S. Demirchyan, and Patras Grishkevichius soon implemented a much harsher policy that resulted in numerous arrests and prison sentences, especially in the Ukraine. The persecution of national dissidents, such as I. Dzyuba, Y. Sverstyuk and V. Chornovil in the Ukraine, did not arouse as much attention in the West as did the dissident trials in Moscow, primarily because they were more removed from the limelight of the world press.

The early 1970s also witnessed anti-Soviet demonstrations in the former Baltic states of Lithuania and Estonia, which, in the Lithuanian case, had to be quelled by Soviet troops. As in neighboring Poland, the Catholic church was closely allied with Lithuanian nationalism, with church papers such as *The Chronicle of the Catholic Church in Lithuania* playing an active political part.

Apart from forceful repression, Russification also manifested itself through cultural and school policy. The Russian language continued to expand its preferential status in non-Russian-speaking parts of the Soviet Union. In the Ukraine, only 20 percent of the population gave Russian as their nationality, yet 40 percent of all school children attended Russian-language schools. In Estonia, mandatory Russian-language instruction began in the second grade of all Estonian language schools, whereas the Estonian language was offered as an elective only, in the fifth grade of Russian-language schools. In the Estonian capital of Tallin 45 percent of native Estonians claimed a knowledge of Russian as against a mere 13 percent of resident Russians who spoke Estonian.

Among aggrieved nationalities, the Soviet Jews emerged as the most problematic group from the standpoint of Soviet officialdom because they, more than others, were seen as transmitters of Western ideas and as causes of internal dissent. As during Zhdanov's purge of the late forties, the Soviet authorities of the seventies took refuge behind the mask of anti-Zionism in combating dissident Soviet Jews, though the attacks were never very far from an open encouragement of latent Russian anti-Semitism.

DISSENT AND CULTURAL DESPAIR

The 1970s, a decade in which Soviet military power reached unprecedented strength, also turned out to be a period of vociferous dissent. Dissent was not new to the Soviet Union. It had surfaced under Khrushchev, though it had then been tolerated only to the extent that it attacked the Stalinist dynamics of Soviet communism, not its ideological premise. Dissent under Khrushchev also did not openly attack Soviet foreign policy to the extent that it would under Brezhnev. There was a student demonstration in Leningrad against Khrushchev's invasion of Hungary in 1956, of which the outside world heard nothing at the time. Soviet intellectuals were similarly critical of the suppression of the Hungarian Revolution, but their protest was private, rather than addressed to a worldwide audience.

Dissident protests against Brezhnev's invasion of Czechoslovakia in 1968 were, by contrast, highly publicized, revealing as never before a solidarity of views between opposition elements in the Soviet Union and the Communist states of Eastern Europe. Soviet physicist Andrei Sakharov declared his solidarity with the liberal reformers of

Czechoslovakia in his essay *Progress, Coexistence and Intellectual Freedom.* General Pyotr G. Grigorenko, soon to emerge as a prominent dissident, also protested the Soviet invasion of Czechoslovakia in a highly visible manner.

The dissident challenge of the 1970s was more difficult to deal with for Soviet authorities because both the internal and external conditions of Soviet power had become more complex. The old method of the Stalinist thirties of physical extermination of known or suspected dissidents could no longer be invoked in the more sophisticated 1970s. With Khrushchev, Brezhnev probably agreed that unfettered violence, once directed against opponents, could easily turn against its own perpetrators. That was the painful lesson of Stalin's rule, which few, even among the most conservative Soviet leaders in Brezhnev's time, were likely to forget.

The End of Slaveholder Socialism

External conditions had also changed, and the Soviet leadership showed itself often quite sensitive to foreign criticism which it might have ignored in the 1940s or 1950s. What Soviet dissident Yuri Orlov chose to call *slaveholder socialism* under Stalin no longer obtained under Brezhnev. Slaveholder socialism, Orlov observed, can be a very stable form of government, if it can be completely isolated from the outside world. With the greater influx of Western correspondents into the Soviet Union since the Helsinki Accord, the Soviet Union had become much more accessible, however, and to some degree accountable for the treatment of its own citizens to the outside world. Many Soviet dissidents, including Solzhenitsyn before his 1973 exile, and Sakharov, were spared a harsher treatment because of the protests of western-based organizations such as Amnesty International or the Authors' League of America. The actions of individual western writers, such as West German authors Heinrich Böll and Günther Grass, also often helped.

The Soviet response to dissent was selective and varied. Dissent, by definition, was not only an embarrassment, but a provocation, under a system which claimed to act not only in the very best interests of all its citizens but in accordance with historical inevitability and law. Dissent, in official Soviet propaganda, thus had to be rationalized either as treason, lunacy, or an act of personal frustration.

Dissent as Madness

Such was in essence the definition of Soviet dissent, given by KGB chief Yuri V. Andropov in an address in 1977. Andropov defined the causes of Soviet dissent as "political and ideological delusions," "religious fanaticism," "nationalist prejudice," "psychic instability," and "personal problems" such as unfulfilled ambitions.

Andropov's definition was based on the description of nervous disorders, as given in the authoritative Soviet work *Nervous and Psychic Diseases* by G. V. Morozov and V. A. Romasenko. Soviet authorities often dealt with dissidents by confining them to mental institutions, in order to cure them of "pathological delusions" mixed with "reformist ideas."

It was part of the effort to cope with dissent that the leadership also emphasized the small size of the dissident movement. The dissidents, in *Pravda's* phrase, were nothing but a "tiny bunch of intellectuals." To some extent, the charge of small numbers was true enough, though it could hardly explain the fact that during the 1970s some 600,000 Soviet Jews applied for emigration visas. Nor should the small number of non-Jewish Soviet dissidents obscure their potential danger to the Soviet rulers. The history of Russian revolutions of the early-twentieth century was not a history of mass parties but of tiny minorities which found a powerful echo among the unorganized masses. No one knows this better than the descendents of the Bolshevik party, which numbered little more than 30,000 people before the tsar was overthrown in 1917.

Anti-Semitism

The Soviet Jews emerged as the largest group of dissidents simply because, forewarned by other experiences of twentieth-century anti-Semitism, they came to regard the anti-Zionist utterances of their leaders as an ill omen for their future in Soviet Russia. The Soviet Jews no longer thought in terms of improving or changing Soviet society through reform, but of leaving it behind in the interest of personal survival or improvement.

Signs of stepped-up anti-Semitism began to mount in Eastern Europe and the USSR particularly after the Arab-Israeli War of 1967. In 1968 Communist propaganda attributed East European "revisionism" primarily to Jewish liberal reformers, such as Czechoslovakia's Eduard Goldstücker, Bohumil Lomsky, Ota Sik, Frantisek Kriegel and Jiri Hajek. Even *Izvestia,* the government newspaper, and *Ogonyok,* the Soviet illustrated magazine, occasionally provided a forum for sharp anti-Zionist and anti-Semitic outbursts. Valery Yemelyanov, a prominent Soviet writer and lecturer, simply called anti-Zionism and anti-Semitism "two sides of the same coin." To Yemelyanov, Sakharov and Solzhenitsyn were "agents of World Zionism." Soviet ideologist Mishin declared in his 1970 book *Social Progress* that the number of Soviet Jews enrolled at Soviet universities was "too large." The Soviet government allowed many Jews to emigrate, though not nearly as many as applied. The year 1979, which marked a new high, witnessed the exodus of 50,000 Soviet Jews.

Other Soviet dissidents were also allowed to leave, if their names had become too well known in the West, if enough pressure was applied, including pressure by prominent spokesmen of Eurocommunism, or if they could be exchanged for Soviet spies or imprisoned Communists in the West. The trading of Soviet dissidents Aleksandr Ginzburg, Mark Dymshits, Eduard S. Kuznetsov, Valentin Moroz and Georgi P. Vins for two Soviet spies, Valdik A. Enger and Rudolf P. Chernyayev, in April 1979, marked one such exchange. Vladimir K. Bukovsky was exchanged in December 1976 for the Chilean Communist leader Luis Corvalan Lepe. Leonid I. Plyushch, Pyotr G. Grigorenko and Andrei Amalrik owed their freedom to emigrate to western pressure.

Bukovsky, Plyushch, and Amalrik produced notable works on present Soviet conditions and their probable future course, including Bukovsky's *Opposition—A New Mental Disease in the Soviet Union* and Amalrik's *Will the Soviet Union Survive until 1984?*

Solzhenitsyn, Sakharov, and Medvedev

However, the most searching questions concerning the Soviet future were asked by the three leading Soviet dissidents, Solzhenitsyn, Sakharov, and Roy Medvedev. The three are in agreement among themselves, as well as with the other dissidents, that the Soviet regime has not done enough in freeing itself from the Stalinist legacy. Some of the dissidents, Roy Medvedev and historian Pyotr Yakir among them, are themselves the children of men who died in the Stalinist purge of the 1930s. In Sakharov's words, only some of the "dirt of Stalin" had been removed, and the people of the USSR were still living in the spiritual atmosphere created by Stalin. The three leading Soviet dissidents have different visions of the future roads of development, however, and their visions reflect, in part, past views on the destiny and purpose of Russia. Sakharov's views, as expressed in *Progress, Coexistence and Intellectual Freedom* (1968), *My Country and the World* (1975), and his now-famous Swedish radio interview of 1973 with reporter Stenholm, evolved from a Marxist reform socialism to a bitterly antisocialist, Western-liberal philosophy. Among Soviet dissidents Sakharov is a "Westerner," who favors Western liberal-democratic political forms and accepts continued industrial growth as vital to Russia's future. To a certain degree Sakharov is a liberal reformer in the tradition of the nineteenth-century Russian Westernizer Alexander Herzen.

Like Sakharov, Solzhenitsyn has rejected Marxism as a socioeconomic system, but he has done so in a much more emphatic manner and with an antiwestern twist. In his *Letter to the Rulers of the Soviet Union,* published in 1973 before his exile, Solzhenitsyn urged the renewal of Russia through Christian morality and a return to a simplistic, agrarian society. Solzhenitsyn's thought reveals many roots derived from the nineteenth-century Russian Slavophiles.

To Solzhenitsyn, Soviet communism of the twentieth century, with all the excesses he so vividly portrayed in *Gulag Archipelago,* was the result of an alien, Western import in the form of Marxist ideology, rather than of nineteeth-century native tsarist autocracy.

Unlike Sakharov and Solzhenitsyn, Roy Medvedev, the dissident historian, had not abandoned faith in Marxism as a font of Soviet socioeconomic renewal. Like the East European reformers of the 1960s, Medvedev visualizes a "socialism with a human face," a synthesis of socialism and democracy. The Russian Orthodox church, in Medvedev's view, has "no future whatever" in the USSR. Like Sakharov, Medvedev hopes that a two-party system will evolve eventually in the Soviet Union. In a sense, Medvedev represents the hopes of the 1917 Socialist revolutionaries, before those hopes were dashed by the realities of Leninism-Stalinism.

Defecting Artists

More embarrassing to the Soviet leadership than the dissent of its intellectuals was the defection of many of its artists to foreign lands. This embarrassment arose partly because the names of the defecting artists were better known to the Soviet public, and partly because of the difficulty of rationalizing cultural despair as an act of ideological treason. The exodus of Soviet artists in the 1970s included not only Solzhenitsyn, himself the greatest living master of the Russian language, but composers, conductors, musicians, painters, sculptors and ballet dancers, a long list of names such as Valery Panov, Galina Ragozina, Mikhail Baryshnikov, Rudolf Barshai, A. Volkonsky, A. Rabinovich, G. Yermolenko, Aleksandr Gleser, and many others.

In a great majority of cases, the motive for emigration was not material betterment, for many of the exiled artists belonged to the privileged elite. In choosing western exile, the artists wished rather to rescue that part of their Russian heritage which they saw endangered or destroyed by the very bureaucracy which, under Brezhnev's "real" socialism, had tried to achieve an identification of Russian nationalism and Soviet communism harder than ever before. The artistic exodus from Soviet Russia of the 1970s was but one symptom of the need for reforms deeper and quicker than the Soviet leaders deemed wise or affordable. The process which Khrushchev began in 1956 thus remained incomplete and inconclusive. Like tsarist Russia in the late nineteenth century, Soviet Russia of the late twentieth century has failed to come to terms with some of its most important internal problems.

In the nineteenth and early twentieth century, reluctant tsars were driven into major democratic changes as a result of humiliating foreign defeats: the Crimean War, before the emancipation of the serfs; the Russo-Japanese War, prior to the limited concessions to representative government and land reform in 1906–1914.

Creeping Despair

The present rulers of Soviet Russia clearly have not overlooked the past lessons and patterns of diminishing tsarist autocracy, and that may well be one of the principal reasons behind their feverish armaments policy. In the perception of the current Soviet leadership there appears to exist a cause-and-effect relationship between overweening external military power and secure internal controls. Hence the reprisals against dissidents, such as Sakharov, who attacked the latest manifestations of Soviet imperial policy such as the invasion of Afghanistan in December 1979.

The danger to the Soviet rulers and to the world at large might well derive, not from external attacks upon the Soviet Union, but from the corrosion of the internal controls through a widening credibility gap, through passive resistance, through cynicism, or simply through despair. The greatest threat to the Soviet system in its present form could well come from the collapse of its ideological integrity before the eyes of its own people. It is fears such as these that make the world's most powerful military establishment react with force against so frail an individual as the aging and ailing Andrei Sakharov.

30

Eastern Europe in the 1970s

THE IMPACT OF THE CZECHOSLOVAK INVASION

The Soviet occupation of Czechoslovakia in August 1968 had been a public demonstration of what Leonid Brezhnev had told the Czechoslovak leaders privately, that the western borders of Czechoslovakia and those of the other bloc nations were also the de facto borders of the USSR. Having gained these borders through its sacrifices in World War II, the Soviet Union intended to stay in Eastern Europe, according to Brezhnev, "forever."

The invasion of Czechoslovakia had further demonstrated that Soviet military action within its own sphere of influence could be undertaken with a minimum of risk, and that Western reaction was not likely to amount to more than verbal protest. Nor did the suppression of the Czechoslovak liberal experiment unduly disturb the earlier pattern of East-West relations which had been in effect since 1953. Western outrage over the Soviet suppression of the East Berlin workers' uprising of June 1953 and over the crushing of the Hungarian Revolution of 1956 had been followed by the relaxed atmosphere of the "spirit of Geneva" in 1955 and the "spirit of Camp David" in 1959. The invasion of Czechoslovakia was similarly soon to be followed by Western initiatives towards détente in the 1970s.

The Western eagerness to seek accommodation with the Soviet Union after each fresh example of Soviet military action in Eastern Europe flowed from a deep longing for the preservation of the peace which Western Europe had found at last under the umbrella of the Atlantic alliance. The desire for peace grew in proportion to the Soviet Union's own mounting military power, which made the alternative of war unacceptable. Parallels with the appeasement policy of the Western democracies during the

1930s were not lacking. When Hitler reoccupied and remilitarized the Rhineland in 1936, Britain acquiesced with the argument that Hitler had not attacked a foreign country, but merely moved into his own "backyard." When Brezhnev occupied Czechoslovakia in August 1968, the Western powers acquiesced, because the Soviet Union had not attacked a NATO country, but had merely moved its forces into an area within its own sphere of influence.

Yet both actions had significant long-term strategic implications not readily perceived at the outset. Hitler's remilitarization of the Rhineland destroyed the credibility of the eastern alliance system of France, setting the stage for the successive destruction of Austria, Czechoslovakia and Poland between March 1938 and September 1939. The Soviet occupation of Czechoslovakia in 1968 altered the strategic balance between the Warsaw Pact and NATO in Soviet Russia's favor, by giving the Soviets an advance position for a surprise attack on NATO, West Germany in particular. The Soviets were able to reap the political benefits of the new imbalance by pressuring West Germany into changing its old policy of revisionism and reunification into a new policy of accommodation with the Soviet Union and abandonment of old territorial claims.

The ideological risks inherent in the Soviet action against the "Prague Spring" also proved to be more manageable than had been assumed. The events of summer 1968 certainly had a disillusioning effect on all those, in the West and the East, who had continued to believe in the ability of institutionalized Marxism to reform itself along Western, liberal lines. Yugoslavia's Milovan Djilas had long since abandoned such beliefs, dismissing the notion of a "Marxist renaissance" as a dream of "Marxist professors." To Poland's leading dissidents, Leszek Kolakowski and Adam Michnik, institutionalized East European Marxism likewise appeared by the end of the 1960s reduced to "questions of power," rather than "intellectual discussion," and to an "empty gesture," unable to mobilize feelings. The great hope of Eastern liberal Communists and Western liberal sympathizers during the 1960s had been the gradual disappearance of ideological antagonisms as part of a common search for common answers to the problems of the industrial societies of the East and West.

The surfacing of Andrei Sakharov, Soviet Russia's famed physicist, as a challenger of Soviet orthodoxy in the summer of 1968 greatly strengthened Western liberal faith in the "convergence theory." As Brezhnev's policy of force against the liberal Czech reformers quickly dashed such hopes, the torch of liberal-Communist synthethis was passed on to the West European Communist parties, whose leaders Enrico Berlinguer, Georges Marchais and Santiago Carrillo soon came to be known under the label of "Eurocommunists."

Eurocommunism

It was the discrediting of Soviet communism as a result of the Prague events which gave Eurocommunism its start as a new and different form of communism. Whatever the tactical motivation of the Italian, French and Spanish Communist parties, they were anxious to separate themselves ideologically from the Soviet model through the repudiation of the concept of the dictatorship of the proletariat and the hegemonial claim of the Soviet Communist party. The Eurocommunists similarly rejected the Soviet economic model as inapplicable to Western Europe because of its distinctly Russian origins in the precapitalist society of 1917 tsarist Russia. Some of the Eurocommunists, such as French Communist Jean Ellenberg, would go so far as saying that neither he nor anyone else he knew of in the French Communist party would care to live in a country such as Soviet Russia. The Eurocommunist professions of Western liberal faith were, and continued to be, the subject of considerable doubt and debate in the west. There is little doubt that they were also an embarrassment for the Soviet Union and an annoyance to some of the East European Communist leaders.

The Eurocommunists championed the cause of East European and Soviet dissidents throughout the 1970s and their criticism succeeded on occasion in obtaining the release of imprisoned or detained dissidents. Louis Aragon, the renowned French writer and member of the French Communist Central Committee, strongly condemned the conviction of the Soviet writers Sinyavski and Daniel in 1969. In 1973 the French Communist party demanded that Solzhenitsyn be allowed to publish in his own country. The Soviet mathematician and dissident Plyushtsh, kept in a mental ward as punishment for his attacks on Soviet policy, was eventually freed in large measure through the efforts of the French Communist party paper *L'Humanité*. The Eurocommunists similarly identified themselves with the signers of the Czechoslovak Charter 77, the most disturbing challenge to the Soviet-installed Husak regime since the Soviet invasion of 1968.

East European Communist reaction to the Eurocommunists was more vehement than the Soviet, especially in Czechoslovakia and Bulgaria. After the Eurocommunists supported the petitioners of *Charter 77,* the Czechoslovak Communist party paper *Rude Pravo* condemned the French Communists as "rightist deviationists." Bulgaria's long-time Communist boss Todor Zhivkov dismissed the entire concept of Eurocommunism as "anti-Soviet" and "bourgeois propaganda." The Soviets attempted to preserve appearances of unity between the ruling communist parties of Eastern Europe and the Eurocommunists of Western Europe, by having representatives of both attend the East Berlin Communist summit of June 1976.

Attended by the leaders of twenty-nine Communist parties, including Brezhnev, the 1976 East Berlin summit was intended both to endorse the policy of détente, as expressed in the 1975 Helsinki Accord, and to reaffirm the Brezhnev doctrine of 1968. Concerning the latter, the East Berlin summit failed to obtain the support of the Eurocommunists, who merely pledged "international voluntary cooperation," based on the "sovereign independence" of the respective Communist parties. The Eurocommunists were equally anxious to demonstrate their ideological apartness from Moscow when stressing at the East Berlin summit the "special conditions and orientation" of the peoples of western Europe.

Having condemned the Soviet occupation of Czechoslovakia in 1968, the Eurocommunists continued to criticize the uses of force, either through proxy or direct action, in Soviet foreign policy. Such was the case both in the Soviet-backed Vietnamese invasion of Cambodia in 1979 and the Soviet invasion of Afghanistan at the turn of 1979–1980. If the phenomenon of Eurocommunism owed its origins at least in part to the Soviet invasion of Czechoslovakia of 1968, then its adverse impact on the Soviet Union showed itself to be more manageable than had originally been supposed. At the outset, there had been speculation in the west that Eurocommunism would develop into an irresistible ideological force, a third Communist model, different from both the Soviet and the Communist Chinese, which the Communist parties of Eastern Europe would eagerly embrace in their own effort at national emancipation from the Soviet tutelage.

Events since 1968 did not support such high expectations. Rather, during the

1970s as before, the Soviet leadership used power as the yardstick and the ultimate criterion of policy. The Eurocommunists had little power in the West and even less power in the East. East European freedom of action remained narrowly defined by the unchanged realities of the Soviet military presence and the growing dependence of the East European economies on Soviet raw materials and energy, especially oil. Nor did the Soviet action against Czechoslovakia unduly disturb the Soviet Union's relationship with Third World countries. As in the case of the suppression of the Hungarian Revolution in 1956, the effect of the 1968 invasion on Third World countries was minimal, because its victim was a European country. The Soviet action of 1968 did not affect their willingness to use Soviet power as a lever against Western interests in Third World areas. Indeed, the occupation of Czechoslovakia may have intensified such willingness, as it demonstrated the decisiveness and effectiveness of Societ foreign policy action, as against the indecision and paralysis of American policy in the Vietnam War.

THE IMPERATIVES OF ECONOMIC GROWTH

Edward Gierek, Poland's Communist leader after the fall of Vladislav Gomulka in December 1970, once characterized the economy as Poland's "only political problem." The definition may have been oversimplified, because the stability of Communist rule, especially in a nation of Poland's make-up, depended on other factors also, such as the nature of state-church relations.

Gierek's definition was accurate to the extent, however, that the Communist regimes were likely to court popular upheavals if economic growth could not be maintained and if minimum expectations of living standards were not met. It was from circumstances such as these that all East European upheavals since 1953 occurred, including those which ousted Gomulka from power in 1970. Gierek himself faced similar threats during the Polish workers' riots at Radom and the Ursus plant in 1976 in response to the government's reducing its subsidies on basic food prices. Compared to the levels of 1945, the Communist regimes of Eastern Europe had many impressive social and economic achievements to their credit in the 1970s. Sizable rural populations had been retrained as an urban industrial work force, and there was considerable progress in the curbing of illiteracy, the emancipation of women and the reduction of infant mortality. Poland, which produced less than 1.4 million tons of steel in 1938, was turning out 12 million tons of steel by the mid-1970s. Polish shipbuilding, which had been in its infancy before World War II, had achieved major world stature with yards at Gdynia, Gdansk, and Szczecin.

Industrial progress was similarly spectacular in other East European economies, some of which were already industrially advanced, such as East Germany, and some of which had been underdeveloped. By the late 1970s Communist Rumania produced as much steel per year as Great Britain had on the eve of World War II. Even Bulgaria, the poorest of the bloc nations and the one least developed industrially, could boast significant gains in agriculture with the formation of large productive cooperatives. Formed out of an initial 13 million individual small farms, the Bulgarian cooperatives, unlike the Soviet collective farm system, became a highly successful form of agricultural organization. With scientific farming, irrigation, and crop specialization, the Bulgarian cooperatives achieved greater productivity and efficiency than was accomplished in the collectivized farm economies of other bloc nations.

With industrial expansion, the bloc economies became increasingly dependent in the 1970s on two major outside sources of support. The Soviet Union, the bloc's principal supplier of raw materials and energy from the outset, acquired new importance with the energy crisis of the 1970s. Soviet oil exports to the nations of *Comecon,* which had totalled 138 million tons for the 1966–1970 period, increased to 238 million tons during 1971–1975. For the Soviet Union, the oil deliveries to *Comecon* not only represented a drain on the USSR's own reserves but, since the 1973 oil crisis, a net loss in hard, convertible Western currency, which could have been obtained through the sale of Soviet oil in the West. During the early 1970s *Comecon* still accounted for about two-thirds of all Soviet oil exports. USSR oil sales to nonsocialist countries began to exceed those to socialist states only by 1976. After the sharp rise in world oil prices in 1973 the Soviet Union continued to deliver oil to *Comecon* at the low, pre-1973 levels until current commitments expired. Beginning in January 1975 the USSR determined oil prices on an annual basis with an immediate increase of more than double the original price. By 1977 there was a further rise of 22.5 percent, bringing prices up to about half the OPEC level. By 1979 Soviet oil prices charged to *Comecon* were within 20 percent of OPEC levels. Increasingly, the Soviet Union urged *Comecon* members to satisfy additional oil needs through direct purchases from OPEC, a difficult alternative in view of OPEC's requiring payment in western currencies.

The Energy Crunch

The energy crunch of the 1970s gave the Soviets new means of pressure and control over the bloc nations. Rumania, whose own dwindling oil output put her out of the foreign oil market, was refused Soviet oil, though not Soviet natural gas, as obvious punishment for her independent foreign policy line. *Comecon's* reliance on Soviet energy also enabled the Soviet Union to demand a greater contribution by *Comecon* nations to the development of the USSR's own energy resources in western Siberia. The USSR attributed its own falling behind western technology in certain areas to its great outlay in developing the newly discovered oil and natural gas deposits in western Siberia during the 1960s. As early as 1969 the USSR thus launched a new program of cooperation with *Comecon,* known as the "Complex Program," which was adopted in July 1971 at the twenty-fifth *Comecon* meeting. Unlike the 1962 *Comecon* program ("Basic Principles of International Socialist Division of Labor") the 1971 program was designed to mobilize *Comecon* resources directly for purposes of Soviet energy development. The 1,600-mile natural gas line from western Siberia to the Czechoslovak border, built by *Comecon* labor and equipment, was one concrete implementation of the 1971 "Complex Program."

Kadarism

Concerning the internal organization of the individual bloc economies, the Soviet Union allowed for considerable leeway in the 1970s, provided that the fundamental political principles of Communist rule, the monopoly of Communist power ("dictatorship of the proletariat"), and obedience to Soviet leadership ("proletarian internationalism") were not compromised. In the development of liberal economic reforms the Hungarians, under the leadership of veteran Communist boss Janos Kadar, went further than most of the other bloc nations. Under the slogan of "socialism of the possible," the Hungarian economist Rezso Nyers instituted a reform program called the "New Economic Mechanism" in the late 1960s, which embodied many of the features of the reforms of Ota Sik, Dubcek's economics minister of the "Prague Spring." Hungary even allowed the return of private enterprise in certain areas, such as crafts and the restaurant business, where state-run enterprises had demonstrably failed to meet demand. Some of the Nyers reforms resulted in sharp wage differences between blue-collar and white-collar workers, which the authorities attempted to curb by placing "socially acceptable limits on the acquisition of property."

The Western Debt

Comecon's reliance on Soviet energy during the 1970s was matched by its increased dependence on Western loan capital for the acquisition of western technology and plant equipment. By the end of the 1970s *Comecon's* debt to the west was variously estimated at between $47 and 54 billion, of which the USSR accounted for a third. Among the bloc nations, Poland's indebtedness was the highest at $13.5 billion.

The massive influx of Western loan capital created a new interdependence between the bloc economies and Western economies, which made the former highly vulnerable to the fluctuations of the latter. The Western recession in the wake of the 1973 Arab oil boycott directly affected the Eastern bloc economies as a result of declining sales of Eastern exports on Western markets. Similarly, the bloc economies did not escape the effects of Western inflation. With the growing need to acquire Western currencies for the repayment of Western loans, the foreign trade patterns for certain bloc nations, notably Rumania, Hungary, and Poland, increasingly shifted to the West. Poland's economic dependence on the West reached a new stage at the end of the decade, when the Polish government, already heavily indebted to the West, agreed to have Western banks monitor its economy as a condition for a new Western bank loan of several hundred million dollars.

The strong economic and financial ties, which developed between the bloc nations and the Western world during the 1970s, resulted in the strong commitment of the bloc nations to the policy of détente. Any disruption of détente through a reckless gesture or action on the part of the Soviet Union, such as the invasion of Afghanistan, evoked consternation which the bloc leaders were barely able to conceal in their public utterances. In this matter, as well as on the subject of increased military expenditures, the Warsaw Pact members were happy to have independent-minded Rumania publicly criticize the Soviet Union. Although none of the other bloc leaders publicly identified with Rumania's denunciation of the Soviet invasion of Afghanistan in January 1980, their silence on the Rumanian accusation was clearly an expression of consent.

If the bloc nations would like the Soviet Union to be less provocative in its dealings with the West, experience has also taught them the limits of their freedom to criticize. The Western powers must take this into consideration as they must appreciate the limits of internal dissent, which the bloc regimes are able to tolerate under conditions of "real" socialism.

THE LIMITS OF DISSENT

If dissent and dissidents became more distinctive features of the Communist regimes in the 1970s than before, the reasons were undoubtedly rooted in part in the promise of a greater exchange of ideas between West and East under the 1975 Helsinki Accord.

In part, dissent reflected a growing generation problem under Eastern communism. The leaders of the East European countries, like those of Soviet Russia, were, for the most part men in their sixties or seventies. By the end of the decade, Bulgaria's Todor Zhivkov was seventy, Hungary's Janos Kadar sixty-eight, Poland's Gierek sixty-seven, and Rumania's Ceausescu a relatively young sixty-two. The average age of Communist party membership in Eastern Europe similarly increased, despite efforts of the leadership to recruit younger members. In Hungary those under twenty-six accounted for a mere 5 percent of total party membership by 1970. In Czechoslovakia, disillusionment over the Soviet occupation of 1968 resulted in a sharp drop in youthful enrolment, the average age of party members being forty-nine by 1971. By the 1970s communism, in Eastern Europe, had been in power long enough to produce a second generation, born after World War II. That generation no longer measured progress against the levels of 1939, or even those of 1949, but against those of the 1970s and of the western world.

The overaged Communist leadership, by contrast, applied the standards of its own youth in judging the "achievements of socialism" and it obviously found them more praiseworthy than did the generation born since Stalin's death. The problem of dissent in Eastern Europe in the 1970s was thus, in part, a problem of generations. "We young people," an eighteen-year-old wrote to the editor of a Sofia newspaper in 1972, "are the owners of the present. The old times are passing into history and you will do us a favor by not reminding us of them over and over again."

As was the case in many other areas, the problem of dissent varied from one country to the next, being considered more serious in some, such as Czechoslovakia, and less so in others, such as Poland and Hungary. The seriousness of the dissident problem in Czechoslovakia was a reflection of the 1968 Soviet invasion. Husak's crackdown against his dissidents was not only in compliance with the Moscow Protocols of August 1968, but an attempt to create conditions which might justify his own request for at least a partial retreat of Soviet forces from Czechoslovakia.

Charter 77

Of the various protests against Husak's policy of "normalization," *Charter 77* was the most damaging and provocative. Presented to the government in January 1977 as a petition signed by well over a thousand persons, *Charter 77* invoked the Helsinki Accord as well as the UN resolution on human rights. Accusing Husak of violations of the civil rights of Czechoslovak citizens, the signers called for a "constructive dialogue" with the government. The Husak regime responded with a mixture of repression, harassment and exile. Husak allowed Zdenek Mlynar, the former first secretary of the CSSR Communist party, to seek political asylum in Austria. Other leading dissidents, such as Jiri Hajek, Dubcek's foreign minister of 1968, Frantisek Kriegel, the playwright Pavel Kohut and the writer Ludvik Vaculik, the author of "2000 Words," were harassed in a subtle campaign of police terror and interrogation. Pavel Kohut, after being allowed to travel abroad, was deprived of his Czechoslovak citizenship in October 1979. October 1979 also witnessed the trial of six leading human rights activists associated with the *Charter 77* movement. Most of the defendants in the Prague trials of October 1979 received lengthy prison terms, including the playwright Vaclav Havel.

Czechoslovak repression was manifested also in the less publicized actions against the arts and the Catholic church. Czechoslovakia's motion picture industry, for a long time among Eastern Europe's finest under such directors as Viri Menzel and Milos Forman, felt the heavy hand of Husak's censors and "literary advisers." Vera Chytilova, whose film *The Apple Game* won high critical acclaim in the West in 1978, had had to wait six years before being granted offical permission to make the film. The plight of the Catholic church in Czechoslovakia received less attention in the West than that of the Church in Poland, partly because there was no similar identification of Czechoslovak nationalism and Catholicism. The Church already a target of strong Communist attack during the time of the Slansky trials of the early 1950s, came under renewed pressure in the Husak era of the 1970s. In a campaign of quiet extinction the Husak regime was gradually reducing the number of state-licensed priests, making it increasingly difficult for Czechoslovakia's Frantisek Cardinal Tomasek to fill parish vacancies after the death of older priests.

Polish Dissidence

Polish authorities, like their Hungarian counterparts, were more tolerant of intellectual dissent than the Czechs. The Gierek regime took little official notice of various "free universities" or "flying universities" in which prominent dissidents, such as historian Adam Michnik, delivered lectures on subjects not taught at the official universities. The Polish authorities also closed their eyes to a series of anti-Soviet and anti-Russian outbursts of Polish nationalism, which usually coincided with anniversaries such as the fortieth anniversary of the outbreak of World War II. The Polish government was much more concerned over workers' unrest caused by meat shortages, and it had to redouble its efforts of finding a new accommodation with the all-powerful Catholic church since the election of a Polish pope in 1978. The papal visit of John Paul II to Poland in June 1979, which it was impossible for the Gierek regime to deny, resulted in certain improvements of the church's position in Communist Poland. The occasion for the papal visit, the death of St. Stanislaus nine hundred years earlier at the hands of King Boleslav, who was himself subsequently overthrown, was itself sufficiently provocative to have contained the seeds of a violent state-church confrontation. John Paul II, who as bishop of Cracow had long experience in dealing with the Communist authorities of his native country, well understood, however, the "Polish realities" of his time. These realities included the survival of Polish Communism under Soviet protection, regardless of the feelings of Poland's devout Catholic community. While pledging "cooperation" and "coexistence" to the Communist regime, the pope also pressed for greater church freedom, for an opportunity to educate the young, and for a social role for the Polish church. Gierek shunned the latter, but he allowed an increase in the number of building permits for new churches in Poland. In a nation that was aroused by the charisma of its own pope and which witnessed a doubling of applicants for the priesthood in 1979, he could hardly have done less.

THE RUMANIAN CHALLENGE AND THE YUGOSLAV QUESTION

During the 1970s Rumania continued its course of national communism under the leadership of party boss Nicolae Ceausescu, independently of Moscow and sometimes in defiance of Moscow. In November 1978 Rumania rejected the Soviet call for increased military spending by the Warsaw Pact members, despite the fact that Rumania's own military budget was among the pact's lowest. Rumania similarly refused to allow its own national forces to be placed under integrated Warsaw Pact command, Ceausescu asserting that the Rumanian army would not "at any time" take orders from the outside. Rumania's defiance on increased arms spending and the integration of the Warsaw Pact command was followed a year later, in November 1979, by Ceausescu's call for an end to both the Warsaw Pact and NATO during his speech at the Rumanian party congress.

In January 1979 Ceausescu denounced the Soviet-backed invasion of Cambodia by Vietnam as a "heavy blow for the prestige of socialism and a threat to détente." In the same month Rumania warmly welcomed the establishment of full diplomatic relations between the United States and Communist China. Rumania likewise refrained from joining in the Warsaw Pact denunciation of Egypt for opening its peace talks with Israel. When the Warsaw Pact nations supported the Soviet position in the UN General Assembly vote on the invasion of Afghanistan, Rumania absented itself from that body. In defying Soviet Russia on virtually every single foreign policy issue, the Rumanians continued to rely on their close relations with Communist China, which were reaffirmed by the visit of Prime Minister Hua Kuo-feng to Bucharest in 1978, as well as the presence of the Chinese Politburo member Ulanhu at the Rumanian party congress of November 1979. Rumania's bold foreign policy line likewise depended on good relations with the United States and the knowledge that Rumania's public utterances often were an expression of the secret desires of the other bloc nations. What the latter dare not say in public because of the presence of strong Soviet military forces on their soil, the Rumanians have openly stated because there are no Soviet troops stationed on theirs.

In its domestic policies, Rumanian national communism has continued its Stalinist practices under the firm hand of Ceausescu, who combined both the presidency and the post of secretary general of the party. If Rumanians have accepted his brand of communism, though by no means enthusiastically, it is because Ceausescu, to many, appeared as the best safeguard against a Soviet invasion, such as Czechoslovakia suffered in 1968. Industrially, Ceausescu's Rumania had many achievements to its credit, though the social cost of industrialization was very high, leaving Rumania one of the poorest countries in Eastern Europe. It was also part of Ceausescu's national communism that Rumania's ethnic minorities, especially the large Hungarian community in Transylvania, numbering some 1.7 million, were subjected to new pressures and discriminations. The dismissal of Karoly Kiraly, the most prominent of ethnic Hungarian Communist leaders in Rumania, from the Council of Minorities in 1978, was an indication of the sharpness of the ethnic conflict. No doubt, Ceausescu wanted to make certain that the Soviets could not use the Hungarian minority as an instrument of internal subversion against the Bucharest regime, much as the Soviets might be tempted to use the diverse nationalities of Yugoslavia in the post-Tito power struggle in that country.

In its endeavor to identify with Rumanian nationalism, Rumanian communism went sometimes to astonishing lengths, allowing even in an oblique fashion the rehabilitation of Rumania's World War II fascist dictator, General Antonescu. In the novel *Delirul* (the delirium), published in 1975, Rumanian author Marin Preda justified Antonescu's attack on the Soviet Union in league with Hitler in 1941 on the grounds that it aimed at the recovery of Rumanian Bessarabia. Antonescu's alliance with Hitler was similarly sanctioned as the lesser of two evils, the alternative being described as Rumania's association with "Freemasons and Bolsheviks."

The Future of Yugoslavia

With the approach of Tito's death in 1980, the future of Yugoslavia, which Tito had ruled for over a third of a century, seemed far from certain. Although Tito had managed to unite the southern Slavs under his own brand of communism more successfully than the ruling Serb dynasty had managed to do between the two world wars, the stength of his unifying role resided more in the leadership qualities of his own person rather than in the institutions of party and state which he created.

Constitutionally, Tito had made provisions for equal representation of Yugoslavia's six national republics and two autonomous regions through the collective presidency under the 1971 constitution. By rotating the leadership position within the collective presidency, no one nationality was to be permitted to dominate the others. Apart from ethnic divisions, Yugoslavia also suffered from religious tensions, particularly between Croation Catholics and Serbian Orthodox Christians, which were closely tied to recent memories of national strife during the turbulent period of World War II. Cardinal Stepinac, the late archbishop of Zagreb, who is still widely revered in Croatia, was to the Serbs a symbol of Croation collaboration with the Nazis because of his announcement of the Croation puppet state in 1941. The passing of Tito's longtime friend and collaborator Edvard Kardelj, a Slovene, in February 1979, was also a severe blow to an orderly succession. Next to Tito, Kardelj enjoyed wide support and recognition among Yugoslavs of all walks of life, because of his authorship of the concept of workers' factory self-management and his pioneering of the Yugoslav policy of nonalignment.

Economically and ideologically the Yugoslav Communist experiment also remained a question mark after thirty years of trial-and-error. The outward appearances of the Yugoslav economy compared favorably indeed with the Communist bloc nations of Eastern Europe. Not only was there an abundance of Western-style consumer articles, but Yugoslavia was the only nation of Eastern Europe whose workers were free to seek employment in the Capitalist West. The earnings of more than 700,000 such workers were of significant help in the Yugoslav balance of payments. Economic decentralization had, in the opinion of some Yugoslav experts, not gone far enough, however, and Edward Kardelj urged further steps in that direction before his death in February 1979. Unemployment also continued to be a serious problem with 700,000 people out of work, as did inflation, foreign indebtedness, and a rising trade imbalance, especially with the nations of the European Economic Community.

Ideologically, the Yugoslav system of communism continued to search for lines of demarcation between liberal communism and Western liberalism, as advocated by such leading Yugoslav dissidents as Milovan Djilas. Both sides in the ongoing ideological dispute were moving into new defensive positions in anticipation of Tito's death. Djilas' attempt to forge a new alliance between Croat and Serbian intellectuals in support of a Yugoslav multiparty system was met by new repression of Djilas himself and the "Praxis group" of liberal university professors.

It was in the realm of foreign policy that Tito's achievements enjoyed the widest support among Yugoslavs, though his accomplishment, being tied to his own personality, might not all outlast his reign. Tito's last years were spent in frequent foreign journeys to the capitals of the superpowers, to Communist China, once his ideological arch-enemy, and to the nonaligned nations of the Third World. Nothing disturbed Tito so much in his final years as the decline of détente and the probability of a new phase in the Cold War. Under a new Cold War the superpowers, in Tito's view, were likely to extend their rivalry into Third World areas, such as Africa—or Yugoslavia itself. Such was the gist of his warnings to both United States and the USSR at the eleventh Yugoslav party congress in June 1978. At the Havana Conference of the Nonaligned Nations in September 1979 Tito used his prestige and influence to stem the tide of Soviet power in Third World countries and to criticize Castro's Cuba in particular for actively supporting Soviet designs in Africa. This was the meaning of Tito's warning at Havana against "alien interests" in the ranks of the nonaligned. Like the Rumanian leaders, Tito also condemned the Soviet-backed invasion of Cambodia by Vietnam. Not ignoring the importance of a secure energy supply independent of the Soviet Union, Tito also visited Iraq, Kuwait, Algeria, and Libya before his death.

31

Détente in Europe:
Ostpolitik and the Helsinki Accord

THE SOCIAL-LIBERAL COALITION IN WEST GERMANY

The West German elections of September 1963 evoked more than the usual interest, because of the anxiety over the strength of the neo-Nazi NPD. If the NPD cleared the 5 percent hurdle and entered parliament, the CDU/CSU-SPD Grand Coalition, which had been formed in 1966 as a safeguard against rising extremism, would certainly have continued in office. If the NPD failed to reach the 5 percent minimum, CDU and SPD were free to resume their accustomed, adversary, parliamentary relationship. In fact, the NPD not only failed to obtain 5 percent of the national vote, but it subsequently lost its representation in the state parliaments of Bavaria and Hesse as well. The liberal Free Democrats (FDP) scored just over 5 percent and thus played again a crucial role between the nearly evenly balanced mass parties, CDU/CSU (46.1 percent) and SPD (42.7 percent).

The New Coalition

By 1969 the consensus between Social Democrats and Free Democrats on important foreign and domestic issues outweighed that between Christian Democrats and Free Democrats, resulting in the SPD-FDP "Social-Liberal" coalition under Chancellor Willy Brandt and FDP chairman Walter Scheel as vice-chancellor and foreign minister.

The coalition had been foreshadowed by the election of Gustav Heinemann (SPD) as president of West Germany earlier in 1969 by the combined votes of FDP and SPD.

In domestic matters, SPD and FDP shared a common commitment to reform in the areas of education, the legal system, and environmental protection, though they failed to develop a common economic and social policy. Initially, FDP representatives hailed the Social-Liberal coalition as an "historic alliance between working class and middle class," but in matters of actual policy the Free Democrat economics ministers Hans Friderichs and his successor Otto Count Lambsdorff continued to uphold laissez-faire principles against Social Democratic pressures for increased social spending. With the broadening of the economic recession at the end of the 1970s SPD-FDP disagreements on social and economic matters intensified to the point where they contributed to the eventual breakup of the coalition government in September 1982.

SPD-FDP agreement was strongest in the field of foreign policy. Both parties believed in the need for a new initiative towards the USSR after the shock of the Czechoslovak invasion of 1968 and after the new administration in Washington had sent clear signals in 1969 of a policy shift away from confrontation and towards détente with the Soviet Union. Both FDP and SPD had freed themselves of old taboos on the German question. The FDP urged recognition of the Oder-Neisse line in 1967 and accepted the reality of two German states the following year. The Soviets hoped to see the kind of Social-Liberal coalition established which materialized in 1969, knowing that it would be more agreeable to a recognition of the German status quo. The Soviet view had been privately communicated by Pyotr Abrassimov, Soviet ambassador to East Germany, to Willy Brandt, some time before 1969 via the Swedish consul general in West Berlin, Sven Backlund.

Willy Brandt

Willy Brandt was a new—and to some, refreshing—change on the West German political scene. Like Adenauer, Brandt had an impeccable political record, having spent the Nazi era in exile, first in Norway, later in Sweden. A Social Democrat from an early age, Brandt left his native Lubeck as a young man in 1933 when most other young Germans of his age either compromised with the new regime or actively supported it. This act of courage earned Brandt as much respect abroad as it continued to earn criticism in some German circles, which characterized his 1933 exile as an act of desertion. Where Adenauer had been widely respected, Brandt was the first German postwar leader to achieve genuine popularity in many parts of Europe, both West and East, as well as in the United States. His prestige was heightened by the award of the Nobel Peace Prize in 1971 in recognition of his efforts towards détente with the USSR and the Communist bloc nations. He was the first German political leader since Stresemann to win the prize, but Stresemann had had to share his with French foreign minister Briand.

Brandt was the first West German leader with whom the Soviets established more than a formal political relationship. When Adenauer visited Moscow in 1955, he and Khrushchev traded accusations of wartime cruelty of their respective countries across the conference table. When Brandt visited Brezhnev at Oreanda in the Crimea in September 1971, Brezhnev also talked about the Second World War. It was not German atrocities, however, that Brezhnev related to his German guest, but the hopelessness with which the Soviets, Brezhnev included, viewed their own situation in 1942 after the fall of the Crimean peninsula. It was no small irony that Brandt, who was seeking détente with the Soviet Union more actively than any other West German chancellor before or since, should have been forced out of office in 1974 as a result of a spy scandal involving Gunther Guillaume, an East German agent who had served as Brandt's close aide for years.

Brandt greatly admired John F. Kennedy and his brother Robert and he borrowed from both the concept of "compassion" as a theme and guide of politics. Even Brandt's own friends would have admitted, however, that he was not a good administrator, and many of his domestic reform programs, launched with high hope and fanfare in 1969, had failed to achieve the expected results by the time of his resignation in 1974. Other programs fell short of expectations despite the more vigorous leadership provided by Brandt's successor, Chancellor Helmut Schmidt, between 1974 and 1982 because of economic difficulties and the growing indebtedness of the West German government.

Educational Reform

Education, the cause of widespread unrest in the sixties, was the first priority of the reform program of the Social-Liberal coalition. The West German "Educational Council" submitted a comprehensive reform program in 1970 which favored the creation of a uniform type of secondary school (*Gesamtschule*), breaking with the central European tradition of dividing children from age ten onwards into preacademic and vocational categories. After much initial enthusiasm, the effort to democratize secondary education failed for lack of interest. The democratization of education on the academic level had been decided on by the conference of West German university presidents in May 1968. The statistics of the reform, which were enacted towards that end during the Social-Liberal tenure between 1969 and 1982, were impressive enough, though they still left many of the problems unsolved. During the decade following 1970, West Germany spent some 26 billion marks on the expansion and construction of university campuses, while the number of faculties increased from 15,000 to over 33,000. Even with expanded facilities, West German universities could not cope with the increase in students seeking admission, and overcrowding continued to be a major problem. On the vocational level, a similar problem existed for youngsters applying for apprenticeships, especially in popular and well-paying crafts and vocations.

Legal Reform

Significant changes were effected in legal reform, the area considered most important by the Social-Liberal coalition after education. Laws affecting marriage and divorce were liberalized, and abortion was legalized within narrowly defined limits. Consumer protection was strengthened. The general thrust of liberal legal reform collided with a sharp increase in political terrorism during the mid-and late 1970s, claiming the lives, among others, of the West German attorney general Buback and of the president of the employers' association, Schleyer. Although terrorism remained limited to a handful of individuals organized in such groups as RAF (Red Army Faction), it commanded great publicity and evoked strong government responses consistent with public demand and expectation. Among the responses was the enactment of antiterrorist laws and the barring from public employment of individuals suspected of disloyalty to the constitutional order of West Germany.

The Environment

Both SPD and FDP were considerably ahead of the general public awareness of environmental problems caused by industrial waste and pollution. The growth-oriented 1950s had created serious environmental problems for German waterways in both East and West Germany, and the River Rhine, recipient of waste materials from the chemical industry especially, stood in danger of ecological collapse. After a good start, environmental reform stagnated with the recession of the late 1970s, when both employers and unions were more concerned with maintaining growth at the expense of all other considerations, including those of the environment. West Germany's expanding nuclear power industry, operating fourteen nuclear plants and planning the opening of another twenty-three, added new problems in the form of nuclear waste storage.

The Economy

The economy proved to be the most difficult of all problems confronting the Social-Liberal coalition and became the immediate cause of its downfall in 1982. The reform programs of 1969 had been based on the tacit assumption that economic growth would continue undisturbed, an assumption based on 7.5 percent GNP growth rate for the year 1969. West German economic growth slumped to 0.5 percent in 1974, the year after the Mideastern oil boycott, and actually declined by 1.6 percent the following year. After a recovery by 1979, economic growth declined once more by 0.2 percent in 1981. The recessions of the seventies and early eighties increased West German unemployment to unprecedented levels, while also increasing public indebtedness. By 1981 unemployment reached 1.2 million, with a further increase to 1.8 million in 1982. Rising unemployment in turn sharpened social tensions, especially between West German and foreign "guest" workers. The "guest" workers, chiefly from Mediterranean countries and Turkey, had been encouraged to come to West Germany during the boom years of the sixties, when labor was scarce and menial, low-paying jobs needed to be filled. With the broadening recession, foreign workers, over a million strong, often became the object of hostility and abuse, not unlike West Indian workers in Britain or Algerian workers in France.

THE NEW *OSTPOLITIK*

Although Brandt suffered several defeats on the domestic front, he managed to carry through on his foreign policy programs, particularly its Eastern dimension, with little or no change from the original concept. The concept was the normalization of relations with Eastern Europe and the Soviet Union and the termination of Cold War tensions with Communist East Germany. Brandt recognized the achievement of Adenauer's foreign policy, which had been the normalization of relations and reconciliation with Germany's former Western enemies. His desire was to achieve a similar reconciliation with the Soviet Union and the nations of Eastern Europe, which had all suffered far more at the hands of Hitler's Germany in World War II than had any Western nation. It was part of Brandt's approach to the Communist powers of Eastern Europe that he accepted a German moral responsibility for the sufferings of the people of Eastern

Europe. Such a note had been conspicuously absent from previous official West German dealings with the USSR.

The Soviets had indicated their willingness to change their policy of threats concerning West Germany, provided that the latter abandoned its revisionist aims, even before the Brandt–Scheel government was formed in October 1969. The resumption of Soviet–West German trade talks at the Hanover Trade Fair in April 1969 was one such indication.

Two Treaties: Moscow and Warsaw

Brandt's reference to the existence of "two states" in Germany in October 1969 and his signing of the nuclear nonproliferation treaty in November 1969 were a suitable beginning to his policy of détente. Between 1969 and 1973 Soviet-German détente was implemented on three interdependent levels, that of Soviet–West German relations, of West German–East European relations, and on the level of West German–East German relations. The Moscow and Warsaw treaties of August and December 1970 represented the chief agreements on the first two levels. The Moscow treaty aimed, according to its wording, at the "normalization of the situation in Europe," by accepting the "actual situation existing in this region." Both sides recognized the existing borders as inviolable, including those between the two German states and the Oder-Neisse. Both promised to desist from the use of force or the threat of force. Concerning Soviet membership in the Warsaw pact and West German NATO membership, the Moscow treaty stressed that the current agreement did not affect bilateral or multilateral treaties previously concluded by either party.

A separate protocol reaffirmed the "rights and responsibilities" of the USSR and the three Western powers concerning Berlin. This was a major gain for West Germany, since East Germany had in times past pressured the Soviets to force the Western powers out of West Berlin altogether.

The Warsaw treaty between Poland and West Germany also confirmed the Oder-Neisse border in addition to acknowledging that Poland had been the first victim of German aggression in World War II. Poland, in turn, promised to let ethnic Germans emigrate to West Germany. It was after the signing of the Warsaw treaty that Brandt made his famous and spontaneous kneel before the monument commemorating the Warsaw ghetto uprising of World War II. The Moscow and Warsaw treaties were followed by similar agreements with other bloc nations. The treaty with Czechoslovakia was delayed until 1973 because of questions relating to the formal status of the 1938 Munich Agreement. The Czechs claimed that the Munich Agreement had never been valid, a claim which raised the possibility that Sudenten Germans, who had fled to West Germany, might still be considered Czechoslovak citizens.

The "Basic Treaty" with East Germany

The normalization of relations between the two German states was, in some ways, the most difficult to accomplish. Ulbricht had always insisted that West German *de jure* recognition of East Germany as a sovereign, separate state must be the first act in any East-West German negotiations concerning other issues. After December 1969 the Soviets no longer supported this view. Though insisting on the acceptance of their own two-state theory, the Soviets tacitly accepted Brandt's thesis, that the two German states were not foreign countries to one another. Their mutual relations, Brandt said, could only be of a special kind. Although there existed two German states, they were both part of the same nation. It may also be assumed that Soviet pressure overruled Ulbricht and paved the way for the exchange of visits between Brandt and his East German counterpart, Premier Willi Stoph, at Erfurt, East Germany on March 19, 1970 and Kassel, West Germany, on May 21. The meetings produced little of substance, but they amounted to a de facto recognition of East Germany by West Germany.

Agreements on transit to West Berlin and on communications between the two German states followed in 1971 and 1972. In November 1972 a "Basic Treaty" (*Grundvertrag*) regulated relations between West and East Germany, though it carefully avoided the term *recognition*. The treaty spoke of the "equal rights" of both states and expressly rejected West Germany's past claim of being the sole legitimate representative of all Germans. Both states agreed to establish "permanent missions" in Bonn and East Berlin, but the term *embassies* was again avoided. Both German states entered the United Nations the following year, thereby symbolizing the end of the German Cold War in its familiar form.

The Four-Power Agreement

Having made peace with Moscow essentially on Moscow's terms, West Germany was rewarded with a four-power agreement on Berlin, concluded on September 3, 1971. In the Berlin Agreement, the four powers, Britain, France, the United States and the USSR pledged to prevent "complications" concerning the situation in Berlin. The Soviets agreed to desist from unilateral action or the use of force. The USSR further guaranteed "unimpeded access" to West Berlin and promised to aid in the easing of travel restrictions of West Berliners to East Germany.

Ostpolitik

Brandt's *Ostpolitik* was generally well received by the West German public, which was inclined to accept his thesis that West Germany had given up nothing which in truth had not already been lost to Germany as a result of the outcome of World War II. The CDU/CSU, now in the unaccustomed role of opposition, did not attack *Ostpolitik* as such, recognizing that some form of accommodation with Moscow was inevitable in the changed climate of the late sixties. CDU/CSU spokesmen did criticize Brandt for not having made as good a bargain with Moscow as might have been achieved according to their own view. CSU leader Franz Josef Strauss maintained in his 1974 Sonthofen speech, that détente, for the Soviets, was essentially a disguise for the establishment of hegemony over Europe. The shift in West German public opinion supported Brandt, however. In public opinion polls of 1951 80 percent of the West German public had refused to recognize the Oder-Neisse line. A similar poll of 1969 revealed a decline in that number to 32 percent. Still, it hurt the Social Democratic party to have to play, once more, the role of the party of renunciation. Again the SPD seemed to be called upon to bear the responsibility for losses incurred by the reckless policy of others, who had preceded them in power. It had been thus in 1918–1919, when the Social Democrats assumed responsibility for the armistice and for the Treaty of Versailles, subsequently the source of bitter nationalist recrimination.

For Germans, the gains of *Ostpolitik* were modest but tangible. For the first time since the end of World War II, West Germans could freely travel to any part of East

Germany, and by the end of the 1970s nearly three million West German visitors had journeyed to Communist East Germany in a single year. For travelers to and from West Berlin the practice of chicanery and deliberate delays was over. Travel restrictions for East Germans were not liberalized nearly to the same degree, for East Germany under détente remained much the same closed society it was before.

Ostpolitik also affected West Germany's relations with her western allies. On the one hand, Brandt's rapprochement with the Soviets was complementary to the larger Nixon-Kissinger design for Soviet-American détente of the early 1970s. Indeed, the multilateral Helsinki Accord of 1975 would hardly have been possible without a prior settlement of West German–Soviet tensions in treaty form. *Ostpolitik,* on the other hand, represented West Germany's first foreign policy initiative, and it was conducted less within the Western alliance framework and more within the domain of specifically German interests than any previous such move. Whenever Germans talked to Russians alone, old suspicions rooted in the history of Weimar foreign policy of the 1920s were likely to resurface. Knowing this, Brandt kept his Western allies fully informed about the progress of his *Ostpolitik,* but he did not seek the Western powers' permission in implementing it.

Some American statesmen, including Secretary of State Henry Kissinger, voiced private concern that *Ostpolitik* could strengthen West German tendencies towards neutralism between the blocs. Others, such as former secretary of state Dean Acheson, former undersecretary of state George Ball, and former U.S. commissioner Lucius Clay thought that Brandt was giving away too much to the Soviets too quickly. President Georges Pompidou of France feared that *Ostpolitik* might actually heighten the chances of German reunification, a prospect that few French citizens relished in private, even if they refrained from saying so publicly in the interest of harmonious relations with West Germany. *Ostpolitik* occasioned strains in the Western alliance only after Willy Brandt's resignation, when Soviet-American relations took a turn for the worse towards the end of the 1970s. Chancellor Schmidt and FDP foreign minister Genscher were reluctant to jeopardize the West German gains of *Ostpolitik* by an unconditional support of U.S. sanctions in the wake of the Soviet invasion of Afghanistan in December 1979 and after the imposition of martial law in Poland in December 1981. Herbert Wehner, the leader of the Social Democratic parliamentary party in the *Bundestag,* coined the term of the *two-leg* foreign policy of West Germany, one leg being the good relations with the West, the other those with the East. If Wehner's two legs were indeed of the same length, West Germany should feel no greater sense of commitment to the West than it does to the East. This was an impression Chancellor Schmidt strove to avoid, though not always successfully. Schmidt hoped that the disturbances over Afghanistan and Poland would remain temporary setbacks of détente, not its final end. Like other European leaders before him, the West German chancellor wished to overcome the division of Europe, a goal he thought attainable through the progressive reduction of armaments of both blocs, both nuclear and conventional, in treaty form. Implicit in Schmidt's thinking was the belief that equality in military strength between the blocs was an essential prerequisite of continued détente. It was for that reason that Schmidt drew the West's attention to the deployment of a new Soviet weapons system in the form of the SS-20 missiles, targeted on Western Europe, during his 1977 speech at the London Institute of Strategic Studies.

Otherwise, *Ostpolitik,* in the view of its West German architects, gave West Germany greater stature and independence in dealing with its western allies. West German–American relations, in particular, had changed since the early sixties, when Chancellor Erhard followed and closely supported American policy, be it in Europe or Southeast Asia. The relationship of Lyndon Johnson and Erhard was not the same as that of Schmidt and Jimmy Carter, or Schmidt and Ronald Reagan. The inclusion of Helmut Schmidt in the western summit of President Carter, President Giscard d'Estaing of France and Prime Minister Callaghan of Britain at Guadeloupe in January 1979 was widely interpreted in West Germany as a significant step towards the elevation of West Germany to an equal footing with the western "Big Three."

DETENTE AND EAST GERMANY

Détente posed new problems also for Communist East Germany. The East German dilemma had always been that East Germany needed West German economic support in order to survive, while it also needed to depict West Germany as a source of evil and potential aggression in order to justify its own Communist regime as the "better" and "peace-loving" government in Germany. The thesis of an aggressive West Germany was not easy to maintain under conditions of *Ostpolitik* and détente, however, when Brezhnev and Chancellor Brandt met in a cordial atmosphere at Oreanda in 1971.

Whenever Soviet leaders had made a move towards normalizing relations with West Germany, East Germany's leaders had asked for and obtained signs of reassurance of continued Soviet support. Such had been the case in 1955, when the USSR established diplomatic relations with West Germany, and again in 1964, before Khrushchev intended to visit West Germany. In 1975, the year of the Helsinki Accord, high point of détente, the Soviets again gave East Germany a new "friendship and mutual assistance pact" with even stronger emphasis on mutual trust and support. The Soviets also upgraded their East German partner in 1976 by staging the summit meeting of Communist party leaders from both Eastern and Western Europe in East Berlin. In addition, the Soviets made increasing use of East German facilities and personnel for training staffs from Third World Soviet client states, such as South Yemen and Angola.

Erich Honecker, Ulbricht's successor as SED leader, quickly proved himself an even more subservient follower of Moscow than his predecessor had been. From May 1971 onwards, East Berlin's party organ *Neues Deutschland* copied Pravda's editorial line even more faithfully than in the past. Honecker stood totally on the Soviet side in the Sino-Soviet conflict. East Germany also assumed new and heavy commitments under *Comecon's* "Complex Program" for the development of USSR energy resources. The chief domestic task, in Honecker's view, was heightened ideological vigilance against the hazards of détente. This meant a campaign against the influence of West German "Social Democratism," against the rekindling of East German hopes of unity with West Germany, and against the notion that the Helsinki Accord had fundamentally altered the relationship between Communist regimes and their subjects. Communist ideology and its dissemination remained, according to Honecker's address before the ninth SED party congress of May 1976, the "centerpiece" of the party's work.

Détente had ended East Germany's isolation in the noncommunist world. When the Helsinki Accord was signed in 1975, East Germany had already established diplomatic relations with 121 nations throughout the world and it had become a member of the UN. Détente had also prompted internal protest, dissent, and a flood of applications for emigration to West Germany. How great was the longing of the East German people for a leader of Willy Brandt's stature and quality was dramatically illustrated during the tumultuous and spontaneous East German demonstrations in support of Brandt, during the latter's brief visit to the East German city of Erfurt in 1970. When Helmut Schmidt visited Honecker at Werbellinsee in December 1981, East German police had cleared the streets of people, who might otherwise have repeated the spectacle of Erfurt of 1970. In order to stifle all German longings of his countrymen, Honecker went to the extreme length of striking the word *German* from public institutions such as the East German Academy of Sciences.

HELSINKI AND THE PROSPECTS OF ACCOMMODATION

The Soviet-German détente of 1970–1972 set the stage for the implementation of détente on a larger, European scale in the form of the Helsinki Accord. Negotiated over a two-year period, the accord was signed on August 1, 1975 by thirty-three European nations, plus the United States and Canada, under the official title, "Final Act of the Conference of Security and Cooperation in Europe (CSCE)".

The accord was divided into three parts ("baskets"). Part One, entitled "Questions Relating to Security in Europe" provided for confidence-building measures, security, and disarmament. Included also in Part One were ten "guiding principles" for the relations between the signatories, stressing sovereign equality, the inviolability of frontiers, nonintervention in internal affairs, human rights, and the peaceful settlement of disputes. Part Two of the Helsinki Accord dealt with cooperation between the signatories in such areas as economics, science, technology and the environment. Part Three, destined to become the most controversial part of the accord, represented the human rights undertaking under the title "Cooperation in Humanitarian and Other Fields."

Although the Helsinki Accord was widely viewed as a kind of substitute peace treaty for Europe, ending both the uncertain state after World War II and the Cold War, the accord expressly denied that it was a treaty under international law. The Helsinki Accord, rather, was a political agreement and a moral commitment on the part of its member states. It made no provision for machinery to enforce the agreement, or even for complaints concerning violations. The accord did provide for a "follow-up conference" to review the past record of the signatories and to assist in the continuation of the détente process in Europe. Otherwise, the signatories promised to implement the provisions of the accord through unilateral, bilateral, and multilateral action. A follow-up conference was duly held in Belgrade in 1977, at a time when the dissident movement in the Communist bloc nations had reached a new level of intensity.

Basket One, in effect, recognized the territorial status quo in Europe, a concession the Western powers had been withholding in theory with regard to the Soviet domination in Eastern Europe since World War II. Basket Two held out the prospect of Western economic and technical assistance, which the USSR had been actively seeking since the start of its détente policy at the beginning of the 1970s. Regarding Basket Three, the Communist bloc had initially strongly opposed any inclusion of human rights provisions and had relented only when the success of the conference itself was at stake. The Soviet attempt to make the actual implementation of the human rights provisions dependent on future negotiations and international agreements, likewise failed. Instead, the Helsinki Accord stressed the equal importance of all its principles, stating that they would be "equally and unreservedly applied."

The Soviet motive for accepting the human rights provisions and, perhaps more importantly, for agreeing that the entire accord be published in its full text in all the signatory nations, may well have been of two opposing kinds. On the one hand, there is reason to believe that Brezhnev may have desired an international Soviet commitment to human rights as a safeguard against a relapse into Stalinism in his own country. The actual extent to which the Soviet leadership would implement the Helsinki human rights provisions would, on the other hand, remain a matter of its own discretion. It would generally be dependent on the climate of East-West relations after the signing of the accord. That was the essence of Brezhnev's remarks in his speech at Tula on January 18, 1977.

If the human rights provisions contained the risk of stirring up internal dissent in the Soviet bloc, it was a risk the Communist leaders clearly thought acceptable. Western involvement in such dissent could, and very soon would be rejected as interference in internal affairs which, the Communist leaders were to point out, was impermissible under Part One of the accord. Ideologically, the Helsinki Accord put no restraints on Moscow. It ruled out force in the relations between the states which had subscribed to it. It did not put restraints on Communist ideological efforts in Europe. It did not, as KGB chief Yuri Andropov emphasized in his April 22, 1976 Moscow speech in honor of Lenin's 106th birthday, "remove the class struggle." The "class struggle," in the official Soviet view, was an historic and unalterable fact, which was beyond the power of any government to eliminate. Politically, the Helsinki Accord likewise appeared advantageous from the Soviet standpoint. The negotiations which preceded the accord between 1973 and 1975 coincided with a shift in American policy, away from Asia and the Vietnam War and back to Europe. The former year, 1973, was advertised by American policy makers as the "year of Europe."

It was also the year of the October War in the Middle East, and the ensuing Arab oil boycott with its disastrous consequences for the industrial nations of Western Europe and Japan. Western Europe shared in the risks of American Mideastern policy without having had the benefit of advance consultation, much less of an active role in shaping that policy.

The Decline of U.S. Prestige

U.S.-West European relations had changed between 1964 and 1973 in other ways as well, as a result of American economic difficulties and the declining value of the U.S. dollar. The North Vietnamese conquest of South Vietnam in April 1975 reaffirmed the impression of American policy failure on a global scale. In between the "year of Europe" and the fall of Saigon was the Watergate scandal and the forced resignation of the American president. The institution of the American presidency, which had been a source of great inspiration in western Europe under Franklin Roosevelt, Harry Truman, and Dwight Eisenhower appeared to have suffered itself irreparable harm. The coincidence of the Helsinki Accord and the decline of American prestige in Western Europe allowed for a new differentiation between Soviet Russia's relationship with Western Europe and with the United States. The Soviets may also have viewed the Helsinki Accord as an opportunity for widening the gap between the United States and Western Europe.

The strength of the Western alliance had always been greatest when Western Europe itself seemed threatened by an aggressive and expansionist Soviet policy. In the Helsinki Accord, the Soviet Union promised peaceful behavior in Europe, but not elsewhere. It was in areas outside Europe that the United States had been suffering major policy reverses in the early and mid-1970s, however, with Europe either critical of U.S. policies, as in Vietnam, or adversely affected by them, as in the Arab oil boycott of 1973.

Finlandization

By obtaining stability in Europe in 1975, largely on the terms it had been seeking since 1955, the Soviet Union was in a better position to accept greater risks outside Europe, as it did with the invasion of Afghanistan or the sponsoring of the Vietnamese invasion of Cambodia. The selection of Helsinki as the site for signing the accord inevitably conjured up images of the eventual ''Finlandization'' of Western Europe. What was usually understood by the term *Finlandization* was the accommodation of Finland to Soviet economic and foreign policy wishes without an internal sovietization of Finland since the Second World War.

The course of events after the conclusion of the Helsinki Accord revealed before long that the risks which the Soviet bloc assumed in making the accord were at least as great as the opportunities it promised. Cooperation and exchanges between the complementary economies of Western Europe and the Soviet Union greatly increased, but so did the expectations of liberalization among the peoples of Eastern Europe. Although the Communist authorities were able to cope with internal dissent in most bloc nations, they failed to do so in Poland at the beginning of the 1980s.

32

Europe Beyond the 1970s

WESTERN GAINS AND WESTERN FEARS

During the first half of the twentieth century an estimated 58 to 60 million people—more than the entire population of the United Kingdom—were killed in two world wars, both of which had had their origins in Europe. Before the first half of the twentieth century was completed, many of Europe's ancient cities, the handiwork and artistry of many generations, had been thoroughly destroyed. From the old St. Petersburg, now Leningrad, in the east; the Benedictine Abbey of Monte Cassino in the south; Dresden in the center; and London and Coventry in the west—to mention but a few—the physical reality of 1945 was one of shattered brick walls and the smell of burnt asphalt, molten in the heat of firebombs and uncontrollable conflagrations. The lone chimney, left standing amidst collapsed walls, had become the symbol of an urban civilization that had failed to meet the challenge of its times.

Since 1945, Europe has been at peace for some forty years, a long period if measured against the frequency of past European conflicts. During the period of peace, most of Europe's shattered cities and edifices were painstakingly rebuilt, some from old blueprints and plans, as in the historic center of Warsaw, the baroque palaces of Dresden, the Winter Palace in Leningrad, the medieval portion of Nuremberg, or the Monte Cassino Abbey, because of the completeness of the war's destruction. East Berlin alone continues to show the scars of World War II firebombing and street fighting, with weeds and trees growing through empty windowframes and shattered staircases in the once magnificent German and French twin cathedrals.

Some of Europe's cities, such as Paris or Frankfurt, have seen their traditional skylines revolutionized through the addition of new skyscraper office buildings which have destroyed the prewar architectural unity in historic downtown areas. Others have witnessed the addition of high-rise social housing satellite towns, with unintended alienating influences on their low-income inhabitants.

Two generations have grown to adulthood since the end of World War II, and their perception of Europe and of Europe's place in the world has often been shaped more by the current problems of their own young lives than by a deeper knowledge or understanding of the forces which very nearly destroyed the civilization of their parents and grandparents during the first half of the century.

Central to such an understanding is the appreciation of the fact that Europe had lost the ability to liberate itself from the forces threatening its destruction in the Second World War, and that liberation depended on the combined efforts of outside forces. The hope that sovereign, united, and democratic Europe could be speedily restored after the war quickly revealed itself as an illusion, which misread the nature of the Soviet system and which ignored the realities of postwar power.

The postwar division of Europe limited by half Europe's ability to learn from its past mistakes and correct its past errors. The current economic difficulties of Western Europe and its quarrels with the United States over matters of defense and trade have tended to obscure, especially to the postwar generations, the significant gains that have been achieved since World War II. The most important gains have been in the areas of increased social awareness and decreased national conflict, which were the areas of prewar European failure and the sources of the two world wars. The gains of European integration have not been as great as was hoped during the optimistic 1950s.

The Failure of Supranationality

The goal of supranationality became a victim of Gaullism in the 1960s, and even purely economic gains have been jeopardized under the strains of renewed economic nationalism as a result of the recession of the early 1980s. Public opinion polls in this period revealed that a mere 16 percent of EEC citizens often thought of themselves as "citizens of Europe," as against 46 percent who said they never did. The figure was much higher in Britain, with 72 percent. In the four EEC countries Greece, Ireland, Denmark, and Britain, fewer than half the people were reported in favor of EEC membership at the beginning of the 1980s. The decline in EEC appeal was due, in part, to the remoteness from public consciousness of the anonymous and faceless EEC bureaucracy in Brussels. The introduction of direct, EEC-wide elections to the European parliament in 1979 has not significantly helped to identify the general public with the goals and spirit of European integration. After more than twenty-seven years of existence, the EEC has yet to devise a common agricultural policy (CAP), which is both satisfactory to farmers and acceptable to such members as West Germany and Britain, the largest contributors to agricultural subsidies under currect rules. Even EEC industrial performance was a cause of disappointment in the early 1980s, after spectacular gains in the 1950s and 1960s, especially in electronics and computer industries. Although the nations of the EEC claimed to be spending twice as much on scientific research as was Japan, they had only 10 percent of the world's computer market at the beginning of the 1980s. Overall, EEC industrial production between 1973 and 1983 grew by 8 percent, as against 26 percent for Japan and 16 percent for the United States over the same period. Most importantly, the EEC failed to develop common organs for the expression of a common political line, especially in foreign policy questions concerning American or Soviet measures. After de Gaulle's exit from the political stage, President Pompidou and Prime Minister Heath had agreed that supranationality could not be instituted by decree, but that it could flow only from a real identity of national interests. It was, however, precisely for lack of such an identity that supranational institutions failed to develop even in the post–de Gaulle era.

The addition in 1974 of a new EEC institution, the European Council, by President Giscard d'Estaing of France and Chancellor Helmut Schmidt of West Germany, consisting of the heads of governments and acting above the EEC Council of Ministers, failed to provide the desired foreign policy coordination among the members of the community.

European Stability

Against the disappointments of integration, however, must be measured the stabilizing and supportive role which the EEC has played in the establishment of democratic governments in the underdeveloped regions of Europe. The European community was not without influence in the overcoming of the Greek military dictatorship of the 1970s and it was an important factor in encouraging the democratic experiments of Spain and Portugal of the late 1970s and early 1980s.

Franco-German Reconciliation

The earlier reconciliation of France and Germany, which was among the original goals of the European federalists, has come to be taken so much for granted that its significance as a major achievement of post–World War II Europe is rarely appreciated. The youth of Western Europe no longer visits each other's capitals as part of invading military columns, but on weekend and vacation trips undertaken for educational or recreational purposes. By the standards of 1914 or 1940, this represents an important gain. In the 1980s one is more likely to encounter bumper stickers on French cars that read "I Like Mozart," than one is apt to see slogans proclaiming messages of past French-German antagonisms.

Ethnic Conflicts

National antagonisms have not entirely disappeared in either part of Europe. In Eastern Europe, there was a brief upsurge of ethnic strife in multinational Yugoslavia after Tito's death, especially between Serbs and the Albanian minority. In Rumania the old feud between ethnic Hungarians and Rumanians continues to be a factor in that country's nationality policy under communism, as it had been before. The friction between Italians and ethnic German South Tyrolese in the *Alto Adige* persists. There have even been increases in regional strife in the democracies both old and new, as among the Scots and the Welsh in the United Kingdom, or the struggle in Northern Ireland, the roots of which are more cultural and religious than they are truly ethnic. In Spain, the problem of Basque separatism resurfaced at the very time of transition from Francoism to Spanish democracy during the 1970s.

The economic recession of the early 1980s has highlighted new national and ethnic problems in Western Europe, stemming from discrimination and violence against foreign workers, principally Algerians in France, Turks in West Germany, Asians, and black West Indians in Britain.

The Growth of Prosperity

The interwar period had been a period of social failure, which undermined democratic stability and contributed to the rise of fascism and communism. The quarter-century following World War II has witnessed, by contrast, an unprecedented growth in west European economic prosperity, with a corresponding increase in democratic strength. In countries of spectacular democratic prewar failure or civil war, Italy, Germany, the Austrian republic, and Spain, the social and political record after World War II has been far more encouraging. However, the postwar prosperity of Western Europe suffered its first major shock as a result of the 1973 Arab oil boycott and the ensuing disarray in Western currencies.

Nuclear Energy

The energy crunch of the 1970s prompted a new surge in West European interest in nuclear energy, just as the first threat of an Arab oil boycott in the wake of the 1956 Suez crisis had prompted the launching of EURATOM in 1957. Significantly, the development of West European nuclear energy in the 1970s resulted less from a coordinated effort of the EEC than it did from individual national policy. By the early 1980s, the share of nuclear energy of total energy needs was 40 percent in France, 25 percent in Belgium, 14 percent each in Britain and West Germany, 9 percent in Spain, 6 percent in Holland and 2 percent in Italy, as against 12 percent in the United States.

Political Change in the 1980s

The economic downturn at the turn of the 1970s and 1980s produced important political changes within the established democracies of Western Europe. In Britain, Conservative rule returned under Prime Minister Margaret Thatcher, while the continued leftward drift of the Labour party resulted in its split into the old Labour party and the newly formed Social Democratic party. In France, Socialist leader François Mitterand succeeded to the presidency after more than two decades of Gaullist and conservative rule. In West Germany, the recession was instrumental in the fall of the Liberal-Social coalition under Helmut Schmidt in 1982 and its replacement by the Conservative-Liberal coalition under CDU leader Helmut Kohl.

The desire to break with the economic policy of the outgoing administration, as a means of overcoming the recession, was a common cause of political change in the three major west European democracies. Mitterand of France—whose government included four Communists, the first to serve in a French government since 1947—began his attack on the recession with a policy of nationalizing more industries and banking on the strength of the argument that nationalized French industries, such as Renault in the automotive branch, were among the most successful in the French economy since 1945. After several franc devaluations and rising foreign trade deficits, Mitterand had to reverse course and search for solutions more along the lines of austerity and the monetarist measures of the Conservative Thatcher government in Britain.

Economic Policies in the 1980s

The search for new and effective economic policies has not been aided by greater clarity in economic theory or a broader consensus among the theorists. The theoretical debate on the best methods for combating the recession of the 1980s closely parallels that of the 1930s on how to overcome the depression. Against the pump-priming theory of John Maynard Keynes are mustered the conservative theories of Friedrich August von Hayek and the monetarist teachings of U.S. economist Milton Friedman, the latter two recipients of the Nobel Prize in economics in 1974 and 1976 respectively. The governments of Western Europe often enough attempted a mix of both sets of economic theories as a basis for practical economic policy. What has changed in a significant way since the depression of the 1930s is the preparation of a much more tightly woven and stronger social net to cushion the impact of economic adversity, because the memory of the exorbitant political price for social inaction in times of severe economic crisis persists. The political price of the recession of the early 1980s, despite record unemployment levels of 10 percent and higher in some of the highly industrialized nations of western Europe, has not reached the alarming levels of the 1930s, though the long-term consequences of a sustained recession must remain a source of concern. The likelihood of democratic failure under the impact of economic crisis may also have been reduced by the longer period of prosperity which has preceded the recession of the 1980s, and by the diminished appeal of ideological alternatives. The depression of the 1930s came on the heels of only a brief five-year period of prosperity, as against the quarter-century of economic progress which preceded the recession of the 1980s. In the 1930s, the model of Soviet communism, building an entire industrial base at a time of Western economic stagnation, exerted often a powerful appeal in the depression-ridden nations of the West. The Western recession of the 1980s, on the other hand, coincided with the spectacle of Communist economic failure, in the Soviet Union itself and among many of the economies of Communist Eastern Europe. No Western economy has yet been driven to the stage where electric power had to be shut off at night, as has occurred in the Rumanian capital of Bucharest and the Yugoslav capital of Belgrade.

Relations with the United States

The early 1980s brought new strains to the relationship of Western Europe and the United States, partly through the issue of defense. The European democracies recognize the historic American contribution to the rescue of twentieth-century European democracy in both world wars, and they appreciate the fact that, since 1941, the American role has been crucial to both the crushing of hegemonial fascism and the curbing of Soviet expansionism. At the same time, the economic, strategic, and psychological relationship between western Europe and the United States has changed since the end of the Second World War and the height of the Cold War with unavoidable consequences for the Alliance.

Economically, the relationship has changed because, recent difficulties notwithstanding, the weight of economic power has shifted in favor of the EEC. In 1950, when European integration took its first concrete steps with the launching of the Schuman Plan, the United States still accounted for 60 percent of world industrial production and for 50 percent of world capital reserves, as against 30 percent of industrial production and 6 percent of capital reserves in 1980.

Strategically, the relationship has changed because the Soviet Union had drawn even in strategic weapons with the United States by the end of the 1970s, and, in the view of some, may have exceeded U.S. strategic weapons power in some areas.

Psychologically, the relationship changed because of the sustained American self-accusation during the Vietnam War, and the succession of American policy failures worldwide after the fall of Saigon in 1975, including the elimination of American influence in Iran and the failure of an effective response to the Soviet invasion of Afghanistan.

Against the broader background of such changes have developed disputes involving trade and fiscal policy, and matters of defense. American complaints concerning subsidized EEC farm exports have been matched by European discomfort over continued high American interest rates, resulting in both the pulling of investment capital out of Europe and the raising of the value of U.S. currency. The latter is of European concern because the price of Mideastern oil continues to be quoted in U.S. currency. Transatlantic disputes have also arisen over the inequality in arms sales between the NATO partners, with the United States selling seven times as much in armaments to the European NATO partners as the other way around. The American response to such complaints has been that the United States spends an estimated $133 billion out of its own annual defense budget to support the defense of western Europe.

Détente

The most important source of West European–U.S. disagreement are relations with the Soviet Union. Since the 1970s, this question has centered around the meaning and the future of détente.

Détente has been a source of disagreement ever since EEC-Soviet relations and Soviet-American relations began to follow different paths, from the late 1970s onward. As against a worsening in Soviet-American relations and a disappointing record of Soviet-American trade, EEC-Soviet commercial and credit transactions significantly increased, culminating in the 1981 pipeline agreement. Under this agreement, the Soviets pledged delivery of Siberian natural gas to western Europe in exchange for west European aid in the building of the pipeline itself.

The punitive American responses to Soviet and Soviet-sponsored actions such as the invasion of Afghanistan in 1979 and the imposition of martial law in Poland in 1981, through embargoes and economic sanctions, raised the broader question of the divisibility or indivisibility of détente. Though publicly disapproving of the Soviet actions, the nations of the EEC were reluctant to uniformly join American initiatives in the imposition of sanctions because they did not wish to jeopardize the recent economic gains and the more relaxed political relations with the Soviet Union in Europe.

Relations with the USSR

The Soviets combined the policy of increased commercial intercourse with western Europe with an increase of their strategic threat to western Europe in the form of a massive deployment of an entirely new missile system, the SS-20 rocket, targeted on western Europe. The combination of increased trade with Europe and of increased threats to Europe coincided with a lessening of the credibility of the U.S. strategic deterrent, because of Soviet Russia's own advances in the realm of strategic missile power. By early 1982, some three hundred Soviet SS-20 missiles, each carrying three nuclear warheads, were targeted on Europe, which had become, in the words of Leonid Brezhnev, the "most fragile and congested habitat" in the world. Large West German population centers such as Hamburg, Brezhnev observed during his November 1981 visit to West Germany, could be wiped out in a single blow.

The European uproar and the bitter controversy over the best response was rooted in the fear which the new Soviet weapon inspired. The Soviet missile, perfected with technology acquired in the West, was not an ordinary replacement of older Soviet medium-range missiles, which had also been targeted on western Europe since Khrushchev's times. Rather, the enhanced accuracy of the new weapon and its mobility increased the likelihood of its actually being used, because of its ability to destroy purely military targets without inflicting massive "collateral" damage to millions of civilians.

The Soviets could have achieved similar results in purely military terms by targeting a portion of their existing intercontinental missiles (ICBMs) on Western Europe without additional cost. That they chose to develop an expensive new medium-range weapons system explained the political message and purposes for which it was designed. The message was that of a selective threat to Western Europe, and later also to Japan and Communist China in the Far East, without the threatened parties having any certainty that the United States, which was beyond the SS-20 reach, would retaliate against the Soviet Union with its own intercontinental missiles.

The initiative for a new deterrent against the Soviet threat thus came from Western Europe, not the United States, a fact nearly forgotten in the ensuing controversy. In December 1979 NATO adopted its "two-track" decision to counter the Soviet threat through the stationing of 572 cruise and Pershing II medium-range missiles, while seeking the limitation of Euro-strategic weapons on both sides through negotiations with the Soviet Union. Such negotiations were begun by the United States and USSR in Geneva in 1981, and they were broken off without results by the Soviet Union two years later, when the stationing of the new U.S. missiles began in Western Europe.

The Antinuclear Movement

Between 1979 and the collapse of the Geneva negotiations in November 1983 the Atlantic Alliance was put under severe strain because of the growth of the antinuclear movement in Western Europe. The movement reflected the anxiety that the work of reconstruction in Europe of nearly forty years might be instantly destroyed as a result of accident, carelessness, or even calculation on the part of the superpowers which, it was feared, might prefer a European nuclear battlefield to one in their own backyards.

Agitation over the missile issue was especially pronounced in West Germany, in part because even before the deployment of the new U.S. missiles, West Germany had more nuclear warheads on its territory than did any other NATO member. In part, West German agitation derived from the fact that the core of the new deterrent, 108 Pershing II missiles, the weapons the Soviets fear the most because of their short flight time of six minutes to Soviet targets, would be stationed exclusively on West German territory. The remaining 464 U.S. cruise missiles were to be scattered, in addition to West Germany, over Britain, Sicily and, pending final consent, Holland and Belgium. Such a deployment made West Germany the potential preferred target of a Soviet preemptive counterstrike.

The West German antinuclear campaign was overwhelmingly directed against the United States, not against nuclear weapons on either side. Its emotionalism and one-sidedness were reminiscent of the campaign against West German rearmament of the early 1950s, and it involved much the same constituency. Prominent in the latter was the West German neutral-nationalist establishment and its mouthpiece, the West German newsmagazine *Der Spiegel,* whose publisher Rudolf Augstein had characterized the United States as an "ally suffered only with nausea" during the Vietnam War. West German neutral-nationalism has shown itself especially susceptible to the Soviet argument that a "special relationship" has existed between Russians and Germans, not merely because of close economic ties, but because of common and mutually afflicted sufferings of the past. From this, the Soviets argued, sprang a special mutual obligation to prevent a recurrence of suffering, such as might happen through the policy of the United States, which was characterized as reckless.

The West German antinuclear campaign yielded the Soviets significant gains, but it also resulted in important losses. Among the gains was the considerable leftward shift of the Social Democratic party, after it had gone into opposition in 1982. With the repudiation of the 1979 NATO "two-track" decision on missile stationing and negotiations, the SPD not only repudiated its own former chancellor Schmidt, but it ended the foreign policy concensus of CDU-SPD, which was basic to West German politics since the late 1950s. The left wing of the SPD, represented by such men as Günther Gaus, former West German representative in East Berlin, and Oskar Lafontaine, the mayor of Saarbrücken, have gone even further and asked for a complete West German withdrawal from NATO. The leftward trend has been further demonstrated by the election of the antinuclear and self-styled environmentalist "green party" to the West German *Bundestag* in March 1983.

At the same time, the missile debate contributed materially to the election victory of CDU chancellor Helmut Kohl in March 1983, as it did to the worst defeat of the Social Democrats in any national election in twenty years. The West German election results of 1983 were as much a vote of nonconfidence in past Social Democratic economic policy, as they were a vote of confidence in the preservation of a strong NATO alliance with a credible response to the Soviet SS-20 threat.

Beyond the confines of German politics, the missile debate of the 1980s also raised broader questions concerning a future restructuring of NATO with an eye on a greater West European role. It was even suggested in 1984 that the NATO supreme command, traditionally in American hands, should go to a European and that the post of NATO secretary general, traditionally occupied by a European, should go to an American.

EASTERN HOPES AND EASTERN DISAPPOINTMENTS

The developments in the Eastern bloc nations at the beginning of the 1980s cannot have been pleasing to Soviet leaders after the Soviet invasion of Czechoslovakia in 1968 was thought to have dealt an effective blow to the twin dangers of East European nationalism and independent-minded East European reform communism. In Czechoslovakia itself, despite the much-publicized flare-up of a native dissident movement in the wake of the Helsinki Accord of 1975, the process of pacification under the firm hand of party boss Gustav Husak appeared to be progressing satisfactorily. Pacification, in Czechoslovakia, meant largely a process of depoliticization as part of an un-official bargain between the people and the Communist party, in which the latter demonstrated its goodwill by providing tolerable living standards. With the claimed per capita income of $2,900 in the late 1970s, Communist Czechoslovakia would indeed appear to have attained respectable living standards which compare favorably even with those in the poorer nations of the EEC. Although the Czechoslovak economy clearly has been allowed to produce more for the consumption of its own citizens than for the benefit of the Soviet economy, Czechoslovakia again is in need of economic reform and investment capital for plant modernization. The failure to provide either will mean before long that the Czechoslovak economy, once more, is operating on borrowed time. Official East European statistics do not always accurately reflect the quality of life, however. Communist East Germany claimed a higher per capita income for the 1970s than Britain's, but few who are familiar with daily living in both countries would declare the quality of life in Communist East Germany superior to that of Britain. It is improbable that one would encounter a restaurant in the west end of London, or for that matter, any restaurant in the British Isles, with signs reading "Today No Potatoes," such as is quite possible in downtown East Berlin at the start of the 1980s. Nor is it likely that one would find only a single type of baby carriage, or only two types of native automobiles with thirty-year old technology, in the streets of British towns and villages.

Hungary in the 1980s

Hungary, under its astute leader Janos Kadar, continued to be an extraordinary example of successful individual economic and social initiative under official communism at the outset of the 1980s. In agriculture, Hungarian cooperatives have been highly successful once allowed to produce for the market, not the bureaucracy, and Hungary has succeeded in becoming a net exporter of food to the tune of $2 billion annually. Hungary's exceptional role in Eastern Europe was further underlined by its becoming a member of the International Monetary Fund and by allowing private enterprise to lease from the state service industries, a total of 16,000 by the early 1980s in areas as widely separated as restaurants, hotels, and even public restrooms. Among East European capitals, none has acquired as much of a Western and easygoing atmosphere as has the Hungarian capital of Budapest, whose restaurants, hotels, and places of entertainment compare favorably with anyone's.

Poland, East Germany, and the Church

Poland became the Soviet Union's major problem in Eastern Europe at the beginning of the 1980s, and there is no guarantee that the problem has yet been solved in a definitive fashion. The roots of the Polish troubles of the 1980s are familiar enough, both with respect to their specifically Polish background as well as in their broader, East European origins. Among the specifically Polish roots is the factor of national Catholicism, which assumed tremendous significance with the 1978 election of a Polish pope, the former Cardinal-Archbishop of Cracow Karol Wojtyla. The first election of an East European to the papacy stimulated not only a religious revival in Catholic Poland, where the church had retained a measure of strength and independence even during the Stalinist 1940s, but also in many other parts of Eastern Europe both Catholic and Protestant. Perhaps not surprisingly, the Hungarian Communist regime again proved the most successful in coping with the new situation by working out a successful coexistence formula with Hungary's Cardinal Laszlo Lekai on the basis of the understanding that in Hungary, both communism and Catholicism were here to stay and must, for that reason, find ways of living together, preferably with the least amount of friction and the greatest amount of cooperation. East Germany's Communist leader Erich Honecker also has attempted, somewhat less successfully, to develop a constructive relationship with the Evangelical church in heavily Lutheran East Germany. The intention was to utilize the Evangelical church as a cushion and a controlling force in the growing peace and antinuclear movement, which East Germany too began to experience at the turn of the 1970s and 1980s, especially among its young people. Moreover, by giving public support to such church-related events as the celebration of Luther's 500th birthday, the Communist regime of East Germany clearly hoped to enhance its prestige and respectability by sharing in the limelight of a religious event of worldwide interest and attention.

Solidarity

In Poland, Wojtyla's elevation to the papacy coincided with the final phase of Edward Gierek's tenure as Communist party leader, which was marked by economic failure. After a very promising beginning in the early 1970s, the ambitious industrial expansion under Gierek failed, because it was heavily dependent on foreign, Western loan capital, and because the goods produced in Poland were not primarily sold in the West, but had to go to Soviet Russia. Polish exports of consumer durables to the USSR increased especially from 1976 onwards, when the rise in world oil prices enabled the Soviet Union to dictate even more unfavorable terms of trade to Poland. Because of increased oil prices, Poland had to pay with larger exports of industrial goods and coal for an unchanged amount of Soviet oil. Polish industrial exports thus not only failed to earn the capital with which to repay Western loans, but they also failed to help raise Polish living standards. Polish workers' morale could be sustained for several years through an abundant food supply at low, heavily subsidized prices. It collapsed when native Polish food, especially meat products, had to be exported to the West in order to earn Western currency. In order to decrease domestic consumption, Gierek did what had caused trouble twice before under Communist rule, in 1956 and 1970; he reduced food price subsidies. The result was unrest among workers in 1976 and on a wider scale in August 1980, from which sprang the trade union Solidarity under Lech Walesa.

The emergence of Solidarity and its ability to extract important concessions from the Communist authorities briefly rekindled hopes among reform Communists that institutionalized Marxism, Czechoslovakia—1968 notwithstanding—was indeed capable of reforming itself. The likelihood of a successful Polish renewal rapidly diminished however, when Solidarity began to raise political demands and call upon workers in other socialist countries—the Soviet Union included—to follow Poland's example of a free labor union.

The Polish challenge of 1980 went to the very root of the Soviet system, echoing tremors that had threatened Lenin's very own leadership in the Soviet Union in its early history, during the Kronstadt Rebellion of 1921. In the context of Eastern Europe, it was also a more complex and dangerous challenge to Soviet rule than those of 1956 or 1968 had been, because the international setting was less favorable to Soviet intervention in 1980. In 1956 and 1968 the Soviets used ongoing Western military operations in other parts of the world, Suez in 1956, Vietnam in 1968, as diversions and propaganda covers for their own military repression in Eastern Europe. The Soviets may, for that reason, have hoped for an American military intervention in Central America in 1980–1981, but were unable to exploit it when it failed to materialize at that time. A further restraining factor was the bad publicity given the Soviet intervention in Afghanistan in December 1979 and its condemnation even in the United Nations General Assembly, where Soviet influence among Third World members had grown significantly. A Soviet military intervention in Poland, quite apart from the risks inherent in Polish resistance, would, furthermore, have defeated the Soviet purpose in the Euromissile controversy at that very time, in which Soviet policy was eager to advertise itself before noncommunist Europe as reasoned and responsible, as against an allegedly irresponsible stand on the part of the United States.

The dangers radiating from Poland through Eastern Europe were, on the other hand, if anything more threatening than those of 1956 or 1968. After Gierek's fall in 1980, no East European Communist party since 1945 had stood similarly discredited and bankrupt before its own people as did the Communist party of Poland.

The crushing of Solidarity through the imposition of martial law on December 13, 1981 by Poland's General Jaruzelski, prime minister and first party secretary both, appeared, from the Soviet standpoint, the least risky solution. It spared Soviet Russia the dangers and embarrassment of a military intervention of its own, and it could be given the appearance of a Polish patriotic action undertaken for the sake of the Polish national interest, not partisan Communist interest. Jaruzelski's action could not hide the incompetence and corruption of the Polish Communist party, whose policies had caused the crisis of 1980 in conjunction with Soviet Russia's own style of economic policy in Eastern Europe. The conferring of the 1983 Nobel Peace prize on Polish labor leader Lech Walesa underscored the failure of Polish communism and, in a wider sense, the failure of the Communist system as such.

Andropov and Chernenko

Impressions of incompetence, corruption and economic failure also overshadowed the final stage of Brezhnev's career, which ended less than a year after the imposition of Polish martial law. The Soviet grain harvest of 1981 was so low that its actual size was not even publicized in the Soviet Union, though Western estimates ranged as low as 160 million tons or, at best, 175 million tons. This compared with the official plan target of 239 million tons, which the eleventh five-year plan had announced as a projected annual average goal for the 1981–1985 period. The summoning of the Polish military as savior of a broken-down Communist system resulted in widespread Western speculation that Brezhnev's death in 1982 would similarly open the gates to a disguised takeover of Soviet Russia by the military. The assumption seemed all the more justified as the Soviet military had gained in prestige with the growth of Soviet armaments and as the vast complex of Soviet defense industry clearly represented the most efficiently run part of the Soviet economy. The elevation of former KGB chief Yuri Andropov to the general secretaryship in 1982 and to the Soviet presidency in 1983 followed perhaps an even deeper logic of the Soviet system, in the sense that the system ultimately relies on inner surveillance and control for its survival. The challenge before Andropov was the same as that before all Soviet leaders since the death of Stalin in 1953, only on a larger scale, because the disillusionment with ideology and party bureaucracy had grown among the ordinary Soviet citizenry with the passage of time. During his brief tenure as Soviet leader from November 1982 to February 1984, Andropov tried to revive sagging Soviet morale through a mixture of economic incentives and a highly visible campaign against corruption in party circles, high and low, as well as through the reimposition of tighter labor discipline among ordinary workers. Even during his short term in office, Andropov's efforts showed promising results in the rise in productivity and the increase in industrial and agricultural output. Whether these changes would move Soviet society appreciably closer to the goal of an ''abundance of material and cultural goods,'' as promised in Khrushchev's still-valid official party program of 1961, is a question which Andropov's successor, Mikhail Gorbachev, who followed Nicolai Chernenko's brief stewardship between 1984–85, must answer during his term of office.

The Nuclear Escalation

When Khrushchev climbed to power thirty years before Andropov died, he boasted of the certainty of the Soviet system's overtaking in economic performance and social services that of the noncommunist world in general, and of the United States in particular. Quite clearly he genuinely believed in his prediction. Since that time, faith in the Soviet system as a more productive one has been increasingly hard to maintain, even among the Soviet Union's most ardent admirers. What has not changed since Khrushchev's time is the existential question, whether armaments, especially nuclear weapons, can be reduced to a level where they would lose both their bankrupting effect on national economies and their everpresent threat of mutual annihilation, either through accident or miscalculation. The developments since the end of the Second World War have been both hopeful and discouraging on this point. They are discouraging because the expenditures for armaments worldwide have continually risen, to the point where a total of $660 billion was spent on armaments in 1982 at a time when nearly half the world's population of 4.5 billion people was judged to be living in poverty and when some 450 million human beings were thought to be suffering from perpetual hunger and malnutrition. By contrast, the world's stockpile of nuclear arms in 1982 had reached a point where their combined explosive force was more than 5,000 times greater than all the munitions spent in the Second World War. By 1982, the world's military expenditures had increased thirteenfold over the level of the mid-1930s, when Europe was heading towards the Second World War. By 1982, the explosive power of nuclear weapons equalled a force of 3.5 tons of conventional TNT explosives for every man, woman and child alive.

Among the most encouraging developments since the end of the Second World War was the fact that the lessons of Europe's greatest failure in the twentieth century, the failure to prevent the outbreak of the First World War in 1914, played a major part in preventing what might well have become the Third World War during the 1960s. John F. Kennedy's successful management of the 1962 Cuban missile crisis was due, in no small measure, to his knowledge of the history of the July crisis of 1914 in Europe.

Suggested Readings

Chapter 1

ALBERTINI, LUIGI, *The Origins of the War of 1914,* 3 vols. (1952–1957). New York: Oxford University Press.

BERGHAHN V. R., *Germany and the Approach of War in 1914.* New York: St. Martin's Press, 1973.

FAY, SIDNEY B., *The Origins of the World War,* 2 vols. New York: Macmillan, 1938.

FEIS, HERBERT, *The World's Banker, 1870-1914.* New York: A. M. Kelley, 1961.

FELDMAN, GERALD D., ed. *German Imperialism 1914-1918.* New York: John Wiley, 1972.

FISCHER, FRITZ, *World Power or Decline.* New York: W. W. Norton, 1974.

HANTSCH, HUGO, *Leopold Graf Berchtold,* 2 vols. Verlag Styria, 1963.

HAYES, CARLTON, J. H., *A Generation of Materialism, 1871-1900.* New York: Harper & Row, 1941.

HINSLEY, F. H., ed. *British Foreign Policy under Sir Edward Grey.* Cambridge University Press, 1977.

LANGER, WILLIAM L., *European Alliances and Alignments, 1871-1890.* New York: Knopf, 1931.

LEE, DWIGHT E., ed. *The Outbreak of the First World War.* Lexington, Mass.: Heath, 1975.

SCHMITT, BERNADETTE E., *The Coming of the War 1914,* 2 vols. New York: Scribner's, 1930.

STAVRIANOS, LEFTAN, *The Balkans 1815-1914.* New York: Holt, Rinehart and Winston, 1963.

STEINER, ZARA S., *Britain and the Origins of the First World War.* New York: St. Martin's Press, 1977.

TAYLOR, A. J. P., *The Struggle for Mastery in Europe: 1848-1918.* Clarendon Press, 1954.

TUCHMAN, BARBARA W., *The Guns of August.* New York: Dell Pub. Co., 1962.

————, *The Proud Tower.* New York: Macmillan, 1966.

Chapter 2

BALDWIN, HANSON W., *World War I.* New York: Harper & Row, 1962.

FALLS, CYRIL, *The Great War.* New York: Putnam, 1959.

GATZKE, HANS W., *Germany's Drive to the West.* Johns Hopkins Press, 1950.

GREBLER, LEO, and WILHELM WINKLER, *The Cost of the World War to Germany and to Austria-Hungary.* New Haven: Yale University Press, 1940.

LIDDELL HART, *The Real War 1914–1918.* Boston: Little, Brown, 1930.

————, *Strategy.* New York: Praeger, 1967.

HORNE, ALISTAIR, *The Price of Glory: Verdun 1916.* New York: St. Martin's Press, 1963.

PITT, BARRIE, *1918: The Last Act.* Cassell, 1962.

RITTER, GERHART, *The Schlieffen Plan.* O. Wolff, 1958.

ROTH, JACK J., ed., *World War I: A Turning Point in Modern History.* New York, 1967.

WOLFF, LEON, *In Flanders Fields.* New York: Ballantine, 1958.

Chapter 3

ADAMS, ARTHUR E., ed., *The Russian Revolution and Bolshevik Victory.* Lexington, Mass.: Heath, 1960.

BERLAU, JOSEPH, *The German Social Democratic Party 1914–1921.* Octagon Books, 1949.

CARR, EDWARD H., *The Bolshevik Revolution,* 3 vols. New York: Macmillan, 1950–1953.

————, *Studies in Revolution.* New York: Barnes and Noble, 1964.

CHARQUES, RICHARD, *The Twilight of Imperial Russia.* Essential Books, 1959.

CROSSMAN, RICHARD, ed., *The God that Failed.* New York: Harper & Row, 1965.

GAY, PETER, *The Dilemma of Democratic Socialism.* New York: Columbia University Press, 1952.

HANAK, HARRY, *Great Britain and Austria-Hungary During the First World War.* New York: Oxford University Press, 1962.

HORN, DANIEL, *The German Naval Mutinies of WW I.* New Brunswick, N.J.: Rutgers University Press, 1967.

KENNAN, GEORGE F., *Russia Leaves the War.* Princeton, N.J.: Princeton University Press, 1956.

LUTZ, R. H., ed., *The Fall of the German Empire,* 2 vols. Stanford University Press, 1932.

MAY, ARTHUR J., *The Passing of the Habsburg Monarchy,* 2 vols. University of Pennsylvania Press, 1966.

MITCHELL, ALLAN, *Revolution in Bavaria, 1918–1919: The Eisner Regime and the Soviet Republic.* Princeton, N.J.: Princeton University Press, 1965.

PLAMENATZ, JOHN, *German Marxism and Russian Communism.* New York: Longman, 1954.

VON LAUE, THEODORE H., *Why Lenin? Why Stalin?* Philadelphia: Lippincott, 1964.

WILSON, EDMUND, *To the Finland Station.* Garden City, New York, 1953.

WOLFE, BERTRAM D., *Three Who Made a Revolution.* New York: Time Inc., 1964.

Chapter 4

ALBRECHT-CARRIÉ, RENÉ, *The Meaning of the First World War.* Englewood Cliffs, N.J.: Prentice-Hall, 1965.

BAILEY, THOMAS A., *Woodrow Wilson and the Great Betrayal.* New York: Macmillan, 1945.

————, *Woodrow Wilson and the Lost Peace.* New York: Macmillan, 1944.

CZERNIN, FERDINAND, *Versailles, 1919.* New York: Putnam, 1964.

LEDERER, IVO JR., ed., *The Versailles Settlement.* Lexington, Mass.: Heath, 1960.

MANTOUX, ETIENNE, *The Carthaginian Peace.* New York: Arno, 1978.

MAYER, ARNO J., *Politics and Diplomacy of Peacemaking: Containment and Counterrevolution at Versailles, 1918–1919.* New York: Knopf, 1967.

THOMPSON, JOHN M., *Russia, Bolshevism, and the Versailles Peace.* Princeton, N.J.: Princeton University Press, 1966.

Chapter 5

BRETTON, HENRY L., *Stresemann and the Revision of Versailles: A Fight for Reason.* Stanford University Press, 1953.

CARR, EDWARD H., *International Relations Between the Two World Wars.* London: Macmillan, 1947.

FELIX, DAVID, *Walter Rathenau and the Weimar Republic: The Politics of Reparations.* Johns Hopkins, 1971.

GALBRAITH, J. K., *The Great Crash, 1929.* New York: Houghton Mifflin, 1955.

HILGER, G. and A. G. MEYER, *The Incompatible Allies: A Memoir-History of German-Soviet Relations, 1918-1941.* New York: Macmillan, 1953.

JACOBSON, JON, *Locarno Diplomacy: Germany and the West, 1925-1929.* Princeton, N.J.: Princeton University Press, 1972.

LAFORE, LAURENCE, *The End of Glory.* Philadelphia: Lippincott, 1970.

MEYER, HENRY C. *Mitteleuropa in German Thought and Action 1815-1945.* Nijhoff, 1955.

WOLFERS, ARNOLD, *Britain and France Between Two Wars.* New York: Harcourt Brace, 1940.

Chapter 6

BAIN, CHESTER A., *Vietnam, the Roots of Conflict.* Englewood Cliffs, N.J.: Prentice-Hall, 1967.

BANCE, A. F., ed., *Weimar Germany: Writers and Politics.* Scottish Academic Press, 1982.

BROGAN, D. W., *France Under the Republic.* Greenwood Press, 1974.

BROOK-SHEPHERD, GORDON, *Dollfuss.* New York: Macmillan, 1961.

BROUÉ, PIERRE and TÉMIME, EMILE, *The Revolution and the Civil War in Spain.* Cambridge, Mass.: The MIT Press, 1972.

CARTER, GWENDOLEN M., *British Commonwealth and International Security.* Greenwood Press, 1971.

CLARK, JON, et al., eds., *Culture and Crisis in Britain in the Thirties.* Lawrence and Wishart, 1979.

COLTON, JOEL, *Léon Blum, Humanist in Politics.* New York: Knopf, 1966.

CRAIG, GORDON, *From Bismarck to Adenauer, Aspects of German Statecraft.* Greenwood, 1979.

DAHRENDORF, RALF, *Society and Democracy in Germany.* New York: Doubleday, 1967.

EKSTEINS, MODRIS, *The Limits of Reason.* New York: Oxford University Press, 1975.

ELLINWOOD, DEWITT, C., and S. D. PRADHAN, eds., *India and World War I.* South Asia Books, 1978.

EYCK, ERICH, *A History of the Weimar Republic,* 2 vols. Cambridge, Mass.: Harvard University Press, 1962.

FISCHER, RUTH, *Stalin and German Communism.* Cambridge, Mass.: Harvard University Press, 1948.

GAY, PETER, *Freud, Jews and other Germans.* New York: Oxford University Press, 1978.

————, *Weimar culture: the Outsider as Insider.* New York: Harper & Row, 1968.

GOPAL, RAM, *British Rule in India.* Bombay: Asia Pub. House, 1963.

HALPERIN, S. WILLIAM, *Germany Tried Democracy.* Archon Books, 1963.

KITCHEN, MARTIN, *The Coming of Austrian Fascism.* McGill-Queen's University Press, 1980.

LACOUTURE, JEAN, *Leon Blum.* New York: Holmes and Meier, 1982.

MACARTNEY, C. A., and A. W. PALMER, *Independent Eastern Europe.* New York: St. Martin's, 1966.

MACK SMITH, DENIS, *Mussolini.* New York: Vintage Books, 1983.

MCKENZIE, JOHN, RICHARD PHILIP, *Weimar Germany, 1918-1933.* Rowman and Littlefield, 1971.

MANSBERGH, NICHOLAS, *The Commonwealth Experience.* New York: Praeger, 1969.

NICHOLLS, A. J., *Weimar and the Rise of Hitler.* New York: St. Martin's Press, 1968.

NOLTE, ERNST, *Three Faces of Fascism.* New York: Holt, Rinehart and Winston, 1969.

RAYMOND, JOHN, ed., *The Baldwin Age.* Dufour Editions, 1961.

RINGER, FRITZ K., ed., *The German Inflation of 1923.* New York: Oxford University Press, 1969.

ROBINSON, RICHARD, A. H., *The Origins of Franco's Spain.* Pittsburgh: University of Pittsburgh Press, 1970.

SALVEMINI, GAETANO, *Under the Axe of Fascism.* H. Fertig, 1969.

————, *The Fascist Dictatorship in Italy.* H. Fertig, 1967.

SCHACHT, HJALMAR, *The Stabilization of the Mark.* New York, 1927.

SERING, MAX, *Germany under the Dawes Plan.* London, 1929.

SHIRER, WILLIAM L., *The Collapse of the Third Republic.* New York: Simon and Schuster, 1969.

STERN, FRITZ, *The Failure of Illiberalism.* New York: Knopf, 1972.

————, *The Politics of Cultural Despair.* New York: Doubleday, 1965.

TAYLOR, A. J. P., *English History, 1914–1945.* New York: Oxford University Press, 1965.

THOMAS, HUGH, *The Spanish Civil War.* New York: Harper & Row, 1977.

THOMSON, DAVID, *Democracy in France since 1870.* New York: Oxford University Press, 1969.

TOMASSON, RICHARD F., *Sweden: Prototype of Modern Society.* New York: Random House, 1970.

WEBER, EUGENE, *Action Française.* Stanford University Press, 1962.

WEISS, JOHN, ed., *Nazis and Fascists in Europe, 1918–1945.* New York: Quadrangle, 1969.

WISKEMANN, ELIZEBETH, *Fascism in Italy: its Development and Influence.* New York: St. Martin's Press, 1969.

WVORINEN, JOHN H., *A History of Finland.* New York, 1965.

Chapter 7

BRACHER, KARL DIETRICH, *The German Dictatorship: The Origins, Structure and Effects of National Socialism.* New York: Praeger, 1970.

CRAIG, GORDON A., *The Politics of the Prussian Army, 1640–1945.* New York: Oxford University Press, 1955.

ELLIS, HOWARD S., *Exchange Control in Central Europe.* Greenwood, 1971.

HALE, ORON J., *The Captive Press in the Third Reich.* Princeton, N.J.: Princeton University Press, 1964.

FEST, JOACHIM C., *Hitler.* New York: Vintage Books, 1975.

HÖHNE, HEINZ, *The Order of the Death's Head.* New York: Coward, McCann, 1970.

MOSSE, GEORGE L., *The Crisis of German Ideology.* New York, 1964.

SCHOENBAUM, DAVID, *Hitler's Social Revolution.* New York, 1967.

SHIRER, WILLIAM L., *The Rise and Fall of the Third Reich.* New York: Simon and Schuster, 1960.

SNELL, JOHN L., ed., *The Nazi Revolution.* Lexington, Mass.: Heath, 1959.

SPEER, ALBERT, *Inside the Third Reich.* New York: Macmillan, 1970.

TOBIAS, FRITZ, *The Reichstag Fire.* New York: Putnam's, 1964.

TOLAND, JOHN, *Adolf Hitler.* New York: Ballantine, 1977.

VON LANG, JOCHEN, ed., *Eichmann Interrogated.* New York: Farrar, Straus and Giroux, 1983.

WHEATON, ELIOT B., *Prelude to Calamity.* New York: Doubleday, 1968.

Chapter 8

BALBANOFF, ANGELICA, *Impressions of Lenin.* University of Michigan Press, 1968.

DEUTSCHER, ISAAC, *Stalin: A Political Biography.* New York: Oxford University Press, 1967.

————, *The Prophet Armed.* New York: Oxford University Press, 1954.

————, *The Prophet Outcast.* New York: Oxford University Press, 1963.

————, *The Prophet Unarmed.* New York: Oxford University Press, 1959.

DRACHKOVITCH, MILORAD, M., ed., *The Revolutionary Internationals, 1864–1943.* Stanford University Press, 1966.

FISCHER, LOUISE, *Men and Politics.* New York: Harper & Row, 1966.

KATKOV, GEORGE, *The Trial of Bukharin.* Briarcliff Manor, N.Y.: Stein and Day, 1969.

MADVEDEV, ROY A., *Nikolai Bukharin.* New York: W. W. Norton, 1980.

PAGE, STANLEY, W., *Lenin and World Revolution.* New York: New York University Press, 1959.

PIPES, RICHARD, *The Formation of the Soviet Union: Communism and Nationalism 1917–1923.* Cambridge, Mass.: Harvard University Press, 1954.

RESHETAR, JOHN S., *A Concise History of the Communist Party of the Soviet Union.* New York, 1964.

SOUVARAINE, BORIS, *Stalin A Critical Survey of Bolshevism.* New York: Arno, 1972.

TROTSKY, LEON, *Literature and Revolution,* University of Michigan Press, 1960.

ULDRICKS, TEDDY J., *Diplomacy and Ideology The Origins of Soviet Foreign Relations 1917–1930.* Beverly Hills, Calif.: Sage Publications, 1979.

Chapter 9

ADAMTHWAITE, ANTHONY, *France and the Coming of the Second World War 1936–1939.* Frank Cass, 1977.

CIENCIALA, ANNA M., *Poland and the Western Powers, 1938–1939.* Boston: Routledge and Kegan Paul, 1968.

EDEN, ANTHONY, *Memoirs: Facing the Dictators.* Houghton Mifflin, 1962.

FEIS, HERBERT, *Three International Episodes.* New York: W. W. Norton, 1969.

HOLBORN, HAJO, *The Political Collapse of Europe.* New York: Knopf, 1960.

KENNEDY, MALCOLM, D., *The Estrangement of Great Britain and Japan, 1917–1935.* University of California Press, 1969.

LEE, DWIGHT E., *Munich: Blunder, Plot or Tragic Necessity?* Lexington, Mass.: Heath, 1970.

LOEWENHEIM, FRANCIS L., *Peace or Appeasement?* Houghton-Mifflin, 1965.

NÉRÉ, J., *The Foreign Policy of France from 1914 to 1945.* Boston: Routledge and Kegan Paul, 1975.

NOUGUERES, HENRI, *Munich.* New York: McGraw-Hill, 1965.

SETON-WATSON, HUGH, *Eastern Europe between the Wars: 1918–1941.* New York: Harper & Row, 1962.

SCHUSCHNIGG, KURT, *The Brutal Takeover.* New York: Atheneum, 1971.

SNELL, JOHN L., *The Outbreak of the Second World War.* Lexington, Mass.: Heath, 1962.

TAYLOR, A. J. P., *The Origins of the Second World War.* New York: Atheneum, 1961.

THORNE, CHRISTOPHER, *The Approach of War, 1938–1939.* New York: St. Martin's Press, 1967.

WANDYCZ, PIOTR S., *France and Her Eastern Allies 1919–1925.* University of Minnesota Press, 1962.

WEINBERG, GERHARD L., *The Foreign Policy of Hitler's Germany.* Chicago: University of Chicago Press, 1980.

WISKEMANN, ELIZABETH, *The Rome-Berlin Axis.* New York: Collins, 1966.

Chapter 10

ACCOCE, PIERRE and QUET, PIERRE, *A Man Called Lucy.* New York: Coward-McCann, 1966.

BALDWIN, HANSON, *Battles Lost and Won.* New York: Harper & Row, 1966.

BOELCHKE, WILLI A., ed., *The Secret Conferences of Dr. Goebbels, the Nazi Propaganda War 1939–1943.* New York: Dutton, 1970.

BUCHANAN, RUSSEL A., *The United States and World War II,* 3 vols. New York, 1964.

CHAPMAN, GUY, *Why France Fell.* Holt, Rinehart and Winston, 1968.

CHURCHILL, WINSTON S., *The Second World War,* 6 vols. Houghton Mifflin, 1948–1953.

CLARK, ALAN, *Barbarossa.* New York: William Morrow, 1965.

COLLIER, B., *The Battle of Britain.* London, 1962.

DALLIN, ALEXANDER, *German Rule in Russia 1941–1945.* 1957.

D'ESTE, CARLO, *Decision in Normandy.* New York: Dutton, 1983.

DORNBERGER, WALTER, *V-2.* New York: Ballantine, 1954.

EISENBERG, AZRIEL, *Witness to the Holocaust.* Pilgrim Press, 1981.

FEIS, HERBERT, *Churchill, Roosevelt, Stalin: The War They Waged and the Peace They Sought.* Princeton, N.J.: Princeton University Press, 1967.

FITZGIBBON, LOUIS, *Katyn.* New York: Charles Scribner's, 1971.

GALLAGHER, MATTHEW P., *The Soviet History of World War II.* New York: Praeger, 1963.

GALLAND, ADOLF, *The First and the Last.* New York: Ballantine, 1954.

GAULLE, CHARLES DE, *The Complete War Memoirs of Charles de Gaulle, 1940–1946.* 3 vols. New York, 1968.

GIBSON, HUGH, ed., *The Ciano Diaries.* New York: Doubleday, 1946.

GILBERT, MARTIN, *Auschwitz and the Allies.* New York: Holt, Rinehart and Winston, 1981.

HAESTRUP, JOERGEN, *European Resistance Movements 1939–1945: A Complete History.* Meckler Publishing, 1981.

HITCHENS, MARILYNN GIROUX, *Germany, Russia, and the Balkans.* Boulder, 1983.

HOESS, RUDOLF, *Commandant of Auschwitz.* World Publishing Co., 1959.

HUGHES, TERRY and JOHN COSTELLO, *The Battle of the Atlantic*. New York: Dial Press, 1977.

JACOBSEN, H. A. and J. ROHWER, eds., *Decisive Battles of WW II*. A. Deutsch, 1965.

JUOZAS, PRUNSKIS, ed., *Lithuania Under Soviet Occupation*. Cicero, 1982.

KOZACZUK, WLADYSLAW, *Enigma*. University Publications of America, 1984.

KROSBY, PETER H., *Finland, Germany, and the Soviet Union, 1940-1941*. University of Wisconsin Press, 1968.

LA GORCE, PAUL MARIE DE, *The French Army*. G. Braziller, 1963.

LANGER, WILLIAM and EVERETT S. GLEASON, *The Undeclared War*. New York: Harper, 1953.

LAQUEUR, WALTER, *The Terrible Secret*. Boston: Little, Brown, 1980.

LEWIN, RONALD, *Ultra Goes to War*. New York: McGraw-Hill, 1978.

LIDDELL HART, *The Liddell Hart Memoirs*, 2 vols. New York: Putnam's, 1965.

————, ed., *The Red Army*. New York: Harcourt, Brace, 1956.

————, *The Rommel Papers*. New York: Harcourt, Brace, 1953.

LOCHNER, LOUIS P., ed., *The Goebbels Diaries 1942-1943*. New York, 1948.

MANSTEIN, ERICH VON, *Lost Victories*. Chicago: Henry Regnery Co., 1958.

MORSE, ARTHUR D., *While Six Million Died*. Overlook Press, 1983.

OVERY, R. J., *The Air War 1939-1945*. Briarcliff Manor, N.Y.: Stein and Day, 1980.

RITTER, GERHARD, *The German Resistance*. Praeger, 1958.

SCHEURIG, BODO, *Free Germany*. Wesleyan University Press, 1969.

SHEPPERD, G. A., *The Italian Campaign*. Praeger, 1968.

STEENBERG, SVEN, *Vlasov*. New York: Knopf, 1970.

THOMPSON, LAURENCE, *1940*. New York: William Morrow, 1966.

TREVOR-ROPER, HUGH, *Blitzkrieg to Defeat: Hitler's War Directives 1939-1945*. New York: Holt, Rinehart, and Winston, 1965.

WEIGLEY, RUSSEL F., *Eisenhower's Lieutenants*. Indiana University Press, 1981.

WEINBERG, GERHARD L., *World in the Balance Behind the Scenes of World War II*. University Press of New England, 1981.

WILMOT, CHESTER, *The Struggle for Europe*. New York: Harper, 1952.

WOODWARD, SIR ERNEST LLEWELLYN, *British Foreign Policy in the Second World War*, H. M. Stationary Office, 1962.

YAHIL, LENI, *The Rescue of Danish Jewry*. Jewish Publications Society of America, 1969.

ZHUKOV, *The Memoirs of Marshal Zhukov*. New York: Delacorte Press, 1971.

Chapter 11

ACHESON, DEAN, *Present at the Creation*. New York: W. W. Norton, 1969.

BALFOUR, MICHAEL, *The Adversaries*. Boston: Routledge and Kegan Paul, 1981.

BALL, GEORGE W., *The Discipline of Power*. Boston: Little, Brown and Co., 1968.

GRAEBNER, NORMAN A., ed., *The Cold War*. Lexington, Mass.: Heath, 1976.

KAPLAN, MORTON A., *The Life and Death of the Cold War*. Nelson Hall, 1976.

LUKACS, JOHN, *A New History of the Cold War*. Anchor Books, 1966.

MASTNY, VOJTECH, *Russia's Road to the Cold War*. New York: Columbia University Press, 1979.

MEE, CHARLES L., JR., *Meeting at Potsdam*. M. Evans and Co., 1975.

NOLTE, ERNST, *Marxism, Fascism, Cold War*. Atlantic Highlands, N.J.: Humanities Press, 1982.

PATERSON, THOMAS G., ed., *The Origins of the Cold War*. Lexington, Mass.: Heath, 1970.

ROTHWELL, VICTOR, *Britain and the Cold War 1941-1947*. Jonathan Cape, 1982.

SMITH, ARTHUR L., JR., *Churchill's German Army*. Beverly Hills, Calif.: Sage Publications, 1977.

WOODHOUSE, C. H., *The Struggle for Greece 1941-1949*. Beekman/Esanu, 1979.

XYDIS, STEPHEN, *Greece and the Great Powers 1944-1947*. Institute for Balkan Studies, 1963.

YERGIN, DANIEL, *Shattered Peace*. Houghton Mifflin, 1977.

Chapter 12

ATONOV-OUSEYENKO, ANTON, *The Time of Stalin.* New York: Harper & Row, 1981.

DUNMORE, TIMOTHY, *The Stalinist Command Economy.* New York: Macmillan, 1980.

GEIGER, KENT H., *The Family in Soviet Russia.* Cambridge, Mass.: Harvard University Press, 1968.

LEONHARD, WOLFGANG, *Three Faces of Marxism.* Holt, Rinehart and Winston, 1974.

ULAM, ADAM B., *Stalin,* New York: Viking, 1973.

Chapter 13

AUTY, PHYLLIS, *Tito.* New York: McGraw-Hill, 1970.

DJILAS, MILOVAN, *Conversations with Stalin.* New York: Harcourt, Brace and World, 1962.

————, *The Unperfect Society.* New York: Harcourt, Brace and World, 1969.

PELIKAN, JIRI, ed., *The Czechoslovak Political Trials 1950-1954.* Stanford University Press, 1971.

Chapter 14

BOWER, TOM, *Klaus Barbie The Butcher of Lyons.* New York: Pantheon, 1984.

EDINGER, LEWIS J., *Kurt Schumacher.* Stanford University Press, 1965.

GIMBEL, JOHN, *The American Occupation of Germany.* Stanford University Press, 1968.

MANN, ANTHONY, *Comeback, Germany 1945-1952.* New York: Macmillan, 1980.

NETTL, J. J., *The Eastern Zone and Soviet Policy in Germany, 1945-1950.* New York: Oxford University Press, 1951.

TAUBER, KURT, P., *Beyond Eagle and Swastika,* 2 vols. Wesleyan University Press, 1967.

Chapter 15

BROMBERGER, MERRY, *Jean Monnet and the United States of Europe.* New York: Coward-McCann, 1969.

GRIMAL, HENRI, *Decolonization, the British, French, Dutch and Belgian Empires 1919-1963.* Westview, 1978.

MONNET, JEAN, *Memoirs.* Garden City, N.Y.: Doubleday, 1978.

SMITH, TONY, *The End of the European Empire,* Lexington, Mass.: Heath, 1975.

Chapter 16

CARILLO, ELISA ANNA, *Alcide de Gasperi; the Long Apprenticeship,* University of Notre Dame Press, 1965.

KOGAN, NORMAN, *A Political History of Postwar Italy.* Pall Mall Press, 1966.

MAMMARELLA, GIUSEPPE, *Italy after Fascism.* University of Notre Dame Press, 1966.

WEBSTER, RICHARD A., *Christian Democracy in Italy 1860-1960.* Hollis and Carter, 1961.

WISKEMANN, ELIZABETH, *Italy since 1945.* New York: Macmillan, 1971.

Chapter 17

FLANNER, JANET, *Paris Journal 1944-1965.* New York: Atheneum, 1965.

GORDON, BERTRAM M., *Collaborationism in France during the Second World War.* Cornell University Press, 1980.

HOFFMANN, STANLEY, et al. eds., *In Search of France.* Cambridge, Mass.: Harvard University Press, 1963.

KNIGHT, FRIDA, *The French Resistance 1940 to 1944.* Lawrence and Wishart, 1975.

LUETHY, HERBERT, *France Against Herself.* New York: Praeger, 1955.

MARSHALL, BRUCE D., *The French Colonial Myth and Constitution-Making in the Fourth Republic.* New Haven: Yale University Press, 1973.

TINT, HERBERT, *France Since 1918.* Batsford B. T., 1970.

Chapter 18

ASTER, SIDNEY, *Anthony Eden.* New York: St. Martin's Press, 1976.

CARLTON, DAVID, *Anthony Eden, A Biography.* Allen Lane, 1981.

COLE, G. D. H., *The Post-War Condition of Britain.* New York: Praeger, 1965.

CROSSMAN, R. H. S., *The Politics of Socialism.* New York: Atheneum, 1965.

FOOT, MICHAEL, *Aneurin Bevan,* 2 vols. Macgibbon and Kee, 1962.

MORGAN, KENNETH O., *Labour in Power, 1945-1951.* Clarendon, 1984.

SELDON, ANTHONY, *Churchill's Indian Summer, The Conservative Government, 1951-1955.* Hodder and Stoughton, 1981.

TAYLOR, A. J. P., et al., eds., *Churchill Revised.* New York: Dial Press, 1969.

WILLIAMS, PHILIP M., *Hugh Gaitskell: A Political Biography.* Jonathan Cape, 1979.

Chapter 19

BLACKSELL, MARK, *Post-War Europe A Political Geography.* Westview, 1978.

FRIEDRICH, CARL J., *Europe: An Emergent Nation?* New York: Harper & Row, 1969.

HARRIS, SIMON, et al., *The Food and Farm Policies of the European Community.* New York: John Wiley, 1983.

SEERS, DUDLEY et al. eds., *Underdeveloped Europe.* Atlantic Highlands, N.J.: Humanities Press, 1979.

Chapter 20

BAUER, ROBERT A., ed., *The Austrian Solution.* University Press of Virginia, 1982.

VALI, A. FERENC, *The Quest for a United Germany.* Johns Hopkins, 1967.

Chapter 21

JORAVSKY, DAVID, *The Lysenko Affair.* Cambridge, Mass.: Harvard University Press, 1970.

MCCAULEY, MARTIN, *Khrushchev and the Development of Soviet Agriculture.* New York: Holmes and Meier, 1976.

MEDVEDEV, ROY A., *Khrushchev.* Blackwell, 1982.

MEDVEDEV, ROY A., and ZHORES A. MEDVEDEV, *Khrushchev: The Years in Power.* New York: Columbia University Press, 1976.

ULAM, ADAM B., *Expansion and Coexistence.* Praeger, 1968.

Chapter 22

BETHEL, NICHOLAS, *Gomulka: His Poland, His Communism.* New York: Holt, Rinehart and Winston, 1967.

FEHÉR, FERENC and AGNES HELLER, *Hungary 1956 Revisited.* George Allen and Unwin, 1983.

FEJTÖ, FRANÇOIS, *A History of the People's Democracies.* New York: Praeger, 1971.

RADVANYI, JANOS, *Hungary and the Superpowers.* Hoover Institution Press, 1972.

REMINGTON, ROBIN A., *The Warsaw Pact.* MIT Press, 1971.

Chapter 23

BUNN, RONALD F., *German Politics and the Spiegel Affair.* Louisiana State University Press, 1968.

KRISCH, HENRY, *German Politics under Soviet Occupation.* New York: Columbia University Press, 1974.

PRITTIE, TRENCE, *Konrad Adenauer 1876-1967.* Tom Stacey, 1972.

SCHOENBERG, HANS W., *Germans from the East.* Nijhoff, 1970.

Chapter 24

BROMKE, ADAM and TERESA RAKOWASKA-HARMSTONE, *The Communist States in Disarray: 1965-1971.* University of Minnesota Press, 1972.

CIEPLAK, TADEUSZ, ed., *Poland Since 1956.* Boston: Twayne Publishers, 1972.

GOLAN, GALIA, *The Czechoslovak Reform Movement.* Cambridge University Press, 1971.

JOHNSON, CHALMERS, ed., *Change in Communist Systems.* Stanford University Press, 1970.

KASER, M. C., ed., *Economic Development for Eastern Europe.* New York: St. Martin's Press, 1968.

MASTNY, VOJTECH, *East-European Dissent 1953-1964.* Facts on File Inc., 1972.

RUBINSTEIN, ALVIN, *Yugoslavia and the Nonaligned World.* Princeton, N.J.: Princeton University Press, 1970.

SHAWCROSS, WILLIAM, *DUBCEK.* New York: Simon and Schuster, 1970.

SKILLING, GORDON H., *Czechoslovakia's Interrupted Revolution,* Princeton, N.J.: Princeton University Press, 1976.

STAAR, RICHARD F., *The Communist Regimes in Eastern Europe,* Stanford University Press, 1967.

WEIT, ERWIN, *Eyewitness.* Deutsch, 1973.

Chapter 25

BRAUN, JOACHIM, *Gustav Heinemann the Committed President,* O. Wolff, 1972.

CROAN, MELVIN, *East Germany.* Beverly Hills, Calif.: Sage Publications, 1976.

GROSSER, ALFRED, *Germany in Our Time.* Praeger, 1971.

HANRIEDER, WOLFRAM F., *The Stable Crisis.* New York: Harper & Row, 1970.

LEGTERS, LYMAN H., ed., *The German Democratic Republic.* Westview, 1978.

SCHNEIDER, EBERHARD, *The G. D. R.* New York: St. Martin's Press, 1978.

SMITH, JEAN E., *Germany Beyond the Wall.* Boston: Little, Brown, 1969.

SOWDEN, J. K., *The German Question 1945-1973.* Bradford University Press, 1975.

ULBRICHT, WALTER, *Whither Germany?* Zeit in Bild Publishing House, 1966.

Chapter 26

ALEXANDRE, PHILIPPE, *The Duel De Gaulle and Pompidou,* Houghton Mifflin, 1972.

COOK, DON, *Charles de Gaulle.* New York: G. P. Putnam's Sons, 1982.

CROZIER, BRIAN, *De Gaulle.* New York: Charles Scribner's Sons, 1973.

DE MÉNIL, LOIS P., *Who Speaks for Europe?* Weidenfeld and Nicolson, 1977.

FREARS, J. R., *France in the Giscard Presidency.* George Allen and Unwin, 1981.

GROSSER, ALFRED, *French Foreign Policy under de Gaulle.* Greenwood, 1965.

HARTLEY, ANTHONY, *Gaullism.* Outerbridge and Dienstfrey, 1971.

HOFFMAN, STANLEY, *Decline or Renewal?* New York: Viking, 1974.

KELLY, GEORGE A., *Lost Soldiers: The French Army and Empire in Crisis 1947-1962,* M.I.T. Press, 1965.

KIEP, WALTER L., *A New Challenge for Western Europe.* Mason and Lipscomb, 1974.

KOLODZIEJ, EDWARD A., *French International Policy under de Gaulle and Pompidou.* Cornell University Press, 1974.

LEDWIDGE, BERNARD, *De Gaulle.* New York: St. Martin's Press, 1982.

PIERCE, ROY, *Contemporary French Political Thought.* New York: Oxford University Press, 1966.

WILLIAMS, PHILIP M. and MARTIN HARRISON, *Politics and Society in de Gaulle's Republic.* Anchor Books, 1973.

Chapter 27

BARCLAY, G. ST. J., *Commonwealth or Europe.* University of Queensland Press, 1970.

CAMPBELL, JOHN, *Roy Jenkins: A Biography,* New York: St. Martin's Press, 1983.

FRANKEL, JOSEPH, *British Foreign Policy 1945-1973.* New York: Oxford University Press, 1975.

GOUGH, IAN, *The Political Economy of the Welfare State.* New York: Macmillan, 1979.

HOLMES, MARTIN, *Political Pressure and Economic Policy: British Government 1970-1974,* Butterworth Scientific, 1982.

HUTCHINSON, GEORGE, *Edward Heath, A Personal and Political Biography.* New York: Longman, 1970.

MACMILLAN, HAROLD, *Pointing the Way, 1959–1961.* New York: Macmillan, 1972.

PORTER, BERNARD, *Britain, Europe and the World 1850–1982, Delusions of Grandeur.* George Allen and Unwin, 1983.

PROUDFOOT, MARY, *British Politics and Government 1951–1970,* Faber and Faber, 1974.

SCHOEN, DOUGLAS E., *Enoch Powell and the Powellites.* New York: St. Martin's Press, 1977.

WILSON, HAROLD, *A Personal Record, The Labour Government 1964–1970.* Boston: Little, Brown, 1971.

Chapter 28

BAKLANOFF, ERIC N., *The Economic Transformation of Spain and Portugal.* New York: Praeger, 1978.

BRUCE, NEIL, *Portugal The Last Empire.* New York: John Wiley, 1975.

BRUNEAU, THOMAS C., *Politics and Nationhood, Post-Revolutionary Portugal.* New York: Praeger, 1984.

CARR, RAYMOND and FUSI, PABLO J., *Spain, Dictatorship to Democracy.* Allen and Unwin, 1979.

DE MACEDO, BRAGA J. and SIMON SERFATY, eds., *Portugal Since the Revolution: Economic and Political Perspectives.* Westview, 1981.

GIANARIS, NICHOLAS, *Greece and Yugoslavia: an economic comparison.* New York: Praeger, 1984.

GRAHAM, LAWRENCE S., and HARRY M. MAKLER, eds., *Contemporary Portugal.* University of Texas Press, 1979.

MCCLELLAN, GRANT S., ed., *Spain and Portugal: Democratic Beginnings.* H. W. Willson, 1978.

PORCH, DOUGLAS, *The Portuguese Armed Forces and the Revolution.* Hoover Institution Press, 1977.

RODGERS, ALLEN, *Economic Development in Retrospect.* V. H. Winston and Sons, 1979.

ROSENTHAL, GLENDA G., *The Mediterranean Basin Its Political Economy and Changing International Relations,* Butterworth Scientific, 1982.

SOARES, MARIO, *Portugal's Struggle for Liberty.* George Allen and Unwin, 1975.

WILLIS, ROY F., *Italy Chooses Europe.* New York: Oxford University Press, 1971.

WOODHOUSE, C. M., *Karamanlis, the Restorer of Greek Democracy.* New York: Oxford University Press, 1982.

Chapter 29

ADOMEIT, HANNES, *Soviet Risk-taking and Crisis Behavior.* George Allen and Unwin, 1982.

AMALRIK, ANDREI, *Will the Soviet Union Survive Until 1984?* Perennial Library, 1970.

BARGHOORN, FREDERICK C., *Détente and the Democratic Movement in the USSR.* New York: Free Press, 1976.

BREZHNEV, L. I., *Socialism, Democracy and Human Rights.* Elmsford, N.Y.: Pergamon, 1980.

GRIFFITH, WILLIAM E., ed., *The Soviet Empire: Expansion and Détente.* Lexington Books, 1976.

GRIGORENKO, PETRO G., *Memoirs.* New York: W. W. Norton, 1982.

KASLAS, BRONIS, J., *The Baltic Nations.* Euramerica Press, 1976.

MEERSON-AKSENOV, MICHAEL, and BORIS SHRAGIN, eds., *The Political, Social and Religious Thought of Russian "samizdat."* Nordland Publishing Co., 1977.

MORTON, HENRY W., and RUDOLF L. TÖKES, eds., *Soviet Politics and Society in the 1970's.* New York: Free Press, 1974.

PARMING, TÖNU and ELMAR JÄRVESOO, *A Case Study of a Soviet Republic: The Estonian SSR.* Westview, 1978.

PIPES, RICHARD, *US-Soviet Relations in the Era of Détente.* Westview, 1981.

REMEIKIS, THOMAS, *Opposition to Soviet Rule in Lithuania 1945–1980.* Institute of Lithuanian Studies Press, 1980.

SAKHAROV, ANDREI D., *My Country and the World.* New York: Knopf, 1976.

SALISBURY, HARRISON E., ed., *Sakharov Speaks.* New York: Vintage Books, 1974.

SHATZ, MARSHALL S., *Soviet Dissent in Historical Perspective.* Cambridge University Press, 1980.

SIMMONDS, GEORGE W., ed., *Nationalism in the USSR and Eastern Europe in the era of Brezhnev and Kosygin.* University of Detroit Press, 1977.

SPECHLER, DINA R., *Permitted Dissent in the USSR*. New York: Praeger, 1982.

STRONG, JOHN W., ed., *The Soviet Union under Brezhnev and Kosygin*. New York: D. Van Nostrand, 1971.

WESTOBY, ADAM, *Communism since World War II*. New York: St. Martin's Press, 1981.

Chapter 30

BRAUN, AUREL, *Romanian Foreign Policy Since 1965*. New York: Praeger, 1978.

————, *Small-State Security in the Balkans*. New York: Barnes and Noble, 1983.

BENDER, PETER, *East Europe in Search of Security*. John Hopkins University Press, 1972.

BROMKE, ADAM and JOHN W. STRONG, eds., *Gierek's Poland*. New York: Praeger, 1973.

CARLTON, DAVID and CARLO SCHAERF, *South-Eastern Europe after Tito*. New York: St. Martin's Press, 1983.

DJILAS, MILOVAN, *Parts of a Lifetime*. New York: Harcourt Brace Jovanovich, 1975.

————, *Tito*. New York: Harcourt Brace Jovanovich, 1980.

FISCHER, LEWIS A., and PHILIP E. UREN, *The New Hungarian Agriculture*. McGill-Queen's University Press, 1973.

GATI, CHARLES, ed., *The Politics of Modernization in Eastern Europe*. New York: Praeger, 1974.

GILBERG, TROND, *Modernization in Romania Since World War II*. New York: Praeger, 1975.

GRAHAM, LAWRENCE S., *Romania: A Developing Socialist State*. Westview, 1982.

HORVAT, BRANKO, *The Yugoslav Economic System*. M. E. Sharpe Inc., 1976.

JEFFRIES, IAN, ed., *The Industrial Enterprise in Eastern Europe*. New York: Praeger, 1981.

KADAR, JANOS, *For a Socialist Hungary*. Corvina Press, 1974.

MELLOR, ROY E. H., *Eastern Europe*. New York: Columbia University Press, 1975.

NATO DIRECTORATE OF ECONOMIC AFFAIRS, *Comecon: Progress and Prospects*. 1977.

NOVE, ALEC, et al., eds., *The East European Economies in the 1970's*. Butterworth, 1982.

PELIKAN, JIRI, *Socialist Opposition in Eastern Europe*. New York: St. Martin's Press, 1973.

RA'ANAN, GAVRIEL D., *Yugoslavia after Tito*. Westview, 1977.

Chapter 31

BALFOUR, MICHAEL, *West Germany, A Contemporary History*. New York: St. Martin's Press, 1982.

BINDER, DAVID, *The Other German: Willy Brandt's Life and Times*. New Republic Book Co., 1975.

HONECKER, ERICH, *Erich Honecker From My Life*. Elmsford, N. Y.: Pergamon, 1981.

KEESING'S RESEARCH REPORT, *Germany and Eastern Europe since 1945*. New York: Charles Scribner's, 1973.

MERKL, PETER H., ed., *West German Foreign Policy*. Chicago Council on Foreign Relations, 1982.

SCHULZ, JACOBSEN et al. eds., *GDR Foreign Policy*. M. E. Sharpe, 1982.

WETTIG, GERHARD, *Community and Conflict in the Socialist Camp*. C. Hurst, 1975.

WINDSOR, PHILIP, *Germany and the Management of Détente*. New York: Praeger, 1971.

Chapter 32

BALASSA, BELA, ed., *European Economic Integration*. North-Holland Publishing Co., 1975.

BAMFORD, C. G., *Geography of the EEC*. MacDonald and Evans, 1983.

BOLTHO, ANDREA, ed., *The European Economy Growth and Crisis*. New York: Oxford University Press, 1982.

BYRNES, ROBERT F., ed., *After Brezhnev*. Indiana University Press, 1983.

CHERNENKO, KONSTANTINE, *Selected Speeches and Writings*. New York: Pergamon, 1982.

CHURCHILL, WINSTON S., *Defending the West*. Arlington House Publishers, 1981.

COLLINS, DOREEN, *The European Communities*, 2 vols. Martin Robertson, 1975.

COSGRAVE, PATRICK, *Margaret Thatcher: A Tory and Her Party*. Hutchinson of London, 1978.

CROOM, HELM, *Crisis in the East European Economy, The Spread of the Polish Disease*. New York: St. Martin's Press, 1982.

FEUCHTWANGER, E. J., and NAILOR, PETER eds., *The Soviet Union and the Third World,* New York: St. Martin's Press, 1981.

FISCHER-GALATI, RADU R. FLORESCU et al. eds., *Romania between East and West.* Boulder: East European Monographs, 1982.

GIERSCH, HERBERT, ed., *The Economic Integration of Israel in the EEC.* J. C. B. Mohr, 1980.

JOHNSON, GALE D., and KAREN M. BROOKS, *Prospects for Soviet Agriculture in the 1980's.* Indiana University Press, 1983.

KAPTEYN, PAUL J. G., ed., *The Social Policy of the European Communities.* A. W. Sijthoff, 1977.

LAIRD, ROY D., et al., eds., *The Future of Agriculture in the Soviet Union and Eastern Europe.* Westview, 1977.

LODGE, JULIET, ed., *Institutions and Policies of the European Community,* New York: St. Martin's Press, 1983.

McCAULEY, MARTIN, ed., *The Soviet Union after Brezhnev.* New York: Holmes and Meier, 1983.

MacSHANE, DENIS, *François Mitterand,* Universe Books, 1982.

MEDVEDEV, ZHORES, *Andropov.* New York: W. W. Norton, 1983.

NATO ECONOMIC DIRECTORATE, *Economic Reforms in Eastern Europe and Prospects for the 1980's.* Elmsford, N.Y.: Pergamon, 1980.

NELSON, DANIEL N., ed., *Romania in the 1980's.* Westview, 1981.

PICKLES, DOROTHY, *Problems of Contemporary French Politics.* Methuen, 1982.

SANTONI, GEORGES, *Contemporary French Culture and Society.* State University of New York Press, 1981.

SCHIAVONE, GIUSEPPE, *The Institutions of Comecon.* New York: Holmes and Meier, 1981.

SCHULTZ, RICHARD H., and GODSON, ROY, *Dezinformatsia.* Elmsford, N.Y.: Pergamon Press, 1984.

SHANOR, DONALD R., *The Soviet Triangle: Russia's Relations with China and the West in the 1980's.* New York: St. Martin's Press, 1980.

STEELE, JONATHAN and ERIC ABRAHAM, *Andropov in Power.* Anchor Press, 1984.

STUART, ROBERT C., ed., *The Soviet Rural Economy.* Rowman and Allanheld, 1984.

VAN BRABANT, JOZEF M., *Socialist Economic Integration.* Cambridge University Press, 1980.

WALLACE, HELEN, et al., eds., *Policy Making in the European Community.* New York: John Wiley, 1977.

Index

A

Abendroth, Wolfgang, 318
Action Française, 78
Addison Act, 72
Adenauer, Konrad, 286
Adenauer's Security Memorandum, 288
Adorno, Theodor, 318
Akhmatova, Anna, 204
Algerian, FLN, 348
Allenby, Sir Edmund, 28
Amalrik, Andrei, 404
Amendola, Giorgio, 372
Amritsar Massacre, 69
Andropov, Yuri V., 403, 439
Andrzejewski, Jerzy, 309
Anglo-German Naval Agreement of 1935, 141
"Angry Young Men," 364
Anschluss, 145
Apel, Erich, 344
Apertura a Sinistra, 372
Appeasement, 144
April Theses, 34

Arias, Gino, 90
Arp, Hans, 5
Aspida Group, 374
Asquith, Herbert, 24
Atlantic, Battle of, 178
Attlee, Clement, 263
Augstein, Rudolf, 340, 436
Auschwitz, 183
Ausgleich, 39
Austrian State Treaty of 1955, 315
Azaña, Manuel, 2

B

Backlund, Sven, 419
Baghdad Pact, 272
Bahr, Egon, 338
Baibakov, Nikolai K., 393
Balabanoff, Angelica, 91
Baldwin, Stanley, 73
Balfour Declaration, 70, 270
Balkan Wars, 7
Ball, George, 424